1989

Dad, & (Grandpa)
Happy Fathers Day
        Love,
    Bob, Anne, Sarah,
    Brian, & Colleen

a treasury of
irish
folklore

a treasury of
irish
folklore

The Stories, Traditions, Legends, Humor, Wisdom,
Ballads and Songs of the Irish People

EDITED WITH AN INTRODUCTION BY

padraic colum

SECOND REVISED EDITION

BONANZA BOOKS
NEW YORK

TO

FREDERICA AND HAROLD LANDON,
TRUE FRIENDS

ACKNOWLEDGMENTS

The editor gives thanks to the two librarians of the American-Irish Historical Society for continuous assistance, and to the editor and members of the staff of Crown Publishers for wise advice and burthen-lifting help.

The editor and publisher wish to thank the following publishers, publications, and individuals for the use of material from contemporary works: Batsford & Co. Ltd.; *Béaloideas,* Journal of the Folklore of Ireland Society; Robert Brennan; Browne & Nolan Ltd.; *The Capuchin Annual;* The Clarendon Press; The Devin-Adair Co.; Myles Dillon; Henry Holt & Co.; Houghton Mifflin Co.; *The Irish Digest; The Irish Sword;* Little, Brown & Co.; Longmans, Green & Co. Inc.; The Macmillan Co.; Harold Matson (Frank O'Connor); David McKay Co., Inc.; Methuen & Co. Ltd.; Frederick Muller Ltd.; Oxford University Press, Inc.; G. P. Putnam's Sons; *Rann,* The Ulster Quarterly of Poetry; Mrs. James Stephens; Beatrice Talbot; The Talbot Press Ltd.; Yale University Press.

This 1983 edition is published by Bonanza Books, distributed by Crown Publishers, Inc., One Park Avenue, New York, N.Y. 10016

Manufactured in the United States of America

LIBRARY OF CONGRESS CATALOGING IN PUBLICATION DATA
Main entry under title:

A Treasury of Irish folklore.

A Reprint. Originally published: 2nd rev. ed. New York :
Crown Publishers, 1967.
Includes index.
1. Folklore—Ireland. 2. Ireland—Social life and customs.
3. Folk-songs, Irish. I. Colum, Padraic, 1881–1972.
GR153.5.T73 1983   398'.09415   83-111818
ISBN: 0-517-420465

h g f e d c

Preface to the Second Revised Edition

The years that have passed since the first publication of *A Treasury of Irish Folklore* have been a time of transition that has affected the traditional lore, that is, the lore handed down from generation to generation in the Irish countryside, more than it has affected any other cultural activity or entertainment—the transition from countryside to towns, from talk by the fireside to oral and visual mass communication.

The century-old type of cottage, clay-built, whitewashed, thatched, is no longer the main feature of the landscape: tiles have taken the place of thatch, some other building material the place of clay; the houses are more convenient and more roomy than the houses we were used to seeing before. Within, the change for the one who has traditional lore in his mind is more significant.

The fire is still on the hearthstones, but the big sods of turf cut on the bog nearby no longer make it; the compressed turf is from the factory that is exploiting the stretches of bog. Electric bulbs have taken the place of candlelight and firelight that gave the walls shadows and the interior a modicum of light. The change is all against neighborly discourse. The younger folk go to the dance hall or the cinema; the older folk stay at home and listen to broadcasts. The isolation that fostered the tale, the song, the piece of local history, the transactions that took on a pattern by being repeated over and over again, have been mitigated. Yet the liveliness of speech, the imaginativeness of phrase, the accomplishment in shaping or relating an incident are still to be noted.

It should be remarked that the epoch of change is also the epoch of gathering. One of the first things that the national government did in Ireland was to set up an Institute of Folklore under a director who is amongst the foremost in the field of European folklore. Through this Institute a rewarding effort has been made to collect and record traditional material: for forty years this collecting and recording has been going on; the result is that the Folklore Institute in Dublin possesses a great collection of the traditional lore of Ireland that is part of the traditional lore of Europe. It has now become evident to scholars in this field that works of interpretation are now due. An example of what should follow on the work of collecting and recording is Maire Mac-Neill's monumental *Feast of Lughnasa*. Meanwhile, local collectors with a knowledge of the tradition are going through the countryside recording what is still current. I have sat with such collectors in cottages and public houses and have been charmed by their interest, their education in everything relating to the material, their ability to draw from a recipient an unflawed piece of traditional lore.

Padraic Colum

Contents

Part I: THE IRISH EDGE

Part II: HEROES OF OLD

Part VI: Ways and Traditions

Part VII: Fireside Tales

Part VIII: THE FACE OF THE LAND

Part IX: BALLADS AND SONGS

Introduction

It has happened at different times to the editor of this collection that, being with a Greek friend when another person revealed himself as of the same nativity, his friend, not always the same one, would ask, "From what place do you come?" The query has the ancientness of the Odyssey—"Where do you come from, stranger?" In the modern instance, the editor, noting a reply that contained a memory-laden place-name—Mitylene, or Samos, or Argos, would be of the opinion that the question asked was less for information than to reach an identification that, recalling perenially beautiful place-names, uplifted the speaker and the hearer. But the query had an everyday significance. "We are separated from other communities in Greece," one friend told him. "We who live on the islands know little about the mainland, and those on the mainland know little of the places across the mountain." Well, even though it relates to practical matters, the query brings out a constituent of the Greek mind—something that arises out of what was important in the days of the epic and is important still—the geographical scene. And even though the query is practical, it must evoke a sense of history as well as scene—the light-waved Mediterranean, the mountains, the divided plain. Here, then, is one stratum of Greek lore.

An Irish person, meeting outside his country one in whom the same nativity is recognized, does not ask, "From what part do you come?" He or she asks, "What name have you?" (In Irish it would be, "What name is on you?") The name given reveals more often than not a stock that can be identified among other Irish stocks, a system of relationships, and very often a territory.* On the threshold of identity there is not for Irish people a consideration of place, but of name, and with the name, local history with its monuments, the castles and keeps that mark conquest and resistance, the older earthen mounds in which abide the fairy folk, the places that have sanctity, notably the holy wells.

Ireland is still a country of country people—farmers living on their acres in cottages built out of materials that are to be found at hand. The country people are not village-dwellers as are the people of the English and French countryside. The houses, apart from each

---

* I am taking the old clan names, the Gaelic names. But it should be remembered that about a sixth of Irish names are of Norman origin—Fitzgerald, Burke, Butler, Power, Grace. But these, too, are of an old stock—the *Sean-Ghaill*—and they can be placed in a history and a territory. There is, of course, a considerable number of English names, some recent and some from far back. There are Scotch and Welsh and some French Huguenot names. In the northeast the bulk of the names are Scottish and English, but in the case of the Scottish, many are of Gaelic origin.

other, each with its own field or fields, give a sense of isolation. An English traveller, a recent one, notes a cottage that "was set in a little island in the bog: by it were two or three little paddock enclosures set about with high dyke banks on which grew willow trees. A little talking brook ran through green mosses by the wall and the shadows of the willow leaves patterned the pink wash of the house with soft blue shadows. The sound of spinning reached us down the sunlit air, rising up to a trembling wail and sinking low again. . . . We came silently to the door over the rushes, and stood as if a spell was over us."*

The Irish landscape where it is most distinctive is stranger than that of any other part of Europe. Water is everywhere—"a land of lakes," as an Irish topographer describes it. There is green of the grass, and always near the grass is the grey of the stones: it is the ever-present greyness—the stones, the massed clouds above—that make people think of Ireland as having a verdure brighter than that of any other country in the world. There is another greyness present, the greyness of ruins that are everywhere—towers, keeps, castles, abbeys, ancient churches. "The whole speaking monuments of the troubled and insecure state of the country from the most remote periods to comparatively modern times," George Borrow noted. And another English traveller, Arthur Young, in the eighteenth century, impressed with the greenness of the country, wrote, "May we not recognize in this the hand of bounteous Providence which has given perhaps the most stony soil in Europe the moistest climate of it. . . . But the rocks are covered with verdure; those of limestone, with only a thin covering of mould, have the softest and most beautiful turf imaginable." The grey walls of the ruins are covered with heavy, wide-leaved ivy. And the sun bursting through the big clouds fills bog or green valley with a rare light—a vibrant, a living kind of light.

But Ireland is not altogether a country of water, grass, bogs and ruins. There is the well-farmed northeast with the industrial city of Belfast; there is the varied east with Ireland's capital city; there is the rich land of the middle south known as "the golden vein"; there are the pastures of Meath; there is the southwest which touched by the Gulf Stream produces some of the flora of the Mediterranean: there the arbutus becomes a great tree; and west and south one sees hedges that are rhododendrons mixed with fuchsias.

The houses that dot the countryside are whitewashed and thatched with straw. They are built of the stiff clay dug nearby; against the whiteness of their limewashed walls is the blackness of the stack of turf or peat, cut in the bog generally convenient to the cottage, the bog being owned or rented as is the land by the various families around. As regards firing, the bog is good to them, for the cut and dried peat makes the most heartening of fires. The fire regulates the culinary as it does the social activities of the house. It is on the hearthstone, level with the floor; over it is the wide chimney, and the glow

---

* Dorothy Hartley: *Irish Holiday*. Robert McBride & Co. New York.

of the burning peat is surrounded by deep ashes; in the morning the ashes are raked off, fresh peat put over the living coals and blown with a bellows, and so the fire is never quenched. Everything social in the ordinary way takes place around the fireside—on occasions one of the rooms becomes a reception room. The visitor is brought at once to the hearth. The neighbours who come in sit by it. When the conversation becomes general, when there is song or story, the gathering becomes the *celidh* or *seanchas*. In the old days when there were many homeless men and women, a sack of leaves or heather-tops was laid within the nook and there the one seeking shelter for the night could sleep. Between the table and the kitchen-dresser couples could dance to the fiddle or the concertina. The year filled with the tilling of the fields and the rearing of stock is diversified by fairs and markets, pilgrimages, or the "pattern" which, much smaller and more local, corresponds to the Breton "pardon," the gathering in honor of a local patron or saint.

A Swedish scholar, Professor Sydov, noting that the traditional culture of Ireland and Gaelic Scotland is amongst the richest and most outstanding in Europe, attributes its rich vitality partly to the fact that the people have been long in possession of their present territory, and partly that there used to be professional narrators—"there being nothing analogous to them in Teutonic territory." The narrator is the shanachie: definitely professional in Gaelic-speaking districts, and less professional as one moves away from such districts, he or she is not only the narrator of stories but the relator of local history which includes genealogies. At an earlier time the shanachie and his or her fireside audience received influences from men who came to the cottages from the outside. "In Ireland," writes the English scholar, Robin Flower, "where the ruin of the seventeenth century scattered the students of the schools among the common folk, the wandering scholar—schoolmaster, poet and musician—was a known figure wherever anything of the old life survived until only the other day." He tells us that "in the peoples' memories two figures of this kind stand out distinct—the witty, inspired, improvising poet, and the poor scholar, travelling from house to house with his bag of books, solving knotty problems with the aid of recondite learning, and often by a parade of scholarship getting the upper hand among a people unlearned, but passionate admirers of printed knowledge and strange tongues." This scholar got a great deal of material from a shanachie in the Blasket Islands off Kerry, a woman, Peg Sayers, and he has this to say of her:

"She has so clean and finished a style of speech that you can follow all the nicest articulations of the language on her lips without any effort; she is a natural orator, with so keen a sense of the turn of a phrase and the lifting rhythm appropriate to Irish that her words could be written down as they leave her lips, and they could have the effect of literature with no savor of artificiality of composition. She is wont to illustrate her talk

with tales long and short which come so naturally along the flow
of conversation, and lighten all her discourse with the wit and
wisdom and folly and vivid incident of the past."*

Her language was Irish (the passage was written twenty years ago
and there is no one now on the Blaskets). As a spoken language Irish
is capable of being eloquent, poetic and witty in a high degree. "The
Gaelic," say the Irish philosopher, Arland Ussher, "is a language of
prodigious diversity of sound and expressiveness of phrase. . . . It
has about twice the number of sounds that other European languages
can boast. . . . As for the expressiveness of the Gaelic folk-idiom,
only the 'Irish-English' of Synge's plays can give strangers some idea
of it; it is a language, if not of a race of poets . . . then at least of a
race which has 'tired the sun with talking,' a language of quips, hyper-
boles, cajoleries, endearments, lamentations, blessings, curses, tirades—
and all very often in the same breath."†

The shanachie, then, seated by the peat fire, receiving attention
and respect, is a central figure in Irish social and cultural history.
The gathering by the fireside makes a pattern for Irish narrative and
discourse in general. Hugh de Blacam writes, "The domestic *seanchas*
of today is the cell on which the living Irish culture is built, or the
channel through which the past flows to inform the future. It may deal
with deep things in the house of the scholar; in the cottage it is satisfied with legendary tales."‡

The Irish have remained an oral rather than a literate people. (It
should be noted that culture does not depend upon reading and writing: the present editor knew an old man, technically an illiterate, who
delighted in repeating passages from an Irish translation of part of the
Iliad.) The schools the people formed without state or church aid,
the "hedge schools," got on largely without books, and this meant that
a great deal of instruction had to be carried in the pupil's memory.
The academic poetry of the seventeenth and eighteenth centuries was
confided to farmers and fishermen; one could hear a recital of the
poems of O'Brudair, O'Rahilly, Merriman in thatched cottages a hundred years after the poets were dead and gone. And that oral memory
held matter that went much further back than the eighteenth and
seventeenth centuries. Robin Flower on the road to Kerry was hailed
by a man digging potatoes in a field. The man came over and talked
to him. "Without further preamble or explanation he fell to reciting
Ossianic lays. For half an hour I sat there while his firm voice went
on. After a while he changed from poetry to prose. . . . I listened spellbound, and as I listened, it came to me suddenly that here on the last
inhabited piece of European land, looking out into the Atlantic horizon, I was hearing the oldest living tradition in the British Isles. So
far as the record goes, this matter in one form or another is older

---

* Robin Flower: *The Western Island.* Oxford University Press. New York.
† Arland Ussher: *The Face and Mind of Ireland.* Devin-Adair Co. New York.
‡ Hugh de Blacam: *Gaelic Literature Surveyed.* The Talbot Press. Dublin.

than the Anglo-Saxon Beowulf, and yet it lives still on the lips of the peasantry, a real and vivid experience, while except for a few painful scholars, Beowulf has long passed out of memory."*

This is Gaelic-speaking Ireland. But although the midland and the eastern counties have ceased to be Gaelic-speaking, the *celidh* or *seanchas* with its lively discourse, its sharp delineations of character, its well-phrased speech keeping some of the Gaelic locutions, still stays. And the formative power of the fireside gathering is strong: books read or stories picked up are turned into familiar patterns. Let us take as an extravagant example of this the paradox of actual persons' adventures reproducing the pattern of a folk-tale.

Three envoys go for conference with the British Prime Minister, David Lloyd George. They are under bonds not to take bite or sup nor sleep a night under a stranger's roof. When they encounter their man he has a salmon in his hands—the Salmon of Knowledge—and is recognizable as the enchanter. The three youths from Erin deliver their message. It takes the heart out of the Enchanter. In the story his groans would split the chair he is seated on. The envoys let us know that they fill the Enchanter's castle.

The editor recalls a story told him in the County Cavan. Its hero was an Irish officer who served in the American Civil War and was subsequently made Governor of Montana, Thomas Francis Meagher. Through misadventure he was drowned in the river. The narrator of the story had read a newspaper account of his death probably forty years before. He knew that Thomas Francis Meagher had been a revolutionist who had, after banishment, found asylum in the United States. The throwing off a ship in the dead of night of a soldier who, according to the story teller's notion, was on his way home to carry on a war of liberation was the climax of the story. "Will they ever find out who did it?" The query was from one who believed that secret and cunning forces were directed against the champion. Later, in the capitol grounds, the editor saw the monument to the first governor of Montana—a soldierly figure on horseback—and he contrasted the solidity of the historic figure with the vulnerability of the folk-hero.

That stories from bookish sources enter the Irish storyteller's repertoire cannot be gainsaid. A listener to a recital, a reader of a collection, often comes on a story out of *The Arabian Nights* or the Bible. Not infrequently in the Journal of the Folklore of Ireland Society, *Béaloideas,* the provenance of a story is given as "The Royal Hibernian Tales" which were in chapbooks distributed by peddlers in the eighteenth century. As these derived from traditional stories, their mere re-telling fitted them into the pattern. But popular books of more recent times also supply characters and incidents. Before the editor read Charles Kickham's *Knocknagow,* people in it were made present to him by a bookless man in County Longford.

All this is to say that there is an apparatus for transmitting tradition, that, as we get it, the tradition has a particular, a pervasive style,

---

* Robin Flower: *The Irish Tradition.* Oxford University Press. New York.

and, further, that that style can impose itself on matter coming from the outside. Irish expression is not exclusively of the countryside. But the culture of the countryside, the traditional culture, creates and fosters that which is most distinctive in Irish expression—the oral, the thing said rather than the thing written, the colorful, the extravagant, the dramatic.

In selecting the matter of this volume from a great concourse of tales, anecdotes and poems, of character and incident, the editor strives to invoke that figure that has such a salient place in Irish tradition—the *seanchaidhe* (shanachie). And he would keep in mind "the witty, inspired, improvising poet, and the poor scholar, travelling from house to house with his bag of books." He would try to keep the oral element dominant, giving a lilt of speech to the main portion of the collection. But there has to be a part that is not visited by the shanachie nor the poet and scholar of the fireside gathering. Irish lore—folklore or just popular lore—is not quite understandable without some knowledge of the development, frustration, and disaster of the community. To supply this knowledge, the editor has to draw from something outside the traditional sources—written history and written biography. He has also to include Irish character and Irish expression as it occurred in other countries. And talking of historians—there is one who is a shanachie among shanachies in the relation of historical episodes, Standish James O'Grady.

History and the perpetuation of an oral tradition may be cause and consequence. The present editor recollects (but he cannot set down the reference) a statement accounting for the fact that Germany preserved into the nineteenth century such a great store of folklore: it was that the Thirty Years' War put Germany back into the heroic age. In Ireland there must have been not one but a few reversions to the heroic age. Tudor warfare in the country gives the impression of more personal kinds of combat than in the rest of Western Europe at the time. The state of the country prevented the Renaissance from affecting ancient modes of feeling and expression that once belonged to the whole of Christendom. Then, with the destruction, expropriation and emigration of the great families who patronized them, the men learned in the old tradition had to betake themselves among the poor and the unlearned to the enhancement, one must believe, of the speech, the poetry, the witty discourse of the peasants' firesides. The sixteenth century ended with the destruction of the Gaelic social system through the unaccountable disaster of Kinsale. But a more dire ruin lay ahead. After the eleven years' warfare that Cromwell put an end to, the population of the country was reduced to one-sixth of what it had been before that warfare started, a reputable historian tells us. Wolf packs went through the length and breadth of the land, attacking debilitated people. How a heritage was passed on to following generations is something historians have left unexplained. Forty years afterwards armies were again engaged at the Boyne, Aughrim and Limerick. This war was followed by a continued emigration of young men to join the armed services on the Continent. Then came penal enactments through which Irish trade was destroyed and Catholics were outlawed—forbidden to give or receive education, to own land, or to enter any profession. This meant that all that was cultivated in "The Hidden Ireland" gathered round the turf fires and that learned poets confided work of an extraordinary mastery of language and verse-technique to schoolless men and women.

Music was part of the inheritance. Collectors got down this music that was composed for the harp and once played before an aristocratic audience. The assembly of tunes from fiddlers and pipers as well as from the last of the harpers made an immense collection. In quantity the unwritten literature, then uncollected, corresponded to the music. But for this material there were no enthusiasts. In the middle of the nineteenth century the whole of this traditional culture—music, unwritten literature, unwritten history—suffered a terrible diminution. The Famine of 1846-47 depopulated whole districts and took the spirit out of the Irish countryside. Writing immediately after that disaster, Sir William Wilde,* who was not only a medical practitioner but an antiquarian and an ethnologist, and who as an Irish speaker had access to the West of Ireland folklore, made this mournful statement.

"With depopulation the most terrific which any country has ever experienced on the one hand, and the introduction of railroads, colleges, industrial and other educational schools on the other—together with the rapid decay of the Irish vernacular, in which the most of our legends, romantic tales, ballads and bardic annals, and vestiges of Pagan rites, and relics of fairy charms were preserved—can superstitious practice continue to exist? But these matters of popular belief and folklore, these rites and legends and superstitions, were, after all, the poetry of the people, the bond that knit the peasant to the soil, and cheered and solaced many a cottier's fireside. . . ."

Forty years after the Famine, scholars began to move into districts where Gaelic was still a vernacular, and to set down the stories, poems, proverbs and charms that were current. An example was given to Ireland by a collector in the other Gaelic territory, by John Francis Campbell (Campbell of Islay), a true Gael whose heart was with the people of the Scottish Highlands and the Islands. His *Popular Tales of the West Highlands* is in every respect the most magnificent assembly of Gaelic folklore accessible in book form. An Irish-American scholar, Jeremiah Curtin, was commissioned by the editor of the New York *Sun* to collect the stories of the Gaelic-speaking districts in Ireland. He did this and published a voluminous collection.† Curtin

---

* Lady Wilde made English versions of some of the stories and proverbs he wrote down in Irish. Sir William and Lady Wilde were the parents of Oscar.

† The stories appeared originally in the Sunday Supplement of the *Sun*, 1892-1893. They were later published in two books: *Myths and Folk-Lore of Ireland* and *Tales of the Fairies and of the Ghost World*.

was one of those terrific Lavengros who can pick up a language by ear and use it extensively in a couple of weeks. He wrote down and translated the Zuni Indian chants; he translated long works from Polish and Russian; it would seem that Irish was just homework for him. Curtin has been blamed by Irish scholars for his inexact renderings of some terms. These are not of frequent occurrence, however. The real defect of his translations comes from his inability to get colloquial charm into his English. Another collector was William Larminie, a poet with a remarkable scholarly equipment: he wrote down in Irish and translated into English stories told in Donegal and Mayo. And then there was that poet and scholar who, when asked at his entrance into Dublin University what languages he knew, replied, "Latin, Greek, Hebrew" and added, "but I dream in Irish." This was Douglas Hyde. He loved and admired the people who held to the unwritten literature, and to him more than to any other person is due the fact that so much of the traditional culture has been saved and that a modern literature in Irish has come into existence. In his translations of folk poetry, particularly in his *Love Songs of Connacht,* he is unrivalled.

By the time a national government had come into being, people were awake to the necessity of getting down all that was left of the narratives, poems, proverbs, charms and histories that were still related orally in Irish and English. It was recognized that the work should be systematic and comprehensive, with headquarters, archives, publications. To serve these ends a Folklore Commission was set up with Professor Delargy as its head; its headquarters is the Folklore Institute in Dublin; a quarterly, *Béaloideas,* is published by The Folklore of Ireland Society in Irish and English, containing oral material as taken down by collectors and reviews of publications dealing with folklore.

This backing of the enterprise of a dozen scholars, this assembling of the lore of the people of the countryside with its enormous number of variants, might seem to be one of the state's less serious undertakings, but as the collection grows and as scholars interpret it, a new conception of the history of the Irish people begins to take shape: one can go beyond this and say that light is thrown on the history of the West European people. For the tradition so tenaciously held in the last outpost of Europe is not merely parochial. It is national, as Professor Delargy says. And this unwritten literature of Ireland once belonged to the whole of Western Europe: it is an international literature, the pre-Renaissance literature of Europe animated by the Gaelic spirit—"a survival of the ancient and mediaeval world of which men read in books, but which we in Ireland have the amazing advantage and privilege of studying at first hand from the living speech of the Irish countryside," to quote Professor Delargy once more.*

As a great deal in this book has another origin, a reader may wonder why so much space has been given in this introduction to the matter of countryside. The reason is—and the repetition may be needed to give the statement its due importance—that to the mind of the editor,

---

* J. H. Delargy: *The Dublin Magazine.* July-September, 1942.

Irish lore when distinctive has the oral style that has been formed or perpetuated in the countryside. This applies to northeast Ulster also. Only a few examples of this lore are given here, not because it is not extensive but because in general it merges with the lore of the rest of the country. Selections which the editor judged to be most distinctive are at the end of the section "The Face of the Land."

When an editor at Crown Publishers invited me to compile for its Folklore series *A Treasury of Irish Folklore*. I was hesitant. "I am not a folklorist," I told the editor, "I am a poet and a teller of stories." "But you are a man of the Irish countryside," he said, "and have an acquaintance with the traditional way of life out of which the folklore came." "But there is the discipline—the special discipline of the folklorist," I told him. "Do you know anyone with that discipline who will compile a treasury of Irish folklore for us?" he asked. I had that privilege. But it was then disclosed that the scholars in that field had commitments that prevented their taking up such a work.

Meanwhile the idea of a treasury of Irish Folklore had been put into my mind. It was seen, however, as a difficult undertaking. The folklore of Ireland—the stories, songs, jests, riddles, usages, charms that make the body of this unwritten literature—is very voluminous. And besides the unwritten literature there is matter that has influenced generations of Irish people that would have to be included in such a treasury—characters, occurrences, anecdotes, speeches, literary creations that have been absorbed into common discourse. And in compiling such a work for an American public, all these matters would have to be put into a perspective, and this would mean the insertion of passages of relevant history.

These difficulties made the assignment so challenging that I decided to take it up. I had had encounters with Irish folklore that gave me insights into the subject; these insights, though coming early in life, had never been lost, and had really never been neglected. I will here refer to their occasions.

Along the main roads of Ireland, ten or twenty miles from each other, are very solid buildings which are now County Homes but before the formation of the Irish State were Workhouses. Originally they were places of shelter for the destitute survivors of the great disaster of the Famine, and afterwards for families evicted from their farms through the operation of bad land laws. My father was master of a Workhouse on the road between Leinster and Connacht. I was born and lived the years of my childhood there. And I came to know as characters the "casuals" who took a night's shelter in the Workhouse. Many of them, men and women, had survived from a time when the folk tradition was pervasive—tinkers, ballad-singers, basket-makers, pipers, fiddlers, men and women itinerants. I must have heard their discourse as I loitered by the gate through which they entered or departed. In this way I became acquainted with ways of living and a fashion of speech and with some of the occupations that belonged to old-time Ireland.

Soon after this initiation I went to live in my grandmother's house on a small farm in County Cavan. The place had ceased to be Irish-speaking, but enough of the past remained to create a familiarity with the old tradition. The entertainment of the evening was the *celidh,* the group round the peat fire made up of visitors who relished conversation and had some pride in their ability to express themselves and to recall interesting personages, interesting episodes in local history. My grandmother knew traditional stories—some that I heard from her were beautiful—but she did not relate them in a professional way. However, her house had one visitor who could do just that, one who was the last shanachie of the district, the last professional storyteller and historian. In his house—it was a tumbledown cabin lighted only by a candle but more often by just the peat on the hearth—I heard stories told in the professional way, with the timing, the gestures, the stresses that belong to an ancient popular art.

And this side of my education was carried on by another person— my uncle-in-law whose business it was to attend the markets in towns around and buy fowl from farmers' wives and daughters, sending them to bigger markets for export. On days when I did not have to go to school, the fowl-buyer would let me come with him to this or that market-town. Such a place would never be without a ballad-singer singing or rather bawling across the street a "come-all-ye" (so called because the opening was generally "Come all ye tender Christians" or "Come all ye true-born Irishman"—one would be pathetic and the other rousing). In these matters the uncle-in-law was a real mentor; jogging home in his cart he would sing a dozen or so ballads out of his own repertoire. Such encounters gave me knowledge of some of the unwritten literature of the people with a good deal of relish for it.

My education in these matters was put on another level when I learned what Irish I know through sitting by firesides in Connemara and having the old folk lesson me with the aid of the books I brought to them—mainly Douglas Hyde's collections of the folk songs of Connacht. Here I realized the truth that is in the simple utterance quoted by him on a page of *The Love Songs of Connacht:*

A tune is more lasting than the voice of the birds,
A word is more lasting than the riches of the world.

Is buaine port ná glor na h-éun,
Is buaine focal na toice an t-saeghail.

Padraic Colum

New York

Part I

THE IRISH EDGE

A Cromwellian Settler Makes an
Irish Testament

"I, John Langley, born at Wincanton, in Somersetshire, and settled in Ireland in the year 1651, now in my right mind and wits, do make my will in my own handwriting. I do leave all my house, goods, and farm at Black Kettle of 253 acres to my son, commonly called 'Stubborn Jack,' to him and his heirs forever, provided he marries a Protestant, but not Alice Kenrick, who called me 'Oliver's whelp.' My new buckskin breeches and my silver tobacco stopper with 'J.L.' on the top I give to Richard Richards, my comrade, who helped me off at the storming of Clonmel when I was shot through the leg. My said son John shall keep my body above ground six days and six nights after I am dead; and Grace Kenrick shall lay me out, who shall have for so doing five shillings. My body shall be put upon the oak table in the brown room, and fifty Irishmen shall be invited to my wake and every one shall have two quarts of the best aqua vitae, and each one one skein, dish and knife before him, and when the liquor is out nail up the coffin, and commit me to the earth whence I came. This is my will; witness my hand this 3rd of March, 1674."

JOHN LANGLEY

From *My Clonmel Scrap Book*, compiled by James White. Dundalgan Press. Dundalk, Ireland.

Introduction

The editor is in a third-class railway carriage on a West of Ireland railway. The man who had left to get some refreshment at a stop comes back with a sandwich in his hand. Looking at it, he says earnestly, "Two slices of stale bread and a slice of ham between like an autumn leaf." Nowhere else, the editor realizes, could one hear such an expression. The passenger is not striving to be witty or humorous. He is passing a judgment on the sandwich in hand. His opinion is in reason, but the expression of that opinion is in terms of imagination.

The editor is seated with a countrywoman at the door of her cottage in an isolated place. Three young girls on their way to a dance come along. They adjust their head-shawls, showing off a little. "They are pretty girls," the editor says to the householder. "If they were hanged for their beauty, they'd die innocent," is her reply. This is a real piece of wit. She did not want to contradict one who is her guest. He has shown, however, that his standard of beauty leaves something to be desired. Her judgment of the beauty under consideration is reasonable, but the expression of it is imaginative.

When one puts imagination at the service of criticism, the result is apt to be a piece of malice, and Irish wit is often malicious. An illustration in a Dublin journal shows two farmers seated on a boundary fence. "I don't see a gap in the moon tonight," one says; and the other answers, "If you did you could let your cows in through it." This strikes at the farmer who would save forage by letting his cows into his neighbor's field through a gapped fence. But the reasonable stated in imaginative terms need not be malicious. To the Irish dramatist with the unlikely name of Dion Boucicault, a lady in New York said, "But you are not really an Irishman, Mr. Boucicault." "Madam, nature did me that honor."

The combination of reason and imagination is not only in the instances of wit and humor—there, of course, being brief, it is most effective; it is in all Irish discourse when that discourse is at its best. To George Berkeley, immaterialism rests on reason. But the argument is demonstrated by his imagination. "All the choir of heaven and the furniture of the earth, in a word, all those bodies which compose the mighty frame of the world, have not any subsistence without a mind." It is a far cry from the philosopher to the comic poet celebrating his Mollie Brallaghan:

The place where my heart was, you might easy rowl a turnip in,
It's the size of all Dublin and from that to the Divil's Glin.

3

The singer takes as reasonable the convention that a girl steals a man's heart. That reasonableness is given an imaginative issue: its outrageousness corresponds with the outrageousness of the convention.

Perhaps we could say that what is startling in Irish wit and humor and exciting in all forms of Irish discourse is the expression of a mind whose spiritual allegiance is to reason and whose linguistic allegiance is to imagination.—P.C.

———

A Man's Life

You see, my boy, a man's life naturally divides itself into three distinct periods. The first is that when he is planning and contriving all sorts of villainy and rascality; that is the period of youth and innocence. The second is that in which he is putting into practice the villainy and rascality he contrived before; that is the prime of life or the flower of manhood. The third and last period is that in which he is making his soul and preparing for another world; that is the period of dotage.

The Nature of Love

Well, now, he was really stupid with love; there wasn't a bit of fun left in him. He was good for nothing on earth but sitting under bushes, smoking tobacco and sighing till you'd wonder where he got the wind for it all. Now you might as well be persuading the birds against flying, or striving to coax the stars out of the sky into your hat, as to be talking commonsense to them that's fairly bothered and bursting with love. There's nothing like it. The toothache and colic together would compose you better for an argument; it leaves you fitted for nothing but nonsense. It's stronger than whiskey, for one good drop of it will leave you drunk for a year, and sick, begorra, for ten; it's stronger than the sea, for it will carry you around the world, and never let you sink in sunshine or in storm; and, begorra, it's stronger than Death himself, for it is not afeared of him, but dares him in every shape. But lovers do have their quarrels sometimes; and, begorra, when they do, you'd almost think they hated one another like man and wife.

Father Prout's Sermon

Somewhere in the Scriptures it is written that whoever gives to the poor lends to the Lord. There are three reasons why I don't tell you exactly where this may be found. In the first place, poor creatures that you are, few of you happen to have the authorized Douay edition, printed and published by Richard Coyne of Dublin, and certified as correct by Archbishop Troy, and the other heads of the Church in Ireland—few among you, I say, have *that*, though I know there is not a house in the parish without a loose song-book or the *History of the Irish Rogues*. In the second place, if ye had it, 'tis few of ye could read it, ignorant haythens that ye are. And in the third place, if every man-jack of ye did possess it, and could read it, (for the church still admits the possibility of miracles), it would not much matter at the present moment, because it happens that I don't quite remember in what part of it the text is to be found—for the wickedness of my flock has affected my memory, and driven many things clean out of my head, which it took me a deal of trouble to put into it when I was studying in foreign parts, years ago. But it don't matter. The fault is not mine, but yours, ye unnatural crew, and maybe you won't find it out, to your cost, before ye have been five minutes quit of this life. Amen.

"He who gives to the poor." Ye are not skilled in logic, nor indeed in anything I know except playing hurley in the fields, scheming at cards in public houses for half-gallons of porter, and defrauding your clergy of their lawful dues. What is worse, there's no use in trying to drive logic into your heads, for indeed that would be the fulfillment of another text that speaks of throwing pearls before pigs. But if ye *did* know logic—which ye don't—ye would perceive at once that the passage I have just quoted naturally divides itself into two branches. The first involves the *giving;* that is, rationally and syllogistically considered, what ye ought to do. And the second involves the *poor;* that is, the receivers of the gifts, or the persons for whom ye ought to do it.

First, then, as to the giving. Now it stands to reason that, as the Scripture says in some other place, the blind can't lead the blind, because maybe they'd fall into the bog-holes, poor things, and get drowned. And so, though there really is wonderful kindness to each

---

"Father Prout" was the invention of the humorous Francis Sylvester Mahony. This piece is not given in *The Reliques of Father Prout,* and so may be by an imitator of Mahony's. The editor took it from an old broadsheet.

other among them, it is not to be expected that the poor can give to
the poor. No, the givers must be people who have something to give,
which the poor have not. Some of ye will try and get off on this head,
and say that 'tis gladly enough ye'd give, but that really ye can't afford
it. Can't ye? If you make up your minds, any one of you, to give up
only a single glass of spirits, every day of your lives, see what it will
come to in the course of a year, and devote *that* to the Church—that is
to the Clergy—and it will be more than some of the well-to-do farmers,
whom I have in my eye at this blessed moment, have had the heart to
give me during the last twelve months. Why, as little as a penny a day
comes to more than thirty shillings in the year, and even that insignificant trifle I have not had from some of you that have the means and
ought to know better. I don't want to mention names, but Tom Murphy of the Glen, I am afraid I shall be compelled to name you before
the whole congregation, some day before long, if you don't pay up
your lawful dues. I won't say more now on that subject, for, as Saint
Augustine says, "A nod's as good as a wink to a blind horse."

Now, the moral of the first part being clearly shown, that all who
can give *ought* to give, the next branch is *to whom* should it be given?
The blessed text essentially states and declares "to the poor." Then
follows the inquiry, who's "the *poor*"? The whole matter depends on
that.

I dare say, ignorant as ye are, some of ye will think it's the beggars
and the cripples, and the blind travelers who contrive to get through
the length and breadth of the country, guided by Providence and a
little dog tied to their fingers by a bit of string. No, I don't want to
say one mortal word against that sort of cattle, or injure them in their
honest calling. God help them. It's their trade, their estate, their occupation, their business to beg—just as much as 'tis Pat Mulcahy's business to tailor, or Jerry Smith's to make carts, or Tom Shine's to shoe
horses, or Din Cotter's to make potheen, and my business to preach
sermons, and save your souls, ye heathens. But these aren't "the poor"
meant in the text. They're used to begging, and they like to beg, and
they thrive on begging, and I, for one, wouldn't be the man to disturb
them in the practice of their profession, and long may it be a provision
to them and to their heirs for ever. Amen.

Maybe, ye mean-spirited creatures, some among you will say that it
is yourselves is "the poor." Indeed, then, it isn't. Poor enough and
niggardly ye are, but you aren't the poor contemplated by holy Moses
in the text. Sure 'tis your nature to toil and to slave—sure 'tis what
ye're used to. Therefore, if any one were to give anything to *you*, he
would not be lending to the Lord in the slightest degree, but throw-

ing away his money as completely as if he lent it upon the security of land that's covered by the lakes of Killarney. Don't flatter yourselves, any of you, for a moment, that you are "the poor." I can tell you that you're nothing of the sort.

Now, then, we have found out who should be the givers. There's no mistake about *that*—reason and logic unite in declaring that every one of you, man, woman and child, should give, and strain a point to do it liberally. Next, we have ascertained that it's "the poor" who should receive what you give. Thirdly, we have determined who are *not* "the poor." Lastly, we must discover who *are*.

Let each of you put on his considering cap and think—well, I have paused that you might do so. Din Cotter is a knowledgeable man compared with the bulk of you. I wonder whether he has discovered who *are* "the poor." He shakes his head—but there is not much in *that*. Well, then, you give it up. You leave it to me to enlighten you all. Learn, then, to your shame, that it's the *Clergy* who are "the poor."

Ah! You perceive it now, do you? The light comes in through your thick heads, does it? Yes, it's I and my brethren is "the poor." We get our bread—coarse enough and dry enough it usually is—by filling you with spiritual food, and, judging by the congregation now before me, it's ugly mouths you have to receive it. We toil not, neither do we spin, but if Solomon in all his glory was not arrayed better than we are, instead of being clothed in vervain and fine linen, 'tis many a time he'd be wearing a threadbare black coat, white on the seams, and out at the elbows. It is the opinion of the most learned scholars and Doctors in Divinity, as laid down before the Council of Trent, that the translation is not sufficiently exact in regard of this text. And they recommend that for the words "the poor" we should substitute "the Clergy." Thus corrected, then the text would read "he who gives to the Clergy, lends to the Lord," which, no doubt, is the proper and undiluted Scripture.

The words of the text are thus settled, and you have heard my explanation of it all. Now for the application. Last Thursday was a week since the fair of Bartlemy, and I went down there to buy a horse, for this is a large parish, and mortification and fretting has puffed me up so, that God help me, 'tis little able I am to walk about to answer all the sick calls, to say nothing of stations, weddings, and christenings. Well, I bought the horse, and it cost me more than I expected, so that there I stood without a copper in my pocket after I had paid the dealer. It rained cats and dogs, and as I am so poor that I can't afford to buy a greatcoat, I got wet to the skin, in less than no time. There you were, scores of you, in the public houses, with the windows up, that all the world might see you eating and drinking as if it was for a wager. And there was not one of you who had the grace to ask, "Father Prout, have you got a mouth in your face?" And there I might have stood in the rain until this blessed hour (that is, supposing it had continued raining until now), if I had not been picked up by Mr. 'Mun Roche, of Kildinan, an honest gentleman, and a hospitable man I must say, though he is a Protestant. He took me home with him, and there, to your eternal disgrace, you villains, I got as full as a tick, and 'Mun had to send me home in his own carriage—which is an everlasting shame to all of you, who belong to the true Church.

Now, I asked, which has carried out the text? You who did not give me even a poor tumbler of punch, when I was like a drowned rat at Bartlemy, or 'Mun Roche, who took me home and filled me with the best of eating and drinking, and sent me to my own house, after that, in his own elegant carriage? Who best fulfilled the Scripture? Who lent to the Lord, by giving to his poor Clergy? Remember, a time will come when I must give a true account of you—and what can I say then? Won't I have to hang down my head in shame, on your account? 'Pon my conscience, it would not much surprise me, unless you greatly mend your ways, if 'Mun Roche and you won't have to change places on that occasion: *he* sit alongside of me, as a friend who had treated the poor Clergy well in this world, and *you* in a certain place, which I won't particularly mention now, except to hint that the little frost or cold you'll have in it, but quite the contrary. However, 'tis never too late to mend, and I hope that by this day week, it's quite another story I'll have to tell of you all. Amen.

The Parish Priest Reproves and Encourages His Flock: A Sermon

But though Father Hannigan had delivered his regular discourse after the first gospel, it was his habit to address a few homely words to the people at the conclusion of the Mass upon which we may call local and individual topics. He now turned round and began in his deep *big* voice, with "Now, what's this I was going to say to ye?"

He pressed the forefinger of his left hand against his temple, as if trying to recall something that had escaped his memory. "Ay! ay! ay! D'ye give up stealing the turf in the name o' God?"

From *Knocknagow, or The Homes of Tipperary*, by Charles J. Kickham, pp. 75-78. James Duffy & Co., Ltd. Dublin. 1887.

"Everyone," he continued after a pause, "must steal turf such weather as this that hasn't it of his own. But sure if ye didn't know it was wrong, ye wouldn't be telling it to the priest. And ye think it would be more disgraceful to beg than to steal it. That's a great mistake. No decent man would refuse his neighbour a hamper of turf such weather as this. And a poor man is not a beggar for asking a hamper of turf such weather as this when he can't get a day's work, and the Easter water bottles bursting. Ye may laugh, but Judy Manogue stopped me on the road yesterday to know what she ought to do. Her bottle of Easter water that she had under her bed was in a lump of ice, and the bottle—a big black bottle that often gave some of ye a headache—and maybe it wasn't without giving more of ye a heartache—before Judy took my advice and gave up that branch of her business: well, the big black bottle was split in two with the fair dint of the frost—under the poor woman's bed. And the Lord knows no Christian could stand without a spark of fire to keep the life in him—let alone looking at a household of children shivering and shaking, and he able and willing to work, and not a stroke of work to be got. But ye all know that stealing is bad, and ye ought fitter make your cases known to the priest, and maybe something might be done for ye. Pride is a good thing—decent, manly pride—and 'twill often keep a man from doing a mean act even when he's sorely tempted. Spirit is a good thing. But, take my word for it, there's nothing like honesty. And poverty, so long as it's not brought on by any fault of his own, need never bring a blush to a man's cheek. So, in the name of God, d'ye give up stealing the turf.

"Father O'Neill is against the beagles. He says 'tis a shame to hear the horn sounding, and see ye scampering over ditches and hedges on the Lord's Day. Well, I don't know what to say to that. 'Tis the only day ye have for diversion of any sort. And as long as ye are sure not to lose Mass, I won't say anything against the beagles. The farmers tell me they don't mind the loss to them to let their sons keep a dog or two. And if ye meet after Mass—mind, I say, *after* divine service—I don't see much harm in it. I'm told, too, that gentlemen of the neighborhood—that is, such of them as *are* gentlemen—don't object to it, as ye are honorable sportsmen and spare the hares. But then there's the hurling. There's a deal of bad blood when ye hurl the two sides of the river. If there's any more of the work that was carried on at the last match, ye'll be the disgrace of the country, instead of being, as ye are, the pride of the barony. 'Tis given up to the Knocknagow boys to be spirited and well-conducted as any in the country."

Father Hannigan turned towards the altar, and Phil Lahy was again advancing with the holy water, but after taking a pinch of snuff he resumed his address.

"I want ye to keep up the good name ye have. And talking of funerals reminds me of your conduct at the burying of that poor man ye brought to Kilrea the week before last. 'Twas a charitable thing to carry him thirteen miles through the teeming rain, and I know ye had pains in your shoulders the next morning after him. 'Twas a charitable thing to lay his poor old bones alongside of his wife and children, as it was his last wish—though he didn't have a chick or child living belonging to him. I say that was a charitable, Christian, Irish act—and may God reward ye for it. But that was no excuse for the way ye be-haved. The parish priest of Kilrea said such a set never came into his parish. And Ould Peg Naughton, that keeps the shebeen house at the church, declared to myself that, though she is there going on fifty-two years, 'twas the drunkenest little funeral she ever laid eyes on. Isn't that a nice cha-rac-ter ye are earning for yourselves? But I hope now you'll remember my words. And now I have one request to ask of ye. I want ye to promise that you'll dig the Widow Keating's stubbles for her. She hasn't a soul to do a hand's turn for her since her boy lost his health. Will ye promise me now that as soon as the weather is fitting ye'll dig the Widow Keating's stubbles? 'Tis short 'twill take ye if ye all join together."

There's Always a Good Reason

The day after my arrival on the Island, Tomas has been fishing all the morning over by Beiginis, and comes into the kitchen early in the afternoon carrying a large bream.

"That's a fine fish you have," I say.

"It's for you, for I thought on the first day of your coming back to the Island you should have a good fish for supper."

I take the fish and lay it down on the table, and begin to thank him in my halting Irish.

"Don't thank me till you've heard all my story," he says.

"Well," I say, "no story could make any difference in my thanks."

"Listen then. When I came back from fishing this morning I had

From *The Western Island, or The Great Blasket*, by Robin Flower, p. 17. Copy-right, 1945, by Oxford University Press, New York, Inc.

two bream, one larger and one smaller. The one there is not the larger of the two."

"How comes that?" I say, smelling a jest in the wind.

"Well, it was this way. I came into my house, and I laid the two fish down on the table, and I said to myself: 'Now which of these two fish shall I give the gentleman from London?' And there came into my head the old saying, 'When the Lord God made Heaven and Earth at the first, He kept the better of the two for himself.' And where could I find a higher example?"

Mr. Dooley on New Year's Resolutions

Mr. Hennessy looked out at the rain dripping in Archery Road, and sighed, "A-ha, 'tis a bad spell iv weather we're havin'."

"Faith, it is," said Mr. Dooley, "or else we mind it more thin we did. I can't remimber wan day fr'm another. Whin I was young, I niver thought iv rain or snow, cold or heat. But now th' heat stings an' the' cold wrenches me bones; an', if I go out in th' rain with less on me thin a ton iv rubber, I'll pay dear f'r it in achin' j'ints, so I will. That's what old age means; an' now another year has been put on to what we had befure, an' we're expected to be gay. 'Ring out th' old,' says a guy at th' Brothers' School. 'Ring out th' old, ring in the new,' he says. 'Ring out th' false, ring in th' thrue," says he. It's a pretty sintimint, Hinnissy; but how ar-re we goin' to do it? Nawthin'd please me betther thin to turn me back on th' wicked an' ingloryous past, rayform me life, an' live at peace with th' wurruld to th' end iv me days. But how th' divvle can I do it? As th' fellow says. 'Can th' leopard change his spots,' or can't he?

"You know Dorsey, iv coorse, th' crosseyed May-o man that come to this counthry about wan day in advance iv a warrant f'r sheep-stealin'? Ye know what he done to me, tellin' people I was caught in me cellar poorin' wather into a bar'l? Well, last night says I to mesilf, thinkin' iv Dorsey, I says: 'I swear that henceforth I'll keep me temper with me fellow-men. I'll not let anger or jealousy get th' betther iv me,' I says. 'I'll lave off all me old feuds; an' if I meet me inimy goin' down th' sthreet, I'll go up an' shake him be th' hand, if I'm sure he hasn't a brick in th' other hand.' Oh, I was mighty compliminthry to mesilf.

From *Mr. Dooley in Peace and War*, by Finley Peter Dunne, pp. 95-99. Copyright, 1898, by Small, Maynard & Co. Boston.

I set be th' stove dhrinkin' hot wans, an' ivry wan I dhrunk made me more iv a pote. 'Tis th' way with th' stuff. Whin I'm in dhrink, I have manny a fine thought; an', if I wasn't too comfortable to go an' look f'r th' ink-bottle, I cud write pomes that'd make Shakespeare an' Mike Scanlan think they were wur-rkin' on a dredge. 'Why,' says I, 'carry into th' new year th' hathreds iv th' old?' I says. 'Let th' dead past bury its dead,' says I. 'Tur-rn ye'er lamps up to th' blue sky,' I says. (It was rainin' like th' divvle, an' th' hour was midnight; but I give no heed to that, bein' comfortable with th' hot wans.) An' I wint to th' dure, an', whin Mike Duffy come by on number wan hundherd an' five, ringin' th' gong iv th' ca-ar, I hollered to him: 'Ring out th' old, ring in th' new.' 'Go back into ye'er stall,' he says, 'an' wring ye'ersilf out,' he says. 'Ye'er wet through,' he says.

"Whin I woke up this mornin', th' pothry had all disappeared, an' I begun to think th' las' hot wan I took had somethin' wrong with it. Besides, th' lumbago was grippin' me till I cud hardly put wan foot befure th' other. But I remimbered me promises to mesilf, and I wint out on th' sthreet, intindin' to wish ivry wan a 'Happy New Year,' an' hopin' in me hear-rt that th' first wan I wished it to'd tell me to go to th' divvle, so I cud hit him in th' eye. I hadn't gone half a block befure I spied Dorsey acrost th' sthreet. I picked up a half a brick an' put it in me pocket, an' Dorsey done th' same. Thin we wint up to each other. 'A Happy New Year,' says I. 'Th' same to you,' says he, 'an manny iv thim,' he says. 'Ye have a brick in ye'er hand,' says I. 'I was thinkin' iv givin' ye a New Year's gift,' says he. 'Th' same to you, an' manny iv thim,' says I, fondlin' me own ammunition. ' 'Tis even all around,' says he. 'It is,' says I. 'I was thinkin' las' night I'd give up me gredge again ye,' says he. 'I had th' same thought mesilf,' says I. 'But, since I seen ye'er face,' he says, 'I've con-cluded that I'd be more comfortable hatin' ye thin havin' ye f'r a friend,' says he. 'Ye're a man iv taste,' says I. An' we backed away fr'm each other. He's a Tip, an' can throw a stone like a rifleman; an', Hinnissy, I'm somethin' iv an amachoor shot with a half-brick mesilf.

"Well, I've been thinkin' it over, an' I've argied it out that life'd not be worth livin' if we didn't keep our inimies. I can have all th' frinds I need. Anny man can that keeps a liquor sthore. But a rale sthrong inimy, specially a May-o inimy,—wan that hates ye ha-ard, an' that ye'd take th' coat off yer back to do a bad tur-rn to,—is a luxury that I can't go without in me ol' days. Dorsey is th' right sort. I can't go by his house without bein' in fear he'll spill th' chimbly down on me head; an, whin he passes my place, he walks in th' middle iv th' sthreet, an' crosses himself. I'll swear off on annything but Dorsey. He's a good man, an' I despise him. Here's long life to him."

A Duel with Words

I was Registrar of the Dublin National Gallery at one time. My man came in and said: "Mr. George Moore to see you, sir." "Ah," said I to myself, "the famous novelist that everybody talks about and nobody reads, and of whom I've never read a word either!" . . . "Show him in," said I.

In ten more seconds George Moore stepped into my lovely office. There were three or four pictures on each of my walls, and a beautiful fire in the grate. Moore looked very carefully at all my pictures before he looked at me, and said: "Ah, copies, I presume."

"I think not," I replied, "but you are more of an expert than I am." Moore sat down. "You are an expert, *ex officio*," said he. "Oh, no," I answered. "I am merely a very superior official: my Director is Quattro-centro and my Board is Byzantine. They are our experts."

An odd thing happens when two writers meet. Without a word being uttered on the subject, each knows in thirty seconds whether the other has ever read a line of his work or not. Neither of us had, and we were both instantly aware that life is not perfect, but, while I was full of patience and hope, Moore was scandalised.

Still, literature was his subject, and this was so in a deeper sense than in any other writer I have ever met. In the way of being dedicated to the craft of writing, Moore was that. He lived for the prose way of thinking—wine, women and murder—and I am sure that when he was asleep he dreamed that he was writing a bigger and better book than any he had yet managed to produce. He loved the art of prose; for poetry he had the traditional reverence that we all have; but I fancy that he had small liking for it.

Poetry presents a problem to the prose men, for it can exist very energetically without character, without humour, it can even get along without action, where prose must have all of these. The novelist may often think of poetry as almost a complete destitution, or as the stock-in-trade of a beggarman: "Poetry is nothing written by no one."

"What are you working at now, Stephens?" said Moore.

From a radio broadcast, by James Stephens in 1949, printed in *The Irish Digest*, April, 1954, pp. 26-28. Dublin. Reprinted by permission of Mrs. James Stephens.

"This morning," I replied, "I translated the *County of Mayo*."

"That is my own county," said he, "and so I am interested. But, my dear Stephens, that poem has been translated so many times already, that you are wasting your, ah, talent, yes, perhaps talent, on a job that every literate person in Ireland has done before you."

"Why, Moore?" said I.

Here he broke in, "Don't you think, Stephens, that I have come to the years in which younger men should address me as Mr. Moore?"

"Certainly, Mr. Moore," said I—and he smiled a grave, fattish and reprobating smile at me.

"You were going to say," he prompted, turning on me his pale fattish face and his sloping, thinnish shoulders, and his air of listening to me almost as through a keyhole.

"Only, sir, that a translation is never completed until it has become a piece of original verse in the new tongue."

"That is an excellent and beautifully impossible definition," said Moore. "Perhaps," he went on, "you would like to say the verses to me. How many are there?" he added hastily.

"Only four," I answered, "and as it is about your own county, sir, you should be the first one to hear them."

"Thank you, Stephens," said he, unnecessarily, for I intended to say that poem to someone. So I said the little poem, and he praised it highly, mainly I think because I had called him "sir."

"I must leave you very soon," said he, "for I have a lunch engagement, but if you ever need literary advice, I hope you will write to me. In fact, I beg that you will do so, for I have a proposition to make to you."

"I am in need of advice right now, Mr. Moore," said I, "and although some might think the matter not literary I consider that everything that has to do with a speech problem has to do with literature."

Moore agreed. "Psychological problems," said he, "are women and religion and English grammar. All other problems are literary. Tell me the matter that is confusing you, Stephens."

"Well, sir," said I, "I have been invited to the first formal dinner party of my life."

"Your first dinner party?" he queried.

"I have eaten," I explained, "with every kind of person and at every kind of table, but I have never dined with anybody."

"At a dinner," said he, "formal or informal, you just eat your dinner."

"Oh, no, Mr. Moore," said I, "the problem has nothing to do with mastication and is quite a troublesome one. I shall be sitting at a strange table and on my right hand there will be a lady whom I have never seen before and may never see again."

"Quite," said he.

"On my left hand," I continued, "there will be another lady whom I've never seen before. In the name of heaven, Mr. Moore, what shall I say to these ladies?"

"Why," said Moore thoughtfully, "this is a problem that never struck me before. It is a very real one," said he, sitting up at me and at it. "If you were an Englishman," he went on, "you could talk a little about the weather, vaguely, you know, a number of Dirty Days and How are You's, and then you could say a few well-chosen words about the soup, and the meat, and subsequently about the pudding—pudding, Stephens."

"Dammit," said I.

"An Irishman," Moore said, "can always find something to say about the cattle, and the crops, the manure, and the . . . No, no," he continued energetically, "no manure—ladies think it is very strange stuff: they prefer to talk about the theaters, actors, I mean, and hats. I'll tell you, talk to the first woman about how pretty her dress is; say that you have never seen so lovely a dress in your life. Then turn to the other hussy, and say that she is the most beautiful person in the room. Admire her rings: don't ask her where she got them: never ask a woman where or how she got anything whatever; questions like that often lead to divorce proceedings. In short, Stephens, talk to them about themselves, and you are pretty safe."

He enlarged on this matter: "You may talk to them about their hair and their eyes and their noses, but," he interrupted hastily, "don't say anything whatever about their knees."

"I will not, Mr. Moore," said I fervently.

"In especial, Stephens, do not touch their knees under any circumstances."

"I will not, Mr. Moore."

"Restraint at a formal dinner party, Stephen, is absolutely necessary."

"I quite understand, sir."

"Moreover, Stephens, women are strangely gifted creatures in some respects, all women have a sense akin to absolute divination about their knees."

"Ah, sir?" I queried.

"When a woman's knee is touched, Stephens, however delicately, the lady knows infallibly whether the gentleman is really caressing her or whether he is only wiping his greasy fingers on her stocking. But

formal dinner parties are disgusting entertainments anyhow. Goodbye,
Stephens."

"Goodbye, Mr. Moore," said I fervently, "and thank you very much
for your help. I shall never forget those ladies' knees."

Moore smiled at me happily, almost lovingly. "Write to me about
this dinner party, Stephens."

"I shall certainly do so, Mr. Moore."

And that was our first meeting.

The Difference Between Youth and Age

. . . He chanced to lift his eyes from the ground and saw, far away, a
solitary figure which melted into the folding earth and reappeared
again in a different place. So peculiar and erratic were the movements
of this figure that the Philosopher had great difficulty in following it,
and, indeed, would have been unable to follow, but that the other
chanced in his direction. When it came nearer he saw it was a
young boy, who was dancing hither and thither in any and every direction. A bushy mound hid him for an instant, and the next they
were standing face to face staring at each other. After a moment's
silence the boy, who was about twelve years of age, and as beautiful as
the morning, saluted the Philosopher.

"Have you lost your way, sir?" said he.

"All paths," the Philosopher replied, "are on the earth, and so one
can never be lost—but I have lost my dinner."

The boy commenced to laugh.

"What are you laughing at, my son?" said the Philosopher.

"Because," he replied, "I am bringing you your dinner. I wondered
what sent me out in this direction, for I generally go more to the east."

"Have you got my dinner?" said the Philosopher anxiously.

"I have," said the boy: "I ate my own dinner at home, and I put
your dinner in my pocket. I thought," he explained, "that I might be
hungry if I went far away."

"The gods directed you," said the Philosopher.

"They often do," said the boy, and he pulled a small parcel from
his pocket.

The Philosopher instantly sat down, and the boy handed him the parcel. He opened this and found bread and cheese.

"It's a good dinner," said he, and commenced to eat. "Would you not like a piece also, my son?"

"I would like a little piece," said the boy, and he sat down before the Philosopher, and they ate together happily.

When they had finished the Philosopher praised the gods, and then said, more to himself than to the boy:

"If I had a little drink of water I would want nothing else."

"There is a stream four paces from here," said his companion. "I will get some water in my cap," and he leaped away.

In a few moments he came back holding his cap tenderly, and the Philosopher took this and drank the water.

"I want nothing more in the world," said he, "except to talk with you. The sun is shining, the wind is pleasant and the grass is soft. Sit down beside me again for a little time."

So the boy sat down, and the Philosopher lit his pipe.

"Do you live far from here?" said he.

"Not far," said the boy. "You could see my mother's house from this place if you were as tall as a tree, and even from the ground you can see a shape of smoke yonder that floats over our cottage."

The Philosopher looked but could see nothing.

"My eyes are not as good as yours are," said he, "because I am getting old."

"What does it feel like to be old?" said the boy.

"It feels stiff like," said the Philosopher.

"Is that all?" said the boy.

"I don't know," the Philosopher replied after a few moments' silence. "Can you tell me what it looks like to be young?"

"Why not?" said the boy, and then a slight look of perplexity crossed his face, and he continued, "I don't think I can."

"Young people," said the Philosopher, "do not know what age is, and old people forget what youth was. When you begin to grow old always think deeply of your youth, for an old man without memories is a wasted life, and nothing is worth remembering but our childhood. I will tell you some of the differences between being old and young, and then you can ask me questions, and so we will get at both sides of the matter. First, an old man gets tired quicker than a boy."

The boy thought for a moment, and then replied:

"That is not a great difference, for a boy does get very tired."

The Philosopher continued:

"An old man does not want to eat as often as a boy."

"That is not a great difference either," the boy replied, "for they both do eat. Tell me the big difference."

"I do not know it, my son; but I have always thought there was a big difference. Perhaps it is that an old man has memories of things which a boy cannot even guess at."

"But they both have memories," said the boy, laughing, "and so it is not a big difference."

"That is true," said the Philosopher. "Maybe there is not so much difference after all. Tell me things you do, and we will see if I can do them also."

"But I don't know what I do," he replied.

"You must know the things you do," said the Philosopher, "but you may not understand how to put them in order. The great trouble about any kind of examination is to know where to begin, but there are always two places in everything with which we can commence—they are the beginning and the end. From either of these points a view may be had which comprehends the entire period. So we will begin with the things you did this morning."

"I am satisfied with that," said the boy.

The Philosopher then continued:

"When you awakened this morning and went out of the house what was the first thing you did?"

The boy thought—

"I went out, then I picked up a stone and threw it into the field as far as I could."

"What then?" asked the Philosopher.

"Then I ran after the stone to see could I catch up on it before it hit the ground."

"Yes," said the Philosopher.

"I ran so fast that I tumbled over myself into the grass."

"What did you do after that?"

"I lay where I fell and plucked handfuls of the grass with both hands and threw them on my back."

"Did you get up then?"

"No, I pressed my face into the grass and shouted a lot of times with my mouth against the ground, and then I sat up and did not move for a long time."

"Were you thinking?" said the Philosopher.

"No, I was not thinking or doing anything."

"Why did you do all these things?" said the Philosopher.

"For no reason at all," said the boy.

"That," said the Philosopher triumphantly, "is the difference between age and youth. Boys do things for no reason, and old people do not. I wonder do we get old because we do things by reason instead of instinct?"

"I don't know," said the boy, "everything gets old. . . ."

How O'Connell Won the Championship of Billingsgate

There was at that time in Dublin, a certain woman, Biddy Moriarty, who had a huckster's stall on one of the quays nearly opposite the Four Courts. She was a virago of the first order, very able with her fist, and still more formidable with her tongue. From one end of Dublin to the other, she was notorious for her powers of abuse, and even in the provinces Mrs. Moriarty's language had passed into currency. The dictionary of Dublin slang had been considerably enlarged by her, and her voluble impudence had almost become proverbial. Some of O'Connell's friends, however, thought that he could beat her at the use of her own weapons. Of this, however, he had some doubts himself, when he listened once or twice to some minor specimens of her Billingsgate. It was mooted once where the young Kerry barrister could encounter her, and some one of the company rather too freely ridiculed the idea of his being able to meet the famous Madame Moriarty. O'Connell never liked the idea of being put down, and he professed his readiness to encounter her, and even backed himself for the match. Bets were offered and taken and it was decided that the matter should come off at once.

The party adjourned to the huckster's stall, and there was the owner herself, superintending the sale of her small wares—a few loungers and ragged idlers were hanging around her stall, for Biddy was a character and in her way was one of the sights of Dublin. O'Connell commenced the attack.

"What's the price of this walking-stick, Mrs. What's-your-name?"

"Moriarty, sir, is my name, and a good one it is; and what have you to say agen it? One-and-sixpence 's the price of the stick. Troth, it's chape as dirt, so it is."

"One-and-sixpence for a walking stick; whew! why, you are not better than an impostor, to ask eighteen pence for what cost you two pence."

Reprinted from *Madden's Revelations of Ireland* in *Irish Wit and Wisdom*, pp. 49-52. P. M. Haverty, Publishers. New York. 1877.

"Two pence, your grandmother! Do you mane to say it's chating the people I am? Impostor, indeed!"

"I protest as I am a gentleman . . ."

"Jintleman! Jintleman! The likes of you a jintleman! Wisha, by gor, that bangs Banagher. Why, you potato-faced pippin-sneezer, when did a Madagascar monkey like you pick up enough of common Christian dacency to hide your Kerry brogue?"

"Easy now, easy now," said O'Connell with imperturbable good humour, "don't choke yourself with fine language, you whiskey-drinking parallelogram."

"What's that you call me, you murderin' villain?" roared Mrs. Moriarty.

"I call you," answered O'Connell, "a parellelogram; and a Dublin judge and jury will say it's no libel to call you so."

"Oh, tare-an'-ouns! Oh, Holy Saint Bridget! that an honest woman like me should be called a parrybellygrum to her face. I'm none of your parrybellygrums, you rascally gallows-bird; you cowardly, sneakin', plate-lickin' blaguard!"

"Oh, not you, indeed! Why, I suppose you'll deny that you keep a hypotenuse in your house."

"It's a lie for you. I never had such a thing. . . ."

"Why, sure all your neighbours know very well that you keep not only a hypotenuse, but that you have two diameters locked up in your garret, and that you go out to walk with them every Sunday, you heartless old heptagon."

"Oh, hear that, ye saints in glory! Oh, there's bad language from a fellow that wants to pass for a jintleman. May the divil fly away with you, you micher from Munster, and make celery-sauce of your rotten limbs, you mealy-mouthed tub of guts."

"Ah, you can't deny the charge, you miserable sub-multiple of a duplicate ratio."

"Go, rinse your mouth in the Liffey, you nasty tickle-pincher; after all the bad words you speak, it ought to be dirtier than your face, you dirty chicken of Beelzebub."

"Rinse your own mouth, you wicked-minded old polygon—to the deuce I pitch you, you blustering intersection of a superficies!"

"You saucy tinker's apprentice, if you don't cease your jaw, I'll . . ." But here she gasped for breath, unable to hawk up more words.

"While I have a tongue, I'll abuse you, you most inimitable periphery. Look at her, boys! There she stands—a convicted perpendicular in petticoats! There's contamination in her circumference, and she trembles with guilt down to the extremities of her corollaries. Ah, you're found out, you rectilinealantecedent, and equiangular old hag! 'Tis with the devil you will fly away, you porter-swiping similitude of the bisection of a vortex!"

Overwhelmed with this torrent of language, Mrs. Moriarty was silenced. Catching up a saucepan, she was aiming at O'Connell's head, when he made a timely retreat.

"You've won your wager, O'Connell, here's your bet," said the ones who proposed the contest.

A Story about King Solomon

"The first person who comes to me with news of my mother's death, I will take his head off," quoth Solomon.

A brother of his, a fool, said that he himself would come with news to Solomon of his mother's death.

All went well until she died.

The brother came with a bag of shore-sand and began throwing it against the window from the outside.

"Who is that?" inquired Solomon.

"You brother, the *amadan!*"

"That is February corn or shore-sand you have," said Solomon. "Have you any other news?"

"The trees are gone!"

"There must have been a great wind. Have you any news except that?"

"Yes, the mill that ground the very first corn for you was broken last night."

"That is the same as saying my mother is dead," replied Solomon.

"The death of your mother is in your own mouth: you can kill yourself now, or not mind it," said the fool, as he departed.

Enri O Muirgheasa, in *Béaloideas*, Journal of the Folklore of Ireland Society. Dublin. 1927. A story told by Thomas Corrigan, the last of the Farnie shanachies.

Mr. Dooley on Criminals

"Lord bless my sowl," said Mr. Dooley, "childher is a gr-reat risponsibility,—a gr-reat risponsibility. Whin I think iv it, I praise th' saints I niver was married, though I had opporchunities enough whin I was a young man; an' even now I have to wear me hat low whin I go down be Cologne Sthreet on account iv th' Widow Grogan. Jawn, that woman'll take me dead or alive. I wake up in a col' chill in th' middle iv th' night, dhreamin' iv her havin' me in her clutches.

"But that's not here or there, avick. I was r-readin' in th' pa-apers iv a lad be th' name iv Scanlan bein' sint down th' short r-road f'r near a lifetime; an' I minded th' first time I iver see him,—a bit iv a curly-haired boy that played tag around me place, an' 'd sing 'Blest Saint Joseph' with a smile on his face like an angel's. Who'll tell what makes wan man a thief an' another man a saint? I dinnaw. This here boy's father wurrked fr'm morn till night in th' mills, was at early mass Sundah mornin' befure th' alkalis lit th' candles, an' niver knowed a month whin he failed his jooty. An' his mother was a sweet-faced little woman, though fr'm th' County Kerry, that nursed th' sick an' waked th' dead, an' niver had a hard thought in her simple mind f'r anny iv Gawd's creatures. Poor sowl, she's dead now. May she rest in peace!

"He didn't git th' shtreak fr'm his father or fr'm his mother. His brothers an' sisters was as fine a lot as iver lived. But this la-ad Petey Scanlan growed up fr'm bein' a curly-haired angel f'r to be th' toughest villyun in th' r-road. What was it at all, at all? Sometimes I think they'se poison in th' life iv a big city. Th' flowers won't grow here no more thin they wud in a tannery, an' th' bur-rds have no song; an' th' childher iv dacint men an' women come up hard in th' mouth an' with their hands raised again their kind.

"Th' la-ad was th' scoorge iv th' polis. He was as quick as a cat an' as fierce as a tiger, an' I well raymimber him havin' laid out big Kelly that used to thravel this post,—'Whistlin' Kelly that kep' us awake with imitations iv a mockin' bur-rd,—I well raymimber him scuttlin' up th' alley with a score iv polismin laborin' afther him, thryin' f'r a shot at him as he wint around th' bar-rns or undher th' thrucks. He slep' in th' coalsheds afther that until th' poor ol' man cud square it with th' loot. But, whin he come out, ye cud see how his face had

From *Mr. Dooley in Peace and War,* by Finley Peter Dunne, pp. 124-129. Copyright, 1898, by Small, Maynard and Co. Boston.

hardened an' his ways changed. He was as silent as an animal, with a sideways manner that watched ivrything. Right here in this place I seen him stand f'r a quarther iv an' hour, not seemin' to hear a dhrunk man abusin' him, an' thin lep out like a snake. We had to pry him loose.

"Th' ol' folks done th' best they cud with him. They hauled him out iv station an' jail an' bridewell. Wanst in a long while they'd dhrag him off to church with his head down: that was always afther he'd been sloughed up f'r wan thing or another. Between times th' polis give him his own side iv th' sthreet, an' on'y took him whin his back was tur-rned. Thin he'd go in the wagon with a mountain iv thim on top iv him, swayin' an' swearin' an' sthrikin' each other in their hurry to put him to sleep with their clubs.

"I mind well th' time he was first took to be settled f'r good. I heerd a noise in th' ya-ard, an' thin he come through th' place with his face dead gray an' his lips just a turn grayer. 'Where ar-re ye goin', Petey?' says I. 'I was jus' takin' a short cut home,' he says. In three minyits th' r-road was full iv polismin. They'd been a robbery down in Halsted Sthreet. A man that had a grocery sthore was stuck up, an' whin he fought was clubbed near to death; an' they'd r-run Scanlan through th' alleys to his father's house. That was as far as they'd go. They was enough iv thim to've kicked down th' little cottage with their heavy boots, but they knew he was standin' behind th' dure with th' big gun in his hand; an', though they was manny a good lad there, they was none that cared f'r that short odds.

"They talked an' palavered outside, an' telephoned th' chief iv polis, an' more pathrol wagons come up. Some was f'r settin' fire to th' buildin', but no wan moved ahead. Thin th' fr-ront dure opened, an' who shud come out but th' little mother. She was thin an' pale, an' she had her apron in her hands, pluckin' at it. 'Gintlemin,' she says, 'what is it ye want iv me?' she says. 'Liftinant Cassidy,' she says, ' 'Tis sthrange f'r ye that I've knowed so long to make scandal iv me befure me neighbors,' she says. 'Mrs. Scanlan,' says he, 'we want th' boy. I'm sorry, ma'am, but he's mixed up in a bad scrape, an' we must have him,' he says. She made a curtsy to thim, an' wint indures. 'Twas less than a minyit befure she come out, clingin' to th' la-ad's ar-rm. 'He'll go,' she says. 'Thanks be, though he's wild, they'se no crime on his head. Is there, dear?' 'No,' says he, like th' game kid he is. Wan iv th' polismin stharted to take hold iv him, but th' la'ad pushed him back; an' he wint to th' wagon on his mother's ar-rm."

"And was he really innocent?" Mr. McKenna asked.

"No," said Mr. Dooley. "But she niver knowed it. Th' ol' man come home an' found her: she was settin' in a big chair with her apron in her hands and th' picture iv th' la-ad in her lap."

How Two Irish Emissaries Came to a British Prime Minister Who Was Also a Fellow-Celt

"What happened?" I asked.

Harry, with his love of the dramatic, re-enacted the scene.

"We arrived at Gairloch, having driven sixty miles in an open car, perished. I said to Joe, 'If he asks me to take a drink, I'll be hard put to it to keep the promise I made to myself.' Outside the house was a *Daily Mail* man who asked us if we were from Ireland. When I said, 'Yes,' he said, 'He'll give you two republics today. He's after catching a ten-pound salmon.' Just then Lloyd George came around a corner of the house, a lively little man with pink cheeks like a baby, clear blue eyes and venerable flowing soft white hair. He literally ran to us, crying, 'Are you the boys from Ireland?' We said we were and he shook our hands warm-heartedly and impulsively. 'Wait till I show you the salmon I caught,' he said. He ran off and returned holding the salmon aloft. 'Isn't it grand?' he cried. He handed the salmon to someone standing by and ushered us into a room. 'Have a drink,' he said. 'I have some good Irish whiskey.' No, we weren't drinking. 'Sherry?' No, no sherry either. 'As you will. Sit down and make yourselves at home. You know I'm always glad to meet an Irishman. I know where I am with them, being a Celt myself. I can never feel the same with these cold-hearted Saxons.' He talked for a while on the superiority of the Celtic character over that of the Anglo-Saxon and then turned to us gleefully, like a boy expecting a new toy.

"Well, I hope you've got good news for me.'

"Joe gave him the letter and he began to read it. His face grew serious as he ran down the page. Still reading the letter, he sat down frowning. Then he collapsed.

" 'My God!' he groaned. 'My God! He can't mean this.' He glanced at the letter again and put his hand wearily to his head. 'After all I said to him he does this to me. You must alter this letter, boys.' Joe

From *Allegiance*, by Robert Brennan, pp. 316-319. Browne & Nolan. Dublin. 1950. Reprinted by permission of the author. As related by Harry Boland to Robert Brennan.

explained that his instructions were not to interpret the contents of the letter. Lloyd George sat for a while as if dazed and I began to pity him. 'A chance missed,' he said and he repeated this three or four times. 'A wonderful chance missed.' He was very sad. 'Here we had a unique opportunity. I was at the head of a coalition government with the Tories in the leash. I could have given de Valera all the realities he wanted, an Ireland with its own Gaelic system of education, its own army and police force, its own flag, its own anthem, the wherewithal to work out its own destiny as a free and independent Gaelic nation, and this man spurns it all for a phrase. I asked him not to use that phrase—a sovereign nation—which means nothing at all if you do not have the essentials. He could have had everything but the name, and he throws it away. He throws me, too, on the scrapheap. Today I was the Prime Minister of the strongest government Britain has had for generations. Tomorrow, when this letter sees the light of day, I will no longer be Prime Minister but merely a country solicitor.' He was pacing up and down, speaking more to himself than to us, the picture of a man in a desperate fix.

" 'What's the alternative?' he went on. 'I resign and let loose the dogs of war in Ireland. No, let the Wilsons, the Birkenheads, and the Churchills have their way. They boast they'll make Ireland a desert and who's going to stop them? Not de Valera! Not me! My power's at an end.'

"All the time we were getting more and more miserable. Lloyd George turned to us.

" 'Could you not appeal to him to alter this letter?'

" 'It would be no use,' Joe said. 'The Dail is meeting today to sanction it.'

"Lloyd George, who had sat down, jumped to his feet excitedly. 'That must be stopped,' he cried. 'That must be stopped at all costs. You must telephone to him. There is too much at stake in this to have it lost over any pettifogging. We can save the day for Ireland and Britain both. We can do it, but that letter must be altered. Look, I'll tell you what I'll do. I'll take the attitude I have not read this letter, you telephone to de Valera telling him to alter it. Get back there and tell him the situation. He must see it. He must see it!'

"We were doubtful, and he said, 'You want to discuss this alone. Very well, I'll go. Ring that bell when you want me!' He went off and left us and there we were with the destiny of a nation in our hands and we had only to ring the bell for the Prime Minister to save it. We decided to telephone Dublin and report what he had said, and we rang the bell. When he came in he was all smiles and encouragement.

" 'Send that message,' he said, 'and believe me, boys, we'll save the day for Ireland.'

"So that's how it happened," concluded Harry. "Is Dev raging?"

"Well, he's knocked about," I said. "He thought you were bringing back the letter."

"No damn fear," said Joe.

In Blackrock, Harry and I invaded Dev's bedroom. He was asleep, but woke up as we entered.

"The message was bungled," said Harry.

Dev glanced at his dejected countenance.

"Don't worry," he said kindly.

"If you knew what he said," began Harry, and Dev stopped him.

"I know," he said, "he told you he was a Celt, he wanted us to have a free Gaelic civilization. He was holding back the British bulldog from destroying us. He said all that to me. He said that if he accepted my terms, he would no longer be Prime Minister, and I said if I accepted less, I would no longer be President of the Irish Republic."

"If he didn't mean what he said," said Harry, "he must be the greatest actor that was ever born."

"Of course he is," said Dev. "After all, the man who beat Clemenceau and Wilson and Orlando is no joke. All right, Harry. There's no harm done. Go and get your breakfast."

Two of a Kind

The individual spoken of drew a chair to the fire, scowling at Barney as if he considered him an intruder. It could be seen at a glance that Dan Brit was not a model of sobriety. After eyeing Barney in silence for a minute, he was turning to the girl to order a pint of porter, when he looked again at him and hesitated. In fact, Dan Brit was debating with himself whether if he ventured to ask Barney to take a drink, Barney was the sort of a person to say afterwards, "Let us have another." And in case he was the man to say so, Dan Brit had his mind made up to call back the girl just as she was going for two pints of porter, saying, "Kitty, I'll take a glass of the old malt; I'm not

---

From *Knocknagow, or The Homes of Tipperary*, by Charles J. Kickham, pp. 189-191. James Duffy & Co., Ltd. Dublin. 1887.

very well today." And so Dan Brit would have a glass of whiskey, price threepence, in exchange for a pint of porter, price three-half-pence; which, in a social and friendly way, and, in the spirit of a "good fellow" he was thinking of pressing Barney to accept at his hand.

And while Dan Brit was pondering the risks to be run in this matter, his eye fell upon Barney's foot on the hob, which object seemed to fascinate Dan Brit and drive all other subjects out of his thoughts for the time being.

"The divil so ugly a foot as that," said Dan Brit solemnly, "I ever see, anyhow."

"There's an uglier one in the house," rejoined Barney.

"No, not in Ireland," returned Dan. "Nor in Europe, Asia, Africa, or America."

"Will you bet a quart of porter?" said Barney.

"That there's not an uglier foot in the house?" exclaimed Dan, staring in astonishment at him.

"Yes," said Barney with spirit, "I'll wager a quart of porter, and let Kitty be the judge, that there's an uglier foot in the house."

"Done!" exclaimed Dan Brit, who grasped the certainty of getting a drink without paying for it. "But will you stake the money?"

"Ay, will I," said Barney, suiting the action to the word, and slapping down the coppers on the chair near him.

"Take the money, Kitty," said Dan Brit, "an' decide the bet."

"What is the bet?" Kitty asked.

It was explained to her; and Kitty shook her head sorrowfully, and told Barney he was always a fool.

"Stake the money yourself," said Barney. And Dan did so.

"Come, give me back that change," said Dan, "an' bring the drink. The bet is mine."

"Wait a bit," returned Barney. "Kitty, give us a peep at your own."

"What impudence you have!" exclaimed Kitty indignantly. "Who dare say a word agin them, I'd like to know." And Kitty exhibited a pair of very presentable feet.

"Begob, Kitty," said Barney with a grin, "if I was dependin' on them, I'd lose my bet."

"An' do you mane to say you haven't lost it?" Dan asked. "Run, Kitty, for the porther."

"Ay, will she; but 'tisn't my money 'll pay for it."

"Didn't you bet there was an uglier foot in the house than that?" And Dan Brit pointed to the foot on the hob.

"I did."

"An' where is it?"

Barney slowly and deliberately drew his other foot from under the chair, and held it up to view.

"Here's your money, Barney," exclaimed Kitty, in an ecstasy of delight. "You won the bet; I'll go for the porter."

Dan Brit's jaw fell down as he stared with open mouth at Barney. And after swallowing his share of the porter, he walked away with an expression of countenance which made Kitty observe that "wan'd think 'twas a physic o' salts he was afther swallyin'."

Irish Justice

It was an abduction case, the offense being of a purely technical character. Having listened patiently to the evidence, the judge, Lord Morris, addressing the Court, said, "I am compelled to direct you to find a verdict of guilty in this case, but you will easily see that I think it a trifling thing which I regard as quite unfit to occupy my time. It is more valuable than yours—at any rate it is much better paid for. Find, therefore, the prisoner guilty of abduction, which rests, mind ye, on four points—the father was not averse, the mother was not opposed, the girl was willing, and the boy conveynient." The judge sentenced him to remain in the dock until the rising of the Court. Hardly had he delivered sentence when, turning to the High Sheriff, Lord Morris said, "Let us go," and, looking at the prisoner, "Marry the girl at once, and God bless ye both."

How the Farmer Got Free Pasturage from the Astronomer

Sir William Rowan Hamilton, the discoverer of the calculus of quaternions, as Astronomer Royal had tenure of some acres of grassland round Dunsink Observatory. To provide milk for his household he put a cow to graze it. In due season the cow's yield lessened. The astronomer consulted a near-by farmer about the decrease. "Why, your cow is just pining away through loneliness," the farmer told him.

From "Obituary of Lord Morris of Killanin," in *The Gael,* October, 1901, p. 321. New York.

By the editor from oral tradition.

"What should I do about it?" "Put more cows to graze with her. But leave that to me," said the farmer, "I have some extra cows I can put with her." "How much will you charge for that?" "Well, seeing it is you, Sir William, I'll loan you my cows without any charge." Very much impressed with the good fellowship of farmers, the astronomer went back to his observatory.

Queen Victoria's After-Dinner Speech

As overheard and cut into lengths of poetry by Jamesy Murphy, deputy assistant waiter at the Viceregal Lodge.

> Me loving subjects, sez she
> Here's my best respects, sez she,
> And I'm proud this day, sez she,
> Of the illigant way, sez she,
> You gave me the hand, sez she
> Whin I came to land, sez she.
> There was some people said, sez she,
> That I was greatly in dread, sez she
> I'd be murthered or shot, sez she,
> As like as not, sez she,
> But 'tis mighty clear, sez she
> 'Tis not over here, sez she,
> I've cause to fear, sez she.
> 'Tis them Belgiums, sez she,
> That's throwin' bombs, sez she,
> And scarin' the life, sez she,
> Out o' me son and the wife, sez she.
> But in these parts, sez she,
> They've warrum hearts, sez she,
> Barrin' Anna Parnell, sez she.
> I dunno, Earl, sez she
> What's come to the girl, sez she,
> An' that other wan, sez she,
> That Maud Gonne, sez she,
> Dressin' in black, sez she,
> To welcome me back, sez she.

From *Prose Poems and Parodies of Percy French*, edited by his sister, Mrs. De Burgh Daly, pp. 55-57. The Talbot Press. Dublin. 1929.

Though I don't care, sez she
What they wear, sez she,
An' all that gammon, sez she,
About me bringin' famine, sez she.
Now Maud 'ill write, sez she,
That I brought the blight, sez she,
Or altered the saysons, sez she
For some private raysons, sez she.
An' I think there's a slate, sez she
Off Willie Yeats, sez she.
He should be at home, sez she,
French polishin' a pome, sez she,
An' not writin letters, sez she,
About his betters, sez she,
Paradin' me crimes, sez she
In the Irish *Times,* sez she,
But what does it matter? sez she
This magpie chatter, sez she,
When that welcomin' roar, sez she,
Came up from the shore, sez she,
Right over the foam, sez she,
'Twas like comin' home, sez she,
An' me heart fairly glowed, sez she,
Along the Rock Road, sez she,
To Buttherstown, sez she,
Till I came to the ridge, sez she,
Of the Leeson Street Bridge, sez she,
An' I was welcomed in style, sez she
By the beautiful smile, sez she,
Of me Lord Mayor Pile, sez she.
Faith, if I'd done right, sez she,
I'd make him a knight, sez she.
Now pass the jug, sez she,
An' fill up each mug, sez she,
Till I give you a toast, sez she,
At which you may boast, sez she.
I've a power o' sons, sez she,
All sorts of ones, sez she,
Some quiet as cows, sez she,
Some always in rows, sez she.
An' the one gives most trouble, sez she,
The mother loves double, sez she.

How Aristotle Outwitted His Wife

It is said that Aristotle was the most learned and knowledgeable man of his time. He had the skill to solve every problem. He knew many things that no one else did. Therefore his name had great fame and renown. But for all his cleverness he failed to cure one thing that happened to him, and that was love. He was in love with a young lady and he could not get any cure for his love but to marry the woman. He was not too long married before his wife noticed that he had much greater fame than she had. Jealousy and envy of her husband seized her, for she desired to get for herself the knowledge and learning of Aristotle.

One day she came to him and spoke softly and gently to him. "We gave each other our love," she said, "when we were young, and now that we are married I want our love to be as it was, and it will not so be henceforth unless I get what I want."

Aristotle spoke to her and asked her what was troubling her.

" 'Tis this," she said. "I will not spend another day with you as your wife unless I get from you your knowledge and learning."

"That is a thing I cannot give you, good woman," said Aristotle. "For it would be death to myself."

"If I do not get it by favor," she said, "I will get it by force." And she fell into a rage and a passion against him.

Aristotle waited awhile in meditation. He said in his own mind that no one had ever overcome a furious woman. Finally he spoke to her.

"I am of a mind to give you my knowledge, but it will take me a day and a night to tell it to you." Joy and jubilation entered her heart and she was quieted.

"Bring here a gray stone," said Aristotle, "and set it down here in my presence." She brought the stone and set it down before him.

"Now, good woman," said he, "you must sit on the stone with your skin touching it."

She was nothing loath. She sat down on the stone without anything between it and her. Then Aristotle began to tell her and she to write. But she was not long sitting on the stone when she complained of the cold going through her.

Robin Flower. in *Béaloideas,* Journal of the Folklore of Ireland Society. Dublin. 1929. A folk tale from the Blasket Islands.

"Never mind that," said Aristotle. "You must suffer to get the knowledge from me."

He did not move from the chair in which he sat but kept on telling and she writing. But she had not written much when the pen fell from her hand.

"I am dying," she said.

"You are not indeed," said Aristotle. "Continue a while; you have not yet all the knowledge."

But if she did, she had not written all the learning and the knowledge when her soul departed from her on the stone.

"So," said Aristotle, "all your knowledge is set aside, for if you had the victory over me I would not have lived."

Irish Bulls: Definition

Blunders in speech used to be called "Irish bulls." A lady seated beside the Provost of Dublin University said, "Dr. Mahaffy, would you tell me what is the difference between an Irish bull and another bull?" "Madam," said Dr. Mahaffy, "an Irish bull is pregnant."

Irish Bulls: Example

In a debate in the Irish House of Commons, Sir Boyle Roache declared, "The profligacy of the age is such that we see little children not able to walk or talk running about the streets and cursing their Maker."

Brendan Behan: Master of the Irish Edge

The first time I encountered Brendan Behan he tried to insult me. The occasion was my appearance at a relative's house on the day of a funeral. His grandmother-in-law, Blanaid Salkeld, a poet and a person whom I liked very much, had died, and I had come to offer my condolence. I hadn't been at the funeral because I had had influenza and

---

By the editor from oral tradition.

Ibid.

By the editor.

the day was rainy. I was talking with Cecil Salkeld, his father-in-law, when Brendan, with other members of the family, came in. "Why weren't you at the funeral?" he demanded. I explained. "She liked you, but why the Hell she liked you I never could make out." He had a bottle of champagne, and he offered me a glass. Now, I don't like drinking champagne at funerals. I made an excuse. "I don't drink in the mornings." He was at a loss as to what further uncomplimentary things he could say to me, but when he had taken his glass he remembered something that made me dislikable to him. There had been an interview with me on the radio, and I had mentioned I was born in a workhouse. To take away the romantic significance that might be attached to such a nativity, I added that my father had been master of the workhouse at the time. "So you're the son of the master," prodded Brendan, and then harangued me about my antiproletarian bias and my snobbishness. His wife and his sister-in-law, the actress Cecelia Salkeld, protested: my remark hadn't any social significance, they maintained. When Brendan was trying to recall something else that would shame me, I said, "I'm glad that your plays are having a success." This was the cue that gave him the punch line: "They're better than your lousy plays, anyway."

But Brendan didn't have anything against me, really. One night, a week after this encounter, I was standing at the corner of Dawson Street waiting for a bus when he and Mrs. Behan came along at the other side of the street. Evidently, seeing me, she nudged him; they came over to me and we greeted each other. "Come and have a drink," he said. I told him I didn't drink at night, rounding off my remark that I didn't drink in the morning. He wasn't annoyed, and I took the opportunity of telling him that I had seen two poems of his, written in Irish, that I admired, one about Oscar Wilde's tomb in Paris, and the other about the Blasket Islands. They were different from the conventional Gaelic poetry. I've forgotten how the scene ended, but I know there were no hard feelings either side.

Our next encounter was in front of Trinity College. He was standing there with a group of Indonesian students around him; they were after him for autographs. As I stood to get a word with him he said to the seekers, "Why don't you ask him for an autograph? He's more famous than I am." Very handsome of Brendan. But the Indonesians did not know me and didn't want to know me, and when I had a few words with Brendan I went on.

We came to meet in pubs, where I listened to his extraordinary discourse or heard him sing ballads. Once his father joined us. He was one of those men who gave a character to Dublin, the artisans from the tenements (he was a house painter) who know poetry, stand up for their

Nationalist opinions, and regard themselves as the truest type of Irishmen. When I mentioned to him jokingly that my acquaintance with Brendan began by his trying to insult me, he was shocked. Insult a poet! Brendan hadn't been brought up to do that!

I was out of Ireland for a while and did not get the history of a libel action in which Brendan had been involved. The case had been through the court. Now, bringing Brendan Behan into court was like bringing an Eskimo into court for putting a madwoman on an ice floe. One might get a verdict against him, but that wouldn't mean anything in terms of his conscience or conduct. "I don't respect the law," he wrote. It is an understatement. Brendan Behan was an anarchist in the complete sense. The only right he stood for was the right of the dispossessed person taking something from the dominating person even by violence or what we might call fraud. The man who was against Brendan won the case with damages. But how get damages from a man who had a contempt for the verdict and would use all his wits to prevent an opponent making a profit out of the transaction? The verdict was only the beginning of the game.

Brendan went into hiding. Back in Dublin, I could not locate him. I mentioned my quest to an American girl poet. She smiled and said, "I'll take you to Brendan." She did. His hideout was in an hospital where, under another name, he was being treated for a chronic disorder. His scheme was to stay there until a play of his was on in a theatre in Iceland. He could get a visa to go there, for the government would take it as a good-will mission to a country that had historic connections with Ireland. And from Iceland he could get to somewhere else. Well, he was a fellow who knew what it was to be on the run!

While I was with him he told me about what had led up to this not unprecedented situation. Never before did I hear a story better told. Nobody could have written it as well as he told it, and if I knew that he himself had published it I would not read the written version. This was a show. It was Brendan Behan dramatizing Brendan Behan in all his rogueries, and it was incomparable. It began with two conspirators taking a dog to a racetrack. Their intentions were dishonest. They would give the dog an injection before they entered him for the course. The stimulus would last for an hour, giving him a vim that would put him ahead on the track. They would collect the bets they had on him and return with a couple of hundred pounds for their gains. The track that the dog was to race on was in the county Kildare.

Over the road they took were streamers announcing—what could be more unexpected?—a rosary marathon. An American priest had come to

Ireland with a project of having a thousand rosaries said in different parts of the country. The Archbishop of Dublin did not favor the idea of this mass prayer production, and so its originator had gone into Kildare to initiate it. The conspirators and the dog went on, and over every road they traveled was the prayerful announcement. The rosary was being publicised, and the dog race wasn't.

They halted to give the dog the stimulus that would put him first on the track. Then they went on to the course and handed over the dog to the attendant. "The race is postponed for an hour," the dog keeper told them. "On account of the rosary. The chapel is over there. We'll have the race when it is over."

Here was a dilemma for the conspirators. The stimulus wouldn't last longer than an hour. Worse than that, the dog would show some aftereffects; a vet would be brought on the scene, the attempted fraud would be discovered, and Brendan and his fellow conspirator would be taken off to gaol.

The bell rang for the rosary in the nearby chapel. "I don't think I'll wait," Brendan told the attendant. "I'll take the dog back with me."

"Oh, no, you won't," said the attendant. "Not till the race is finished. The dog's in my charge now, and he'll have to stay where he is."

The two conspirators went off to consult. What could they do to prevent discovery and gaoling, not to mention an attack by angry sportsmen? The sensible thing would be to get into their car and get back to Dublin, leaving the dog impounded. But Brendan Behan had his wits to fall back on. He went to the attendant again.

"I should tell you," said he, "that that dog has the worst bark of any dog in Ireland. If you leave him there he'll start barking and howling."

"I can't help that," said the man in charge. "I get him on the track after the rosary is over, and that's all I can do about it."

"It's on my conscience," said Brendan. "I've brought him where hundreds of people will be here for their devotions. I warn you that at the most sacred part of the rosary, he'll bark in a way that will disturb not only one congregation, but every chapel in the countryside." The attendant, his mind more on the rosary than on the race, went to the kennels and came back with the dog. Holding him by the scruff of the neck, he threw him at Brendan. "Take your bloody dog to hell out of this," he said, as the sound of the first prayers came to them.

Brendan wrote the story. He mentioned his fellow conspirator by a name that was identifiable. Hence the action for libel. Hence Brendan's waiting to get to Iceland on a good-will mission. As he told it, it was the best-told story I ever heard.

The Widow Malone

Did you hear of the widow Malone,
Ohone!
Who lived in the town of Athlone,
Alone!
Oh! she melted the hearts
Of the swains in them parts—
So lovely the widow Malone,
Ohone!
So lovely the widow Malone.

Of lovers she had a full score
Or more;
And fortunes they all had galore,
In store;
From the minister down
To the Clerk of the Crown,
All were courting the widow Malone,
Ohone!
All were courting the widow Malone.

But so modest was Mistress Malone,
'Twas known
No one ever could see her alone,
Ohone!
Let them ogle and sigh,
They could ne'er catch her eye—
So bashful the widow Malone,
Ohone!
So bashful the widow Malone.

Till one Mr. O'Brien from Clare—
How quare!
It's little for blushing they care
Down there—
Put his arm round her waist,
Took ten kisses at last—

First quoted in *Charles O'Malley, The Irish Dragoon*, by Charles Lever, Vol. I, pp. 148-149. The Pearson Publishing Co. New York. 1872.

"Oh," says he "you're my Molly Malone—
                My own!"
"Oh," says he, "you're my Molly Malone!"

And the widow they all thought so shy,
                My eye!
Ne'er thought of a simper or sigh—
                For why?
But, "Lucius," says she,
"Since you've now made so free
You may marry your Molly Malone,
                Ohone!
You may marry your Molly Malone."

There's a moral contained in my song,
                Not wrong,
And, one comfort, it's not very long,
                But strong:
If for widows you die,
Learn *to kiss*, not to sigh,
For they're all like sweet Mistress Malone!
                Ohone!
Oh! they're very like Mistress Malone!

A Few Jigs and Reels

The Irishman half drunk, the Englishman fed, the Scotsman hungry
—that's how they are at their best.*

                *   *   *   *

Three things that could be bettered without being improved: poor
clothes on a drunken man; a plain wife married to a blind man; a
wooden sword in the hand of a coward.†

                *   *   *   *

The lake is not encumbered by the swan; nor the steed by the bridle;
nor the sheep by the wool; nor the man by the soul that is in him.

A hound's tooth, a thorn in the hands, a fool's retort are the three
sharpest things of all.

---

* From oral tradition. † From *A Miscellany of Irish Proverbs,* compiled by
Thomas F. O'Rahilly. The Talbot Press. Dublin. 1922.

The son's seat in his father's house is broad and steady, but the father's seat in the son's house is cramped and rickety.

Idleness is the fool's desire.

Long loneliness is better than bad company.

Contentions are better than loneliness.‡

*   *   *   *

The parson complained to my friend that he had never heard what he had so often heard of—the wit of the Irish peasant. "But you have never spoken to an Irish peasant?" "No." "Then let us try the next one we meet." The next man they met was leading by the halter a horse with a white blaze on his face which suggested to the parson the mild remark, "What a white face your horse has!" "Faith, then, it's your own face would be white if your neck had been so long in a halter!" retorted the man in a tone which suggested that the wish was father to the thought.

The Dean, a septuagenarian, broke off a conversation in order to hurry after a passing tram, to the amazed admiration of an old beggar woman. "Look at the ould dane," she cried, more to herself than to Father Ryan, "skipping about like a newly-married flea!"§

*   *   *   *

When Flanagan was a young boy, he used to sell papers on the streets of Dublin. One day an elderly gentleman approached him and said:

GENT: My dear young boy, will you kindly show me the way to the General Post Office?

FLAN: I will to be shu-er. Go straight down along dere, take th' first turn to th' right, an' den to th' left, and yew can't miss it.

GENT: Thank you, my boy. Tell me, have you no better clothes to wear?

FLAN: Sorra stitch, sir.

GENT: Oh, that's a pity. Have you no boots?

FLAN: Boo-wits, deedin' I haven't.

GENT: That's very sad, very sad indeed. Have you no home, my boy?

FLAN: Meself and me little bruder, we live in an ow-el garret.

---

‡From *Ancient Cures, Charms and Usages of Ireland,* by Lady Wilde. Ward & Downey. London. 1890. §By Richard Ashe-King, in *The Gael,* May, 1903. New York.

GENT: Oh, dear, oh dear. Your parents are not living then?

FLAN: No, sir, they're both dead, God rest dere souls.

GENT: Well, now, my boy, how would you like to come to a nice home where you would get plenty of food, clothes, boots, in fact, surrounded by all the grand things of life?

FLAN: Be begob, dat'd be grand.

GENT: Very good, my son. I will take you to that grand place, and not alone will I give you all these splendid things, but at the same time I will show you the way to Heaven.

FLAN: Ho! Ho! Is that so? An' sure yew don't know th' way to the Post Office yerself, yew dirty oul eejit.¶

A Poet Makes His Own Epitaph

Four Oonas, four Mauryas, four Aunias, four Nuras,
Four fours of the finest maids in the four Fourths of Ireland—
Four boards that are laid to make four sides of my coffin,
Four nails to each board—the women who refused me their loves.

¶From *Recitations, Monologues, and Character Sketches,* by Val Vousden. Walton's. Dublin. [no date]

Attributed to Thomas Costello, seventeenth century.

Part II

HEROES OF OLD

The Celts

Great were their deeds, their passions and their sports;
    With clay and stone
They piled on strath and shore those mystic forts,
    Not yet o'erthrown;
On cairn-crowned hills they held their council-courts;
    While youths alone,
With giant dogs, explored the elk resorts,
    And brought them down.

Of these was Finn, the father of the bard,
    Whose ancient song
Over the clamour of all change is heard,
    Sweet-voiced and strong.
Finn once o'ertook Grania, the golden-haired,
    The fleet and young;
From her the lovely, and from him the feared,
    The primal poet sprung.

Ossian! Two thousand years of mist and change
    Surround thy name—
The Fenian heroes now no longer range
    The hills of fame.
The very names of Finn and Goll sound strange—
    Yet thine the same—
By miscalled lake and desecrated grange—
    Remains, and shall remain!

Thomas D'Arcy McGee

From *The Oxford Book of Irish Verse*. London. 1958.

Introduction

"Overwhere. Gaunt grey ghostly gossips growing grubber in the glow." With this sentence on page 594 of *Finnegans Wake*, the dimness of a country's prehistory is evoked. Great slabs of stone stand on stone supports—cromlechs or dolmens. They are all we can make out in "the spearsprid of dawn fire." In the case of Ireland we can see something besides the cromlechs and the cairns—gold—treasuries of rings that were currency and well-wrought golden ornaments. The National Museum in Dublin has a great collection of them. And then we get to know that Ireland was the Klondike of a Europe that is known only to archeologists—the Europe of the time when the navies of Tarshish—that is, the ships equipped to sail from Tyre to Tartessus in Spain—traded with the West.

In the first line of what purports to be an account of the successive colonization of Ireland there is the glint of gold. Nemed and his men came out of the Caspian Sea and into the Northern Ocean. "There appeared to them a golden tower on the sea close by them. Thus it was: when the sea was in ebb the tower appeared above it, and when it flowed it rose above the tower. Nemed went with his people towards it for greed of the gold." These Nemedians fought with the Fomorians for possession of Ireland and came under Fomorian oppression. Then came the Firbolg. After them, the Tuatha De Danann who took the land from the Firbolg. Then came "Sons of Mil," the Gaels, or, as they alternatively named themselves, the Scots, who displaced the De Danann and became the dominant people in Ireland. Their language, a variant of the Celtic language spoken in Gaul and Britain and once in Northern Italy, an Indo-European language which had Latin as a close relative, became the language of Ireland, Gaelic Scotland, and the Isle of Man.

The account of the various colonizations is given in a composition of the seventh century—*Leabhar Gabhála, The Book of Invasions*. It is an academic production directed (1) towards giving a common ancestry to the dynastic people and (2) towards linking up with world history as it was known at the time the beginning of the history of Ireland. But in this scenario a few genuinely traditional items have found a place—Amergin's magic chants and the talismans the Tuatha De Danann brought with them to Ireland from their abandoned cities.

In *The Book of Invasions*, "The Children of Mil" are represented as coming immediately from Spain. Their leaders are shadowy. Mil or Miledh is the Latin "Miles," a soldier; his wife is Scota, a feminization of the name by which the Romans knew the Gaels, Scot; his two sons are Eber and Eremon, both meaning "The Irishman." When it became necessary to include some outside families in the Milesian genealogies (Mil, by the way, never reached Ireland) a new ancestor was brought on the scene, Ith, the brother of Mil and the uncle of Eber and Eremon, the representatives of the northern and southern halves of Ireland on whom the original genealogies converged.

The function of the poet who accompanied the invaders is evident: it is to utter magic songs that would overawe the elemental beings who would prevent a fresh occupation of the land.

THE CELTS

No intelligent person takes literally racial names attached to population-groups—Latin, Slav, Nordic, Celtic, Anglo-Saxon. There were never unmixed races in any European country, and certainly there are none now. But there are cultural inheritances and distinctive attitudes, and if we are vigilant about it we may give groups with recognizable inheritances and attitudes an ancestral name.

In this sense we can name the hereditary Irish people Celtic. We may note, too, that practically all the place names in Ireland—this applies to the partitioned northeast as well as to the main part—are Celtic; that the bulk of the personal names in the main part are Celtic, and that in the northeast, in sections that are not Catholic, there is a large proportion of Celtic names deriving from Scot ancestry. And more vital than nomenclature is the historical fact that until the middle of the nineteenth century three-fourths of the population of Ireland spoke one of the extant Celtic languages, Gaelic. Leaving the very doubtful issue of race aside, the Ireland that is presented in these pages is Celtic by culture.

"They shook all empires but they founded none," Mommsen, the German historian, said of the Celts. A French scholar, Professor Hubert,* qualifies this statement. The Celts of Gaul stabilized the weakening Roman Empire and enabled it to hold up against the people who were ultimately to destroy it—the German tribes—and in doing this they helped to spread a civilizing influence. They were not capable of making Celtia into an empire, but they had enough feeling for wide organization and social culture to recognize these in the Roman Empire and to give that empire their very effective support. They were looked upon as barbarians by the Greeks and Romans, but barbarians of a superior kind; they were ranked above the Germans,

---

* Professor Hubert's books are *The Rise of the Celts*, published by Alfred Knopf, and *The Decline of the Celts*, published in the History of Civilization series. They are of great interest to those who want to know about our Celtic ancestors and also to those who want to know about Europe before the Mediterranean domination.

Ligurians, Iberians. On contemporaries who observed them or reflected on their polity and on their leaders, they left an impression of remarkableness for their military prowess and their individuality. The Celts had notions about another world which interested Latin thinkers. They were literate, too: when Julius Caesar with much advertised slaughter broke up the immigration of the Helvetii into Gaul he found a census of the immigrants written in Greek characters.

In Gaul, the Celts, according to Professor Hubert, "built their own houses and cities; they arranged the country to suit themselves, and as they arranged it so it still remains, for wherever the Celts established themselves permanently, without exception the French have remained. . . . The origin of the French nation goes back to the Celts. Behind them there is a formless past, without history or even a name." The French are a Celtic people, speaking Latin with a Celtic accent and in accordance with Celtic psychology, Professor Hubert maintains. In Gaul the place names are compounded with *magus,* meaning a plain or open field (in Ireland, Mayo, Maynooth), and this designates "settlements in the plains, probably agricultural." In Spain into which the Celts also penetrated, place names are usually compounded with *briga,* which is the Gallic equivalent of the German *burg.* This shows a situation different from that in Gaul: it "tells of insecurity, a state of war or danger of war, and we can imagine the Celts of Spain who had conquered only the least attractive parts of the country, scattered in the midst of Ligurian tribes, driven off, but still formidable, and keeping watch on the Iberian or Tartessian states whose military power is always represented as considerable in the earliest writers."

Where was the original home of the Celts? Not in Gaul, for there though the names of towns and villages are Celtic, the names of rivers and hills are from another language. But in what is now Germany the names of rivers, hills, forests are Celtic. This shows that the earliest settlements there were Celtic. Professor Hubert notes:

> Now the names given to the land and its natural features are the most enduring of place names. The first occupants of a country always pass them on to their successors. . . . The names of places and peoples which have been enumerated cover the southwestern corner of Germany. The area in which they are found is a vast irregular triangle with one point on the Rhine near Cologne and another beyond Bohemia.

At one time the Celtic and Germanic peoples neighbored each other, the Celtic being the people with the more advanced social and political forms. This is shown by the Celtic words in the Germanic languages. "Gothic *reika,* 'prince,' and *reiki,* 'kingdom,' come from the Gaulish *rix* and *rigion* (Irish *riga),* not from the Indo-European *rex* and its associated words."

It is Professor Hubert's theory (among Celtic scholars he is alone in holding it) that the Celtic people who lived by the North Sea, breaking off from the Celtic stock in the Bronze Age, became the Gaels (scholars write it "Goidels"). They were farmers and stock-raisers who did not live in villages but in houses in the middle of their fields as in Ireland today. They hired ships from a neighboring seafaring people and sailed for a new home, leaving, of course, a remnant behind: these were absorbed in the German expansion. According to this story, the Gaels would have had no share in the great events of the Celtic expansion; they would have been long settled in Ireland by the time the people whom the Greeks named Celts and the Romans Gauls made their contact with the Mediterranean powers.

The Goidelic is one branch of the Celtic family; the Brythonic is the other. It should be explained that "Brythonic" does not necessarily have to do with Britain; it has, in terms of the Celticists, more to do with Gaul. The distinction has to do with language. The language of Britain and Gaul has a "P" sound in it; the language of Ireland, Highland Scotland, and the Isle of Man has instead of a "P," a "Q," or, as it is written now, a "C." The word for "son" in Welsh is "map," which is the "ap" of familiar Welsh names—ap Rhys or Price, ap Howell or Powell; while the word for "son" in Gaelic is the familiar Irish or Scots "mac." The "P" using were the Continental, the "Q" using, the insular Celts.

If we accept the theory that the Gaels went into Ireland in the Bronze Age we can understand their attaining such homogeneity at the beginning of Irish history: a single language is spoken throughout the country, and although it is recognized that there are racial groups that are not Gaelic, these groups are in a framework of a Gaelic polity. This is not the case in Britain or Gaul. According to Professor Hubert, the incoming Gaels gave Ireland its name: Piera, a name from an Indo-European root expressing fatness or fertility (the Greek home of the Muses had the same name), and from Piera is derived Eiru, Hibernia, Juvernia, and the Welsh Iwerddon. Irish scholars do not accept this derivation.

The distinguished Irish scholar, Professor MacNeill, maintains that the Celts did not arrive in Ireland until the Iron Age, and did not completely establish themselves there until the second century A.D. Who were the people who were there already, the people who gave a name to the country? They were the ancient Hesperian people whose present-day representatives, Professor MacNeill holds, are the Basques. The Gaels imposed their language upon them, but took over certain of their institutions. Another Irish authority, Professor O'Rahilly, puts the arrival of the Gaelic-speaking Celts at a date even later than Professor MacNeill's. For the original home of these invaders, Professor O'Rahilly goes as far as Switzerland: they were the Helvetii whose planned emigration Caesar broke up. According to the census that his intelligence service got hold of, there were over three hundred thousand people in the movement: the Roman legions could not have destroyed all of them. A remnant went on, reached western Gaul, and got shipping for Ireland where, with their iron weapons, they were able to establish themselves in a short time. Who were the people who were in Ireland before these Celts? Celts speaking another idiom, Professor O'Rahilly says. They were Brythonic-speaking, their language being of the same type as that of the Welsh and Bretons of today.

Long before the Roman legions subjugated Gaul, in the golden age of Greece, a sensational event was noted in "the news that came to Pontus simultaneously with the event, that an army from the land of the Hyperboreians had taken a Greek city named Rome, situated near the Great Sea." These Far Northerners were the Celts under Brennus who had his name from the war god Bran. At the other end of the Mediterranean, a city that was really Greek, Marseilles, barely escaped being taken by another army of the same people: envoys returning from making a thank-offering at Delphi for that deliverance heard of the taking of Rome. The Celts were across the Pyrenees at the same time as they were across the Alps. And in the East they threw a colony into Asia Minor which retained its Celtic language until the fourth century of our era: the trophy we know as "The Dying Gaul" was put up to commemorate a victory won over the Celts in that part of the world. On the neck of the dying warrior is the torque, the collar of twisted gold specimens which we can look at in the National Museum of Ireland. And even as we dismiss the idea of race, we are forced to admit that the Eurasian warrior of the Greek sculptor might be an Irishman of today. Speaking of the culture of La Tene which is supposed to have ended with the conquest of Gaul, Professor Hubert says, "The last heir of that art, which was crossed about the sixth century with Germanic art, is the art of Ireland of the time of Charlemagne, with its illuminated manuscripts and its gorgeous gold work."

THE NAME "IRELAND"

The name "Ireland" comes from the Scandinavians: it is the native name "Eire" with "land" added. "Eire," anciently "Eiru," has a dative case "Eirinn," and this is often wrongly used as a nominative. Two scholars, Sir John Rhys and Henri Hubert, think the name comes from the Indo-European "Piera." Professor MacNeill thinks it is from a community in the southwest, the "Ivernian." In poetry two other names are used—"Banba," signifying Ireland in the heroic sense, and "Fola," signifying Ireland in the intellectual sense: thus the poets write of "the heroes of Banba" and "the scholars or poets of Fola."

THE PROVINCES OF IRELAND

The division of Ireland is fourfold, four provinces—Ulster in the north, Munster in the south, Leinster in the east, Connacht in the

west. As in the case of the name of the country, three of the provinces
in their non-Gaelic forms have Scandinavian terminations. Connacht
(sometimes written Connaught) retains its ancient name; the native
names for the other provinces are Ulaidh (Oola), Mumhan (Muan),
Leighean (Lehan). Originally the division was fivefold (the Irish word
for province means "Fifth") and in prehistoric times it was sevenfold.
And so the present-day provinces do not actually correspond with the
older divisions. The war, for instance, between Ulaidh and Connacht
was not a war between Ulster as we see it on the map and Connacht
as we see it on the map, although the two royal sites, Emain Macha
(Armagh) and Cruachan are in present-day Ulster and Connacht. In
the fifth century certain kings formed a royal domain in what is now
the county Meath and set up a royal residence there, Tara (Tearach).
In speaking of the geography of early and medieval Ireland, it should
not be forgotten that part of Scotland (Alba) was included in the
Gaelteacht, Gaeldom.

The Irsh Epic

More than any other European cycle outside the Greek, the stories
of the early Iron Age in Ireland have epical character and epical scope.
The inclusive narrative that is named the *Táin Bó Cúalnge, The
Cattle Raid of Cooley,* is in prose with verse-passages that give brilliancy to the narrative but only stylize some preceding or succeeding
passage.

The long episode given here, the Combat at the Ford, is the central
incident in the Táin. The events leading up to it are these: Deirdre,
her husband, Naisi, and his two brothers have been brought back to
Ireland by promises of safety made by King Concobar. Fergus, the
most chivalrous of Concobar's generation, has pledged himself for their
safety. But despite his own and Fergus' pledges, Concobar has Naisi
and his brothers (the Sons of Usnach) slain and Deirdre taken to his
house. This leads to defection from the heroic companionship. Fergus,
with other of the Ulster heroes, takes service with Maeve, a queen of
the West.

But the narrative has another point of departure. There is the
humorous and extravagant competition between Maeve and her husband, or rather her consort, as to their respective possessions. Maeve
matches Ailill, but then it is discovered that one of her bulls, scorning
to be under the charge of a woman, has left her herd and joined Ailill's.
This the queen cannot bear. The most famous bull in Ireland is in
possession of the Ultonians, and Maeve sends envoys to procure him.
But the arrogance of the envoys forces a break in the negotiations.
They are sent back to Maeve without the bull.

Another story claims our attention at this point. An Ulster land-
owner has a mysterious woman come to his house; he takes her as his
wife, and, as is usual in the story of the Supernatural Bride, he is for-

bidden to speak of her. But at an assembly of the men of Ulster he boasts of his wife, even going so far as to say she could race Concobar's horses. He is seized and would be put to death unless his wife makes good his boast. She is pregnant, but nevertheless races Concobar's horses. She dies at the end of the course and puts a curse on the men of Ulster: it dooms the men of Concobar's dominion to the debility of a woman in childbirth on certain occasions.

Maeve decides to invade Ulster, not only for the purpose of carrying off the bull but of humiliating Concobar who was a former husband of hers. She times her expedition to coincide with the debility of the Ulster warriors.

But the prize of the war, the meed of victory, as the translators of Homer put it, is only a great bellowing bull! This is where the Irish conception fails to come within measurable distance of the Greek. The Helen-Deirdre theme which should have gone to universalize the Irish story becomes marginal. And so, in spite of the magnificence, charm, and enchantment of certain of the episodes, in spite of the humor and sportsmanship that make it unique in early literature, the famous bull has stamped the Táin into a pastoral civilization.

Maeve assembles a mighty army; it includes not only her own levy with the Ulster refugees, but forces from all the other provinces, and even the professional Gaulish soldiers settled in Leinster. Cu Chullain, either because he is not of Ulster descent or because his semi-divinity immunizes him, is not afflicted by the curse. He takes it on himself to guard the ford across which Maeve's army has to push. As one hero to others, he offers single combat, and he cannot be swept aside until the series of duels is decided by his death. Maeve, one guesses, would have made little of the chivalric code if Fergus had not been there to press for its observance. Champion after champion engages Cu Chullain and is overcome.

It is at this stage that Ferdiad is brought on to fight Cu Chullain. They have been comrades in arms, trained together by a woman-warrior. Every inducement is offered to Ferdiad to take up Cu Chullain's challenge, the greatest being marriage with Finnabair, Maeve's daughter (although it is not so stated, Ferdiad, the chief of a vassal people, must have been moved by the prospect of having a princess from one of the great lineages for wife, apart from Finnabair's evident winningness). As in the fight between Achilles and Hector we feel that there is something unfair about this match: after all, like Achilles, Cu Chullain is semi-divine, and as Achilles has divine armor, so Cu Chullain has a secret weapon which ultimately he will use: it is a curious weapon, launched by the foot down a running stream.

It is a long time since the stories about the Ultonian hero were formed into an epic-tale—probably thirteen hundred years. The history of Western Europe had its beginning after that, and with this fact in mind we are startled to learn that, only forty years ago, an episode out of the career of Cu Chullain was being recited by the peat fire by a man who bore the unbardic name of James Kelly. As the Cu Chullain of this episode is the Cu Chullain of the folk, the living Cu Chullain, we place him before the Cu Chullain of the written stories.

In 1904 Stephen Gwynn had James Kelly in non-colloquial Irish recite to him the lay of Cu Chullain's tragic encounter with his son. He published his translation of the lay in an essay entitled "The Life of a Song." What is given here are extracts from the essay and from the translation of the lay.

The story of Deirdre had currency in Scotland as a folk tale, but not in Ireland. The version given here is nineteenth century and is from literary sources. . . . In early Irish story-telling there is a particular oddness which makes a modern retelling difficult; it has to be said that in "Deirdre of the Sorrows" the difficulty has not been fairly met.

The heroes are subject to prohibitions—*geasa*. These could be taken for points of honor—they are acted on as if they were points of honor —except that they are imposed from the outside, and, as far as we can make out, are purely arbitrary. Predictability is a large ingredient in story-telling, and anything that takes from predictability in the conduct of the characters is a defect. The *geasa*, or prohibitions, do that.

In "Deirdre of the Sorrows" the nineteenth-century poet and antiquarian, Sir Samuel Ferguson, romanticizes the *geis* in one case and in another leaves it unexplained. Deirdre in the old story is determined to take a young rather than an elderly husband; she forces the elopement on Naisi by putting him under *geis*—he must not leave her in Connor's territory. The crisis in the story—Fergus delaying for a feast instead of going ahead with the people who have placed themselves under his protection—is due to another prohibition: he must not refuse a feast offered him by one of the Red Branch. The duel between Cu Chullain and his son is also due to a prohibition—the prohibition laid on the young man against telling his name and race. In this case, however, the prohibition becomes meaningful in terms of narrative: the fact that the young man knows who his antagonist is, knows, too, that his own destruction will be direful to that antagonist, gives something over and above what is in the theme of the combat between father and son; and makes the story that was related by James Kelly more poignant than its Iranian parallel, "Sohrab and Rustum."

"The Pillow Talk" and "The Combat at the Ford" are translated directly from the Irish text of the Book of Leinster by the American scholar, Joseph Dunn. Only the first half of "The Pillow Talk" is given, enough to project what is the greatest creation of old Irish literature, the personality of Medb. In Professor Dunn's translation, the old forms of the names are kept: the name now written "Maeve" appears as "Medb." On the other hand, in "Deirdre of the Sorrows" the name "Concobar" is given in its modern form "Conor."

"The Pillow Talk" is abbreviated and so is "The Combat at the Ford"—this mainly by leaving out the verse passages in it. The literateurs of Gaelic Ireland did not consider verse a proper medium for narrative. But when in the course of a narrative they came to incidents or speeches that were susceptible of brilliant treatment, they put them into verse. The verse usually repeats what had been said in prose. So in this presentation there are two reasons for leaving out the verse passages: one is that the effects that the verse was designed for, effects of brilliancy, can hardly ever be carried into translations, and the other reason is that the verse, repeating what has been said before, interrupts the narrative. However, there is one poem in "The Combat at the Ford" that should be retained: it is Cu Chullain's lament over Ferdiad. This is a superb example of a mode that the early Irish poets were the first to exploit—the dramatic lyric; besides, it brings out an element which makes the Táin remarkable among early compositions—the element of chivalry.

Its tone is fiercely provincial, but we can see that the Táin is in process of being made into a national epic. All references to attack on or defeat of Tara have been suppressed; Cu Chullain's body is buried in Ulster's Emain Macha, but his head is buried at Tara. He proclaims himself a national hero when, on taking arms, he "swears by the gods my people swear by, I care not if my life has only the span of a day and a night if my deeds be spoken of by the men of Ireland."

INTRODUCTION TO THE STORIES ABOUT FINN

Fian, Fianna: According to Professor MacNeill the word means something like *vassal,* and this scholar suggests that the Fianna were levies conscripted from a subject population. Their leaders (Finn MacCuhal is the outstanding one) have no territorial lordship; they move readily from place to place; they support themselves, as would a dispossessed people in an uncrowded country, by the chase; they are hunters when they are not fighters. And Finn is no aristocratic hero as Cu Chullain is: he is a folk hero, crafty as well as brave, vindictive as well as generous. His saga came to exceed in popularity that of Cu Chullain's; it was developed in every part of Ireland as well as in Gaelic Scotland. It had advantages over the Cu Chullain saga in that it was not written down, that it had no fixity of text. And it was not so tragic as aristocratic sagas tend to be; it had room for humor. Then, unlike Cu Chullain, Finn lived to the prime of manhood and had sons and grandsons; he had a more complete and many-sided life than the short-lived and singular Cu Chullain. The Finn saga came out of the folk, and to a large extent it was developed by the folk.

But it also came into the courts. A time came when the courts of southern Ireland tired of hearing about the exploits of the northern heroes and wanted to have a saga of their own. Their story-tellers brought Finn forward and built him up as a national hero, the guardian of the high-kingship. But even while they did this they kept the northern saga in mind, making some of the new court stories reflect some of the old. The elderly Finn's passion for Grania, her elopement with the youthful Dermott, reflects the elderly Concobar's passion for Deirdre and her elopement with the youthful Naisi. Dermott, like Cu Chullain, is related to the Divine Folk—his protector is Angús, god of Love and Youth. But the tone of the two stories is so different that their resemblance is not apparent: the King of Ireland's daughter is a modern person compared to the rhymer's daughter, and her story is romantic rather than heroic.

This story is crucial in the Finn saga; after this episode there is dissension in the Fianna. Finn has shown himself ready to put his passion for Grania above the interest of the companionship. Then the King of Ireland, Cormac's son Cairbry, turns on the Fianna and destroys them. Oscar, Finn's grandson, the most sympathetic of the Fianna falls at the battle of Gowra. Oisin goes into the Land of Youth. Tara, too, fades out of the stories. The high-kingship remains, but after the time of Niall (fifth century), it alternates between the northern and southern branches of his descendants and different royal sites are taken over. Its prestige goes, and Tara is abandoned.

The eclipse of Tara and the Fianna puts the story-tellers into a reminiscing mood, and out of that mood comes the great story of Oisin's sojourn in the Land of Youth and his return to Ireland. He comes back to an Ireland in which the Fianna are no longer remembered. He meets Saint Patrick, is well entreated, and, greatly to the saint's satisfaction, to him relates the old Pagan stories. This friendship between the new-coming saint and the long-surviving hero dramatizes the reconciliation of Paganism and Christianity which was without parallel in any other country.

(*Note:* English renderings of ancient Irish names, naturally, vary considerably, and of course there is no "official" or "correct" spelling of any of them. In this book, the original author's spelling has been preserved, and so such names as Cu Chullain may appear in several different ways, but of course are always easily recognizable.) —P.C.

The Tuatha De Danaan

The Tuatha De Danaan lived in the northern isles of the world, learning lore and magic and druidism and wizardry and cunning, until they surpassed the sages of the arts of heathendom. There were four cities in which they learned lore and science and diabolic arts, to wit, Falias and Gorias, Murias and Findias. Out of Falias was brought the Stone of Fal, which was in Tara. It used to roar under every king that would take the realm of Ireland. Out of Gorias was brought the Spear that Lug had. No battle was ever won against it or him who held it in his hand. Out of Findias was brought the Sword of Nuada. When it was drawn from its deadly sheath, no one ever escaped from it, and it was irresistible. Out of Murias was brought Dagda's Cauldron. No company ever went from it unthankful.*

The Magic Song Amergin Utters Against the Wind Raised by the De Danaan

I invoke the land of Ireland,
Much-coursed be the fertile sea,
Fertile be the fruit-strewn mountain,
Fruit-strewn be the showery wood,
Showery be the river of water-falls,
Of water-falls be the lake of deep pools,
Deep-pooled be the hill-top well,
A well of tribes be the assembly,
An assembly of the kings be Tara,

From *Ancient Irish Tales*, edited by Tom Peete Cross and Clark Harris Slover, p. 28. Copyright, 1936, by Henry Holt & Co., Inc. New York.
* The names of the cities are evocative enough to fill three lines of Yeats's:
       The towery gates of Gorias,
       And Findias and Falias,
       And long-forgotten Murias.

Ibid., p. 19.

53

Tara be the hill of the tribes,
The tribes of the sons of Mil,
Of Mil of the ships, the barks,
Let the lofty bark be Ireland,
Lofty Ireland, darkly sung,
An incantation of great cunning;
The great cunning of the wives of Bres,
The wives of Bres of Buaigne;
The great lady Ireland,
Eremon hath conquered her,
Ir, Eber have invoked for her.
I invoke the land of Ireland.

The Invaders of Ireland

Sometime in the nineteenth century an anonymous versifier—he
was probably a hedge schoolmaster—put into street-ballad form the
successive conquests and colonization, thereby giving an item of interest to the fireside while presenting the reader with a sequence of
names that occur in Irish tradition and modern Irish poetry.

Should any inquire about Eirinn,
It is I who can give him the truth
Concerning the deeds of each daring
Invader, since Time was a youth.

First Cassir, Bith's venturesome daughter,
Came here o'er the Eastern Sea;
And fifty fair damsels she brought her
To solace her warriors three.

Bith died at the foot of his mountain,
And Ladra on top of his height;
And Cassir by Boyle's limpid fountain,
Ere rushed down the Flood in its might.

Taken by the editor from a 1913 ballad-sheet.

For a year, while the waters encumber
The Earth, at Tul-tunna of strength,
I slept, none enjoyed such sweet slumber
As that which I woke from at length.

When Partholan came to the island
From Greece, in the Eastern Land,
I welcomed him gaily to my land,
And feasted the whole of his band.

Again, when Death seized on the strangers
I roamed the land, merry and free,
Both careless and fearless of dangers,
Till blithe Nemid came over the sea.

The Firbolgs and roving Firgallians
Came next like the waves in their flow;
The Firdonnans arrived in battalions,
And landed in Erris—Mayo.

Then came the wise Tuatha de Danaans,
Concealed in black clouds from their foe;
I feasted with them near the Shannon,
Though that was a long time ago.

After them came the Children of Milé,
From Spain, o'er the Southern waves;
I lived with the tribes as their Filea
And chanted the deeds of their braves.

Time ne'er my existence could wither,
From Death's grasp I always was freed,
Till Patrick the Christian came hither
To spread the Redeemer's pure creed.

My name it is Fintan, the Fair Man,
Of Bochra, the son—you must know it:
I lived through the Flood in my lair, man;
I am now an illustrious poet.

The Duel of Cu Chullain and His Son

Cu Chullain, the Achilles of Irish epic, was famous from the day in boyhood when he got his name by killing, bare-handed, the smith's fierce watchdog that would have torn him. The ransom (penalty) for the killing was laid on by the boy himself, and it was that he should watch Culann's house for a year and a day till a pup should be grown to take the place of the slain dog. So he came to be called Cu Chullain, Culann's Hound, and by that name he was known, when, as a young champion, he set out for the Isle of Skye, where the warrior witch Sgathach (from whom the island is called) taught the crowning feats of arms to all young heroes who could pass through the ordeals she laid upon them.

There was no trial that Cu Chullain could not support, and the fame of him drew on a combat with another Amazonian warrior, Aoife, and she gave love to her conqueror—whose passion for the fierce queen was not enough to keep him from Ireland. When he made ready to go, the woman told him that a child was to be born of their embraces, and she asked what should be done with it. "If it be a girl, keep it," said Cu Chullain, "but if a boy, wait till his thumb can fill this ring"—and he gave her the circlet—"then send him to me." So he departed, leaving wrath behind him.

The child born was a son, and Aoife reared him and taught him all the feats of arms that could be taught to a mortal, except one only, and of that feat only Cu Chullain was master; there would be none could kill him but his own father. And when the boy had learnt all and was a perfect warrior, Aoife sent him out to Ireland under a pledge to refuse his name to any that should ask it, well knowing how the wardens of the coast would stop him on the shore. It fell out as she purposed. The young Connlaoch defeated champion after champion till Cu Chullain went down, and was recognized by his son. But the pledge tied Connlaoch's tongue, and only when he lay dying, slain by the magic throw which Aoife had withheld from his knowledge, could he reveal himself to his father.

Cu Chullain says:
> "Champion, tell your story,
> For I see your wounds are heavy;
> 'Twill be short ere they raise your cairn,
> So hide your testament no longer."

By Stephen Gwynn, in *The Gael*, April, 1904, pp. 143-145. New York.

Connlaoch says:

> Let me fall on my face,
> For methinks 'tis you are my father,
> And for fear lest men of Eire should see
> Me retreating from your fierce grapple,
> I took pledges to my mother
> Not to give the story to any single man,
> If I would give it to any under the sun,
> It is to your bright body I would tell it.
> I lay my curse on my mother,
> That she put me under pledge;
> But if it were not for the feat of magic
> I had not been got for nothing."

Cu Chullain says:

> I lay my curse on your mother,
> For she destroyed a multitude of young ones;
> And because the treachery that was in her
> Left your smooth flesh reddened."

Then comes, with the boy's dying word, the revelation of the most tragic moment in the fight.

> "Cu Chullain, beloved father,
> Is it not a wonder you did not know me
> When I cast my spear crooked and feebly
> Against your bush of blades."

Where will you find a finer stroke of invention. The boy, tongue-tied by his pledge, knows his father and feels his defense falling against the terrible onset; he would not, if he could, be the victor, but he thinks of a way within the honor of his bond which may awaken knowledge of him; and he casts his javelin with a clumsiness not to be looked for in the champion "that tied Conall." It is useless, the battle madness is in Cu Chullain, he thinks only of conquest, an end to the supple, quick parrying, and he throws the *gae bulga,* a spear of dragon's bones glistening with points (his "bush of blades"), with the magic cast that there is no meeting. And now there is nothing left to him but the lamentation:

"Och! Och! Great is my madness!
I lifting here my young lad!
My son's head in my one hand,
His arms and his raiment on the other.

"I, the father who slew his son,
May I never throw spear nor noble javelin;
The hand that slew its son,
May it win torture and sharp wounding.

"The grief for my son I put from me never,
Till the flagstones of my side crumble,
It is in me, and through my heart,
Like a sharp blaze in the hoary hill grasses.

"If I and my heart's Connlaoch
Were playing our kingly feats together,
We could range from wave to shore
Over the five provinces of Erin."

Pillow Talk

Once on a time, when Ailill and Medb had spread their royal bed
in Cruachan, the stronghold of Connacht, such was the pillow-talk
betwixt them:
Said Ailill, "True is the saying, O woman, 'She is a well-off woman
that is a rich man's wife.' "
"Aye, that she is," answered the wife; "but wherefore say'st thou
so?"
"For this," Ailill replied, "that thou art this day better off than the
day that first I took thee."
Then answered Medb, "As well-off was I before I ever saw thee."
"It was a wealth, indeed, we never heard nor knew of," said Ailill;
"but a woman's wealth was all thou hadst, and foes from lands next
thine were wont to carry off the spoil and booty that they took from
thee."
"Not so was I," said Medb; "the High King of Erin himself was

---

From *Táin Bó Cúalnge* (*The Cattle Raid of Cooley*), translated by Joseph Dunn,
pp. 1-4. David Nott & Co. London. 1914.

my father, Eochaid Feidlich son of Finn son of Finnen son of Finnguin son of Rogen Ruad son of Rigen son of Blathacht son of Beothacht son of Enna Agnech son of Angus Turbech. Of daughters had he six: Derbriu, Ethne and Ele, Clothru, Mugain and Medb, myself, that was the noblest and seemliest of them all. It was I was the goodliest of them in bounty and gift-giving, in riches and treasures. It was I was best of them in battle and strife and combat. It was I that had fifteen hundred royal mercenaries of the sons of aliens exiled from their own land, and as many more of the sons of freemen of the land. These were as a standing household-guard," continued Medb; "hence hath my father bestowed one of the five provinces of Erin upon me, that is, the province of Cruachan: wherefore 'Medb of Cruachan' am I called. Men came from Finn son of Ross Ruad, king of Leinster, to seek me for a wife, and I refused him; and from Cairbre Niafer son of Ross Ruad, king of Tara, to woo me, and I refused him; and they came from Conchobar son of Fachtna Fathach, king of Ulster, and I refused him likewise. They came from Eochaid Bec, and I went not; for it is I that exacted a peculiar bride-gift, such as no woman ever required of a man of the men of Erin, namely, a husband without avarice, without jealousy, without fear. For should he be mean, the man with whom I should live, we were ill-matched together, inasmuch as I am great in largess and gift-giving, and it would be a disgrace for my husband if I should be better at spending than he, and for it to be said that I was superior in wealth and treasures to him, while no disgrace would it be were one as great as the other. Were my husband a coward, it were as unfit for us to be mated, for I by myself and alone break battles and fights and combats, and it would be a reproach for my husband should his wife be more full of life than himself, and no reproach our being equally bold. Should he be jealous, the husband with whom I should live, that too would not suit me, for there never was a time that I had not one man in the shadow of another. Howbeit, such a husband have I found, namely thyself, Ailill son of Ross Ruad of Leinster. Thou wast not churlish; thou wast not jealous; thou wast not a sluggard. It was I plighted thee, and gave purchase price to thee, which of right belongs to the bride—of clothing, namely, the raiment of twelve men, a chariot worth thrice seven bondmaids, the breadth of thy face of red gold, the weight of thy left forearm of white bronze. Whoso brings shame and sorrow and madness upon thee, no claim for compensation or satisfaction hast thou therefor that I myself have not, but it is to me the compensation belongs," said Medb, "for a man dependent upon a woman's maintenance is what thou art."

"Nay, not such was my state," said Ailill; "but two brothers had

I; one of them over Tara, the other over Leinster; namely Finn over Leinster and Cairbre over Tara. I left the kingship to them because they were older but not superior to me in largess and bounty. Nor heard I of a province in Erin under woman's keeping but this province alone. And for this I came and assumed the kingship here as my mother's successor; for Mata of Muresc, daughter of Matach of Connacht, was my mother. And who could there be for me to have as my queen better than thyself, being, as thou wert, daughter of the High King of Erin?"

"Yet so it is," pursued Medb, "my fortune is greater than thine."

"I marvel at that," Ailill made answer, "for there is none that hath greater treasures and riches and wealth than I: indeed, to my knowledge there is not."

The Combat at the Ford

The four great provinces of Erin were side by side and against Cu Chulainn from Monday before Samain (Hallowe'en) to Wednesday after Spring-beginning, and without leave to work harm or vent their rage on the province of Ulster, while yet all the Ulstermen were sunk in their nine days' pains, and Conall Cernach sought out battle in strange foreign lands paying the tribute and tax of Ulster. Sad was the plight and strait of Cu Chulainn during that time, for he was not a day or a night without fierce, fiery combat waged on him by the men of Erin, until he killed Calatin with his seven and twenty sons and Fraech son of Fidach and performed many deeds and successes which are not enumerated here. Now this was sore and grievous to Medb and to Ailill.

Then the men of Erin took counsel who should be fit to send to the ford to fight and do battle with Cu Chulainn to drive him off from them.

With one accord they declared that it should be Ferdiad son of Damon son of Daire, the great and valiant warrior of the Fir Domnann, the horn-skin from Irrus Domnann, the irresistible force, and the battle-rock of destruction, the own dear foster-brother of Cu Chulainn. And fitting it was for him to go thither, for well-matched and alike was their manner of fight and of combat. Under the same instructress had they done skillful deeds of valor and arms, when learning the art

---

Ibid., pp. 217-267.

with Scathach and with Uathach and with Aife. Yet was it the felling of an oak with one's fists, and the stretching of the hand into a serpent's den, and a going into the lair of a lion, for hero or champion in the world, aside from Cu Chulainn, to fight or combat with Ferdiad on whatever ford or river or mere he set his shield. And neither of them overmatched the other, save in the feat of the *gae bulga* (bag-spear) which Cu Chulainn possessed. Howbeit against this, Ferdiad was horn-skinned when fighting and in combat with a warrior on the ford; and they thought he could avoid the *gae bulga* and defend himself against it, because of the horn about him of such kind that neither arms nor multitude of edges could pierce it.

Then were messengers and envoys sent from Medb and Ailill to Ferdiad. Ferdiad denied them their request, and dismissed and sent back the messengers, and he went not with them, for he knew wherefor they would have him, to fight and combat with his friend, with his comrade and his fosterbrother, Cu Chulainn.

Then did Medb despatch to Ferdiad the druids and the poets of the camp, and lampooners and hard-attackers to the end that they might make the three satires to stay him and the three scoffing speeches against him, to mock at him and revile and disgrace him, that they might raise three blisters on his face,—Blame, Blemish, and Disgrace, that he might not find a place in the world to lay his head, if he came not with them to the tent of Medb and Ailill.

Ferdiad came with them for the sake of his own honor and for fear of their bringing shame on him, since he deemed it better to fall by the shafts of valor and bravery and skill than to fall by the shafts of satire, abuse, and reproach. And when Ferdiad was come into the camp, Medb and Ailill beheld him, and great and most wonderful joy possessed them, and they sent him to where their trusty people were, and he was honored and waited on, and choice, well-flavored strong liquor was poured out for him until he became drunken and merry. Finnabair, daughter of Ailill and Medb, was seated at his side. It was Finnabair that placed her hand on every goblet and cup Ferdiad quaffed. She it was that gave him three kisses with every cup that he took. She it was that passed him sweet-smelling apples over the bosom of her tunic. This is what she ceased not to say, that her darling and her chosen sweetheart of the world's men was Ferdiad. And when Medb got Ferdiad drunken and merry, great rewards were promised him if he would make the fight and combat.

When now Ferdiad was satisfied, happy and joyful, Medb spoke, "Hail now, Ferdiad. Dost thou know the occasion wherefor thou art summoned to this tent?"

"I know not, in truth," Ferdiad replied; "unless it be that the nobles of the men of Erin are here. Why is it a less fitting time for me to be here than any other good warrior?"

"It is not that, indeed," answered Medb, "but to give thee a chariot worth four times seven bondmaids, and the apparel of two men and ten men, of cloth of every color, and the equivalent of Mag Muirthemne of the rich soil of Mag Ai, and that thou shouldst be at all times in Cruachan, and wine be poured out for thee there; the freedom of thy descendants and thy race forever, free of tribute, free of rent, without constraint to encamp or take part in our expeditions, without duress for thy son, or for thy great-grandson, till the end of time and existence; this leaf-shaped golden brooch of mine shall be thine, wherein are ten-score ounces, and ten-score half-ounces, and ten-score scruples, and ten-score quarters; Finnabair, my daughter and Ailill's, to be thy own wife, and my own most intimate friendship, if thou exactest that withal."

"He needs it not," they cried, one and all; "great are the rewards and gifts!"

[Such lavish rewards, with sureties, were not enough to persuade Ferdiad to fight Cu Chulainn, until Medb tried a trick.]

"Ye men," said Medb, in the wonted fashion of stirring up disunion and dissension, as if she had not heard Ferdiad at all, "true is the word Cu Chulainn speaks."

"What word is that?" asked Ferdiad.

"He said, then," replied Medb, "he would not think it too much if thou shouldst fall by his hands in the choicest feat of his skill in arms, in the land whereto he should come."

"It was not just for him to speak so," said Ferdiad; "for it is not cowardice or lack of boldness that he hath ever seen in me by day or night. And I speak not so of him, if it be true that he spoke so, I will be the first man of the men of Erin to contend with him on the morrow, how loath soever I am to do so!"

And he gave his word in the presence of them all that he would go and meet Cu Chullain. For it pleased Medb, if Ferdiad should fail to go, to have them as witnesses against him, in order that she might say that it was fear or dread that caused him to break his word.

[Cu Chulainn, when warned by his friend and master Fergus, of the impending fight with Ferdiad, expressed his dismay.]

"As my soul liveth, it is not to an encounter we wish our friend to come, and not for fear, but for love and affection of him; and almost

I would prefer to fall by the hand of that warrior than for him to fall by mine."

"It is just for that," answered Fergus, "that thou shouldst be on thy guard and prepared. Say not that thou hast no fear of Ferdiad, for it is fitting that thou shouldst have fear and dread before fighting with Ferdiad. For unlike to all whom it fell to fight and contend with thee on the Cattle-Raid of Cooley on this occasion is Ferdiad son of Daman son of Daire, for he has a horny skin about him in battle against a man, a belt, equally strong, victorious in battle, and neither points nor edges are reddened upon it in the hour of strife and anger. For he is the fury of the lion, and the bursting of wrath, and the blow of doom, and the wave that drowns foes."

"Speak not thus!" cried Cu Chulainn, "for I swear by my arms of valor, the oath that my people swear, that every limb and every joint will be as a pliant rush in the bed of a river under the point of the sword, if he show himself to me on the ford! Truly I am here," said Cu Chulainn, "checking and staying four of the five grand provinces of Erin from Monday at Samain till the beginning of spring, and I have not left my post for a night's disport, through stoutly opposing the men of Erin on the Cattle-Raid of Cooley. And in all this time, I have not put foot in retreat before any one man nor before a multitude, and methinks just as little will I turn in flight before him."

* * * * *

And Cu Chulainn reached the ford. Ferdiad waited on the south side of the ford; Cu Chulainn stood on the north side. Ferdiad bade welcome to Cu Chulainn. "Welcome is thy coming, O Cu Chulainn!" said Ferdiad.

"Truly spoken has seemed thy welcome always till now," answered Cu Chulainn; "but to-day I put no more trust in it. And, O Ferdiad," said Chu Chulainn, "it were fitter for me to bid thee welcome than that thou should'st welcome me; for it is thou that art come to the land and the province wherein I dwell; and it is not fitting for thee to come to contend and do battle with me, but it were fitter for me to go to contend and do battle with thee. For before thee in flight are my women and my boys and my youths, my steeds and my troops of horses, my droves, my flocks and my herds of cattle."

"Good, O Cu Chulainn," said Ferdiad; "what has ever brought thee out to contend and do battle with me? For when we were together with Scathach and with Uathach and with Aife, thou wast not a man worthy of me, for thou wast my serving-man, even for arming my spear and dressing my bed."

"That was indeed true," answered Cu Chulainn; "because of my youth and my littleness did I so much for thee, but this is by no means my mood this day. For there is not a warrior in the world I would not drive off this day in the field of battle and combat."

It was not long before they met in the middle of the ford. And then it was that each of them cast sharp-cutting reproaches at the other, renouncing his friendship.

*   *   *   *   *

"Too long are we now in this way," said Ferdiad; "and what arms shall we resort to to-day, O Cu Chulainn?"

"With thee is thy choice of weapons this day until night-time," answered Cu Chulainn, "for thou are he that first didst reach the ford."

"Rememberest thou at all," asked Ferdiad, "the choice of arms we wont to practice with Scathach and with Uathach and with Aife?"

"Indeed, and I do remember," answered Cu Chulainn.

"If thou rememberest, let us begin with them."

They betook them to do their choicest deeds of arms. They took upon them two equally-matched shields for feats, and their eight-edged targets for feats, and their eight small darts, and their eight straight swords, with ornaments of walrus-tooth, and their eight lesser ivoried spears which flew from them and to them like bees on a day of fine weather.

They cast no weapons that struck not. Each of them was busy casting at the other with those missiles from morning's early twilight until noon at mid-day, and while they overcame their various feats with the bosses and hollows of their feat-shields. However great the excellence of the throwing on either side, equally great was the excellence of the defense, so that during all that time neither bled nor reddened the other.

"Let us cease now from this bout of arms, O Cu Chulainn," said Ferdiad; "for it is not by such our decision will come."

"Yea, surely, let us cease, if the time hath come," answered Cu Chulainn.

Then they ceased. They threw their feat-tackle from them into the hands of their charioteers.

"To what weapons shall we resort next, O Cu Chulainn?" asked Ferdiad.

"Thine is the choice of weapons until nightfall," answered Cu Chulainn, "for thou art he who didst first reach the ford."

"Let us begin, then," said Ferdiad, "with our straight-cut smooth-hardened throwing-spears, with cords of full-hard flax on them."

"Aye, let us begin then," assented Cu Chulainn.

Then they took on them two hard shields, equally strong. They fell to their straight-cut, smooth-hardened spears with cords of full-hard flax on them. Each of them was engaged in casting at the other with the spears from the middle of noon till yellowness came over the sun at the hour of evening's sundown. However great the excellence of the defense, equally great was the excellence of the throwing on either side, so that each of them bled and reddened and wounded the other during that time.

"Wouldst thou fain make a truce, O Cu Chullain?" asked Ferdiad.

"It would please me," replied Cu Chullain; "for whoso begins with arms has the right to desist."

"Let us leave off from this now, O Cu Chulainn," said Ferdiad.

"Aye, let us leave off, if the time has come," answered Cu Chulainn.

So they ceased; and they threw their arms from them into the hands of their charioteers.

Thereupon each of them went toward the other in the middle of the ford, and each of them put his hand on the other's neck and gave him three kisses in remembrance of his fellowship and friendship. Their horses were in one and the same paddock that night, and their charioteers at one and the same fire; and their charioteers made ready a litter-bed of fresh rushes for them with pillows for wounded men on them. Then came healing and curing folk to heal and cure them, and they laid healing herbs and grasses and a curing charm on their cuts and stabs, their gashes and many wounds. Of every healing herb and grass and curing charm that was brought from the fairy-mounds of Erin to Cu Chulainn and was applied to the cuts and stabs, to the gashes and many wounds of Cu Chulainn, a like portion thereof he sent across the ford westward to Ferdiad, to put on his wounds and his pools of gore, so that the men of Erin should not have it to say, should Ferdiad fall at his hands, it was more than his share of care had been given to him.

Of every food and of every savory, soothing and strong drink that was brought by the men of Erin to Ferdiad, a like portion thereof he sent over the ford northwards to Cu Chulainn; for the purveyors of Ferdiad were more numerous than the purveyors of Cu Chulainn. All the men of Erin were purveyors to Ferdiad, to the end that he might keep Cu Chulainn off from them. But only the inhabitants of Mag

Breg were purveyors to Cu Chulainn. They were wont to come daily, that is, every night, to converse with him.

They bided there that night. Early on the morrow they arose and went to the ford of combat.

"To what weapons shall we resort on this day, O Ferdiad?" asked Cu Chulainn.

"Thine is the choosing of weapons till night-time," Ferdiad made answer, "because it was I had my choice of weapons yesterday."

"Let us take, then," said Cu Chulainn, "to our great, well-tempered lances to-day, for we think that the thrusting will bring nearer the decisive battle to-day than did the casting of yesterday. Let our horses be brought to us and our chariots yoked, to the end that we engage in combat over our horses and chariots on this day."

"Good, let us do so," Ferdiad assented.

Thereupon they took full-firm broad-shields on them for that day. They took to their great, well-tempered lances on that day. Either of them began to pierce and to drive, to throw and to press down the other, from early morning's twilight till the hour of evening's close. If it were the wont of birds in flight to fly through the bodies of men, they could have passed through their bodies on that day and carried away pieces of blood and flesh through their wounds and their sores into the clouds and the air all around. And when the hour of evening's close was come, their horses were spent and the drivers were wearied, and they themselves, the hero warriors of valor, were exhausted.

"Let us give over now, O Ferdiad," said Cu Chulainn, "for our horses are spent and our drivers tired, and when they are exhausted, why should we too not be exhausted?" And in this manner he spoke, and uttered these words at that place:

> We need not our chariots break—
> This, a struggle fit for giants.
> Place the hobbles on the steeds,
> Now that the din of arms is over!

"Yea, we will cease, if the time has come," replied Ferdiad. They ceased then. They threw their arms away from them into the hands of their charioteers. Each of them came towards his fellow. Each laid his hand on the other's neck and gave him three kisses. Their horses were in the one pen that night, and their charioteers at one fire . . . etc.

They abode there that night. Early on the morrow they arose and repaired to the ford of combat. Cu Chulainn marked an evil mien and a dark mood that day beyond every other on Ferdiad.

"It is evil thou appeareast to-day, O Ferdiad," said Cu Chulainn; "thy hair has become dark to-day, and thine eye has grown drowsy and thine upright form and thy features and thy gait have gone from thee!"

"Truly not for fear nor for dread of thee has that happened to me to-day," answered Ferdiad; "for there is not in Erin this day a warrior I could not repel!"

"Alas, O Ferdiad," said Cu Chulainn, "a pity it is for thee to oppose thy fosterbrother and comrade and friend on the counsel of any woman in the world!"

"A pity it is, O Cu Chulainn," Ferdiad responded. "But, should I part without a struggle with thee, I should be in ill repute forever with Medb and with the nobles of the four great provinces of Erin."

"A pity it is, O Ferdiad," said Cu Chulainn; "not on the counsel of all the men and women of the world would I desert thee or would do thee harm. And almost would it make a clot of gore of my heart to be combating with thee!"

* * * * *

"How much soever thou findest fault with me to-day," said Ferdiad, "for my ill-boding mien and evil doing, it will be as an offset to my prowess." And then he said, "To what weapons shall we resort to-day?"

"With thyself is the choice of weapons to-day until night-time come," replied Cu Chulainn, "for it was I that chose on the day gone by."

"Let us resort, then," said Ferdiad, "to our heavy, hard-smiting swords this day, for we trust that the smiting each other will bring us nearer to the decision of battle to-day than did our piercing each other yesterday."

"Let us go, then, by all means," responded Cu Chulainn.

Then they took two full-great long-shields upon them for that day. They turned to their heavy, hard-smiting swords. Each of them fell to strike and to hew, to lay low and cut down, to slay and undo his fellow, till as large as the head of a month-old child was each lump and each cut, each clutter and each clot of gore that each of them took from the shoulders and thighs and shoulderblades of the other.

Each of them was engaged in smiting the other in this way from the twilight of the early morning till the hour of evening's close. "Let us leave off from this now, O Cu Chulainn!" said Ferdiad.

"Aye, let us leave off if the hour is come," said Cu Chulainn.

They parted then, and threw their arms away from them into the hands of their charioteers. Though in comparison it had been the meeting of two happy, blithe, cheerful, joyful men, their parting that night was of two that were sad, sorrowful, and full of suffering. They parted without a kiss, a blessing, or any other sign of friendship, and their servants disarmed the steeds and the heroes; no healing nor curing herbs were sent from Cu Chulainn to Ferdiad that night, and no food nor drink was brought from Ferdiad to him. Their horses were not in the same paddock that night. Their charioteers were not at the same fire.

They passed that night there. It was then that Ferdiad arose early on the morrow and went alone to the ford of combat, and dauntless and vengeful and mighty was the man that went thither that day, Ferdiad the son of Daman. For he knew that that day would be the decisive day of the battle and combat; and he knew that one or the other of them would fall there that day, or that they both would fall. It was then he donned his battle-garb of battle and fight and combat. He put his silken, glossy trews with its border of speckled gold next to his white skin. Over this, outside, he put his brown-leathern, well-sewed kilt. Outside of this he put a huge, goodly flagstone, the size of a millstone, the shallow stone of adamant which he had brought from Africa, and which neither points nor edges could pierce. He put his solid, very deep, iron kilt of twice molten iron over the huge goodly flag as large as a millstone, through fear and dread of the *gae bulga* on that day. About his head he put his crested war-cap of battle and fight and combat, whereon were forty carbuncle-gems beautifully adorning it and studded with red-enamel and crystal and rubies and with shining stones of the Eastern world. His angry, fierce-striking spear he seized in his right hand. On his left side he hung his curved battle-sword, which would cut a hair against the stream with its keenness and sharpness, with its gold pommel and its rounded hilt of red gold. On the arch-slope of his back he slung his massive, fine, buffalo shield of a warrior whereon were fifty bosses, wherein a boar could be shown in each of its bosses, apart from the great central boss of red gold. Ferdiad performed divers brilliant manifold marvellous feats on high that day, unlearned of any one before, neither from foster-mother nor from foster-father, neither from Scathach nor from Uathach nor from Aife, but he found them of himself that day in the face of Cu Chulainn.

Cu Chulainn likewise came to the ford, and he beheld the various, brilliant, manifold, wonderful feats that Ferdiad performed on high. "Thou seest yonder, O Loeg my master, the divers bright, numerous, marvellous feats that Ferdiad performs one after the other, and therefore, O Loeg," cried Cu Chulainn, "if defeat be my lot this day, do thou prick me on and taunt me and speak evil to me, so that the more my spirit and anger shall rise in me. If, however, before me his defeat takes place, say thou so to me and praise me and speak me fair, to the end that greater may be my courage."

"It certainly shall be done so, if need be, O Cucuc," Loeg answered.

Then Cu Chulainn, too, girded on his war-harness of battle and fight and combat about him, and performed all kinds of splendid, manifold, marvellous feats on high that day which he had not learned from anyone before, neither with Scathach nor with Uathach nor with Aife.

Ferdiad observed those feats, and he knew they would be plied against him in turn.

"What weapons shall we resort to to-day?" asked Cu Chulainn.

"With thee is the choice of weapons till night-time," Ferdiad responded.

"Let us go to the Feat of the Ford, then," said Cu Chulainn.

"Aye, let us do so," answered Ferdiad. Albeit Ferdiad spoke that, he deemed it the most grievous thing whereto he could go, for he knew that Cu Chulainn used to destroy every hero and every battle-soldier who fought with him in the Feat of the Ford.

Great indeed was the deed that was done on the ford that day. The two horses, the two champions, the two chariot-fighters of the west of Europe, the two bright torches of valor of the Gael, the two hands of dispensing favor and of giving rewards and jewels and treasures in the west of the northern world, the two veterans of skill and the two keys of bravery to the Gael, the man for quelling the variance and discord of Connacht, the man for guarding the cattle and herds of Ulster, to be brought together in an encounter as from afar, set to slay or to kill each other, through the sowing of dissension and the incitement of Ailill and Medb.

Each of them was busy hurling at the other in those deeds of arms from early morning's gloaming till the middle of noon. When mid-day came, the rage of the men became wild, and each drew nearer to the other.

Thereupon Cu Chulainn gave one spring once from the bank of the ford till he stood upon the boss of Ferdiad son of Daman's shield, seeking to reach his head and to strike it from above over the rim of the shield. Straightway Ferdiad gave the shield a blow with his left elbow, so that Cu Chulainn went from him like a bird onto the brink of the ford. Again Cu Chulainn sprang from the brink of the ford, so that he lighted upon the boss of Ferdiad's shield, that he might reach his head and strike it over the rim of the shield from above. Ferdiad gave the shield a thrust with his left knee, so that Cu Chulainn went from him like an infant onto the bank of the ford.

Loeg espied that. "Woe, then, O Cu Chulainn," cried Loeg, "it seems to me the battle-warrior that is against thee hath shaken thee as a woman shakes her child. He has washed thee as a cup is washed in the tub. He hath ground thee as a mill grinds soft malt. He hath pierced thee as a tool bores through an oak. He hath bound thee as the bind-weed binds the trees. He hath pounced on thee as a hawk pounces on little birds, so that no more hast thou right or title or claim to valor or skill in arms till the very day of doom and of life, thou little imp of an elf-man!"

Thereat for the third time Cu Chulainn arose with the speed of the wind, and the swiftness of a swallow, and the dash of a dragon, and the strength of a lion into the clouds of the air, till he alighted on the boss of the shield of Ferdiad son of Daman, so as to reach his head that he might strike it from above over the rim of his shield. Then it was that the warrior gave the shield a violent powerful shake, so that Cu Chulainn flew from it into the middle of the ford, the same as if he had not sprung at all.

It was then the first distortion of Cu Chulainn took place, so that a swelling and inflation filled him like breath in a bladder, until he made a dreadful, many-colored, wonderful bow of himself, so that as big as a giant or a sea-man was the hugely-brave warrior towering directly over Ferdiad.

Such was the closeness of the combat they made, that their heads encountered above and their feet below and their hands in the middle over the rims and bosses of their shields.

Such was the closeness of the combat they made, that their shields burst and split from their rims to their centers.

Such was the closeness of the combat they made, that their spears bent and turned and shivered from their tips to their rivets.

Such was the closeness of the combat they made, that the boccanach and the bannanach (the puck-faced sprites and the white-faced sprites) and the spirits of the glens and the uncanny beings of the air screamed from the rims of their shields and from the guards of their swords and from the tips of their spears.

Such was the closeness of the combat they made, that the steeds of the Gael broke loose affrighted and plunging with madness and fury, so that their chains and their shackles, their traces and their tethers snapped, and the women and children and the undersized, the weak and the madmen among the men of Erin broke out through the camp southwestward.

At that time they were at the edge-feat of the swords. It was then Ferdiad caught Cu Chulainn in an unguarded moment, and he gave him a thrust with his tuck-hilted blade, so that he buried it in his breast, and his blood fell into his belt, till the ford became crimsoned with the clotted blood from the battle-warrior's body. Cu Chulainn endured it not under Ferdiad's attack, with his death-bringing, heavy blows, and his long strokes and his mighty middle slashes at him.

Then Cu Chulainn bethought him of his friends from the fairymound and of his mighty folk who would come and defend him and of his scholars to protect him, whenever he would be hard-pressed in the combat. It was then that Dolb and Indolb arrived to help and to succor their friend, namely Cu Chulainn, and one of them went on either side of him and they smote Ferdiad, the three of them, and Ferdiad did not perceive the men from the fairy-mound. Then it was that Ferdiad felt the onset of the three together smiting his shield against him, and thence he called to mind that, when they were with Scathach and Uathach, learning together, Dolb and Indolb used to come to help Cu Chulainn out of every stress wherein he was.

Ferdiad spoke; "Not alike are our foster-brothership and our comradeship, O Cu Chulainn."

"How so, then?" asked Cu Chulainn.

"Thy friends of the fairy-folk have succored thee, and thou didst not disclose them to me before," said Ferdiad.

"Not easy for me were that," answered Cu Chulainn, "for if the magic veil be once revealed to one of the sons of Mil, none of the Tuatha De Danann will have power to practice concealment or magic. And why complainest thou here, O Ferdiad?" said Cu Chulainn; "thou hast a horn skin whereby to multiply feats and deeds of arms on me, and thou hast not shown me how it is closed or how it is opened."

[Ferdiad now had the upper hand. But Cu Chulainn called for his *gae bulga*.]

When Ferdiad saw that his gillie had been thrown and heard the *gae bulga* called for, he thrust his shield down to protect the lower part of his body. Cu Chulainn gripped the short spear that was in his hand, cast it off the palm of his hand over the rim of the shield and over the edge of the corselet and hornskin, so that its farther half was visible after piercing Ferdiad's heart in his bosom. Ferdiad gave a thrust of his shield upwards to protect the upper part of his body, though it was help that came too late. Loeg sent the *gae bulga* down the stream, and Cu Chulainn caught it in the fork of his foot, and when Ferdiad raised his shield Cu Chulainn threw the *gae bulga* as far as he could cast underneath at Ferdiad, so that it passed through the strong thick, iron apron of wrought iron, and brake in three parts the huge, goodly stone the size of a millstone, so that it cut its way through the body's protection into him, till every joint and every limb was filled with its barbs.

"Ah, that blow suffices," sighed Ferdiad. "I am fallen of that! But, yet one thing more: mightily didst thou drive with thy right *foot*. And it was not fair of thee for me not to fall by thy *hand*."

* * * * *

Thereupon Cu Chulainn hastened towards Ferdiad and clasped his two arms about him, and bore him with all his arms and his armor and his dress northwards over the ford, so that it would be with his face to the north of the ford, in Ulster, the triumph took place and not to the west of the ford with the men of Erin. Cu Chulainn laid Ferdiad there on the ground, and a cloud and a faint and a swoon came over Cu Chulainn there by the head of Ferdiad. Loeg espied it and the men of Erin all arose for the attack upon him.

"Come, O Cucuc," cried Loeg; "arise now from thy trance, for the men of Erin will now come to attack us, and it is not single combat they will allow us, now that Ferdiad son of Daman son of Daire is fallen by thee."

"What availeth it me to arise, O gillie," said Cu Chulainn, "now that this one is fallen by my hand? . . . Ah, Ferdiad, greatly have the men of Erin deceived and abandoned thee, to bring thee to contend and do battle with me. For no easy thing is to contend and do battle with me on the Cattle-Raid of Cooley!"

* * * * *

"Good, O Cucuc," said Loeg, "let us leave this ford now; too long are we here!"

"Aye, let us leave it, O my master Loeg," replied Cu Chulainn. "But every combat and battle I have fought seems a game and a sport to me compared with the combat and battle of Ferdiad."

Cu Chullain's Lament Over Ferdiad

> Play was each, pleasure each,
> Until Ferdiad faced the beach;
> Dear that pillar of pure gold

From *Bards of the Gael and Gall, Examples of the Poetic Literature of Erinn,* by George Sigerson, p. 119. Charles Scribner's Sons. New York. 1907.

Who fell cold beside the ford.
Hosts of warriors felt his sword,
     First in battle's breach.

Play was each, pleasure each,
Until Ferdiad faced the beach;
Lion fiery, fierce and bright,
Wave whose might no thing withstands,
Sweeping, with the shrinking sands,
     Horror o'er the beach.

Play was each, pleasure each,
Until Ferdiad faced the beach;
Loved Ferdiad, dear to me;
I shall dree his death for aye—
Yesterday a mountain, he,
But a shade to-day.

Deirdre of the Sorrows

The nobles of Ulster were feasting in the house of Felimy, the son of Dall, the rymer of King Conor. Then was the wife of Felimy busied in attendance on her guests though shortly to become a mother. Cups and jests go round, and the house resounded with the revel. Suddenly the infant screamed in the womb of its mother, and the bitter pains of childbirth fell upon her. Then arose Cathbad the Druid, and prophesied, as she was borne away—"Under thy girdle, O woman, screamed a woman child, fair-haired, bright-eyed, beautiful—a virgin who will bring sorrow on Ulster—a birth fatal for princes—a child of disaster: let her name be Deirdre." Then sat they all in amaze till the infant was brought in; and it was a female child; and Cathbad looked upon it, and again prophesied—

When Cathbad ceased, the nobles present with one voice cried out that the child should not live; but Conor taking the child from Felimy, commanded that she should be cared for by his own people; and when the baby was nursed, he sent her to be brought up in a

From *Hibernian Nights' Entertainment*, by Sir Samuel Ferguson, pp. 16-31. P. M. Haverty, Publishers. New York. 1872.

lonely fort, where she should never see man till he might make her his own wife. Here Deirdre dwelt till she had grown to be the most beautiful maiden in all Ireland; and never yet had seen a man, save one aged and morose tutor. But on a certain day in winter, when her tutor was slaying a calf before the gate of the fort, to prepare food for her, she saw a raven drinking the blood from the snow. Then said she to her nurse, "Lovely, in truth, were the man marked with these colors—body like the snow, cheeks like the ruddy blood, and hair black as the wing of the raven—ah, Lewara, are there such men in the world without?" "Many such," said Lewara, "but the fairest of all is in the king's house —Naisi, the son of Usnach." "Alas!" cried Deirdre, "if I get not sight of that man I shall die!" Then her nurse plotted how she should bring Naisi and Deirdre together.

Now on a certain day, Naisi was sitting in the midst of the plain of Eman, playing on a harp. Sweet, in truth, was the music of the sons of Usnach. The cattle listening to it, milked ever two-thirds more than was their wont; and all pain and sorrow failed not to depart from whatsoever man or woman heard the strains of that melody. Great also was their prowess. When each set his back to the other, all Conor's province had been unable to overcome them. They were fleet as hounds in the chase: they slew deer with their speed.

Now, then, as Naisi sat singing on the plain of Eman, he perceived a maiden approaching him. She held down her head as she came near him, but passed without speaking. "Gentle is the damsel who passeth by," said Naisi. Then the maiden looking up, replied, "Damsels may well be gentle where there are no youths." Then Naisi knew that it was Deirdre, and great dread fell upon him. "The king of the province is betrothed to thee, oh damsel," he said. "I love him not," she replied, "he is an aged man: I would rather love a youth like thee." "Say not so, oh, damsel," said Naisi; "the king is a better spouse than the king's servant." "Thou sayest so," replied Deirdre, "that thou mayest avoid me." Then plucking a rose from a briar, she flung the flower to him, and said, "Now art thou ever disgraced if thou rejectest me." "Depart from me, I pray then, damsel," said Naisi. "Nay," replied Deirdre, "if thou dost not take me to be thy wife, thou art dishonored before all the men of thy country: and this I know from my nurse Lewara." Then Naisi said no more; and Deirdre took his harp, and sat beside him, playing sweetly. When the men of Ulster heard the delightful sound, they were enchanted. But the sons of Usnach rushed forth, and came running to where their brother sat, and Deirdre with him. "Alas," they cried, "what hast thou done, O brother? Is not this the damsel fated to ruin Ulster?" "Ah, me!" said

Naisi. "I am disgraced before the men of Erin for ever, if I take her not after that which she hath done." Then he told them the tale of what had happened. "Evil will come of it," said the brothers. "I care not," said Naisi. "I had rather be in misfortune than in dishonor. We will fly with her to another country."

They then took counsel together, and for the love they bore to Naisi, resolved to accompany him wheresoever he might go. So that night they departed, taking with them three times fifty men of might, and three times fifty women, and three times fifty greyhounds, and three times fifty attendants; and Naisi took Deirdre to be his wife. Then being pursued by Conor, who was greatly enraged at the loss of his betrothed spouse, they wandered hither and thither over Erin, in constant danger. . . . At length, weary of wandering through Erin, they came into the realm of Alba, and made their home in the midst of a wild therein.

There, when the chase of the mountain failed them, they fell upon the herds and cattle of the men of Alba; and the fame of their exploits reaching the ears of the king of that country, they were received into friendship and allegiance by him. But upon a certain day, when the king's steward made a circuit of the palace, early in the morning, he saw Naisi and Deirdre asleep in their tent. Then said he to the king, "O, king, we have at last found a meet wife for you. There is in the bed of Naisi, son of Usnach, a woman worthy of the sovereign of the west of the world; let Naisi be slain, O king, and marry thou the woman thyself." "Nay," said the king, "do thou first solicit her in private." It is done so. Deirdre informs Naisi of all this; and, moreover, how the son of Usnach would be put forward into danger till he should be slain, that the king might wed her being left without her husband. "Away, therefore," she said, "for if we depart not to-night, you will be slain to-morrow." Then the sons of Usnach departed from the palace of the king of Alba, and went into a distant island of the ocean.

Upon a certain day, King Conor was feasting with the nobles in the mansion of Emania, and there was sweet music and delight among all present. And after the bards had sung, in delightful measures, their branches of kindred and boughs of genealogy, King Conor raised his royal voice and said: "I would know of you, princes and nobles, whether you have ever seen a feast better than this, or a mansion better than the mansion of Emania?" "We have seen none," they replied. "And again," said Conor, "I would fain know of you, if there be anything whatsoever here wanting," "Nothing," they replied. "Say not so," said Conor, "I well know what is here wanting; the presence of the three renowned youths, the martial lights of the Gael, the three noble sons of Usnach, Naisi, Aini, and Ardan. Alas, that they should be absent from us for the like of any woman in the world! Hard bested they are, and outlawed in an island of the ocean, fighting with the men of the king of Alba. Sons of a king indeed they are, and well could they defend the sovereignty of Ulster—I would they were with us." Then the nobles replied and said: "Had we dared to speak our thoughts, this is what we would ourselves have said; and moreover that had we but the three sons of Usnach in the country, Ulster alone would not be inferior to all the rest of Erin: for, men of might they be, and lions for valor and prowess." "Let us then," said Conor, "dispatch messengers to Alba, to the island of Loch Etive, to the fastness of the clan Usnach, to solicit their return." "Who can give sufficient surety of safety to induce the sons of Usnach to come into thy kingdom?" asked they. "There are three only of all my nobles," said Conor, "on whose guaranty against my anger, the sons of Usnach will trust themselves; and they are Fergus, Cuchullan, and Conell Carnach: one of these will I send upon this message."

Then taking Conell Carnach into a place apart, Conor asked him what he would do if he should send him for the sons of Usnach, and that they should come to harm while under his pledge of safe conduct. "Whomsoever I might find injuring them," said Conell Carnach, "on him would I straightway inflict the bitter pain of death." "Then can I perceive," said Conor, "that dear to you I myself am not." A like question asked Conor of Cuchullan, and of him received a like answer. Then called he apart Fergus, the son of Roy, and in like manner questioned him; this said Fergus in answer. "Thine own blood I shed not; but whomsoever else I should find doing injury to those in my safe conduct him would I not permit to live."

"Then," said Conor, "I perceive thou lovest me. Go thou to the clan Usnach, and bring them to me on thy guaranty; and return thou by the way of Dun Barach, but let not the sons of Usnach tarry to eat meat with any till they come to the feast I shall have prepared for their welcome in Emania. Give me thy pledge to do this." Then Fergus bound himself by solemn vow to do the king's commands, and so returning together, they joined the other nobles and bore away that night in feasting and delight. The king, however, called Barach into a place apart, and asked him had he a feast prepared at his mansion? "I have a feast prepared in Dun Barach," said Barach, "to which thou and thy nobles are ever welcome." "Let not Fergus then depart from thy mansion," said Conor, "without partaking of that feast on his return from Alba." "He shall feast with me for three days," replied Barach, "for we are brothers of the Red Branch, and he is under vow not to refuse my hospitality." Next morning Fergus, with his two sons, Buini Borb and Illan Finn, and Cailon the shield-bearer, bearing his shield, departed from Emania for pleasant Alba. They sailed across the sea until they came to Loch Etive, to the island of the sons of Usnach. Here dwelt the clan Usnach in green hunting booths along the shore.

And Deirdre and Naisi sat together in their tent, and Conor's polished chess-board between them, and they played at chess. Now when Fergus came into the harbor, he sent forth the loud cry of a mighty man of chase. And Naisi hearing the cry, said, "I hear the call of a man of Erin." "That was not the call of a man of Erin," replied Deirdre, "but the call of a man of Alba." Then again Fergus shouted a second time. "That was surely the cry of a man of Erin," said Naisi. "Nay, 'twas not, indeed," replied Deirdre; "let us play on." Then, again, Fergus shouted a third time, and Naisi knew that it was the cry of Fergus, and he said, "If the son of Roy be in existence, I hear his hunting shout from the loch; go forth, Ardan, my brother, and give our kinsman welcome." "Alas!" said Deirdre. "I knew the call of Fergus from the first." "Why didst thou then conceal it, my queen?" said Naisi. Then Deirdre answered, "Last night I had a dream. Three birds came to us from the plains of Emania, having each a drop of honey in its beak; and they departed from us, having each a drop of blood in place of the drop of honey." "And how dost thou read that dream, O princess?" said Naisi. "That Fergus cometh with false messages of peace from Conor," she replied, "for sweeter is not honey than the message of peace of the false man." "Nay, think not so," said Naisi; "Fergus is long in the port: go, Ardan, meet him quickly, and guide him to our tent." Then Ardan went and welcomed Fergus, and embraced him and his sons, and kissed them and demanded of them the news from Erin. "Good news," said Fergus. "Conor hath sent us to be your warranty of safe conduct, if you will return to Emania." "There is no need for them to go thither," said Deirdre, "greater is their own sway in Alba than the sway of Conor in Erin." "To be in one's native land is better than all else," said Fergus, "for of little worth are power or prosperity to a man if he seeth not each day the land that gave him birth." "True, it is," said Naisi, "dearer to me is Erin than Alba, though in Alba I should enjoy more fortunate estate than in Erin." "Put your trust in me," said Fergus, "I pledge myself for your safe conduct." "Let us go then," said Naisi, "we will go under Fergus's safe conduct to our native land."

They whiled away that night until the dawning of next day; then went they down to their ships and set sail across the sea.

*   *   *   *   *

By this time they had reached the port of Dun Barach; and Barach himself meeting them upon the shore, welcomed Fergus and his sons, and the sons of Usnach, and Deirdre also, with kisses eager and affectionate. Then Barach said to Fergus—"Tarry, and partake of my feast; for I will not let thee part from me for three days without breaking thy vow of brotherhood and hospitality." When Fergus heard this, he became crimson red, for anger, from head to foot, and thus he said— "Thou has done ill, O Barach, to ask me to thy feast, knowing, as thou dost, that I am bounden to Conor not to let the sons of Usnach, who are under my safe-conduct, tarry night or day for entertainment from another, till they reach Emania, where he hath his banquet prepared to welcome them." "I care not," said Barach, "I lay thee under the ban of our order if thou rejectest my hospitality." Then Fergus asked of Naisi what he should do? and Deirdre answered—"Thou must either forsake Barach or the sons of Usnach: it were truly more meet to forsake thy feast than thy friends who are under thy protection." "Neither Barach nor the sons of Usnach will I forsake," said Fergus; "for I will remain with Barach, and my two sons, Illan Finn and red Buini Borb, shall be your escort and pledge of safe conduct, in my stead, to Emania." "We care not for thy safe conduct," said Naisi; "our own hands have ever been our pledge of protection"; and he departed from Fergus in great wrath; and Ardan, and Ainli, and Deirdre, and the two sons of Fergus followed him, and they left Fergus sad and gloomy behind them.

Then said Deirdre—"I would counsel that we go to the isle of Rathlin, and abide there till Fergus shall be free to accompany us; for I fear this safe conduct will not long protect us." Then did Naisi and the sons of Fergus reproach her, and they said they would not take that counsel, and go forward to Emania even as they were. "Alas!" said Deirdre; "would that I had never left the long-grassed Alba!" But when they had come to Fincairn watch-tower, in the mountain of Fuadh, Naisi perceived that Deirdre did not accompany them, for sleep had fallen upon her; and on returning he found her in a deep slumber in the valley; and when she was awakened, she arose in grief and fear. "Alas!" she said, "I dread treachery: I had a dream, and in my vision I beheld Illan Finn fighting for us, and Buini Borb idle, and his head on Buini Borb, and Illan Finn's trunk headless." "Thy lips are lovely, but thy prophecy, nought save evil," said Naisi. "Let the vengeance of thy lips fall on the stranger. I fear not treachery. Let us on." And so they went on till they came to Ardsallagh; and then Deirdre said to Naisi—"I see a cloud over Emania, and it is a cloud of blood. I counsel you, O sons of Usnach, go not to Emania without Fergus; but let us go to Dundalgan, to our cousin Cuchullan, till Fergus shall have fulfilled his obligation to Barach." "I fear not," said Naisi; "let us proceed." Then again Deirdre cried—"O! Naisi, look at the cloud over Emania: it is a cloud of blood; gore drops fall from its red edges. Ah me! go not to Emania to-night; let us go to Dundalgan—let us take shelter with Cuchullan." "I fear not," said Naisi; "I will not hear thy counsel; let us proceed." "Grandson of Roy," said Deirdre, "seldom have we not been of one accord before—I and thou, Naisi! This had not been so that day when Lewara led me to your seat upon the plain of Emania." "I fear not," said Naisi; "let us on!" "Sons of Usnach," again said Deirdre, "I have a signal by which to know if Conor designs treachery against us. If we be admitted into the mansions of Emania, Conor designs not harm toward us; if we be lodged apart, in the mansion of the Red Branch, then doth Conor surely meditate us evil." By this they were arrived before the gates of Emania. Then Naisi knocked at the gate, and the door-keeper demanded who was without? "Clan Usnach and Deirdre," replied Naisi. Then were they conducted towards the house of the Red Branch, by Conor's orders. " 'Twere better to take my counsel even yet," said Deirdre, "for evil is surely now designed for us." "We will not do so," said Illan Finn, the son of Fergus; "coward-liness hath never been known of the sons of my father. I and Buini Borb shall go with you to the Red Branch." Then moved they on to the house and entered it; and attendants brought them rich viands and sweet wines, until all were satisfied and cheerful, save only Deirdre and the sons of Usnach; for they partook not of much food or drink, being weary from their journey, and in dread of their lives. Then said Naisi, "bring hither the chessboard, that we may play": and he and Deirdre played upon the polished chessboard.

And now when Conor knew that Deirdre was in the Red Branch, he could not rest at the feast, but said—"Whom shall I find that will do my errand to the Red Branch, to tell me whether her beauty lives upon Deirdre; for, if her own face and figure live upon her, there is not in the world a woman more beautiful than she." Then said Lewara, the nurse, "I will do thine errand." For she dearly loved both Naisi and Deirdre, whom she, at first, had brought together. Then Lewara, coming to the Red Branch, found Naisi and Deirdre with the polished board between them, playing at chess; and she gave them kisses eager and affectionate, and said, "Alas! my children, you do not well to spend your time in games and pleasure, while Conor cannot rest for the thoughts of the treachery he designs you. Wo is me, this night will be a black night for the clan Usnach, if ye bar not fast your doors and windows, and fight not courageously, O sons of Fergus, and manfully defend your charge till Fergus himself cometh." Then shed she bitter tears, and returned to the mansion of Emania; and Conor asked what tidings. "Tidings of good and of evil," replied Lewara; "and my good tidings are, that the sons of Usnach are three of the most valiant and noble; of the most excellent form and aspect of all the men in the world; and that, with their help, thou mayest henceforth sway all Erin, if thou wilt; and my evil tidings are, that she, who at her departure from Erin was the fairest of women, is now bereft of her own form and aspect, and is lovely and desirable no longer." Then Conor's wrath and jealousy abated, and he went on feasting until a second time he thought of Deirdre, and he said, "Whom shall I find to bring me true tidings from the Red Branch? is there any here will do my errand truly?" Then none of the nobles answered; for they feared to abet the king, in violating the pledge of Fergus, as they dreaded he now meditated to do. Then said Conor to one of his people, "Knowest thou who slew thy father, O Trendorn?" "Naisi Mac Usnach slew my father, and my three brothers," replied Trendorn. "Go thy way, then," said Conor, "and bring me true tidings of Deirdre, whether her beauty still live upon her; for, if it doth, there is not on the ridge of earth a woman lovelier than she." Then Trendorn went to the Red Branch, and found one window unfastened, and looked through it, and saw Naisi and Deirdre within, and the polished board between them, and they playing. And Deirdre said to Naisi, "I see one looking at us through the window." Thn Naisi flung the chessman he held in his hand at the spy, and dashed his eyes out of the head of Trendorn. And Trendorn went to Conor, and told him, and Conor cried aloud, "This man who hath maimed my servant would himself be king!" Then asked he, what tidings of Deirdre? "Such beauty liveth upon her," said Trendorn, "that there is not on the ridge of earth a woman so beautiful." As Conor heard this his jealousy and hatred were renewed, and he rose from the table in great wrath, and cried that the sons of Usnach had sought to slay his servant, and called upon his people to go and assault the Red Branch, and bring them forth, that they might be punished.

Then came the troops of Ulster to the Red Branch, and sent forth three dreadful shouts about it, and set fire and flames to the doors and windows. And the sons of Usnach, when they heard the shouts, demanded who were without, "Conor and Ulster," cried the troops, and shouted fearfully. "Villains," cried Illan Finn, "would ye break my father's pledge?" "Ravishers and villains," cried Conor, "would ye abet the seducer of my wife?" "Ah me," said Deirdre, "we are betrayed, and Fergus is a traitor." "If Fergus hath betrayed you," said Red Buini Borb, "yet will not I betray you"; and he threw open the gates, and went forth with his men, and slew thrice fifty men of might abroad, and made dreadful confusion among the troops. Then Conor demanded who made that havoc of his people, and Buini answered, "I, Red Buini Borb, the son of Fergus." "Hold thy hand," said Conor, "and I will bestow upon thee the territory of Slieve Fuadh." Then Buini Borb held back his hand from the carnage, and demanded, "Wilt thou aught else?" "I will make thee mine own prime councillor," replied Conor; and Buini Borb desisted from the slaughter, and went his way. But his territory was made that night a desert; and it is called Dalwhiuny to this day, a wild moor on the mountains of Fuadh. When Deirdre saw that Buini Borb had deserted them, she said, "Traitor father, traitor son: Well knew I that Fergus was a traitor!" "If Fergus was a traitor," said Illan Finn, "yet will not I be a traitor: while liveth this small straight sword in my hand, I will not forsake the sons of Usnach!" Then Illan Finn went forth with his men and they made three swift onslaughts round about the mansion, and slew thrice an hundred men of might abroad, and came in again where Naisi sat playing at chess with his brother Ainli, for the sons of Usnach would not let their calm hearts be troubled by that alarm. Then taking torches, Illan Finn and his men went forth a second time, and slew their men of might abroad, and drove the bearers of the flame and fire from around the mansion. Then it was that Conor cried, "Where is my own son Fiara Finn?" "I am here, my king," cried Fiara. "As I live," said Conor, "it was on the same night that thou and Illan Finn were born; go then and do battle with him manfully. And as he is clad in his father's arms, clothe thou thyself in mine. Take Ocean, Flight, and Victory—my shield, my spear, and my claymore, and do good battle for your father with this son of Fergus." Fiara then arrayed himself in his father's noble and bright armour, and went to the Red Branch, and did good battle with Illan Finn. They fought a fair fight, stout and manly, bitter and bloody, savage and hot, and vehement, and terrible, till Illan Finn beat down Fiara, so that he forced him to crouch beneath the shelter of his shield. Then the waves round the blue rim of Ocean roared, for it was the nature of Conor's shield that it ever resounded as with the noise of stormy waves when he who bore it was in danger. And the three chief seas of Erin roared with all their waves responsive to the shout of Ocean. The wave of Tuath, and the wave of Cliona, and the wave of Inver-Rory roared around Erin for the danger of Fiara. Conell Carnach sitting on the rock of Sanseverick heard the tumult from Loch Rory and the sea, and taking his arms and calling his men of might, came towards Emania, where he knew that Conor, his sovereign, was in peril. There, on the open field before the mansion of Red Branch, they found Fiara Finn sore pressed by his adversary, and, coming behind him, he thrust his sword through the heart of Illan Finn, whom he knew not, for he had not yet beheld his face. "Who hath pierced me at my back?" asked Illan Finn, "when he might have had fair battle, face to face, had he sought it?" "Nay, rather, who art thou?" said Conell. "Illan, the son of Fergus," replied Illan Finn; "and art thou Conell Carnach?—Alas, it is even so. Evil is the deed thou hast done, Conell, to slay me while defending the clan Usnach, who are in the Red Branch under my father's pledge of safe conduct from Alba." "By my hand of valour," cried Conell, "this shall not be unavenged," and he struck Fiara Finn a sharp stroke, where he stood, and lopped away his head from his beard and went thence in great wrath and sorrow. The weakness of death then fell darkly upon Illan, and he threw his arms into the mansion, and called to Naisi to fight manfully, and expired.

And now the men of Ulster came again to assault the Red Branch, and to set fire and faggots to the doors. Then forth came Ardan and his men and put out the fires, and slew three hundred men of might abroad, and made sore havoc of Conor's people. Naisi himself came forth with his men the last third of the night, and ere day dawn had slain two hundred and driven all the troops from around the mansion. And at dawn, Conor brought all the men of Ulster, and he and the clan Usnach, with their men, joined battle on the plain and fought a fierce fight until broad day. And the battle went against the men of Ulster; and till the sands of the sea, the leaves of the forest, the dewdrops of the meadows, or the stars of heaven be counted, it is not possible to tell the number of heads and hands, and lopped limbs of heroes, that then lay bare and red from the hands of Naisi and his brothers and their people on that plain. Then Naisi came again into the Red Branch to Deirdre, and she encouraged him and said: "We will yet escape: fight manfully and fear not." Then the sons of Usnach made a phalanx of their shields, and spread the links of their joined bucklers around Deirdre, and bounding forth like three eagles, swept down upon the troops of Conor, making sore havoc of his people in that onslaught. Now when Cathbad the Druid saw that the sons of Usnach were bent on the destruction of Conor himself, he had recourse to his acts of magic; and he cast an enchantment over them, so that their arms fell from their hands, and they were taken by the men of Ulster, for the spell was like a sea of thick gums about them, and their limbs were clogged in it that they could not move.

Then was there no man in the host of Ulster, that could be found who would put the sons of Usnach to death, so loved were they of the people and nobles. But, in the house of Conor was one called Maini Rough Hand, son of the king of Lochlin; and Naisi had slain his father and two brothers; and he undertook to be their executioner. So the sons of Usnach were there slain: and the men of Ulster, when they beheld their death, sent forth three heavy shouts of sorrow and lamentation. Then Deirdre fell down beside their bodies, wailing and weeping, and she tore her hair and garments, and bestowed kisses on their lifeless lips and bitterly bemoaned them. And a grave was opened for them, and Deirdre, standing by it, with her hair dishevelled, and shedding tears abundantly, chanted their funeral song.

> The lions of the hill are gone,
> And I am left alone—alone—
> Dig the grave both wide and deep,
> For I am sick, and fain would sleep.
>
> The falcons of the wood are flown,
> And I am left alone—alone—
> Dig the grave both deep and wide,
> And let us slumber side by side.
>
> The dragons of the rock are sleeping,
> Sleep that wakes not for our weeping,
> Dig the grave and make it ready,
> Lay me on my true love's body!

* * * * *

The High-Kingship

The high-kingship of Ireland developed out of the kingship of Tara in what is now the county of Meath. The possessors of Tara would have been wealthy amongst the early kings, for it is an eminence over a grass land that has always been famous for cattle-raising. But Tara had also associations that would give its kings prestige. Nearby are the great mounds that had been the burial chambers and temples for a Bronze Age people. There was the Brugh, or Dwelling of Angus, a divinity associated with youth and love. Now, as Professor MacAlister has

---

By the editor.

shown in *Tara, a Pagan Sanctuary,* its early kings were priest-kings of a kind we can discern in prehistoric Greece, Italy, and other countries: they were representatives of the divinity that brought about agricultural increase, and their proper office was the performance of the rites that promoted fertility. The divine folk lived in the Brugh. From it came the brides of the kings' ritual marriages. Perhaps the substantiality of what may be called the background of these women comes from the fact that they could be thought of as having a habitation. The sacred king had to have everything about him auspicious: he had to be sound, uninjured, and of a fine appearance. So it is with the early kings of Tara.

Conn, his son Art, his grandson Cormac, and his great grandson Cairbry form a dynasty at Tara that, compared with the kings before them, has the look of a political kingship. This was around A.D. 200. Cormac made Tara a social as well as a political center by building the great Hall of Assembly in which outstanding personages among the nobility and the learned classes were entertained during the sacred festivals; he also made the lesser kings lodge their youthful princes in Tara as hostages.

It is possible that in Cormac's time there were influences from Roman Britain; some scholars see in Tara's famous hall a reproduction of a Roman building and in the Fian who guarded it a reproduction of the Roman Legion. The Hall of Assembly left ridges that can still be seen and measured. A plan of the interior has come down to us with even a list of dishes that were served to the different grades of nobility, professional classes, and royal attendants. There was a bulge in the center, and there the king, queen, and princes had their seats commanding the upper and lower portions of the hall.

With Cormac the story of Tara begins. He was the son of Art whose father was Conn of the Hundred Battles or the Hundred Battalions, and his mother's name was Etain. His father, going into battle, foretold his death to Etain, and knowing that she had conceived, told her to bring her son for fosterage to a friend whom he named, Lugna.

Cormac

Etain was then pregnant and resolved to go to the house of Lugna Fer Tri so that her child should be born there. When she reached his

From *The Cycles of the Kings,* by Myles Dillon, pp. 23-25. Geoffrey Cumberlege, Oxford University Press. London and New York. 1946.

country the birth-pains seized her, and she got down from her chariot and was delivered of a son on a bed of fern. A peal of thunder greeted his birth, and Lugna, hearing this, knew that it was for the birth of Cormac, son of the true prince Art, and he set out in search of him.

Etain slept after her delivery, and entrusted the boy to her maid till they should continue their journey. The maid fell asleep, and a she-wolf came and carried off the child to her lair in the place now known as Cormac's Cave. Lugna came to where she lay, and she told him all that had happened. He brought her to his house, and proclaimed that whosoever should find tidings of the child should obtain in reward whatever he asked.

Grec MacArod was abroad one day, and coming upon the cave, he saw the whelps playing before it and the child creeping among them. He brought the news to Lugna, and was granted the territory where the Grecraige now dwell. The child and the whelps were brought home from the cave, and the child was named Cormac, for that was the name his father had given him. He was the delight of many for his beauty and grace and dignity and strength and judgment.

One day, as he was playing with Lugna's sons, he struck one of them. The lad exclaimed that it was too much to suffer a blow from one whose race and kindred were unknown, save that he was a fatherless child. Cormac complained to Lugna, and Lugna told him that he was the son of the true prince Art, son of Conn of the Hundred Battles, and that it was prophesied that he should steer his father's rudder, for there would be no prosperity in Tara until he should reign there. "Let us go," said Cormac, "to seek recognition in my father's house in Tara." "Let us go then," said Lugna.

They went to Tara, and MacCon welcomed them and took Cormac into fosterage. There was a woman hospitaller in Tara at that time named Bennaid. Her sheep grazed the queen's woad. MacCon awarded the sheep to the queen in compensation for the grazing of the woad. "No," said Cormac. "The shearing of the sheep is enough in compensation for the grazing of the woad, for both will grow again." "It is a true judgment!" said all. "It is the son of a true prince who has given judgment!" The side of the house on which the false judgment had been given fell down the slope. It will stay thus for ever. That is the Crooked Mound of Tara.

The men of Ireland expelled MacCon and gave the kingship to Cormac. Everything prospered while he lived. His wolves remained with him, and the reason for the great honor he received was that he had been reared by wolves.

Tara was restored by Cormac so that it was grander than ever before, houses, fences, and buildings. Well was it with Ireland in his time. The rivers teemed with fish, the woods with mast, the plains with honey, on account of the justice of his rule. Deer were so plentiful that there was no need to hunt them. Cormac built the noblest building that ever was raised in Tara. Though he was opposed by the Ulstermen, he was never deprived of the kingship till his death. He died in the *raith* of the hospitaller in Cletech when a salmon bone stuck in his throat.

Cormac ordered that he should not be buried in Bruig na Boinne, for he did not adore the same god as those who were buried there. He ordered his burial in Ros na Rig with his face due east towards the rising sun.

Instructions of a King

"O Cormac, grandson of Conn," said Carbery, "what were your habits when you were a lad?"
"Not hard to tell," said Cormac.

> I was a listener in woods,
> I was a gazer at stars,
> I was blind where secrets were concerned,
> I was silent in a wilderness,
> I was talkative among many,
> I was mild in the mead-hall,
> I was stern in the battle,
> I was gentle towards allies,
> I was a physician of the sick,
> I was weak towards the feeble,
> I was strong towards the powerful,
> I was not close lest I should be burdensome,
> I was not arrogant though I was wise,
> I was not given to promising though I was strong,
> I was not venturesome though I was swift,
> I did not deride the old though I was young,
> I was not boastful though I was a good fighter,
> I would not speak of anyone in his absence,

From *Selections from Ancient Irish Poetry*, translated by Kuno Meyer, pp. 105-106. Constable & Co. Ltd. London. 1911.

I would not reproach, but I would praise,
I would not ask, but I would give,
For it is through these habits that the young become
old and kingly warriors."

"O Cormac, grandson of Conn," said Carbery, "what is the worst thing you have seen?"

"Not hard to tell," said Cormac. "Faces of foes in the rout of battle."

"O Cormac, grandson of Conn," said Carbery, "what is the sweetest thing you have heard?"

"Not hard to tell," said Cormac.

"The shout of triumph after victory,
Praise after wages,
A lady's invitation to her pillow."

Dermott and Grania

It was very early in the morning; the place was under Finn Mac-Cuhal's court, Almu in Leinster; the people were Finn himself and two of his captains who had found him roaming around between the light and dark.

"What is the cause of this early rising of yours, Finn?" one asked him.

"He is wont to be without slumber and sweet sleep," said Finn, "who lacks a fitting wife. When that is the case a man is lonely and restless. Anyway, it has been so with me since Maignes, the daughter of Garad, died."

"What is it compels you to be without a wife or mate?" they said to him. "You had a wife before Maignes, and a wife before her again. And there is no woman or maiden on the green-sodded island of Eirinn, whom, if you turned your eyes on her, we would not bring you."

"And I," said one, "could show you a maiden who beyond everyone else would be a fitting wife for you."

"Whom have you in mind?" Finn asked.

"The daughter of the King of Ireland, Grania."

From *The Frenzied Prince, Being Heroic Stories of Ancient Ireland*, told by Padraic Colum, pp. 123-139. Copyright, 1943, by David McKay Co. Philadelphia.

Finn became thoughtful. After a while he said, "There have been variance and distance between King Cormac and myself this while back, and if a refusal was given me by him there would be the width of the Shannon between us. Would you," he said to the two before him, "go to Tara and speak to King Cormac about the affair? If he refuses, no one need ever hear of it."

"We will go to Tara," the two said, "and you, Finn, say nothing about what we've gone for unless we are favored by King Cormac."

The two who spoke to Finn that early morning were Oisin the poet, Finn's son, and Duanach MacMorna the druid. It is not told how they fared till they reached Tara. But reach Tara they did; they were brought before King Cormac.

"There is not a king's son, a hero, nor a champion in Ireland to whom my daughter has not given a refusal of marriage," said the king when they told him of their errand. "And each and every one of them," he said, "lays the blame on me for the refusal."

It was easy to be seen that the king was troubled about the matter. "I invite you to visit my daughter," he said, laying his hands on the shoulders of the envoys. "It is better you should hear her own words than that Finn MacCuhal should have any ill-feeling against myself."

So he brought Oisin and Duanach MacMorna into the women's quarters and into Grania's own bower with its window of blue glass. And he had Grania bring in bread and meat and wine so that they might feast and become familiar together. He himself sat on the couch beside his daughter.

"Here, O Grania," said King Cormac, "are two of the people of Finn MacCuhal. They have come to ask that you consider Finn for a husband. What answer do you want to give, my daughter?"

"If he be a fitting son-in-law for you, why should he not be a fitting husband for me?" Grania answered.

"There is no *if* about it as far as I'm concerned," said the king. To that Grania made no answer.

She had a thin strip of gold about her head and a piece of amber at her neck, and MacMorna the druid thought that, like the amber and gold, Grania was fine and rare but unreckonable in their possessions. She was tired of being with her women, he thought.

Oisin the poet took stock of Grania so that he might be able to speak of her when he went back to Almu. She was young to be in the place his own mother had been in, Oisin considered. She was younger than the other two wives Finn had had even when they were at their youngest. Her fingers with their reddened nails were long; her hands were long; she was long from ankle to knee, from knee to thigh. Her lips were red but very thin, her eyes were bright but not deep. She looked on them and looked on her father very steadily but as one who kept her own thought.

She would be a fit wife for Finn, Oisin told himself, for she was fair in her looks and knowledgeable in what she said, and in every way showed the dignity of a king's daughter.

All went well; they feasted and became familiar. King Cormac looked cheerful when he appointed an evening for Finn and his people to come to a feast in Tara when, in the presence of Finn's people and the nobles and chiefs of Cormac's territory, Grania's hand would be placed in Finn's.

"I have never looked at Finn," said Grania. "Which of you two is he like?"

"He should be like me," said Oisin, "seeing I'm his son."

"Yes," said Grania, "Finn has a son who has reached an age when he can be as famous as you are, Oisin."

Then Oisin and MacMorna went back to Almu in Leinster, and came into Finn's court there, and told him of the favorable reception that had been given them, and told him of Grania's looks and manners and words. Afterwards Finn announced the feast they had been invited to in Tara, and when the Fian knew what the feast was towards, they raised three shouts around their captain, Finn MacCuhal.

Now as everything wears away so the space of time between then and the time of the feast wore away, and the day come when Finn with his chosen chieftains left Almu for Tara. A joyous and colorful band, they crossed the plain of Leinster and nothing is told of them until they entered the Midcuartha, Cormac's great hall in Tara.

The King of Ireland sat in the raised part that in the shape of a bow was midway in the hall, commanding the upper and lower parts. His wife sat at his left shoulder and his daughter Grania sat at her left shoulder. Finn MacCuhal sat on the king's right shoulder and the druid MacMorna sat beside him.

Across the hall Cairbry, Cormac's son, sat with Oisin beside him. And in the body of the hall were the captains of the Fian and the nobles of Ireland, each according to his rank and his patrimony.

Without clamour or disturbance all were served.

Between those who were beside the king there was gentle discourse. Duanach MacMorna, as the feast went on, chanted for Grania the songs and verses and melodious poems of her fathers and ancestors, the lays of their home place, Cruachan, from whence the kings of Ireland had come to Tara.

After listening to these for a while, Grania said:

"What is the reason for Finn's coming to Tara this night?"

"If it is not known to you," said the druid, "do not wonder if it is not known to me."

"I desire to hear it from you."

"It is to ask for yourself as a wife and a mate that Finn has come to Tara."

"I marvel that it is not for the like of Oisin he would ask me," said Grania, "for it is fitter I should be with the like of him than be with a man as old as my father."

The druid kept silent at that, and Grania said:

"Who is the warrior who is just below Oisin's place?"

"Goll MacMorna, the active and soldierly."

"Who is that graceful man at the shoulder of Goll?"

"Caelte MacRonan."

"Who is the haughty looking warrior at MacRonan's shoulder?"

"MacLugaid who is sister's son to Finn MacCuhal."

"Who is the young warrior at the other side of Oisin? I mean the one with the ruddy cheeks and the curling black hair."

"He is Dermott, grandson of Duivna, favored of women and maidens, and a mortal whom Angus of the Brugh greatly cherishes."

"That must set O'Duivna well apart from the rest of you," said Grania. "No one else of the Fian, I think, is cherished by an immortal. Who is at Dermott's shoulder?"

"Diorruing. He is a very skilful leach."

"What a goodly company is here!" said Grania.

"But chief of all is the one at your father's shoulder."

"Ah, Finn!" said Grania. "Do not think you have to remind me of Finn."

But as if she had been reminded of him she called to her special handmaid and had her bring her the jewelled goblet that was in her bower behind the dais, her own goblet. The handmaid brought it and Grania filled it.

"Take the goblet to Finn first," she said to her handmaid, "and ask him to take a draught out of it, and let him know that it is sent by me." The goblet contained a drink for nine times nine men. In the liquor Grania put a cunning drug.

Finn laughed as he took a draught out of it. But soon he fell into a stupor and then into a slumber. The goblet was handed around. Cormac took the goblet and drank and he, too, fell into a slumber; so did Cormac's wife, Queen Eitche.

"Take the goblet to Cairbry and ask him to drink out of it; tell him it comes from Grania, and ask him to give the goblet to the nobles by him."

The handmaid did as Grania bade her.

After he had drunk out of it Cairbry was hardly able to pass the goblet on to those next him. All who drank out of the goblet fell into a deep slumber.

Thereupon Grania left her place and went to where Dermott was. She stood beside him and she said:

"Wilt thou receive courtship from me, O Dermott?"

"I may not," said Dermott, "seeing you are betrothed to my chieftain, Finn."

"That has not yet been," said Grania. "Wilt thou receive courtship from me, O'Duivna?"

"I will not, Grania, because thou dost not know me, having seen me only this once."

"I have seen you before, O'Duivna, and on a special occasion. It was at the hurling match between the Fian and the men of Tara when you saved the match for the Fian by breaking two goals against my brother Cairbry. Wilt thou receive courtship from me?"

"I will not. Finn would be humbled by that, and I am not one to humble my chieftain."

"Then," said Grania, "I lay obligations on you, obligations that bind you through the force of ancient Druidism, O'Duivna. I lay obligations on you to take me out of this house tonight before Finn MacCuhal and the King of Ireland come out of their slumber."

"Wicked are you to lay obligations of the kind upon me," Dermott cried. "And why do you lay them on me rather than on the sons of kings and high princes who are in this royal house tonight?" he added questioningly.

"Because there is no man in all Ireland I would have take me except you, Dermott O'Duivna. You and my father were watching the match that I saw through my window of blue glass. One of the champions of the Fian was stricken and the game was going against them. Then you sprang up, took the hurling-bat from one who was there, went into the game and won it for the Fian. I never gave my love to any man from that time to this but to you alone, Dermott, and I never will no matter what comes or goes."

"Oisin," said Dermott, "what can I do about the obligations that have been laid upon me?"

"It is part of your honor now to keep these obligations," Oisin said. "Go with Grania, but keep yourself well against the wiles and force of Finn."

"What counsel do you give me, Caelte?"

"I have a fitting wife, and yet I had rather than the wealth and fame of the world that it had been to me that Cormac's daughter proffered love."

"What counsel, O Diorruing, do you give?"

"Go with Grania though death come out of it and I come to grieve because of that."

"Is that the counsel of all of you?"

"It is," said Oisin, and all the others said it with him.

Then Dermott stretched out his hands and took farewell of Oisin and the chiefs of the Finn. It was no wonder he wept then; he was leaving that great companionship forever.

Now on the night that Finn was in Tara, it was he who kept the keys of the rampart, and so none could leave the royal precinct. Dermott looked to the dais where the king and queen, Finn and MacMorna were in slumber and to the other parts of the hall where those who had been given the goblet slept.

They would wake up, Dermott thought, and find himself and Grania in the hall, for there was no way of their getting beyond the rampart. Grania led Dermott up to the royal seat. Outside it was her own bower. They went through it and into a garden that was closed with a wicket gate.

"It is against my obligations as one of the Fian," said Dermott, "to go through the low gate."

But Grania went to the other side of the wicket and called to him.

"I know, O Grania," said Dermott heavily, "that the course you face towards is not for a king's daughter. I know not what nook or corner or distant part of Ireland I can take you to that would be safe from MacCuhal's vengeance."

"It is certain I will not come back," said Grania, "and that I will not part from you until death parts me from you."

"Then I will not tell you to come back," said Dermott. He put his hands on the staves of his two spears and rose and vaulted across the wall. He was on the grass-green ground of the plain beyond the rampart. Grania was beside him.

"Forward, O Grania," said Dermott as he folded her cloak about her. "We must be far away and well hidden by the time Finn MacCuhal takes his weapon in his hand."

They in the hall wakened in the early day and it was not long before it was disclosed to Finn and the others that Grania and Dermott had stolen away together. Finn stood looking into the goblet that held the draught Grania had sent him. Cormac and Cairbry went from the hall,

but still Finn stood looking into the goblet. The women wailed for
Grania gone, but Finn stayed movelessly there. The rest of the Fian
gathered together and went out on the rampart, but Finn still stood,
and still looked into the goblet. But at last he went outside and summoned his trackers; he bade them follow Dermott and Grania and
show him the place where they were. He took his weapon then, and,
giving a command to the troop of the Fian that were there, went
with them after the trackers.

Dermott and Grania had gone a mile beyond Tara when Grania
said:

"I am wearying, O'Duivna."

"Your father's mansion is not far behind," Dermott said. "Bethink
you, Grania! I can bring you back without Finn or your father knowing that we went on this way."

"No, but do this, O'Duivna," said Grania. "Go back to where my
father's horses are, their chariots beside them. Take horses and a
chariot and come back to this place where I shall wait for you."

Dermott went. He yoked a chariot to a pair of horses and drove
back to where he had left her. Grania had remained there. He lifted
her into the chariot and drove on through the darkness, facing towards the west. The sun rose and Dermott hurried the horses on. It
was full day when they came to the River Shannon. Dermott led one
horse across and left the other to stray up or down the bank. The
chariot he broke up and threw pieces of it into deep parts of the
river. He lifted Grania up and carried her across the ford. And now
they were in Connacht where there were many unknown and hidden
places.

Finn's trackers, when they came to the river, had no more traces
they could follow. But Finn told them he would hang them each side
of the ford unless they found track again. What could they do but
go up and down like hounds until they found it?

So they followed Dermott and Grania, the trackers and Finn with
the troop he had with him. But Oisin took Bran, Finn's wise hound,
and set her upon the track, knowing that if she came upon the pair
she would warn them that pursuers were coming on them. Bran came
to where Dermott and Grania were resting and put her head on
Dermott's bosom.

"This is Finn's hound and the Fian are near us," he said.

Grania shook at the thought that she would be taken from Dermott
and that he would be slain before her eyes. "Take warning and fly,"
she cried. And those two who now knew that in all the world they
had only each other headed away from whence Bran came. They fled

from hiding place to hiding place that day and the next day and the day after that. But though the trackers came close to them Dermott's comrades of the Fian always found ways of warning them when pursuit was gaining on them.

A day came when part of a forest they were lurking in was nearly surrounded and the trackers had sworn to Finn they would bring Dermott's head to him, Caelte had his great-voiced henchman raise the Fian hunting-cry.

They slipped out of the forest and found badgers' holes that they hid in.

Finn went back to his court in Almu. But his jealousy about Grania and his hatred of Dermott did not abate. He put a ban upon Dermott as an outlaw in hiding from him and as a forest freebooter.

Then Dermott and Grania had respite from pursuit. The chieftain of a territory they came into permitted them to build a bothie and to hunt and fish and gather the wild fruit in his territory. Twelve moons they lived there.

One evening Dermott was strewing rushes and the soft tops of pine trees for a bed, and Grania was cooking salmon by a stream; they saw a shining figure in the glade and Dermott knew him for Angus, his fosterer. And when he had greeted them Angus, looking on them with grave and kindly gaze, said:

"The counsel I give you is that you flee from this place and from every place that you are known in, and in your going here and there never to go into a cave in which there is but one passage, never to go on an island that has but one channel between it and the land. Whatever place you cook your meal in, there eat it not; whatever place you eat in, there sleep not; whatever place you sleep in, there eat not on the morrow."

Angus went from them and at the first light Dermott and Grania left the place that had sheltered them. The wild deer was their meat and the water of the springs was their drink. They roamed Ireland while Dermott made a living by the strength of his hand and the temper of his sword.

As for Finn MacCuhal, he gave his counsel to one person only, to his woman-spy and tracker, Deirdu. She went up and down Ireland for him, finding out about Dermott and Grania, where they sheltered, who were their friends and unfriends. And by Deirdu he sent message to ancient enemies of his clan, men of the broken Clan Morna, who would gladly make peace with him.

Then one day when the chief battalion of the Fian stood with him at Almu they beheld a troop coming towards them.

"Our fathers were at the battle of Cnucha and the slaying of Cuhal," they said, "and now we want to make peace and obtain from Finn the places in the Fian that our fathers had."

"You must give compensation for the slaying of Cuhal," Finn answered them.

"We have no gold nor silver nor herds of cattle to give, Finn."

"Ask no compensation of them," said Oisin to his father. "Their fathers fell at Cnucha, and that should be compensation enough for the slaying of your father."

"It seems to me," said Finn, "that if anyone should slay me it would be an easy matter to satisfy my son in the matter of compensation. But for all that, none shall come into the Fian without giving me compensation."

"What compensation would you have us make, Finn?" asked the leader of the troop.

"I ask the head of a warrior," said Finn.

"I will give you good counsel," said Oisin, speaking to the troop whose fathers had been at the battle of Cnucha, "return to where you were reared and do not ask peace of Finn as long as you live. It is no light matter to get for Finn what he will ask of you. Return."

"Nay," said the leader of those dull-witted men, "our hearts are set on joining the Fian, and we will make the compensation that Finn asks of us."

When no one was beside them Finn told them what compensation he wanted from them: the head of Dermott O'Duivna.

Then one day Finn saw coming towards him his woman-tracker Deirdu, her legs failing, her tongue raving, her eyes dropping out of her head, and he knew that the day of his vengeance had come. Dermott and Grania, the woman told him, had taken refuge in the Fortress of the Ancient people, and Clan Morna were closing round that ring of stones.

Forthwith Finn summoned certain battalions of the Fian and they went swiftly towards the fortress of Da Both. Clan Morna were there. They told him that the one whose head they would bring him was within the ring of standing stones and that there was a woman with him.

"Foul fall the friends of Dermott O'Duivna for his sake," said Finn.

"Dermott O'Duivna is not there," said Oisin, "and it is a mark of your envy and jealousy, Finn, to think that he would put himself in such a place."

Then Finn lifted up his voice, and cried:

"Which of us is the truth with, O Dermott, myself or Oisin?"

And the answer of Dermott came back:

"Thou didst never err in thy judgment, Finn."

And the battalion of the Fian and the troop of Clan Morna with Finn himself standing amongst them saw Dermott stand on one of the stones of the fortress; they saw him raise Grania beside him; they saw him give her three kisses while Finn stood there. Stings of jealousy went into the heart of Finn and he swore that Dermott should give his life for those kisses.

But now Dermott, his armour on, his sword in hand, came to one of the openings in the fortress. "Who is outside?" he asked.

"No foe, Dermott, for here is Oisin. Come out to us and none will dare do thee hurt or harm."

"I will not break out until I find what opening Finn himself is at."

"Caelte is here," was said to him at another opening. "Come amongst us and we will fight and die for your sake."

"No," said Dermott, "for I will not have Finn harry you because of your well doing to myself."

To the third, to the fourth, to the fifth opening Dermott went. At the sixth he was told that the Clan Morna were there.

"Unvaliant ye are, O ye of the lie and the tracking, and it is not from fear of your hand," said Dermott, "but from disgust of you I will not go out."

He went to the seventh, and when he asked who were at that opening he heard Finn MacCuhal's voice.

"Here am I with my own henchmen, and if you should come amongst us we promise to cleave your bones asunder."

"I pledge my word," said Dermott, "that the gate that you are at, O Finn, is the very gate that I shall go through."

He turned to take farewell of Grania, and he saw beside her the shining figure of Angus of the Brugh. He knew that Grania would be taken to safety. If he were not slain by Finn and his henchmen he would be with Grania again.

"I shall put my mantle over her and depart from this without the knowledge of Finn or the Fian of Ireland," Angus said.

As for Finn, he charged his troop to let Dermott take three steps towards them. But, with his hands on the staves of his spears, Dermott vaulted across the wall and beyond Finn's troop. Standing away from them, his shield before him, his sword in his hand, he said:

"There never came on thee, Finn, battle or combat, strait or extremity in my time that I would not adventure into for thy sake and the sake of the Fian. And I swear that if thou dost attack me I shall avenge myself and thou shalt not get my head at a little cost."

"Dermott has spoken truth," said Oisin, "and it is to meet that you, Finn, spare him and forgive him."

"I will not," answered Finn.

Then only the troop of Clan Morna would make the attack on Dermott. The battalions of the Fian stood by, their arms on the ground. But the troop of Clan Morna were engaged against him, and rushed upon him.

Dermott, sword in hand, passed through them as a wolf through a flock of sheep.

When Finn would go into the battle, the Fian linked their shields together and held him back. Then when the Fian drew off and the troop of Clan Morna had no more battling, Finn looked on a heap of slain and saw that Dermott was not amongst them.

Deirdu who had searched the fortress came to tell him that Grania was not to be found.

Then Finn knew all he had lost: Cormac's daughter, the trust his companions had had in him, the faith in himself that he had held since the night he had saved Tara from the Goblin. So much had Grania taken from him when she had sent him the goblet to drink out of. And his heart was still unforgiving.

As for Dermott he went to the Brugh of Angus by the Boyne. Outside it two figures stood, Angus and Grania. The life of Grania almost fled through her mouth when she saw Dermott with all the marks of combat upon him. Angus washed out his wounds and gave him a new garb and brought him and Grania into his mansion.

Later Grania went back to Tara and the King of Ireland endeavored to make peace between Dermott and Finn MacCuhal. It went hard with Finn to make peace, but he knew that he could not keep up the feud with Dermott since his own Fian would not support him in it. He agreed to the terms that Dermott proffered and he lifted the ban.

These were the terms that Finn MacCuhal and King Cormac made with Dermott O'Duivna: The district which his father owned he was let have, and the district of Cos Corann was given by King Cormac as a dowry to Grania. In his own patrimony Dermott built a great house.

The Death of Dermott

In the Great House he built, the house that was named Rath Grania, Dermott O'Duivna lay. In the dark of night he wakened out of his

Ibid., pp. 141-150.

sleep, starting with such violence that Grania had to hold him.

"What has come into your mind?" she asked, her arms about him.

"It seemed to me that I heard the baying of a hound."

"But it is night," said Grania.

"It is night," said Dermott, "but I heard that baying only now. I wonder at the baying of a hound that seems hunting in the night."

But Grania quieted him, singing to him the sleep-song that she had sung on a night of their flight from Finn:

> Sleep, although the wild-duck, deeming
> That the fox is stepping near,
> Guides her brood from out the shallows
> To the middle of the mere.

Dermott slept, but he heard again the baying of the hound; with a start he wakened, and again Grania quieted him with her sleep-song:

> Sleep, although the linnet rustles
> From that rounded nest of hers,
> She should keep her head enfolded—
> Nothing but the ivy stirs!

He slept again, and when he wakened it was daylight. He stood on the middle of the floor as if listening for something. His own hound, Mac an Cuill, ran whimpering about the yard.

"I will go seek the hound whose voice I heard last night," Dermott said to Grania.

"I would not have you go," Grania said. "I pray you not to go anywhere today." She put her arms about him. "Do not go where I cannot see you today," she said.

But Dermott would not have her hold him. "What should I be doing in Rath Grania on a day of May when the bushes are in blossom?" was all he asked.

"That is not why you go, Dermott," Grania said.

"I will be more content," he said, "when I look from the top of Ben Gulban and know what the hound was hunting in the night."

Grania knew she could not stay him when he spoke in that way. She watched him as he made ready to betake himself from Rath Grania. As he was fastening his belt she said: "I would have you arm yourself with your great sword, the Moralltach, today."

"It is too heavy," Dermott said. "I will take my smaller sword, the Begalltach."

"In that case," said Grania, "let your spear be the great one, the Gae Derg."

"What beast could I use the Gae Derg on?" answered Dermott. "I am going hunting; I will take Mac an Cuill with me on a leash."

"When if not today," said Grania, "could we talk to our household about the feast we should give for the King of Ireland and Finn and the chiefs of the Fian? Let us arrange that today, and you, Dermott, can go hunting on Ben Gulban tomorrow."

"It is well bethought of," said Dermott, "but today is a good day for hunting and tomorrow will not be a bad day to talk about the giving of a feast."

So Dermott left Rath Grania.

All alone, leading his hound and armed with his lesser sword and his lesser spear he went up the slopes of Ben Gulban. When he reached the top there was one standing there as if waiting for him, a man with a single hound beside him. The man was Finn MacCuhal.

Dermott O'Duivna did not salute him as Finn was wont to be saluted by men of the Fian. He spoke only to ask if he were holding a chase on the hill. And Finn, looking at Dermott's hound and sword and spear answered that not he, but certain captains of the Fian were holding a chase on Ben Gulban.

"They hunt the Boar of Ben Gulban," Finn told him. "They are foolish to do that. Already the boar has wounded a score of the beaters."

"I heard a hound baying in the night," said Dermott, "and that was what brought me here."

"Leave the hill to the boar and his hunters, O'Duivna," said Finn. "I do not want you to be here."

"Why should I leave the hill?" Dermott answered. "I have no dread of a boar."

"You should have," said Finn, "for you are under prohibitions about hunting a boar."

"My father was cursed on account of a boar," said Dermott, "I know that."

"The curse was to fall on your father's son and on no one else, O'Duivna," Finn said. "It has been told you by me, remember."

"Even so," said Dermott, "it would be craven of me to leave the hill before I had sight of the boar. Here I stay. But would you leave your hound with mine?"

Finn did not answer. He went down the side of the hill and his hound followed him, leaving Dermott a solitary man with the hound Mac an Cuill beside him. There was a tearing noise and Dermott knew that the Boar of Ben Gulban was coming up the hill, and he knew that none was in pursuit of him because there was no baying of hounds behind him. No men, no hounds were there to hem him round.

Dermott unslipped Mac an Cuil. But the hound cowered before the bristled, gnashing brute.

He slipped his finger into the string of his lesser spear, the Gae Bwee, and made a careful cast. The spear struck the boar between his little eyes. But not a single bristle was cut, not a gash or scratch was made upon him.

"Woe to him who heeds not the counsel of a good wife," said Dermott O'Duivna to himself.

He drew the Begalltach from his belt and struck the wild boar. But even then the boar pitched him so that he fell along the bristly back. Then the boar turned and crashed down the side of the hill. He rushed back and reached the summit again. There he pitched Dermott down and gored and ripped him. And Dermott lay on the ground not able to raise himself, writhing with the pain of his deep, wide wounds.

On the track of the boar came the hunters; Finn and four chiefs of the Fian with them. They found Dermott where he was lying; and Oisin and Caelte raised him up.

"What grief to see a hero torn by a pig," said Oisin. "What grief to us to see Dermott O'Duivna in this plight."

"I grieve," said Finn, "that the women of Ireland are not here to gaze on him and to see the beauty and grace they found in him spoiled by the pig's gashes."

"Finn has come," said Dermott, knowing his voice, "and it is in his power to heal me."

"It is in Finn's power to heal Dermott," said the other chiefs of the Fian.

"I am no leach," said Finn.

"It was granted to thee, Finn, by the Women of the Green Mantles," said Dermott, "that a draught of water carried in thy hands would heal a wounded man."

"It is true what Dermott says," said Oisin, Finn's son.

"I can give the draught only to such as are deserving of it from me. What would all of you have? O'Duivna is not deserving that I should bring him water in my palms," said Finn MacCuhal harshly.

"I am well deserving of it, and you know that well, Finn," said Dermott. "Whatever you might do for me would be only a repayment for what I have done for you. When your bitter enemies cast firebrands on a house you were feasting in, I was not backward in willingness to relieve you. I bade you stay within enjoying your heady drinks while I went forth and slew men and quenched the flames. You were not surly when I came back to you. If I had asked you for a drink then you would have given it to me."

"Unfaithfulness changes everything, O'Duivna," said Finn, "and the world knows that you were unfaithful to me. You bore Grania away from me in the presence of the men of Ireland."

"I do not regret that I took Grania, Finn," said Dermott, "and it has been told you by men you can believe that Cormac's daughter put me under bonds to take her away. And that is not what you should remember.

"You should bring me a drink in your palms because of your remembrance of the time when you were beleaguered in the Brugh of the Rowan Tree, and I hastened to your relief, and by my fortune and valour brought you a goblet I had taken from your beleaguerers. I gave you that goblet in token of a victory that saved you, Finn. You should remember that and not harden your heart against me. Many a valiant man has fallen by your hand and there are others who will fall. There will be reckoning for you and the Fian. Not for you do I grieve, but for Oisin and Oscar and the rest of the brave and faithful companionship. I know that you, Oisin, will be left to lament over the Fian."

Oisin said, "I will not allow you, Finn, to withhold a drink of water from Dermott O'Duivna. And I say now that if any other prince in the world should think of doing O'Duivna such treachery there should leave this hill only whoever of us had the strongest hand. Heed what I say, and bring the water in your palms without delay."

"I know not where the wells are on this mountain," said Finn.

One of the Fian said, "Nine paces from you is a well of clear water."

Finn MacCuhal went to the well and raised the full of his hands of the water.

He turned to where Dermott O'Duivna lay. But he had not gone more than four paces when he let the water slip through his hands.

When they stepped towards him angrily he went back and took his palms' full of water out of the well. But even as he turned round he thought upon Grania and let the water slip through his hands. Dermott sighed piteously when he saw that.

"We will not stand here and see such treachery done," they said, and Oisin, Oscar, Caelte and Lewy's son put their spears against Finn MacCuhal. Then Finn for the third time lifted water from the well. But as Finn stood above him, his hands held out stiffly, life parted from the body of Dermott O'Duivna.

There was silence on the top of the hill until Dermott's hound, Mac an Cuill, coming back, stood above Dermott's body and bayed long and loud. Oisin and Oscar, Caelte and Lewy's son stood there, no sighs nor groans coming from them although their hearts were wrung. They looked on Dermott who had had such grace and vigour and accomplishment, and thought about by-gone days and the joyousness that had been in the Fian, the sport, the spirit, and the companionship.

Finn MacCuhal went from them and stood beside the well. And seeing him there Caelte said, "No draught can heal you, Finn, nor make you any different from what we now know you to be: a cunning man, caring for your own ends only—you that were our mainstay."

Oisin said, "Ignobly you have done, Finn, and we never can have reverence for you again."

Lewy's son said, "The strength of the Fian will go because of this, but as you, Finn, planted the acorn, bend the oak yourself."

But Oscar thought of the affection that Angus bore to Dermott, and he cried out:

> "Raise, raise the cry for him, ye Danaan hosts,
> For Dermott with the weapons laid across,
> And place him in your green, smooth-sided Brugh:
> But we will keep the sorrow of his loss."

Then the four covered Dermott with their mantles and set a guard of the Fian around him.

Then to where Finn was standing Dermott's hound, Mac an Cuill, went, and Finn put a leash on him and held him. But his own hound stayed away from Finn.

Grania was standing on the ramparts when she saw the chiefs of the Fian coming towards Rath Grania, and she recognized them: Finn, Oisin, Oscar, Caelte, and Lewy's son, and she knew that the hound that Finn led was Dermott's. A chill went through her body. "If Dermott were alive it is not Finn who would lead Mac an Cuill," she said to herself.

When they came to where she stood they told her, "Dermott is dead, slain by the Boar of Ben Gulban."

She fainted, hearing that.

And when her senses came back to her and she knew that what she had heard was true, she raised a cry that was heard at the furthest end of the stronghold, so that her women and retainers who were there came to the rampart.

Then wailing went up from his household for Dermott O'Duivna.

Still Finn held Mac an Cuill. Grania asked him to let go the hound, but Finn said, "It is little enough I recovered from Dermott O'Duivna whom I fostered and made a hero of, and this hound of his I shall keep."

Oisin went and took the leash out of Finn's hand and brought Mac an Cuill to Grania. She sent the retainers to Ben Gulban to bring the dead back to Rath Grania. But that they did not do, for Dermott's body had been taken away by Angus Og.

As for Finn MacCuhal, he went back to Almu. Gloomy indeed were the days there, for there was no longer trust between the Fian and their chieftain.

When another season had passed, Finn, without the knowledge of his captains and without making any farewells to them, left Almu. To Rath Grania he went. And as he was alone and unarmed he was permitted to enter.

When Grania came to where he was, Finn told her he had come to offer a peace, and, when they had grown, to give her sons a place in the Fian.

At first Grania would not listen to him. But then she listened and he told her how Dermott's sons would be looked up to in the Fian. "But who will guarantee that?" Grania asked him.

"Yourself, Grania," Finn said. "For there is no man more fit for you to marry than myself, and there is no woman in Ireland more fit to be the wife of Finn MacCuhal than you." Grania would not listen to him at first, but then she listened, and in more and more fervent words he told her how much he loved her.

A day came when the captains of the Fian saw a pair coming towards Almu, and one was Finn, and the other, when the pair came nearer, they knew for Grania. Thereupon the captains of the Fian gave three shouts of derision and mockery. Grania bent her head in shame. But Finn took her hand and led her into the great hall of Almu.

At the banquet that night Oisin said to his father, "We trow, Finn, that from this time on you will keep Grania fast."

Whatever was meant by that, Finn did keep Grania, and Grania seemed to like being kept fast by the Chieftain of the Fian. She and Finn stayed together until one of them died. And though there was no longer that spirit amongst the Fian that Oisin and Caelte remembered, they all had to stand together, for now Cormac's son, Cairbry, stirred against them.

The Gruff Gillie

If anyone asked who was the best-looking and the most pleasant-spoken amongst the Fian, the answer was easy: he was Dermott O'Duivna. And if anyone asked who was the most unseemly and the most scurrilous-tongued in the three battalions, the answer, too, was easy: he was Conan Baldhead. It was a spectacle to see two such figures together, the handsome Dermott and the cross-eyed Conan.

But it was not when the white shields were against their shoulders and the helmets were on their heads that one beheld the unlikeness that made even the hounds and horses gaze and gaze. It was when, their nine months' service to the King of Ireland rendered, the Fian went to hunt the deer in Munster, making their camp at Knockany. They went there after the harvest month, the three battalions with their hounds, their horses, and their gillies. One year Finn appointed Conan the master of the camp and Dermott the starter of the chase.

When the baying of the full-grown hounds and the yelping of the whelps were filling the camp, Dermott came to Finn and told him that an uncouth-looking fellow was on his way towards them.

"If his looks don't belie his voice," said Finn, "he must be an outlandish kind of fellow." He said this because a big, bawling, brawling voice was now in their ears.

Into the camp came a shambling fellow leading a shambling horse. His chest was as wide as a door, and a pair of big, hairy knees appeared under his tunic; he was wide-mouthed and gap-toothed and his head was as shaggy as a wolf's fell. An iron-mounted club was in his hand, and with it he struck the side of his horse making a sound that was like a wind tearing down a sail. The horse's ribs showed through its flea-bitten hide. It was a long horse, or, rather, a long mare, with a back like the ridge of a house. The Fian who were around thought that with every next blow of the iron-shod club she would be knocked over on the green.

And then the pair stood there, the halter on the ground, the iron-shod club held in one hand while with the other the fellow scratched the back of his head, and the mare's head hung to the ground.

"You're Finn MacCuhal," he bawled, bending his knee to the chief of the Fian. "And you're Conan," he said to the bald-headed, cross-eyed

Ibid., 91-105.

camp-master, "because you couldn't look like that and be anybody else except Conan."

"Your business, lout?" roared Conan.

"It's about getting a place in your Fian," said the fellow. "That is, if I can find out what wages you pay a lad like me."

"Does a horse-boy come with you?" Finn asked.

"Horse-boy?" said the fellow. "If I had a horse-boy he would have to get a bit out of everything I get to eat. Believe you me, Finn," said he, clapping his stomach, "I have an appetite that won't let me give anything to anyone else. I'm a Fomorian, I am," said he, "and we Fomorians do without horse-boys. And as for my mare, she's a kindly beast, and I like to keep her under my own control."

With that he picked up the rope and held the mare as if he was afraid some one of the Fian was going to take her from him.

The beaters and the stalkers were standing around, holding the hounds on their leashes, all looking at the long, knobby, down-looking mare and the outlandish-looking fellow that held her. The mare wheezed and her head dropped lower.

"Who are you?" asked Finn.

"I'm known east and west and south and north as the Gruff Gillie," he said, "or, if you like, the Rough Gillie, or the Tough Gillie. I'm called that because I've notions of my own what to do and no master that I've ever had has been able to change them. And you," said he to Finn and to the rest of the Fian who were coming out of their bothies, "don't ever try to get me to do things that I don't want to do."

"Shall we take the Gruff Gillie for a camp-servant?" said Finn to the Fian who were around.

The hounds were baying and the three battalions of the Fian felt in a sporting humor as did Finn himself. "Aye, aye," they cried. "Take him for a gillie."

"Conan," ordered Finn, "take the gillie's mare to the grazing-ground. And you, O'Duivna," he said, "have your horn ready to blow for the best chase that was ever on Knockany."

Conan, abusing everyone, led the knobby, long-backed, knock-kneed mare to the grazing ground, and the Gruff Gillie, using his club for a pole, vaulted about with the joy, it would seem, of getting a place with the Fian of Ireland. It was a sight that made all forget the prospect of the chase of Knockany. But one man did not forget it; he was Dermott; he stood there, the horn in his hands, impatient to blow it.

"Isn't it nice to have bald-headed Conan for my horse-boy?" shouted the gillie as he vaulted with his club.

The horses in the grazing-ground raised their heads and sniffed as the queer-looking mare was brought amongst them. It was plain they had never seen the like of her. When Conan let go of the rope she stood with her head hanging as if she were ready to die on her four legs. The fine racers and hunters belonging to the chiefs of the Fian came around her.

Then suddenly the gillie's mare shot out her hind-legs and struck a horse belonging to Caelte full on the jaws, knocking it sideways. Then screaming and kicking she tore through the others, biting this one, kicking the other. The horses of the Fian scattered all over the grazing-field. The hounds barked, the men shouted, the horses screamed, and above all the sounds was the wheezing of the Gruff Gillie's mare.

Finn shouted an order to Conan. Conan grabbed the rope and dragged the mare from the grazing-field. "May you get as knobby and as knock-kneed, Finn," said he, "for letting the man and beast stay amongst us."

"I dare you to lay a hand on my mare," bawled the gillie. "I dare you, Conan."

Conan went on the mare's back. "I'll ride her out of this," said he. But the mare lay down, Conan on her back, and not for all the kicks he gave her would she rise again.

The Fian, their hands on their knees, laughed at Conan straddling the long mare, all except Dermott who stood with the horn in his hands.

"She's used to bigger weight than yours, manikin," bawled the gillie. "If a few of the lads get on her back she'll rise quick enough."

One, and then another, of the Fian got on the mare's back. Thirteen crowded behind Conan Baldhead. Suddenly the mare scrambled to her feet, and everybody laughed louder than before to see so many on that long back, holding her mane and holding each other. She stumbled on for a bit and the sight was so comic that the stalkers and beaters and gillies of the camp laughed in the faces of the Fian.

"Well, there's one thing I won't let the Fian of Ireland do and that is make a mock of my mare," bawled the Gruff Gillie. "That's not what I came here for. I'll go away, so I will, and I'll take my mare with me. And this will be a lesson to all honest Fomorians not to hire themselves to any pack of Irish."

With the club in his hand the gillie walked away, bawling in front of his stumbling mare. He walked fast and she went a bit fast, too. He broke into a trot and she picked up to a trot, too.

"And that's all I've got from the Fian," he shouted back to them. "Mockery! Not even a meal."

"We're wasting a fine morning, Finn," said Dermott, fidgeting with the horn. All of the three battalions were on the ground now, and the hounds could hardly be held. A stag was out up there, and they knew it. But Conan was shouting from the back of the mare:

"We can't get off! Come on and stop the mare!"

The Gruff Gillie took to running, and the mare with the fourteen on her back ran, too.

As she ran she became more and more of a steed. There were no longer hollows in her sides; her head went up, and she came to look, not only a big, but a gallant and good-looking mare.

"A murrain on you, Finn," shouted Conan. "Why don't you stir yourself? Or would you have us in the next townland before you move?"

The Gruff Gillie dropped his club, put his arms to his sides, and began to run. The mare stretched out her legs and went faster and faster, the fourteen making a jig-jog on her back.

Conan let a great bawl out of him.

"What sort of a captain are you, Finn MacCuhal, to let your men be carried off before your eyes?"

"Rescue!" cried Finn.

"Rescue!" cried Dermott. "Rescue, rescue!" shouted the others. With Finn at their head all made off after the mare and the Gruff Gillie. Down hollow and up height the mare went, the gillie before her, the Fian after her. One of the Fian who had been standing by when the fourteen got on the mare was able to keep up with her: he was Liagan the Swift.

Finn and the others kept on, racing as they had never raced before. It was a chase they hadn't reckoned on, but it was a chase indeed. Here and there they had a glimpse of their quarry as the mare topped a hill or swam a river. No stag had ever brought them as far as the mare, and she was still going on.

But the chase could not be given up; if he left Conan and the others in the power of a wild man, a Fomorian, Finn could never hold up his head again, let alone keep the chieftainship of the Fian of Ireland. He and his followers had to keep up the chase, no matter how long, no matter how breath-depriving, no matter how heart-breaking it was.

They burst at last into the ravines of Kerry, and there was the sea before them. They gasped out something like a cheer, for the Gruff Gillie and his mare would have to halt now. But he didn't. He took hold of the rope and went into the sea. The mare with the fourteen of the Fian on her back went into the sea, too.

Liagan took hold of the mare's tail. And as swiftly as they had raced, so swiftly did the gillie and his mare swim out, fourteen on her back and one holding to her tail.

"We'll have to follow them," Finn said when he and his companions reached the beach. "We're sworn to rescue any of the Fian that are in danger. Take a breath now and give our shout so that Conan and the others will know that we'll be after them." As soon as their breath came back to them, the Fian on the beach gave a shout that went across the sea and maybe came to the ears of the fifteen that were on the back and at the tail of the mare that, as it was easy to see now, was an ordinary mare no more than her master was an ordinary gillie.

The next part of the adventure was Dermott O'Duivna's. The Fian cut down trees and made a raft. When that was done they made sails out of their mantles, put on board the venison they had killed, took water, and sailed across the sea. At the end of a day they made a landfall. A high cliff went up from a narrow strand. To climb it they would have to make ladders and hack out footholds. Dermott would not wait for all this to be done: the most sure-footed of the Fian, he climbed the cliff and came up on a high land where there was a wood with a mountain back of it.

He went through the wood, following a path that led to a well. Above it, hanging from a branch, was a drinking-horn half covered with silver and lavishly ornamented. And the well was very clear, but so deep was its water that Dermott could not see to the bottom. It was a well that held him in wonder.

But after a while he took the horn, dipped it in the well, and drank from it.

As he did, there came a murmur from the well. Then there was a sound of branches being pulled aside and Dermott saw coming towards him a champion who had sword and shield and helmet, and whose face had a frown of anger.

"So," he said, "without my leave you take my drinking-horn and drink from my well? This is not to be borne." And as the champion came towards Dermott he drew his sword.

Dermott was amazed that a stranger should be treated in so uncourteous a fashion. All he had done was to take a drink of water from a well in a wood, and whose leave did he have to ask for that? Still, he would have liked to have shown the Champion of the Well that there was no impudent intent in what he had done. But he came towards him so furiously that there was nothing for Dermott to do but draw his own sword.

They fought for long. But for all his fierceness the Champion of the Well was not the equal in strength or swordsmanship of one of the

Fian. Dermott would have overcome him, but suddenly the champion flung his sword into the well and plunged in himself. Dermott watched him sink through the water. So deep down did he go that sight of him was lost.

The next day Dermott hunted a deer in the wood. He killed it, hung the meat and made a fire. Then when he had cooked and eaten his meat he went to the well, took the drinking-horn, dipped it in and took a draught of the water.

No sooner had he done this than a murmur came from the well; there was a sound of branches being struck aside, and he saw the Champion of the Well coming towards him.

"So," he cried, "it is not enough that you should use my drinking-horn and take a draught out of my well, but you must kill my deer also!"

Dermott held up his hand in token of friendliness. But it was no use; with sword drawn the champion came to him.

Dermott drew his sword; the two fought beside the well. But the strength and skill that men of the Fian had to have were not in the Champion of the Well. Suddenly, as on the day before, he flung his sword into the well, and before Dermott could hold him, he plunged into it. And, as before, Dermott watched him sink down until he went out of sight.

He rested there. The next day Dermott cut from the hung meat, cooked it and ate. Then he went to the well wondering what adventure would befall him.

Nothing happened until he took down the drinking-horn, and, dipping it in, drank the water of the well. Then, as before, a murmur came from the well, there was a sound of one making his way through branches, and the Champion of the Well came towards him, his sword drawn.

"So," he cried, "you will not be gone from my well!"

They fought as before. Dermott, dropping his own sword, sprang to hold him when the champion flung his sword into the well. But pulling him with him the champion plunged in. Down they sank. And when his senses were leaving him, Dermott was drawn through a passage of stone that went upward and found himself in the court-yard of a fortress. Armed men were there.

"Keep this one here," the Champion of the Well said to them, "it may be that he is the only one of the Fian of Ireland that the King of Sorca has been able to bring against me." He went into the fortress then, and the men kept a watch on Dermott.

As for Finn and the men who were with him, they made ladders and hacked out footholds, they climbed the cliff and came where Dermott left tokens of his movements. They came to the well, and standing around it, they raised the Fian's shout. They waited for Dermott's coming. And then they heard a shout, and out of a cave in the mountain a single horseman came towards them.

He saluted Finn. "I will reveal myself," he said. "I am Abartach, the King of Sorca. I came to you as the Gruff Gillie so that I might draw Finn and the Fian of Ireland to my help. I am threatened by the King of Land-under-Wave who would take from me the treasures that make me supreme in Faerie—the Spear, the Stone and the Caldron."

"Why should we fight on your side against the King of Land-under-Wave?" Finn asked him.

"Bethink thee, Finn," said the one whom they had known as the Gruff Gillie. "You have heard of Sorca and you have heard of Abartach."

He had; Finn knew he had. But what had he heard of Sorca and Abartach? Who had spoken these names? His mother? Bovmall? His uncle Crimmall? Someone talking beside a fire while a child listened. A story about help or hospitality given to his father. It was enough, that memory. Finn promised Abartach his help.

The King of Sorca brought them into the cave. Then they went down through passages in the earth. After what seemed to be a day's travel they came to a fortress. There Finn and the Fian were royally entertained. A feast was given them and there was the music of harps and the chanting of poetry. But Dermott was not with them, and Finn and his companions were downcast because of that.

As for Dermott he stayed in the courtyard of the fortress, disarmed but unguarded. The men were called to form an army that was to march away. Dermott, having eaten a meal they left for him, slept. In a dream he thought that a fair young woman came to him and stood above him. He wakened, and it was as he had dreamed.

"Take me to where your chieftain, Finn, is," she said to Dermott.

She had the three colors—the whiteness of snow, the redness of blood, the blackness of the raven that drinks the blood that has flowed upon the snow. She was noble in her stature and graceful in her movements. She told Dermott that she loved Finn because of all she had heard about him, and longed to be with him in Ireland.

She was the sister of the King of Land-under-Wave; it was with him, as Champion of the Well, that Dermott had fought. Moriah was the fair young woman's name.

Dermott told her he did not know where Finn was. Moriah knew.

He was in the fortress of the King of Sorca, and she, going with him, would show Dermott how to come to his chieftain. She led him out of the fortress and along a hidden path and brought him to where the army of the King of Sorca was arrayed.

Dermott saw his comrades of the Fian of Ireland, and he saw Finn upon a hillock, looking over the lines of battle. Dermott went to him, and his chieftain was as glad to see him as if already he had won the battle. Moriah stayed where Dermott had placed her; under a rowan tree, with a ring of shields around her.

And then the army of the King of Sorca, with Finn leading it and the Fian strengthening it, went into battle with the army of the King of Land-under-Wave. The armies fought and neither yielded to the other. Dermott sought out the enemy king. They fought as they had fought beside the well, and no more this time than the other times were the strength and the swordsmanship of the King of Land-under-Wave equal to Dermott's.

Dermott's sword pierced his shield, and the king fell upon his knee. That was the end of the battle.

Lifting up their king the army of Land-under-Wave drew back. "The treasures that make the supreme King of Faerie are Abartach's, are Abartach's," they cried as they drew back.

A feast was given for the Fian by King Abartach, and Dermott brought Moriah to it and placed her beside Finn. Even if he hadn't won a victory Finn would have been happy to have one so fair and so gracious beside him.

When the harps played Moriah chanted a poem; it was a poem of her own and it was meant for Finn only. It told how she, a maiden of Land-under-Wave, had heard of his deeds and had loved him for what she had heard of him. And it seemed as if Finn forgot he was a warrior and remembered that he was once a poet. Anyway, when the harps sounded again he chanted a poem to Moriah.

"And I will be with you in Ireland," she said to him, and her face had all happiness in it.

In the morning Finn and the Fian stood on the narrow strand and looked towards Ireland. Moriah, lifted up on shields, looked over, too.

"What wages, Finn, would you have me give you?" Abartach asked.

"I do not remember that I paid you any wages," Finn answered, "and so there is nothing due from you to me."

"Speak for yourself, Finn," said Conan sourly.

"Speak you for the Fian, Conan," said the King of Sorca. "What wage would you have me give them?"

"Bring your mare here, and let fourteen women of your kingdom get on her back, and over with them to Ireland and across it. And let your own mare (I mean your queen) hold on where Liagan held."

The fourteen who had been on the mare cheered Conan's words. Abartach smiled. "Behold your men, Finn!" he said.

Finn looked to his men and his men looked to Finn. When they turned round again they were no longer on the narrow strand but on a wide beach with the hills of Kerry before them. And Abartach was no longer beside them.

"Back to the Hill of Almu and to our own homes," Finn commanded. His arm was around Moriah. He lifted her on his shield to give her a glimpse of Ireland. And then with shouts and songs they all marched towards Finn's house on the Hill of Almu.

The Return of Oisin and His Meeting with Saint Patrick

Precisely twelve men stood in a half-circle round a block of granite, in a valley which, because of the exceeding beauty of the song of multitudes of thrushes, to which its peculiar properties gave a rich depth and passion, had been named Gleann-n-Smol by the first human traveler that had wandered that way in the beginning of time. The block of granite was vast. It was hewn square and trimmed craftily. It stood exactly in the corner of a great clearing where the sod had been cut away to its bed of gravel at the base of the mountainside. It lay grey and comely in the soft evening light, shining against the orange gravel clearing that stretched like an inhuman wound by the pale green of the verdure into which it had been cut.

Certain signs of recent removal lay about it—several strands of coarsely twisted rope, splintered timber, and torn clothing stained with blood. The grass below it had been trampled into mire. Yet the twelve men, standing in a half-circle, did not look triumphant, as at a task finely accomplished. They did not even look cross, like men well rid at last of one vexed work. One and all, they had the look of men in a dream, snared by some inner mystery that had left them astonished.

They were of all sorts and sizes, these twelve men. There were young men in the flower of youth. There were old men, chewing the withered fruit of wisdom. There were middle-aged men, who, being neither in-

From *The Return of the Hero,* by "Michael Ireland" (Darrell Figgis), pp. 1-24. Chapman & Dodd. London. 1923.

toxicated by the fragrance of flowers nor reflective with the bitter-sweetness of their chewing, had a hard and grim expression on their faces. There were tall men. There were no short men, but there were men not so tall as others. They were all sweating, and they were all bemused, a state of the body and a state of mind that are not often found at the one moment together among men—or, for that matter, among women.

Then one of them spoke. He was a middle-aged man, which accounted for his being the first to revive. He was, in fact, the most middle-aged of all the men. The signs of his revival were the cross and cantankerous lines that appeared across his brows. And this is what he said: "If I were in drink now I'd have said . . ."

He did not complete the sentence. He fell back into the silence from which he had risen, and the cross and cantankerous lines were washed out by the original wonder of his reflections. The evening forgot his deep, resounding complaint. No one spoke. No one stirred.

Then at last an old man said: "What would you have said?"

"It is no matter," the other replied, "what I would have said. I would have said it just the same."

"I wouldn't doubt you," said the next oldest of the middle-aged men along the line. "Not what I wouldn't have done the same."

But the first speaker said nothing, and remained lost in the power of the light that had apparently lured his eyes. Notwithstanding this, the silence was now restless. It was like the silence of a sleeper first stirring himself into life, lying on the borderland of sleep and wakefulness. The restlessness passed over the twelve men in waves till at last a young man burst into speech. He was a very young man. His face was sanguine; it was also pleasantly sunburnt; and his voice, that cried out abruptly, was full of the infinite yearning always associated with his time of life. He said: "Where is the beautiful hero that came riding out of the western world on a steed of surpassing vigor?"

All the others looked askance at him, awkwardly, when he made this sudden exclamation.

"There doesn't be such things," said the most middle-aged man among them. "And, anyway, it's against religion to believe that there is."

This was a most remarkable saying. For whereas all the young men of the twelve looked as if they were religious in one way, and whereas all the old men looked religious in another way, none of the middle-aged men looked as if they were religious in any way at all. They all looked too beset with merely worldly care, and this was especially true of the speaker. So that it was not surprising when an old man said:

"All harm from him, anyway, whether or no. We'd have been another week getting that old block of stone into its place but for him."

"That's true," said one, looking at his torn vest and bruised arm.

"It's true without doubt," said another, looking at the shaft of a broken pole he still held in his hand.

"Haven't we the proof of him?" said a third, about whose arms were still coiled the strands of severed rope.

"He came with a face like the dawn of day," said the first young man. "He came with hair like the rays of the sun and with eyes bright and blue like the sky. There were never flowers like the color of the clothes he wore. His steed was powerful and vigorous like original strength. He filled the valley with his presence when he came coursing down the ways of the world."

"How he laughed when he saw us toiling with that old boulder," said an old man. " 'Is this the kind of men there are in Ireland?' says he. 'Wait till I set it for you,' says he."

"His voice was like the music all other musics seek to be," said a young man quite ecstatically, and then became suddenly silent.

An old man said: "He came beside me like a mountain for height and the west wind for speed. He lifted the cornerstone in his two hands and threw it where it is now with one turn of his hands and he leaning out from the saddle over the side of his steed. Didn't I near fall with the power of my strength gone from the cornerstone?"

"That's all very well," said a middle-aged man. "But where is he now? Will you tell me that?"

"He went through the air with that clap of thunder," said a young man.

"Will you have sense and not be forever talking," said an old man. "That was no clap of thunder. That was the bursting of his saddle-girth with the weight of the boulder. Didn't I see him with these two eyes put out that proper leg of his to steady himself on the earth and leap back to his place, the way he wouldn't fall? Clap of thunder, in-deed! 'Tis the chief fault of young men that they are young."

"It may be," said the young man. "But I heard a lament like all the sorrows of the world crying out . . ."

He got no further. He was interrupted by the most middle-aged man of them all.

"There doesn't be such things. It's against religion to say there is. And if there is itself, who'd believe us? And if there were any to be-lieve us, who'd own it? It was ourselves put that cornerstone for the new church where it is. True or false, it'll be a likelier tale for us to bear if we all say the same thing. . . ."

At this precise moment a prodigious groan broke out from behind them. It was like the bellow of a deer driven to bay and beset by hounds, for though it was full of pain, it was, however, majestic and most musical. All the twelve men, with their different sorts and sizes, and according to their different heights and manners and speeds and temperaments, at once turned round together. And there, stretched upon the grass, lay a man of enormous age and stature. His groan had been caused by his efforts to raise himself to a sitting position.

The twelve men gathered round the curious figure stretched on the grass. With remarkable agreement they let their astonishment emerge through their open mouths; and as they kept their mouths open while the stretched figure was occupied, with the most alarming groans, in lifting himself upon his arms, it is to be concluded that their astonishment did not cease to issue during all that time.

Never could imagination have conceived an appearance of such age as that figure presented. A long, untidy beard of the purest white flowed down over his breast like a stream of snow among withered winter flowers. There were more lines, puckers, and wrinkles on the leathery skin of his face than an astrologer could have devised in drawing the most complicated horoscope. His white, abundant hair still swept the grass gently as he lifted himself painfully upon his elbows. He was inconceivably withered and shrunken, and his skin hung in loose folds about him. He looked as if his frame, through long periods of time, had retreated upon itself, shuddering as it went. Yet, shrunken though he was, and withered though he was, it was apparent that he was fully more than twice as tall as the tallest of the twelve men.

His clothes were as aged as himself. They were not worn; they were merely withered. They were not frayed with use; they were simply faded with time. They were like flowers that still recalled summer's profusion of color though at the point of crumbling into original dust. A mantle fell over his shoulders that unquestionably had one time been purple. It fell to his ankles, and opened in front to display a silken tunic embroidered with gold. This tunic was now cream, though it may once have been white, and the embroidery was wrought in sinuous whorls that flowed endlessly and gracefully and returned upon their beginnings. The gold was faded. It was, in fact, old gold. The tunic fell to his knees, and was caught about his waist with a golden girdle wrought and jeweled to match the great broach that clasped the mantle upon his left shoulder. Beneath the tunic was a vest of many colors, all faded now like the dreams of youthful splendor. His shoes were also shrunken and withered. They were held together in comely shape by the silver chasing with which they had been worked, and

which now tore the retreated leather. Yet they had not retreated as
fast or as far as the feet within them, for they hung loosely at the
end of the bony shanks from which the windings had fallen, and were
coiled about the ankles. In like manner the band of gold that had
clasped his brow had fallen off, and lay at a distance on the grass.

"In the name of God," said the oldest of the twelve men, devoutly
crossing himself, "what is this at all?"

"The saints preserve us," said the middle-aged man, also crossing
himself, "but there'll be trouble on the head of this day, I suppose."

"Where is the beautiful hero that came riding from the western
world?" said the youngest of the twelve men.

After these remarkable sayings the silence was only broken by the
woeful creaking of aged joints as the stranger succeeded at last in
poising himself upon his hams. He then attentively regarded the
twelve men. They were restive under that regard, for the wonder it
expressed was the wonder of a scornful mind.

The stranger opened his wrinkled lips to speak, but at first there
only came from them a sound like the western wind through winter's
woods. Twice he essayed to govern that rushing sound, and then these
words were framed in a mighty whisper: "This should be Gleann-na-
Smol, but who are ye at all?"

"Good neighbors," said an old man, and repeated: "Good neighbors.
You're very heartily welcome, whoever you are. I'll suppose we'll know
sometime, and it wouldn't be right to trouble you now."

"Dare you ask who I am?" said the stranger, and the twelve men
were shaken by the sudden bellow of his indignation. "I am Oisin."

"Didn't I say," said the middle-aged man, "that there'd be trouble
at the head of this day?" He did not speak in protest. He spoke with
religious resignation.

"Which Oisin might that be?" said the same old man who had
spoken before. "It isn't a familiar name in this part of the country,
though it's a very good name."

The stranger who was called Oisin looked at him in astonishment.
"Ah, the Battle of Gowra ruined us, and those who lived after didn't
escape the Battle of Cnoc-an-Air," he said, and he fell into lamentations that lasted a considerable time.

The twelve men courteously did not break in upon those lamentations, and it was as well they did not, for they would not have been
able to make themselves heard. Then when the stranger's sorrow had
somewhat abated he turned to them and said: "Is this Ireland of the
heroes and the mighty men?"

"I suppose it is," said one distressfully.

"It is Ireland, anyway," said an old man with conviction.

"It is Ireland, O Oisin," a young man said simply and proudly.

Oisin looked long at the last speaker, and were his gaze divisible into parts, one-third of those parts would have uttered approval, whereas two-thirds would have been loud with scorn. Those aged eyes became almost young again as they flashed inspection of the youth from crown to toe. Then the aged head shook from side to side in a dejected manner.

"It is not as it was in my time, for Banba is diminished, and Fodhla is shorn of her beauty. The vigor of youth, where is it, and where have they fled, the splendor and stature of men in their strength? Has the oak become like the ash, and does the elm sway like the spruce that the tribes of Ir and Heremon should have passed into the likeness of these twelve mannikins that I see before me? Is the eagle of Gullion become a kite, and is the hawk no more than the magpie? Ochone, O Finn, my father, Finn the wise, the son of the mighty Cumhal. Ochone, O Oscar, my darling, who slew Meargach of the spears when there was none other to prevail against him. And ochone, O Caoilte, my comrade, and the ranks of the great Fianna. Would that I were with ye wherever ye are, instead of in the company of these mannikins, for sweet Eire was littler to us in a single day's hunting than Gleann-na-Smol is great to them. Whither shall I find you, O Heroes, and where are you to be discovered, O Mighty Men? Ochone, that I am from you, and that I am left after."

It was in this manner that he made lament for a little while; and as he did so, the oldest of the twelve men drew near to him.

"Is it of the Fianna of Ireland you speak?" said this oldest man. "And were you indeed of that company?"

Oisin made no answer, but looked at him in sorrowful pride.

"Because," continued the old man, "it is many hundreds of years since they were in Ireland by all accounts."

Oisin looked at him in stern reproof. "We," he thundered, "the Fianna that is, never used to tell untruth, and falsehood was never attributed to us. By truth and the might of our hands we came safe out of every conflict. There were but few left after the woeful field of Gowra, but take me to them, for it is plain to see that ye are but of the Fir Bolg and the sprites and lying goblins of the Glens."

Even as he spoke he heard the thin sound of a bell behind him; and as all the twelve men were looking that way, he, too, turned to see what it might be had attracted their attention.

To Oisin it seemed that he had never seen anything more remarkable than this procession. It was led by diminutive children in white robes. Their shrill voices were singing a most mournful tune with incredible slowness. They were followed by bearded men, also in white robes and also singing, whose voices mixed incongruously with the piercing tones of the children. It was not a dirge they were singing. It had not the splendor, not the abandon, of a dirge. But it was very like a dirge. Other children came, swinging golden vessels, and Oisin's nostrils were assailed by a sharp aromatic odor.

Then other men followed, who had heavily brocaded decorations thrown over their white robes like the armor worn by warriors overseas who were not quick enough to avoid the lurching spear. Chief among these he noticed one of a grave and dignified aspect. In his right hand he carried a strange weapon, the like of which Oisin had never seen. For the greater part of its length it was shaped like a spear, except that it was too weighty for the man who bore it with difficulty. Besides, it was curved into a pattern at the top, and whoever saw a spear curved into a pattern where it should have been barbed and sharp? It might have been a shepherd's crook, to which it bore a distant resemblance. But whoever saw a shepherd's crook wrought in costly gold, and of so unwieldly a size? Yet there was something about this man that moved to respect. He was the tallest man Oisin had yet seen, and he bore his body with the authority of a noble mind. A grey pointed beard flowed down to the arch of the solar plexus; for, as a warrior, Oisin had already noted carefully where the solar plexus was. His eyes were grey. They were grey like a well-tempered sword, and their glance was as menacing when the pensive lids lifted, and the grey eyes flashed towards him in enquiry. Decidedly he was an unusual man, and Oisin quickened with affection for him.

Saint Patrick

What do most of us know about the apostle with the adopted Roman name whose memory has been cherished for over fifteen hundred years by Irish people? For most of us the picture of a white-bearded personage banishing a wriggling snake covers a great deal of what we know about him. Or else we see him as an open-air preacher holding up a shamrock by way of illustrating the doctrine of the Trinity. This second image can be more easily disposed of. Undoubtedly he was a

---

By the editor.

strong Trinitarian (Churchmen had to be strong for this point of faith in the fifth century), but it is unlikely that Patrick would have made use of such an inadequate illustration: Irish people wore the shamrock because it had a resemblance to a cross; its association with the Trinity is through an afterthought. The first image, the one that has the snake in it, requires a little more comment.

There were never any snakes in Ireland, and so our saint was under no necessity to banish them. Now the Norse word for "toad" is "paud"; coming to Ireland they noticed there were no such creatures there. They heard of a man whose name was "Paudrig," and they thought that this name meant "toad-expeller," and out of that misunderstanding came the legend of Patrick's banishing not only toads but snakes. Of course that helped to add veneration to his name, for the snake was the emblem of evil. And so the most popular of the stories about Ireland's apostle has a Norse and not an Irish origin.

We have to get past both the shamrock and the snake to perceive what sort of a man the apostle really was. He was a man of great conviction, great energy, great charity; he combined great visionary power with a practical sense and a soldierly audacity; he could have been a good general and a remarkable poet. He was a saint because he loved men and loved God. He brought Christianity to a people *ubi nemo ultra erat*—"beyond which no man dwelt." Beyond the limit of the Roman world was a country that had not known the Roman order. Patrick who had been a captive in that land, who knew its people and their language, dedicated his prime of life to making himself fit for missionary service in it. In a vision he saw one coming to him with papers bearing the inscription "the voice of the Irish"; he felt himself possessed by a spirit urging him to go back amongst a people who had held him as a slave.

He belonged to the time of Saint Ambrose, Saint Augustine, Pope Leo the Great, to the period of important Church councils. As a missionary he was the accredited representative of a Church that had a great organization, a highly developed doctrine, a remarkable personnel. He was associated with a group of Churchmen who were striving to bring a new order into Europe. There was a conference at which the project of a mission to Ireland was discussed. Patrick knew he was the man for the mission: his captivity in the country, his knowledge of the language, the voices that had come to him made him know himself as the man singled out by God for this work. How terrible his disappointment must have been when, on the advice of one whom he had trusted, he was passed over and another missionary was sent to Ireland. At the end of his life, even when he knew he had done the work that had been appointed to him, he remembered the bitterness of that disappointment. But the first missionary failed; then he was consecrated bishop and commissioned to go to Ireland. Patrick was about forty-five years of age then.

His conversion of Ireland was not a local event; ultimately it was a European event. Christopher Dawson in one of his essays has shown us that it was only when Churchmen were forced away from the typical organization of Christianity, the Greek and Roman urban organization, that they were able to deal with the barbarians of the North. Well, Patrick went into a country that had no towns, no urban life; he had to build up a church that was different in its organization from the churches of Romanized Europe. In after centuries the Irish missionaries and the Saxon missionaries who had been trained by them were able to reach hunters, fishers, and tillers by being able to think, speak, and act like them.

A hump-shaped eminence of basalt with scant herbage and scrub upon it—this is Slieve Mis, or Slemish, and we come upon it suddenly as we pass from Antrim into Down. It was from the slopes of this eminence that the youthful captive who afterwards took the name of Patrick watched over his master's flocks or droves. Often he prayed up there; his prayers were said in frost and hail and snow, sometimes as many as a hundred a day. And then he made an escape from the place. When he returned to Ireland, a bishop and a missionary of Rome, he went towards this mount, sailing up the river we see, the river Quoile. The ruler of the territory, believing that his former captive was returning with strange, immense powers and with vengeance in his heart, fired his house and gave himself to the flames. Then another local magnate presented the missionary with a barn; in it he celebrated Christian rites, establishing his first church in Ireland. Years later, an old man, he came back to the place of his first foundation; he died here and was buried nearby.

Often, as a youthful captive who was swineherd or shepherd, he must have climbed these rugged slopes to look towards the land from which he had been taken. The Roman communities in Britain, although a doom hung over them, to him represented civilization. His dream was to return. Once he heard a directing voice; he made a flight; he found a ship (helped, Oliver St. John Gogarty has suggested, by an "underground") about to sail from Ireland. After he came to it he had moments of tragic suspense. He was willing to work his passage to the port to which the vessel was bound. His proposal was entertained by the mariners, but afterwards the ship-master objected, saying sharply,

"Nay, in no wise shalt thou come with us." The disappointment, coming as the end of his captivity seemed to be in sight, was bitter. He turned away from the mariners to seek shelter. As he went he prayed, and before he had finished his prayer he heard one of the crew shouting behind him, "Come quickly, for they are calling you." The shipmaster had been persuaded to forego his objection, and Patrick, now about twenty-one years of age, set sail from Ireland in rough company.

The ship, the cargo, and the voyage were as strange as any romance-writer need devise: dogs were part of the cargo—great Irish wolf-hounds. The crew wished to enter into a compact of friendship with him, but he refused; probably it involved some Pagan rite. They reached port (on the continent) and then made a journey overland; they wandered through a desert country for eight and twenty days; many of the dogs became exhausted and were left to die on the road. What was the desert land they traversed? Probably Southern Gaul. "It was the last night of the year 406 that the Vandals, Suevi, Alans, and Burgundians burst into Gaul." The picture of the desolation that he gives has helped Professor MacNeill to date Patrick's journey.

Apparently Patrick and his company went into Italy; afterwards he wandered back to the South of France. For a while he stayed at the monastery of Lerens; then, after great labors, he won home again to his friends in Britain.

PATRICK TAKEN CAPTIVE

Patrick's native place according to the Irish scholar, Eoin MacNeill, was Abergavenny, in the country that is now Wales. Here, along ways that still communicated with the Roman center, lived communities loyally Roman, devotedly Christian. Patrick spoke the language of the British Celts as well as the Latin tongue. But at the time he was taken captive—he was fifteen then, it is surmised—he had not been trained in the schools. He speaks in his Confession of his inability to write good Latin, "apologizing that he has not had the double advantage that others (of his calling and station) have had, who, as is most fitting, have been educated in sacred literature, and have not lost the Latin speech of their childhood, but have rather constantly acquired a more refined use of it, whereas he, as his style, he says, betrays, was forced in his youth to adopt a strange language in place of Latin." "His style, indeed, suggests," remarks Professor MacNeill, "that, like many a candidate for examination in our time, his conscious weakness in Latin composition caused him to fill out his sentences with phrases taken from other writings, and not always apt to express the intended sense." Well, on this Roman and Christian community that still had communication with the Roman center, Irish raiders descended in 401. The raiders were probably under the command of the high-king Niall. "The object of the raid was to secure a large booty in slaves and other things of value." The household of the decurion Calpurnius hardly survived the raid: its youthful heir (Patrick) was carried off together with its man-servants and maid-servants. Thousands of captives were brought from Britain by these particular raiders. They were sold as slaves, Patrick tells us, and scattered among many tribes, even to the farthest part of Ireland.

At the time he began his mission, the most powerful king in Ireland was Laegaire (Leary), the second in succession from Niall who had carried Patrick over thirty years before. Laegaire claimed to be Ard-ri, high-king or emperor of the Irish, and his seat was at Tara. Patrick went to Tara and preached before him. Laegaire did not adopt the new creed, but he put no obstacles in the way of Patrick's mission.

He sat with three kings to revise the laws of Ireland. That revision was an acknowledgment that his mission had been successful, for it was to incorporate teachings in the national law. But still Patrick looked on himself as an exile and a man of little account. The world that he felt he belonged to—the world of his father, the decurion— was perishing in his sight: the Roman legions had been withdrawn from Britain, and Germanic Pagans with Gaels and Picts were rending what had been left of the Roman order. Nay, Christianity itself was no restraint upon men who had knowledge of the Latin language and who claimed some shadow of Roman authority. The soldiers of the King of North Britain massacred Patrick's converts and mocked the envoy whom he had sent to rebuke them. "In hostile guise they are dead while they live, allies of Scots and apostate Picts, as though wishing to gorge themselves on the blood of innocent Christians whom I in countless numbers begot to God and confirmed in Christ." So Patrick writes in one of the great letters that have come down to us from those days, his letter to Coroticus. This was a British prince who had raided Ireland and carried off as captives a number of converts, youths and maidens. We today might think that that would be a commonplace of the fifth century, something that a busy man would hardly get wrought up about, like the bombing of a town in our day. But injustice and violence would always be battled against by Patrick. With an indignation that makes us ashamed of our own lukewarmness, he denounces the tyrant of that day. "You deliver the members of Christ as it were to a house of ill-fame. What manner of hope in God have you, or any who cooperate with you? God will judge."

Through fifteen hundred years the Christianity that was the core of Patrick comes over to us. "Aye, and where shall Coroticus with his most villainous followers, rebels against Christ, where shall they see themselves, who distribute baptized damsels as rewards, and that for the sake of miserable temporal things which verily pass away in a moment like a cloud of smoke which is dispersed by the wind." Then he makes appeal to all whom his letter may reach "That they may liberate the baptized captive women whom they have taken, so that they may deserve to live to God and be made whole here and in eternity."

In that letter comes the bitter cry of the exile, although perhaps twenty years had been spent in labor in Ireland and he was now an old man. "Did I come to Ireland without God or according to the flesh? Who compelled me—I am bound by the spirit—not to see any of my kinsfolk? Is it from me that I show godly compassion towards the nation who once took me captive and harried the men-servants and maid-servants of my father's house? I was free-born according to the flesh. I am born of a father who was a decurion, but I sold my nobility, I blush not to state it, nor am I sorry for it, for the profit of others."

When he died many communities contended for the glory of having his burial in their grounds. Tradition says that, leaving it to Providence to resolve their claims, the bier was laid on a wagon to which four white oxen were yoked: from the church that was his first foundation, the oxen with their burthen were turned and were permitted to fare on without human direction. On a slope above the river Quoile they stayed and there, in Downpatrick, the body of Patrick was laid in earth. A community grew up around the burial place, and the round tower that still stands was raised. The National Museum in Dublin has the little bell that he held in his hand when he summoned his congregation in the Ireland of fifteen hundred years ago—always and by all visitors it is looked at with special reverence. Beside it is a reliquary made in honor of the saint by one of the Norman lords of the West of Ireland—one of the De Berminghams. It is covered over with the figures of the French saints who were thought most of at the time—one thinks of how present Patrick is in comparison with any of them, and of how deep is the veneration in which he has been held by all comers into Ireland. "I, Patrick, a sinner, the most rustic, and the least of all the faithful, and in the estimation of very many deemed contemptible."

Saint Colum-cille Foretells What Saint Patrick Will Do for the Men and Women of Ireland on the Day of Judgment

Before they went to visit certain of the saints of Ireland, Colum-cille (Saint Columba) and Bauheen, his cousin, betook themselves to Armagh, that place that was consecrated by Saint Patrick and in which the bell that he blessed was still rung. It was on a Sunday, and they walked near the church that Saint Patrick had founded and the grave-yard where his close companions were laid. Suddenly the ground gaped, the headstones fell, the cairns crumbled. The book he was reading Bauheen dropped into a grave that burst open; he scrambled down to get it and was struck on the head with the broken arm of a stone cross. He tried to pull himself out by gripping a branch, but the tree fell down on him.

"Why doesn't he do something to give his companions quiet and peace in their graves?" Bauheen said when he got the earth out of his mouth.

"Whom do you speak of?" Colum-cille asked, drawing his companion out of the way of a yew-tree that heaved itself at them.

"Patrick," said Bauheen, rubbing the sore place on his elbow. "Are we not in his stead? And why doesn't he do something to give his companions quiet and peace in their graves?"

"If you knew what Saint Patrick will do for the people of Ireland on the Day of Doom . . ."

"There," said Bauheen, as the branch of a lifted thorn-bush poked itself into Colum-cille's eyes, "I knew you'd get it, too."

"Nevertheless, you must not belittle Patrick, the protector of the people of Ireland," said Colum-cille, and he made two long jumps and got out of the graveyard, Bauheen with three jumps coming behind him.

"If you knew as I know what effort he will make on the Day of the Last Judgment for the people of Ireland, you would not murmur against Saint Patrick," Colum-cille said when they were out of the graveyard.

"Tell me, then," said Bauheen, "what effort he will make for the people of Ireland on that Last Day?"

From *The Legend of Saint Columba*, by Padraic Colum, pp. 57-62. Copyright, 1935, by The Macmillan Co. New York.

"Some part of it I can tell you, but not all," said Colum-cille. "Harken, Bauheen, to what I shall deliver to you, and never afterwards let a word pass your lips in belittlement of Patrick."

Away from the place of gaping graves and crumbling cairns and breaking crosses they seated themselves, and under the shade of a well-rooted ash-tree Colum-cille told his companion this prophetic story.

"The men and women of Ireland will assemble themselves at Clonmacnoise . . ." Colum-cille began.

"At Clonmacnoise?" said Bauheen in great surprise.

"At Clonmacnoise," said Colum-cille decidedly. "They will do that in honor of the greatest saint living in Ireland at the present time— Saint Ciaran. There the folk of Ireland will assemble themselves on the Day of Doom. And to Clonmacnoise, Patrick will go. Seeing him the people will know him for their leader. He will strike the bell that he broke upon the demons when he banished them from the mountain. At the sound of that bell the men and women of Ireland will crowd towards their leader, and lucky will they feel on that day, they who were truly followers of Patrick, who kept his feast-day with alms-giving and his good-will belittled never."

"Amen!" said Bauheen.

Colum-cille went on. "With Patrick we shall march, all of us. We shall journey to where Saint Martin has his station. With him we shall join and thence go to where the most holy Peter and the most holy Paul have their place. Guided by these two primal saints we shall make our way to Mount Olivet.

"Saint Peter, Saint Paul and Saint Martin will go to where Our Lord is enthroned. But with us, the men and women of Ireland, Patrick will stay. He will be seated on a chair of gold above the throng. Summoning Saint Ailbe to him, he will send him with seven bishops to the feet of our Lord on Mount Sion."

"Tell on," urged Bauheen.

"He will send Ailbe to inquire what will Our Lord has towards the men and women in his charge. And when he has bade him welcome to Ailbe, Our Lord will say, 'Where is the lightning-flash of the Western World? He is long in appearing before us.'

" 'What is Thy word for him, O Lord?' " Ailbe will ask.

" 'Many sinners are with him,' Our Lord will say. 'My word to him is this: leave behind ere coming before us all those who have wrought evil in their lives.'

" 'How shall I say that to Patrick, O Lord,' Ailbe will say. 'Thou knowest he whom Thou hast named the Lightning-flash of the Western World is a wrathful and quick-tempered man.'

" 'Nevertheless, thou shalt take My word back to him,' the Lord will say.

"With trepidation Ailbe will salute Patrick and say, 'I have had converse with Our Lord, and He bade me to tell thee to leave behind ere thou goest before Him all who have wrought evil in their lives.'

" 'It appears I have not been given even the beginning of a welcome to Mount Sion,' Patrick will say, 'And you, Ailbe, have failed me in this.'

"Then he will speak to Ciaran, Cainneach, and myself, and declare that all the people of Ireland, sinners as well as sinless, must be with him when he goes before Our Lord. He would have none parted from him until he had spoken on their behalf.

"He will send Munda to Mount Sion then, Munda who was his companion when he came to make Ireland Christian. It will be Munda's duty to remind Our Lord that a promise was made to Patrick on his coming to our land—a promise that he would be the advocate for all our people on the Day of Judgment.

" 'You who come from Patrick are not negligent in reminding Us of the promise made to him,' Our Lord will say. And he shall tell Munda that his word to Patrick is that he will have to put out of his following all who wrought evil in their lives."

"And then . . .?"

"Then," said Colum-cille, "I shall find myself beside the golden chair on which Patrick is seated, and I shall hear myself being directed to go unto Our Lord on Mount Sion, but what I am being told to say or do, I shall not be able to recollect, for the sound of all the waves of the world will be in my ears. I shall find myself standing at the feet of Our Lord, and when He speaks to me I shall be able to speak of one thing only, namely, of Patrick's great love for all the people of Ireland, sinners at well as sinless, the love that brought him to keep a long and wasting fast upon the mountain that is named Cruachan, to the end that no one born in Ireland after the coming of the Faith should lose utterly the friendship of Our Lord. And this being said there will be such a silence that I will believe that sound has utterly departed from the world. And then I shall hear Our Lord make answer, and he will say: 'We will consult with the Nine Hierarchies of Heaven about what We shall do about this Patrick and his following.' And he shall say to me in a kindly voice, 'Go back to him, and bid him come to Us with the whole of the host that is his people. Ah, but tell him, too, that he will have to do this. . . .' "

Thereupon Colum-cille paused, and Bauheen, in great anxiety, asked him: "What will Patrick have to do for the people of Ireland upon that Day?"

Colum-cille opened his mouth to speak. But at that moment the bell of Armagh that is called the Bernan, sounded.

"That stroke is to remind us," said Colum-cille, "that it is fitter for us to be inside Saint Patrick's church, praying as Saint Patrick taught us to pray, than to be foretelling what he will do for us on the Day of Judgment."

"But what will he do for us on the Day of Judgment?" Bauheen asked as they went over the ground that was hollow and lumpy but no longer heaving.

"God decreed that the bell should be struck at this moment to forbid my telling what more the Lightning-flash of the Western World will do for the people of Ireland on the Judgment Day," Colum-cille said, and saying this, he and Bauheen went into the church and listened to the hymn that was being sung in praise of Saint Patrick.

How Colum-cille Saved the Poets' Guild

Colum-cille, holding himself responsible for a battle waged against the high-king, exiled himself, making a vow that he would not look upon the land of Ireland or the face of anyone dwelling in Ireland for the rest of his life. However, two questions came up in which Colum-cille had a vital interest: the first was the relation of the Irish kingdom in Alba, Dalriada, to the King of Ireland, and the second was the proposed dissolution of the guild of poets. Colum-cille was a member of the guild, and as head of the monastic settlement in Iona he was the mediator between the Gaels of Ireland and the Gaels of Scotland. The angel who attended him took means to make it clear to him that it was his duty to go to Ireland and attend the council at which these questions were to be debated.—P.C.

In the night the angel stood beside where Colum-cille lay. In his hand he held a book of crystal. He motioned to put the book in Colum-cille's hand and have him open and read it. But Colum-cille would not take the book, he knew that what was written therein was a sentence which he had no wish to obey.

Ibid., pp. 106-117.

The angel went and the night passed. And on a second night the angel appeared with the crystal book and proffered it to him. But Colum-cille would not take it, and the angel went and the night passed. On a third night he came again and held the book to him. Colum-cille kept his hand away from it. Then the angel took a scourge from out of the folds of his garments and struck Colum-cille on the side with it. The stroke the angel dealt did him much hurt, and on the morning he saw a welt left by the stroke—it was all down his right side.

He repented that he was disobedient to Axal's will; he prayed that the angel might come to him again. And when on a fourth night the angel held the crystal book to him, he took it in his hand and opened it; he read the sentence that was therein. It was: "Prepare to return to thine own land and stay there for a while."

So Colum-cille knew he would have to go back to Ireland in spite of the vow he had made not to look on the face of a man or woman standing on Irish ground. And soon afterwards it was made known to him that the King of Ireland, Ae MacAinmire, had summoned a council to meet at Drumceat. Envoys came to Iona from the people of Ireland telling him of their sorrow because of his absence, begging him to return, and, for their sake, take part in the council. King Aedan of Dalriada came to Iona to urge him to come with him to Ireland.

Colum-cille resolved that all the time he would be in Ireland his cowl would be drawn down over his eyes so as to keep his vow he would look on no man or woman in Ireland. And when that tall figure with face half covered by a cowl stepped on the green where the council was being held, there was an outburst of welcome from all the gathering. The King of Ireland's son, Donald, came to meet him and escort him to the pavilion where the kings and princes and high prelates held their session. The King of Ireland rose up and welcomed him and welcomed King Aedan, and the welcome he gave to Colum-cille was not less than the welcome he gave to King Aedan.

Aedan spoke to the council, advocating that the King of Ireland should forego his power of going into Dalriada. The men of Ireland murmured in opposition to this. Then a man who was learned in history and affairs spoke: Colman was his name. And Colman said that the King of Ireland should renounce his right of going into Dalriada, but that the men of Dalriada should pay him tribute, and that if the King of Alba went to the aid of the King of Ireland, the men of Dalriada should supply him with ships and give rations to his army.

Colum-cille then spoke to the council. And so loving were the men of Ireland to him and so trustful of his judgment that they were ready to be ruled by what he said. And what he said was all in support of

Colman's argument. Many spoke against Colman and Colum-cille as against Aedan, but they were not able to remove from the minds of most of the council the effect produced by the deep voice and the solemn words that came from the man with the cowl down over his eyes. At the end of the day the King of Ireland and his own councillors agreed to renounce the right of going into Dalriada and to accept the tribute and service that were offered in return for that renunciation. The King of Ireland and the King of Alba joined their hands together while Column-cille said words that were to be long remembered: "Let there be peace in perpetuity between the men of Eirinn and the men of Alba."

It was then that the council came to deal with the case of the poets of Ireland. Colum-cille made plea that their order should not be abolished nor their guild dissolved, and that none of them should be banished out of Ireland.

"It is no easy thing to maintain them," said King Ae. "Their guild is too ungovernable; their demand upon rulers and people are exorbitant. You know very well, Colum-cille, that unless they are given large donations they make reviling and scoffing verses on people. I myself have suffered from their satire. This broach of mine, which is the handiwork of the greatest of artificers and which has been a treasured possession in my family for many generations, has been made the subject of a very mocking ballad. And," said Ae MacAinmire, " 'tis very little would start them deriding the crown that is upon my head." When he said this, the blind Dallan Forgail, the Chief Poet of Ireland, groaned aloud, turning his head this way and that way to find out if there was anyone in the council who was favorable to the poets.

Then Colum-cille, as one belonging to the guild of poets, stood up and spoke. He said: "A skull dug out of a hill is all that is Cormac MacAirt—a skull and a lettering upon a stone. But Cormac MacAirt, the noble, the generous, the beautiful, goes among us, making everyone of us strive to be of his pattern. And what has made Cormac a pattern to men? Not his possessions, for they are long since gone. The praises the poets gave him are Cormac's lasting possession, and it is the poets who have given Cormac the life he has for us. If there had been no poets to praise him, that king, like many another, would now be only a skull and lettering upon a stone."

When Colum-cille said this, a prelate answered: "We have other things to think of besides fables, Colum-cille."

Then, his voice rising to a chant, Colum-cille answered:

If the poets' verse be fable,
Then is all your knowledge fable.
All your rights and state and power,
And this drifting world is fable.

For their fable which is lasting
Give the fable that is passing!
Kingly scarlet, scholars' blue
Will make no show in hereafter.

God has dowered sons of Adam
With a craft for them to work on;
Honor then the craft that's proven,
Give the craftsman means to live by.

When Colum-cille had spoken in this wise the mind of the council was no longer hardened against the poets. Then it was agreed that whatever judgment Colum-cille gave, the council and the guild of poets would abide by it. Colum-cille gave this judgment:

That the principal poet of one district should not go into another district for goods or preferment without leave of his lord; that if he made a poem that was of interest to the people of another district, the lord of that district would send his principal poet to meet him at the border and have him recite the poem. And if he judged it worthy, that other poet was to reward him who made it and bring it back to his lord. And if this other poet did not find it worthy, the one who made it was to go back without any reward.

That the poets were no longer to go about in bands, quartering themselves for long seasons on this or that ruler; that none of them should be banished; that their privileged order should be kept in existence, and that their guild should not be dissolved.

The council accepted this judgment and the poets were content with it. Their franchise was curtailed, but they had still their guild; their order remained a privileged one, and, happily, none of them were banished out of Ireland.

The next day the head professor of every grade of the Bardic Assembly came and recited a poem of eulogy of Colum-cille. Standing before him, one and then the other of them recited his praise. And when he heard the praises of himself chanted by the poets of Ireland, the heart of Colum-cille swelled and his mind became lit up, and such was his exultation that the air above his head became filled with evil spirits who gloated over his loss of humility and his access of vainglory.

Bauheen, his tight-lipped cousin, who was beside him, perceived this; he rebuked him sharply, telling him that it was not right that he should take such account of the world's praises, and that he should consider only his duty to God. And when he heard that rebuke and knew its justice, Colum-cille covered his head with his mantle and wept sorely, repenting of the vanity that he had given way to. As he wept, the evil spirits that were above his head dispersed, leaving the air clear.

It was then that Colum-cille made his last address to the poets of Ireland, their faces unseen by him. He told them that they were not to write down the praises that they had made, and that they were not to make them known to men.

"But," said Bauheen to him afterwards, "it is known that the Chief Poet of Ireland, Dallan Forgail, is making a eulogy of you. You have done nothing to withhold him from doing this."

"Service for service—it is that that keeps a folk together, cousin Bauheen," said Colum-cille cheerfully. "It is right that the Chief Poet of Ireland should make a eulogy of me on account of the benefit I have done his order."

"But then," said Bauheen, "everybody will be reciting Dallan's poem and Alba and Ireland will be filled with your praise. How will you be able to keep your humility with such urgings to vainglory?"

Colum-cille smiled on his cousin. "Dallan is a very skilled poet," he said, "and I have asked him to use all his art in making this commemorative poem. And I promise you, Bauheen, that no more plentiful than hornless piebald cows are the men in Ireland and Alba that will be able to comprehend much less remember the poem that Dallan uses all his skill in the making of."

And so it came to be. Dallan's poem was praised by every poet in Ireland because of the strangeness of its rhythm and the depth and density of its references. "Amra," which means "strange," is the title that that poem of Dallan's is known by. We have been told that a scholar in Armagh got the first part of the poem by heart, and he was so bent on knowing the second part that he made a pilgrimage to the tomb of Colum-cille, and prayed and fasted there to the end that his mind might be so illuminated that he would be able to memorize the second part. In the morning he was able to repeat the second part and he jumped about with joy. But when he tried to repeat the first part he found that he could not bring the lines of it together. Fast and pray as he might, he was never able to get into his mind any but the first or second part: never the whole of the "Amra" did that man know. If the scholar had been a drunken fellow, we have no doubt but by the grace of Colum-cille, his patron, he would have been able to get by heart the whole of Dallan Forgail's eulogy.

Brian Boru

Near the mouth of the Shannon is the site of a stronghold famous in Irish history and poetry, Kincora. No remains of it are left. At the end of the tenth century, it was the stronghold of a king who, basing his power on Ireland's great waterway, the Shannon, strove bravely and wisely to establish a state that would be strong enough in the face of actual and imminent invasions to permit the country to develop her own civilization. The king was Brian, who was named "Boru" after the adjacent village where he was born.

The eighth, ninth, and tenth centuries form a period in which Northern and Western Europe were harried and partially conquered by Scandinavian invaders, Danes and Norse, a people still Pagan and fiercely anti-Christian. They founded kingdoms in England, Scotland, France. In Ireland they encountered a more established order than in any country they had yet entered, and they were not able to make, as they made in King Alfred's England, any large conquest. The high-king of Ireland, symbol of an historical unity, was able to keep a prestige that gave the country a morale. But the raids and invasions that kept up for generations made for greater devastation. The wealth of the country was plundered; churches and schools were destroyed; books, as representing a form of life the invaders were especially inimical to, they destroyed wherever found, generally sinking them in lakes: the round towers were built in this period to provide places where the treasures of the monastery and the books of its schools could be secured—places that could not be entered or burnt by plunderers. The invasions of the Scandinavians are marked by flights of scholars from Ireland.

Towards the end of the ninth century the Norse and Danes were beginning to settle down along the coasts, but their presence meant constant warfare and disruption in the country. At the time when young Brian came on the scene, the Scandinavians occupied a camp in the area now covered by the city of Limerick. They were formidable neighbors to the small Irish states. "Their pine woods," says an historian, "supplied them with timber for stout vessels, and from the

By the editor.

mines of Upsala they had iron and copper for the chains and anchors of their ships, for their heavy swords, their spear and arrow points and headpieces and shields, and all the armor which was later the wonder and admiration of the Irish."

The Scandinavians in the place that is now Limerick were just across the river from a state that was about half the size of the present county Clare. The people of that state were named "Dal Gas," a name which has been modernized "Dalcassian." The young king of this state, Mahon, made a peace with the Scandinavians. But his younger brother, Brian, refused to be bound by the peace. "However small the injury he might do to the foreigners, he preferred it to peace," says the historian of his deeds. He went into the forests and waste places with a small band of followers and kept up a warfare. And so, like many other kings who stand out as champions of their people, Brian's early training was in rugged places and with followers, looked upon as outlaws, who shared his hardships.

When there were few left of his band he came back to his brother's house, and the makers of his saga have made a dramatic scene out of the meeting of the younger and elder brother. The saga-maker left it in prose which a modern poet, Alice Milligan, has changed into verse:

Brian of Banba, all alone, up from the desert places,
Came to stand where the festal throne of the lord of Thomond's race is,
Came after tarrying long away till his cheeks were hunger-hollow,
His voice grown hoarse in a hundred fights where he called on his men
    to follow.
He had pillowed his head on the hard tree-roots, and slept in the sun
    unshaded,
Till the gold that had shone in his curls was gone, and the snow of his
    brow was faded;
And where he came he was meanliest clad, 'midst the nobles of the
    nation;
Yet proudly he entered among them all, for this was his brother's
    banquet-hall,
    And he was a Prince Dalcassian!

Mahon, King of the Dal-Cas, throned in his palace proudly,
Drank the mead from a costly glass, whilst his poet harping loudly,
Traced in song his lineage long to the times of ancient story,
And praised the prowess of Cennedi's sons, and counted their deeds
    of glory.

And chanted the fame of the chieftains all, the banquet-board surrounding—
But why does he turn to this stranger tall? for whom is his harp now
sounding?
"The King," he says, "is a champion bold, and bold is each champion
brother,
But Brian, the youngest, is bravest and strongest, and wiser than any
other."

The King rose up on his royal throne, and sorrowful was his gazing,
And greatly the envy grew in his heart at the sound of such high
appraising;
For Mahon had dwelt in a palace fair, at peace with the land's invader,
While Brian lurked in the wild-cat's lair, and slept where the she-wolf
laid her.
Mahon was clad in a robe of silk, a gift of a Dane chief's sending;
The only cloak that Brian had was torn by the brambles' rending.
Mahon had called for the mead and wine from the hands of those who
hasted;
But the thin cold wine that the swan-flocks sip was the only wine that
Brian's lip
For a year and more had tasted.

"Brian, my brother," said the King, in a tone of scornful wonder,
"Why dost thou come in beggar-guise our palace portals under?
Where hast thou wandered yester-year? On what venture of love hast
thou tarried?
Tell us the count of thy prey of deer, and what cattle-herds thou hast
harried.
Where is the mantle of silken fold, and the jeweled brooch that bound
it?
In what wager lost was the band of gold that once thy locks sur-
rounded?
Where hast thou left the courtly train that befitteth thy princely
station?
The hundred high-born youths I gave, the chosen sons of the chieftains
brave
Of the warriors Dalcassian?"

"I have hunted no deer since yester-year, I have harried no neighbor's
cattle,

1 have wooed no love, I have joined no game, save the kingly game of
　　battle;
The Danes were my prey by night and day, in their forts of hill and
　　hollow,
And I come from the desert-lands alone, since none are alive to follow.
Some were slain on the plundered plain, and some in the midnight
　　marching.
Some were lost in the midnight floods, and some by the fever parching;
Some have perished by wounds of spears, and some by the shafts of
　　bowmen;
And some by hunger and some by thirst, and all are dead; but they
　　slaughtered first
　　Their tenfold more of their foemen."

The King leaped down from his cushioned throne and grasped the
　　hand of his brother:
"Brian, though youngest, thou'art bravest and strongest, and nobler
　　than any other;
So choose at thy will of my flocks on the hill, and take of my treasures
　　golden,
Were it even the ring on my royal hand, or this broidered cloak I am
　　rolled in."
Brian smiled: "You will need them all as award of bardic measure;
I want no cattle from out your herds, no share of your shining treasure;
But grant me now"—and he turned to look on the listening warriors'
　　faces—
"A hundred more of the Clan Dal Cas, to follow me over plain and
　　pass:
To die, as fitteth the brave Dal Cas, at war with the Outland races."

After this encounter Mahon joined with Brian in the war against
the foreigners, and, becoming ambitious through the success the Dal
Cas achieved, laid claim to the important kingship of Cashel. The
Danes were driven out of the southwest; Mahon was murdered by
Irish rivals, and Brian, around the age of forty, made himself King of
Cashel and dominated the whole south of Ireland. The contemporary
high-king was Maelseachlainn whose name is often written Malachi.
He had defeated the foreigners at Tara; he had taken their stronghold
of Dublin and brought away two famous trophies, the sword of
Carlus and the torque of Tomar. He and Brian divided Ireland be-
tween them, Malachi taking the northern half and Brian the southern
half.

The kingdom of Leinster, included in the southern half, made an alliance with the Norse of Dublin, and declared war. Brian, with the support of Malachi, defeated the Leinstermen and the Norse and took Dublin. And now the time had come for Brian to initiate a policy unique in the history of Ireland. The example of Charlemagne was before him; through the school in Clonmacnoise which had contact with the school Charlemagne set up in Paris, the idea of an imperial power that could check the invasions of the Scandinavians and advance a Christian civilization was familiar to learned men in Ireland. Brian embodied the idea. He made an alliance with the defeated Norse. Gathering all his forces he marched on Tara and demanded that Malachi acknowledge him as high-king. Malachi went into Brian's camp and accepted gifts from him—a token of submission. Brian, now king of Ireland, permitted Malachi to style himself king of Tara.

But it was evident that he intended to create a kingship of a new order. In the northern metropolis, Armagh, his secretary wrote his title in words that can still be read—"Imperator Scotorum"—"Emperor of the Gaels." He claimed possession of all the southern fortresses; he attempted to weaken the northern dynasts by recognizing the petty kingdoms from which they drew tribute. Knowing that the Norse and Danes could not be driven out, he inaugurated a policy of drawing them into the political and social life of the country.

But in striving to establish a dominant state in Ireland, Brian had a more difficult task than an able and ambitious dynast in any other part of western Europe would have had. The whole constitution of Irish society was opposed to centralized authority: Irish society was at once vital and strongly traditional. It would have taken two or three generations of resolute and enlightened leadership to make that society favorable to an order inaugurated by a king from an obscure stock in an obscure part of Ireland.

Twelve years after he had declared himself "Imperator Scotorum," Brian had to face an invasion of Ireland. He was in his seventieth year. The Norse and the Irish accounts of the battle that ensued show a woman working to bring about the invasion. She was Gormlai, the sister of the King of Leinster, the mother of Sigtrygg, the Norse king of Dublin: she is called Kormlada in the Njal Saga. Gormlai brought about a new alliance between the Norse and Leinstermen. She prevailed upon her son to gather forces that could be great enough to overthrow Brian's. And when Sigtrygg told her he had secured the help of Earl Sigurd with the promise of the kingdom of Ireland and herself for wife, "she was well pleased, but said they must gather greater forces still." Earl Brodir was summoned to join Earl Sigurd.

The Norse of Dublin with the Leinstermen and the Vikings from overseas made a force of about twenty thousand men—a great force for those days. Brian had the men of Munster and Connacht; he had the support of Malachi with the men of Meath; he had Scottish allies. The fighting took place in what is now covered by the northern streets of Dublin: the Viking ships lay off Clontarf, and the retreat to them was across a weir. In Irish history the battle is "The Battle of Clontarf"; in the Norse saga it is "The Battle of Dublin."

Earl Brodir's mail-clad men were greatly dreaded by the Irish who still fought in their tunics. They were the right wing of the Norse army with Earl Sigurd and the Orkney and Shetland men. Murrach, Brian's son, led the wing opposed to this powerful force: he had the home-forces, the men of the Shannon side, and was supported by the Scottish allies. The Norse center was made up of the men of Leinster and other Irish forces, and it was opposed by the Munster forces. The Norse left was made up of the men of Dublin, and was opposed by the Connacht forces.

Brian's center, broken by the men of Leinster, was saved by the arrival of Malachi with the men of Meath. The battle went on. Murrach's onslaught on the Norse right wing was so vigorous that the mail-clad fighters were dispersed. Brodir was forced into a near-by wood. Tordelbach, Brian's grandson, who is named Kerthialfad in the Njal Saga, strove with Earl Sigurd.

Sigurd, had he won this battle and set himself up as King of Ireland, could have claimed kinship with an Irish dynastic family, for his mother was Eithne, daughter of the king of Ossory. It was she who wove the magic banner that he carried. The Earl's Saga tells how he went to his mother for advice about the battle he was going into, telling her that there would be no less odds against him than seven to one. She answered, "I had reared thee up long in my wool-bag had I known that thou wouldst like to live forever. . . . Better it is to die with honor than to live with shame. Take thou here hold of this banner which I have made for thee with all my cunning, and I ween it will bring victory to those before whom it is borne, but speedy death to him who bears it." Now Brian's grandson, a youth of fifteen, came against him, the Njal Saga tells, "so fast that he laid low all who were in the front rank, and he broke up the array of Earl Sigurd right up to his banner, and slew the banner-bearer.

"Then he got another man to bear the banner, and there was a hard fight. Kerthialfad smote the man his death-blow at once, and so on, one after another, all who stood near him.

"Then Earl Sigurd called on Thorstein, the son of Hall of the Side, to bear the banner, and Thorstein was just about to lift the banner, but Asmund the White said, 'Don't bear the banner! For all who bear it get their death!' 'Hafrn the Red,' called the Earl, 'bear the banner!' 'Bear thine own devil thyself,' answered Hafrn. Then the Earl said, ' 'Tis fit that the beggar should bear his own bag,' and with that he took the banner from the staff and put it under his cloak."

Seeing that the battle was going against him, Sigurd formed the design of capturing or killing Brian. He drew Brodir from the near-by wood to join with him. Breaking through the lines they slew the king's guards. His son and grandson hurried to where Brian was in a shelter. Sigurd with his banner was killed. But Brodir, breaking into the "shieldburg," slew the king. Then, surrounded by foemen, Brodir was slain by an unknown hand.

The battle was over; the King of Ireland had won over the Norse and their Irish allies; the Vikings had retreated to their ships. But Brian was dead. His son, Murrach, engaging in single combat with a Viking, lost his life, and Tordelbach, his grandson, was slain in the water beside the Viking ships. None were left of those who might have carried on Brian's policy.

The song which is given in the Njal Saga, the song which Darraud had heard the weird women sing, was prophetic for Ireland:

> Now new-coming nations
> That island shall rule,
> Who on outlying headlands
> Abode ere the fight;
> I say that king mighty
> To death now is done,
> And low before spear-point
> That Earl bows his head.
>
> Soon over all Ersemen
> Sharp sorrow shall fall.
> That woe to those warriors
> Shall wane nevermore:
> Our woof now is woven,
> Now battlefield's waste,
> O'er land and o'er water
> War tidings shall leap.*

---

* Translated by Sir George Dasent, in *The Saga of Burnt Njal.*

Their defeat seemed portentous to the Scandinavians whose swords and axes had hewed out victories from Iceland to Normandy and from Caithness to Constantinople. Earl Sigurd had such foreboding that for long he was steadfast against obeying King Sigtrygg's summons. And after Brodir had resolved to go, a shower of boiling blood fell upon him and his men; their axes and spears fought of themselves; ravens flew at the men and pressed them so hard that they had to keep them off with sword and shield. In Iceland, on the day of the battle, blood came on the priest's stole. In the Orkneys a chieftain saw the apparition of Earl Sigurd and rode forward to meet it—"men saw that they met and rode under a brae, but they were never seen again." In the Southern Islands, Earl Gilli dreamt that a man came to him from Ireland and sang runes about the battle. In Caithness a man saw folk riding twelve together to a bower; he looked through the window slit and saw women weaving: men's heads were the weights of the looms, men's entrails were the warp and woof, a sword was the shuttle, the reeds were arrows. And as they wove, the women chanted a lament for "the sword-bearing rovers" which the man who watched learned by heart.

But this was not the finish of a career that had had a creative idea. One side of the pattern given by Charlemagne, the political side, had been torn up; the other side, the cultural side, remained and had a living influence for centuries. Centers of learning had been destroyed, libraries had been pillaged, learned men had fled the country. In the years of peace in his stronghold by the Shannon, Brian planned a revival of learning. Historians who were close to him tell us he "sent professors and masters to teach wisdom and knowledge and to buy books beyond the seas." A new learned order was instituted by him. Up to the tenth century learning had been fostered in the monasteries. A new learned order, a lay order, now took over, an order that is associated in its beginnings with the Shannon settlements. This was the Bardic Order that influenced Ireland directly for five centuries and left a tradition that had longer-lasting influences.*

---

* "They correspond in a way to the university man, but their fixed place in society was higher than any that his attainments alone have ever been able to secure for the university man in England. They were, indeed, until the fall of the old Irish order and intellectual aristocracy, with all the privileges and, no doubt, many of the prejudices of a caste."—Robin Flower: *The Irish tradition*. Oxford University Press, New York, Inc.

The Unbroken Line of O'Briens

The O'Briens divided into several branches, the chief being the O'Briens, of Ara, north of County Tipperary; of Connagh, in the east of County Limerick; of Pobelbrien, where their main stronghold was at Carrigconnell, on the River Shannon; of Aherlow, in County Tipperary, and of Comaragh, in County Waterford, where they had extensive possessions in the valley between Dungarvan and the Suir.

The place of inauguration of the O'Briens, as Kings and Princes of Thomond, was at Tullagh, County Clare, and their motto or war-cry was "Lamb Laidir An Uachdar," or "The Strong Hand Uppermost." On their armorial ensigns were three lions, which were on the standards of Brian Boru and borne by his men at the Battle of Clontarf.

In modern times the O'Briens were Earls of Inchiquin, Marquises of Thomond and Barons of Burren, in County Clare. Many of them were distinguished commanders in the Irish brigades in the service of France under the titles of Earls of Clare and Counts of Thomond. Today, the present Baron of Inchiquin, Sir Donough Edward Foster O'Brien, has his seat at Dromoland Castle, Newmarket-on-Fergus, County Clare, thus maintaining an unbroken line of male descent from Brian Boru.

From "If Your Name Is O'Brien," by V. J. Ryan, in *The Irish Digest*, March, 1950, p. 94. Dublin.

Part III

GREAT CHIEFS AND UNCROWNED KINGS

Letter from
Hugh O'Neill, Earl of Tyrone,
to Sir John McCoughleyn

Our greetings to you, McCoughleyn. We have received your letter, and what we make out from it is that you offer nothing but sweet words and procrastination. For our part in the matter, whatever man would not be on our side and would not spend his efforts for the right, we take it that that man is a man against us. For this reason, whatever you yourself are doing well, hurt us as much as you are able, and we shall hurt you to the best of our ability, with God's will.

O'NEILL

At Knocduffmaine, 6th Feb. 1600.

From *A Celtic Miscellany: Translations from the Celtic Literatures,* by Kenneth Hurlstone Jackson. Harvard University Press. Cambridge. 1951.

Introduction

To leave a blank between the eleventh and the fifteenth century seems to imply that nothing that affected the people of Ireland happened in that long interval. On the contrary, events that had the greatest import for them happened in these centuries. But, as far as the knowledge of this editor goes, these great events left no deposit that has been drawn upon in the formation of popular tradition. They belong exclusively to history.

The events are the Norman invasion; the acceptance by the Irish princes of the Plantagenet assumption of the Lordship of Ireland; the abolition of the High-Kingship; the Irish resurgence and the stoppage of the Norman spread in the west and south; the attempt to set up Edward Bruce as King of Ireland and the consequent war that all but destroyed the early Norman and English settlements in Ireland; the adoption by certain of the great Norman families of Irish law with the Gaelicization of their names; the reduction of English power in Ireland to Dublin and a strip of country alongside—the Pale.

From then until the close of the sixteenth century when medieval Ireland that contained in itself so much of an earlier Ireland was destroyed, the country outside the Pale was governed by great magnates of Norman and Gaelic names. If Ireland had been isolated from the expanding state on the east, there would have emerged from this feudalism some paramount lord who would have made himself king. As the fifteenth century progresses we note that the scene is set for such a play. But time is running out. The Tudor monarch in England is forming the Renaissance great state. In Scotland the great magnates are losing to the monarch. And this rising monarchy could strengthen itself against English encroachment by an alliance with a group of Irish magnates, and, by giving support to one of them, make Ireland a kingdom. This seems to be the purport of the play that is being offered towards the end of the fifteenth century. But the Scots lose Flodden Field, and thereafter Tudor power overshadows Scotland and Ireland.

Of an age stirring with such drama, the four personages described by different historians are representative. Here is the Norman-Irish Fitzgerald who had the kingship in his grasp but fell back on the part of the last of the barons. Here is the Gaelic O'Neill, haughty, humorous, politic, a good ruler of his own people, but too private-minded for the great role that soon it would be too late to enact. And later, on a narrowed stage but still representative, Grania O'Malley who shows us what stuff there was in the ruling stock at the time, and Brian O'Rourke who, if he did nothing else, showed how indomitable these old chieftains were.—P.C.

Garret More Fitzgerald, Earl of Kildare

Henry VII had already realized in a meeting with Garret More that, "since all Ireland cannot rule this man, this man must rule all Ireland," and so he restored Kildare as deputy, giving him further in marriage as his second wife his own cousin, Elizabeth St. John, and pardoning the whole body of his supporters. Kildare ruled Ireland for the rest of his life, and the bridling of the Dublin parliament even made him still more master, for as long as the King approved, he could manage it and legislate in it as he wished. Save for that, all his former powers were restored and so was Anglo-Irish control in Dublin. All the highest offices in Church and State (saving those of bishops and of chancellor, treasurer, and the chief judges) were in the appointment of Kildare; he spent whatever revenues of state there were, commanded its forces, named the constables of the royal castles, and used the royal artillery for his own purposes. In the north he protected the interests of his nephews, sons of Conn More O'Neill, though the second of these, the famous Conn Bachach, did not become O'Neill till 1519. A fine family grew up around him, and through his five daughters he allied himself with the great houses of Gael and Gall. One married Ulick Burke of Clanrickard; another Donal MacCarthy Reagh; another Mulrony O'Carroll; another the Lord of Slane; a fifth, Margaret, Sir Piers Butler who, on the death of his father, James, in 1478, became head of the Polestown Butlers and deputy for the absent Earl of Ormond.

In these years in which he was left in charge of Ireland, Garret More, both as deputy and earl, marched over more of Ireland than any viceroy had done for generations, bringing local chiefs into vassalage, securing the succession of the O'Neill or the O'Kelly he favored, and blowing down with royal artillery the castles of private opponents. Ireland had found in him an "uncrowned king," and though she was divided into local combinations, at least they revolved round the great names of Geraldine, Butler, Burke, and O'Brien. The culmination of these armed confederacies was seen in the year 1504. In the west Garret More's great opponent was Ulick Burke, his own son-in-law, who was usurping the royal town of Galway and had ill-treated his wife, Kildare's daughter. It came to a battle in which the summons of Kildare was answered by O'Donnell, O'Neill, O'Kelly, the Mayo Burke and the

From *A History of Ireland*, by Edmund Curtis, pp. 154-158. Methuen & Co., Ltd London. 1936.

English of the Pale, and that of Clanrickard by O'Brien and the chiefs of Ormond and Connacht. In all, Kildare mustered an army of English and Irish as would have conquered the Pale in twenty-four hours, had he but dared to claim the Crown of Ireland. On August 19, 1504, some ten thousand men faced one another on the low eminence of Cnoc Taugh near Galway, armies medievally equipped with bows and bills, spears and swords, light horsemen and heavy axe-men, and so desperate was the fighting that out of Clanrickard's nine battalions of gallowglasses, eighteen hundred men, only the remnant of one battalion, escaped alive.

It was a famous victory, and Kildare entered Galway in glory, but though it was reported to the King as a great triumph for the English cause in Ireland, it was but the final explosion of a long feud and the crushing of a great rival. The ability of Garret More cannot be doubted, nor can his popularity with both the races of Ireland, but though he was a secret Yorkist and wished to be a king-maker, he was not one of those Bruces or Vasas who have dared to set themselves at the head of a new and independent nation.

Kildare, indeed, realized that a new age had come with the failure of the Yorkist hope and the coming of the Tudors, nor could he ignore the news that in 1499 King James of Scotland brought the lordship of the Isles to an end after two centuries and a half of independence by hanging its lord, John MacDonnell, and three of his sons. The moral was that both in England and Scotland the day of a new and powerful monarchy had come.

In 1505 Hugh Oge O'Donnell succeeded his father as overlord of Tyrconnell, Sligo, Fermanagh, and Leitrim. His race had been allied with Kildare for some forty years against Clanrickard and other enemies, and Kildare and he became the chief leaders of a movement to unite Scotland and Ireland against England with the possible hope of a Yorkist restoration. . . . O'Donnell was that new type of Irish chief who could travel and speak other languages, he visited Rome in 1510, and, later, on his return was knighted by the King in London, but he did not hesitate to enter into communication with James IV, King of Scots, Henry's enemy, who thought of attacking England through Ireland. But before this design ripened the Great Earl himself was dead.

It was in a petty skirmish with the O'Mores of Leix that Garret More's long life ended. He was trying one of the King's new guns upon them, and in return one of them shot him with one of their new muskets. On September 3, 1513, the Earl was dead, and six days later the King of Scots was slain with all his chivalry at Flodden Field, while

O'Donnell could only write from Donegal to Henry to clear himself from suspicion.

Garret More came nearer to being accepted King of Ireland than any man since the Conquest, and his popularity lasted for forty years of his rule. He is described as "a mighty man of stature, full of honor and courage, open and plain, hardly able to rule himself when he was moved to anger, easily displeased and soon appeased, of the English well beloved, a good justiciar, a suppressor of rebels and a warrior incomparable." Under him, though the union of the two races was not operated, there was a growing sense of new nationality, and Gaelic chiefs and old English lords allied and intermarried openly. The influence of the Renaissance was seen in Ireland in the founding of Kilkenny School by Piers Butler, in a splendid college in Maynooth, built by the Great Earl, and the fine library, both of manuscripts and books, that the Earl and his son had in their Maynooth castle. It was a flowering time also for Gaelic culture which both races honored, and if Ireland was dominated by a numerous and powerful aristocracy without a king, at least civilization under them had a noble and generous character.

The power of the Geraldine had extended itself over the Pale, and over a large part of Leinster and is expressed in the *Red Book of Kildare,* a great family rental drawn up for Garret More. This power rested on affection and loyalty as well as on force, and even after the fall of the Geraldines in 1534 a Dublin official could write to Thomas Cromwell: "This English Pale, except in towns and a few of the possessioners, be so affectionate to the Geraldine for kindred, marriage, fostering, and adherence, that they covet more to see a Geraldine to reign and triumph than to see God come among them."

Shane O'Neil

Justice has never been done to Shane O'Neil. That the English should have maligned him goes without saying, for he was one of the most formidable enemies they ever had in Ireland. But that his own countrymen should not have defended him is stranger. The fact is we have, in the main, been disposed to accept the English estimate of Shane. We have been rather inclined to regard him as a desperate character, a great fighter, but a man possessing no real intellectual

By Barry O'Brien, in *The Gael,* May, 1904, pp. 175-176. New York.

qualities. Mr. Froude, summing up the English opinion, describes Shane as "an adulterous, murdering scoundrel"—strange words, it will be admitted, from the panegyrist of Henry VIII.

Shane's matrimonial arrangements were unquestionably irregular. He ran away with another man's wife, which was certainly unjustifiable, but he ran away with the husband at the same time, which was at least original. But more of this anon. That he was a "murderer," Mr. Froude gives no proof whatever. Of course he refers to the death of Matthew O'Neil, Shane's illegitimate brother. But there is no evidence to show that Matthew was "murdered." He was killed in a quarrel between his people and Shane's people; but however the matter was brought about there is no evidence to show that Shane was present, or that he had anything to do with the business.

Shane O'Neil was something more than a mere fighter. He was a man of real intellectual force. He proved himself the equal of Elizabeth's generals on the field, and of her statesmen in negotiation. Nor is there evidence wanting to show that the great Queen herself appreciated his vigor and finesse. At all events, she recognized that he was a power in his own province, and she put forth all her strength—or main—to crush him. He hurled defiance at England at a time when England was hurling defiance at Europe.

Shane came of a good stock—O'Neils upon one side, Geraldines on the other; for his father, Con Bacagh, had married Alice, daughter of the Earl of Kildare.

From the beginning his path was strewn with trouble. In 1541-2, Con Bacagh had, with other Irish chiefs, made submission to Henry VIII, renouncing his title of "The O'Neil" and receiving the "Earldom of Tyrone" instead, with Matthew next in line. Shane, who was younger than Matthew, but the eldest of the legitimate children, protested against the injustice which had thus been done to him, and finally persuaded his father to right the wrong. Matthew was disinherited and Shane confirmed in his position. Matthew appealed to the English. The English espoused his cause. Con was invited to Dublin castle to discuss the subject. But once there, he was held fast. Treacherously entrapped, he was made a prisoner. Shane protested, and demanded his father's release. The government refused, and Shane declared war.

In 1551, Sir James Croft, the Lord Deputy, sent an army into Ulster to crush him. The English began their operations by attacking Shane's allies—the MacDonnells of Antrim in Rathlin Island. The MacDonnels were victorious, and Croft's army was annihilated. In 1522 another army was sent to the north; it was routed by Shane's allies near Belfast. Matthew O'Neil advanced to the help of the English; Shane suddenly fell upon him, and scattered his forces to the winds. Yet a third attempt was made; it also ended in failure. Negotiations were then opened with Shane, but nothing came of them. "We found nothing in Shane," said the English ambassadors, "but pride and stubbornness." At length Croft retired from the combat, released Con Bacagh, and left Shane master of the situation.

For about six years there was peace between Shane and the English. Con Bacagh had been again invited to Dublin Castle where he remained until his death in 1559. In the same year Matthew O'Neil had been killed in an encounter between Shane's people and his own— killed in battle, Shane said.

Shane, now repudiating the English title of "Earl of Tyrone," adopted the old Irish title of "The O'Neil," and was elected Chief of his Clan. The English Government took alarm. Shane had again flouted them. In defiance of English law, according to which the eldest son of Matthew was now Baron of Dungannon, he had himself according to Irish law been elected Chief of the Clan. It was clear that he meant to hold his own, and to withstand the English to the last. In these circumstances, the Lord Justice, Sir Henry Sidney, resolved to bring the recalcitrant Ulster Chief to book. He marched with an army to Dundalk, and "summoned" Shane to appear before him. Shane, with that touch of humor which is so delightful in his dispatches, calmly ignored the "summons," but invited Sidney to his house, where there was to be an interesting function in a few days, viz., a christening. In fact, Shane said he would be delighted if the Lord Justice would stand sponsor for the young O'Neil. Sidney was, perhaps, a humorist, and might have been tickled by the situation, or with Croft's example before him, he might have thought it wiser, on the whole, to test Shane in conciliatory spirit. In any event, he accepted the invitation, and visited Shane's castle.

Sidney seems to have been well pleased with his visit, and was apparently captivated by this "adulterous murdering scoundrel." He and Shane discussed the whole situation amicably. Shane said, in effect, that Matthew O'Neil *père* was a bastard. That being so, his eldest son could not inherit. Shane, on the other hand, was admittedly the legitimate son, and had been elected, according to Irish law, Chief of the Clan. This was Shane's case. Doubtless, Sidney reminded Shane, as Elizabeth herself reminded him subsequently, that Con Bacagh had acknowledged Matthew; and Shane, in all probability, said to Sidney, as he subsequently said to Elizabeth, with characteristic humor, that his father "was too good a gentleman to deny any child that was sworn to him." In the end Sidney seems to have been quite won over by Shane, and promised to present his case in a favorable light to the Queen. Sidney was a peaceful man; he also appreciated Shane's abilities.

Everyone is familiar with Henry VII's answer to those who told him that all Ireland could not govern the Earl of Kildare. "Then," said the King, "let the Earl of Kildare govern all Ireland."

Sidney probably at that time thought that the best solution of the Ulster difficulty would be to let Shane rule Ulster, provided he could be got to acknowledge Elizabeth as his sovereign—a concession Shane was ready enough to make, for it in reality meant little to him. As long as he could rule Ulster he did not care what Elizabeth called herself, and to rule Ulster he was resolved.

By the end of 1559 Sidney was, however, recalled, and the Earl of Sussex became Lord Deputy. Sussex despised the methods of Sidney. He had methods of his own—the arm of the soldier, the dagger or the poisoned cup of the assassin. He tried all and he failed in all. At the outset, however, Elizabeth, whether through policy, through fear, or merely as a blind, advised peace. Shane was in possession, she said; he was legitimate; let him be. Then an interesting correspondence passed.

It is strange that Shane, unaccustomed to courts (as he himself tells us he was) yet knew how to write like a courtier. Of course, he had never seen Elizabeth, and yet he played on her foibles as if he knew every turn of her mind. He flattered, he cajoled, was submissive, firm, always most respectful, and deferential; but ever driving his points most irresistibly home. It was an age of dishonest diplomacy. Perhaps every age is an age of dishonest diplomacy. Shane was, at all events, a master of the craft. When I say that he was a match for Cecil and Bacon with their own weapons, I shall, perhaps, have said all that is necessary to give an accurate idea of the diplomatic skill of Shane O'Neil.

Elizabeth summoned him to London to justify the position he had taken up. He replied to this "summons," and the letter is a good specimen of his epistolary style. I shall take a single paragraph. He begins with deference and, it may be, with veiled sarcasm, humoring the while the vanity of her Majesty. He says: "And now that I am going over to see you, I hope you will consider that I am but rude and uncivil and do not know my duty to your Highness, nor yet your Majesty's law, but am brought up in wildness far from all civility." He then proceeds more boldly, revealing the true character of "Shane the Proud." "Yet have I a good will in the commonwealth of my country; and please your Majesty to send over two commissioners that you can trust and will take no bribes or otherwise be imposed upon, to observe what I have done to improve the country, and to hear what my accusers have to say." Having boldly thrown down this challenge, he adds with defiance: "Then let them go into the Pale and hear what the people say of your soldiers, with their horses, and their dogs, and their concubines. Within this year and a half three hundred farmers are come from the English Pale, to live in my country, where they can be safe."

This single paragraph marks the character and the abilities of Shane. It is a dispatch written with the spirit of a ruler of men. Courteous, skillful, dignified, bold; challenging inquiry, exposing the English methods of bribery and falsehood; denouncing the government of the Pale.

"Within this year and a half three hundred farmers are come from the English Pale, to live in my country, where they can be safe." This is not the language of a vassal. It is the language of one sovereign conveying rebuke to another in courtly and dignified phraseology.

Nor did Shane write without warrant. Sidney had visited Shane's country, and reported that Tyrone was so "well inhabited as no Irish county in the realm was like it." Campion, a contemporary authority, wrote: "[O'Neil] ordered the north so properly that if any subject could prove the loss of money or goods within the precincts he would assuredly either force the robber to restitution, or at his own cost redeem the harm to the losers' contention."

And Campion adds: "Sitting at meals, before he put one morsel in his mouth, he used to slice a portion above the daily alms, and send it to some beggar at his gate, saying it was meet to serve Christ first."

Shane having challenged Elizabeth to send commissioners to his country, and having exposed her own methods of government in the Pale, states, as a condition precedent to his visit to England, that he will need an advance of 3,000 pounds "to pay my expenses in going over to you, and when I come back I will pay your deputy three thousand pounds Irish, such as you are pleased to have current here," and he, adopting the role of courtier once more, ends by adding: "Also I will ask your Majesty to marry me to some gentlewoman of noble birth meet for my vocation."

While Elizabeth corresponded with Shane in a friendly spirit, she was really contemplating his destruction. Mr. Froude does not blink the fact. He says: "For Shane the meaning of his summons to England was merely to detain him there 'with gentle talk' till Sussex could return to his command and the English army be reinforced. Preparations were made to send men and money in such large quantities that rebellion could have no chance; and so careful was the secrecy which was observed to prevent Shane from taking alarm that a detachment of troops sent from Portsmouth sailed with sealed orders, and neither men nor officers knew that Ireland was their destination until they had rounded Land's End."

It was doubtless hoped that while the fleet was on its way to Ireland, Shane would be on his way to England, and that thus Tyrone, in the absence of its chief, would be at the mercy of Sussex's soldiers. But either Shane was, in some unaccountable manner, put upon his guard, or the natural shrewdness of the man kept him out of danger. At all events he did not move. He was expected daily in Dublin to start on his journey to London, but he constantly gave some excuse. "At one time his dress was not ready, at another he had no money, and pressed to have his loan of three thousand sent to him. He was polite; he was courteous; he was friendly; but he stopped in Tyrone."

Meanwhile Sussex had returned to his command, and he laid a deep scheme for the destruction of Shane. He resolved to raise up the rival princes of Ulster against the Chief of Tyrone, and he employed the familiar methods of bribery and corruption. O'Reilly of Brefney was made an Earl. O'Donnell of Tyrconnell was promised an Earldom. Means were used to draw away the Scots from their alliance with O'Neil. Then a grand combined attack was to be made upon the arch enemy. O'Donnell and O'Reilly were to march on Tyrone from the west, the Scots were to fall upon the "rebel" from the north and east, while Sussex would advance from the south to give him the coup de grace. It was a well-laid scheme. But the gods smiled on Shane. Mars fought upon his side, and even Cupid flew to his assistance.

O'Donnell was married to the sister of the Earl of Argyle, popularly called the "Countess of Argyle," a woman who has been described as "not unlearned in Latin," speaking French and Italian; and "counted sober, wise, and no less subtle." It was Sussex's calculation that with the O'Donnell, representing a powerful Irish clan, and the Countess of Argyle, representing the Scots, as his allies, the way for destruction of Shane would be made easy. But Sussex counted without his host. The Countess of Argyle loved Shane O'Neil; and for aught we know to the contrary, however we have no evidence on the point, may have revealed Sussex's plot to him. In any case, Shane was forearmed. Suddenly he dashed into O'Donnell's country and ravaged it with fire and sword. Then he swooped down upon O'Donnell and carried him and the Countess off. Fifteen hundred Scots surrounded the lady, but not one of them raised a hand against Shane. It was a master stroke. With O'Donnell in his hands, the Clan O'Donnell was paralyzed. With the Countess in his hands, the Scots' alliance was made safer than ever. Sussex accepted defeat, and did not move a man out of the Pale to molest the invincible Chief of Tyrone.

Grace O'Malley, Irish Sea Queen

Her proper name in Irish was Grainne Ni Mhaille; Grania Uaile is the popular form; and Grace O'Malley is the polite English form, which, I daresay, the lady herself never heard.

It is strange we find no reference to Grania in what may be called our National Annals. Neither in the *Annals of Lough Ce,* nor in the *Annals of the Four Masters,* nor in the *Annals of Clonmacnoise,* do we find the slightest reference to Grania, because I daresay the official chroniclers would not recognize any female chieftain as head of her tribe. It is to the State Papers we must go to get authentic information about Grania—that is to say, to the letters written to the Privy Council in Ireland or in England, by the statesmen of Queen Elizabeth who visited Connaught. Above all, we have one invaluable document, written in July, 1593, containing Grania's answers to eighteen questions put to her by the Government about herself and her doings, the authenticity of which cannot be questioned, and which gives us the most important facts in her personal history.

The O'Malleys had from immemorial ages been lords of the Owles, or Umhalls—that is, the country all around Clew Bay, now known as the baronies of Burrishoole and Murrisk. It is said they derived their descent not from Brian the great ancestor of the Connaught kings, but from his brother, Orbsen; and hence they are set down in the *Book of Rights* as tributary kings to the provincial kings of Connaught. In the middle of the thirteenth century they were driven out of a good portion of the northern Owle by the Burkes and Butlers, but still retained down to the time of Grania some twenty townlands, or eighty quarters in Burrishoole, and held more of it as tenants to the Earl of Ormond. Grania tells us that O'Malley's barony of Murrisk included all the ocean Islands from Clare to Inisboffin.

As Bingham describes Grania in 1593 as the "nurse of all rebellions in Connaught for the last forty years," she must have been born about the year 1530, before Henry VIII had yet changed his religion.

From a lecture delivered by Archbishop Healey in the Town Hall, Westport, Ireland, January 7, 1906. Printed in a pamphlet published by The Catholic Truth Society. Dublin.

It is highly probable that Grania was fostered on Clare Island, which belonged to her family, and it was doubtless here she acquired that passionate love of the sea, as well as that skill and courage in seafaring which made her at once the idol of her clansmen and the greatest captain in the western seas.

"*Terra Marique Potens,*" was the motto of her family, and Shane O'Dugan tells us that there never was an O'Malley who was not a sailor, but not one of them all could excel Grania in sailing a galley or ruling a crew. This open-air life on the sea, if it did not add to her beauty, gave her great strength and vigor. Sydney, the Lord Deputy, who met her in Galway in 1576, describes her, when she must have been about middle age, as "famous for her stoutness of courage, and person, and for sundry exploits done by her by sea." Whatever literary education she got in her youth she probably received from the Carmelite Friars on Clare Island, but I suspect, although she was afterwards married to two of the greatest chiefs in the West, that Grania knew more about rigging and sailing a galley than she did of drawing-room accomplishments.

It is not unlikely that Grania was an heiress, and though she could never, according to the Brehon Law, become "the captain of her nation," especially after marriage, she still seems to have always retained the enthusiastic love and obedience of her clansmen, especially in the islands. She must, of course, get a husband, and so they chose a fitting help-mate for a warrior Queen in the person of Donall an Chogaidh O'Flaherty, of Bunowan, in the barony of Ballynahinch. He was in the direct line descendant of Hugh Mor and was the acknowledged heir to the headship of all the western O'Flahertys, and certainly after the death of Donall Crone ought to be the Chief Lord of all Connemara, although Teige na Buile contested his claims.

This alliance, therefore, united in the closest bonds of friendship the two ruling families of Murrisk and Ballynahinch, with nothing but the narrow estuary of Leenane Bay, or rather the Killery, between them. Moreover, it made the united tribes chief rulers of the western seas, so that when Grania sailed away from her island home, with the sea-horse of O'Malley and the lions of O'Flaherty floating proudly fore and aft from the mast-heads of her galleys, the young sea-queen must have been a happy bride, and expected happy days in her new home at Bunowan Castle.

By this her first marriage, Grania tells us she had two sons, Owen and Morogh. Her eldest son, Owen, she said, was always a good and loyal subject, in the time of Sir Nicholas Malby, and also under Sir Richard Bingham, until the Burkes of McWilliam's country and the

Joyces began to rebel. Then Owen, for the better security of himself, his flocks and his herds, did, by direction of Sir R. Bingham, withdraw into a strong island. At the same time a strong force was sent under the lead of Capt. John Bingham (brother of Sir Richard) to pursue the rebels—the Joyces and others. But missing them, they came to the mainland—right against the said island—where her son was, calling for victuals, whereupon the said Owen came with a number of boats, and ferried all the soldiers over to the island, where they were entertained with the best cheer that could be provided. That very night Owen was apprehended by his guests, and tied with a rope together with eighteen of his chief followers. In the morning the soldiers drew out of the island 4,000 cows, probably by ropes, 500 stud mares and horses, and 1,000 sheep, leaving the rest of the poor people on the island naked and destitute. The soldiers then brought the prisoners and cattle to Ballynahinch, where John Bingham halted. The same evening he caused the eighteen prisoners to be hanged, amongst whom there was an old gentleman of four score and ten years, Theobald O'Toole by name. The next night a false alarm was raised in the camp at midnight, when Owen, who was lying fast bound in the tent of Captain Grene O'Molloy, was murdered with twelve deadly wounds, and so, miserably ended his life.

This murder of Owen, eldest son of Grania Uaile, is one of the ugliest deeds of Bingham's black record in Connaught. It was not directly his own doing, but it was the doing of his brother and agent, Captain John Bingham. It was one of those utterly cruel and treacherous deeds which still tend to preserve bitter memories in the hearts of the western Gael.

After the death of her husband, Donall O'Flaherty, Grania probably returned to Clare Island, where she felt most secure and most at home. It is probable she took her young daughter with her, for Bingham expressly tells us that the Devil's Hook of Corraun, their near neighbor in Clare Island, was her son-in-law. She doubtless made Clare Island her headquarters, and either built or strengthened the castle which still stands on a cliff over the little harbor. It was admirably situated close to the beach, on which her galleys were drawn up under her own eyes, so that when opportunity offered they were easily run down to the shore, and she would thus be ready to make her swoop on any part of the western coast without difficulty. With the Devil's Hook at Darby's Point or Kildavnet, and her cousins or nephews at Murrisk, and she herself at Clare, Grania held a very strong position against all her foes. But she was not content with one or two strongholds; she had at least half a dozen. At this time the Castle of Belclare was not in her hands. It belonged first to McLaughlin O'Malley, chief of the name, and then to Owen Thomas O'Malley, who dwelt there in 1593. There is reason to think that Grania had also the Castle beyond Louisburgh at Carramore, of which only traces now exist. It would be a useful stronghold to secure her passage to and from Clare Island. Then tradition connects her with the castle of Kildavnet, which she probably built to secure the passage through Achill Sound. It was thoroughly suited for that purpose, with deep water and secure anchorage against every wind and sea. Moreover, she took care to ally herself closely with the lord on the other side. This was Richard Burke, whom the Dublin officials called the Devil's Hook, which was an attempt at translating his Irish nick-name, Deamham an Chorain, the Demon of Corraun, because he was lord of that wild promontory, and I daresay, always ready for any wild deed. Grania gave her daughter in marriage to this Devil's Hook, so between them they were able to hold command of Achill Sound and Clew Bay. It is likely she gave him the ward of the Castle of Kildavnet. But she was not content with commanding the south entrance. From her castle of Doona, which, it is said, she seized by stratagem, she held control of the whole of Blacksod Bay.

Grania was not content with all these castles. She also got possession of Carrigahowley—more politely called Rockfleet—in this way. It appears that it belonged to Richard Burke, as sub-tenant to the Earl of Ormond, commonly called Richard an Iarainn, or as the English writers call him, Richard in Iron, because he always wore a coat of mail. His mother was an O'Flaherty, and so he was closely connected with the family of her late husband, and he resolved to marry the young and enterprising widow; nor was Grania unwilling, for so she would become mistress of Carrigahowely, which suited her well. She became, in fact, both master and mistress, for Sir Henry Sydney, the Deputy, tells us, that when he came to Galway in 1576, there came to visit him there "a most famous feminine Sea-Captain called Grania O'Malley, and she offered her services to me wherever I would command her, with three galleys and 200 fighting men, either in Ireland or in Scotland. She brought with her her husband, for she was, as well by sea as by land, more than master's mate to him. He was of the Nether Burkes, and now I hear is McWilliam Eoghter, called by nickname Richard in Iron."

The Deputy clearly saw that Grania was master both on land and sea, but he made a knight of Richard in Iron, which greatly pleased that worthy himself, and Grania also, for she was now Lady Burke, although we never heard of her being called by that name, either in history or fiction.

This passage also shows that Grania had several large galleys, capable of carrying sixty or seventy men each, with twenty or thirty oarsmen to work them. With such a fleet at her disposal, well manned, and well equipped too from the spoils of the sea, Grania was more than able to hold her own against all comers, even against the much larger English vessels which dared not follow her into the creeks and island channels of Clew Bay. I am inclined to think that she and her seamen were not very scrupulous in differentiating their enemies; in fact she tells us herself, in reply to the Government interrogatories, that her former trade for many years was what she calls "maintenance by land and sea"; that is, she lifted and carried off whatever came handy on sea or shore from Celt or Saxon. We know for certain that she raided Aranmore more than once, and even the great Earl of Desmond's territory at the mouth of the Shannon.

She was once more to set up at her old trade. It would appear she now made Carrigahowley her headquarters. The cruelty and greed of Sir R. Bingham drove the Mayo Burkes into rebellion in 1586; and the murder of her eldest son, already described, caused Grania to give her sympathies, and, to some extent, her help to the rebels. Her own statement is that after the death of her last husband "she gathered together all her own followers, and with 1,000 head of cows and mares she departed" (no doubt from her husband's residence), and became a dweller in Carrigahowley at Burrishoole. After the murdering of her son Owen, the rebellion being then in Connaught, Sir Richard Bingham granted her letters of protection against all men, and willed her to remove from her late dwelling at Burrishoole, and come and dwell under him (somewhere near Donomona or Castlebar). In her journey as she travelled she was encountered by five bands of soldiers under the leading of John Bingham (who had already caused her son to be murdered), and thereupon she was apprehended and tied with a rope—both she and her followers; at the same instant they were spoiled of their said cattle, and of all that they ever had besides the same, and brought to Sir Richard, who caused a new pair of gallows to be made for her last funeral, when he thought to end her days; but she was set at liberty on the hostage and pledge of one Richard Burke, otherwise called the 'Devil's Hook'—that is, Richard of Corraun, her own son-in-law."

"When she did rebel," she adds, "fear compelled her to fly by sea to Ulster, and there with O'Neill and O'Donnell she stayed three months, her galleys in the meantime having been broken by a storm. She returned then to Connaught, and in Dublin received her Majesty's gracious pardon through Sir John Perrott, six years ago, and was so made free. Ever since she dwelleth in Connaught, a farmer's life, very poor, bearing cess, and paying her Majesty's composition rent, having utterly given over her former trade of maintenance by land and sea."

It is quite clear from the State Papers, although not expressly stated, that Grania did visit London, and had an interview with Queen Elizabeth, probably in 1593. In July of that year she had petitioned the Queen and Burghley for maintenance, and begged the Minister to accept the surrender of her sons' lands—that is her sons by both husbands—and grant them a patent for their lands on surrender. She also asked her Majesty's license to prosecute all her Majesty's enemies with fire and sword—a bold demand for an old lady over sixty, with sons and grandsons; but she knew it would please the Queen, and if granted would give her once more a free hand on the western coasts. It was at this very time that Bingham, in a letter to the Privy Council, describes Grania as "a notable traitress, and the nurse of all the rebellions in the province for forty years." Grania renewed her petition to Burghley two years later (in 1595), "to be put in quiet possession of a third of the land of both her late husbands." She certainly went to London in 1593, in the month of August, as Bingham's letter of September 19th shows, and if she went to London, no doubt she saw the Queen and her Minister, for nothing else would or could have induced her to go there at all.

Unfortunately we have, so far as I know, no authentic account of this famous interview at Hampton Court. The two queens at this time were about the same age, and neither of them could be vain of her personal charms, for both were in the sere and yellow leaf. We may be sure they eyed each other with great curiosity, and took wondering note of each other's queenly raiment. The dialogue, too, must have been interesting, though doubtless carried on through an interpreter, for as Grania's husband, the late McWilliam knew no English, but was well skilled in Latin and Irish, we may fairly conclude that Grania, too, had no Beurla. There is reason to think that the English Queen granted Grania her requests, and sent her home rejoicing.

Grania, as she always preferred, travelled by sea, and on her homeward voyage landed, it is said, at Howth, no doubt to procure supplies. Tired of the sea, and perhaps hungry too, she sought admission to Howth Castle during the dinner hour, but she found all the doors closed, and was not admitted to the Castle. This was not the Irish hospitality that Grania was accustomed to in the West, so she was wrathful, and happening to meet the young heir of Howth with his nurse in the grounds, she carried off the boy to her galley, and made all sail straightway for Clew Bay. The Lord of Howth, great nobleman as he was, found it necessary to come to terms with Grania, and the child was restored, not on ransom, but on condition of the Lord of Howth promising to keep his door open during dinner, and have a cover always set for the chance wayfarer by land or sea. More power to Grania for teaching them that lesson of hospitality! Such is the story, of which the strongest proof is the fact that this custom has been for centuries undoubtedly observed at Howth Castle, and that a picture in the Castle Hall depicts the whole scene of Grania's exploit; but there is no really authentic evidence of the truth of the story.

In her own day, and with her own weapons by land and sea, as Bingham said, for more than forty years she fought a stubborn fight on the shores and islands of Clew Bay. Her memory still clings as close as their sheltering ivy to the old castles that she built. Almost everything around Clew Bay is associated with her memory. Her undying presence still haunts its shores and islands.

Brian of the Ramparts O'Rourke

In Bingham's time the strongest chief in the west of Ireland was the O'Rourke, Brian na Murtha, Lord of Leitrim. This chieftain was a tall and remarkably handsome man. His most distinguishing characteristic was pride. All the lord deputies and presidents who had anything to do with him remarked upon this trait. "He was the proudest man with whom I had to do in my time," wrote Sir Henry Sidney. "The proudest man who walks upon the earth today," wrote Malby. "The proud beggar—the insolent, drunken, proud beggar!" wrote the fiercer and more abusive Bingham. As to the charge of drunkenness, I can only say this: I have myself seen in the Record Office, at the Four Courts, this man's signature written when he was quite old, at the foot of a certain State document, and I never saw more exquisite calligraphy. The characters are small, regular, and of most delicate formation.

When Bingham came into the Province, O'Rourke had been several times in rebellion, and had always beaten the Government. Then, when Perrott was made Viceroy, O'Rourke at once made his submission to Perrott. He recognized the heir of Henry VIII as his lawful superior, and shaped his course accordingly. Besides, he liked Perrott and Perrott liked him. Perrott induced him to join in the "composi-

By Standish O'Grady, in *The Gael,* February, 1901, pp. 42-43. New York.

tion" of Connaught and lay down his O'Rourkeship with all its privileges and powers. Then he legally ceased to be a chieftain and became only a great landlord. He retained a great deal of Leitrim in his own hands, and received fixed rents from the proprietors of the remainder. When his friend Perrott departed, O'Rourke was left face to face with Bingham whom he disliked and despised.

During the Armada winter he received and sheltered some Spanish sailors. The Government demanded their surrender with the intention of hanging them as they had hanged all the rest. O'Rourke replied that it did not consist with his honor as a gentleman or his dignity as a prince to surrender men whom he had admitted to the rites of hospitality. Bingham now, without notice, collected his forces and fell upon him. Bingham thought to surprise him in his castle on the shores of Lough Gill, but as snow lay on the ground, Bingham's people were seen, and in short, this swoop on Bingham's part came to nothing. O'Rourke then went into rebellion, and as a preliminary desired his sheriff to shift somewhere else for an office. His eldest son was at the time a student at Oxford. O'Rourke sent one of his gentlemen, Charles Trevor, thither secretly. Young O'Rourke, afterwards celebrated as Brian Oge of the Battle-Axes, ran away from Oxford in company with Trevor, and came home through Scotland and Ulster. He immediately took the field as one of his father's chief lieutenants.

In this rebellion O'Rourke stirred up North Connaught, and kindled a fierce flame of war. He sent for all the wood-kerne and bad subjects and licensed them to make prey within the borders of Bingham's presidency. In reply to a letter from Perrott he said he would be under the government of no man in the land save the Viceroy. The Government sent commissioners to treat with him—judges and bishops. O'Rourke received them *en roi*. He did not stir from his place to meet them or once remove his cap from his head. He regarded himself as a sovereign prince owning no superiors on earth save the Queen and her deputy.

Eventually, Bingham having beaten the North Connaught insurgents, invaded Breffney, or the Breffney O'Rourke's country, in three divisions. O'Rourke's own feudatories revolted against him, and the constable of his forces turned traitor and joined Bingham. O'Rourke now went into the north to his ally, the McSweeny, Red Hugh's foster father. Red Hugh was at this time prisoner in Dublin Castle. McSweeny, hardly knowing how he was to deal with this extraordinary proud and haughty being, in the end surrendered to him his own chieftainship. O'Rourke would not be chieftain without exercising a chief's functions, and actually hanged some of McSweeny's own kinsmen. Eventually he went to Scotland to seek aid from some of the great Scotch nobles. He was there arrested by James VI, who in pursuit of some tortuous State policy sent him forward to London as a present to the Queen. He was brought before the council, Cecil, Walsingham and the rest. The council looked at their remarkable captive so long known to them by report, now seen at last in the flesh, and the captive looked at the council, so long known to him, man by man. He stood erect, not a joint bending in back or knee, with his hat on, as when at Dromahaire he received the Commissioners of the Viceroy, a captive but also a king.

"Why don't you kneel?" asked one of the council, when they began to recover from the curious dramatic influence of the nature of the situation. He spoke in Latin, a tongue almost as familiar as Irish to the elder generation of the Irish and Norman-Irish chiefs. *"Cur genua non flectis?"* "I am not so used. *Non sum ita facera solitus."* "Are you not used to kneel before pictures? *Genua coram nonne es solitus imaginibus flectere?"*

"Yes, of God's saints—between whom and *you* there is much difference, *multum distat."*

Dismissed by the council, he was a second time brought from the Tower of the Court of Queen's Bench to be tried before a jury on the charge of high treason.

The indictment having been read and translated for his benefit, for he did not understand English, Brian refused to plead save on four conditions:

(1) The assistance of an advocate.

(2) The affidavits forwarded out of Ireland to be put in my hands.

(3) The presence and examinations in court of the persons who swore the affidavits.

(4) The Queen in person to preside as judge at my trial.

"The fellow with a barbarous insolence," writes Camden, "refused to plead save on these conditions."

The first three everyone will agree to have been mere justice. In the fourth we see the well-known pride of the man, surely an honorable pride, self-respect of an admirable and even heroic sort. To no jury of the fat and greasy sort would he make his defence, but to his liege and sovereign. All those Irish princes in the midst of their most furious rebellions never denied that the Queen was their sovereign. They rebelled against her officers and presidents, such as Bingham, who came with their intolerable wrongdoings between them and their Queen. I am surprised that the Queen did not pardon him. She understood Ireland well enough to know that men might rebel against her officers and yet entertain feelings of loyalty and regard for herself.

In O'Rourke's case, her mind seems to have been preoccupied by an outrageous slander. It was charged against him that he had dragged the Queen's picture at the heels of his warhorse, and that he had stood by and approved while his men thrust their battle-axes through it. Bingham, mendacious as well as ferocious, sent this story to London. Great attempts were made to get it proved, but not the slightest evidence of any sort or description in support of the charge could be discovered. The nearest thing to evidence was the following: An image of the Virgin Mary was discovered in his country, and an ultra-clever official *deemed* that this image might have been assumed by the chieftain to be the effigy of the Queen and might have been treated in the manner described. But he confesses, honest man, that there were no marks of thrustings or slashings upon it. This was the nearest thing to evidence.

The charge was, of course, a vile slander. No man of O'Rourke's type, indeed no Irish gentleman of the period, could have stooped to such low rascal insolence.

To O'Rourke's most reasonable demands the Chief Justice replied that they could not be granted, adding further that if he persisted in his refusal to plead, he would be obliged to consider the charge of high treason as proved, and proceed to pass sentence of death.

"You will do as you please," replied the prince. *Facies ut tua est voluntas.*

The Chief Justice sentenced him to death. He was led from the court, and a few days afterwards was beheaded at Tyburn. Such was the end of Brian-of-the-Ramparts, the first cousin of Red Hugh. There is surely something very refreshing in this proud refusal of the O'Rourke to plead his cause before a hired brehon and a parcel of money-grubbing London shopkeepers. His own chief tenants charged with treason were judged by himself, or a court of his chieftains over which he presided. He would accept no lower tribunal for himself, though his head should roll for it.

O'Rourke's last recorded speech was also highly characteristic. At the time of his execution there was a very vile Irish ecclesiastic in London, Miler Magrath, Archbishop of Cashel, a most sordid and knavish creature, an awful devourer of Church property—a perfect glutton in that way. In the next generation Strafford compelled his sons and nephews to disgorge a great deal of it. This ecclesiastical rascal, seeing a fellow-countryman led to the scaffold, thought to join the procession, and administer religious consolation, by the way, to the chieftain.

O'Rourke looked askance at Miler, and for the last time unclosed his laconic lips.

"I think," said he, "thou art a Franciscan who has broken thy vows."

Such was the exit of Brian-of-the-Ramparts O'Rourke, the proudest man who walked upon the earth in his day.

He was succeeded by his son Brian-of-the-Battle-axes, who fixed himself in the Iron Mountains (Silabh an Iarann) and thence waged truceless war with Bingham, beat Bingham, recovered his father's territory, and did some considerable things in his day. Indeed, a foray on his territory by Bingham, wherein his milch cows were driven from his lawn (an intolerable insult) was the proximate cause of the Nine Years War.

The Nine Years' War: Its Leaders and Battles

The policy of the English court with regard to the magnates who were the actual rulers of the country outside the English Pale was to get from each and every one of them something which the representatives of the realm had never yet given—a whole-hearted recognition through the Parliament in Dublin of the English sovereign as effective ruler of Ireland. Such recognition had become less possible through the fact that the sovereign would have to be recognized not only as the head of the realm but the head of the church. Neither the Gaelic chiefs, the Norman-Irish nobles, nor even the older English settled in Ireland (the poet Richard Stanihurst would be representative of such families) could be brought round easily to doing this. On the practical level, then, English policy was directed towards preventing alliances among the magnates or the emergence of any personage who might get to such eminence as to draw a considerable part of the country to him and enable him to form an alliance with Scotland, France or Spain. The usual method used by the vigilant and adroit English agents in Ireland was to divide the great houses by setting up one branch against another or one member against another: such a person might be made a dependent on English power, and, in return for the backing of his privileges, put his armed levies at the disposal of the Crown. If the splitting up of a ruling family could not be effected, more strong-arm methods were used.

By the editor.

And this brings us to the entrance into Irish history of two famous personages, each of whom had received characteristic treatment through English statecraft—Hugh O'Neill and Hugh O'Donnell.

At this stage Ulster was more of a center of resistance to English infiltration than any other part of Ireland. Its paramount princes, cherishing a descent from a dynasty that had lasted five hundred years, the dynasty of Niall, had a kingly consciousness. These Ulster dynasts were just across from Scotland and so were at the receiving end for the soldiery from the Hebrides who regularly took service with the Irish lords. The violent suppression of what was called "The Desmond Rebellion" with the extirpation of the heads of the House of Kildare had left the Ulster principalities strong *vis-à-vis* the rest of Ireland. But the principalities were divided. There was a feud between O'Donnell and O'Neill, and inside each family there were members who found or would find advantage in favoring the Crown.

O'Neill's territory was Tir-Eoin, the modern county of Tyrone; O'Donnell's territory, Tir-Connail, the modern county of Donegal. We have heard of Matthew O'Neill. Denounced by Shane as a bastard, he had taken the English title of Baron of Dungannon. His son, Hugh, was taken to England, fostered in one of the great English houses, lived as a young man in contact with the court, and received the training of a young English noble of the time. It was expected that he would get an English cast of mind. Let us say that, brought up outside Ireland, he got the Renaissance cast of mind.

It would be of immense interest to know how a young Irish noble responded to the life of the higher circles in Elizabethan England. That we have no way of knowing. He was a great personage for the English of his time. When Drayton came to write of momentous events they include:

> Tyrone his peace to gain,
> The quiet end of that long-living Queen,
> The King's fair entry and the peace with Spain.

Hugh O'Neill, Earl of Tyrone to the English and "The O'Neill" to the Irish was a man of two worlds. He kept English people close to him. His second wife was Mabel Bagnal, sister of Marshal Bagnal, an English commander in Ireland. The enmity between O'Neill and Bagnal gives personal drama to the campaign in which each was leader.

Younger than O'Neill was the cadet of the O'Donnell family whose name, too, was Hugh. In him were the two Gaelic strains, that of Ireland and that of Scotland. From his adolescence Hugh Roe O'Donnell was remarkable. The bright hair from which he derived his nickname ("Ruadh" or "Red") enhanced the vividness of his appearance, and this vividness went with a quickness that all who encountered him remarked—a quickness of movement and of thought. He understood war, but he did not, as O'Neill did, understand policy. His career could be used as an illustration of the murkiness of the English design in Ireland. Held in captivity as a youth, he was poisoned while a refugee in Spain by an English agent who happened to be Anglo-Irishman.

The Two Hughs

Near Rathmullan, on the western shore of Lough Swilly, looking towards the mountains of Innishowen, stood a monastery of Carmelites and a church dedicated to the Blessed Virgin, the most famous place of devotion in Tyrconnell, whither all the clan-Connell, both chiefs and people, made resort at certain seasons to pay their devotions. Here the young Red Hugh, with Mac Swyne of the battle-axes, O'Gallagher of Ballyshannon, and some other chiefs, were in the summer of 1587 sojourning a short time in that part to pay their vows of religion; but not without stag-hounds and implements of chase, having views upon the red-deer of Fanad and Innishowen. One day, while the prince was here, a swift-sailing merchant ship doubled the promontory of Dunaff, stood up the lough, and cast anchor opposite Rathmullan; a "bark, black-hatched, deceptive," bearing the flag of England, and offering for sale, as a peaceful trader, her cargo of Spanish wine. And surely no more courteous merchant than the master of the ship had visited the north for many a year. He invited the people most hospitably on board, solicited them, whether purchasers or not, to partake of his good cheer, entertained them with music and wine, and so gained very speedily the good will of all Fanad. Red Hugh and his companions soon heard of the obliging merchant and his rare wines. They visited the ship, where they were received with all respect, and, indeed, with unfeigned joy; descended into the cabin, and with connoisseur discrimination tried and tasted, and finally drank too deeply; and at last when they would come on deck and return to the shore, they found themselves secured under hatches; their weapons had been removed; night had fallen; they were *prisoners* to those traitor Saxons. Morning dawned,

From *The Story of Ireland,* by A. M. Sullivan, pp. 241-264. M. H. Gill & Son, Ltd. Dublin. 1905.

and they looked anxiously towards the shore; but, ah! where is Rath-mullan and the Carmelite church? And what wild coast is this? Past Malin and the cliffs of Innishowen; past Benmore, and southward to the shores of Antrim and the mountains of Mourne flew that ill-omened bark, and never dropped anchor till she lay under the towers of Dublin. The treacherous Perrott joyfully received his prize, and "exulted," says an historian, "in the easiness and success with which he had procured hostages for the peaceable submission of O'Donnell." And the prince of Tyrconnell was thrown into "a strong stone castle," and kept in heavy irons three years and three months, "meditating," says the chron-icle, "on the feeble and impotent condition of his friends and relations, of his princes and supreme chiefs, of his nobles and clergy, his poets and professors."

Three long and weary years—oh! but they seemed three ages!—the young Hugh pined in the grated dungeons of that "Bermingham Tower," which still stands in Dublin Castle yard. "Three years and three months," the old chroniclers tell us—when hark! there is whis-pering furtively betimes as young Hugh and Art Kavanagh, and other of the captives meet on the stone stairs, or the narrow landing, by the warders' gracious courtesy. Yes; Art had a plan of escape.

It is even so. And now all is arranged, and the daring attempt waits but a night favourably dark and wild—which comes at last; and while the sentries shelter themselves from the pitiless sleet, the young fugi-tives, at peril of life or limb, are stealthily scaling or descending bastion and battlement, fosse and barbican. With beating hearts they pass the last sentry, and now through the city streets they grope their way south-wards; for the nearest hand of succour is amidst the valleys of Wick-low. Theirs is a slow and toilsome progress; they know not the paths, and they must hide by day and fly as best they can in the night-time through wooded country. At length they cross the Three Rock Moun-tain, and look down upon Glencree. But alas! Young Hugh sinks down exhausted! Three years in a dungeon have cramped his limbs, and he is no longer the Hugh that bounded like a deer on the slopes of Glen-vigh! His feet are torn and bleeding from sharp rock and piercing brambles; his strength is gone. He exhorts his companions to speed onwards and save themselves, while he awaits succour if they can send it. Reluctantly, and only yielding to his urgent entreaties, they de-parted. A faithful servant, we are told, who had been in the secret of Hugh's escape, still remained with him, and repaired for succour to the house of Felim O'Tuhal. Felim was known to be a friend, though he dared not openly disclose the fact. But now "the flight of the pris-oners had created great excitement in Dublin, and numerous bands were despatched in pursuit of them." It was next to impossible—certainly full of danger—for the friendly O'Tuhal, with the English scouring-parties spread all over hill and vale, to bring in the exhausted and helpless fugitive from his hiding place, where nevertheless he must perish if not quickly reached. Sorrowfully and reluctantly Felim was forced to conclude that all hope of escape for young Hugh this time must be abandoned, and that the best course was to pretend to discover him in the copse, and to make a merit of giving him up to his pursuers. So, with a heart bursting with mingled rage, grief, and despair, Hugh found himself once more in the grip of his savage foes. He was brought back to Dublin "loaded with heavy iron fetters," and flung into a narrower and stronger dungeon, to spend another year cursing the day that Norman foot had touched the Irish shore.

There he lay until Christmas Day, 25th December, 1592. Henry and Art O'Neill, fellow-prisoners, were on this occasion companions of Hugh's flight. In fact the lord deputy, Fitzwilliam, a needy and corrupt creature, had taken a bribe from Hugh O'Neill to afford opportunity for the escape. Hugh of Dungannon had designs of his own in desiring the freedom of all three; for events to be noted further on had been occurring, and already he was, like a skilful statesman, preparing for future contingencies. He knew that the liberation of Red Hugh would give him an ally worth half Ireland, and he knew that rescuing the two O'Neills would leave the government without a "queen's O'Neill" to set up against him at a future day. Of this escape Haverty gives us the following account:

"They descended by a rope through a sewer which opened into the Castle ditch; and leaving there the soiled outer garments, they were conducted by a young man, named Turlough Roe O'Hagan, *the confidential servant or emissary of the Earl of Tyrone,* who was sent to act as their guide. Passing through the gates of the city, which were still open, three of the party reached the same Slieve Rua which Hugh had visited on the former occasion. The fourth, Henry O'Neill, strayed from his companions in some way—probably before they left the city—but eventually he reached Tyrone, where the earl seized and imprisoned him. Hugh Roe and Art O'Neill, with their faithful guide, proceeded on their way over the Wicklow mountains towards Glenmalure, to Feagh Mac Hugh O'Byrne, a chief famous for his heroism, and who was then in arms against the government. Art O'Neill had grown corpulent in prison, and besides been hurt in descending from the Castle, so that he became quite worn out from fatigue. The party were also exhausted with hunger, and as the snow fell thickly, and their clothing was very scanty, they suffered additionally from intense cold.

For awhile Red Hugh and the servant supported Art between them; but this exertion could not long be sustained, and at length Red Hugh and Art lay down exhausted under a lofty rock, and sent the servant to Glenmalure for help. With all possible speed Feagh O'Byrne, on receiving the message, despatched some of his trusty men to carry the necessary succour; but they arrived almost too late at the precipice under which the two youths lay. 'Their bodies,' say the Four Masters, 'were covered with white-bordered shrouds of hailstones freezing around them, and their light clothes adhered to their skin, so that, covered as they were with the snow, it did not appear to the men who had arrived that they were human beings at all, for they found no life in their members, but just as if they were dead. On being raised up, Art O'Neill fell back and expired, and was buried on the spot; but Red Hugh was revived with some difficulty, and carried to Glenmalure, where he was secreted in a sequestered cabin and attended by a physician."

O'Byrne brought them to his house and revived and warmed and clothed them, and instantly sent a messenger to Hugh O'Neill (with whom he was then in close alliance) with the joyful tidings of O'Donnell's escape. O'Neill heard it with delight, and sent a faithful retainer, Tarlough Buidhe O'Hagun, who was well acquainted with the country, to guide the young chief into Ulster, where O'Neill received them right joyfully. And here "the two Hughs" entered into a strict and cordial friendship, and told each other of their wrongs and of their hopes. O'Neill listened, with such feelings as one can imagine, to the story of the youth's base kidnapping and cruel imprisonment in darkness and chains; and the impetuous Hugh Roe heard with scornful rage of the English deputy's atrocity towards Mac Mahon, and attempts to bring his accursed sheriffs and juries amongst the ancient Irish of Ulster. And they deeply swore to bury for ever the unhappy feuds of their families, and to stand by each other with all the powers of the North against their treacherous and relentless foe. The chiefs parted, and O'Donnell, with an escort of the Tyrowen cavalry, passed into Maguire's country. The chief of Fermanagh received him with honour, eagerly joined in the confederacy.

We may conceive with what stormy joy the tribes of Tyrconnell welcomed their prince; with what mingled pity and wrath, thanksgiving and curses, they heard of his chains, and wanderings, and sufferings, and beheld the feet that used to bound so lightly on the hills, swollen and crippled by that cruel frost, by the crueller fetters of the Saxon. But little time was now for festal rejoicing or the unprofitable luxury of cursing; for just then, Sir Richard Bingham, the English leader in Connaught, relying on the irresolute nature of old O'Donnell, and not aware of Red Hugh's return, had sent two hundred men by sea to Donegal, where they took by surprise the Franciscan monastery, drove away the monks (making small account of their historic studies and learned annals), and garrisoned the buildings for the queen. The fiery Hugh could ill endure to hear of these outrages, or brook an English garrison upon the soil of Tyrconnell. He collected the people in hot haste, led them instantly into Donegal, and commanded the English by a certain day and hour to betake themselves with all speed back to Connaught, and leave behind them the rich spoils they had taken; all which they thought it prudent without further parley to do. And so the monks of St. Francis returned to their home and their books, gave thanks to God, and prayed, as well they might, for Hugh O'Donnell.

During the four years over which the imprisonment of Red Hugh extended, important events had been transpiring in the outer world; and amidst them the character of Hugh of Dungannon was undergoing a rapid transmutation. We had already seen him cultivating friendly relations with the neighbouring chiefs, though most of them were in a state of open hostility to the queen. He, by degrees, went much farther than this. He busied himself in the disloyal work of healing the feuds of the rival clans, and extending throughout the north feelings of amity—nay, a net-work of alliances between them. To some of the native princes he lends one or two of his fully trained companies of foot; to others, some troops of his cavalry. He secretly encourages some of them (say his enemies at court) to stouter resistance to the English. It is even said that he harbours Popish priests. "North of Slieve Gullion the venerable brehons still arbitrate undisturbed the causes of the people; the ancient laws, civilization, and religion stand untouched. Nay, it is credibly rumoured to the Dublin deputy that this noble earl, forgetful apparently of his coronet and golden chain, and of his high favour with so potent a princess, does about this time get recognized and solemnly inaugurated as chieftain of his sept, by the proscribed name of *"The O'Neill"*; and at the rath of Tulloghoge, on the Stone of Royalty, amidst the circling warriors, amidst the bards and ollamhs of Tyr-eoghain, "receives an oath to preserve all the ancient former customs of the country inviolable, and to deliver up the succession peaceably to his tanist; and then hath a wand delivered to him by one whose proper office that is, after which, descending from the stone, he turneth himself round thrice forward and thrice backward," even as the O'Neills had done for a thousand years; altogether in the most un-

English manner, and with the strangest ceremonies, which no garter king-at-arms could endure.

While matters were happening thus in Ulster, England was undergoing the excitement of apprehended invasion. The Armada of Philip the Second was on the sea, and the English nation—queen and people —Protestant and Catholic—persecutor and persecuted—with a burst of genuine patriotism, prepared to meet the invaders. The elements, however, averted the threatened doom. A hurricane of unexampled fury scattered Philip's flotilla, so vauntingly styled "invincible"; the ships were strewn, shattered wrecks, all over the coasts of England and Ireland. In the latter country the crews were treated very differently, according as they happened to be cast upon the shores of districts amenable to English authority or influences, or the reverse. In the former instances they were treated barbarously—slain as queen's enemies, or given up to the queen's forces. In the latter, they were sheltered and succoured, treated as friends, and afforded means of safe return to their native Spain. Some of these ships were cast upon the coast of O'Neill's country, and by no one were the Spanish crews more kindly treated, more warmly befriended, than by Hugh, erstwhiles the queen's most favored *protégé*, and still professedly her most true and obedient servant. This hospitality to the shipwrecked Spaniards, however, is too much for English flesh and blood to bear. Hugh is openly murmured against in Dublin and in London. And soon formal proof of his "treason" is preferred. An envious cousin of his, known as Shane of the Fetters—a natural son of Shane the Proud, by the false wife of O'Donnell—animated by a mortal hatred of Hugh, gave information to the lord deputy that he had not only regaled the Spanish officers right royally at Dungannon, but had then and there planned with them an alliance between himself and king Philip, to whom Hugh—so said his accuser—had forwarded letters and presents by the said officers. All of which the said accuser undertook to prove, either upon the body of Hugh in mortal combat, or before a jury well and truly packed or empanelled, as the case might be. Whereupon there was dreadful commotion in Dublin Castle. Hugh's reply was—to arrest the base informer on a charge of treason against the sacred person and prerogatives of his lawful chief. Which charge being proved, Shane of the Fetters was at once executed.

After this comes Hugh O'Neill's romantic marriage. We quote from Haverty's narrative.

"This man—the marshal, Sir Henry Bagnal—hated the Irish with a rancour which bad men are known to feel towards those whom they have mortally injured. He had shed a great deal of their blood, obtained a great deal of their lands, and was the sworn enemy of the whole race. Sir Henry had a sister who was young and exceedingly beautiful. The wife of the Earl of Tyrone, the daughter of Sir Hugh Mac Manus O'Donnell, had died, and the heart of the Irish chieftain was captivated by the beautiful English girl. His love was reciprocated, and he became in due form a suitor for her hand; but all efforts to gain her brother's consent to this marriage were in vain. The Irish prince and the English maiden mutually plighted their vows, and O'Neill presented to the lady a gold chain worth one hundred pounds; but the inexorable Sir Henry removed his sister from Newry to the house of Sir Patrick Barnwell, who was married to another of his sisters, and who lived about seven miles from Dublin. Hither the earl followed her. He was courteously received by Sir Patrick, and seems to have had many friends among the English. One of these, a gentleman named William Warren, acted as his confidant, and at a party at Barnwell's house, the earl engaged the rest of the company in conversation while Warren rode off with the lady behind him, accompanied by two servants, and carried her safely to the residence of a friend at Drumcondra, near Dublin. Here O'Neill soon followed, and the Protestant bishop of Meath, Thomas Jones, a Lancashire man, was easily induced to come and unite them in marriage the same evening. This elopement and marriage, which took place on the 3rd of August, 1591, were made the subject of violent accusations against O'Neill. Sir Henry Bagnal was furious, was henceforth his most implacable foe, and the circumstance was not without its influence on succeeding events."

By this time young Hugh Roe O'Donnell was made the O'Donnell with the ancient ceremonies of his race.

The young chief did not wear his honours idly. In the Dublin dungeons he had sworn vows, and he was not the man to break them; vows that while his good right hand could draw a sword, the English should have no peace in Ireland. Close by the O'Donnell's territory, in Strabane, old Torlogh Lynagh O'Neill had admitted an English force as "auxiliaries" forsooth. "And it was a heartbreak," says the old chronicler, "to Hugh O'Donnell, that the English of Dublin should thus obtain a knowledge of the country." He fiercely attacked Strabane, and chased the obnoxious English "auxiliaries" away, "pardoning old Torlogh only on solemn promise not to repeat his offence. From this forth Red Hugh engaged himself in what we may call a circuit of the north, rooting out English garrisons, sheriffs, seneschals, or functionaries of what sort soever, as zealously and scrupulously as if they were plague-pests. Woe to the English chief that admitted a queen's sheriff within his territories! Hugh was down upon him like a whirlwind!

O'Donnell's cordial ally in this crusade was Maguire, lord of Fermanagh, a man truly worthy of such a colleague. Hugh of Dungannon
saw with dire concern this premature conflict precipitated by Red
Hugh's impetuosity. Very probably he was not unwilling that O'Donnell should find the English some occupation yet awhile in the north;
but the time had not at all arrived (in his opinion) for the serious and
comprehensive undertaking of a stand-up fight for the great stake of
national freedom. But it was vain for him to try remonstrance with
Hugh Roe, whose nature could ill brook restraint, and who, indeed,
could not relish or comprehend at all the subtle and politic slowness
of O'Neill. Hugh of Dungannon, however, would not allow himself at
any hazard to be pushed or drawn into open action a day or an hour
sooner than his own judgment approved. He could hardly keep out of
the conflict so close beside him, and so, rather than be precipitated
prematurely into the struggle which, no doubt, he now deemed inevitable, and for which, accordingly, he was preparing, he made show
of joining the queen's side, and led some troops against Maguire. It
was noted, however, that the species of assistance which he gave the
English generally consisted in "moderating" Hugh Roe's punishment
of them, and pleading with him merely to sweep them away a little
more gently; "interfering," as Moryson informs us, "to save their lives,
on condition of their instantly quitting the country!" Now this seemed
to the English (small wonder indeed) a very queer kind of "help." It
was not what suited them at all; and we need not be surprised that
soon Hugh's accusers in Dublin and in London once more, and more
vehemently than ever, demanded his destruction.

It was now the statesmen and courtiers of England began to feel that
craft may overleap itself. In the moment when first they seriously contemplated Hugh as a foe to the queen, they felt like "the engineer hoist
by his own petard." Here was their own pupil, trained under their own
hands, versed in their closest secrets, and let into their most subtle arts!
Here was the steel they had polished and sharpened to pierce the heart
of Ireland, now turned against their own breast! No wonder there was
dismay and consternation in London and Dublin—it was so hard to
devise any plan against him that Hugh would not divine like one of
themselves! Failing any better resort, it was resolved to inveigle him
into Dublin by offering him a safe-conduct, and, this document notwithstanding, to seize him at all hazards. Accordingly Hugh was duly
notified of charges against his loyalty, and a royal safe-conduct was
given to him that he might "come in and appear." To the utter astonishment of the plotters, he came with the greatest alacrity, and daringly
confronted them at the council-board in the Castle! He would have

been seized in the room, but for the nobly honourable conduct of the
Earl of Ormond, whose indignant letter to the lord treasurer Burleigh
(in reply to the queen's order to seize O'Neill) is recorded by Carte:—
"My lord, I will never use treachery to any man; for it would both
touch her highness's honour and my own credit too much; and whosoever gave the queen advice thus to write, is fitter for such base service
than I am. Saving my duty to her majesty, I would I might have revenge by my sword of any man that thus persuaded the queen to write
to me." Ormond acquainted O'Neill with the perfidy designed against
him, and told him that if he did not fly that night he was lost, as the
false deputy was drawing a cordon around Dublin. O'Neill made his
escape, and prepared to meet the crisis which now he knew to be at
hand. News soon reached him in the north that large reinforcements
were on their way from England, that garrisons were to be forced upon
Ballyshannon and Belleek, commanding the passes into Tyrconnell,
between Lough Erne and the sea. The strong fortress of Portmore also,
on the southern bank of the Blackwater, was to be strengthened and
well manned; thus forming, with Newry and Greencastle, a chain of
forts across the island, and a basis for future operations against the
north."

There was no misunderstanding all this. "It was clear that, let King
Philip send his promised aid, or send it not, open and vigorous resistance must be made to the further progress of foreign power, or Ulster
would soon become an English province." Moreover, in all respects,
save the aid from Spain, Hugh was well forward in organization and
preparation. A great Northern Confederacy, the creation of his master-
mind, now spanned the land from shore to shore, and waited only for
him to take his rightful place as leader, and give the signal for such a
war as had not tried the strength of England for two hundred years.

At last the time had come; and Dungannon with stern joy beheld
unfurled the royal standard of O'Neill, displaying, as it floated proudly
on the breeze, that terrible *Red Right Hand* upon its snow-white folds,
waving defiance to the Saxon queen, dawning like a new Aurora upon
the awakened children of Heremon.

With a strong body of horse and foot, O'Neill suddenly appeared
upon the Blackwater, stormed Portmore, and drove away its garrison,
as carefully as he would have driven poison from his heart; then
demolished the fortress, burned down the bridge, and advanced into
O'Reilly's country, everywhere driving the English and their adherents
before him to the south (but without wanton bloodshed, slaying no
man save in battle, for cruelty is nowhere charged against O'Neill); and

finally, with Mac Guire and Mac Mahon, he laid close siege to Monaghan, which was still held for the queen of England. O'Donnell, on his side, crossed the Saimer at the head of his fierce clan, burst into Connaught, and shutting up Bingham's troops in their strong places at Sligo, Ballymote, Tulsk, and Boyle, traversed the country with avenging fire and sword, putting to death every man *who could speak no Irish*, ravaging their lands, and sending the spoil to Tyrconnell. Then he crossed the Shannon, entered the Annally's, where O'Ferghal was living under English dominion, and devastated that country so furiously, that "the whole firmament," says the chronicle, "was one black cloud of smoke."

This rapidity of action took the English at complete disadvantage. They accordingly (merely to gain time) feigned a great desire to "treat" with the two Hughs. Perhaps those noble gentlemen had been wronged. If so, the queen's tender heart yearned to have them reconciled; and so forth. Hugh, owing to his court training, understood this kind of thing perfectly. It did not impose upon him for a moment; yet he consented to give audience to the royal commissioners, whom he refused to see except at the head of his army, "nor would he enter any walled town as liege man of the queen of England." "So they met," we are told, "in the open plain, in the presence of both armies." The conditions of peace demanded by Hugh were:

1. Complete cessation of attempts to disturb the Catholic Church in Ireland.

2. No more garrisons—no more sheriffs or English officials of any sort soever to be allowed into the Irish territories, which should be unrestrictedly under the jurisdiction of their lawfully elected native chiefs.

3. Payment by Marshal Bagnal to O'Neill of one thousand pounds of silver "as a marriage portion with the lady *whom he had raised to the dignity of an O'Neill's bride.*"

We may imagine how hard the royal commissioners must have found it to even hearken to these propositions, especially this last keen touch at Bagnal. "The rebels grew insolent," says Moryson. The utmost that could be obtained from O'Neill was a truce of a few days' duration.

Early in June, Bagnal took the field with a strong force, and effecting a junction with Norreys, made good his march from Dundalk to Armagh. The castle of Monaghan, which had been taken by Con O'Neill, was now once more in the hands of the enemy, and once more was beseiged by the Irish troops. Norreys, with his whole force, was in full march to relieve it; and O'Neill, who had hitherto avoided pitched battles, and contented himself with harassing the enemy by continual

skirmishes in their march through the woods and bogs, now resolved to
meet this redoubtable general fairly in the open field. He chose his
ground at Clontibret, about five miles from Monaghan, where a small
stream runs northward through a valley enclosed by low hills. On the
left bank of this stream the Irish, in battle array, awaited the approach
of Norreys. We have no account of the numbers on each side, but when
the English general came up, he thought himself strong enough to force
a passage. Twice the English infantry tried to make good their way
over the river, and twice were beaten back, their gallant leader each
time charging at their head, and being the last to retire. The general
and his brother, Sir Thomas, were both wounded in these conflicts, and
the Irish counted the victory won, when a chosen body of English horse,
led on by Segrave, a Meathian officer, of gigantic bone and height,
spurred fiercely across the river, and charged the cavalry of Tyrowen,
commanded by their prince in person. Segrave singled out O'Neill, and
the two leaders laid lance in rest for deadly combat, while the troops on
each side lowered their weapons and held their breath, awaiting the
shock in silence. The warriors met, and the lance of each was splintered
on the other's corselet, but Segrave again dashed his horse against the
chief, flung his giant frame against his enemy, and endeavored to un-
horse him by the mere weight of his gauntletted hand. O'Neill grasped
him in his arms, and the combatants rolled together in that fatal
embrace to the ground. There was one moment's deadly wrestle and a
death groan: the shortened sword of O'Neill was buried in the Englishman's groin beneath his mail. Then from the Irish ranks arose such a
wild shout of triumph as those hills had never echoed before—the still
thunder-cloud burst into a tempest—those equestrian statues become
as winged demons, and with their battle cry of *Lamh-dearg-aboo,* and
their long lances poised in eastern fashion above their heads, down
swept the chivalry of Tyrowen upon the astonished ranks of the Saxon.
The banner of St. George wavered and went down before that furious
charge. The English turned their bridle-reins and fled headlong over
the stream, leaving the field covered with their dead, and, worse than
all, leaving with the Irish that proud red-cross banner, the first of its
disgraces in those Ulster wars. Norreys hastily retreated southwards,
and the castle of Monaghan was yielded to the Irish.

This was opening the campaign in a manner truly worthy of a royal
O'Neill. The flame thus lighted spread all over the northern land.
Success shone on the Irish banners, and as the historian informs us, "at
the close of the year 1595, the Irish power predominated in Ulster and
Connaught."

Over several of the subsequent engagements in 1596 and 1597 I must pass rapidly, to reach the more important events in which the career of O'Neill culminated and closed. At length in the summer of 1598, he seems to have thrown aside all reliance upon foreign aid, and to have organized his countrymen for a still more resolute stand than any they yet had made against the national enemy.

The Battle of the Yellow Ford

In the month of July, 1598, Hugh O'Neill sent messengers to Phelim MacHugh, then chief of the O'Byrnes, that he might fall upon the Pale, as they were about to make employment in the north for the troops of Ormond, and at the same time he detached fifteen hundred men and sent them to assist his ally, O'More, who was then beseiging Porteloise, a fort of the English in Leix. Then he made a sudden swoop upon the castle of Portmore, which, says Moryson, "was a great eyesore to him, lying upon the chiefe passage into his country," hoping to carry it by assault.

Ormond now perceived that a powerful effort must be made by the English to hold their ground in the north, or Ulster might at once be abandoned to the Irish. Strong reinforcements were sent from England, and O'Neill's spies soon brought him intelligence of large masses of troops moving northward, led by Marshal Sir Henry Bagnal, and composed of the choicest forces in the queen's service. Newry was their place of rendezvous; and, early in August, Bagnal found himself at the head of the largest and best appointed army of veteran Englishmen that had ever fought in Ireland. He succeeded in relieving Armagh, and dislodging O'Neill from his encampment at Mullaghbane, where the chief himself narrowly escaped being taken, and then prepared to advance with his whole army to the Blackwater, and raise the siege of Portmore. Williams and his men were by this time nearly famished with hunger; they had eaten all their horses, and had come to feeding on the herbs and grass that grew upon the walls of the fortress. And every morning they gazed anxiously over the southern hills, and strained their eyes to see the waving of a red cross flag, or the glance of English spears in the rising sun.

O'Neill hastily summoned O'Donnell and MacWilliam to his aid,

From *Emerald Gems: A Chaplet of Irish Fireside Tales, Histories, Domestic and Legendary,* compiled from Approved Sources, pp. 391-396. Thomas B. Noonan & Co. Boston. 1878.

and determined to cross the marshal's path, and give him battle before he reached the Blackwater. His entire force on the day of battle, including the Scots and the troops of Connaught and Tyrconnell, consisted of four thousand five hundred foot and six hundred horse; and Bagnal's army amounted to an equal number of infantry, and five hundred veteran horsemen, sheathed in corselets and head-pieces, together with some field artillery, in which O'Neill was wholly wanting.

Hugh Roe O'Donnell had snuffed the coming battle from afar, and on the 9th of August joined O'Neill with the clans of Connaught and Tyrconnell. They drew up their main body about a mile from Portmore, on the way to Armagh, where the plain was narrowed to a pass, enclosed on one side by a thick wood, and on the other by a bog. To arrive at that plain from Armagh, the enemy would have to penetrate through wooded hills, divided by winding and marshy hollows, in which flowed a sluggish and discolored stream from the bogs; and hence the pass was called *Beal-an-atha-buidhe,* "the mouth of the yellow ford." Fearfasa O'Clery, a learned poet of O'Donnell's, asked the name of that place, and when he heard it, remembered (and proclaimed aloud to the army) that St. Bercan had foretold a terrible battle to be fought at a yellow ford, and a glorious victory to be won by the ancient Irish.

Even so, Moran, son of Maoin! and for thee, wisest poet, O'Clery, thou hast this day served thy country well, for, to an Irish army, auguries of good were more needful than a commissariat: and those bards' songs, like the Dorian flute of Greece, breathed a passionate valor that no blare of English trumpets could ever kindle.

Bagnal's army rested that night in Armagh, and the Irish bivouacked in the woods, each warrior covered by his shaggy cloth, under the stars of a summer night; for to "an Irish rebel," says Edmund Spenser, "the wood is his house against all weathers, and his mantle is his couch to sleep in." But O'Neill, we may well believe, slept not that night away. The morrow was to put to proof what valor and discipline was in that Irish army, which he had been so long organizing and training to meet this very hour. Before him lay a splendid army of tried English troops, in full march for his ancient seat of Dungannon, and led on by his mortal enemy. And O'Neill would not have had that host weakened by the desertion of a single man, nor commanded—no, not for his white wand of chieftancy—by any leader but this his dearest foe.

The tenth morning of August rose bright and serene upon the towers of Armagh and the silver waters of Avonmore. Before day dawned the English army left the city in three divisions, and at sunrise they were winding through the hills and woods behind the spot where now stands the little church of Grange.

The sun was glancing on the corselets and spears of their glittering cavalry; their banners waved proudly, and their bugles rang clear in the morning air, when suddenly from the thickets on both sides of their path, a deadly volley of musketry swept through their foremost ranks. O'Neill had stationed here five hundred light-armed troops to guard the defiles; and in the shelter of thick groves of fir-trees they had silently waited for the enemy. Now they poured in their shot, volley after volley, and killed great numbers of the English. But the first division, led by Bagnal in person, after some hard fighting, carried the pass, dislodged the marksmen from their position, and drove them backwards into the plain. The center division, under Cosby and Wingfield, and the rear-guard led by Cuin and Billing, supported in flank by the cavalry under Brooke, Montacute, and Fleming, now pushed forward, speedily cleared the difficult country, and formed in the open ground in front of the Irish lines. "It was not quite safe," says an Irish chronicler (in admiration of Bagnal's disposition of his forces), "to attack the nest of griffins and den of lions in which were placed the soldiers of London." Bagnal, at the head of his first division, and aided by a body of cavalry, charged the Irish light-armed troops up to the very intrenchments, in front of which O'Neill's foresight had prepared some pits, covered over with wattles and grass, and many of the English cavalry, rushing impetuously forward, rolled headlong, both men and horses, into these trenches, and perished. Still the marshal's chosen troops, with loud cheers and shouts of "St. George for merry England!" resolutely attacked the intrenchment that stretched across the pass, battered them with cannon, and in one place succeeded, though with heavy loss, in forcing back into their defenders. Then first the main body of O'Neill's troops was brought into action, and with bagpipes sounding a charge, they fell upon the English, shouting their fierce battle-cries—"Lamh-deargh!" and "O'Donnell aboo!" O'Neill himself, at the head of a body of horse, pricked forward to seek out Bagnal amid the throng of battle; but they never met: the marshal, who had done his devoir that day like a good soldier, was shot through the brain by some unknown marksman. The division he had led was forced back by the furious onslaught of the Irish, and put to utter rout; and, what added to their confusion, a cart of gunpowder exploded amid the English ranks, and blew many of their men to atoms. And now the cavalry of Tyrconnell and Tyrowen dashed into the plain and bore down the remnant of Brooke's and Fleming's horse; the columns of Wingfield and Cosby reeled before their rushing charge; while in front, to the war-cry of "Bataillah-aboo!" the swords and axes of the heavy-armed gallowglasses were raging among the Saxon ranks. By this time the cannon were all taken; the cries of "St. George" had failed, or turned into death shrieks; and once more England's royal standard sank before the Red Hand of Tyrowen.

Twelve thousand gold pieces, thirty-four standards, and all the artillery of the vanquished army, were taken. Nearly three thousand dead were left by the English on the field. The splendid army of the Pale was in fact annihilated.

Beal-an-atha-buie, or, as some of the English chronicles call it, Blackwater, may be classed at one of the great battles of the Irish nation; perhaps the greatest fought in the course of the war against English invasion. Other victories as brilliant and complete may be found recorded in our annals; many defeats of English armies as utter and disastrous; but most of these were, in a military point of view, not to be ranked for a moment with the "Yellow Ford." Very nearly all of them were defile surprises, conducted on the simplest principles of warfare common to struggles in a mountainous country. But Beal-an-atha-buie was a deliberate engagement, a formidable pitched battle between the largest and the best armies which England and Ireland respectively were able to send forth, and was fought out on principles of military science, in which both O'Neill and Bagnal were proficient. It was a fair stand-up fight between the picked troops and chosen generals of the two nations; and it must be told of the vanquished on that day, that, though defeated, they were not dishonored. The Irish annals and chants, one and all, do justice to the daring bravery and unflinching endurance displayed by Bagnal's army on the disastrous battlefield of Beal-an-atha-buie.

The fame of this great victory filled the land. Not in Ireland alone did it create a sensation. The English historians tell us that for months nothing was talked of at court or elsewhere throughout England, but O'Neill and the great battle on the Blackwater, which had resulted so disastrously for "her Highness." Moryson himself informs us that "the general voyce was of Tyrone amongst the English after the defeat of Blackwater, as of Hannibal amongst the Romans after the defeat at Cannæ." The event got noised abroad, too; and in all the courts of Europe Hugh of Tyrone became celebrated as a military commander and as a patriot leader.

O'Neill and His National Confederacy Against Essex

So irresistible was the inspiration of Hugh's victories in the north, that even the occupied, conquered, broken, divided, and desolated south began to take heart and look upward. Messengers were despatched to Hugh entreating him to send some duly authorised lieutenants to raise the standard of Church and Country in Munster, and take charge of the cause there. He complied by detaching Richard Tyrrell, of Fertullah, and Owen, son of Ruari O'Moore, at the head of a chosen band, to unfurl the national flag in the southern provinces. They were enthusiastically received. The Catholic Anglo-Norman lords and the native chiefs entered into the movement and rose to arms on all sides. The newly-planted "settlers," or "undertakers" as they were styled—(English adventurers amongst whom had been parcelled out the lands of several southern Catholic families, lawlessly seized on the ending of the Desmond rebellion)—fled pell mell, abandoning the stolen castles and lands to their rightful owners, and only too happy to escape with life. The Lord President had to draw in every outpost, and abandon all Munster, except the garrison towns of Cork and Kilmallock, within which, cooped up like prisoners, he and his diminished troops were glad to find even momentary shelter. By the beginning of 1599, "no English force was able to keep the field throughout all Ireland." O'Neill's authority was paramount—was loyally recognized and obeyed everywhere outside two or three garrison towns. He exercised the prerogatives of royalty; issued commissions, conferred offices, honours, and titles; removed or deposed lords and chiefs actively or passively disloyal to the national authority, and appointed others in their stead. And all was done so wisely, so impartially, so patriotically —with such scrupulous and fixed regard for the one great object, and no other—namely, the common cause of national independence and freedom—that even men chronically disposed to suspect family or clan selfishness in every act gave their full confidence to him as to a leader who had completely sunk the clan chief in the national leader. In fine, since the days of Brian the First, no native sovereign of equal capacity —singularly qualified as a soldier and as a statesman—had been known in Ireland. He omitted no means of strengthening the league. He renewed his intercourse with Spain; planted permanent bodies of troops

From *The Story of Ireland,* by A. M. Sullivan, pp. 272-278. M. H. Gill & Son, Ltd. Dublin. 1905.

on the Foyle, Erne, and Blackwater; engaged the services of some additional Scots from the Western Isles; improved the discipline of his own
troops, and on every side made preparations to renew the conflict with
his powerful enemy. For he well knew that Elizabeth was not the
monarch to quit her deadly grip of this fair island without a more
terrible struggle than had yet been endured.

The struggle was soon inaugurated. England—at that time one of
the strongest nations in Europe, and a match for the best among them
by land and sea, ruled over by one of the ablest, the boldest, and most
crafty sovereigns that had ever sat upon her throne, and served by
statesmen, soldiers, philosophers, and writers, whose names are famous
in history—was now about to put forth all her power in a combined
naval and military armament against the almost reconstituted, but as
yet all too fragile, Irish nation. Such an effort, under all the circumstances, could scarcely result otherwise than as it eventually did; for
there are, after all, odds against which no human effort can avail and
for which no human valour can compensate. It was England's good
fortune on this occasion, as on others previously and subsequently, that
the Irish nation challenged her when she was at peace with all the
world—when her hands were free and her resources undivided. Equally
fortunate was she at all times, on the other hand, in the complete
tranquillity of the Irish when desperate emergencies put her on her
own defence, and left no resources to spare for a campaign in Ireland,
had she been challenged then. What we have to contemplate in the
closing scenes of O'Neill's glorious career is the heroism of Thermopy-
lae, not the success of Salamis or Plataea.

Elizabeth's favourite, Essex, was despatched to Ireland with *twenty
thousand* men at his back; an army not only the largest England had
put into the field for centuries, but in equipment, in drill, and in
armament, the most complete ever assembled under her standard.
Against this the Irish nowhere had ten thousand men concentrated
in a regular army or movable corps. In equipment and in armament
they were sadly deficient, while of sieging material they were altogether
destitute. Nevertheless, we are told "O'Neill and his confederates were
not dismayed by the arrival of this great army and its magnificent
leader." And had the question between the two nations depended
solely upon such issues as armies settle, and superior skill and prowess
control, neither O'Neill nor his confederates would have erred in the
strong faith, the high hope, the exultant self-reliance that now animated them. The campaign of 1599—the disastrous failure of the
courtly Essex and his magnificent army—must be told in a few lines.
O'Neill completely outgeneraled and overawed or overreached the

haughty deputy. In more than one fatal engagement his splendid force was routed by the Irish, until, notwithstanding a constant stream of reinforcements from England, it had wasted away, and was no longer formidable in O'Neill's eyes. In vain the queen wrote letter after letter endeavouring to sting her quondam favourite into "something notable"; that is, a victory over O'Neill. Nothing could induce Essex to face the famous hero of Clontibret and the Yellow Ford, unless, indeed, in peaceful parley. At length having been taunted into a movement northward, he proceeded thither reluctantly and slowly. "On the high ground north of the Lagan, he found the host of O'Neill encamped, and received a courteous message from their leader, soliciting a personal interview. At an appointed hour the two commanders rode down to the opposite bands of the river, wholly unattended, the advanced guards of each looking curiously on the uplands."

O'Neill, ever the flower of courtesy, spurred his horse into the stream up to the saddlegirths. "First they had a private conference, in which Lord Essex, won by the chivalrous bearing and kindly address of the chief, became, say the English historians, too confidential with an enemy of his sovereign, spoke without reserve of his daring hope, and most private thoughts of ambition, until O'Neill had sufficiently read his secret soul, fathomed his poor capacity, and understood the full meanness of his shallow treason. Then Cormac O'Neill and five other Irish leaders were summoned on the one side, on the other Lord Southampton and an equal number of English officers, and a solemn parley was opened in due form." O'Neill offered terms: "first, complete liberty of conscience; second, indemnity for his allies in all the four provinces; third, the principal officers of state, the judges, and one-half the army to be henceforth Irish by birth." Essex considered these very far from extravagant demands from a man now virtually master in the island. He declared as much to O'Neill, and concluded a truce pending reply from London. Elizabeth saw in fury how completely O'Neill had dominated her favourite. She wrote him a frantic letter full of scornful taunt and upbraiding. Essex flung up all his duties in Ireland without leave, and hurried to London.

The year 1600 was employed by O'Neill in a general circuit of the kingdom, for the more complete establishment of the national league and the better organization of the national resources. "He marched through the center of the island at the head of his troops to the south," says his biographer, "a kind of royal progress, which he thought fit to call a pilgrimage to Holy Cross. He held princely state there, concerted measures with the southern lords, and distributed a manifesto announcing himself as the accredited Defender of the Faith." "In the beginning

of March," says another authority, "the Catholic army halted at Inniscarra, upon the river Lee, about five miles west of Cork. Here O'Neill
remained three weeks in camp consolidating the Catholic party in
South Munster. During that time he was visited by the chiefs of the
ancient Eugenian clans—O'Donohoe, O'Donovan, and O'Mahoney.
Thither also came two of the most remarkable men of the southern
province: Florence McCarthy, lord of Ourberry, and Donald O'Sullivan, lord of Bearhaven. McCarthy, "like Saul, higher by the head and
shoulders than any of his house," had brain in proportion to his brawn;
O'Sullivan, as was afterwards shown, was possessed of military virtues
of a high order. Florence was inaugurated with O'Neill's sanction as
McCarthy More, and although the rival house of Muskerry fiercely
resisted his claim to superiority at first, a wiser choice could not have
been made had the times tended to confirm it.

While at Inniscarra, O'Neill lost in single combat one of his most
accomplished officers, the chief of Fermanagh. Maguire, accompanied
only by a priest and two horsemen, was making observations nearer to
the city than the camp, when Sir Warham St. Leger, marshal of
Munster, headed out of Cork with a company of soldiers, probably on
a similar mission. Both were in advance of their attendants when they
came unexpectedly face to face. Both were famous as horsemen and for
the use of their weapons, and neither would retrace his steps. The Irish
chief, poising his spear, dashed forward against his opponent, but received a pistol shot which proved mortal the same day. He, however,
had strength enough left to drive his spear through the neck of St.
Leger, and to effect his escape from the English cavalry. St. Leger was
carried back to Cork where he expired. Maguire, on reaching the camp
had barely time left to make his last confession when he breathed his
last. This untoward event, the necessity of preventing possible dissen-
sions in Fermanagh, and still more the menacing movements of the
new deputy, lately sworn in at Dublin, obliged O'Neill to return home
earlier than he intended.

The Battle of the Curlew Mountains

In treating of the fall of Queen Elizabeth's favorite, Robert, Earl
of Essex, historians have not at all recognized his very bad record as
Chief Governor of Ireland.

By Standish O'Grady, in *The Gael*, July, 1903, pp. 201-214. New York.

They may say he did nothing, but in fact he did a great deal less, for he was beaten by the insurgent lords at many points.

As he marched through the Queen's country, young O'More, lord of that region, routed his rear guard and plundered his baggage in the Pass of Plumes. At Askeaton, County Limerick, he was beaten by the Geraldines and driven out of West Munster. The sons of Feagh Mac-Hugh defeated his cavalry in one battle and his infantry in another. Finally, his lieutenant, Sir Conyers Clifford, President of Connacht, was first beaten by Red Hugh at Ballyshannon and afterwards beaten disastrously in the Curlew Mountains.

With such an Irish record it is not surprising that on his return to England his reception should have been so cold. I propose here to give a sketch of this latter battle, partly to enable the reader to form some idea of the curiously embroiled and intertangled relations of the chieftainry with each other and with the state, and partly with the purpose of illustrating the war-methods of the sixteenth century as practiced in Ireland.

When the "Nine Years' War" broke out, Sir Richard Bingham was master of all Connacht. Presently he came into collision with Red Hugh, and Red Hugh beat him. Red Hugh was only a boy, yet he beat the veteran and shook most of Connacht loose from his control.

When Essex came into Ireland, Bingham was hopelessly beaten and could hardly venture to show himself outside the gates of Athlone. The Burkes of Clanricarde and the O'Briens of Thomond, two zealous Royalist clans, alone kept the Queen's flag flying in the open, and Red Hugh was destroying them. Then the Queen recalled Bingham in disgrace. He was brought to London as a state prisoner pursued by an infinity of complaints urged against him by chieftains of the West, and Sir Conyers Clifford appointed President of Connacht simultaneously with the appointment of Earl of Essex as Lord Lieutenant of that realm.

Clifford seems to have been a man of signal nobility of character. "The Four Masters" declare that "there did not come of English blood into Ireland in the latter times a more worthy person." His reputation preceded him, and on his arrival a considerable proportion of the western lords who had been previously in rebellion and allies of Red Hugh waited upon him and tended him their allegiance.

So without striking a blow, Clifford recovered immediately the greater portion of the province. Then at the head of a considerable army he marched northwards for the invasion of Tyrconnel but did not succeed. Red Hugh beat him at Ballyshannon, drove him back and resumed his operations in Connacht.

The County of Sligo was one of the divisions of Connacht in which the change produced by the coming of Clifford was not felt. It was still strongly held by Red Hugh's lieutenants. In 1598 Clifford flung into that county a young royalist chieftain and a body of horse with the object of exciting there a rebellion of Red Hugh's feudatories. A cavalry battle ensued in which the Royalists were overthrown by Red Hugh's horse, and the leader of this forlorn hope, in fact the O'Conor Sligo, was driven within the fortress of Collooney and there besieged by Red Hugh.

Partly to relieve him, partly to deliver another great stroke at Red Hugh, Clifford mustered his forces at Athlone. When all was in readiness Clifford rose thence and marched to Boyle, a strong town in the north of Roscommon, close to the frontiers of Sligo.

Between Roscommon and Sligo lay the Curlew Mountains, on the north side of which all the country was held by Red Hugh, except Collooney, which he was blockading. Clifford's force numbered 2,500 infantry and 300 horse. It consisted of Connacht-Irish, Meath-Irish, and regulars. The regulars were, for the most part, Irish, too, but officered to some extent by English gentlemen. The Connacht and Meath contingents represented the military quotas which those provinces were bound to furnish for war.

On demand under certain conditions, all the nobles and landowners were bound to "rise out," as the phrase ran, at the head of a fixed body of foot and horse, well equipped, and serve at their own expense for forty days. To our notions Clifford's army on this occasion was absurdly small. But in the sixteenth century such a force was not small, but, on the contrary, a great host.

The State was seldom able to put into the field for active service an army of more than 4,000 men nor the insurgent chiefs one of greater dimensions. When at Kinsale the contending powers severally brought all their forces to a head, out of the whole of Ireland there were but some six or seven thousand effective men on each side.

At the head of this force, Clifford, on the 13th of August, marched through the gates of Boyle in the midst of mild weather and heavy pouring rain. The army had come that day from the town of Roscommon and entered Boyle wet and weary, thinking only of supper, rest, and sleep. Clifford took up his quarters in the monastery there. The rest of his army was billeted throughout the town.

Monastery and town must have been of considerable capacity, for I find a little later a garrison of 1,500 men posted there. Clifford's army, I say, expected to sleep comfortably in Boyle that night, but they did not. Shortly after their arrival the army was on march again, moving silently through darkness and rain towards the Curlew Mountains. Why, we shall see presently.

When Red Hugh heard of this invasion he lay, with cavalry only, blockading the castle of Collooney. Within that castle was the O'Conor Sligo. Hugh was very anxious to lay his hands upon O'Conor Sligo, who had, for a long time, given him a great deal of trouble. Hearing the tidings, Hugh wrote to Tyrone to come and help; Tyrone came by forced marches, but was unable to help. He came too late.

Hugh also sent the usual war-summons to all his feudatories and captains, and all these being near came to him at once. These were O'Dogherty, the three M'Sweeny's, O'Boyle, O'Byrne, M'Clancy, O'Gallagher, and others. His army when assembled consisted of about 2,500 men, horse and foot. We see here a proof of Red Hugh's military power. On the sudden, he was able to draw together a force as great as that of the Queen's President of Connacht. Nor was it in any respect less efficient. Hugh now rose from Collooney, but left behind him 200 horse to continue the blockade.

To the command of this force, he appointed his cousin, *Nial Garv*, i.e., Nial the Rough. I notice him particularly, for it was this rough cousin whose defection a little afterwards broke Red Hugh's brilliant career. Nial Garv rebelled against Red Hugh, became the "Queen's" O'Donnell, and led a great Queen's party in the northwest. He was a violent, headstrong, implacable young man, and most furious both in speech and demeanor.

As Hugh Roe with the bulk of his army marches southwards from Collooney, imagine Nial Garv with his 200 horsemen moving round that fortress through the trees and Nial's fierce and strident voice uplifted at times ringing out words of menace and command. That young man, afterwards the Queen's O'Donnell, was certainly the roughest, ruggedest, and most bull-headed and bull-hearted creature to be found anywhere at this time.

RED HUGH BLOCKS THE CURLEWS

Hugh Roe at the head of the rest of his army marched straight forward to the Curlews, going with his accustomed velocity, and encamped on the northern slopes of the same. From Boyle two roads led through the mountains into Sligo. One of these was circuitous, rugged, and easily defended. It was unlikely that Clifford would try to force the Curlews by this road, nevertheless Hugh blocked it with 300 picked men, pikes and guns, no cavalry. He himself leading the bulk of his forces, and a considerable body of churls bearing spades and axes advanced from his camp along the direct road till he came to the blackened ruins of a castle which once commanded a gorge on the sudden slope of the mountains.

This castle had been erected by Bingham both for the defense of the Pass and as a fetter on the warlike MacDermot clan who then occupied this region. Shortly after the breaking out of the war it had been stormed and burnt by the chief of this clan, MacDermot of the Curlews, a brave man, not at all so rude and wild as one might imagine, as the reader will discover later on. At this point Red Hugh determined to fight with Clifford, and to that end ordered the erection there of a barricade with double flanks. This was early on the morning of the 13th, and at the time Clifford was marching out of Roscommon along the road to Boyle. The morning was bright and fine, but the atmosphere was suspiciously transparent. From the mouth of the gorge, through a small opening in the trees, the walls, towers, and turrets of Boyle could be seen distinctly, white and glistening in the sunlight. Red Hugh, who was on horseback, and surrounded by his chiefs and principal officers, stood still for a while, and regarded it intently.

This young man, now for many years the terror of all Royalists in the West, was only twenty-six years of age, and looked even younger than he was, so clear and fresh was his complexion, so vivid his countenance, so alert and rapid was he in all his movements. Yet he was no boy, but already a skillful commander in the field, and a strong and resolute administrator. Then he bade his men fall to, and the adjoining woods rang with the noise of axes, and presently sounded with the crash of falling timber. Meanwhile the gorge was alive with spadesmen laboring diligently under the direction of the young chief's engineers, and gradually the barricade began to assume form.

Once for all, let me warn the reader against the ignorant notion that the armies of the insurgent lords were the rude crowds of what are vaguely known as kerne. They were armies in the proper sense of the word, armed, directed, and handled according to the best military methods in vogue at the time.

Shortly after noon, the sky became overcast, and at two o'clock the rain fell and continued to fall. At four there was the sound of the firing of heavy ordnance from the direction of Boyle; it was the garrison of Boyle saluting the army of the President. The flashes were quite visible. Red Hugh believed that Clifford, after a short halt, would roll forward again, and force the passage of the Curlews. The probability also was that he would advance by the direct road.

Should he prefer the more circuitous route, Hugh believed that the three hundred planted there would retard his advance sufficiently to enable himself to transfer his army by the nearest cross-country ways, and fight Clifford upon that road at a point which he had already settled in his mind. Clifford, in fact, was not aware that Red Hugh was in this neighborhood at all; for Hugh had come from Collooney with extraordinary celerity, Clifford imagined that he had only to do with MacDermot of the Curlews, Hugh's marcher-lord in this region.

Behind the barricade Hugh's people stood under arms, the gunmen forward with matches already lit, behind them the battle and on the wings kerne, *i.e.*, light foot, armed only with swords and javelins. His few horsemen were posted under shelter of a wood on the right of the barricade. Presently the whole of Clifford's army reached Boyle, and instead of advancing, as Red Hugh firmly expected, entered Boyle, presumably for a short rest and for refreshment. Now, however, hour succeeded hour, and there was no sign of the emergence of Clifford's people from Boyle. On the contrary, as night fell, Hugh's scouts came in with the intelligence that all the bugle notes heard in the town indicated that the Royalist army would pass the night there.

The rain now began to fall in torrents, and the wind rose to a storm howling in the forest, and whistling round the crags of the mountainsides. It grew dark two hours before darkness was due. Red Hugh now determined to lead his army back to camp, leaving a force of gunmen to hold the barricade as well as they could in the event of a night attack. Such an attack might possibly be delivered, but was he to keep his army here all night under arms waiting for an assault which might never come? In that event his tired men would have to contend in the morning with Clifford's well-rested and refreshed forces. . . . Hugh bade the officer in charge of the barricade send a swift mounted messenger to him at the first sign of the approach of Clifford's men, bade the bugles sound retreat, and rode away with his army, winding darkling, through the wild Curlews.

THE QUEEN'S M'SWEENY

Red Hugh did not succeed in bringing all his soldiers back to camp. Shortly after that sounding of the trumpets, there emerged, from the woods on the right side of the barricade, three men wearing brazen morions, two with guns on their shoulders, who stepped down the slope quickly, going in the direction of Boyle. The man who had no gun was a gentleman of the M'Sweenys.

His name is unknown, but his purpose is well known. He was about to change sides and ally himself with the cause of the Queen. He believed that his change of ideas would be peculiarly welcome to the Queen's people just now, because he brought with him important intelligence. He could tell them that the narrow gorge at the head of Curlew Pass was undefended, that Hugh Roe, trusting to the wetness and blackness of the night, had marched back to camp, and that if they wished to do a good stroke upon him, now was the time. He could have access to the English commander, for his kinsman, Sir Miler M'Sweeny, was with him in Boyle.

No one can study the history of Elizabethan Ireland without being amazed and disgusted at the choppings and changings which marked the careers of nearly all the chieftains. Granuaile's son fought first for Hugh Roe and then for the Queen, and changed sides twice after that. His rival, the land Burke, now with Hugh Roe, was once a pillar of the Queen's cause in Mayo.

Nial Garv, now in rebellion, will one day be a pillar of the Queen's cause in the northwest, and before the end of the war will be in rebellion again. O'Conor Sligo, now a Queen's man blockaded in Collooney, will presently be Red Hugh's man, and in a year or two the Queen's man again, so that Red Hugh will have to seize and imprison him and give his lordship to his brother. But in each case there is an explanation, and if one looks closely into the explanation, one does not find the apparent treacheries so very surprising.

* * * *

So these three men stepped from the slopes of the Curlews, crossed the wet plain, presented themselves to the sentinels at Boyle, and were led into Sir Miler's presence. To him they explained the situation. By him it was also explained to Sir Conyers and his officers, with the result that in a short time the bugles rang out, and all Boyle sounded with the noise of military preparation. In spite of darkness and teeming rain, Clifford's army got on march again, and rolled through the night towards the pass in the Curlew Mountains, which, as we know, was now practically undefended.

Brian Ogue of the Battle-Axes

When Hugh Roe arrived at his camp he found himself reinforced by the arrival of the Lord of Leitrim, the O'Rourke, Brian Ogue of the Battle-Axes. It was he whose milch cows Bingham had seized upon the lawn at Dromahaire. It was he who, by exacting vengeance on the Binghams for that insult, had unintentionally kindled all the north into rebellion, and so precipitated the Nine Years' War. He arrived in camp leading a little army of horse and foot, and amongst the foot 160 big gallow-glasses clad in shirts of glittering chainmail, and carrying long battle-axes. As these gallow-glasses played a great part in the Battle of the Curlew Mountains, the reader must not forget them.

* * * *

But now arrived visitors of a different sort. Horsemen galloped up to the great central tent, and springing swiftly from the saddle, announced that the enemy was on the march, and at their ease, crossing or about to cross the strewn timber. The war would not now be fought where the advantage was with the northerns, but on this side of the selected point and on even terms.

A swift shadow crossed the face of the young prince at these ill tidings. Had he known that this blow came from his own revolted vassal, Sir Miler, it would probably have been deeper. But quickly recovering himself, he invented new plans and sent out new orders. "Breakfast at once for the whole army," was the first of these; surely a good beginning for a day which promised to be one of long and continued battle. Breakfast, too, was doubly necessary this morning, for his devout warriors were hollow-bellied enough after yesterday's severe abstinence. . . .

"Soldiers, through the help of the Holy Virgin, Mother of God, we have, ere this, at all times conquered our heretic foe. Today we will annihilate him. In her name yesterday we fasted. Today we celebrate her feast. So then in the Virgin's name, let us bravely fight and conquer her enemies."

Shouts and clash of arms proved that he had touched the right chord in the hearts of these simple warriors, for whom the Middle Ages had by no means passed away, but who were still as devout, and in the old way, as their forefathers of the days of the Crusaders.

With banners waving, war-pipes screaming, MacDermot and his 600 men marched straight into the mountains. Rain still fell, but not heavily. After him, at a slower pace, followed Brian Ogue and his gallow-glasses, over whom waved the O'Rourke banner, showing the lions of the house of Breffney surmounted by a mailed hand grasping a dagger.

As MacDermot and Brian Ogue disappeared, folded away and hidden in the hollows of the hills, Red Hugh and his host also advanced till they reached a point at which Clifford's progress might best be obstructed. The point selected by Red Hugh for fighting the Battle of the Curlew Mountains was one where cavalry would not operate, and where his flanks could not be turned. He sent his war-horses to the rear and dismounted his lancers, for he was resolved to put his whole strength into the contest at this selected point.

Here he was rejoined by the 300 whom he had previously planted as a guard upon that unused and circuitous road, and where their presence was no longer necessary. Having made all his dispositions, he and his chief officers rode forward to the track of MacDermot and Brian Ogue, to see how matters fared in the hills, whence probably sounds of firing already came.

Red Hugh expected that he would soon be joined by his skirmishers, falling back before Clifford's advance.

CLIFFORD ENTERS THE CURLEWS

To return to Clifford. The three deserting M'Sweenys arriving at Boyle informed their dear lord, Sir Miler, that the Curlews were undefended, Hugh Roe having marched back to camp. Sir Miler brought the news to Clifford. Clifford sent out the necessary orders. . . . The tired soldiers had to buckle on their war gear again and face once more the raging elements.

Soon the whole army, horse, foot, and carriages were again upon the road. The wall and towers of monastery Boyle were left behind and Clifford's host rolled along the great road leading into Ulster across the Curlews, men and horses plodding wearily forward through the miry ways and driving rain. Clifford, by Sir Miler's advice, avoided the unfrequented way which Red Hugh had beset with 300 men. At the foot of the Curlews he bade Markham halt with the horse in a green pasture. Day now dawned, not rosy-fingered, but wet exceedingly.

It was about this time that at the other side of the Curlew mountains the conviction arose in a certain redhead there that Clifford would not march that day. The army now began to ascend the Curlews in three divisions. The vanguard was commanded by Sir Alexander Ratcliffe, son of the Earl of Sussex, the battle, *i.e.*, the strong central division, by Clifford himself. The rear-guard was brought up under Sir Arthur Savage, captain of a Norman-Irish sept of the County of Down.

About a quarter of a mile from the mouth of the passage, Ratcliffe came upon "a barricado with double flanks," in fact, the woody obstruction at which Red Hugh had intended to dispute the passage of the Curlews. There were a few sentries there who discharged their muskets and fled. The place was practically undefended.

Opening a passage through the barricado, Sir Conyers placed guards upon the same with the instructions that they were not to stir until they should hear from him again, which they never did. On the right flank of their half-ript barricado he put Lieutenant Rogers and his company, on the left Ralph Constable, an officer held in high and deserved honor "for his virtue."

Not far from Constable and on the same flank he posted Captain Walter Flood and Captain Windsor. Each of these captains had forty men. There were 160 in all, Ralph Constable being chief in command. Should the army suffer a disaster in the mountains, the Governor believed that Constable would hold the half-barricaded gap and check the onrush of the pursuers. He was a prudent general and looked behind as well as before.

Having made these sensible arrangements, Clifford led his army into the heart of the Curlews. The Curlews were not so much mountains as great bleak highlands of a boggy character like nearly all Irish highlands and hills, a fact which accounts for the softness and rounded beauty of our mountain scenery. Presently, still ascending, the army came upon a great expanse of brown moorland looked down on by distant hills. A grey road traversed the bog and at the further end stopped short suddenly in a green wood. The wood blocked the view northwards. Clifford could not tell what was going on at the other side of that wood.

The road was not straight but swerved considerably, resembling a well-bent bow. It was bordered by some ground, moderately firm, studded with yellow furze, whence its name *Bohar-buidhe* or the Yellow Road. As string to this bent bow there ran straight across the bog a sort of causeway, not exactly a way, but more of the nature of firm ground, rough and obstructed. Its course was traceable by the eye, for it was greener than the surrounding bog. This causeway, leaving the regular road at a certain point, fell in again with the road well on this side of the wood; let the reader remember this rough causeway intersecting the bend of the road.

The army went by the road advancing as before in three separate divisions. Sir Alexander Ratcliffe was in the van, Clifford in the battle, Sir Arthur Savage leading the rear column. Carts and horses, mules and *garrans* bearing panniers filled the spaces between the columns. Here in fact went the baggage, ammunition, and provisions.

RATCLIFFE CLEARS THE BOHAR-BUIDHE WOOD

So over the vast brown bog the Royalist army, minus the cavalry, wound its way slowly towards the wood. Below them lay Constable and his 160 guarding the barricado. Below these, again, Clifford's cavalry stood their ease at the foot of the hills southwards. The passage of the

Curlews was not yet achieved nor a point reached at which horse could be anything but a danger and encumbrance.

It was now morning. The pouring rain of the previous night gradually ceased, the sky cleared and the sun rose. The peasantry who from the hills watched the army saw the glittering of armor and weapons with eyes friendly or hostile as the Queen's host slowly threaded the brown bog curving round towards the wood where all believed that the Battle of the Curlew Mountains would now be lost or won.

*   *   *   *   *

Flocks of crying curlews, scared by the sound and glitter, rose here and there, settling down at greater distances. All eyes were now fixed on the wood. It was obviously the next point and Sir Conyers thought the last point at which the passage of the Curlews could be disputed with any advantage to the northerns.

All believed that this wood was filled with Red Hugh's warriors, and that the battle would be fought amid its depths. It was August 14th, and here as elsewhere autumn was laying its fiery finger on the leaves, upon the mountain ash chiefly, a tree very common in primeval Irish woods—also the first which yields itself to autumnal painting.

Nor were Clifford's conjectures quite wrong, though too far from quite right. As Ratcliffe approached the wood, the still quiet groves of it became suddenly alive. From some half thousand matchlocks scattered along its edge, each gunman there posted well behind a protecting tree, tongues of fire flashed out through the leaves and scrub, bullets of lead and iron began to rain into Ratcliffe, and smoke concealed all greenery. Hoarse voices in Gaelic shouted words of command, for here was the MacDermot, with Red Hugh's 600 arquebus men, archers, and musketeers. The Battle of the Curlew Mountains had begun.

Forthwith Ratcliffe formed his column for attack, light troops forward, gallow-glasses behind, and plunged into the smoke regardless of the fast-flashing tongues and the raining bullets. This firing suddenly ceased. If there was any fighting it was mostly unseen and hand-to-hand amid the trees. I believe there was not much. As bold Ratcliffe and his men with a shout plunged into and through the wood, firing as they went, MacDermot and his men began to pour out at the other side.

Although the wood might have been successfully maintained had Red Hugh concentrated all his forces there in time, it was not maintainable by such strength as MacDermot had at his command. I may mention here casually that Boyle had been the capital of the Mac-

Dermot nation till fierce Bingham took it from them, and, the Queen being agreeable, conferred it upon himself, and that the Boyle monastery was a foundation of the same family. So MacDermot had in this war something to fight for beyond glory.

MacDermot, however, could not hold the wood. He fell back, he and his gunmen, retreating upon Brian Ogue, who also with his gallowglasses fell back northwards, and nearer to Red Hugh's camp, far enough, at least, not to subject themselves to any very deadly fire on the part of Ratcliffe's men, who now emerged, cheering, on the northern boulders of the same, probably sending thence a volley by way of military farewell into MacDermot's rear.

Ratcliffe had cleared out the *Bohar-buidhe* wood in fine style, opening up, so far, the passage of the Curlews. From the wood, which was half a mile in depth, the road still running northwards and Colloney-wards, now traversed another brown bog and, along this moving off leisurely and in good order, Ratcliffe saw MacDermot and the expelled gunmen retreating in the wake of Brian Ogue of the Battle-Axes with his small but formidable-looking cohort of mailed gallow-glasses trailing their long battle-axes.

Beaten so far were the northerns, but obviously not beaten to flight. Genial Homer would have pictured MacDermot and Brian Ogue as two raw-devouring lions beaten off from the cattle-fold, but retreating slowly, looking around and askance, not being at all terrified in their minds. . . .

As soon as Clifford learned that Red Hugh's people had been driven out of the wood and that the way was cleared, he despatched a messenger with orders to Markham . . . and the Queen's horse began to get under way. Meantime the invading army was traversing the dangerous *Bohar-buidhe* wood.

*   *   *   *   *

Savage and the rear-guard were probably still among the trees when the sound of fresh firing in front proved that Ratcliffe and the van were already engaged with the enemy, opening a mile or two more of the wild road through the Curlews. The army as it emerged from the wood observed the same order of advance, Ratcliffe with his gunmen and light troops still in the van.

The road now traversed another bog, bare, too, save that there was on the eastern side, that to Ratcliffe's right, another wood, lying rather further than a calyver's shot from the road. Upon this road MacDermot's men were still in view and also, as Ratcliffe soon perceived, deploying for fight, "not at all terrified in their minds."

The left wing of MacDermot's little army abutted on and was protected by the wood. His right leaned upon the hillside, for the road at
this point skirted the mountain. . . .

Ratcliffe also drew out his men and disposed them in fighting order.
There was no opportunity for maneuvering and nice feats of generalship. It was a fair and even duel between the gunmen of both armies.

MacDermot's men had the advantage of the ground, for they were
more inured to fighting in such an element than regular troops. Ratcliffe's, on the other hand, were superior in numbers, and furnished
probably with a better style of weapon. Moreover, MacDermot's 600
were not all gunmen. With them were interspersed bowmen, Scots for
the most part, Red Hugh's maternal kindred, and javelin-men who
hurled their spears exactly like the warriors of the Iliad, casting with
great force and accuracy to an extraordinary distance.

Remember, too, that Elizabethan firearms were very different towards ours. Good armor could resist the impact of their bullets and
their range was very short. So javelin-men, Homeric spear-casters
trained from childhood to the practice of the art, were of considerable
service when the opposing ranks came into some relative nearness.

Behind Ratcliffe's fast deploying men the rest of the Royalist army
stood "refused," waiting till he should disperse this obstruction and
clear the way once more. Immediately behind him was the first division
of the convoy, then the main battle under the President, then the
second convoy, after which Savage and the rear guard still struggling
through the *Bohar-buidhe* wood.

THE FIGHT ON THE BOG SIDE

Now began in right earnest the conflict which is called the Battle of
the Curlew Mountains. Many a battle had been fought upon this famous road as far back as the bright semi-fabulous epic of Queen Maeve,
and far beyond. By this road Ulster invaded Connacht, and Connacht,
Ulster. Here defenders had the advantage, and many a fierce conflict
had been fought and won upon these brown bogs.

*   *   *   *   *

The Royalist vanguard, now well deployed, soon settled down steadily to their warlike work—steadily, though the nature of the ground
was anything but favorable to straight shooting, and many a brave
soldier, as he leveled his piece, found it hard even to keep his feet in
the yielding soil. Under the eyes of the President and the whole army,
Ratcliffe's men deployed, took rank, and fired; loaded, advanced, and

fired again, ever advancing and ever firing, and the Tir-Conallians, despite their showers of arrows and spears, and the "thick volleys of red-flaming flashes" with which they responded, began to fall back, their steady ranks wavering, trembling, as it were, towards breakage and dispersion.

The men had not expected that they would be required to fight *a outrance* with Clifford's whole army now fast emerging from the wood, and getting into position behind their vanguard. They believed, and no doubt rightfully believed, that their commander's instructions had been to fight and fall back, and expected momentarily to hear the bugles sing retreat. But MacDermot perceived that his handful might even so, by determined valor, defeat and destroy all Clifford's army.

Could he but beat Ratcliffe, and the vanguard, and drive them back in confusion upon the convoy, and then double up the convoy and the vanguard together upon the battle, what might not happen on such obstructed ground to an army left bare of its horse and encumbered with its own weight?

At all events he saw this opportunity, and would not have the bugles sing retreat at all, but advance, if anything, and the war-pipes shriek only battle and onfall. Nothing loath, the pipers stepped out and played.

They were brave men, these pipers. The modern military band retires as its regiment goes into action. But the piper went on before his men and piped them into the thick of battle. He advanced, sounding his battle-pibroch, and stood in the ranks of war while men fell round him. Derrick in his *Image of Ireland,* about this date, gives a woodcut representing a battle. In the foreground of the Irish lies a slain figure reflecting little credit on the artist, but under which Derrick writes "pyper," well aware that the fall of the musician was an event second only to that of a considerable officer. So in the State Papers we often read such entries as this:

"Slew Hugh, son of Hugh, twenty-five of his men, and two pipers."

"Slew Art O'Connor and his piper."

An illegitimate brother of Black Thomas of Ormond gives a long list, name by name, of the rebels whom he slew. Divers pipers are specially mentioned, and in such a manner as to indicate that the slayer was particularly proud of such achievements.

So here upon the brown bog Red Hugh's pipers stood out beyond the men sounding wild and high the battle-pibrochs of the north with hearts and hands brave as any in the wild work, and the bugles sang only battle, rang battle, onfall, and victory in men's hearts and ears, and the awful music of the oaths outsang all other sounds, outpealed the buglecalls and battle-pibrochs, the thundering of the captains rose above the thundering of the guns.

Up and down, to and fro, ran these, adjuring and menacing, striking and heading back the runaways. Hither and thither with swords drawn ran the Irish officers, MacDermot, lord of the Curlews, and Red Hugh's foster-brother, McSweeny of the Battle-Axes, and the two O'Gallaghers, Eocha and Tully. To and fro, up and down the wavering ranks they rushed thundering abuse, protestations, and many a fierce Irish oath and curse; raising high the sacred name of Mary. *Mary,* and not *O'Donnell-a-boo* seems to have been the war-cry that day.

Behind the wavering gunmen stood the lowering mailed figure of the young Oxonian, Brian Ogue and his century and a half of ranked gallow-glasses, their long weapons leveled, not likely to show cowards any mercy. Silent and steady they stood to rear of all the battle clangor and confusion, a mass, though a small one, of valor educated and trained to the point of perfection; clad in complete steel, ready to go on or go back at a word from their young chieftain, not at all ready to lose rank in either movement—flower of the Brennymen, "very great scorners of death."

And again rearward upon some eminence stood Red Hugh. If we could only contrive to see him, with his blue flashing eyes and notoriously fiery locks escaped from the helmet and falling on his mailed shoulders, his countenance which "no one could see without loving," not now soft, bright, and amiable, as the "Four Masters" beheld it when they were boys, but stern and minatory. Somewhere far off stood Red Hugh with his brothers, brave Rory, afterwards Earl, one of the two who made the Flight of the Earls and closed a great chapter of Irish history; and Manus, the well-beloved, who was to die at home in Tir-Connall, slain by the hand of his own rough cousin *Nial Garv;* and *Cath-Barr,* "Top of Battle," youngest of the famous four.

THE ROLE OF THE BARDS

Then near at hand, just in the rear of the fighting men, rode O'Rourke's bard, and MacDermot's, and Red Hugh's, as close as they might go to the field of battle, noting who were the brave and who the recreant. The public entertain a very false notion of the medieval bard. They picture him as an old, bent man, with flowing white beard, sad, bowed down in spirit, but flashing up under the influence of liquor and the spell of poetic rage, a humble wight receiving gifts which were a sort of alms. Such is our modern romantic conception of the bard.

The real bard was a high-spirited, proud, and even wealthy man, chief of a sept, and lord of extensive estates, holding the same by right and not by grace. He had men of war to wait on him, though he himself wore no arms, for fighting was not his function but the causing of others to fight well. He carried no harp, and no orphan boy carried one for him, and though he made poems and knew poems by the hundred, he was no reciter. He went to the wars as an observer and watcher, and men feared him. Somewhere, I say, in the neighborhood of the battle, such bards, mounted on fleet steeds, watched the progress of the fray, noting who were the heroes and who the poltroons.

And still in the brown bog the captains thundered and the bugles rang battle, and the banners waved defiance and advance, the war-pipes sounding their shrillest and maddest, the brave pipers standing out well in advance of the fighters. Again, through the hearts of the wavering Tir-Connallians the fading battle-fire blazed out anew; again, with firm mien and unbroken ranks, they stood steady to their war-work and hurled their rain of spears and arrows, and leveled and fired their "perfectly straight and straight-aiming guns" upon the advancing Royalists.

MacDermot's Breaks the Battle on the Queen's Host

Once again Red Hugh's men stood steady and unwavering under the Royalist fire, returning the same and with interest. The Royalists had a long and wet march, and were not in such good condition as Red Hugh's fresh and well-breakfasted troops. Now in their turn, they, too, began to slack fire, to waver in their ranks, and finally to retreat upon the pike men, probably throwing them, too, into disorder. The Tir-Connallians pressing forward began to rain their bullets into the dense ranks of the Queen's gallow-glasses of the first division, who had neither cavalry nor musketeers to sweep back their assailants. So the latter at their ease poured volley after volley upon the resisting mass.

Ratcliffe, seeing that his gunmen were now beaten past the rally, sought to organize a charge of his gallow-glasses, crying loudly that he would head the charge himself, calling all true men to follow, and even summoning individuals by name out of the wavering and confused ranks. Meantime Red Hugh's "fulminators" were pouring into the struggling crowd out of which Ratcliffe sought to disengage the braver elements and fashion a forelorn hope.

Having in some sort compassed his purpose, though already suffering from a shot in the face, he was leading them on "with unconquerable resolution" when his leg was broken by a gun-shot which called him to a sudden halt. So while the blood of his first wound ran down his face, stood Ratcliffe supported in the arms of two of his officers, and in this situation roared to Henry Cosby who seems to have been next in command, directing him to lead the charge, but perceiving him slack and as he was being withdrawn out of fire, he called anew to his lieutenant: "I see, Cosby, that I must leave thee to thy baseness, but will tell thee ere I go that it were better for thee to die in the hands of thy countrymen than at my return to perish by my sword."

But Cosby went not on. He was son of Francis Cosby of Stradbally Hall in O'More's country, Cosby of the decorated tree and brother of Alexander (as it was surmised) so cleverly dodged the wild cutting and slashing of Rory Ogue by using his comrade as a shield. Cosby came not on but the Tir-Connallians did. They drew close, archers, cross-bowmen, casters, and gunmen, ranked before this jammed mob of soldiers, and slaughtered at their leisure, while flaming Ratcliffe was being carried to the rear, and cowardly Cosby "showed slackness" in leading the forlorn group which his brave commander had disengaged and fashioned out of the clubbed vanguard.

THE BRENNY MEN LET LOOSE

This was the moment for a cavalry charge, which, under such conditions, would have cut the vanguard to ribbons. But cavalry there were none on either side. Neither Clifford nor Red Hugh would trust their precious cavalry in these bogs and obstructions. But in the rear of MacDermot's men there was something as good, better in such ground as this. Here in shiny ranks stood O'Rourke's Brenny men standing at their ease watching the fray, waiting for one word from their chief. At last the word came, literally a word. Brian Ogue, in tones not familiar to the class-rooms of Oxford, shouted *Farragh*.

"Farragh," he cried now, not Ferio, and like hounds slipped from the leash, O'Rourke's Brenny men went upon the Queen's vanguard. Only 160, but mailed gallow-glasses, picked men and strong, the flower of Breffney, all in rank perfectly fresh, eager as hounds certain of victory. MacDermot's gunmen and archers gave way to the right hand and to the left, opening out like folding-doors as the Brenny men, with a shout which at such an instant changed fortitude to alarm and alarm to panic terror, went upon the foe.

The battle harvest was ripe and these were the reapers; ripened, if I may say so, by that rain of darts and spears and that heat of "red-flaming flashes" and fiery balls of lead. Guess how coward Cosby, who showed slackness in charging the gunmen, met this forward-sweeping wave of steel, with its crest of glittering axes. Cosby and his forlorn men quickly fell back as if there were any hope in demoralized numbers, terrified yet more by the retreat of the only corps which still showed some rudiments of formation.

The vanguard was hopelessly clubbed, gunmen and halberdiers inextricably tangled. Nor at this juncture had they a leader to disentwine the tangle and pull the lines straight and distinct. The vanguard was captainless, reduced to that state by Ratcliffe's broken leg and Cosby's lily heart. Brave men, surely abundant enough even now in this wild moment, had no chance, mobbed, overborne by the cowards unable to find each other out in the press and stand together disengaged from the ruck. What chance ever have the brave left captainless—what fate but to be trampled down by the fools and cowards?

Had that random bullet but spared their captain's shank-bone things might have been so different. Were he at this moment to return as he had promised, run his blade through Cosby for a swift and salutary beginning, he, standing clear of the chaos, would have gathered all these to himself, crying to them in general and calling men by their names. . . .

To left and right MacDermot and his gunmen opened out like double-doors unfolding as Brian Ogue went into the Queen's vanguard. To right and left they opened and now poured in their fire transversely on either flank of the struggling mass, while in front Brian Ogue and his reapers fell to the despatch of their red work. A moment the raised axes, razor-sharp and bright, glistened in the sun, and then fell ringing with dry clangor or more horribly silent, rising not so bright, rising and falling like lightning, such a war harvest to be reaped, such battle-fury in men's hearts, and such an opportunity!

And on the flanks MacDermot volleyed transversely, and soon his spear-hurlers clutched sword and fell on, and the gunmen slung by the slow calyver, gripped swordhilt and did likewise.

Not long the struggle under such conditions. Back rolled the vanguard, back where Clifford was ranking his men and making his dispositions, seeing how matters went in front. Back rolled the vanguard effusing afar their own panic, back in the first instance on the forward convoy. Here the peasant drivers cut their wagon traces, mounted, and ran, and the trains of mules and pack-horses stampeded, and amid this confusion the flying vanguard tumbled into, through and over the battle, while brave Clifford did all that man could do to stem the raging storm, and MacDermot's prophetic soul was justified by the event. He had doubled back the vanguard and the first convoy upon the battle. And the battle, too, was broken and rolled back on the second convoy and the rear guard.

CLIFFORD'S HEROIC DEATH

At this moment a cry arose: "The President is dead!" The President had gone down in the midst of the raging flood but he was not killed. His horse was shot, and he had fallen. He was soon on his feet again roaring commands and encouragements to his own men, so far as they were still rational beings, endeavoring in vain to restore the fight, commanding, entreating, doing all that a brave man could do. "There had not come of the English into Ireland in the latter days a better man."

Seeing the day utterly lost, two of his Irish officers, the lieutenant of Captain Burke, name not given, and Sir Miler McSweeney urged him to leave the field.

Overcome with wrath and shame, he declared, Roman-like, that he would not overlive that day's ignominy. But that affection which moved Sir Miler McSweeny to use entreaties persuaded him now to practice force, by which they carried him from the pursuing rebels some few paces, when enraged by the wildness of his men, he broke from them in a fury, and made head to the whole troop of pursuers, in the midst of whom he was when struck through the body with a bullet. He died fighting, consecrating by an admirable resolution the memory of his name to immortality.

Yet even after Clifford's death, his division, or parts of it, rallied and fought on. Savage and the rear-guard managed to keep their ranks while the roaring deluge of flight and panic terror raged past them. There was tough fighting, or, at all events, resistance of some sort, after the fall of Clifford, and before the best materials of the Queen's host gave way utterly, and the rout became universal.

Savage, I feel sure, played a brave part; I should be much surprised if he did not, for gallantry was in his blood. Four centuries had elapsed since the founder of the clan Savage marched from Dublin with the great John de Courcy and a handful of Norman knights and archers to the conquest of Ulster, and did conquer Ulster.

* * * * *

Savage, surely, like Clifford and Ratcliffe, did his best to save the battle, but at last all broke and fled. Brian Ogue's battle-axes going like smith's hammers or the flails of thrashing men on their rear and MacDermot volleying from right to left, and all solid companies getting broken up and swept away by the torrents of panic-stricken humanity.

So at last the whole of the Queen's host was reduced to chaos, stream-ing madly away, and the Battle of the Curlew Mountains was fought and lost and won. On rushed the fugitives, disappearing not too rapidly within that half mile of autumnal forest. The road was choked with baggage wagons, provisions, camp furniture, impediments of various kinds, and the running mass of men collided and jostled against each other and the trees, as the Royalists retraveled these primeval soliti-tudes, while battle-axe and sword and calyver and pistol played ever on their rear.

MARKHAM STRIKES IN WITH THE QUEEN'S HORSEMEN

As the runaways emerged from the southern fringes of the forest, a sight was presented fit to recall a sense of shame and obedience to their captains to the minds of men not utterly frenzied and unmanned by fear. Before them if they could see anything for fright lay the great brown bog threaded by its narrow white road gorse-fringed, and on the road the clear midday sunlight glancing from bright morions and armor, the Earl of Southampton's horses advancing under the com-mand of Sir Griffin Markham; quietly, leisurely, following Sir Conyers under full belief that the passage of the Curlews had been forced, riding four or five abreast along the road wound through the great bog that intervened between the wood and the "barricado with double flanks."

What a spectacle for their brave commander when the wood sud-denly began to spout its rills and torrents of wild runaways, kerne, gallow-glasses, musketeers, common soldiers and officers tumbling out thence in every direction, falling into peat-holes, and rising and run-ning, the better part without weapons, many tearing off and flinging away their armor as they ran.

Markham, a brave man who had a head for war and also an eye in his head, at a glance took in the situation and decided swiftly on his course. When he first witnessed this extraordinary spectacle far out in front at the other side of the great bog, *viz.*, the green wood vomiting at a hundred points the whole Royalist army which was to have con-quered North Connacht, he was not far from that "barricado with the double flanks," and advancing along the main road which served so much, stretching across the bog like a bent bow. But besides this wheel-way there was, as formerly mentioned, another way more direct.

It was a mere continuity of moderately firm ground, rocky and furze-strewn, solid enough for his purpose, which fell in with the main road at this side of the wood. Quickly taking in the situation, he advanced

as well as he could, and as swiftly, along this rough short-cut by which
the panic-stricken army did not run, and which was open to his use.
They, poor wretches, for the most part, poured along and on both sides
of the main road.

So avoiding that shameful torrent of wild humanity, he and his
dragoons by this short-cut struck in upon the main road behind them,
between the runaways and the pursuers. Here Markham formed his
men on the road and on both sides of it, the ground being firm enough,
and charged MacDermot and his gunmen, now disordered in pursuit;
charged them, and also broke them, cutting them down in all directions or driving them into the wood and far out into the wetnesses of
the bog.

Now was the time for Captain Burke, Sir Miler McSweeny or some
other brave and competent officer to take charge of that roaring flood
of ruin, and reorder such of its elements as were not utterly demoralized; for the pursuit was stayed, and the pursuers in their turn overthrown by brave Markham and the cavalry.

COUNTER-CHARGE BY BRIAN OGUE

Markham's spirited charge gave the opportunity of converting the
rout into a victory. MacDermot and his gunmen were now shattered
and dispersed, driven out into the bog on both sides of that firm
ground where Markham had charged. But now while the Royalist
dragoons rushed along, sabring and spearing, their ranks quite disordered in pursuit, and while some stood firing pistol shots at the gunmen out in the bog, Markham and his horse came full tilt upon a new
and unexpected foe.

From the wood emerged Brian Ogue with his century and a half of
heavy-armed foot, steady, ranked, in perfect order. Fearing the event,
Brian Ogue kept his gallow-glasses well in hand, and here, following
with slow deliberate foot in the rear of the kerne, emerged to sight.
From the green forest came to sudden view that formidable phalanx,
their shining battle-axes now dull enough.

The Royalist horse were now charged in front by Brian Ogue, while
MacDermot's gunmen closing in from the bog fired transversely
through their ranks on each side. Markham and the horse could not
win the battle alone. Then as now, horse were no match for foot that
would keep their ranks and decline to be frightened by mere show and
glitter.

Charged by Brian Ogue, Markham could not stand the impact of
the Brenny men. Down tumbled horses and their riders to the cleaving

of Brian Ogue's battle-axes. Markham, too, was utterly routed, so routed that he lost "all his pennons and guidons." Brian Ogue handled the Queen's horsemen that day better than I think he ever handled Lily's irregular Latin verbs at Oxford.

There was another Oxford man, but of the Queen's Irish in this battle, Richard Burke, Lord Dunkellin, chief designate of the High Burkes. Brian Ogue in this melee received two wounds, one in the hand and another in the leg. Markham did not escape without receiving some tokens. He had the small bone of his right arm broken with the stroke of a bullet and his clothes torn by another.

So the cavalry, too, broke and fled, following the fugitives, and again the flood of flight and chase rolled down the slopes of the Curlews. The guard so prudently placed at the barricado participated in the disgraceful rout, which was perhaps the most remarkable example of cowardice in this whole shameful business.

They were 160 in number and might have held the pass for hours against any army unprovided with artillery. Clifford had not destroyed the barricade, but merely opened a passage through it. The gap was narrow enough for defense and not wide enough for the torrent of ruin which now sought to pour through. Some wiser than the rest climbed over the rampart and the bristling palisades. Most of the fugitives rushed at the open passage and blocked it. But for the relief afforded by Markham there would have been an awful slaughter here.

Of the beaten army the Meath Irish fared worst. The great mass of the army were Connacht Irish, who were well acquainted with the Curlews and knew good paths over the bogs and through the hills. Many of their officers and lords had, I suppose, been often here hawking. The Meath Irish knew nothing of the country, and so thought of nothing save of rushing straight along by the way they came. The few English soldiers here shared their fate. They were certainly few.

* * * * *

These timber barriers which the Royalists had passed so joyfully that morning proved now an obstacle to their flight. Here those who still kept their weapons flung them away, and here also quantities of clothes and armor were found. The pursuers consisted only of 600 fulminators, now reduced to less than 400, and Brian Ogue's century and a half of gallow-glasses. But resistance was never thought of.

From the mountains the mingled flood of chase and panic-flight rolled on towards the town of Boyle, execution never ceasing, for Sir Griffin seems not to have been able again to get his cavalry in order.

Through the gates of Boyle it poured, and kept pouring, till the gates had to be closed against the foe.

Red Hugh's lieutenants and their warriors encamped that night under or not far from the walls, and one of the most remarkable battles recorded in Irish history came to an end. In war there is a great deal of luck, and we may observe, too, that scratch armies are admirably fitted for the losing of battles.

Here were Meathian Irish and Connacht Irish—men one might almost describe, such was the disjointed state of the land, as of different nationalities; here veterans of the army of Essex, and soldiers drawn from the garrisons; here, finally, were English soldiers mixed with Irish, and the Irish for the most part not regulars, only the rising-out of Meath and Connacht, that is to say, the local gentry and their followings. Yet the little band of conquerors was a scratch army, too, so from any point of view it must be accounted a most glorious victory.

The battle was won by 600 musketeers and archers, and a company of Brenneian gallow-glasses. A very remarkable battle in every way; lost to the Crown seemingly through the cowardice of the Royalist vanguard, or, shall we say, of Henry Cosby, who, we may hope, got well killed. In this battle were slain of the Royalists one thousand four hundred, no quarter being given. MacDermot and Brian Ogue lost in killed and wounded only 240 men. The baggage, standards, etc., and nearly all the arms of the invading army fell into the hands of the conquerors.

When in reading English history we perceive the intense wrath felt in London against the Earl of Essex and his conduct of the Irish wars, we must remember the sense of imperial humiliation which was felt at a defeat such as the foregoing sustained under his government. The Nine Years' War is throughout a wonder, miraculous everywhere. From beginning to end the insurgent lords lost only one battle, the Battle of Kinsale. Yet they were beaten!

CLIFFORD DECAPITATED

Brian Ogue, as stated, received two bullet wounds during his victorious tussle with Markham and the horse. He rode or was borne in a litter homewards to the camp along that corpse-strewn road. His scratches don't seem to have troubled him much. He paused as he went, scrutinizing with deliberation the bodies of those who by their superior armor seemed men of rank, and which were exhibited to him as he passed. Amongst them he was shown the familiar features of Sir Conyers Clifford, President of Connacht.

He knew him well. He had been to visit him on his first coming into his presidentiad, and had only been prevented from allying himself and his Breffneian nation with the Queen's cause by the stern menacing attitude towards him by Red Hugh. He ordered his attendants to behead Clifford, and sent the head forward as a trophy and a token to Red Hugh. The decapitation of slain foes was a universal custom of the age. Had Brian Ogue fallen, Clifford would have decapitated him.

Among the rows of heads which adorned the battlements of Dublin Castle at this moment was the tarred head of Brian Ogue's own father, the brave proud Brian na Murtha. Clifford's head was forwarded to Red Hugh in the north; his body was conveyed south to MacDermot, to the Castle of Gaywash, hard by Boyle, where McDermot and his army were now encamped.

I like Brian Ogue and am sorry, custom or no custom, that he ordered the decapitation of Clifford. My regret has been anticipated by the "Four Masters."

Red Hugh sent a swift detachment of horse with Clifford's head to Collooney, to Nial Garv, his cousin in command there. Nial Garv, demanding a parley with the defenders of the Castle, informed Sir Donough of the defeat of the Royalists, and in proof of the statement exhibited the head of the slain general. That was enough. Sir Donough gave up Collooney, himself and its defenders as prisoners without demanding terms, for his condition was desperate.

Shortly after Red Hugh himself appeared upon the scene, and held a long colloquy with his captive. The result of the conference was that Sir Donough undertook to transfer his allegiance from the Queen to Red Hugh, and to hold all Sligo from him on the same terms that his ancestors used to hold it from Red Hugh's ancestors. Hugh reinvested him in the lordship of Sligo, presented him with horses, cattle, sheep, and ploughs and all manner of farm instruments, and even with a population, so that in a short time the wasted land became once again an inhabited, industrious, and well-settled principality.

The Disastrous Battle of Kinsale

There now appear before us two remarkable men whose names are prominently identified with this memorable epoch in Irish history—

From *The Story of Ireland,* by A. M. Sullivan, pp. 278-285. M. H. Gill & Son, Ltd. Dublin. 1905.

Mountjoy, the new lord deputy; and Carew, the new lord president of Munster. In the hour in which these men were appointed to the conduct of affairs in Ireland, the Irish cause was lost. Immense resources were placed at their disposal, new levies and armaments were ordered; and again all the might of England by land and sea was to be put forth against Ireland. But Mountjoy and Carew alone were worth all the levies. They were men of indomitable energy, masters of subtlety, craft, and cunning, utterly unscrupulous as to the employment of means to an end; cold-blooded, callous, cruel, and brutal. Norreys and Bagnal were soldiers—able generals, illustrious in the field. Essex was a lordly courtier, vain and pomp-loving. Of these men—soldier and courtier—the Irish annals speak as of fair foes. But of Mountjoy and Carew a different memory is kept in Ireland. They did their work by the wile of the serpent, not by the skill of the soldier. Where the brave and manly Norreys tried the sword, they tried snares, treachery, and deceit, gold, flattery, promises, temptation, and seduction in every shape. To split up the confederation of chiefs was an end towards which they steadily laboured by means the most subtle and crafty that human ingenuity could devise. Letters, for instance, were forged purporting to have been written secretly to the lord deputy by the Earl of Desmond, offering to betray one of his fellow confederates, O'Connor. These forgeries were "disclosed," as it were, to O'Connor, with an offer that he should "forestall" the earl, by seizing and giving up the latter to the government, for which, moreover, he was to have a thousand pounds in hand, besides other considerations promised. The plot succeeded. O'Connor betrayed the earl and handed him over a prisoner to the lord deputy, and of course going over himself as an ally also. This rent worked the dismemberment of the league in the south. Worse defections followed soon after; defections unaccountable, and, indeed, irretrievable. Art O'Neill and Nial Garv O'Donnell, under the operation of mysterious influences, went over to the English, and in all the subsequent events, were more active and effective than any other commanders on the queen's side! Nial Garv alone was worth a host. He was one of the ablest generals in the Irish camp. His treason fell upon the national leaders like a thunderbolt. This was the sort of "campaigning" on which Mountjoy relied most. Time and money were freely devoted to it, and not in vain. After the national confederation had been sufficiently split up and weakened in this way—and when, north and south, the defecting chiefs were able of themselves to afford stiff employment for the national forces, the lord deputy took the field.

In the struggle that now ensued O'Neill and O'Donnell presented one of those spectacles which, according to the language of the heathen classics, move gods and men to sympathy and admiration. Hearts less brave might despair; but *they,* like Leonidas and the immortal Three Hundred, would fight out the battle of country while life remained. The English now had in any one province a force superior to the entire strength of the national army. The eventful campaign of 1601, we are told, was fought out in almost every part of the kingdom. To hold the coast lines on the north—where Dowcra had landed (at Derry) four thousand foot and four hundred horse—was the task of O'Donnell; while to defend the southern Ulster frontier was the peculiar charge of O'Neill. "They thus," says the historian, "fought as it were back to back against the opposite lines of attack." Through all the spring and summer months that fight went on. From hill to valley, from pass to plain, all over the island, it was one roll of cannon and musketry, one ceaseless and universal engagement; the smoke of battle never lifted off the scene. The two Hughs were all but ubiquitous; confronting and defeating an attack to-day at one point; falling upon the foes next day at another far distant from the scene of the last encounter! Between the two chiefs the most touching confidence and devoted affection subsisted. Let the roar of battle crash how it might on the northern horizon, O'Neill relied that all was well, for O'Donnell was at his post. No matter what myriads of foes were massing in the south, it was enough for O'Donnell to know that O'Neill was there. "Back to back," indeed, as many a brave battle against desperate odds has been fought, they maintained the unequal combat, giving blow for blow, and so far holding their ground right nobly. By September, except in Munster, comparatively little had been gained by the English beyond the successful planting of some further garrisons; but the Irish were considerably exhausted, and sorely needed rest and recruitment. At this juncture came the exciting news that—at length!—a powerful auxiliary force from Spain had landed at Kinsale. The Anglo-Irish privy council were startled by the news while assembled in deliberation at Kilkenny. Instantly they ordered a concentration of all their available forces in the south, and resolved upon a winter campaign. They acted with a vigour and determination which plainly showed their conviction that on the quick crushing of the Spanish force hung the fate of their cause in Ireland. A powerful fleet was sent round the coast, and soon blockaded Kinsale; while on the land side it was invested by a force of some fifteen thousand men.

This Spanish expedition, meant to aid, effected the ruin of the Irish cause. It consisted of little more than three thousand men, with a good supply of stores, arms, and ammunition. In all his letters to Spain, O'Neill is said to have strongly urged that if a force under five thousand men came, it should land in *Ulster,* where it would be morally and materially worth ten thousand landed elsewhere; but that if Munster was to be the point of debarkation, anything less than eight or ten thousand men would be useless. The meaning of this is easily discerned. The south was the strong ground of the English, as the north was of the Irish side. A force landed in Munster should be able of itself to cope with the strong opposition which it was sure to encounter. These facts were not altogether lost sight of in Spain. The expedition as fitted out consisted of six thousand men; but various mishaps and disappointments reduced it to half the number by the time it landed at Kinsale. Worse than all, the wrong man commanded it: Don Juan D'Aquilla, a good soldier, but utterly unsuited for an enterprise like this. He was proud, dour-tempered, hasty, and irascible. He had heard nothing of the defections and disasters in the south. The seizure of Desmond and the ensnaring of Florence McCarthy—the latter the most influential and powerful of the southern nobles and chiefs—had paralyzed everything there; and Don Juan, instead of finding himself in the midst of friends in arms, found himself surrounded by foes on land and sea. He gave way to his natural ill-temper in reproaches and complaints; and in letters to O'Neill, bitterly demanded whether he and the other confederates meant to hasten to his relief. For O'Neill and O'Donnell, with their exhausted and weakened troops, to abandon the north and undertake a winter march southward was plain destruction. At least it staked *everything* on the single issue of success or defeat before Kinsale; and to prevent defeat and to insure success there, much greater organization for cooperation and concert, and much more careful preparation, were needed than was possible now, hurried southward in this way by D'Aquilla. Nevertheless, there was nothing else for it. O'Neill clearly discerned that the crafty and politic Carew had been insidiously working on the Spanish commander, to disgust him with the enterprise, and induce him to sail homeward on liberal terms. And it was so. Don Juan, it is said, agreed, or intimated that if, within a given time, an Irish army did not appear to his relief, he would treat with Carew for terms. If it was, therefore, probably disaster for O'Neill to proceed to the south, it was certain ruin for him to refuse; so with heavy hearts the northern chieftains set out on their winter march for Munster, at the head of their thinned and wasted troops. O'Donnell, with his habitual ardour, was first on the way. He was joined by Felim O'Doherty, MacSwiney-na-Tuath, O'Boyle, O'Rorke, the brother of O'Connor Sligo, the O'Connor Roe, Mac Dermott, O'Kelly, and others; mustering in all about two thousand five hundred men. O'Neill, with MacDonnell of Antrim, MacGinnis of Down, Mac-

Mahon of Monaghan, and others, marched southward at the head of between three and four thousand men. Holy Cross was the point where both their forces appointed to effect their junction. O'Donnell was first at the rendezvous. A desperate effort on the part of Carew to intercept and overwhelm him before O'Neill could come up was defeated only by a sudden night-march of *nearly forty miles* by Red Hugh. O'Neill reached Belgooley, within sight of Kinsale, on the 21st December.

In Munster, in the face of all odds—amidst the wreck of the national confederacy, and in the presence of an overwhelming army of occupation—a few chiefs there were, undismayed and unfaltering, who rallied faithfully at the call of duty. Foremost amongst them was Donal O'Sullivan, Lord of Beare, a man in whose fidelity, intrepidity, and military ability, O'Neill appears to have reposed unbounded confidence. In all the south, the historian tells, "only O'Sullivan Beare, O'Driscoll, and O'Connor Kerry declared openly for the national cause" in this momentous crisis. Some of the missing ships of the Spanish expedition reached Castlehaven in November, just as O'Donnell, who had made a detour westward, reached that place. Some of this Spanish contingent were detailed as garrisons for the forts of Dunboy, Baltimore, and Castlehaven, commanding three of the best havens in Munster. The rest joined O'Donnell's division, and which soon sat down before Kinsale.

When O'Neill came up, his master-mind at once scanned the whole position, and quickly discerned the true policy to be pursued. The English force was utterly failing in commisariat arrangements; and disease as well as hunger was committing rapid havoc in the besiegers' camp. O'Neill accordingly resolved to *beseige the beseigers* to increase their difficulties in obtaining provision or provender, and so cut up their lines of communication. These tactics manifestly offered every advantage to the Irish and allied forces, and were certain to work the destruction of Carew's army. But the testy Don Juan could not brook this slow and cautious mode of procedure. "The Spaniards only felt their own inconveniences; they were cut off by the sea by a powerful English fleet, and," continued the historian, "Carew was already practising indirectly to their commander his 'wit and cunning' in the fabrication of rumours and the forging of letters. Don Juan wrote urgent appeals to the northern chiefs to attack the English lines without another day's delay; and a council of war of the Irish camp, on the third day after their arrival at Belgooley, decided that the attack should be made on the morrow." At this council, so strongly and vehemently was O'Neill opposed to the mad and foolish policy of risking an engagement which, nevertheless, O'Donnell, ever impetuous, as violently sup-

ported, that for the first time the two friends were angrily at issue, and
some writers even allege that on this occasion question was raised between them as to who should assume commander-in-chief on the morrow. However this may have been, it is certain that once the vote of
the council was taken, and the decision found to be against him,
O'Neill loyally acquiesced in it, and prepared to do his duty.

On the night of the 2nd January (new style)—24th December old
style, in use among the English—the Irish army left their camp in
three divisions; the vanguard led by Tyrrell, the centre by O'Neill,
and the rear by O'Donnell. The night was stormy and dark, with continuous peals and flashes of thunder and lightning. The guides lost
their way, and the march, which even by the most circuitous route
ought not to have exceeded four or five miles, was protracted through
the whole night. At dawn of day, O'Neill, with whom were O'Sullivan
and Campo, came in sight of the English lines, and to his infinite
surprise found the men under arms, the cavalry in troops posted in
advance of their quarters. O'Donnell's division was still to come up,
and the veteran earl now found himself in the same dilemma into
which Bagnal had fallen at the Yellow Ford. His embarrassment was
perceived from the English camp; the cavalry were at once ordered to
advance. For an hour O'Neill maintained his ground alone; at the end
of that time he was forced to retire. Of Campo's 300 Spaniards, 40
survivors were with their gallant leader taken prisoners; O'Donnell at
length arrived and drove back a wing of the English cavalry; Tyrrell's
horsemen also held their ground tenaciously. But the rout of the
centre proved irremediable. Fully 1,200 of the Irish were left dead on
the field, and every prisoner taken was instantly executed. On the
English side fell Sir Richard Graeme; Captains Danvers and Go-
dolphin with several others, were wounded; their total loss they stated
at two hundred, and the Anglo-Irish, of whom they seldom made count
in their reports, must have lost in proportion. The earls of Thomond
and Clanricarde were actively engaged with their followers, and their
loss could hardly have been less than that of the English regulars.

On the night following their defeat, the Irish leaders held council
together at Innishannon, on the river Bandon, where it was agreed that
O'Donnell should instantly take shipping for Spain to lay the true
state of the contest before Philip the Third; that O'Sullivan should
endeavor to hold his castle of Dunboy, as commanding a most important harbour; that Rory O'Donnell, second brother of Hugh Roe,
should act as chieftain of Tyrconnell, and that O'Neill should return
into Ulster to make the best defence in his power. The loss in men was

not irreparable; the loss in arms, colours, and reputation, was more painful to bear, and far more difficult to retrieve.

Irish War-Cries

There was no more effective incentive to noble effort and heroic endeavor than the various war-cries or battle slogans of Irish chiefs and clans. High above the din of battle, the wild and often fierce shouts of defiance from lusty lungs carried far more terror to the enemy than the rudest shock of arms, and inspired more courage and valiant endeavor than even the greatest leader's personality could hope to inspire. The simplest and principal of these war-cries in ancient Erin was that of *Faire, Faire,* signifying "to watch," or "be on your guard," literally to "look out," as modern parlance expresses it. This was, in a sense, a precautionary signal, yet from this word *Faire* (commonly written Farrah), the modern exclamation "Hurrah" is supposed to have been derived. Another and more general cry was *a buaidh,* signifying "to the victory." This cry is invariably written *aboo,* a phonetic rendering of the original Gaelic phrase. The latter phrase was added to the name of the chief, the tribe, or the clan in the following manner: O'Neill *abu* (the battlecry of the immediate followers of the O'Neill); *Clann conail abu* (the tribe name of the septs, of which the O'Canainains, O'Mulroys, and, later, the O'Donnells were chiefs). The phrase *abu* or *a buaidh* is very commonly and incorrectly rendered in English "for ever." The phrase *go brath* is capable of such a translation, but not *abu;* which means "to victory." This practice gained an extraordinary impetus at the time of the Crusades throughout the then civilized world, the English, French, and Spanish nations adopting it. Its spread became eventually universal; and the battlecry has been perpetuated to the present day. Napier, in his *History of the Peninsular War,* says: "Nothing so startled the French soldiery as the wild yell [*fag an bealach,* "clear the way"] with which the Irish soldier sprang to the charge."

Historic Fontenoy furnishes a striking instance of the inspiring effect of the war-cry. The Irish brigade under command of O'Brien (Lord Clare) ordered as a forlorn hope by Marshal Saxe to save what seemed to him almost certain and disastrous defeat, rushed at their foes with the cry, *Cuimhnidh ar Luimneach, agus ar Fheille na Sacsanach*

From *The Gael,* March, 1899, pp. 11-12. New York.

("Remember Limerick, and Saxon Faith"), utterly routing the allied forces of English, Dutch, Hanoverian, and Austrians under Cumberland.

Heraldry has done much to perpetuate these old war-cries in the form of "mottoes" appended on ribbons and affixed to the blazon of arms. In these cries is found the origin of the use of such mottoes, which are an elaboration of the original war-cry.

The following will serve as illustration:

O'Beirne, chief of Hy-Birn, county Roscommon: Use the motto adopted by the O'Beirne of Spain, *Fuimus*: "We have been."

O'Breen, chief of Luigne or Leyney, county Westmeath: *Comhrac an ceart!* "Fight for the right."

O'Brien, Munster's ancient kings: *Lamh laidir a-n uachdar,* "The strong hand uppermost." This is also borne by the O'Kennedys, the senior branch of the sept.

Burke, or De Burgo: The followers of Richard de Burgo, or Burke, second Earl of Ulster, adopted the Irish language, customs, and dress, and, following the Irish custom (because he was red-haired), styled their chief *Ricard earla ruadh,* or "Richard the Red Earl." Their war-cry was *Gall ruadh abu!* "The red stranger to victory."

MacCartan, chiefs of Kinelarty, county Down: *Buailim-se,* "I strike."

MacCarthy, Prince of Desmond, whose battlecry was *Lamh laidir abu,* "The strong hand to victory." The MacCarthy Reagh and other branches of the family also use this on their arms as a motto. The Latin motto, *Fortis, ferox et celer,* "Strong, fierce and swift," is also used, and that of *Forti et fideli nihil difficile,* "Nothing is difficult to the strong and faithful."

MacCoghlan, Lords of Delvin, King's county: *Ceart na suas,* "Justice, not urbanity."

O'Concannon, chiefs of Hy-Diarmada in ancient Connaught: *Conn gan on,* "Wisdom without guile."

O'Connell, chief in Kerry: *Ciall agus neart,* "By reason and strength."

O'Connor, kings of Connaught: *O Dhia! gach an cathair,* "Oh! God to each [of us] a fortress."

Dayton-Fitzgerald: *Shanet abu!* "Shanet to victory." This was the war-cry of the "Desmond" Fitzgeralds, and is borne as a motto by the families of Vesey-Fitzgerald, Foster-Vesey-Fitzgerald, Fitzgerald of Kilcourcy and of Adelphi, county Clare, and other branches; whilst those of the "Geraldine" of Leinster-Fitzgeralds and its offshoots invariably use the war-cry *Crom abu!* "Crom to Victory!" Crom castle was an ancient stronghold of the Fitzgerald family in Limerick.

O'Doherty, lords of Innishowen, county Donegal: *Ar-n-duthchas,* "For our [birthplace] inheritance."

O'Donnell, princes of Tir Conail: Their war-cry was *O'Dombhnaill abu!* "O'Donnell to victory!" The motto borne with arms is *In hoc signo vinces,* "In this sign, conquer." Also borne by the O'Donnells of Spain and Austria.

O'Donovan, lords of Clann Cahill, county Limerick: *Giolla ar n-Namhuid abu!* "Servant of our enemy to victory!" *i.e.,* a successful fighter. The motto *Vir super hostem* ("A man above an enemy," *i.e.,* generous to foes) is sometimes used on arms.

O'Dunne, chiefs of Hy-Riagain, Queen's county: *Mullach Eireann abu!* "The summit of Erin to victory!" A cry adopted from top or summit of Slieve Bloom Mountains (Ard Eireann), on the borders of King's and Queen's counties, and lying in the ancient possessions of the O'Dunnes.

O'Farrell, princes of Annally: *Bhris me mo ghreim,* "Active am I in my task," in allusion to crest.

Fitzpatrick, or MacGiolla Padraig, princes of Ossory: *Ceart laidir abu!* "Right is strong in victory."

Fleming, Lord Slane, a title now abeyant: *Bhear na righ gan,* "May the King live forever." A relic of Jacobite days.

O'Fogarty, lords of Eliogarty, county Tipperary: *Fleadh agus failte,* "A banquet and a welcome."

Fox, lords of Teffia and chiefs of Kilcourcy: *Sionnach abu!* "The fox to victory!" This war-cry is derived from the fact that the head of the sept of O'Catharnaigh (O'Kearney) was styled *An Sionnach* ("the fox"), and his descendants take their family name from him.

McGarry, lords of Dal Buinne, county Antrim: *Fear garbh a' maith,* "A rugged man, but excellent in battle," *i.e.,* a good fighter.

O'Gorman, chiefs in Queen's county and county Clare: *Tosach cathad agus deineachad air,* "First in the battle, and last in the fight." This is often rendered in Latin: *Primi et ultimi in bello.*

Grace: This Norman-Irish sept of Kilkenny used as war-cry, *Gras aig abu!* "Valiant [generous] Grace to Victory."

O'Halloran, lords of Clann *Ferghail:* This war-cry was *Clann Fearghail abu!* "Clann *Ferghail* to victory!" The motto used on arms is *Lotaim agus marbhaim:* "I wound and I kill."

O'Hagan, lords of Tullaghoge, county Tyrone: *Buaidh no bas,* "Victory or death."

O'Hanley, chief in Roscommon: *Saigheadoir collach abu!* "Victory to the valiant archer [slayer] of the boar."

O'Hanrahan, chiefs in Corcaree, county Westmeath, and in Tipperary: *An Uachdar,* "The uppermost."

Hussey, baron Galtrim: *Ceart direach abu!* "Strict justice in victory."

Kavanagh (senior branch of the McMurroughs, kings of Leinster): *Siothchain agus fairsinge,* "Peace with plenty." This is rendered in Latin *Fortis et hospitalis.*

O'Leary, chiefs of *Hy-Laoghaire,* now "Iveleary," county Cork: *Laidir is e lear righ,* "Strong is the sea-king."

Magawley, lords of Calry, county Westmeath: Many of the parent branches blazon the motto *Dulce periculum* ("Danger is sweet") with their armorial bearings. Valerio Magawley-Cerati, Count of the Holy Roman Empire of Austria (his birthplace), is a scion of the ancient house of Calry. By reason of such descent, and to emphasize that fact, he had confirmed to him and his heirs the right to bear the arms of the clan *MacAmhalghaidh,* with the motto, *Lamh dhearg abu!* "The red hand to victory."

MacMahon, lords of Farney, county Monaghan: *So dorn do na dubfhuiltibh,* "Here is the fist [hand] for the dark-blooded," *i.e.,* the traitor or enemy. It is also used in Latin, *Manus haoc inimica tyrannis* ("This hand is an enemy to tyrants").

Mahon, of Roscommon (a Roscommon, branch of the Ulster MacMahons): *Buaidh go brato!* "Victory forever."

O'Mahoney, chiefs in Cork and Kerry: *Lasair romhuinn a buaidh!* "Flame before us to victory."

O'Meagher, chiefs of Ikerrin, county Tipperary: *Meagher go brath,* "Meagher Forever." Their motto, "Brave as a Lion—Bold as a Hawk."

O'Molloy, hereditary standard bearers to the Ardrigh in Ireland: *Gearr aige agus doghadh buaidh,* "Short in action and mischievous in victory."

O'More, prince of Leix: *Connlan abu,* "The hero to victory."

O'Neill, prince of Tirowen: *Lamh dearg Eirinn,* "The red hand for Erin." The arms of the O'Neill is the red sinister hand which the O'Neill alone bears properly. Those who are descended from his race use a red dexter hand. The red hand is the badge of the ancient Clanna Ruadri (clan Rory) of Ulster. The O'Neills appropriated it at the expulsion of the Irian septs (of which were the clan Rory) by the Hermonian power.

O'Rourke, prince of Breffney: *Buaidh!* "To victory." This is borne by the O'Rourkes of France also.

O'Shaughnessy, chiefs of Cineal Hugh, county Galway: *Buailim se,* "I strike him."

O'Sullivan Mor: *Lamh foisneach abu!* "The quiet [gentle] hand to victory."

MacSwinney, chiefs of Donegal and Cork: *Tuaghan tulaigh abu!* "The axe of the hillock to victory!"

Woulfe (anciently the sept O'Mictire): *Guileann uasal,* "The noble whelp." The name Mictire means "Son of the Craftsman."

Mottoes in England and Ireland are not necessarily hereditary, and unless attached to or in any way forming a part of the arms or crest may be altered, assumed, or discarded at the will of the bearer.

Part IV

IRELAND WITHOUT LEADERS

The Last Soldier-Leader

"With Owen O'Neill passed away the greatest Irishman of his period. He had sacrificed a splendid position in the Spanish army to come to Ireland, where he was rewarded with distrust and dislike. His career is one of the greatest tragedies in the history of Ireland. Landing there only to find that the movement he had helped to plan was on the verge of extinction, he, by his personality and strength, organized and resuscitated his despairing party. Among Irish generals he only was able to make headway against his enemies. When the break-up of the Confederation came he found himself not only fighting the English and Scots, but also the armies of his countrymen in the South. In the campaign against the armies of Inchiquin, Preston, Clanricarde and Jones, with the Scots under Monroe in his rear, he showed that the reputation which he had won in Flanders was not unearned. To have brought off his army unscathed from the midst of so many enemies was one of the most remarkable feats in history.

From *O'Neill and Ormond,* by Diarmid Coffey. Maunsel & Company. Dublin. 1914.

Introduction

The debacle of Kinsale meant the breakup of Gaelic Ireland. Lands were no longer held by the old tenures and the old allegiances were whittled away. O'Neill, some time after he had signed the Articles of Mellifont, left Ireland with some of his kinsmen and with some of the lords who were allied to him. This "Flight of the Earls" is a puzzling episode. O'Neill believed that a conspiracy was in existence to put him on trial that would have an ignominious execution at the end. But he must have known, too, that his flight with kinsmen and friends would be as morally devastating as a lost battle. Such indeed was the case. Not the Battle of Kinsale but the Flight of the Earls impressed itself on the peoples' memory. Now comes an emigration of leading members of the historic families. Spain is hospitable to them, and they take military service mainly in the Spanish Netherlands.

To the Ireland of the time, the depression and emigration of the leading families meant more than the destruction of an aristocracy would have meant to any other country in western Europe. The whole social system depended on the great families: it was they who supported the scholars, musicians, poets, law officers. The disappearance of an historic family left a blank in the countryside.

This might have eventuated in the disappearance of the whole national tradition; however, there were men in Ireland who were able to make a new line of defense, a spiritual line of defense. These were the scholars who set down in Irish *Forus Feasa ar Eirinn* and the work that we now name *The Annals of the Four Masters,* Geoffrey Keating and the Franciscans, Michael O'Clery, Peregrine O'Clery, Fearfeasa O'Mulcrony, Peregrine O'Duigenan. The object of these scholars was to give to the Irish people—how easily they might have been left without it—a sense of the dignity of their country. Without these devoted scholars Ireland would indeed have been the Celtic fringe of another land. It fell to the scholars rather than the poets to do this; the scholars had a national outlook while the poets were attached to particular families. However, in the seventeenth and eighteenth centuries the poets were to supply a vision that kept the spirit alive in the country.

In the history presented by Geoffrey Keating and the scholars whom we know as the Four Masters, much—indeed, in the case of the Annals—the greater part is derived from epic and saga material. This, of course, does not detract from either work as an image of the Ireland that is gone but that will be looked back to with pride and renewed hope. There is a remarkable spirit of generosity in the contemporary and the near-contemporary parts of the Annals. Every English soldier and administrator whose conduct showed any degree of fairness is praised to the full. "For the glory of God and the honor of Ireland": this is a translation of a line from the dedication of the Annals. It is incidental there. But those who know of the Annals as a sort of legendary book think of it as a single line dedication. If it were, it would have been the most comprehensive dedication in literature: the work is worthy of such a dedication.

On the Continent the Irish were not a mere soldiery. Don Philip O'Sullivan in Madrid wrote in Latin a fascinating account of the Nine Years' War for the sons of its veterans. Irish scholars took over a college in Salamanca University,* and in Louvain in the Spanish Netherlands, Irish scholars gave and received instruction.

When Hugh O'Neill and his fellow expatriates died in Rome, the bard of the O'Donnells addressed to the Lady Nuala O'Donnell a Lament for the Princes in which they are mourned for as the last "of the line of Conn." Twenty years after that elegy was uttered a soldier appeared who was to show that line at its noblest.

OWEN ROE O'NEILL AND OLIVER CROMWELL

The place was Arras, the time 1640. Arras was a place difficult to defend against the French, one of those commanders was to be known in history as the great Conde. A force of Spaniards and Irish held it until they were permitted to march out with the honors of war. Their commander was "Don Eugenio O'Neill, Irish colonel, a man of great experience," says the Spanish record.

In Irish history Don Eugenio is known as Eoghan (Owen) O'Neill, and, on account of the color of his hair, "Ruadh" or "red"—Owen Roe O'Neill. He was the son of Hugh O'Neill's younger brother, and had a command in the war that ended with the debacle of Kinsale: he was sixteen at the victory of the Yellow Ford and twenty at the defeat at Kinsale. Subsequently he took service with the Spaniards, serving as so many of the Irish did at the time in the Netherlands.

Owen was a man of the new time, a military officer, not a hereditary chieftain. He was an Irishman rather than a Gael. Many Irish Catholics of Norman and English descent were coming into the Netherlands, and O'Neill made an effort to get them into Irish regiments. He was an O'Neill, an Ulsterman, but on another side he went back to the Fitzgeralds; he was a grandson of the great Earl of Kildare. His wife, Lady Rose O'Doherty, was the granddaughter of Shane O'Neill. She was a great lady and a heroine in her own right.

As a soldier whose experience was noted, he might have become a

---

* The Irish government has just returned to the Spanish this college—a beautiful building known as "The College of the Irish Nobles."

Spanish grandee and appeared, as his undistinguished cousin did, in a Velasquez painting. Under his quiet and patient exterior there was a dream, a dream that he was to speak of on his dying bed—to lift the oppression from his own country and then to help drive the Turks out of Europe. His house in Brussels was an Irish headquarters; he kept in touch with all that was happening in Ireland and with various forces in Europe.

An ill-organized insurrection in Ulster brought O'Neill with seasoned troops on the Irish scene. Sometime afterwards a government was set up in Kilkenny. O'Neill placed himself under it.

The government was the Council of the Catholic Confederation: it was in Catholic interests but Royalist Protestants were favorable to it because it was counter-Puritan, counter-Parliamentarian. It was recognized abroad. However, it was a government that was riddled with weaknesses. Its one asset was the armed forces it assembled, but that asset it proceeded at once to dissipate by setting up four separate commands—Ulster, Munster, Connacht, and Leinster. The Ulster command went to O'Neill, but the important one, the Leinster command, went to one who had been his rival in the Netherlands where his reputation was low, to General Preston. The Connacht command went to an English Catholic, Lord Castlehaven, whose main concern was the restitution of his property. The Royalists kept an army under Lord Ormond, an opportunist Irishman of Norman descent, a Butler. The Parliamentarians had an army under General Jones, while the Scots in Ulster had an army under an officer who had been trained in Sweden, General Munroe.

In England the Puritans were a rising power, in Scotland the Covenanters were dominant. In Ireland the Catholic Confederation was made up of Gaelic and Norman-Irish and Anglo-Irish elements. Its business was to keep in existence the Three Kingdoms with a Stuart king at their head. It was made up of magnates who wanted security for their landed property, freedom of religion, the right to set up their own schools, entry into the university and an untrammelled commerce. They were moderate and they were compromising, and against them were set the aggressiveness of the Parliamentarians in England and the Covenanters in Scotland who were out to destroy Catholicism, root and branch.

From its establishment there were tensions within the Council set up by the Catholic Confederation. The Anglo-Irish who dominated it distrusted the Gaelic party who, they suspected, looked to France or Spain rather than to Royalist England; next to a complete defeat by the Puritans they dreaded a victory by a representative of the Old Irish. They kept O'Neill in Ulster until it was necessary to bring him closer to headquaters to repair Preston's defeat. Meanwhile they gave away their military power for treaties that could never be kept.

In this war two actions stand out—O'Neill's brilliant victory over the Scottish general at Benburb, and, at the end of the war, his nephew's, young Hugh O'Neill's, defense of Clonmel against Cromwell. And the knightly character of Owen Roe stands out against the murk of ineptitude and intrigue that hangs over the later history of the Confederation.

The state of war lasted eleven years. Seventy thousand troops—an immense force in those days—were sent into Ireland, most of them were killed or taken prisoner. Ireland lost five-sixths of her population. We need not be incredulous of such mortality, for in those days armies lived off the country which in protracted warfare meant that famine succeeded famine. A man might travel twenty or thirty miles, says Prendergast, the reputable historian of *The Cromwellian Settlement,* and not see a living creature. Homeless children were picked up and sold to slavers. Wolves roamed over Ireland, preying on debilitated people. Looking back on this time the Irish people found their bitterest imprecation in "The curse of Cromwell," and, remembering the gloomy troopers who took possession of confiscated lands, they said of one who was forbidding, "The drop of Cromwell is in him."

But such summaries do not make for sensible history. Cromwell's own campaign in Ireland was short and brought to a conclusion a war that had lost its objectives. And there was no organization, no leader with whom the English dictator could make a tolerable peace.

And yet when this has been said there is something particularly sinister about the English Parliamentarian subjugation of Ireland: it is not in the fact that their generals had prisoners hanged and that they refused the usual quarter to the inhabitants of towns they entered. It is in the fact that they commercialized the war. It was financed by London merchant-companies on the security of land bonds, which meant that those who held bonds took possession of lands and dwellings leaving their former owners without means of subsistence. Men, women, and children went in payment, too; prisoners taken in captured towns, children roaming the countryside were sold to those who transported them to the West Indies, to work as slaves in the plantations.* Cromwell landed in August; in November, Owen Roe O'Neill died on the island of Lough Oughter in county Cavan. With the remnant of his army his nephew made a stand at Clonmel.

It seems odd to envisage Owen Roe O'Neill and Oliver Cromwell sitting down together to make a settlement. Yet if Owen Roe had had his uncle's sense of political expediency, and, unmindful of the Council in Kilkenny, had held a strong force in Ulster, this might have even-

---

* This traffic may have begun with the picking up of vagrant youngsters. But the Cromwellian soldiery would have had no scruple about "breaking and entering" to get them. They had to have booty, and Irish youngsters had become booty. Sir William Petty estimated that six thousand young boys and girls were transported to the plantations. This is likely to be a conservative estimate.

tuated. Cromwell's General Monk had opened negotiations with him. Munroe, whom he had defeated at Benburb, wrote to him in friendly terms; so did Coote, another Puritan general.

The conquest which the Plantagenet Kings and the Tudor State had tried to effect was now accomplished. "The brethren of the Covenant and the sword," writes Carlyle in his preface to one of the volumes of the writings and speeches of Oliver Cromwell, "looked forward to the acomplishment of a dream which they had long entertained, the vision of a rich and fertile country, a promised land, which should be the prize of victory and whose estates should be enjoyed by the conquerors. In that spirit Cromwell and his men approached their task." After Cromwell's conquest, the Irish champions are outlaws and men who were trained in isolated parts of the country—scholars, poets, minstrels.—P.C.

Dedication of *The Annals of the Four Masters*

"It is self-evident, wherever nobility and honor flourish, that nothing is more glorious or more worthy of praise than to revive the knowledge of ancient authors and of the illustrious personages and nobles of former times, so that succeeding generations might cherish the memory of their ancestors.

"I, Michael O'Clerigh, a poor brother of the Order of Saint Francis, have come before you, O noble Farrell O'Gara, knowing what grief and sorrow it was to you (for the glory of God and the honor of Ireland) that the race of the Gael has passed under a cloud of darkness, and that no memorial remains of our saints and virgins, our bishops, abbots, and church dignitaries, our kings and princes, lords, chieftains, and men of learning. I explained to you that I thought I could get the assistance of the chroniclers whom I most esteemed to compile a book of annals, in which the aforesaid matters might be put on record; and that, should they not be written down now, they would not again be discovered to be put on record until the end of the world."

Dudley Mac Firbis

Dubhaltach Mac Firbisigh, or, as the name is Anglicized, Donald or Dudley Mac Firbis, was born about 1585 at Lecain, in the county Sligo. According to Eugene O'Curry, he "appears to have been intended for the hereditary profession of antiquarian and historian, or that of the *Fenechas,* or ancient laws of his native country (now improperly called the Brehon Laws). To qualify him for either of these ancient and honorable professions, and to improve and perfect his education, young Mac Firbis appears at an early age to have passed into Munster, and to have taken up his residence in this school of law and history, then kept by the Mac Eagans of Lecain, in Ormond, in the present County of Tipperary. He studied, either before or after this, in Burren, in the present county of Clare, at the no less distinguished legal and literary school of the O'Davorens, where we find him with many other

---

A compendium of Irish history completed in 1632.

By Charles O'Farrell, in *The Gael*, June, 1901, pp. 173-174. New York.

young Irish gentlemen about the year 1595, under the presidency of Daniel O'Davoren."

Dudley Mac Firbis' studies were not confined to the ordinary branches of education obtainable through the medium of his native language, but included also Greek and Latin.

After the completion of his education we have no account of Mac Firbis until the year 1645, when he seems to have been settled in Galway, where he made the acquaintance of the learned Roderick O'Flaherty, author of *Ogygia* and Dr. John Lynch, author of *Cambrensis Eversus,* to both of whom he acted as Irish tutor, affording them besides much valuable assistance in the prosecution of their historical studies.

At this period Mac Firbis commenced his important work on Irish genealogies, which occupied five years, as he states he finished it in 1650 at the College of St. Nicholas, Galway. O'Curry in speaking of this work says:

"This book is, perhaps, the greatest national genealogical compilation in the world, and when we remember his great age at the time of its compilation, and that he neither received nor expected reward from anyone, that he wrote this book (as he himself says), simply for the enlightenment of his countrymen, the honor of his country, and the glory of God, we cannot but feel admiration for his enthusiasm and piety, and veneration for the man who determined to close his life by bequeathing this precious legacy to his native land."

In 1652 on the surrender of Galway to the Parliamentary Forces, Dr. Lynch fled to France, and Mac Firbis lost one of his best and most steadfast friends. He continued, however, under adverse circumstances to apply his honest zeal and active industry to the task of transferring and restoring into permanent form the contents of manuscripts falling into decay. After a few years as a transcriber, his prospects assumed a brighter aspect. Sir James Ware, impressed with the importance of securing the services of one so thoroughly acquainted with the language, history, and antiquities of his country as Mac Firbis had the reputation of being, employed him, in the year 1655, to collect and translate from the Irish annals, materials for the composition of his learned works on the antiquities and Ecclesiastical History of Ireland.

The death of his patron having put a stop to his labors in Dublin, Mac Firbis appears to have returned to Sligo, his native place, where he lived in great poverty during the remaining years of his life. He had outlived many of his friends who had encouraged and assisted him in former years; others, like Dr. Lynch, had sought safety in flight from the vengeance of their successful opponents in the civil war which then distracted the country; of those who remained behind, the majority, including the learned Roderick O'Flaherty, heir to a handsome patrimony, were reduced by confiscation to a state of poverty hardly less intense than that into which Mac Firbis was plunged.

The death of Mac Firbis was sudden and violent. In the year 1670 while traveling to Dublin he was assassinated at Dunflin, in the county Sligo. The circumstances attending the event are thus narrated by Professor O'Curry:

"Mac Firbis was at that time under the ban of the penal laws, and, consequently, a marked and almost defenseless man in the eye of the law, while the friends of the murderer enjoyed the full protection of the constitution. He must have been then past his eightieth year, and he was, it is believed, on his way to Dublin, probably to visit Robert, the son of Sir James Ware. He took up his lodgings for the night in the village of Dunflin, in his native county. While sitting and resting himself in a little room of the shop, a young gentleman of the Crofton family came in, and began to take some liberties with a young woman who had care of the shop. She, to check his freedom, told him that he would be seen by the old gentleman in the next room; upon which, in a sudden rage, he snatched up a knife from the counter, rushed furiously into the room, and plunged it into the heart of Mac Firbis. Thus it was that, at the hand of a wanton assassin, this great scholar closed his long career—the last of the regularly educated and the most accomplished master of the history, antiquities, and laws and language of ancient Erin."

Owen Roe O'Neill's Speech at Benburb

Owen Roe O'Neill addresses his troops before the battle of Benburb: a British officer's account.

... Then there was an intermission on both sides, being preparing to fight more close, on which MacArt (Owen Roe O'Neill) spoke these words, as I was told, or to that effect.—

"Gentlemen and Fellow Soldiers! Know that those who stand before

From *History of the War in Ireland, from 1641-1653*, by a British officer of the regiment of Sir John Clotworthy. Dublin. 1873.

Quoted in *Ireland from the Flight of the Earls to Grattan's Parliament*, a documentary record compiled and edited by James Carty, pp. 65-66. C. J. Fallon, Ltd. Dublin. 1949.

you ready to fight are those that banished you, your Wives and Children from your Lands and Houses, and make you seek your Bread and Livelihood in strange places. Now you have Arms in your hands as good as they have, and you are Gentlemen as good as they are. You are the Flower of Ulster, descended from as Ancient and Honourable a Stock of People as any in Europe. This Land you and your Predecessors have possessed for about three thousand years. All Christendom knows your quarrel is good—a Fight for your native Birthright and for the Religion which your Forefather professed and maintained since Christianity came first to this Land.

"So now is the time to consider your distressed and slavish condition; you have Arms in your Hands, you are as numerous as they are; and now try your Valour and your Strength on those who have banished you, and now resolve to destroy you Bud and Branch. So let your Manhood be seen by your push of Pike; and I will engage, if you do so, by God's assistance and the Intercession of His Blessed Mother, and all the Holy Saints in Heaven, that the Day will be your own. Your word is *Sancta Maria;* and so in the Name of the Father, Son and Holy Ghost advance, and give not Fire until you are within Pike length."

Which accordingly was observed. At which time the Sun and Wind were against them, and blew the Smoke in their faces, so that for a little moment the Musketeers could not see. At which charge the Scottish and British officers stood it Manfully, and left not their Ground until they were beaten down by push of Pike. But their men did not back them so vigorously as they should . . . the Irish Pikes were longer by a foot, and far better to pierce, being four square and small and the others' Pikes broad-headed which are the Worst in the world.

An Officer Describes the Rout at Benburb

The rout began two hours before night, in which the enemy left very rich booty of all sorts, which hindered the execution much, by the soldiers falling to plunder. My lord Montgomery was taken pris-

From *A Journal of the Most Memorable Transactions of General Owen O'Neill and His Party, from the year 1641 to the year 1650,* faithfully related by Colonel Henry McTully O'Neill, who served under him.

Ibid., p. 64.

oner and so was Major Cocheran; Captain Hamilton, with several other officers slain, with four thousand private men on the spot; and in the pursuit that night and the next day, about one hundred and fifty soldiers were taken prisoners, and dismissed with a pass. To the best of my memory upwards of twenty colours were taken, their artillery (being four field-pieces) with most of all their tents, arms and baggage left behind (except Sir James Montgomery's regiment on their right who escaped). . . . Next day O'Neill ordered my lord Blayney's and Captain Hamilton's corpses to be interred in Benburb church with the proper ceremonies. . . .

Oliver Cromwell Reports on the Taking of Drogheda (Tredah)

It hath pleased God to bless our endeavours at Tredah. After battery, we stormed it. The enemy were about 3,000 strong in the town. They made a stout resistance, and near 1,000 of our men being entered, the enemy forced them out again. But God giving a new courage to our men, they attempted again, and entered, beating the enemy from their defences. The enemy had made three entrenchments, both to the right and left of where we entered; all which they were forced to quit. Being then entered, we refused them quarter; having the day before summoned the town. I believe we put to the sword the whole number of the defendants. I do not think thirty of the whole number escaped with their lives. Those that did, are in safe custody for the Barbadoes. . . . I wish that all honest hearts may give the glory of this to God alone, to whom indeed the praise of this mercy belongs.

[He told the Council that 3,000 at least, besides some women and children, were, after the assailants had taken part and afterwards all the town, put to the sword on 11th and 12th September; at which time Sir Arthur Aston, the governor, had his brains beat out, and his body hacked and chopped to pieces.]

From a letter to the Hon. John Bradshaw, Esq., President of the Council of State. Dublin, September 16, 1649.
Ibid., p. 70.

Pierce Ferriter, Outlaw Hero

We know a good deal about Pierce Ferriter. The scion of a distinguished Norman-Irish family, he had an estate in Kerry. He was a leader in the war that Cromwell ended; his estate was confiscated and he was condemned to death. It is at this stage, when he is a "man on his keeping" that he becomes the hero of stories told in Kerry and the Blaskets. He was hanged by the party of soldiers that captured him. Pierce Ferriter, like his English Cavalier contemporaries, was a poet, a wit, and a swordsman. His charming poem to Meg Russell, an English girl who entered aristocratic circles, shows how close Royalist Irish and English were before the Puritans gained the ascendency.

The scholar who wrote down the folk-tale in which he figures says little about his poetry. He was a poet of distinction, much more open to European influences than the Irish poets who were his contemporaries. To readers of Anglo-Irish literature, his name is known through his "Lament for Sir Maurice Fitzgerald."—P.C.

"I remember well," he went on, "how once, when we were digging a grave, we found shaped stones below the earth, and there were marks of lime on the stones. It was said that Pierce Ferriter had his castle there, a place that he could fly to when the chase was too hot upon his heels."

"Pierce Ferriter?" I [Robin Flower] cried. "That would be the poet?"

"The poet it was, and, beyond being a poet, he was many other things too. He had done many deeds out of the way, things that didn't please the King and his people. So the watch was out after him, and before they caught him in the end, and hanged him, he had many a shift to keep his feet free of them. They did their best to come up with him, but he was too clever for them for a good while. He had this castle built on the brink of the cliff, and he used to live in it; but when the chase was too near to him he had another place, a cave in the hill that neither deer nor eagle could come at.

"A day of the days, on an early morning of summer, he was living lightly in his castle, and he put his head out and what should he see but the guard right over against him. Terror seized him that he should

From *The Western Island, or The Great Blasket*, by Robin Flower, pp. 86-90. Copyright, 1945, by Oxford University Press, New York, Inc.

be out so early in the morning, and he had no time to think of a shift. He said to himself that the best thing he could do was to yield himself up to them and take things easily. He told their captain that, if it was he they wanted, he was well pleased to go with them, for he had been too long on his keeping, escaping from them, and he would rather go with them to suffer all they could do to him than live the life he had been living any longer. They were pleased enough, for they had thought he would fall to fighting with them as he had done often enough before. They agreed together, and Pierce said to them that maybe they had been out and about without food and drink too long, and that he would give orders for dinner to be made ready for them, if they wished. The captain said it was so and they had good need of it. Pierce told the girl to get dinner ready, and he bade them come along with him to the crest of the hill, where they might have a fine view while the dinner was preparing. He told them to throw away their guns and not to be bothered carrying them. Finding him fine and easy in the morning, they were fine and easy with him, too, and did whatever he told them. They threw aside their guns, and before they went to the hill, Pierce spoke aside to the girl and told her not to spare water on the guns when they were out of sight. This girl Pierce had was no fool, for if she had been he wouldn't have had her.

"Off they went, they climbed the hill and they spent a good time walking on the hill till they thought it was time for the dinner to be ready. Then they turned back to the castle. When they were drawing near to it, Pierce said he would go in front, for the way in was rather troublesome. So he went in before them, and when he was inside there was a corner of the castle above the cliff with only room for one man at a time to go the way. The next man wouldn't know whereabouts in the castle the man in front would have stopped. When the first man came by the corner where Pierce was, Pierce thrust at him with a piece of wood and with that thrust sent him down the cliff, and the next man after him, and so with all who came in to the last man, none of them knowing where the man before had gone, till there were fifty men lying in the creek, dead corpses in a heap. Pierce did well that day, but he wouldn't have been so comfortable in his castle if he had known that the pursuit was so near upon his heels."

"Well," said I, as the tale ended, "that was a bad day for the soldiers."

"It was so," said he, "but it would have been as bad a day for Pierce if he hadn't had his wits about him."

"And have you any tale," I said, "of Pierce's cave back in the hill?"

"Yes," he answered, "it was there that he made his verse of poetry."

"And what verse was that?"

"Wait and you will hear it in its right place in the tale. For every tale has its order, and it's a poor story-teller that would put the end before the beginning."

"Follow on with you then," said I, "and I will wait for the verse to the end."

"Well, whenever Pierce felt the pursuit coming too close to him he would fly to this cave that was in the steepest and the worst cliff in the Island. There's many a man in the Island to-day that couldn't walk in the place where it is. However, he was often lonely in it in days of storm and wild weather. The great sea would come up to it, and he could hear the noise of the swell roaring below it. The place where this cave is is a great wide flagstone, with a hole going into it below, and a fine uneven space within. Six feet from it there was a great gush of spring water running down very convenient for him. There was a constant drip falling from the middle of the stone that roofed it, and it was always a marvel to him why that drip should be in the heart of the stone while all the rest of the cave was as dry as a fox's earth. A day of the days he was lying his length in it and this drip fell down on him, and he made this verse that follows:

" 'Hast Thou no pity, O God, that I lie this way,
Lonely and cold, and hardly I see the day;
The drip from the heart of the stone never stilled in my ear,
And the voice of the sea at my feet ever echoing near?"

I wrote down the verse, leaving the tale to be recorded at another time. The day of which I speak was in the spring of the year. The turf had been cut and laid out to dry on the slope of the hill, and was now ready to be built into a rick. Tomas rose, and going to the dresser at the bottom of the kitchen by the door poured out a glass of milk for me. I drank it, and we went out together into the warm sun of midday. Up through the village we climbed at the slow Island pace. For nobody ever hurries there, the leisurely amble of the ruminating donkeys setting the pace for the deliberative activities of the day.

Tomas's rick lies but a little way round the shoulder of the hill, and arrived there, I sat upon a broad stone fallen from the base of the rick, while he built up the turf from the little piles of sods upended against one another, which covered the ground.

Long practice has made all the actions of the Island economy unconscious, and his hands worked lightly and certainly of themselves, while his mind and his talk still dwelt upon Pierce Ferriter and his wild doings. For in the people's tradition Pierce had degenerated strangely from the gallant figure of history, the poet chieftain whose memory stands out with a kind of heroic grace from the turbulent background of the wars of '41. His poems are a strange blend of the laments and eulogies and satires of the Irish tradition and the love-lyrics of the European fashion, strangely transmuted by the alchemy of the Irish mind, which in translating never leaves anything as it finds it, but mixes inevitably a strong infusion of the native idiom and vision with whatever foreign matter comes its way. His deeds are written in the melancholy history of the seventeenth century:

> He lived a life of sturt and strife
> And died by treachery.

All this is changed once more in the simple tradition of the country-side. His actual poems are for the most part forgotten, though fragments are remembered here and there, and I have been told that even in far Donegal one of his poems has been in our day taken down from living lips. But for the most part he has become a center for the drifting verses which have no discoverable father, and many of his actions, too, have decorated other heroes before the powerful magic of his personality drew them to himself. He has become the typical "man on his keeping," the hero of a hundred evasions, a fellow of infinite resource and wile, always giving the slip to the noose which hangs waiting for him, and which will have him in the end. But, when the end comes—the gallows on the Hill of the Sheep in Killarney—his gay gallantry flashes out at the last, and he flings away his hope of life on a point of honor. A priest had given him, the tale goes, a fragment of the consecrated wafer, and promised him that while he held the holy bread under his tongue he would not die. Thrice they made to hang him, but thrice the rope broke. By the law of the gallows he was now free, but as he went away a sudden thought came to him. "I will never live," he cried, "to be called the leavings of a rope," and he turned back, and spitting out the charmed fragment, he submitted his neck again, and now for the last time, to the strangling noose.

The Rapparees

Righ Shemus he has gone to France and left his crown behind;
Bad luck be theirs, both night and day, putting running in his mind;

A peasant ballad of 1691, by Charles Gavan Duffy. In *Ballad Poetry of Ireland*, pp. 203-205. Ford's National Library. New York. 1886.

Lord Lucan followed after with his Slashers brave and true,
And now the doleful keen is raised—"What will poor Ireland do?
What must poor Ireland do?
Our luck," they say, "has gone to France—what can poor Ireland do?"

Oh! Never fear for Ireland, for she has sojers still.
For Rory's boys are in the wood and Remy's on the hill;
And never had poor Ireland more loyal hearts than these—
May God be kind and good to them, the faithful Rapparees—
The fearless Rapparees!
The jewel were you, Rory, with your Irish Rapparees!

Oh, black's your heart, Clan Oliver, and colder than the clay!
Oh, high's your head, Clan Sassanach since Sarsfield's gone away!
It's little love you bear to us, for the sake of long ago—
But hold your hand, for Ireland still can strike a deadly blow—
Can strike a mortal blow—
Och, *dar-a-Criost,* 'tis she can still,
Can strike a deadly blow.

The Master's bawn, the Master's seat, a surly bodach fills;
The Master's son, an outlawed man, is riding on the hills.
But, God be praised, that round him throng as thick as summer bees,
The swords that guarded Limerick's wall—his faithful Rapparees!
His loving Rapparees!
Who dare say "No" to Rory Oge, with all his Rapparees!

Black Billy Grimes of Latnamard, he racked us long and sore—
God rest the faithful hearts he broke!—we'll never see them more.
But I'll go bail he'll break no more while Trugh has gallows trees;
For why? he met one lonely night, the fearless Rapparees—
The angry Rapparees!
They never sin no more, my boys, who cross the Rapparees!

Now Sassanach and Cromweller, take heed of what I say—
Keep down your black and angry looks that scorn us night and day;
For there's a just and wrathful Judge that every action sees,
And He'll make strong to right our wrong the faithful Rapparees!
The men who rode by Sarsfield's side, the roving Rapparees!

Turlough O'Carolan

There can perhaps be no greater entertainment than to compare the rude Celtic simplicity with modern refinement. Books, however, seem incapable of furnishing the parallel; and to be acquainted with the ancient manners of our own ancestors, we should endeavour to look for their remains in those countries which, being in more measure retired from an intercourse with other nations, are still untinctured with foreign refinement, language, or breeding.

The Irish will satisfy curiosity in this respect preferably to all other nations I have known. They in several parts of the country adhere to their ancient language, dress, furniture, and superstitions; several customs exist among them that still speak their original; and in some respects Caesar's description of the ancient Britons is applicable to them.

Their bards, in particular, are still held in great veneration among them; those traditional heralds are invited to every funeral, in order to fill up the intervals of the lament with their songs and harps. In these they rehearse the actions of the ancestors of the deceased, bewail the bondage of their country under the English government, and generally conclude with advising the young men and maidens to make the best use of their time, for they will soon, for all their present bloom, be stretched under the table, like the dead body before them.

Of all the bards the country ever produced, the last and the greatest was Carolan the Blind. He was at once a poet, a musician, a composer, and sung his own verses to his harp. The original natives never mention his name without rapture; both his poetry and his music they have by heart. . . . His songs in general may be compared with those of Pindar, as they have frequently the same flights of imagination; they are composed merely to flatter some man of fortune upon some excellence of his stable, as in Pindar, another for his hospitality, a third for the beauty of his wife and children, and a fourth for the antiquity of his family. Whenever any of the original natives of distinction were assembled at feasting or reveling, Carolan was generally

---

O'Carolan was born in 1670 and died in 1738. He was an accomplished harpist, composed in a new style, wrote poetry that is elegant and graceful, not rhapsodic in the bardic style. Oliver Goldsmith, who wrote this piece (Essay XX) about him could not have known him, as O'Carolan died when Goldsmith was ten years of age. But it is likely that his family had been in houses that the popular poet and musician frequented.

there, where he was always ready with his harp to celebrate their praises. He seemed by nature formed for his profession; for as he was born blind, so also he was possessed of a most astonishing memory, and a facetious turn of thinking, which gave his entertainers infinite satisfaction. Being once at the house of an Irish nobleman where there was a musician present who was eminent in his profession, Carolan immediately challenged him to a trial of skill. To carry the jest forward, his lordship persuaded the musician to accept the challenge, and he accordingly played over on his fiddle the whole piece after him, without missing a note, though he had never heard it before; which produced some surprise; but their astonishment increased when he assured them he could make a concerto in the same taste himself, which he instantly composed; and that with such spirit and elegance, that we may compare (for we have it still) with the finest compositions of Italy.

His death was not more remarkable than his life. Homer was never more fond of a glass than he; he would drink whole pints of Usquebaugh,* and, as he used to think, without any ill consequence. His intemperance, however, in this respect, brought on an incurable disorder; and when just at the point of death, he called for a cup of his beloved liquor. Those who were standing round him, surprised at the demand, endeavoured to persuade him to the contrary; but he persisted, and, when the bowl was brought him, attempted to drink, but could not; wherefore, giving away the bowl, he observed with a smile that it would be hard if two such friends as he and the cup should part at least without kissing; and then he expired.

O'Carolan's Address to Cian O'Hara's Cup

> Were I west in green Arran,
> Or south in Glanmore,
> Where the long ships come laden
> With claret in store;

---

* Uisge batha: The water of life: the word "whiskey" is a corruption of it.

From *Lays of the Western Gael and Other Poems*, translated by Sir Samuel Ferguson, p. 150. Sealy, Bryers & Walker. Dublin. 1897.

Yet I'd rather than shiploads
Of claret, and ships,
Have your white cup, O'Hara,
Up full at my lips.

But why seek in numbers
Its virtues to tell,
When O'Hara's own chaplain
Has said, saying well—
"Turlough, bold son of Brian,
Sit ye down, boy, again,
Till we drain the great cupaun
In another health to Cian."

Costello and the Fair Oona

I do not think that there is any love song more widely spread throughout the country and more common in the mouth of the people than the poem which Tumaus Loidher (strong Thomas) Costello, or Coisdealbhach (foot-shaped?), as the name is often written, composed over the unfortunate and handsome girl Una MacDermott, to whom he had given love. There was no man in Ireland in his time of greater strength and activity than this Tumaus, and that was why he got his nick-name of Tumaus Loidher. The Shanachies used never to be tired of telling wonderful stories about him. He lived in the time of Charles II, I think, and his people had much land, but after Cromwell's coming to Ireland they lost the greater portion of it, and it came into the possession of the Dillons in the counties Sligo and Mayo. This Tumaus Loidher was that quick that he would overtake a three-year-old colt that never had been bridled, and he was that strong that as often as ever he got a hold of his mane he would hold him, without allowing him to get away. They say that this was the first great deed that he performed: When he was a boy growing up, about seventeen years of age, there came a champion or bully to the town of Sligo, and he put a challenge under (*i.e.* challenged) the whole county, looking for a man who would go to wrestle or contend with him. The custom which they had at that time was, that the city into which a champion of this sort would come, was obliged to sup-

From *Amhrain Gradh Chuige Connacht, The Love Songs of Connacht,* translated by Douglas Hyde, pp. 47-61. Gill & Son, Ltd. Dublin. 1905.

port and maintain the champion until they could find another man who would beat him at wrestling.

The day came when the whole county gathered together to Sligo to see was there any man who would go wrestling with the champion, and Costello's father's brother was going there likewise. Tumaus asked him to allow him to go with him, and after long entreaty he gave him leave. When they came to Sligo there were multitudes there before them, and they went out on the lawn or meadow where the champion was. Everyone who was going wrestling with him he used to be throwing him and hurling him on the ground, and there was no man able to stand before him. Young Costello's uncle saw Tumaus quivering and boiling. "What's on you?" (What's the matter with you?) says he. "Ora," says he, "let me go to wrestle with him." "You great fool," says the uncle to him, "what's that you're saying? Do you want the champion to kill you?" "He won't kill me," says the lad; "I am stronger than he." "Let me feel your arms," says the old man. Tumaus stretched them out, and the muscles that were in them were as firm and hard as iron. The lad was beseeching the old man, and asking permission of him until he was tired at last, and gave him permission to go fight with the champion. There was no other man coming forward at this time, for the champion had beaten them all, as many as went wrestling with him, and the other people were afraid. Costello stood out then and said, "I'll go wrestling with you." The champion laughed when he saw the young gossoon going out against him, and he said, "If you're wise, little gossoon, you will stay where you are, and you won't come fighting with me." "I'll do my best with you, anyhow," says Tumaus.

Now this was the way it was customary with them to make a wrestling at this time; that was, to bind a girdle or belt of leather round about the body of the two men, and to give each man of them a hold on the other man's belt, and when they would be ready and the word would be given them they would begin wrestling. When the great multitude saw the belt going on young Tumaus, they cried out not to let him go fight, for they were afraid he would be killed, for this champion killed a good many people before that, and they thought there was no likelihood that a soft young boy like Tumaus would bring his life away from him; but Tumaus would not listen to them, for he felt himself that he was stronger than the people thought. The old uncle was shedding tears when he saw that it was no good for him to be talking to him.

The leather belt went on him then, and the champion got a firm hold of it, and he got a good hold of his enemy's belt. The order was then given them to begin on one another. When he got the word Tumaus suddenly drew in his two hands that were fastened in his enemy's belt towards himself, but the champion never put a stir out of himself. Tumaus got a leverage on him and gave him the second squeeze, but the enemy did not stir. "Dear uncle," said Tumaus, "what's on this man that he is not wrestling with me; loose him from me till we see?" Then the people came up and they loosed the hands of the champion from the belt where they were fastened, and on the spot the man fell back, and he cold dead; his back-bone had been broken with the first squeeze that Tumaus gave him.

That was the first hero-feat that Tumaus ever performed, and he himself understood then that he was stronger than other people. A smith bet with him one day that he would make four horse-shoes which he would neither bend nor straighten, but that he must put the four shoes together when trying to bend them. What did the smith do but put steel into them in place of iron. Tumaus came, and he took the shoes in his hand, and he gave them a squeeze; but he never stirred them. He gave them the second squeeze, but there was no good for him in it. "By my hand, then," says he, "it's well you made them. I must take off my cotamore (great coat) to it." He threw the cotamore off him and he gave them the third tightening, but he could not bend them, because it was steel was in it; however, he made pieces of them in his two hands as if they were glass. The smith was standing at the door, as he was afraid that the shoes might break, although it was an impossibility, as it seemed to him; but as soon as he saw them breaking, out with him, and he pulled the door after him. Then Costello took a flame of wrath when he saw the trick the smith played him, and he turned round and hurled the pieces of steel that were in his hand out after the smith, and he flung them with such strength that he drove them out like bullets through the door.

The old people have, or they had fifteen years ago, so many stories about the adventures and deeds of Tumaus Loidher, that were I to begin on them, and were I able to tell them as I heard them, I would never cease telling of them, and for that reason I shall only speak here of the occasion on which he composed the poem I am about to give on Una* MacDermott.

Una gave him love, and he gave love to Una. The Costello was not rich, but MacDermott had much riches and land, and he ordered his

---

* Una is pronounced "Oona" not "Yewna" as so many people now call it. This beautiful native name is now seldom heard.—D. H.

daughter Una not to be talking or conversing with Tumaus Loidher, because he never would allow her to marry him. There was another man in it who was richer than the Costello, and he desired that she should marry this man. When he thought, at last, that his daughter's will was sufficiently broken and bent by him, he made a great collation, or feast, and sent an invitation to the gentlemen of the whole county, and Tumaus Loidher was among them. When the dinner was finished they began drinking healths, and MacDermott said to his daughter: "Stand up and drink the health of that person whom you like best in this company," because he thought she would drink the health of that wealthy man he had laid out for her as a consort. She took the glass and stood up, and drank a drink on Tumaus Loidher Costello. When the father saw her doing that anger came upon him, and he struck her a blow of his palm on the side of the head. She was ashamed, and tears came into her eyes, but she was too high-spirited to let the people see that she was crying at the blow her father gave her, and she lifted a snuff-box and put a pinch of it to her nose, letting on that it was the strong snuff that knocked the tears out of her. Tumaus Loidher left the room upon the spot. It was anent the occurrence that happened there, that he spake this rann amongst many others—

> Is it not courteously the child of the white breasts said it,
> Wringing her two hands and smoothing her fingers,
> Putting a shadow upon the reason, and she in pain,
> And bitter destruction on it! it was a strong snuff.

After that Una MacDermott was stricken sick with the love she gave him, and she was getting no relief or cure at all from anything, and she was so bad at last that she was not able to leave her bed. Then, and not till then, MacDermott gave her leave to call to herself the Costello. Una sent for him, and he came, and they guided him to Una's chamber, and her soul came again to her with satisfaction of mind when she saw him. The joy that was on her at seeing him did her so much good that she at last fell into a pleasant quiet sleep, the first sleep she had got for months, and he sitting beside her bed, and she holding his hand in her own hand. He sat there for a good while, but as she was not awaking and as he was loath to be remaining there, he loosed his hand out of her hand, and went out of the room and down the stairs. He found nobody at all in the house, and he was ashamed to remain in it by himself. He called to his servant to saddle the horse and be going. He then got on his horse and rode slowly, slowly, from the house, thinking every moment that he would be sent for, and that they would ask him to return; accordingly, he remained near the house, but there was no messenger coming to call him back. His servant was tired waiting for him to go on, and he thought it long the time that his master was riding without going far from the house. He began to say to his master that MacDermott's people were only humbugging him, and he put it into his head that they were doing an act of treachery on him. Costello did not at first believe that it was so, but when no one was coming to him, while the servant kept continually putting this suspicion into his head, he began, himself, to believe it, and took his vow and oath by God and Mary that he would never again turn back and never speak a word to Una or one of MacDermott's people unless he should be called back before he went across the ford of the little river, the Donogue. When he did go into the river he would not go across it, and he remained in the water for half an hour or more, ever hoping that a messenger might come after him. Then the servant began to revile him: "I think it a great wonder," he said, "for a gentleman like you to be cooling in this water for any woman at all in the great world; is it not small your pride, to endure a disgrace like that?" "That's true for you," said the Costello, and he drove his horse up upon the bank. Scarcely was he up on the dry ground when there came a messenger after him in a full run from Una, calling to him to come back to her quickly; but the Costello would not break his vow, and he did not return. After Costello's going from her, Una did not awake for an exceedingly long time. On awaking of her at last, airy and light, the first thing she did was to send for the Costello, but he was gone. She frightened at that, and sent a messenger after him, but the messenger did not come up with him in time. Costello took then a flame of anger and struck a fist upon the servant who gave him the bad advice, so that he killed him of that blow.

It was not long after this that grief and melancholy preyed so much upon Una that she withered away and found death. Nothing at all that was on the world could give any comfort to the Costello after that. Una was buried in a little island in the middle of Lough Cé, and Costello came to the brink of the lake the night after her burial and swam out to the island, and threw himself down upon her grave, and put the night past, watching and weeping over her head. He did the same thing the second night; he came the third and spake above her grave, as I heard it—

"O fair-haired Una, ugly is the lying that is upon you,
On a bed narrow and high among the thousand corpses,
If you do not come and give me a token (?), O stately woman, who
was ever without a fault,
I shall not come to this place for ever, but last night and to-night."

Or, as I found this stanza in a very ill-written manuscript, the only
one in which I ever did find it:

"Unless thou givest me thy hand, O stately woman who did no
evil,
My shadow shall not be seen upon this street for ever but to-night."

No sooner did he say that than he felt Una rising up, and striking
a light blow of her palm upon his cheek, and he heard a voice like
Una's, saying, "Come not," and he then departed satisfied, without
returning for ever.

The rest of the life of Tomaus Loidher was as wonderful as this
story, and the old people in the Counties Roscommon and Sligo used
to have as many stories about him as would keep a person listening
to them for an entire night, but I did not collect them all when I was
able, and now I cannot find them. He found death at last. There
was a man of the Ruanes, and the Dillons promised him a reward if
he would kill him, and he loosed a bullet at him from behind a turf
clamp and killed him. He was lying for three days on the ground
without any person to take him up, for they were afraid of him. On
account of this deed the Costellos who came after him would not
allow any man of the name of Ruane to live on their estate. But some
say that it was his brother, Dooaltagh, or Dudley, the dim-eyed, who
died in this manner.

I shall now give the stanzas which the Costello made about Una
MacDermott as I heard them from many people. The country people
say that they are in "cramp-Irish," and that there was never yet found
a piper or a fiddler to play them on the pipes or the fiddle! There
are a great many stanzas in the poem, but I never got the whole of
them or the half. I heard these stories about Tomaus Loidher from
Shamus O'Hart, from Walter Scurlogue (or Sherlock), both of them
dead now, and from Martin O'Brennan, or Brannan, in the County
Roscommon, but I got some of the verses from a man in the island
of Achill who had never heard any talk about Tomaus Loidher.

When he died he was buried, as he himself directed, in the same
grave-yard and island in which Una was buried, and there grew an

ash-tree out of Una's grave and another tree out of the grave of
Costello, and they inclined towards one another, and they did not
cease from growing until the two tops were met and bent upon one
another in the middle of the graveyard, and people who saw them
said they were that way still, but I was lately on the brink of Lough
Cé and could not see them. I was not, however, on the island.

FAIR UNA

O fair Una, thou blossom of the amber locks,
Thou who art after thy death from the result of ill counsel,
See, O love, which of them was the best of the two counsels,
O bird in a cage, and I in the ford of the Donogue.

O fair Una, thou has left me in grief twisted,
And why shouldst thou like to be recounting it any more for ever?
Ringleted *cooleen* upon which grew up the melted gold,
And sure I would rather be sitting beside thee than the glory of heaven.

O fair Una, said he, of the crooked skiffs(?)
And the two eyes you have the mildest that ever went in a head,
O little mouth of the sugar, like new milk, like wine, like *b'yore*,
And O pretty active foot, it is you would walk without pain in a shoe!

O fair Una, like a rose in a garden you,
And like a candlestick of gold you were on the table of a queen,
Melodious and musical you were going this road before me,
And it is my sorrowful morning-spoil that you were not married to
    your dark love.

O fair Una, it is you who have set astray my senses;
O Una, it is you who went close in between me and God,
O Una, fragrant branch, twisted little curl of the ringlets,
Was it not better for me to be without eyes than ever to have seen you?

It's wet and cold was my visit to the village last night,
And I sitting up on the brink of the couch by myself,
O brightness without gloom, to whom the many were not betrothed
    but [only] I,
Wherefore proclaimest thou not the cold of the morning to myself.

There are people in this world who throw disrepect upon an empty
    estate

[Having] a quantity of worldly good [themselves], though they have
  them not lastingly,
Complaint over [lack of] goods or lament for land I would not make;
I would rather than two sheep if I had Una (*i.e.* "a lamb," a play on
  the word).

I found the following four stanzas in a bad manuscript in which
were only a few of the above verses. I never heard these other four
myself. It is plain it was not the Costello who made the last one of
them, at all events.

Stand ye and look ye is my very love a-coming,
She is like a ball of snow and like bee's honey which the sun would
  freeze
Like a ball of snow and like bee's honey the sun would freeze;
And my portion (*i.e.* my love) and my friend, it is long that I am
  alive after you.

O Una, O friend, and O golden tooth,
O little mouth of honey that never uttered injustice,
I had rather be beside her on a couch, ever kissing her,
Than be sitting in heaven in the chair of the Trinity.

I passed through the byre of my friends last night;
I never got any refreshment or [even] the wetting of my mouth.
'Twas what the frowning high-shouldered (?) girl said, and madder on
  her fingers,
"My three pities that it was not in a solitude I met yourself."

Four Unas, four Annies, four Marys and four Noras,
The four women, the four finest were in the four quarters of Fola
  (Ireland)
Four nails and four saws to four boards of coffin,
Four hates on the four women who would not give their four loves
  off their four kisses.

The Truth about Fontenoy

Of late years doubts have been expressed as to the extent of the
participation of the Irish Brigade in the battle of Fontenoy, and it

From "The Irish Brigade at Fontenoy," by Sir Charles Petrie, in *The Irish Sword*,
the Journal of the Military Historical Society of Ireland, Vol. I (1951-52), pp. 166-
172. Dublin.

may not be uninteresting to reexamine the problem in the light of a recent visit to the battlefield.

First of all, there is the traditional view of Fontenoy, namely that the charge of the Irish Brigade at a critical moment saved the day for France.

What is more, this interpretation has very substantial backing, for the first thing that Louis XV did when the British and Hanoverian column had been driven from the field was to ride down the Irish lines and tell the troops that he owed the victory to them.

Then there is the testimony of the French commander-in-chief himself, the Maréchal de Saxe, for immediately after the battle he wrote in a private letter, "The Irish Brigade, which was in front, behaved as bravely as possible." Lastly, there is the fact that the only English colour taken on this occasion was captured by Sergeant Wheelock of Bulkeley's Regiment.

More recently, however, contrary opinions have been expressed, and they are summed up in the latest edition of *Chambers's Encyclopaedia,* where it is stated, "A legend arose that the Irish Brigade saved the situation for France. This is incorrect: the credit is due to the Régiment Normandie under Lowendahl."

Clearly, therefore, the authorities are divided, and it will be well in the interest of historical truth to find out which view is correct, if that be possible.

The fighting took place on Tuesday, May 11th, 1745, and it was one of the engagements in the War of the Austrian Succession.

The campaign of 1745 saw the French in the field early, and their first act was to lay siege to Tournai. The English and Dutch set out to relieve the town, and the French waited for them on the plateau at Fontenoy.

Both armies were between 50,000 and 60,000 strong, and if there was a slight advantage in numbers it was in favour of the French. Louis XV was in the field with his troops, but the commander-in-chief was Maréchal de Saxe, the greatest soldier of the day. He was at this date only forty-nine years old, but his health was none too good, and throughout the battle of Fontenoy he was in considerable physical pain.

The Irish Brigade was serving with the French army, and it consisted of the regiments of Clare, Ruth, Lally, Berwick, Dillon and Bulkeley, amounting to a total strength of 3,870. There was also one Irish cavalry regiment, namely Fitz-James's.

On the other side were what for the sake of convenience may be described as the Allies, and they were a composite force of English,

Hanoverians, Dutch, and Austrians in varying proportions. The English troops represented the flower of the British army, and included the Brigade of Guards. This mixed force was commanded by a young man of twenty-four, the Duke of Cumberland, a younger son of George II.

Cumberland seems to have stumbled on the French position without realising how strong it really was. On the other hand, de Saxe was perfectly informed about everything that the Allies were doing. In consequence he was able to compel his enemies to fight on ground of his own choosing, where he was ready to receive them.

Tournai was effectively masked with a force of 21,000 men, and with the French field army de Saxe took up position on a cultivated plateau five miles to the south-west of the beleaguered town.

In the centre of de Saxe's line was the village of Fontenoy, while his left rested on Barri wood and his right on Antoing and the Scheldt. Both Fontenoy and Antoing were strongly fortified.

The French position having been selected in this way, de Saxe proceeded to strengthen it with a number of redoubts which were to prove one of the decisive factors in the battle.

The reason he adopted this course was his belief that French infantry could not be relied upon to meet a hostile charge in line.

The French reserves were on the left flank, covered by Barri wood. In the first line of these reserves were the six regiments of the Irish Brigade; to the left of them were the Régiments Royal Corse and Normandie, and to the right was Royal Vaisseaux.

Behind the Irish were the Régiments Hainault, Royal Infanterie, Soissonais, and La Couronne, and behind them again two lines of cavalry regiments, the extreme left being occupied by the Carabiniers.

On the night of May 10th a strong enemy reconnaissance drove the French outposts back in the centre, and de Saxe was compelled to burn and evacuate a group of cottages about half-a-mile from Fontenoy.

Some squadrons of Dutch cavalry also deployed on the French right flank, but these incidents had no real effect upon de Saxe's dispositions, especially as Cumberland made no effort to occupy Barri wood, an omission which was to cost him very dear on the following day. By night every French unit was in position, and the King and the Dauphin rode down the lines to deafening shouts of "*Vive le Roi.*"

The battle may be said to have begun at six o'clock on the morning of the 11th with a half-hearted attempt by the British to capture Barri wood, which by this time was firmly held by the French; but it was repulsed without any great difficulty.

In another part of the field the Dutch attacked Fontenoy and Antoing, but they had not taken the trouble to reconnoitre their objectives, which were hidden from them by the nature of the ground, and so they were quite unaware of the immense strength of the positions they were assaulting. Accordingly, the attackers were greeted with a terrific discharge of grape-shot and musketry, which soon proved to be more than they could stand.

By 11 o'clock in the morning the position thus was that the Allied assaults had failed miserably. Cumberland, therefore, had the choice of beating an ignominious retreat or of making a frontal attack on the French lines. He decided to make the frontal attack, but to combine it with another Dutch attempt on Fontenoy.

The Dutch on this occasion were supported by two English battalions, but all the same they were again repulsed with heavy loss.

Cumberland then gave the order to advance; he took his place at the head of the first line, though as commander-in-chief it would have been more convenient had he been in a position to observe the progress of the battle as a whole. Sixteen thousand men, the flower of the British army, began to move forward up the slope to Fontenoy, raked by a murderous fire from the French redoubts.

Whole ranks were swept away, but still the dense mass continued to press forward over the heaps of dead and dying, while the sergeants dressed the ranks with their long halberds as if they were on parade.

It was without question one of the most memorable feats of valour in military history, for in spite of the terrible flanking fire from the redoubts, and of the efforts of one French regiment after another, the British moved steadily on, until they stood proudly in the centre of the French position, apparently masters of the battlefield.

Up to this moment the Irish Brigade as a whole had not been engaged, though for some unexplained reason the Dillon Regiment had been detached from it, and ordered to charge in company with Normandie and Royal Vaisseaux.

Irish valour, however, in this instance was unavailing, and the Dillon Regiment would seem to have suffered substantial casualties.

The battle had thus reached a stage in which victory would clearly incline to the side which displayed the greater initiative, and it soon transpired that this would not be the Allies. The garrison of Tournai remained quiescent, though an effective diversion might have been made: while the Dutch on the left gave no sign.

As for Cumberland, although his men were temporary masters of the battlefield, he himself seems to have lost control of the battle, probably because he was too far in front to see it as a whole. All he did was to order the cavalry to come to his assistance, a step which he should have taken much earlier in the day.

The Allied horse accordingly advanced but the fire from the redoubts was too much for the Austrians and Dutch, who thereupon bolted. This threw the English cavalry into confusion; and though they rallied in due course, they were soon hurled back again by another tide of fugitives.

Eventually some useful work was done by three regiments, namely the Blues, the Scots Greys, and the Royals, but the hour for useful cooperation was past, and the cavalry effected little in support of the advance of the infantry.

Such being the case, if any initiative was to come it must clearly be from the French, and they did not prove wanting. The guns were duly brought up, and a salvo of grape-shot cut lanes in the solid mass of human flesh which was the Allied column.

There was naturally some confusion in the British ranks, and de Saxe saw his chance. He ordered not only Dillon's Regiment, but Normandie and Royal Vaisseaux, to charge again, and he threw in the other five still fresh regiments of the Irish Brigade.

They attacked the British right flank, while the Gardes Francaises and Suisses, together with a number of line regiments, assailed the left flank. Finally, the Maison du Roi charged the British front.

This was too great a concentration of force to be resisted, and the British fell back, though at no point did their retreat degenerate into anything resembling a rout.

Such in its main outlines was the battle of Fontenoy and the part played by the Irish Brigade. The tribute paid to their behaviour by the King of France and Maréchal de Saxe has already been quoted, and both were in a position to know the truth. The leading English authority on the battle, the late Francis Henry Skrine, takes the same line in his *Fontenoy and the War of the Austrian Succession,* where he says, "Among French infantry regiments those of the Irish Brigade stood first. Their desperate valour was a factor of great importance in our disaster."

In so far as the criticism of the services of the Irish Brigade is honest, it probably springs from a confusion between the first charge of the Dillon Regiment, with Normandie and Royal Vaisseaux, and the subsequent charge of the Irish Brigade as a whole. On the earlier occasion, as we have seen, the Irish attack was repulsed, while the second onslaught was successful.

If further testimony is required for the important part played by the Irish Brigade, it lies in the rewards which were distributed by King Louis XV upon an unprecedented scale.

The commanding officer of Berwick's Regiment was promoted Brigadier, and the Lieutenant-Colonels of Bulkeley's and Ruth's were given pensions of 1,000 and 600 livres respectively. Crosses of St. Louis were distributed lavishly, and wounded officers received gratuities of 200 to 600 livres.

Sergeant Wheelock, of Bulkeley's Regiment, was promoted to the rank of Second Lieutenant by the King in person on the field of battle for his capture of an enemy flag.

It may be worthy of mention in this connection that one of the fruits of the French victory at Fontenoy was the capture of Ghent, and in the town was found a vast quantity of British stores. Among these was a large amount of cloth, and this was duly made into uniforms for the Irish Brigade.

The Irish casualties totalled 274 officers, non-commissioned officers, and men killed, and 382 wounded, or 656 casualties in all, which was a very high proportion indeed of the 3,870 who went into action.

Fontenoy ranks among the most murderous conflicts of the 18th century. In all, the French lost over 7,000 officers and men in killed and wounded and this represented a little more than 12 per cent. of the total number engaged. The Allied losses were about the same.

In a sense the Irish Brigade never fully recovered from the War of the Austrian Succession, for the losses at Fontenoy and at Laffeldt, two years later, were not wholly replaced from Ireland, and in part at any rate the strength was brought up to establishment by the inclusion of men who were not of Irish origin.

An Irish Priest Administers the Last Sacrament to the King of France

The Abbé Edgeworth belonged to a family, the most famous member of which was Maria (but Maria's remarkable father was famous in his day). He was brought up in France where his family (not Maria's) emigrated on becoming Catholic. He had a small property in Ireland from which came the name he used most in France—"de Firmont." After the execution of Louis XVI he was asked to take the office of almoner to Louis XVII then living in exile, and during the ascendency of Napoleon, he lived with that wandering court in the most dreary parts of Europe, an unfitting life for one who wanted to

Quoted in *The Abbé Edgeworth,* by M. V. Woodgate, pp. 86-109, 111. Browne & Nolan, Ltd. Dublin. 1945.

be an active priest. Through the rascality of his agent he was deprived of his property in Ireland and so was left destitute among destitute people. While attending liberated prisoners of war he caught jail fever, which brought about his death in 1807. A more devoted priest and a better Christian than the Abbé Edgeworth, it would be difficult to imagine.—P.C.

I found all the Ministers assembled. Consternation appeared on their countenances. As soon as I entered, they arose, and all surrounded me with eagerness. The Minister of Justice first addressed me. "Are you," said he, "the Citizen Edgeworth de Firmont?" I replied that I was. "Louis Capet," continued the Minister, "having expressed to us his desire to have you near him at his last moments, we have sent for you to know whether you consent to the service he requires of you." I replied, that since the King had signified his wishes, and named me, it became my duty to attend him. "Then," pursued the Minister, "you will go with me to the Temple, whither I will conduct you." And immediately taking a bundle of papers from the table, he whispered a moment to the other Ministers, and going out in haste, ordered me to follow him.

* * * * *

An escort of horse waited for us at the door with the Minister's carriage, into which I got and he followed me. At this time all the Catholic clergy of Paris were dressed like other citizens, so that I was not in clerical dress, but recollecting what I owed to the King, who had been accustomed to such costume, and to religion itself, which received for the first time a sort of homage from the new government, I thought I ought on this occasion to resume the exterior marks of my station. At least to make the attempt appeared to me a duty. I mentioned it to the Minister before we quitted the Tuileries, but he rejected my proposition in terms that prevented my further insisting on it, though without using any offensive language towards me.

Our drive to the Temple passed in gloomy silence. Two or three times, however, the Minister made an attempt to break it. He drew up the carriage windows and exclaimed, "Great God, with what a dreadful commission I am charged! What a man!" added he, speaking of the King. "What resignation! What courage! No! Human nature alone could not give him such fortitude. He possesses something beyond it." Such expressions gave me an excellent opportunity for speaking some unwelcome truths, but I hesitated an instant what course I should pursue. For I reflected that my first duty was to afford

the King the religious consolation he had so earnestly desired, and
that by giving vent to the indignation the conduct of my companion
and his associates had inspired me with, I should probably be forbidden to approach my royal master. I therefore resolved on absolute
silence. The Minister seemed to comprehend my motive, and said not
a word during the remainder of the drive.

We arrived at the Temple, and the first gate was instantly opened
to us. But when we reached the building that separates the court from
the garden, we were stopped; and before we could proceed, it was
necessary that the commissaries of the tower should come and examine
us, and ascertain our business. Even the Minister seemed subject to
this form.

We waited for the commissaries near a quarter of an hour without
speaking to each other. At last they appeared. One of them was a
young man of about seventeen or eighteen and they saluted the Minister as an acquaintance. He told them in a few words who I was and
the nature of my mission. He made a sign to me to follow them, and
we all together crossed the garden to the tower.

Here the scene became horrible beyond description. The door of the
tower, though very narrow and very low, opened with a terrible
noise. It was loaded with iron bolts and bars. We passed through a
hall filled with guards into a still larger hall, which appeared from its
shape to have been once a chapel. There the commissaries of the Commune, who had custody of the King, were assembled and I could not
discover in their countenances that embarrassment or consternation
which had struck me in the Ministers. There were about twelve of
them, mostly in the dress of Jacobins.

Their air, their manners, their *sang-froid* all denoted them to be
men of desperate minds, who did not shrink from contemplation of
the blackest crimes.

But in justice I ought to say that this is not a portrait of them all;
and I thought I could discover some, who had been induced from the
weakness of their character to associate with the rest. Whatever might
be their respective feelings, they were all taken indiscriminately by the
Minister into a corner of the apartment, where he read to them in a
low voice the papers which he had brought from the Tuilleries.

When he had done, he turned suddenly to me, and desired me to
follow him, but this the council opposed by acclamation. Again they
assembled in a corner of the hall, deliberating some time in whispers.
The result was that one-half of the assembly accompanied by the Minister went upstairs to the King, while the other half remained to guard
me.

When the doors were carefully closed, the oldest of the commissaries approached me with a polite but embarrassed air, spoke of the terrible responsibility he was under and begged a thousand pardons for the liberty he was obliged to take. I guessed that this preamble was to end in my being searched, so I anticipated him by saying, that since the reputation of M. de Malesherbes could not excuse him from this formality, I could not flatter myself that when I came to the Temple an exception would be made in my favor. I assured him I had nothing about me that could be suspected, but added that he was welcome to satisfy himself. Notwithstanding this declaration, the search was made with rigor. My snuff-box was opened, the snuff examined, and a little pencil case, which happened to be found in my pocket, was carefully inspected to discover whether it concealed a *poignard!*

They paid no attention to any papers I had about me, and finding everything else unexceptionable, they renewed the excuses with which they had begun, and invited me to sit down; but I had scarcely done so, when two of the commissaries, who had gone up to the King, came to tell me that I was allowed to see him. They conducted me up a winding staircase, which was so narrow that two persons could hardly pass each other. At certain intervals barriers were placed across the stairs, and at every barrier stood a sentinel. These men were actual *sans culottes,* and almost all drunk. The shouts they made, re-echoing through the vaults of the Temple, were quite horrible.

When we reached the apartment of the King, all the doors of which were open, I perceived him in a group of eight or ten persons. It consisted of the Minister of Justice, accompanied by some members of the Commune, who came to read to him the fatal decree, which sentenced him to death on the following day. He was calm and tranquil, even with an aspect of benignity, while not one of those who surrounded him had an air of composure.

As soon as he saw me, he waved his hand for them to retire. They obeyed in silence. He himself shut the door after them, and I found myself alone with my sovereign.

Till this moment I had been able to command the various emotions with which I had been agitated; but at the sight of a prince, who had been once so great, and who was now so unfortunate, I was no longer master of myself. I could not restrain my tears, and I fell at his feet without the power of utterance. This touched him more than the decree which he had just heard. He answered my tears only by his own; but soon resuming all his firmness. "Forgive me," said the King, "forgive me, sir, a moment's weakness, if such it can be called. For a long time I have lived among enemies, and habit has in some degree familiarized me to them, but when I behold a faithful subject, this is to me a new sight, a different language reaches my heart, and in spite of my utmost efforts, I am melted."

Saying these words he kindly raised me from the ground, and let me into his closet that he might speak more freely, for from his chamber all he said was overheard. This closet or cabinet was built in one of the turrets of the Temple. It had neither hangings nor ornament. A bad stove served for a fireplace, and the only furniture was one table and three leather chairs. There, making me sit down near him, "Now, sir," said he, "the great business of my salvation is the only one which ought to occupy my thoughts. The only business of real importance! What are all other subjects compared to this? This must, however, be delayed for a few moments, because my family are coming to take leave of me for ever. In the meantime, here is a paper that I wish you to read." As he spoke, he drew from his pocket a sealed paper, and broke it open. It was his will, which he had made in the month of December, at a period when he was uncertain whether any religious assistance would be allowed to him in his last moments.

* * * * *

This most interesting conversation was interrupted by one of the commissaries, who came to inform the King that his family were coming down, and that he was at length permitted to see them. At these words he appeared extremely agitated, and he broke from me with precipitation. . . . Even I, though shut up in the cabinet where the King had left me, could easily distinguish their voices, and I was involuntarily in some degree witness to the most touching scene I ever heard. It would be impossible for me to describe this agonizing interview. Not only tears were shed, and sobs heard, but piercing cries, which reached the outer courts of the Temple. The King, the Queen, Monseigneur the Dauphin, Madame Elizabeth, Madame Royale, all bewailed themselves at once, and their voices were confounded. At length their tears ceased, for their strength was exhausted. They then spoke in a low voice and with some degree of tranquility.

* * * * *

One thought had strongly weighed upon my mind since I had been so near the King. I determined to procure the means of administering the Sacrament to his Majesty, at any risk to myself, since he had been so long deprived of receiving it. . . . I proposed it to him, but though he desired it most ardently, he seemed afraid of compromising my safety. I entreated him to give me his consent, promising that I would conduct myself with prudence and discretion. He at length yielded. "Go, sir," said he, "but I very much fear you will not succeed, for I know the men with whom you have to deal. They will grant nothing which they can refuse."

Fortified by this permission, I desired to be conducted to the hall of council, and there I made my demand in the name of the King. The proposal, for which the commissaries of the tower were not prepared, disconcerted them extremely, and they sought for different pretexts to elude it. "How could they find a priest at that hour, and when they had got one, how obtain all that was necessary?" "The priest is already found," I replied, "for I am he. And as for the rest, the nearest church will supply all that is necessary, if you will make the application. You will consider that my demand is just, and that it would be against your own principles to refuse me."

One of the commissaries instantly, though rather in guarded terms, insinuated that my request was only a snare, and that under the pretense of giving Communion to the King, I intended to poison him. "History has furnished us with examples enough of this kind to make us circumspect," said he. I looked steadily in the face of this man and replied, "The strict search I underwent as I came in here ought to convince you that I do not carry poison. If then to-morrow any is found, it must be from you that I shall have received it. All that I demand for the celebration of the Mass must pass through your hands.". . . A quarter of an hour passed, and I was again brought into the chamber, where the President thus addressed me, "Citizen Minister of Religion, the council have taken into consideration the request that you have made in the name of Louis Capet, and since they deem his request conformable to the law, which declares all forms of worship are free, they consent to it. Nevertheless, we exact two conditions. The first that you draw up instantly an address containing your demand, signed by yourself; and the second that your religious ceremonies should be conducted by seven o'clock tomorrow at the latest, for at eight precisely Louis Capet must set out for the place of execution." These last words were said like all the rest with a degree of cold-blooded indifference, which characterized an atrocious mind.

* * * * *

At five o'clock he arose and dressed as usual. Soon after he sent for me, and I attended him for near an hour in the cabinet, where he had received me the evening before. When I retired, I found an altar completely prepared in the King's apartment. The commissaries had executed to the letter everything I had required of them. They had even done more that I had asked, I having only demanded what was indispensable. The King heard Mass. He knelt on the ground without cushion or desk. He then received the Sacrament, after which ceremony I left him for a short time at his prayers. He soon sent for me again and I found him seated near the stove where he could scarcely warm himself. . . . Morning began to dawn, and the drums sounded in all the sections of Paris. An extraordinary movement was heard in the tower—it seemed to freeze the blood in my veins. But the King, more calm than I was, after listening to it for a moment, said to me without emotion, " 'Tis probably the National Guard beginning to assemble." In a short time detachments of cavalry entered the court of the Temple, and the voices of officers and the trampling of horses were distinctly heard. The King listened again, and said to me with the same composure, "They seem to be approaching.". . . We heard another knock at the door—it was to be the last. It was Santerre and his crew. The King opened the door as usual. They announced to him (I could not hear in what terms) that he must prepare for death. "I am occupied," he said with an air of authority. "Wait for me. In a few minutes I will return to you." Then, having shut the door, he knelt at my feet. "It is finished, sir," said he. "Give me your last benediction, and pray that it may please God to support me to the end."

He soon arose, and leaving the cabinet, advanced towards the wretches who were in his bedchamber. . . . "Are there amongst you any members of the Commune? I charge them to take care of this paper." It was his will. One of the party took it from the King. "I recommend also to the Commune Clery, my valet de chambre. I can do no more than congratulate myself in having had his services. They will give him my watch and clothes; not only those I have here, but those that have been deposited at the Commune. I also desire that in return for the attachment he has shown me, he may be allowed to enter into the Queen's—into my wife's—service." He used both expressions. No one answering, the King cried out in a firm tone, "Let us proceed," at which words they all moved on.

The King crossed the first court, formerly the garden, on foot. He turned back once or twice towards the tower, as if to bid adieu to all most dear to him on earth; and by his gestures it was plain that he was then trying to collect all his strength and firmness. At the entrance of the second court a carriage waited, two gend'armes held the door. At the King's approach one of these men entered first, and placed himself in front. The King followed and placed me at his side. At the back of the carriage the other gend'arme jumped in last and shut the door. . . . The King, finding himself seated in the carriage where he could neither speak to me nor be spoken to without witnesses, kept a profound silence. I presented him with my breviary, the only book I had with me, and he seemed to accept it with pleasure. He appeared anxious that I should point out to him the psalms that were most suited to his situation, and he recited them attentively with me. The gend'armes, without speaking, seemed astonished and confounded at the tranquil piety of their monarch to whom they doubtless never had approached so near.

The procession lasted almost two hours. The streets were lined with citizens, all armed, some with pikes and some with guns, and the carriage was surrounded by a body of troops, formed of the most desperate people of Paris. As another precaution they had placed before the horses a great number of drums, intended to drown any noise or murmur in favor of the King. But how could they be heard? Nobody appeared either at the door or windows, and in the streets nothing was to be seen but armed citizens. Citizens, all rushing towards the commission of a crime, which perhaps they detested in their hearts. . . .

As soon as the King had left the carriage, three guards surrounded him, and would have taken off his clothes, but he repulsed them with haughtiness. He undressed himself, untied his neckcloth, opened his shirt and arranged it himself. The guards, whom the determined countenance of the King had for a moment disconcerted, seemed to recover their audacity. They surrounded him again, and would have seized his hands.

"What are you attempting?" said the King, drawing back his hands. "To bind you," answered the wretches. "To bind *me*," said the King with an indignant air. "No, I shall never consent to that. Do what you have been ordered, but you shall never bind me." The guards insisted. They raised their voices, and seemed to wish to call on others to assist them.

Perhaps this was the most terrible moment of this most dreadful morning. Another instant, and the best of Kings would have received from his rebellious subjects indignities too horrid to mention—indignities that would have been to him more insupportable than death. Such was the feeling expressed in his countenance. Turning towards me, he looked at me steadily, as if to ask my advice. Alas! it was impossible for me to give any, and I only answered by silence. But as he continued the fixed look of inquiry, I replied, "Sire, in this new insult, I only see another trait of resemblance between your Majesty and the Saviour Who is about to recompense you." At these words he raised his eyes to heaven with an expression that can never be described. "You are right," he said. "Nothing less than his example should make me submit to such degradation." Then, turning to the guards, "Do what you will. I will drink of the cup even to the dregs."

The path leading to the scaffold was extremely rough and difficult to pass. The King was obliged to lean on my arm, and from the slowness with which he proceeded, I feared for a moment that his courage might fail. But what was my astonishment, when arrived at the first step, I felt that he suddenly let go my arm, and I saw him cross with a firm foot the breadth of the whole scaffold, silence by his look alone fifteen or twenty drums that were placed opposite to him, and in a voice so loud that it must have been heard at the Pont Tournant, I heard him pronounce distinctly these memorable words, "I die innocent of all the crimes laid to my charge. I pardon those who have occasioned my death, and I pray to God that the blood you are now going to shed may never be visited on France."

He was proceeding when a man on horseback in the national uniform waved his sword, and with a ferocious cry ordered the drums to beat. Many voices were heard at the same time encouraging the executioners. They seemed re-animated themselves, and seizing with violence the most virtuous of Kings, they dragged him under the axe of the guillotine, which with one stroke severed his head from his body. All this passed in a moment. The youngest of the guards, who seemed about eighteen, immediately seized the head, and showed it to the people as he walked round the scaffold. He accompanied this monstrous ceremony with the most atrocious and indecent gestures.

At first an awful silence prevailed. At length some cries of *"Vive la Republique"* were heard. By degrees voices multiplied, and in less than ten minutes this cry, a thousand times repeated, became the universal shout of the multitude, and every hat was in the air.

The narrative proper ends here, but the Abbé added something more in a letter he wrote to his brother. The blood of the King saturated his clothes, and as he stood on the scaffold an auction of the King's belongings was held—his hat and handkerchief. Then followed singing and dancing to the *Marseillaise*. The Abbé wrote:

"Then, indeed, I thought it time to quit the scaffold. But casting my eyes round about, I saw myself invested by twenty or thirty thousand men in arms, and to pierce the crowd seemed to me a foolish attempt. However, as I must take that party, or by remaining to share the public joy, my only resource was to recommend myself to Providence, and to steer my course towards the side on which the ranks seemed to have less depth. All eyes were fixed upon me, as you may suppose, but as soon as I reached the first line, to my great surprise, no resistance was made. The second line opened in the same manner, and when I got to the fourth or fifth, my coat being a common surtout (for I was not permitted on this occasion to wear any exterior marks of a priest), I was absolutely lost in the crowd, and no more noticed than if I had been a simple spectator of a scene, which forever will dishonor France."

The Abbé Mac Geoghegan to the Irish Troops in the Service of France

Europe, towards the end of the last century, was surprised to see your fathers abandon the delights of a fertile country, renounce the advantages which an illustrious birth had given them in their native land, and tear themselves from their possessions, from kindred, friends, and from all that nature and fortune had made dear to them; she was astonished to behold them deaf to the proposals of a liberal usurper, and, following the fortunes of a fugitive king, to seek with him in foreign climes, fatigues, and danger, content with their misfortune, as the seal of their fidelity to unhappy masters.

France . . . gladly opened to them a generous bosom, being persuaded that men so devoted to their princes would not be less so to their benefactors; and felt a pleasure in seeing them march under her banners. Your ancestors have not disappointed her hopes. Nervinde, Marseilles, Barcelona, Cremona, Luzara, Spire, Castiglione, Almanza, Villa Viciosa, and many other places, witnesses of their immortal valour, consecrated their devotedness for the new country which had adopted them. France applauded their zeal, and the greatest of monarchs raised their praise to the highest pitch by honoring them with the flattering title of "his brave Irishmen."

The example of their chiefs animated their courage: the Viscounts Mountcashel and Clare, the Count of Lucan, the Dillons, Lees, Rothes, O'Donnells, Fitzgeralds, Nugents, and Galmoys opened to them on the borders of the Meuse, the Rhine and the Po, the career of glory,

From *The History of Ireland Ancient and Modern,* Taken from the most Authentic Records, and Dedicated to the Irish Brigade, by the Abbé Mac Geoghegan, translated from the French by Patrick O'Kelly, pp. 5-7. Printed for the author of the translation by T. O'Flanagan. Dublin. 1831.

whilst the O'Mahonys, MacDonnels, the Lawlesses, the Lacys, the Burkes, O'Carrols, Croftons, Comerfords, Gardners, and O'Connors crowned themselves with laurels on the shores of the Tagus.

The neighbouring powers wished to have in their service the children of these great men: Spain retained some of you near her throne. Naples invited you to her fertile country; Germany called you to the defence of her eagles. The Taafs, the Hamiltons, O'Dwyers, Brownes, Wallaces and O'Neills supported the majesty of the Empire, and were entrusted with its most important posts. The ashes of Mareschal Browne are every day watered with the tears of the soldiers to whom he was so dear, whilst the O'Donnells, Maguires, Lacys, and others endeavoured to form themselves after the example of that great man.

Russia, that vast and powerful empire, an empire which has passed suddenly from obscurity to so much glory, wished to learn military discipline from your corps. Peter the Great, that penetrating genius and hero, the creator of a nation which is now triumphant, thought he could not do better than confide that essential part of the art of war to the Field Mareschal de Lacy, and the worthy daughter of that great emperor always entrusted to that warrior the principal defence of the august throne which she filled with so much glory. Finally, the Viscount Fermoy, general officer in the service of Sardinia, has merited all the confidence of the crown.

But why recall those times that are so long past? Why do I seek your heroes in those distant regions? Permit me, gentlemen, to bring to your recollection that great day, forever memorable in the annals of France; let me remind you of the plains of Fontenoy, so precious to your glory; those plains where in concert with chosen French troops, the valiant Count of Thomond being at your head, you charged, with so much valour, an enemy so formidable; animated by the presence of the august sovereign who rules over you, contributed with so much success, to the gaining of a victory, which, till then, appeared doubtful. Lawfeld beheld you, two years afterwards, in concert with one of the most illustrious corps of France, force entrenchments which appeared to be impregnable. Menin, Ypres, Tournay saw you crown yourselves with glory under their walls, whilst your countrymen, under the standards of Spain, performed prodigies of valour at Campo Sancto and at Valetri.

The Irish College in Paris was the one tangible boon that accrued to them from these victories; it was given the Irish refugees as a charity rather than as a reward for two generations of military service.

Michael Dwyer

The insurrection of 1798 was best sustained in the eastern counties of Wicklow and Wexford. Of the impromptu leadership in Wicklow three showed themselves as resourceful—Michael Dwyer, Billy Byrne of Ballymanus, and Myles Byrne. Myles Byrne managed to get out of the country after the insurrection had been quelled, became a colonel in the Napoleonic armies, and lived to write an excellent account of what might have been a war of independence if the insurrectionists had any extent of country to fall back on. The gentleman-farmer, Billy Byrne of Ballymanus, was hanged. His resourcefulness enabled Michael Dwyer to make a deal with the government by which a possible death penalty was commuted to banishment, but banishment to Australia which was then at the ends of the earth and known only as a convict settlement.

It is extraordinary that in 1934 Padraig O'Tuathal was able to obtain an Ediphone recording of the recollections of one for whom the insurrection and the adventures of its leaders were household matters. Mrs. O'Tool of Ballinglen whose recollections were recorded was eight years of age when her grandfather died, her grandfather who had taken a prominent part in the insurrection. By the fireside in the Wicklow farmhouse, away from the stir of national and international events, the lives of her grandfather's comrades must have been realized by her with great distinctness. And Mrs. O'Tool embodied a tradition, the *Seanchas,* the oral history which was to be related dramatically, of course, but responsibly, too. Checked against written sources, what she tells about the insurrection in Wicklow is substantially accurate.

What she related, what is recorded of her recollections, is more than is given here. Padraig O'Tuathal got down in these Wicklow traditions a family saga of the greatest interest to those who want to know how the people of the Irish countryside lived and reacted to public affairs. The publication of them is an earnest of what the Folklore Commission can accomplish in the field of social history.

And it also shows the competence of the shanachie. Mrs. O'Tool would not have regarded herself as a professional storyteller—probably there was no one in her time in County Wicklow who was looked upon as a storyteller of the type of Peg Sayers in the Blasket Islands.

From *Béaloideas,* Journal of the Folklore of Ireland Society. Dublin. 1929.

Nevertheless she gives us a narrative in which incident and character become memorable. One would give a good deal of Irish fiction for that exchange between the Presbyterian insurrectionist who goes to Mass with Michael Dwyer and the priest who remonstrates with them for bringing guns into the chapel—"It is not always we have a rebellion, Father. Go on with the Mass!"—P.C.

On one occasion Dwyer and my grandfather and Hugh Byrne of Monaseed and poor McAllister—I am troubled to the heart when I think of poor McAllister; he was a true man—well, the four of them were in a cave on Lugnaquilla when the daylight came. By and by the sun shone in through the heather which hung over the hole they crept in. They were as comfortable as the day is long lying in a big bundle of clean straw and good bedclothes that was brought from a farmer's house; and the farmer's house was my great-grandfather's. They were brought from a farmer's house near to the mountain and placed there designedly for the boys. So the four awoke, and they began to talk, and they got up and struck their flints and steel 'cause there was no matches. Then they lit their pipe, each of them, and they commenced to smoke and to talk as happy as the day is long, when a robin came in—and a robin is unusual so high up in the mountain, you know—a robin flew in, and she jumped around the quilt over them, and one grabbed at her, and another, and she flew out from the whole of them, and it wasn't two minutes till she came in again, and when she came in she bustled and set herself just as if she was going to jump at them, and she got wicked looking and: "O!" says they, "there is something in this." The four jumped to their feet, and one of them put his head through the hole and he pulled back excited. "O!" he says, "the hillsides is red with soldiers." "Which will we lie in," says another, "or will we get out? If they have bloodhounds we're found out." "That's right," says they, and they all jumped to their feet, and the bloodhounds came in to the bed, but they dragged on their breeches and put their hats on them, and out they went with their guns. Dwyer whipped his seawhistle and he whistled, and he could be heard, I suppose, in Arklow, and they fired off their three shots, and the soldiers turned around and they ran for their lives, and they never got time to look back till they fell over Lugnaquilla, and they told when they got below that the hills was full of rebels.

There was a woman who used to deal in carrying bread around to the farmers herself and selling it to the women and children and otherwise, and when '98 broke out she was a valiant heroine woman and should be good, should have been of good blood or she wouldn't have been so sound as she was, for she never divulged it, and she carried scores and maybe hundreds of back-loads of powder to the boys and a dozen of penny buns put in over the pack, and no one ever detected it that she carried back loads of powder to the boys during the whole year of '98 and was never detected. Her name was never made known afraid they might find out what she was at, and she would have got a horrid death, but, thanks to God! she didn't—she was never known by anything but the "Walking Magazine."

One Sunday morning Dwyer and McAllister were at Mass in Knockananna Chapel, and they brought their guns with them and left them by the wall. The priest remonstrated with them and said that the House of God was no place to bring guns, but McAllister who was a Presbyterian but used to go to Mass with Dwyer said: "It is not always we have a rebellion, Father. Go on with the Mass!" And the priest did so.

During the Mass a neighbour came to Dwyer and said that he had been at the window and that the chapel yard was full of soldiers, and Dwyer picked out two clever young fellows and he told them for to go away to a field a distance from the chapel-yard but in sight of it, and says he: "Take off your coats."

He told them to run along the field in their shirts as fast as they could, and he picked out two or three more young chaps of boys that were clever enough to understand him, and he told them to go down beside the soldiers and stand looking down at this field and to cry out each one in surprise and wonder: "There they go! There they go!" And they did so, and the soldiers asked them who did they mean by there they go, and they told them—all cried out: "Dwyer and Mc-Allister! Dwyer and McAllister!" The soldiers started for to overtake Dwyer and McAllister, and they failed on it for Dwyer and McAllister was hid in the chapel and when the soldiers cleared out they cleared out and went their way in peace and quietness. The soldiers went out across the fence and they came on the two boys that ran, and they sitting with their coats on, and they smoking their pipes, and they asked them did they see two men running through the fields, and they said "No," that they were not long there. So Dwyer and McAllister walked off in safety and left the poor lads wandering about to look for them.

Dwyer was near being captured in Imaal after that when the soldiers came to a house where he was, but he got out and into a piggery behind a big old sow, and when the soldiers came in the sow sat up on her hind legs and made battle with them, and Dwyer gave her a little stab now and then behind backs and they prodded at her with their bayonets, and she groaned at them fearful wicked, and by and by they got tired and said he wasn't there at all.

Dwyer and my grandfather and the boys went on to a friend's place in the Churches, and there was a born cripple lodging at the house, and no one mistrusted anything about him. He was at one side of the kitchen and they were at the other talking over their plans, and Dwyer said that he would get into St. Kevin's Bed and let the soldiers surround him, and the boys could surround them and he would fire off a shot as a signal.

So the cripple gathered up the whole story, and when he got up the next morning and got in his box where there were four dogs drawing him—it was a strange sight to see—he got on to the camp, and he informed on the poor fellows, and told every word he heard the night before. He informed on them, and when he mentioned St. Kevin's Bed the English officer said he knew nothing about St. Kevin's Bed, and the cripple brought the soldiers on to show them where St. Kevin's Bed was, and when he came there he pointed it out to them. But Dwyer rose up on his elbow when he saw him, and he let fly at him, and he blew him out of the old box. The soldiers took flight then, and got away with their lives. So when Dwyer expected they'd be surrounding him backwards he jumped into the lake which was never done since nor before by any man.

When Dwyer was after being married to his wife, a beautiful woman, Doyle, an officer came from Humewood Camp where they were staying—several of them and a lord—an English lord, lord Huntley and this old officer came to Mrs. Dwyer in the absence of Dwyer, and he asked her to come out on the road that he wanted to speak to her. He was very nice to her, and he made her great promises. He told her that there was as good men in England as Dwyer—she should have been cool—it wasn't I was in it!—I suppose he meant to give her the pick of an Englishman, and as well that she'd never want, that she'd have money at her command every place she'd go; he'd promise her that she'd never want for money, and he told her that there was as good men in England as Dwyer. If she'd just let him know where was Dwyer everything 'd be right, and then he looked around him and he said: "Maybe, Mrs. Dwyer, you wouldn't like to be seen speaking to me here on the road? If you'd come down to yonder grove beside the Slaney at the dusk of night, such an evening as there was moonlight, we would have a private conversation where there'd be no one to see us." Mrs. Dwyer agreed with him and said she would go, and when Dwyer came home she told him the whole story. Dwyer told her that they'd save her the journey, that he'd go and have a loving chat with this old officer, and he said to her to dress him in her grey cloak, as there was cloaks with a big hood at the back worn by girls in them days. So she dressed Dwyer in the grey cloak which covered him down to the feet, and he started to have a loving conversation with the old officer. He went down to the bank of the Slaney, and he made himself as small as he could, and he sat down concealed in his grey cloak. The old officer stepped out of the grove and gently tipped him on the shoulder to have the loving chat with Mrs. Dwyer, and to his great surprise Dwyer jumped to his feet and whipped hold of him by the throat, and threw him into the Slaney, and hammered him against the stones there till he had him boneless and senseless and lifeless, and he laid him down there beside the Slaney. He was brought off by the soldiers and buried and they made no fuss about him at all.

Two neighbours of Dwyer's went to the Glen of Imaal and advised him to surrender and not to give the English Government the pleasure of arresting him and hanging him as a dog, after all his bravery and the good acts he had done. He told them that he'd never go into Humewood to lay down his arms to a British subject, that he'd suffer death a thousand times before he'd do it, and he'd stay where he was and give them more of it. So the two men importuned him not to venture his life altogether, and that they'd go into Humewood and propose to Hume that he'd have to come out to meet Dwyer, to come to some settlement, that he wouldn't go into Humewood, that he'd never do it. Hume agreed to come out, and that he'd bring no guard of soldiers with him, nor to come by day, and he done neither, but he brought two farming men like what they were along with him and they put on Imaal Gap after nightfall, and when they were drawing near Hume got a bit shaky about Dwyer and he cried out: "Was that Dwyer?" and Dwyer said it was, and he asked him: "Dwyer have you got arms on you?" "I have," says Dwyer, "but they won't affect you tonight." So they drew near to each other, and Hume mentioned a number of the transports abroad, but Dwyer told him if he made up his mind to go anywhere he'd go where he liked, and if not he'd stay at home and give them more of it. Hume, delighted to hear of a chance of getting shut of him at all, to get him out of Ireland, threw up his arms and he said: "All right, Dwyer, all right. Go where you please. We'll send you anywhere."

So Dwyer said he'd to to Sydney in Australia, and if they did not send him there he'd go nowhere at all but would stay at home and give them more of it. So they sent him to Sydney in Australia, and he brought his pike along with him.

Billy Byrne of Ballymanus

In the year of '98, my boys, we got reason to complain
When we lost our chief commander, Billy Byrne was his name.
He was took in Dublin City and brought off to Wicklow Gaol,
And to our great misfortune, for him they'd take no bail.

When he was taken prisoner the lot against him swore
That he a Captain's title upon Mount Pleasant bore,
Before the King's grand army his men he did review
And with a piece of cannon marched on for Carrigruadh.

When the informers they came in
There was Dixon, Doyle and Davis and likewise Bid Doolin.
They thought it little scruple his precious blood to spill
Who never robbed nor murdered nor to any man did ill.

It would melt your heart with pity how these traitors did explain
That Byrne worked the cannon on Arklow's bloody plain.
They swore he worked the cannon and headed the pikemen,
And near the town of Gorey killed three loyal Orangemen.

They swore he had ten thousand men all ready at his command,
All ready for to back the French as soon as they would land.
They swore he was committed to support the United cause.
The Judge he cried out "Guilty," to be hanged by coercion laws.

One of those prosecutors I often heard him tell,
It was at his father's table he was often treated well,
And in his brother's kitchen where many did he see.
The Byrnes were well rewarded for their civility.

My curse light on you, Dixon, I ne'er will curse your soul,
It was at the Bench at Wicklow you swore without control.
The making of a false oath you thought it little sin,
To deprive the County Wicklow of the flower of all its men.

Ibid.

Where are you, Matthew Davis, or why don't you come on,
To prosecute the prisoner who now lies in Rathdrum?
The devil has him last chained repenting for his sins,
In lakes of fire and brimstone and sulphur to the chin.

When the devil saw him coming he sang a merry song,
Saying "Welcome, Matthew Davis, what kept you out so long?
Where is that traitor, Dixon, to the Crown so loyal and true?
I have a warm corner for him and, of course, Bid Doolin too."

Success to Billy Byrne! May his name forever shine,
Through Wicklow, Wexford and Kildare and all along the line.
May the Lord have mercy on his soul and all such souls as he,
Who stood upright for Ireland's cause and died for Liberty!

The Battle of Ballygullen

At dawn of day on the 4th of July, after our reconnoitring parties
had returned, our army was roused from its slumber and left its bivouac
to take up a military position on a small hill just over Ballyfad.

With Esmond Kyan and other officers, I was at the head of our
column. We were going in front to choose out the situation. All at
once, on reaching this rising ground, we found ourselves enveloped
in a thick fog which, as we advanced, became so dense that we could
not distinguish anything at upwards of twenty feet distance. After
marching some time thus, we heard a volley of musketry, the balls of
which came whistling over our heads and through our ranks. We knew
that this volley came from the enemy's advance guard, frightened at
the noise of our approach and wishing to give the alarm to their own
troops who were following. They must have feared falling into an
ambuscade in the fog.

We returned immediately to Ballyfad and took another direction,
as we could not distinguish the force of the enemy until the fog would
disappear and the day become brighter. In retracing our way down
the hill, we met numbers of our men going astray from the main body
on account of the fog. However, all soon fell in with their ranks, and
the division moved in perfect order along the high road to Gorey.

From *Memoirs of Miles Byrne, Chef de Bataillon in the Service of France*, edited
by His Widow, pp. 273-283. Gustave Bossange et Cie. Paris. 1863.

After we had marched about a mile in this direction, the fog began to clear and the morning became bright. All at once we noticed a large division of the English army, horse, foot and artillery, following our column about two musket shots distant from our rear-guard. This division was commanded by General Sir James Duff and, since he did not accelerate his march to attack us, it was evident that he was waiting for other divisions to come to his assistance before he risked battle.

Our division was marching in perfect order; the men were calm, but anxious for the command to halt and begin battle. They were continually looking behind them at the mass of red coats, glittering arms and banners, following on the same road, and flanked by a big force of cavalry which, however, did not attempt to charge our rear-guard. Our generals, therefore concluding that Sir James Duff was merely waiting for reinforcements, decided to risk a general action.

When our column had made more than two miles on the Gorey road, it turned to the right by a narrow cross-road leading to the town-land of Ballygullen, and continued for about a mile in this direction, the English following at the same distance. The Irish column then halted and formed its line of battle quickly and with great skill. Our gunmen took position behind fences on both sides of the road, while some of our pikemen, moving along with well-mounted men at their head, gave the impression that the march was being continued in the usual way. This induced the English cavalry to advance and follow as they had been doing all the morning.

Our men behind the fences allowed the cavalry to come very near the line. It was intended to let them pass on and to get them between two fires, but the impatience of our marksmen could not be restrained any longer. They began a well-directed fire on the cavalry, which was thrown into great disorder and fled, large numbers being killed and wounded.

General Duff, seeing his cavalry attacked and dispersed so suddenly, marched rapidly forward with all his forces and deployed his column. Then commenced the Battle of Ballygullen, the last regular one we fought in the County of Wexford.

The greatest bravery and generalship was displayed. Our gunmen boldly kept their position under the heaviest fire; being good marks-men, every shot either killed or wounded, and they continued this fire until their last cartridge was spent. Then a large body of pikemen, headed by almost all the chiefs, marched forward to turn the left flank of Duff's army, and to intercept his communications with Gorey. To avoid being turned, he had to fall back on the Gorey road. Thus we succeeded in making the enemy quit the field. But knowing that other divisions would soon arrive to Duff's assistance, we were unable to avail of our victory fully by pursuing and pressing home our advantage.

We had great numbers killed and wounded in this battle, which lasted two hours, and was fought with equal bravery on both sides.

Our generals, having seen that the wounded were carried away to safety, gave orders to rally and make a halt on a rising ground about half a mile from the field of battle. They wished to prepare to meet any divisions of the enemy which might be coming from Carnew, Ferns and other places. This pause also gave time to our men in the rear to rejoin their respective corps, which they did at their ease, unmolested by the enemy's cavalry which had now completely disappeared from view.

It was during the short rest taken by our army after this battle that I had my last talk with brave Anthony Perry. When I came up, he was lying on the ground holding his horse by the bridle. I sat down beside him, holding mine in the same manner. He seemed exhausted. I asked him what plan we should now follow. He replied that all the leaders believed that it would be madness to remain any longer in Wexford, overrun as it then was with English troops. They had therefore resolved to march to the Wicklow Mountains and there manoeuvre, gaining time until supplies of arms and ammunition would come from France or elsewhere.

When our men were rested and rallied, we marched off on the Ferns road, as if to attack that town. An English division, marching from the town to attack us, retreated as soon as the news of General Duff's defeat was known. We did not see their scouting parties in front, rear, nor on our flanks the rest of the day. But they were certainly ready to receive us in their garrison strongholds, which we, through want of artillery and ammunition, could not hope to capture.

After passing Cranford, we turned to the right from the Ferns road. We passed by Buckstown House, where I saw my dear mother and sister for an instant only. They, with many other females, had taken refuge in this mansion.

It was decided to make a night march in order to baffle the enemy. Our column was to march on to Wingfield and thence along the road to Kilpipe and Aughrim, that is, by the straight way which leads to Glenmalure and the Wicklow Mountains. I wish to be particular about tracing this route; some historians have stated that, after the Battle of Ballygullen, our division marched to Carrigrew and there dispersed. Far from thinking of dispersing, our men were flushed with the hope that something good was still in store for them. Never did I see them march and keep together better than they did all that day, both before and after the battle.

As Ballygullen was the last pitched battle we fought in County Wexford, I feel it but just to say that I never saw more bravery than was shown on this occasion by our leaders and men. Throughout the campaign, want of ammunition was our chief misfortune. The search for it led us to attack towns where we suffered severe losses which could have been avoided if we had had plenty of powder and ball.

I have been frequently asked if our failure was not in great measure to be attributed to the want of experienced officers in our army. Certainly, such officers are the soul of every army, and no one can esteem their worth more than I do. But it was a depôt of military stores we wanted most; we had a host of leaders who showed talents of the first order for the field. Alas! we had no friendly foreign countries to furnish us with those military stores so necessary for carrying on a war of independence, and such as the Greeks received in their struggle from every country in Europe as well as from America.

Scarcity of ammunition and our despair of getting fresh supplies decided us to march, after the Battle of Ballygullen, to the Wicklow Mountains, there to defend ourselves as best we could until our situation would improve. Another reason for this march was the lack of food in Wexford. The county had been ravaged in all directions. Last season's provisions were wholly consumed, and the new crops were still unfit for use. Though we could procure cattle, we could seldom halt and wait long enough to have them killed and the meat cooked for eating.

When I look back, I am really astonished that we bore up against hunger and fatigue, particularly on the day of the Battle of Bally-gullen. This day began at dawn, and with marching, countermarching and fighting, terminated only with a weary night march. The march was not impeded by the enemy, but our long fast caused many men to go right and left away from the main body in search of something to eat.

When we had passed Kilpipe, a brave young fellow, handsome and well mounted, rode up to me on the road. His name was Tom Woodburn. He proposed that I should go to my step-sister's house at Ballintemple, a mile away, where I could get rest and refreshment. He himself wished to stay for the night with her father-in-law, Mr. Doyle, whom he knew and whose house was but two fields from hers. I reluctantly consented to this plan, and we went to Ballintemple.

It is one of the acts of my life which frets me most when I look back. My brother-in-law, who had taken no part in the Insurrection, ran a chance of being shot or transported had I been found in his house. He was the father of six children, the eldest of them being only ten years old. How cruel it would have been had these poor children been left fatherless on my account!

My sister and her husband were terrified when they saw me. They told me that their place had been searched by the yeomen cavalry almost every day since the Battle of Arklow. These yeomen were almost sure to call and search next day.

After eating a meal which I much needed, I retired to one of the out-houses—not the stable, for that was the first place the cavalry would search to see if any horses there might suit them. I soon fell asleep, un-conscious of my danger.

At the dawn of day my poor sister, who had spent the night watch-ing and listening while I slept, woke me and led me a little distance from the house. On the hill opposite I saw at once, quite plainly, a horseman. At the same time we heard the noise of cavalry coming up the valley to the house. My sister pointed out to me the way to escape. One minute later I would have been shot or a prisoner. I crossed a field, got over a high fence and remained concealed until my dear sister came in about an hour and told me that the danger was over for the moment. The Orange cavalry had visited every part of her dwelling and out-houses. At her father-in-law's house they had cap-tured poor Thomas Woodburn, tied him neck and heels, and carried him off to Arklow or perhaps shot him on the way.

I asked my sister to send for a young man called Larry Lorgan, who had been wounded at the Battle of Arklow and had remained in hiding ever since. He immediately came to me, and we decided that during the day he would tell all the men in hiding who wished to join our army to assemble late in the evening. I undertook to lead them to our camp, which should now be on the way to Glenmalure.

At dusk he brought to the meeting place ten or twelve poor fellows, badly armed but determined to fight their way. I took leave of my poor sister and set out with my small detachment. All of them seemed de-lighted to get away from the misery of lying in hiding. They were cheered at the prospect of joining the main body again and, since most of them knew the country we had to march through, there was no need for guides.

We were joined on the way by many of our men who from fatigue had remained behind the army. At Aughrim several fine fellows came out of their hiding places and marched with us. But we could not find out definitely what direction the main body of our army had taken. We resolved to fight our way to Glenmalure without delay.

Next morning, to our great sorrow, Larry Lorgan was killed in a skirmish with a body of enemy cavalry. After this unfortunate incident we resumed our march. We arrived early that day in Glenmalure, and there I met great numbers of County Wexford men, all of whom were, like myself, at a loss to know what direction our main army had taken. We decided to organize ourselves as best we could, and to remain in Glenmalure until we might learn where Garret Byrne and the other chiefs had pitched their camp.

Glenmalure provided some food resources. Flocks of sheep grazed on the mountains arounds, but the want of salt and vegetables was sorely felt. No bread could be got for any money, and the potatoes, being unripe, were unfit for use. Thus, we had to go far away on night expeditions to get oatmeal and salt.

Here I first saw the brave, intrepid Michael Dwyer. He had already acquired a great reputation in this mountainous district. Every time the cavalry tried to reconnoitre the position near the entrance to the Glen, he was sure to be on their flank or in ambuscade, before daylight, awaiting their arrival. Both he and his followers were from this country, and were very good marksmen. They took delight in terrifying the cavalry, who wheeled about and fled the moment a shot was fired at them. So, by reason of Dwyer's bravery, we were perfectly safe at night, to rest and recover from the fatigues of our Wexford campaign.

The famous Holt had just arrived in the Glen. Worth special mention is a night expedition which we made under his command, and during which we encountered, suddenly, near the bridge of Greenan, an enemy army marching from Rathdrum to reconnoitre our position in the Glen. Hearing the noise of our column's advance, the enemy delivered a fierce discharge from their pistols, and then awaited in silence our approach.

I shall never forget Holt's presence of mind in this danger. He cried out with the voice of a Stentor, ordering our pikemen to march in a body across the bridge. In the same loud voice he ordered the gunmen to wade across the river and attack the enemy's flanks. The enemy, apparently terrified, retreated in disorder to Rathdrum, while we, on our side, had the greatest trouble in rallying our men and keeping them from disbanding. However, after some time panic subsided and we rallied again on the road and returned to the Glen.

Glenmalure is nearly three miles long. The little river, Avonbeg, coming down from high mountains, runs through it. There were several houses on each side of the river, and in those houses our men could cook the mutton which they got in abundance. They found timber for pike handles in the rafters of the smelting house belonging to the lead mines. Soon we were fairly well armed with pikes, though still badly provided with firearms and ammunition.

Sad tidings now reached us of the defeat and complete dispersal of our main army, which had marched into the Counties of Meath, Louth and Dublin. The chiefs of the Glen held a meeting, and resolved in consequence to defend the Glen more carefully than ever.

Among those who escaped to Glenmalure from the Boyne were Esmond Kyan and my brother Hugh. The former would not stay with us. He insisted on returning to Wexford, where he expected to get a safe hiding-place. Alas! he was hanged and gibbeted like the other patriots whose heads already decorated the public buildings in the town of Wexford.

Had Father Kearns and Anthony Perry reached Glenmalure, they would have been able to make use of the great advantages these Wicklow Mountains offered against the enemy. But they were doomed not to die the death of soldiers. They were both captured and hanged at Edenderry.

Lord Edward Fitzgerald

In 1773 the Duke of Leinster, father of Lord Edward, died, and the Duchess, shortly after, married a Scottish gentleman, Mr. Ogilvie, with whom she had her family removed to a house near Aubigny, in France, lent them by her brother, the Duke of Richmond.

Here the military education of little Edward was begun; he erected forts in the orangery, surveyed and drew maps of the fields about, and generally so threw himself, heart and soul, into the study of his future profession, that when the family returned to England, in 1779, he, then hardly sixteen years of age, was able to direct the pitching and laying out of a camp by the Sussex militia, of which the Duke of Richmond was colonel.

In 1780 he obtained a lieutenancy in the Ninety-sixth Regiment of foot, only to effect an exchange (as that regiment was not going into active service) into the Nineteenth, with which he went to Charleston, South Carolina, during the first year of the American Revolution, and

By Geraldine M. Haverty, in *The Gael*, September, 1901, pp. 293-296. New York.

took for a short time a most energetic part in the campaign about that city.

* * * * *

Some have been inclined to think that the future patriot received his first conceptions of sympathy with the cause of liberty during this sojourn in a country fighting for its freedom: there is no reason to think so. A brief campaign, harried by a victorious foe, and only a few months before the watchman's cry of "Past one o'clock and Cornwallis is taken!" echoed through the night in the streets of Philadelphia, presented little opportunity for the study of political problems, and, had his thoughts been turned in that direction, he could hardly have decided to enter Woolwich to complete his education as an officer of the British army, which he did, not long after his return to England.

* * * * *

During his subsequent sojourn in Canada, whither he went with his regiment, a lady's name appears constantly in his home letters, and her marriage during his absence was a severe blow to his trusting and affectionate heart.

He was learning other things in the New World, however—the virtues of republican independence, a love of freedom from the trammels and artificialities of military life, and his letters are full of enthusiastic admiration for the simple, hardy life of the frontiersman.

Here he was adopted by the Bear tribe of Indians.

* * * * *

A visit to Paris in 1792, during which he spent much time in the company of Thomas Paine, brought him in contact with the leading spirits in the movement for French liberty, which association in the intoxicating atmosphere of republicanism then gathering all Europe in its folds, all combined to develop in him the principles of national liberty and the deep love of his native land which had hitherto been unaccounted in his career.

It was at a banquet given in honor of the victories of the French arms, that he, in company with some others, formally renounced his title, and drank a toast: "The speedy abolition of all hereditary titles and feudal distinctions," which gave an opportunity for his enemies at home to procure his summary dismissal from the British army.

In the career of this brilliant young patriot, love and adventure always went side by side, and it was almost immediately after he had thus definitely proclaimed his political sentiments, that he met and fell in love with the beautiful Pamela, daughter of the Duke of Orleans and Madame de Genlis, who passed as the adopted daughter of that lady, under the name of Mademoiselle Sims.

Their first meeting was romantic; he saw her at the opera, was struck by her resemblance to a dear friend long dead, Mrs. Sheridan, who had long wished that these two should meet. But that had been prevented by Fitzgerald's professed antipathy to "learned women," among whom he counted Madame de Genlis.

Their mutual attraction was all that their dead friend could have wished, and in less than a month after their first meeting they were married in Paris, and Mademoiselle Sims became Lady Edward Fitzgerald, the renunciation of his title having been apparently a passing flash of republicanism, which was suffered to fade into oblivion.

Lord Edward took his bride to London, where she was welcomed by his indulgent mother; they then proceeded to Dublin, where they plunged anew into the sea of controversy regarding religious liberty which was beating about Parliament.

Although he delivered some fiery speeches in the House, and took a deep interest in the political struggle which was now being carried forward, Lord Edward did not identify himself with the United Irishmen for some years. He spent his time in a pleasant, quiet, domestic manner at different country places, gardening and writing long letters to his mother, in which nothing seemed further from his thoughts than the idea of engaging in any revolutionary struggle.

He formally joined the United Irishmen early in 1796, and was in the same year entrusted with a mission from that body to the French Directory, and from that time he was deeply concerned in all matters pertaining to the Rebellion.

On the 28th of April, 1798, Arthur O'Conor, probably Fitzgerald's most intimate associate in these affairs, was arrested with Father Quigley, at Margate, England, on their way to France, and incriminating papers being found upon them, they were committed to the Tower on a charge of high treason. In consequence of these discoveries the office of the *Press,* in Dublin, was entered and searched, and Fitzgerald and Mr. Sampson were found there.

Events now showed that the struggle with or without French aid must soon come, and Lord Edward's military training became useful in the organization of a revolutionary staff with officers in each county, acting under regular instructions drawn up by himself.

The fervent patriotism and absolute loyalty of the members of the

United Irishmen, which alone could have permitted so large and scattered a body of men to carry on operations under the very eyes of the government, had given the leaders a perfect trust in the integrity of their followers. Hence, the implicit confidence reposed in a few traitors such as Reynolds. It takes all kinds of men to make up a revolution, and probably there were many good men and true whose outward character was no more prepossessing than his. Though suspected and disliked by some of the party, yet he was granted admission into their most secret councils.

Dr. MacNevin writes of Reynolds: "My opportunity enabled me to know that he was given to lying, much of a glutton, and both expensive and avaricious, qualities I have never seen belong to a man of firm resolution, generous purpose, integrity and courage."

* * * * *

On Monday, March 12th, acting under the direction of Reynolds, who had been summoned to a special council, Major Swan, accompanied by thirteen sergeants, went to the house of Oliver Bond, and by means of the password "Where's McCann? Is Ivers from Carlow come?" obtained admission and arrested all who were assembled. Fortunately, neither MacNevin, Sampson, Emmet, nor Fitzgerald was there; the three first were shortly after arrested elsewhere, but Fitzgerald escaped, and went into hiding. His house was searched, and poor Pamela, ill and frightened, gave up all papers.

Her husband preserved his freedom for a few months, by rapidly changing his places of concealment, going first to the house of a widowed lady, Mrs. Dillon, near the Grand Canal, where, it is recorded, so light-hearted was he that on his walks after dark with a little child, the two could be heard laughing and talking for some distance.

* * * * *

From Mrs. Dillon's house, that retreat being in danger of discovery, he fled for shelter to the home of Mr. Murphy, in Thomas Street, between which place and the houses of two other gentlemen, Mr. McCormick and Mr. Moore, he passed his time in safety until May.

These houses were chosen because their owners belonged to a class of citizens who had most in common with the uprising, and through whom Lord Edward could hold frequent communication with the moving spirits in the enterprise to which his enthusiasm and authority and soldierly training were of such inestimable value. The plan was, when they had gained over a sufficient number of the militia (who were already much disaffected), to organize a supplement to their own untrained forces (the hope of aid from France having dwindled to a mere chance of obtaining some skilled officers) that Lord Edward should raise his standard at Leinster, and take Dublin with the lord-lieutenant and other government officials.

Though searched for with eagerness by the government, he still continued to direct operations from his retreat, and the anxiety for his capture became so strong that 1,000 pounds was offered for his apprehension. His family, meanwhile, imagined him safe out of the country, and though wondering at the reward, felt no fears for his safety.

He had retired for a while to the country, but, the date for the general uprising being set for the night of the 23rd of May, and his personal assistance being required in Dublin, Fitzgerald accordingly returned, and traveling for the last time through his old hiding places, finally arrived at Mr. Murphy's house, where his uniform, of dark green and crimson, was brought to him and concealed by Mr. Murphy in an outhouse.

Treachery was now doing its work; the government was advised of the whereabouts of the noble fugitive, who had so long evaded them, and it was on the afternoon of the 19th of May, just after dinner, when Lord Edward had gone up to his room and was lying on his bed, that the house was abruptly entered by Major Swan and a man named Ryan, who was the printer of an Orange newspaper and a captain of yeomanry.

Mr. Murphy, who was speaking to his guest, was disturbed by the tramping of feet upon the stairs, and turning, confronted the intruders. Lord Edward started to his feet, whereupon Swan fired a pistol at him, which not taking effect, he struck Murphy in the face, and hustled him from the room. Ryan, meanwhile, had attacked Fitzgerald, who had produced a small crooked dagger which he kept about him. A desperate struggle ensued, during which Ryan received a wound which afterwards proved fatal. Major Swan having placed guards about the house now hurried up into the room with a party of soldiers, and firing, shot Lord Edward in the arm, compelling him to drop his dagger.

It required the united efforts of the party to subdue their prisoner; they finally held him down with their muskets crossed, a drummer having meanwhile wounded him in the neck with a sword.

He was carried to the castle, and thence to Newgate, under a strong force of soldiery.

Here he remained, wounded and ill, and under the fearful strain and fever consequent on his wounds his mind became unbalanced.

His knowledge of the execution of young Clinch, just outside his cell, and the cruelty which prohibited any of his family and friends from visiting him in his prison, contributed in no small measure to his illness and misfortune.

Pamela, the "poor, pale, pretty little wife," as he used to call her, in a very low condition from fright and illness, had been taken away to England, as there was no chance of her being of any use in Ireland, and there was much suspicion and prejudice against her on account of her French connections.

It was not until the evening before he died that his aunt, Lady Louisa Connolly, hearing through another late prisoner in Newgate of his dangerous condition, made a desperate and successful effort to see him. Failing with Lord Camden, she hastened to Lord Clare, who, overcome by her violent entreaties, consented to go with her to Newgate and procure admission to the prisoner.

She took with her Lord Henry Fitzgerald, brother of the patriot. Lady Louisa wrote an account of this visit, in which she describes the pleasure of Lord Edward at their visit, but adds that "his senses were much lulled."

He died in convulsions caused by his wounds about two hours after the visitors had departed, a sad ending for one of his temperament.

He loved the open strife of the battlefield, and the soldier's life; he died in prison. He had dearly loved his family and friends, and had died away from them, attended only by unfriendly prison guards. Freedom, gaiety, and pleasure he had loved, and his last hours were lonely, dark, and miserable.

Moore tells us how he once hastened after him in the street, "desirous," as he says, "of another look at one whose name had, from my school days, been associated in my mind with all that was noble, patriotic and chivalrous. Though I saw him but this once," he continues, "his peculiar dress, the elastic lightness of his step, his fresh, healthful complexion, and the soft expression given to his eyes by their long, dark eyelashes, are as present and familiar to my memory as if I had intimately known him."

John Philpot Curran

The sparkling wit, the brilliant orator, the enthusiastic advocate, the extraordinary humorist, the flashing conversationalist was with all

By Charles O'Hanlon, in *The Gael*, February, 1900, pp. 52-54. New York.

one of the most devoted, true-hearted patriots and statesmen ever given birth to. He was born on the 24th day of July, 1750, at the little town of Newmarket, in the County of Cork. His father, James Curran, was Seneschal of the manor court of Newmarket, and was a man of moderate acquirements and of very limited circumstances. His mother, whose maiden name was Philpot, was of a very respectable family, and possessed of rare mental endowments. Curran was accustomed to say: "The only inheritance I can boast of from my poor father, was the very scanty one of an unattractive face and person like his own, and if the world has ever attributed to me something more valuable than face and person, or than earthly wealth, it was that another and a dearer parent gave her child a portion from the treasures of her mind."

. . . The early career of the wayward, witty, and erratic village-boy, bore with it the usual sparkling coruscations of genius. In all youthful sports and pastimes, young Curran took the lead, and on one occasion became the unknown spokesman to an itinerant Punch and Judy show, to the great amazement of the audience, who were puzzled at the intimate knowledge which Mr. Punch seemed to possess of all the salient and comic points of Village gossip. . . .

His course in college was marked with social and convivial powers; wit, comicality, and impudence, yet with great love of classical lore and literature. Having qualified for a master's degree, in 1773, he left college, and entered as a law student in the Middle Temple, London.

To the lamentations of a woman at an Irish wake, Curran attributed his great love of oratory. His first attempts at public speaking were utter failures, not only from confusion and precipitation of utterance, whence he derived the cognomen of "Stuttering Jack Curran," but from a nervous paralysis, to which the most imaginative minds are subject on first encountering the gaze of a large audience.

Five years later he appeared in a cause célèbre at the Cork assizes. It was a singular case, and served to display the courage that was his distinguishing characteristic. A Catholic peasant had fallen under the censure of the Church. His sister was the mistress of a territorial magnate, Lord Doneraile. She begged his lordship to force the parish priest to remove the censure. Lord Doneraile, accompanied by a military fire-eater, Captain St. Leger, called upon the priest. The priest would not yield, and Lord Doneraile horsewhipped him. An action for assault was the result. But there was not a member of the Munster circuit who would hold a brief against the great nobleman. The story of the outrage shocked Curran. He volunteered his services. They were accepted.

Taking into account the prostrate condition of the Catholics at that period, the bigotry of Protestant juries, and the extraordinary circumstance of a poor priest suing for justice against a Protestant lord, the success of Curran, in obtaining a verdict with thirty guineas damages for his client, was regarded by the general public as the highest proof of forensic ability and eloquence. In his appeal to the jury he described Mr. St. Leger, who was a relative of Lord Doneraile's, and who had recently retired from a regiment that had been ordered on actual service, as "A renegade soldier, a drummed-out dragoon, who wanted the courage to meet the enemies of his country in battle, but had the heroism to redeem the ignominy of his flight from danger by raising his arm against an aged and unoffending minister of religion, who had just risen from putting up before the throne of God a prayer of general intercession, in which his heartless insulter was included." The result was a duel in which Curran declined to return his adversary's innocuous fire. These circumstances established a lasting claim to the homage and admiration of his enthusiastic countrymen for the Protestant advocate, and they ever after regarded him as one of themselves.

Curran's practice at the bar grew rapidly, and he soon rose to the front rank in his profession. He had all the qualities of a great advocate. He was eloquent, judicious, painstaking, good-tempered; quick to see the faults in an adversary, and always ready to turn them to the best advantage; a master of invective and a master of humor; able to amuse, coax, convince; a favorite alike with judges who were not corrupt; and with juries who wished honestly to do their duty; a popular orator and a perfect cross-examiner.

* * * * *

As a cross-examiner, indeed, Curran's skill was unrivalled. He was ingenious, witty, trenchant, raking a witness by a fire of raillery or overwhelming him by a series of perplexing questions. "My lord," cried one of his victims, "I cannot answer Mr. Curran, he is putting me in such a doldrum." "A doldrum," exclaimed the judge; "what is a doldrum, Mr. Curran?" "Oh, my lord," replied Curran, "it is a common complaint with persons like the witness. It is a confusion of the head, arising from a corruption of the heart."

* * * * *

A barrister entered the hall with his wig very much awry, and of which he was not at all apprised, he was obliged to endure from almost every observer some remark on its appearance, till at last addressing himself to Mr. Curran, he asked him, "Do you see anything ridiculous in this wig?" The answer instantly was, "Nothing but the head."

Bills of indictment had been sent up to a grand jury in the finding of which Curran was interested. After delay and much hesitation, one of the grand jurors came into court to explain the reason why it was ignored. Curran, very much vexed by the stupidity of this person, said, "You, sir, can have no objection to write upon the back of the bill ignoramus, for self and fellow-jurors; it will then be a true bill."

* * * * *

There was one Irish judge—*mirabile dictu*—a dull, black-letter lawyer, who did not relish his wit. On one occasion, when Curran rose to cross-examine a witness, the witness laughed. "What are you laughing at?" said Curran. "Let me tell you that a laugh without a joke is like—is like—" "Is like what, Mr. Curran," growled the judge. "Like a contingent retainer, my lord, without any particular estate to support it," was the reply.

"How do you get your living?" Curran asked a witness. "Please, sir, I keep a racket court," was the answer. "So do I," said Lord Norbury (himself a bit of a wit) in allusion to the uproar caused by Curran's sallies and, indeed, by his own jokes.

Curran Defends the Rebels

It was by his defense of the United Irishmen, however, that Curran's fame was established. The United Irish Society, originally a constitutional body, ultimately became a revolutionary organization, whose object was the separation of Ireland from England by force of arms.

Curran was more than the advocate of the United Irishmen. He was their friend. Though himself not a separatist, he sympathized with their aspirations, and admired the courage and self-sacrifice with which they devoted themselves to the national cause. His task was difficult, even perilous, but he risked everything for his clients. "In the days," says Charles Phillips, "from which he dates his glory, peril beset his path, armed men composed his auditory, exasperated authority denounced his zeal, and faction scowled upon the dauntless advocate it burned to make its victim."

Ibid., pp. 54-55.

One of the judges—Lord Carleton—warned him that if he defended Samuel Neilson—one of the founders of the United Irish Society—he would lose his silk gown. "Well, my lord," said Curran, "his Majesty may take the silk, but he will leave the *stuff* behind."

In 1794 he defended Hamilton Rowan for seditious libel. The United Irishmen of Dublin had issued an address, in 1792, to the Volunteers, beginning, "Citizen soldiers," condemning the policy of the government, advocating the claims of the Catholics, and calling on the nation "to arm" in defense of its liberties.

Mr. Lecky has described Curran's speech for the defense as "one of the most eloquent speeches ever delivered at the Bar." When he rose, the court was filled with troops. He said, "Gentlemen of the jury, when I consider the period at which this prosecution is brought forward; when I behold the extraordinary safeguard of armed soldiers resorted to—no doubt for the preservation of peace and order—when I catch, as I cannot but do, the throb of public anxiety which beats from one end to the other of this hall . . . it is in the honest simplicity of my heart I speak when I say that I never rose in court of justice with so much embarrassment as upon this occasion."

The finest passage in the speech—one of the finest passages, perhaps, in any speech ever delivered at the Bar—was on the justice of "universal emancipation," and when Curran issued into the street afterwards, his appearance was the signal for a popular ovation.

He himself has described the scene. The people gathered around him. He feared that they might take him off his legs and carry him on their shoulders about the town. He begged them to "desist." "I laid great emphasis," he says, "on the word desist, and put on my best suit of dignity. However, my next neighbor, a gigantic, brawny chairman, eyeing me with somewhat of contemptuous affection from top to toe, bellowed out to his companions, 'Arrah, blood and turf, Pat, don't mind the little crayture; here, pitch him up this minute upon my shoulder,' which was accordingly done."

In 1798, Curran defended the brothers Sheares for high treason. They were the sons of a banker in Cork. Both were educated at Trinity College, Dublin; both were United Irishmen; both were members of the Bar. John, the younger of the two, aged thirty-two, took an active part in the movement. He was an organizer, and stood high in the confidence of his leaders. Henry, aged forty-five, was not equally implicated. Indeed, the principal evidence against him was a treasonable proclamation found in his desk. It was written by John and put in the desk without Henry's knowledge.

An unscrupulous scoundrel named Armstrong (Captain Armstrong) wormed himself into the confidence of the brothers, and betrayed them. He received the sum of 29,000 pounds—spread over a period of sixty years—for this act of infamy. The trial took place on July 4, amid a scene of intense public excitement and anxiety. The judges acted like partisans, and no consideration was shown either to the prisoners or their counsel. After a continuous sitting of sixteen hours, Curran asked for a short adjournment.

"I protest," he said, "I have sunk under this trial. If I must go on, the court must bear with me. I will go on until I sink; but after a sitting of sixteen hours with only twenty minutes' interval, I should hope it would not be thought an obtrusive request to ask for a few hours' interval of repose and recollection." "What say you, Mr. Attorney-General?" said the judge. "My lords," said the Attorney-General (Toler, afterwards Lord Norbury), "I cannot consent." "We think it better to go on, Mr. Curran," said the judge, hinting at the same time that much had been conceded to the prisoners.

Curran: "Gentlemen of the jury, it seems that much has been conceded to us. God help us. I do not know what has been conceded to me; if so insignificant a person may have extorted the remark. Perhaps it is a concession that I am allowed to rise in such a state of mind and body, of collapse and deprivation, as to feel but a little spark of indignation, raised by the remark that much has been conceded to the counsel for the prisoners! Much has been conceded to the prisoners. Almighty and merciful God, who lookest down upon us, what are the times to which we are reserved, when we are told that much has been conceded to prisoners who are put upon their trial at a moment like this—of more darkness and night of the human intellect than a darkness of the natural period of twenty-four hours—that public convenience cannot spare a few hours to those who are accused for their lives, and that much has been conceded to the advocate almost exhausted in the poor remarks that he has endeavored to make upon it. My countrymen, I do pray you by the awful duty which you owe your country—by that sacred duty which you owe your character—and I know how you feel it—I do beseech you by Almighty God to have mercy upon my client—to save him, not from the consequences of his guilt, but from the baseness of his accusers, and the pressure of the treatment under which I am sinking."

On Friday morning, at eight o'clock, the jury returned a verdict of guilty. Then the court adjourned for a few hours. At 3 P.M. the prisoners were sentenced to death. On Saturday morning they were hanged.

In July '98, Curran defended Oliver Bond, a wealthy Dublin merchant (though a native of Ulster) and a United Irishman. He was one of the most powerful men in the organization. It was at his house that the Leinster Directory used to hold their meetings. Through the treachery of an informer—Reynolds—the house was surrounded by military in March '98, and the members of the Directory seized. According to the practice of the times, the court was filled with soldiers.

While Curran was addressing the jury, there was a sudden clash of arms. "What is that?" he cried. Those who were nearest to him scowled fiercely at him, as if they would do him violence. "You may assassinate, but you shall not intimidate me," cried the fearless advocate. So great was the turmoil, that he had to resume his seat. Three times he rose, and three times he had to sit down before he could be heard. "I have very little, scarcely any hope," he said, "of being able to discharge my duty to my unfortunate client—perhaps most unfortunate in having me for his advocate. I know not whether to impute these inhuman interruptions to mere accident; but I greatly fear they have been excited by prejudice."

Curran was a member of the Irish House of Commons—from 1783 to 1797—but his political speeches are not remarkable. He was, of course, a staunch Nationalist, and resisted the union like all the incorruptible Irishmen of the day.

* * * * *

The Volunteers were disbanded, and the Parliament was destroyed. When all was over, Curran was standing one day outside the Parliament buildings. A nobleman—who had been ennobled because he had voted for the Union—came up and said, "Curran, what do they mean to do with that useless building? For my part, I hate even the sight of it." "I do not wonder," rejoined Curran. "I never yet heard of a murderer who was not afraid of a ghost."

* * * * *

"Is that hung beef, Mr. Curran?" said Lord Norbury (familiarly known as the "hanging judge") to Curran at a Viceregal dinner party. "No, my lord," was the reply; "your lordship hasn't tried it."

Curran and a friend were walking together one day at Cheltenham. An Irish acquaintance who aped English manners was seen coming along lolling his tongue out in a remarkable fashion. "What on earth does he mean by that?" said the friend. "He's trying to catch the English accent," said Curran.

Curran and Robert Emmet

One dark shadow hangs over the life of Curran—the fate of Robert Emmet, the brother of one of the most gifted of the United Irishmen, Thomas Addis Emmet, and himself an enthusiastic rebel, the leader of the hopeless attempt which a handful of men made to seize Dublin Castle in 1803. Emmet loved Curran's daughter Sarah. They were engaged to be married.

Curran knew nothing of the facts. He saw Emmet frequently at his house, but suspected nothing. Then the rising came. After its suppression Emmet could have escaped. But he wished to see Sarah Curran once more. He concealed himself in a house near Curran's. He wrote to Sarah—tried to see her. Then his hiding place was discovered. He was arrested. His relations with Sarah Curran became public. Curran's house was searched for papers, and Curran himself had to undergo an examination before his inveterate enemy, Lord Clare. Curran was indignant. He refused to defend Emmet, refused even to see the doomed rebel.

"I did not expect you," wrote Emmet, "to be my counsel. I nominated you because not to have done so might have appeared remarkable. Had Mr. B—— been in town, I did not wish even to have seen you, but as he was not I wrote to you to come to me at once. I know that I have done you a very severe injury, much greater than I can atone for with my life; that atonement I did offer to make before the Privy Council by pleading guilty, if those documents were suppressed."

Then, referring to his love for Sarah Curran, and to Curran's refusal to see him, he concluded:

"I know not whether this" (his love for Sarah) "will be any extenuation of my offense—I know not whether it will be any extenuation of it to know that if I had the first 'situation' in the land in my power at this moment I would relinquish it to devote my life to her happiness. I know not whether success would have blotted out the recollection of what I have done; but I know that a man with the coldness of death on him need not be made to feel any other coldness, and that he may be spared any addition to the misery he feels not for himself but for those to whom he has left nothing but sorrow."

On September 20, 1803, Emmet was hanged; he was only twenty-four. Sarah Curran spent the rest of her days in England, where she died in 1808. Moore has enshrined her memory in immortal lines:

Ibid., pp. 55-56.

She is far from the land where her young hero sleeps,
    And lovers around her sighing;
But coldly she turns from their gaze, and weeps,
    For her heart in the grave is lying.
She sings the wild songs of her dear native plains,
    Every note which he loved awaking;
Ah! little they think, who delight in her strains,
    How the heart of the minstrel is breaking.

He had lived for his love, for his country he died,
    They were all that to life had entwined him;
Nor soon shall the tears of his country be dried,
    Nor long will his love stay behind him.
Oh! make her a grave where the sunbeams rest
    When they promise a glorious morrow;
They'll shine o'er her sleep, like a smile from the West,
    For her own loved island of sorrow.

Robert Emmet, on Being Found Guilty of Treason*

My Lords:—What have I to say why sentence of death should not be pronounced on me according to law? I have nothing to say that can alter your predetermination, nor that it will become me to say with any view to the mitigation of that sentence which you are here to pronounce, and I must abide by. But I have that to say which interests

---

From *The World's Famous Orations*, Williams Jennings Bryan, editor-in-chief, Vol. VI, pp. 137-148. Copyright, 1906, by Funk & Wagnalls Co. New York.

* Delivered at the Session House in Dublin before the court which had convicted him of high treason, September 19, 1803. Emmet, at that time only twenty-three years old, had taken part in a rebellion against the government. The famous address here given was an impromptu one, delivered while Emmet stood forward in the dock in front of the bench. Curran's daughter, to whom Emmet was engaged, and of whom Moore wrote the poem beginning, "She is far from the land where her young hero sleeps," two years afterward married an officer of some distinction in the Royal Staff Corps, Major Sturgeon. She died in Sicily a few months later—it is said of a broken heart.

Born in 1778, died in 1803; became a leader of the United Irishmen, and in 1803 led an unsuccessful rising in Dublin; escaping to the mountains he returned to Dublin to take leave of his fiancée, Sarah Curran, daughter of the orator, and was captured and hanged.—W.J.B.

me more than life, and which you have labored (as was necessarily your office in the present circumstances of this oppressed country) to destroy. I have much to say why my reputation should be rescued from the load of false accusation and calumny which has been heaped upon it. I do not imagine that, seated where you are, your minds can be so free from impurity as to receive the least impression from what I am going to utter—I have no hopes that I can anchor my character in the breasts of a court constituted and trammeled as this is—I only wish, and it is the utmost I expect, that your lordships may suffer it to float down your memories untainted by the foul breath of prejudice, until it finds some more hospitable harbor to shelter it from the storm by which it is at present buffeted.

Was I only to suffer death after being adjudged guilty by *your* tribunal, I should bow in silence, and meet the fate that awaits me without a murmur; but the sentence of law which delivers my body to the executioner, will, through the ministry of that law, labor in its own vindication to consign my character to obloquy—for there must be guilt somewhere: whether in the sentence of the court or in the catastrophe, posterity must determine. A man in my situation, my lords, has not only to encounter the difficulties of fortune, and the force of power over minds which it has corrupted or subjugated, but the difficulties of established prejudice: the man dies, but his memory lives. That mine may not perish, that it may live in the respect of my countrymen, I seize upon this opportunity to vindicate myself from some of the charges alleged against me. When my spirit shall be wafted to a more friendly port; when my shade shall have joined the bands of those martyred heroes who have shed their blood on the scaffold and in the field, in defense of their country and of virtue, this is my hope: I wish that my memory and name may animate those who survive me, while I look down with complacency on the destruction of that perfidious government which upholds its domination by blasphemy of the Most High—which displays its power over man as over the beasts of the forest—which sets man upon his brother, and lifts his hand in the name of God against the throat of his fellow who believes or doubts a little more or a little less than the government standard—a government which is steeled to barbarity by the cries of the orphans and the tears of the widows which it has made.*

I appeal to the immaculate God—I swear by the throne of Heaven,

---

* At this period Lord Norbury interrupted Emmet, saying severely, that the mean and wicked enthusiasts who felt as he did "were not equal to the accomplishment of their wild designs."—W.J.B.

before which I must shortly appear—by the blood of the murdered patriots who have gone before me—that my conduct has been through all this peril and all my purposes, governed only by the convictions which I have uttered, and by no other view, than that of their cure, and the emancipation of my country from the superinhuman oppression under which she has so long and too patiently travailed; and that I confidently and assuredly hope that, wild and chimerical as it may appear, there is still union and strength in Ireland to accomplish this noble enterprise. Of this I speak with the confidence of intimate knowledge, and with the consolation that appertains to that confidence. Think not, my lords, I say this for the petty gratification of giving you a transitory uneasiness; a man who never yet raised his voice to assert a lie, will not hazard his character with posterity by asserting a falsehood on a subject so important to his country, and on an occasion like this. Yes, my lords, a man who does not wish to have his epitaph written until his country is liberated, will not leave a weapon in the power of envy; nor a pretense to impeach the probity which he means to preserve even in the grave to which tyranny consigns him.*

Again I say, that what I have spoken, was not intended for your lordship, whose situation I commiserate rather than envy—my expressions were for my countrymen; if there is a true Irishman present, let my last words cheer him in the hour of his affliction.†

I have always understood it to be the duty of a judge when a prisoner has been convicted, to pronounce the sentence of the law; I have also understood that judges sometimes think it their duty to hear with patience, and to speak with humanity; to exhort the victims of the laws, and to offer with tender benignity his opinions of the motives by which he was actuated in the crime, of which he had been adjudged guilty: that a judge has thought it his duty so to have done, I have no doubt—but where is the boasted freedom of your institutions, where is the vaunted impartiality, clemency, and mildness of your courts of justice, if an unfortunate prisoner, whom your policy, and not pure justice, is about to deliver into the hands of the executioner, is not suffered to explain his motives sincerely and truly, and to vindicate the principles by which he was actuated?

My lords, it may be a part of the system of angry justice, to bow a man's mind by humiliation to the purposed ignominy of the scaffold;

---

* Here he was again interrupted by the court.—W.J.B.

† Again Emmet was interrupted, Lord Norbury saying he did not sit there to hear treason.—W.J.B.

but worse to me than the purposed shame, or the scaffold's terrors, would be the shame of such unfounded imputations as have been laid against me in this court: you, my lord [Lord Norbury], are a judge, I am the supposed culprit; I am a man, you are a man also; by a revolution of power, we might change places, tho we never could change characters; if I stand at the bar of this court, and dare not vindicate my character, what a farce is your justice? If I stand at this bar and dare not vindicate my character, how dare you calumniate it? Does the sentence of death which your unhallowed policy inflicts on my body, also condemn my tongue to silence and my reputation to reproach? Your executioner may abridge the period of my existence, but while I exist I shall not forbear to vindicate my character and motives from your aspersions; and as a man to whom fame is dearer than life, I will make the last use of that life in doing justice to that reputation which is to live after me, and which is the only legacy I can leave to those I honor and love, and for whom I am proud to perish. As men, my lord, we must appear at the great day at one common tribunal, and it will then remain for the searcher of all hearts to show a collective universe who was engaged in the most virtuous actions, or actuated by the purest motives—my country's oppressors or——*

My lord, will a dying man be denied the legal privilege of exculpating himself, in the eyes of the community, of an undeserved reproach thrown upon him during his trial, by charging him with ambition, and attempting to cast away, for a paltry consideration, the liberties of his country? Why did your lordship insult me? or rather why insult justice, in demanding of me why sentence of death should not be pronounced? I know, my lord, that form prescribes that you should ask the question; the form also presumes a right of answering. This no doubt may be dispensed with—and so might the whole ceremony of trial, since sentence was already pronounced at the castle, before your jury was impaneled; your lordships are but the priests of the oracle, and I submit; but I insist on the whole of the forms.

I am charged with being an emissary of France! An emissary of France! And for what end? It is alleged that I wished to sell the independence of my country! And for what end? Was this the object of my ambition? And is this the mode by which a tribunal of justice reconciles contradictions? No, I am no emissary; and my ambition was to hold a place among the deliverers of my country—not in power, nor in profit, but in the glory of the achievement! Sell my country's independence to France! And for what? Was it for a change of masters?

---

* Here Emmet was told to listen to the sentence of the law.—W.J.B.

No! But for ambition! O my country, was it personal ambition that could influence me? Had it been the soul of my actions, could I not by my education and fortune, by the rank and consideration of my family, have placed myself among the proudest of my oppressors? My country was my idol; to it I sacrificed every selfish, every endearing sentiment; and for it, I now offer up my life. O God! No, my lord; I acted as an Irishman, determined on delivering my country from the yoke of a foreign and unrelenting tyranny, and from the more galling yoke of a domestic faction, which is its joint partner and perpetrator in the parricide, for the ignominy of existing with an exterior of splendor and of conscious depravity. It was the wish of my heart to extricate my country from this doubly riveted despotism.

I wished to place her independence beyond the reach of any power on earth; I wished to exalt you to that proud station in the world.

* * * * *

Be yet patient! I have but a few words more to say. I am going to my cold and silent grave: my lamp of life is nearly extinguished: my race is run: the grave opens to receive me, and I sink into its bosom! I have but one request to ask at my departure from this world—it is the charity of its silence! Let no man write my epitaph: for as no man who knows my motives dare now vindicate them, let not prejudice or ignorance asperse them. Let them and me repose in obscurity and peace, and my tomb remain uninscribed, until other times, and other men, can do justice to my character; when my country takes her place among the nations of the earth, then, and not till then, let my epitaph be written. I have done.*

The Story of Sarah Curran

Among the many pathetic figures in the galaxy of Irish heroines stands the slender and drooping form of Sarah Curran, daughter of

---

* At his execution Emmet, in passing out of his cell, met the turnkey who had been kind to him. Fettered as he was he could not shake hands with him, but instead kissed him on the cheek. The turnkey is said to have fainted then and there and not to have recovered until after Emmet was hanged and his head severed from his body.—W.J.B.

By Geraldine M. Haverty, in *The Gael*, March, 1901, pp. 96-98. New York.

John Philpot Curran, and betrothed of the ill-fated young patriot, Robert Emmet.

Her fate was the more touching because of the extreme gentleness of her character, and the utter lack of glory or excitement in her life of great sorrow. Hers was a passive and unmarked career. Heroine she could scarcely be called, save for the ennobling influence of a great trouble.

A lonely childhood was hers. Her mother had deserted husband and children when Sarah was but a mere child, and this unhappy act had the effect of making the father, for a period at least, treat his children with marked coldness and severity. As they grew up, we have little evidences that he was a most affectionate and attentive parent, but it is, nevertheless, true that Sarah, at least, seemed to feel the effect of these early years of sternness. Hers was a peculiarly timid and reserved nature, and it was this very fear and timidity that was the cause of much of the trouble that overwhelmed her in later years.

It was at a ball given in her honor at the house of Mr. Lambart, Rath Castle, in Wicklow, that Sarah Curran and Robert Emmet first met. The meeting was signalized on his side by the sudden development of a passion that was as lasting as it was fiery. Sarah, on the contrary, was quite untouched. She was either indifferent to the handsome and dashing young patriot, or, else, was afraid of him. A delicate flower was she, pale and slender, with a crown of golden hair, and a refined patrician style of face and manner. Barely seventeen, unused to the world, and much in awe of her father, it might be easily guessed that she hesitated to encourage the addresses of any suitor, especially one who would prove so unpleasing to her father, as a visionary, reckless, and extremely revolutionary young student.

In Trinity, where Emmet was a student, he was at this time somewhat under a cloud, on account of his known political opinions. A formal investigation had been made by the Chancellor (afterwards Lord Clare) in which all the students were examined under oath.

One writer says:

"There were a few—amongst the number poor Robert Emmet—whose total absence from the scene, as well as the silence that followed the calling out of his name, proclaimed how deep had been his share in the transactions now to be inquired into."

* * * * *

It was just at this period of his career that he met Sarah Curran, and another incentive to action was added to his violent patriotism, in the shape of an ambition to win honors and triumphs which he could lay at the feet of his gentle lady. "I must make myself worthy of the woman of my choice," he said to a confidante, "and the glory which sheds its lustre on the husband shall reflect its splendor on the wife."

At first, she gave him no encouragement whatever. His frequent visits to her father's house (where he was always welcome, his father and Curran having been close friends) were probably attributed by the unobservant parent to a natural pleasure taken in his own society by ambitious or admiring friends.

It was not until after he had returned from Paris, whence he should have sailed to join his brother, Thomas Addis, in America, and his secret plots and affiliations being in part discovered, he was in some danger, that sympathy began to enlist her affections.

"Afterwards," Emmet writes in his letter to Curran after his arrest, "I had reason to suppose that discoveries were made, and that I should be obliged to quit the kingdom immediately, and I came to make a renunciation of any approach to friendship that might have been formed. . . . I then for the first time, found, when I was unfortunate, by the manner in which she was affected, that there was a return of affection, and that it was too late to retreat."

Among the predominant traits in Robert Emmet's character, and the ones which most certainly foiled his plans and made him an easy prey to the spies and informers of the day, were his simplicity and unsuspicious truthfulness. He was "confident of success," says Madden, "exaggerating its prospects, extenuating the difficulties which beset him, judging of others by himself, thinking associates honest who had seemed so, and animated, or rather inflamed, by a burning sense of the wrongs of his country, and an enthusiasm in his devotion to what he considered its rightful cause."

It is strange that he should not have given a thought to the danger to which he was exposing a young and very innocent and simple-minded girl. If Sarah Curran had any ideas of patriotism, she never seemed to have expressed them. She was not the stuff of which patriots are made. The task of braving her lover's departure probably had far greater terrors for her than had the project of defying the whole British government for her lover. Yet her constancy was unswerving. She carried on a constant correspondence with him, through the medium of Miss Lambart, whose part in the matter was, to say the least, injudicious. Finally, the storm broke. The little insurrection, so excellently planned, so ill carried out, was soon over. The lack of anything like concerted action was evident. The Wicklow men, not being ordered, had not arrived; the Kildare men were turned back;

the Wexford contingent came and remained waiting for orders, which never came. Other bodies of men were waiting in convenient places for signals which were not given. All this gives evidence of traitors in the ranks, and when, to crown all, a false alarm "The army is upon us" was suddenly given, Emmet determined to sally forth, and meet death in the street, if need be, rather than remain cooped up in ignorance. Even yet, all might have been saved, had it not been for the murder of Lord Kilwarden; but, on hearing of that lamentable act, the unhappy leader gave up all hope, and fled precipitately.

Curran's first news of the whole business was gained next morning, when he found a detachment of soldiers, under Major Sirr, waiting for him outside "The Priory," with the information that they were to search his house for evidences of complicity in the transactions of the preceding night.

"Almost thunderstruck," says Curran, "I at once proffered every facility in my power. To my utter amazement a correspondence of which I had not even a suspicion was discovered." A severe blow this to a man of Curran's prominence in public matters.

The unfortunate prime mover in the matter was lying hidden at Harold's Cross, a spot halfway between Dublin and "The Priory." He might have escaped, had it not been for a Quixotic resolution of seeing once more his lady-love, and personally begging her forgiveness for the calamities he had brought upon her. Even after his discovery and arrest, he, with characteristic simplicity, entrusted a letter addressed to Sarah, to a person employed about the jail. The unknown messenger pocketed the money, given by Emmet, and promptly delivered the letter to the authorities. On hearing this, the unhappy young conspirator, in despair lest he should still further have committed her in the eyes of the law, addressed a letter to the government in which he engaged himself to submit to his fate without one word in his own defense, provided the letter was suppressed.

Curran's refusal to defend Emmet can hardly be wondered at, in view of the circumstances and of the fact that he himself stood on delicate ground in Irish matters. His fellow-lawyers, however, stood by him to a man, with the exception, of course, of Fitzgibbon, afterwards Lord Clare, long a bitter rival of the brilliant advocate.

The trial and sentence, however, were but a foregone conclusion. "Pray do not attempt to defend me," Emmet said to his counsel Barrowes. "It is all in vain."

* * * * *

Sarah Curran failed, slowly but surely, after the tragic death of her lover. She left her father's house not as some have said, because ordered by him (Curran was not a hard-hearted man, and had been very fond of this delicate, timid child) but for various reasons—change of air, and separation from the scenes of so much sorrow. She stayed at Cork, with some Quaker friends named Penrose. She was petted and consoled by all who knew her, but the memory of the gallows and the nameless grave of her beloved seemed always before her mind. She moved like a shadow among the gayest scenes.

Washington Irving says: "She did not object to frequent the haunts of pleasure but she was as much alone there as in the depths of solitude. She walked about in a sad reverie, apparently unconscious of the world about her."

The story of one so true and tender could not but excite interest in a country remarkable for enthusiasm. It completely won the heart of a brave officer, who paid his addresses to her, and thought that one so true to the dead could not but prove affectionate to the living. She declined his attentions, for her thoughts were irrevocably engrossed by the thought of her former lover. He, however, persisted in his suit. He solicited, not her tenderness, but her esteem. He was assisted by her conviction of his worth, and her sense of her own destitute and dependent situation, for she was existing on the kindness of friends. In a word, he succeeded in gaining her hand, though with a solemn assurance that her heart was unalterably another's.

The marriage was thus recorded in the *Hibernian Magazine*: "February, 1806, at Cork, Captain R. H. Sturgeon, of the Royal Staff Corps, and nephew to the late Lord Rockingham, to Miss Sarah Curran, daughter of John P. Curran."

The fact that the marriage took place at Cork, instead of at her father's house, as well as Irving's conviction that she was living on the charity of friends, seems to indicate that her father had really cast her off. Her husband took her to Italy, in the vain hope of reviving her wasted strength and repairing her broken heart, but nothing could cure her silent and devouring melancholy. "She tried to be an exemplary wife, but was never a happy one." A little incident which happened months after her marriage showed how deeply her thoughts were rooted in the past.

A portrait of Emmet, as he appeared at his trial, had been painted by George Petrie, from sketches which he had taken at the time.

The artist's little son, alone in the studio one day, saw a closely veiled lady enter, who did not notice this boy, but walked up to the easel, and after gazing long in silence on the pictured face, broke into a passion of grief which seemed to the frightened child, crouching in his corner, to last an hour. After this burst of sorrow was over, she controlled herself and left the room. Long afterwards, the boy learned from his father that the visitor had been Sarah Curran, coming by appointment, to see her dead love's portrait, on condition that she should meet no member of the family.

. . . If her family had really been estranged from her in life they at least received her after her death, for she was buried at Newmarket in the same tomb with Curran's mother, Sarah Philpot. Her husband was killed six years later, in the war of 1814.

Wolfe Tone, on Being Found Guilty of Treason*

I mean not to give you the trouble of bringing judicial proof to convict me legally of having acted in hostility to the government of his Britannic majesty in Ireland. I admit the fact. From my earliest youth I have regarded the connection between Great Britain and Ireland as the curse of the Irish nation, and felt convinced that, while it lasted, this country could never be free nor happy. My mind has been confirmed in this opinion by the experience of every succeeding year, and the conclusions which I have drawn from every fact before my eyes. In consequence, I was determined to employ all the powers which my individual efforts could move, in order to separate the two countries. That Ireland was not able to herself to throw off the yoke, I knew; I therefore sought for aid wherever it was to be found. In

---

From *The World's Famous Orations*, William Jennings Bryan, editor-in-chief, Vol. VI, pp. 132-136. Copyright, 1906, by Funk & Wagnalls Co. New York.

* Addressed to the court-martial assembled to try him in the Dublin barracks in November, 1798. Tone is described as having been "dressed in the French uniform; a large cocked hat with broad gold lace and the tri-colored cockade; a blue uniform coat with gold-embroidered collar and two large gold epaulettes; blue pantaloons with gold lace garters at the knee, and short boots bound at the top with gold lace." He was found guilty and sentenced to death on his own confession. His request that he might be shot, instead of hanged, and thus die a soldier's death, was refused. While awaiting execution he committed suicide in order to escape the gallows.

The Irish revolt had begun in the year of Tone's arrest and conviction—1798. It was suppressed about a year later after many thousands of lives had been lost on each side.

Born in 1763, died in 1798; promoted and served in the Expedition of Hoche to Ireland in 1796; captured on a French squadron bound for Ireland in 1798; on being sentenced to death, he committed suicide.—W.J.B.

honorable poverty I rejected offers which, to a man in my circumstances, might be considered highly advantageous. I remained faithful to what I thought the cause of my country, and sought in the French Republic an ally to rescue three millions of my countrymen.

Attached to no party in the French Republic—without interest, without money, without intrigue—the openness and integrity of my views raised me to a high and confidential rank in its armies. I obtained the confidence of the executive directory, the approbation of my generals, and I will venture to add, the esteem and affection of my brave comrades. When I review these circumstances, I feel a secret and internal consolation, which no reverse of fortune, no sentence in the power of this court to inflict, can deprive me of, or weaken in any degree. Under the flag of the French Republic I originally engaged with a view to save and liberate my own country. For that purpose I have encountered the chances of war among strangers; for that purpose I repeatedly braved the terrors of the ocean, covered, as I knew it to be, with the triumphant fleets of that power which it was my glory and my duty to oppose. I have sacrificed all my views in life; I have courted poverty; I have left a beloved wife unprotected, and children whom I adored fatherless.

After such a sacrifice, in a cause which I have always considered—conscientiously considered—as the cause of justice and freedom, it is no great effort, at this day, to add the sacrifice of my life.

But I hear it is said that this unfortunate country has been a prey to all sorts of horrors. I sincerely lament it. I beg, however, that it may be remembered that I have been absent four years from Ireland. To me those sufferings can never be attributed. I designed by fair and open war to procure a separation of two countries. For open war I was prepared, but instead of that a system of private assassination has taken place. I repeat, while I deplore it, that it is not chargeable on me. Atrocities, it seems, have been committed on both sides. I do not less deplore them. I detest them from my heart; and to those who know my character and sentiments, I may safely appeal for the truth of this assertion: with them I need no justification. In a case like this success is everything. Success, in the eyes of the vulgar, fixes its merits. Washington succeeded, and Kosciusko failed.

After a combat nobly sustained—a combat which would have excited the respect and sympathy of a generous enemy—my fate has been to become a prisoner, to the eternal disgrace of those who gave the orders. I was brought here in irons like a felon. I mention this for the sake of others; for me, I am indifferent to it. I am aware of the fate which awaits me, and scorn equally the tone of complaint, and that of supplication. As to the connection between this country and Great Britain, I repeat it—all that has been imputed to me (words, writings, and actions), I here deliberately avow. I have spoken and acted with reflection, and on principle, and am ready to meet the consequences. Whatever be the sentence of the court, I am prepared for it. Its members will surely discharge their duty—I shall take care not to be wanting in mine.

I wish to offer a few words relative to one single point—the mode of punishment. In France our *emigrees,* who stand nearly in the same situation in which I now stand before you, are condemned to be shot. I ask that the court adjudge me the death of a soldier, and let me be shot by a platoon of grenadiers. I request this indulgence rather in consideration of the uniform I wear—the uniform of a *chef de bridage* in the French army—than from any personal regard to myself. In order to evince my claim to this favor, I beg that the court may take the trouble to peruse my commission and letters of service in the French army. It will appear from these papers that I have not received them as a mask to cover me, but that I have been long and *bona fide* an officer in the French service.

I have labored to create a people in Ireland by raising three millions of my countrymen to the rank of citizens. I have labored to abolish the infernal spirit of religious persecution, by uniting the Catholics and Dissenters. To the former I owe more than ever can be repaid. The services I was so fortunate as to render them they rewarded munificently; but they did more: when the public cry was raised against me—when the friends of my youth swarmed off and let me alone—the Catholics did not desert me; they had the virtue even to sacrifice their own interests to a rigid principle of honor; they refused, tho strongly urged, to disgrace a man who, whatever his conduct toward the government might have been, had faithfully and conscientiously discharged his duty toward them; and in so doing, tho it was in my own case, I will say they showed an instance of public virtue of which I know not whether there exists another example.*

---

* This paragraph in Tone's speech was long suppressed, being first published in 1859, with the "correspondence" of Cornwallis, the lord-lieutenant of Ireland of 1790.—W.J.B.

Part V

NEW LEADERS AT HOME AND ABROAD

Demolishment

"Here I would conclude with our buildings, but when I look
about I cannot but bewail the desolation which civil rebellion hath
procured. It looks like the later end of a feast. Here lieth an old
ruined castle like the remainder of a venison pasty, there a broken
fort like a minced pie half subjected, and in another place an old
abbey with some turrets standing like a carcase of a goose broken up.
It makes me remember the old proverb: it is better to come to the
end of a feast than the beginning of a fray."

Justice Luke Gernon

Written by Justice Luke Gernon, an English resident in Ireland (1620). From
Ireland from the Flight of the Earls to Grattan's Parliament, compiled and
edited by James Carty. C. J. Fallon. Dublin. 1949.

Introduction

Not all political leaders have the sort of personality that makes such impact on the people as to give them the status of heroes. Ireland produced two that had this sort of personality: O'Connell and Parnell. The Parnell who appears in the piece below is Parnell on the defensive; he has been discredited by a divorce action and public opinion is being whipped up against him. But it is this Parnell, the Parnell within a year of his death, fighting for a leadership that he knows is essential to the cause, who makes the greatest impression on the public mind—the tragic hero. In the United States the exiled revolutionist, Thomas Francis Meagher, hoists the green flag on battlefields fought over by the Federal army. At home and abroad an array of colorful characters give a sense of adventurousness and high-spiritedness to a people engaged in a national struggle that has its rises and falls.—P.C.

Daniel O'Connell

Prince Puckler-Muskau visited him in his home in Kerry when, then around fifty, O'Connell was an outstanding European figure, with victory in sight for the great movement he headed—Catholic Emancipation. The German prince thought he looked like a general of Napoleon's: "The resemblance is indeed more striking by the perfection with which he speaks French." A generation earlier and Daniel O'Connell would probably have been in the French army: his uncle, Count O'Connell, was the last Colonel of the Irish Brigade in the service of France.

Puckler-Muskau noted the histrionic quality that was in O'Connell —a quality that probably went to make him the great advocate that he was. His manners which were very democratic had something of the stage in them. "They do not conceal his very high opinion of himself and are occasionally tinged with what an Englishman would call vulgarity." The sculptor of the heroic statue of him in Dublin was aware of this histrionic quality: with his cloak thrown back from his shoulder he has O'Connell enact the Chieftain.

"The Liberator!" Irish people of the last two generations have difficulty in realizing what that popularly conferred title meant. They know that the O'Connell epoch ended in disaster. His constitutionalism ("the golden link of the Crown") was ignored by the British and came to be bitterly rejected by the Irish. His dissociation of politics from the national tradition is for the generations influenced by the Gaelic League incomprehensible. With Irish as a native speech and addressing vast crowds for whom it was native, he never used Irish publicly, snubbed people who presented him with works in Irish, and let it be understood that he would welcome the demise of the language. Yes, at the moment it is hard to recover what "The Liberator" meant for the people of the sixties, seventies, and eighties.

Yet O'Connell was an uplifting force for Ireland, and it is not too much to say that he was a precipitating force in Europe. He took democracy out of what in modern terms would be the "cells" and brought it into the open. What in Europe was an affair of secret societies, he turned into immense demonstrations—a hundred thousand rent-paying farmers stretching round a platform from which a

---

By the editor.

great Parliamentarian told them he could drive a coach-and-four through any act of Parliament.

Certain understandable things made O'Connell curb the revolutionary movement that his demonstrations tended to; and this, in the second part of his career, led to national frustration. Only a forceful movement could have saved Ireland from the disaster that was just round the corner, and the man who had already won Catholic Emancipation would not and could not sponsor forcefulness. Essentially a man of the feudal age, he had been appalled by the excesses of the revolution in his second country, France. The peasant rising in Ireland in 1798 had only resulted in severer repression. As a lawyer and a Parliamentarian, he had too great a faith in Constitutionalism. Then he had a private reason for discounting the use of arms: his shot had put his antagonist on his deathbed, in a duel he had been forced into. Always histrionic, O'Connell wore a black glove on the hand that had held the pistol, and always humane, he gave a pension to the family of the man whose death was due to him.

"The great tragedian and the great comedian of the Irish race," Yeats said, comparing Parnell with O'Connell. But to understand how the great comedian affected the country, we have to place him in his epoch. Ireland was still under the Penal Laws when he came on the scene: Irish Catholics might not own land, educate their children at home or abroad, carry a sword as gentlemen did in those days, own a horse worth ten pounds or over, nor take a place in the Legislature. However, the harshness of the laws was mitigated by the natural kindliness of people: there were still Catholic gentry: they held their ancestral estates through the good-hearted contrivance of Protestant neighbours in whose names the title-deeds to many ancient estates were held and who never reneged on their trusts; and as for education, no one informed when the sons of neighbouring families went to schools abroad. Very often a Protestant gentleman would have a priest come to his house as a tutor (Oliver Goldsmith was taught French by a priest). A Protestant young man who had had a Catholic nurse would recognize the nurse's son as his foster-brother, and in Ireland in those days the tie of fosterage was strong. Below the gentry there were agrarian middlemen who lived well, and in many parts of the country there were farmers under decent landlords who were prosperous. But the generality of the people of the countryside, the tenant-farmers, were as burthened as the French peasants of the old regime. The rents they paid were exorbitant and could be increased at the will of the landlord; one-tenth of their produce every year went to the upkeep of a church that in most places had no congregation; they were expected to be quite abject when paying rents or asking for a renewal of lease. And the rents, uneconomic as they were, and the tithes to the Established Church were not the only exactions that the family of the tenant-farmer had to put up with. Says Thady in Maria Edgeworth's *Castle Rackrent*, "duty fowls and duty turkeys and duty geese came as fast as we could eat 'em, for my lady kept a sharp look-out, and knew to a tub of butter everything the tenant had, all round. They knew her way, and what with fear of driving for rent, and Sir Murtagh's lawsuits, they were kept in such good order, they never thought of coming near Castle Rackrent without a present of something or other—eggs, honey, butter, meal, fish, game, grouse, and herrings, fresh and salt, all went for something. As for their young pigs, we had them, and the best bacon and hams they could make up, with all the young chickens in spring."

The abjectness of people without any security and brought close to destitution was what O'Connell first of all had to cope with. He belonged to the Catholic gentry, was educated in France, and at the outset of his career showed himself as an advocate and an orator of mark. Those who profited by the system that left the great part of the population helpless and near destitute insolently named themselves "The Ascendancy." It was to denude this "Ascendancy" of their social, moral, and intellectual authority that O'Connell used his immense powers. And it is as the destroyer of "The Ascendancy" that he becomes the folk-hero of modern Ireland—"The Liberator."

"To upraise and vindicate them!" This in the words of his son was how the people, who thronged round his carriage and went down on their knees to invoke blessings and mercies on him, regarded O'Connell's labors. And if we would witness these labors at their noblest we should read with imagination and some historical perception his conduct of the defence of John Magee, on trial for a libel on the Viceroy. The Attorney General had packed the jury; not only were Catholics excluded, but all Protestants—and they were numerous in Dublin—who were known to be liberal or patriotic. That the case was lost before it was pleaded, O'Connell knew. But like the man of genius that he was, he turned what might have been looked on with consternation into opportunity—the opportunity of arraigning the court, and beyond the court "The Ascendancy" which had put itself in a place where it could be stripped, not only of moral, but of legal authority.

O'Connell's procedure was magnificent: with his tremendous vituperative powers he could have brought the court down into the gutter. But that would have been only a partial victory. A superiority was to be asserted. And so against the ignobility of "The Ascendancy" appears the dignity of those whom they would control. Grandeur enters the courtroom: it is the grandeur of O'Connell's mind and O'Connell's style, but it appears as the grandeur of a people.

O'Connell's defence of John Magee forces a comparison with Curran's defence of Peter Finerty. Personally, the editor, if a choice could have been made, would prefer to have heard Curran. Using the word in its widest sense, Curran was more spiritual than O'Connell and he had the supreme gift of the orator—the power to throw out phrases that stay in the memory; when he spoke for Peter Finerty he spoke not only with the accomplishment of the advocate, not only with the inner conviction of the poet that he was, but with the exaltedness of the prophet. As a performance, however, O'Connell's defence—or, rather, his arraignment—cannot be surpassed. Curran, speaking at an earlier time, could appeal to the eighteenth century's rationalities. O'Connell, speaking at a time of bitter partisanship, speaking, too, as a half outlaw, had hurdles to surmount. The performance he gave and sustained, even as a feat of physical endurance, was tremendous. Here, indeed, he was the up-raiser and the vindicator of "the Irishry."

Parnell has come into Irish folklore and so has Dean Swift, but O'Connell was born and reared to be in folklore. That the belated heroic age persisted around his patrimony up to the time he was born, we know from the dirge his aunt made for her husband. He was an officer in the Imperial army, but when he returned to Ireland he could be allowed the condition of gentleman only by sufferance. Part of the condition was to have a horse that exceeded the value of ten pounds. In a dispute about such a mount, Art O'Leary was shot to death by one who ranked as gentleman. The dirge that "Dark Ellen" made for him in Irish might belong to the time of Queen Gormlai, but Gormlai would not be so unrestrained. Daniel O'Connell of Derrynane, in Kerry (Daniel was the English of Donhnal, Donald, anciently a royal name) lived in a time when the unwritten literature of the countryside was still vigorous: in that literature he appears in various roles.

There is the story of his being entertained in the house of an English personage. A ready-witted table-maid as she passes him a dish addresses him in Irish; when he replies in Irish, she warns him that poison is prepared for him—"There is salt in your cup to slay the hundreds!"—She is the giant's or the enchanter's daughter whose wit saves the hero. There is, amongst others, the story in which he appears as the shrewd adviser whose recommendation to do something fantastic saves the applicant from an enormous penalty. And he is even able to win a victory over a notorious virago in the manner of the folk Aristotle.

Historically, O'Connell was the last of the orators in the Greek and Roman style who made public opinion by the voice. His voice was a magnificent organ but it is difficult to believe it reached all of the hundred thousand people who, it is reported, stretched all around him in the open air at Tara.

Having gained Catholic Emancipation, he attempted to gain Repeal of the Union which meant the restoration of the Irish Parliament by the means that availed before, pressure through great popular demonstrations. In this he failed. The end of his career came when, rather than involve them with the military, he ordered the throngs, that were converging on the place he had appointed, back to the counties they had marched from. It was a retreat witnessed by the whole of Ireland, and it took the spirit out of the country. There was a split in the national forces; then came the Famine, and, as if to close an epoch with fitting mournfulness, O'Connell's death in Genoa.

O'Connell at the Hill of Tara

"O'Connell resembles Luther," observes Lecky; "In each was the same instinctive tact in governing great masses of men, the same calculated audacity, the same art in inspiring and retaining confidence."

He inspired and ruled the "monster meetings."

"The greatest of all these meetings, perhaps the grandest display of the kind that has ever taken place was held around the Hill of Tara. According to very moderate computations, about a quarter of a million were assembled there, to attest their sympathy with the movement. The spot was well chosen for the purpose—Tara of the Kings, the seat of the ancient royalty of Ireland.

It was on this spot that O'Connell, standing by the stone where the kings of Ireland had been crowned, sketched the coming glories of his country. Beneath him, like a mighty sea, extended the throng of listeners. They were so numerous that thousands were unable to catch the faintest echo of the voice they loved so well; yet all remained passive, tranquil, and decorous."

From *The Gael*, January, 1901, p. 15. New York.

O'Connell's Speech in the Magee Case

I consented to the adjournment yesterday, gentlemen of the jury, from that impulse of nature which compels us to postpone pain; it is, indeed, painful to me to address you; it is a cheerless, a hopeless task to address you—a task which would require all the animation and interest to be derived from the working of a mind fully fraught with the resentment and disgust created in mine yesterday, by that farrago of helpless absurdity with which Mr. Attorney-General regaled you.

But I am now not sorry for the delay. Whatever I may have lost in vivacity, I trust I shall compensate for in discretion. That which yesterday excited my anger, now appears to me to be an object of pity; and that which then roused my indignation, now only moves to *contempt*. I can now address you with feelings softened, and, I trust, subdued; and I do, from my soul, declare, that I now cherish no other sensations than those which enable me to bestow on the Attorney-General and on his discourse, pure and unmixed compassion.

It was a discourse in which you could not discover either order, or method, or eloquence; it contained very little logic, and no poetry at all; violent and virulent, it was a confused and disjointed tissue of bigotry, amalgamated with congenial vulgarity. He accused my client of using Billingsgate, and he accused him of it in language suited exclusively for that meridian. He descended even to the calling of names: he called this young gentleman a "malefactor," a "Jacobin," and a "ruffian," gentlemen of the jury; he called him "abominable," and "seditious," and "revolutionary," and "infamous," and a "ruffian" again, gentlemen of the jury; he called him a "brothel keeper," a "pander," "a kind of bawd in breeches," and a "ruffian" a third time, gentlemen of the jury.

I cannot repress my astonishment, how Mr. Attorney-General could have *preserved* this dialect in its native purity; he has been now for

From *The Select Speeches of Daniel O'Connell, M.P.*, edited by his son John O'Connell, Esq., pp. 244-304. James Duffy & Sons. London. [no date]

It was on Tuesday, 27th July, the second day of the proceedings, that he was called upon to speak. We quote the ample report of the *Evening Post*.

At eleven o'clock, the Chief Justice took his seat in the court, which was crowded from an early hour, public expectation being much excited and interested, with respect to the proceedings and the issue of the day.

Mr. O'Connell rose and spoke as follows.—J. O'C.

nearly thirty years in the class of polished society; he has, for some years, mixed amongst the highest orders in the state; he has had the honour to belong for thirty years to the first profession in the world— to the only profession, with the single exception, perhaps, of the military, to which a high-minded gentleman could condescend to belong— the Irish bar. To that bar, at which he has seen and heard a Burgh and a Duquery; at which he must have listened to a Burston, a Ponsonby, and a Curran; to a bar which still contains a Plunket, a Ball, and despite of politics, I will add, a Bushe. With this galaxy of glory, flinging their light around him, how can he alone have remained in darkness? How has it happened, that the twilight murkiness of his soul, has not been illumined with a single ray shot from their lustre? Devoid of taste and of genius, how can he have had memory enough to preserve this original vulgarity? He is, indeed, an object of compassion, and, from my inmost soul, I bestow on him my forgiveness, and my bounteous pity.

* * * * *

But, to be serious. Let me pledge myself to you that he imposes on you, when he threatens to crush the Catholic Board. Illegal violence may do it—force may effectuate it; but your hopes and his will be defeated, if he attempts it by any course of law. I am, if not a lawyer, at least, a barrister. On this subject I ought to know something, and I do not hesitate to contradict the Attorney-General on this point, and to proclaim to you and to the country that the Catholic Board is perfectly a legal assembly—that it not only does not violate the law, but that it is entitled to the protection of the law, and in the very proudest tone of firmness, I hurl *defiance* at the Attorney-General!

I defy him to allege a law or a statue, or even a proclamation that is violated by the Catholic Board. No, gentlemen, no; his religious prejudices—if the absence of every charity can be called anything religious—his religious prejudices really obscure his reason, his bigoted intolerance has totally darkened his understanding, and he mistakes the plainest facts and misquotes the clearest law, in the ardour and vehemence of his rancour. I disdain his moderation—I scorn his forbearance—I tell him he knows not the law if he thinks as he says; and if he thinks so, I tell him to his beard, that he is not *honest* in not having sooner prosecuted us, and I challenge him to that prosecution.

It is strange—it is melancholy, to reflect on the miserable and mistaken pride that must inflate him to talk as he does of the Catholic Board. The Catholic Board is composed of men—I include not myself

—of course, I always except myself—every way his superiors, in birth, in fortune, in talents, in rank. What! Is he to talk of the Catholic Board lightly? At their head is the Earl of Fingal, a nobleman whose exalted rank stoops beneath the superior station of his virtues—whom even the venal minions of power must respect. We are engaged, patiently and perseveringly engaged, in a struggle through the open channels of the constitution for our liberties. The son of the ancient earl whom I have mentioned cannot in his native land attain any honourable distinction of the state, and yet Mr. Attorney-General knows that they are open to every son of every bigoted and intemperate stranger that may settle amongst us.

But this system cannot last; he may insult, he may calumniate, he may prosecute; but the Catholic cause is on its *majestic march;* its progress is rapid and obvious; it is cheered in its advance, and aided by all that is dignified and dispassionate—by everything that is patriotic—by all the honour, all the integrity of the empire; and its success is just as certain as the return of to-morrow's sun, and the close of to-morrow's eve.

We will—we must soon be emancipated, in despite of the Attorney-General, aided as he is by his august allies, the aldermen of Skinner's-alley. In despite of the Attorney-General and the aldermen of Skinner's-alley, our emancipation is certain, and not distant.

I have no difficulty in perceiving the motive of the Attorney-General, in devoting so much of his medley oration to the Catholic question, and to the expression of his bitter hatred to us, and of his determination to ruin our hopes. It had, to be sure, no connection with the cause, but it had a direct and natural connection with you. He has been, all his life, reckoned a man of consummate cunning and dexterity; and whilst one wonders that he has so much exposed himself upon those prosecutions, and accounts for it by the proverbial blindness of religious zeal, it is still easy to discover much of his native cunning and dexterity. Gentlemen, he thinks he knows his men—he knows you; many of you signed the no-Popery petition; he heard one of you boast of it; he knows you would not have been summoned on this jury, if you had entertained liberal sentiments; he knows all this, and, therefore, it is that he, with the artifice and cunning of an experienced *nisi primus* advocate, endeavours to win your confidence, and command your affections by the display of his congenial illiberality and bigotry.

You are all, of course, Protestants; see what a compliment he pays to your religion and his own, when he endeavours thus to procure a verdict on your oaths; when he endeavours to seduce you to what, if you were so seduced, would be perjury, by indulging your prejudices, and flattering you by the coincidence of his sentiments and wishes. Will he succeed, gentlemen? Will you allow him to draw you into a perjury out of zeal for your religion? And will you violate the pledge you have given to your God to do justice, in order to gratify your anxiety for the ascendancy of what you believe to be his church? Gentlemen, reflect on the strange and monstrous inconsistency of this conduct, and do not commit, if you can avoid it, the pious crime of violating your solemn oaths, in aid of the pious designs of the Attorney-General against Popery.

Oh, gentlemen! it is not in any lightness of heart I thus address you —it is rather in bitterness and sorrow; you did not expect flattery from me, and my client was little disposed to offer it to you; besides, of what avail would it be to flatter, if you came here pre-determined, and it is too plain that you are not selected for this jury from any notion of your impartiality?

But when I talk to you of your oaths and of your religion, I would full fain I could impress you with a respect for both the one and the other. I, who do not flatter, tell you, that though I do not join with you in belief, I have the most unfeigned respect for the form of Christian faith which you profess. Would that its substance, not its forms and temporal advantages, were deeply impressed on your minds! then should I not address you in the cheerless and hopeless despondency that crowds on my mind, and drives me to taunt you with the air of ridicule I do. Gentlemen, I sincerely respect and venerate your religion, *but* I despise and I now apprehend your prejudices, in the same proportion as the Attorney-General has cultivated them. In plain truth, every religion is good—every religion is true to him who, in his due caution and conscience, believes it. There is but one bad religion, that of a man who professes a faith which he does not believe; but the good religion may be, and often is, corrupted by the wretched and wicked prejudices which admit a difference of opinion as a cause of hatred.

The Attorney-General, defective in argument—weak in his cause, has artfully roused your prejudices at his side. I have, on the contrary, met your prejudices boldly. If your verdict shall be for me, you will be certain that it has been produced by nothing but unwilling conviction resulting from sober and satisfied judgment. If your verdict be bestowed upon the artifices of the Attorney-General, you may happen to be right; but do you not see the danger of its being produced by an admixture of passion and prejudice with your reason? How difficult is it to separate prejudice from reason, when they run in the same direction. If you be men of conscience, then I call on you to listen to me, that your consciences may be safe, and your reason alone be the guardian of your oath, and the sole monitor of your decision.

I now bring you to the immediate subject of this indictment. Mr. Magee is charged with publishing a libel in his paper called the *Dublin Evening Post*. His lordship has decided that there is legal proof of the publication, and I would be sorry you thought of acquitting Mr. Magee under the pretence of not believing that evidence. I will not, therefore, trouble you on that part of the case; I will tell you, gentlemen, presently, what this publication is; but suffer me first to inform you what it is not—for this I consider to be very important to the strong, and in truth, triumphant defence which my client has to this indictment.

Gentlemen, this is *not* a libel on Charles Lennox, Duke of Richmond, in his private or individual capacity. It does not interfere with the privacy of his domestic life. It is free from any reproach upon his domestic habits or conduct; it is perfectly pure from any attempt to traduce his personal honour or integrity. Towards the man, there is not the least taint of malignity; nay, the thing is still stronger. Of Charles Duke of Richmond, personally, and as disconnected with the administration of public affairs, it speaks in terms of civility and even respect, it contains this passage which I read from the indictment:—

"Had he remained what he first came over, or what he afterwards professed to be, he would have retained his reputation for *honest open hostility*, defending his political principles with firmness, perhaps with warmth, but without rancour; the supporter and not the tool of an administration; a mistaken politician, perhaps, but an honourable man and a respectable soldier."

The Duke is here in this libel, my lords—in this libel, gentlemen of the jury, the Duke of Richmond is called an honourable man and a respectable soldier! Could more flattering expressions be invented? Has the most mercenary Press that ever yet existed, the mercenary Press of this metropolis, contained in return for all the money it has received, any praise which ought to be so pleasing—"an honourable man and a respectable soldier?" I do, therefore, beg of you, gentlemen, as you value your honesty, to carry with you in your distinct recollection, this fact, that whatever of evil this publication may contain, it does not involve any reproach against the Duke of Richmond, in any other than in his public and official character.

*   *   *   *   *

When the art of printing was invented, its value to every sufferer—its terror to every oppressor, was soon obvious, and means were speedily adopted to prevent its salutary effects. The Star-Chamber—the odious Star-Chamber, was either created, or at least, enlarged and brought into activity. Its proceedings were arbitrary—its decisions were oppressive, and injustice and tyranny were formed into a system. To describe it to you in one sentence, it WAS A PREMATURELY PACKED JURY. Perhaps that description does not shock you much. Let me report one of its decisions which will, I think, make its horrors more sensible to you—it is a ludicrous as well as a melancholy instance.

A tradesman—a ruffian, I presume, he was styled—in an altercation with a nobleman's servant, called the swan, which was worn on the servant's arm for a badge, a goose. For this offence—the calling a nobleman's badge of a swan, a goose, he was brought before the Star-Chamber—he was, of course, convicted; he lost, as I recollect, one of his ears on the pillory—was sentenced to two years' imprisonment, and a fine of £500; and all this to teach him to *distinguish swans from geese.*

I now ask you, to what is it you tradesmen and merchants are indebted for the safety and respect you can enjoy in society? What is it which has rescued you from the slavery in which persons who are engaged in trade were held by the iron barons of former days? I will tell you; it is the light, the reason, and the liberty which have been created, and will, in despite of every opposition, he perpetuated by the exertion of the Press.

Gentlemen, the Star-Chamber was particularly vigilant over the infant struggles of the Press. A code of laws became necessary to govern the new enemy to prejudice and oppression—the Press. The Star-Chamber adopted, for this purpose, the civil law, as it is called—the law of Rome—not the law at the periods of her liberty and her glory, but the law which was promulgated when she fell into slavery and disgrace, and recognized this principle, that the will of the prince was the rule of the law. The civil law was adopted by the Star-Chamber as its guide in proceedings against and in punishing libellers; but, unfortunately, only part of it was adopted, and that, of course, was the part least favourable to freedom. So much of the civil law as assisted to discover the concealed libeller, and to punish him when discovered, was carefully selected; but the civil law allowed truth to be a defense, and that part was carefully rejected.

* * * * *

Amongst the means taken to raise money in Ireland, for James the First, and his son Charles, a proceeding called "a commission to inquire into defective titles," was invented. It was a scheme, gentlemen, to inquire of every man what right he had to his own property, and to have it solemnly and legally determined that he had none. To effectuate this scheme required great management, discretion, and integrity. First, there were 4,000 excellent horse raised for the purpose of being, as Strafford himself said "good lookers-on." The rest of the arrangement I would recommend to modern practice; it would save much trouble. I will shortly abstract it from two of Strafford's own letters.

The one appears to have been written by him to the Lord Treasurer; it is dated the 3rd December, 1634. He begins with an apology for not having been more expeditious in this work of plunder, for his employers were, it seems, impatient at the melancholy waste of time. He then says—

"Howbeit, I will redeem the time as much as I can, with such as may give furtherance to the king's title, *and will inquire out* FIT MEN TO SERVE UPON THE JURIES."

Take notice of that, gentlemen, I pray you; perhaps you thought that the "packing of juries" was a modern invention—a new discovery. You see how greatly mistaken you were; the thing has example and precedent to support it, and the authority of both are, in our law, quite conclusive.

The next step was to corrupt—oh, no, to interest the wise and learned judges. But commentary becomes unnecessary, when I read for you this passage from a letter of his to the King, dated the 9th of December, 1636:—

"Your Majesty was graciously pleased, upon my humble advice, to bestow four shillings in the pound upon your Lord Chief Justice and Lord Chief Baron in this kingdom, fourth of the first yearly rent raised upon the commission of defective title, which, *upon observation, I find to be the best given that ever was.* For now they do intend it, with a care and diligence, such as if it were their own private, and most certain gaining to themselves; every four shillings once paid, shall better your revenue for ever after, at least five pounds."

Thus, gentlemen of the jury, all was ready for the mockery of law and justice, called a trial.

Now, let me take any one of you; let me place him here, where Mr. Magee stands; let him have his property at stake; let it be of less value, I pray you, than a compensation for two years' imprisonment; it will, however, be of sufficient value to interest and rouse all your agony and anxiety. If you were so placed here, you would see before you the well-paid Attorney-General, perhaps, malignantly delighted to pour his rancour upon you; on the bench would sit the corrupt and partisan judge, and before you, on that seat which you now occupy, would be placed the packed and predetermined jury.

I beg, sir, to know what would be your feelings, your honour, your rage; would you not compare the Attorney-General to the gambler who played with a loaded die, and then you would hear him talk, in solemn and monotonous tones, of his conscience? Oh, his conscience, gentlemen of the jury!

But the times are altered. The Press, the Press, gentlemen, has effectuated a salutary revolution; a commission of defective titles would no longer be tolerated; the judges can no longer be bribed with money, and juries can no longer be—— I must not say it. Yes, they can, you know—we all know they can be still *inquired out*, and "packed," as the technical phrase is. But *you*, who are not packed, *you*, who have been *fairly* selected, will see that the language of the publication before us is mildness itself, compared with that which the truth of history requires—compared with that which history has already used.

*   *   *   *   *

Let me transport you from the heat, and fury of domestic politics; let me place you in a foreign land; you are Protestants, with your good leave, you shall, for a moment, be Portuguese, and Portuguese is now an honourable name, for right well have the people of Portugal fought for their country, against the foreign invader. Oh! how easy to procure a similar spirit, and more of bravery, amongst the people of Ireland! The slight purchase of good words, and a kindly disposition, would convert them into an impenetrable guard for the safety of the Throne and State. But advice and regret are equally unavailing, and they are doomed to calumny and oppression, the reality of persecution, and the mockery of justice, until some fatal hour shall arrive, which may preach wisdom to the dupes, and menace with punishment the oppressor.

In the meantime I must place you in Portugal. Let us suppose for an instant that the Protestant religion is that of the people of Portugal —the Catholic, that of the government—that the house of Braganza has not reigned, but that Portugal is still governed by the viceroy of a foreign nation, from whom no kindness, no favour has ever flowed, and from whom justice has rarely been obtained, and upon those unfrequent occasions, not conceded generously, but extorted by force, or wrung from distress by terror and apprehension, in a stinted measure and ungracious manner; you, Protestants, shall form, not as with us in Ireland, nine-tenths, but some lesser number, you shall be only four-fifths of the population; and all the persecution which you have your selves practiced here upon Papists, whilst you, at the same time, accused the Papists of the crime of being persecutors, shall glow around; your native land shall be to you the country of strangers; you shall be aliens in the soil that gave you birth, and whilst every foreigner may, in the land of your forefathers, attain rank, station, emolument, honours, you alone shall be excluded; and you shall be excluded for no other reason but a conscientious abhorrence to the religion of your ancestors.

* * * * *

Is there amongst you any one friend to freedom? Is there amongst you one man, who esteems equal and impartial justice, who values the people's rights as the foundation of private happiness, and who considers life as no boon without liberty? Is there amongst you one friend to the constitution—one man who hates oppression? If there be, Mr. Magee appeals to his kindred mind, and confidently expects an acquittal.

There are amongst you men of great religious zeal—of much public piety. Are you sincere? Do you believe what you profess? With all this zeal—with all this piety, *is* there any conscience amongst you? *Is* there any terror of violating your oaths? Be ye hypocrites, or does genuine religion inspire ye? If you be sincere—if you have conscience—if your oaths can control your interests, then Mr. Magee confidently expects an acquittal.

If amongst you there be cherished one ray of pure religion—if amongst you there glow a single spark of liberty—if I have alarmed religion, or roused the spirit of freedom in one breast amongst you, Mr. Magee is safe, and his country is served; but if there be none—if you be slaves and hypocrites, he will await your verdict,* and despise it.

O'Connell's Last Case

A thrilling account of Daniel O'Connell's last case, that of the "Doneraile Conspiracy," is here given: An unpopular Irish magistrate had been murdered and the resulting investigation unearthed a conspiracy to kill a number of oppressive local magnates. One hundred and fifty persons were indicted, and were to be tried in three batches.

---

* And slaves, hypocrites, and bigots they proved themselves, by finding a verdict for the Crown.—J. O'C.

From *The Gael*, March, 1901, p. 101. New York.

In the defence of the first batch, Daniel O'Connell was not engaged, and they were all convicted and sentenced, lads and aged men together, to execution within the week. The remaining prisoners and their friends, seized with panic, sent an urgent messenger from Cork to Derrynane, ninety miles away, and O'Connell hastened to the rescue.

There was not a moment to spare, as the judge had refused to delay the opening of the second trial for his arrival. Traveling in a light gig with relays of horses, and scarcely stopping for rest or food, O'Connell traversed the frightful Kerry roads at full speed, and at length arrived in the courthouse square flogging his exhausted horse, which dropped dead between the shafts as he descended, hailed by a crowd of thousands with wild shouts: "He's come! He's come!"

Amid a frantic uproar of cheers, he was swept into the courtroom, where the opposing lawyer, Mr. Doherty, was addressing the jury.

The solicitor-general turned white. The cloud of despair lifted from the faces of the prisoners in the dock. O'Connell at once bowed to the judges, and apologized for not appearing in wig and gown. He also craved permission to refresh himself in court. A bowl of bread and milk was brought, and as he ate, a young barrister on either side of him poured into each ear an account of all that had been done, and how the case stood.

It was a contrast, the big, massive counsellor snatching his hasty breakfast, and the graceful, aristocratic Mr. Doherty, talking in the most refined way to the court. As he laid down a doctrine of law, O'Connell, with marked contempt, cried out, with his mouth full of bread and milk: "That's not law!"

Again and again he interrupted, but always the decision of the judges upheld him and affirmed the error of his antagonist. He was still more successful when the witnesses fell into his hands for cross-examination. They told or tried to tell the same story on which the former prisoners had been convicted; but O'Connell so badgered, tripped, and terrified them that their evidence went hopelessly to pieces.

"Wisha, thin," cried one of them hysterically, visibly trembling, "God knows 'tis little I thought I'd meet you here this day, Counsellor O'Connell! May the Lord save me from you!"

The jury could not agree, though locked up and starved for a day and a half. Nor were the accused tried again, for the third batch having received meanwhile a full acquittal, the government despaired of conviction and they were discharged, while the sentence of the unfortunates already condemned to be hanged was commuted to transportation.

Blind Raftery

Dr. Hyde said he wanted to speak of one of the most remarkable men of whom he had ever found traces in the West of Ireland, and one of the strangest poets that ever wrote a verse or composed a stanza. The man whom he was going to speak of was one of those many geniuses of whom Ireland still remained in almost complete ignorance —a man whose life and deeds and works could only have been recovered by the longest and closest and most diligent searching amongst the old people of a generation who had now almost passed away.

The hero of the paper was a man who could neither read nor write. He had no access to books of any kind, or to any form of literature, except what, his eyes being blind, he was able to pick up through his ears as he traveled from peasant's cottage to peasant's cottage with his bag over his shoulder, picking up, as he went, his day's meal. Proceeding, Dr. Hyde went on to describe how he first came upon traces of Raftery.

About twenty years ago, when he was a gossoon, he was going out one frosty morning with his gun on his shoulder and his dog at his heel, when he saw an old man sitting at the door of a cottage singing to himself an old Irish song, which, as it afterwards turned out, was Raftery's "County of Mayo." The old man, at his request, taught him the song, and he went his way. It was fully twelve years after when he again came on traces of the poet, who he did not know at the time had written the song.

He was one day in the Royal Irish Academy poking through some old manuscripts that were lying there rotting on the shelves, when he came upon a little manuscript written in a shaky, scrawling hand, containing a number of poems ascribed to a man called Raftery, and amongst them the very song that he had learned that blessed morning long ago. Seven years more elapsed before he came on what the African hunter would call a "hot spoor" of Raftery. He had taken a house in Blackrock, and was walking down to the station one morning when he met an old blind man begging alms. Having given him a penny and passed on about a hundred yards, it struck him suddenly that he should have addressed the old man in Irish. He turned back, and having addressed the old man again, found he could speak excellent Irish.

From a report on a lecture, "A Famous Mayo Poet," given by Dr. Douglas Hyde, in *The Gael*, April, 1903, pp. 115-116. New York.

He conversed with him for an hour, and amongst the things they talked about was Raftery.

The old man gave him minute directions as to a little house in a village in Southern Galway into which Raftery had been taken to die. Three or four years ago, Dr. Hyde went on to say, he found himself in the locality denoted, and going ten or twelve miles out of his way actually found the identical old man who had tended Raftery on his sick bed, had called in the priest for him, and had seen him die. Everybody in the village knew something about him, but nobody had written down his poems. The old man indicated a place where he had heard there was a man who had Raftery's poems written down in a book. He went there and found that the man had gone to America twenty years before and taken the book with him. He was directed to another house where the poems were, but with the same luck—the man had taken the book with him to America fifteen years ago.

With the aid of some of the people he was able to get some of Raftery's poems, and took them down. With the help of Lady Gregory he was able to find out a third manuscript belonging to an old stonecutter, which contained fifteen or sixteen poems in addition to those he had already got. Then he came back to the Royal Irish Academy, but could not get a trace of the old manuscript he had seen many years ago. The index and catalogue afforded him no assistance, because, said Dr. Hyde, since the death of O'Curry they had left it in exactly the condition that that great Irishman had let it pass from his hands uncompleted. But after two whole days' search he again found the little roll of paper, and discovered that it contained twenty poems, several of which he had not got before.

Other poems had been got from Miss McManus, the editor of the *Gaelic Journal,* the town clerk of Tuam, and Father O'Looney, of Loughrea. One was obtained from a pawnbroker in Dublin, and several more came from out of the way directions. Altogether he had collected forty-five poems that everybody believed were lost and gone.

Dr. Hyde, in the concluding portion of his paper, described Raftery and the times he lived in, as illustrated by his poems, many of which he read out in Gaelic and in English. Born between 1780 and 1790, he saw the light first near Kiltimagh, his parents being very poor people. Smallpox deprived him of his sight early in life, so that he had never any better occupation with which to make a living, than that of fiddler. Yet, though absolutely destitute and practically dependent on alms, no poet of the people had ever exercised so widespread influence upon those among whom he lived. It was only in Ireland that the poems and life of such a man could have been all but abso-

lutely lost, and it was passing curious that their recovery should have
been the result of the mere accident of a man walking back a hundred
yards to give a penny to a blind beggar.

Raftery the Poet

Once, at a wedding where he was playing the fiddle, a newcomer
asked, "Who is the old fellow over there"? Raftery answered:

> I am Raftery the Poet
> Full of hope and love
> With eyes that have no light,
> With gentleness that has no misery.
>
> Going west upon my pilgrimage
> By the light of my heart,
> Feeble and tired
> To the end of my road.
>
> Behold me now,
> And my face to the wall,
> A-playing music
> Unto empty pockets.*

THE COUNTY OF MAYO†

Now, coming on Spring, the days will be growing,
And after Saint Bride's Day my sail I will throw;
Since the thought has come to me I fain would be going,
Till I stand in the middle of the County Mayo!

The first of my days will be spent in Claremorris,
And in Balla, beside it, I'll have drinking and sport,
To Kiltimagh, then, I will go on a visit,
And there, I can tell you, a month will be short.

---

* Translated by Douglas Hyde.
† Translated by Padraic Colum.

I solemnly swear that the heart in me rises,
As the wind rises up and the mists break below,
When I think upon Carra, and on Gallen down from it,
The Bush of the Mile, and the Plains of Mayo!

Killeadean's my village, and every good's in it;
The rasp and blackberry to set to one's tooth;
And if Raftery stood in the midst of his people,
Old age would go from him, and he'd step to his youth!

The Last Gleeman

Michael Moran was born about 1794 off Black Pitts, in the Liberties of Dublin, in Faddle Alley. A fortnight after birth he went stone-blind from illness, and became thereby a blessing to his parents, who were soon able to send him to rhyme and beg at street corners and at the bridges over the Liffey. They may well have wished that their quiver were full of such as he, for, free from the interruption of sight, his mind became a perfect echoing chamber, where every movement of the day and every change of public passion whispered itself into rhyme or quaint saying. By the time he had grown to manhood he was the admitted rector of all the ballad-mongers of the Liberties. Madden, the weaver; Kearney, the blind fiddler from Wicklow; Martin, from Meath; M'Bride, from heaven knows where; and that M'Grane, who in after days, when the true Moran was no more, strutted in borrowed plumes, or rather in borrowed rags, and gave out that there had never been any Moran but himself, and many another, did homage before him, and held him chief of all their tribe.

Nor despite his blindness did he find any difficulty in getting a wife, but rather was able to pick and choose, for he was just that mixture of ragamuffin and of genius which is dear to the heart of woman, who, perhaps because she is wholly conventional herself, loves the unexpected, the crooked, the bewildering. Nor did he lack, despite his rags, many excellent things, for it is remembered that he ever loved caper sauce, going so far indeed in his honest indignation upon one occasion as to fling a leg of mutton at his wife. He was not, however,

From *The Celtic Twilight*, by William Butler Yeats, pp. 79-90. A. H. Bullen, Ltd. London. 1902.

much to look at, with his coarse frieze coat with its cape and scalloped edge, his old corduroy trousers and great brogues, and his stout stick made fast to his wrist by a thong of leather: and he would have been a woeful shock to the gleeman MacConglinne, could that friend of kings have beheld him in prophetic vision from the pillar stone at Cork. And yet though the short cloak and the leather wallet were no more, he was a true gleeman, being alike poet, jester, and newsman of the people. In the morning when he had finished his breakfast, his wife or some neighbour would read the newspaper to him, and read on and on until he interrupted with, "That'll do—I have me meditations"; and from these meditations would come the day's store of jest and rhyme. He had the whole Middle Ages under his frieze coat.

He had not, however, MacConglinne's hatred of the Church and clergy, for when the fruit of his meditations did not ripen well, or when the crowd called for something more solid, he would recite or sing a metrical tale or ballad of saint or martyr or of Biblical adventure. He would stand at a street corner, and when a crowd had gathered would begin in some such fashion as follows (I copy the record of one who knew him), "Gather round me, boys, gather round me. Boys, am I standin' in puddle? Am I standin' in wet?" Thereon several boys would cry, "Ah, no! Yez not! Yer in a nice dry place. Go on with *St. Mary*; go on with *Moses*"—each calling for his favourite tale. Then Moran, with a suspicious wriggle of his body and a clutch at his rags would burst out with, "All me buzzim friends are turned backbiters"; and after a final "If yez don't drop your coddin' and diversion I'll lave some of yez a case," by way of warning to the boys, begin his recitation, or perhaps still delay, to ask, "Is there a crowd round me now? Any blackguard heretic around me?"

The best-known of his religious tales was *St. Mary of Egypt*, a long poem of exceeding solemnity, condensed from the much longer work of a certain Bishop Coyle. It told how a fast woman of Egypt, Mary by name, followed pilgrims to Jerusalem for no good purpose, and then, turning penitent on finding herself withheld from entering the Temple by supernatural interference, fled to the desert and spent the remainder of her life in solitary penance. When at last she was at the point of death, God sent Bishop Zozimus to hear her confession, give her the last sacrament, and with the help of a lion, whom He sent also, dig her grave. The poem has the intolerable cadence of the eighteenth century, but was so popular and so often called for, that Moran was soon nicknamed Zozimus, and by that name is he remembered. He had also a poem of his own called *Moses*, which went a little nearer poetry without going very near. But he could ill brook solemn-

ity, and before long parodied his own verses in the following ragamuffin fashion:

> In Egypt's land, contagious to the Nile,
> King Pharaoh's daughter went to bathe in style.
> She tuk her dip, then walked unto the land,
> To dry her royal pelt she ran along the strand.
> A bulrush tripped her, whereupon she saw
> A smiling babby in a wad o' straw.
> She tuk it up, and said with accents mild,
> "Tare-and-agers, girls, which av yez owns the child?"

His humorous rhymes were, however, more often quips and cranks
at the expense of his contemporaries. It was his delight, for instance,
to remind a certain shoemaker, noted alike for display of wealth and
for personal uncleanness, of his inconsiderable origin in a song of
which but the first stanza has come down to us:

> At the dirty end of Dirty Lane,
> Liv'd a dirty cobbler, Dick Maclane;
> His wife was in the old king's reign
>   A stout brave orange-woman.
> On Essex Bridge she strained her throat,
> And six-a-penny was her note.
> And Dickey wore a bran-new coat,
>   He got among the yeoman.
> He was a bigot, like his clan,
> And in the streets he wildly sang,
> O Roly, toly, toly raid, with his old jade.

He had troubles of divers kinds, and numerous interlopers to face
and put down. Once an officious peeler arrested him as a vagabond,
but he was triumphantly routed amid the laughter of the court, when
Moran reminded his Worship of the precedent set by Homer, who was
also, he declared, a poet, a blind man, and a beggarman. He had to
face a more serious difficulty as his fame grew. Various imitators
started up on all sides. A certain actor, for instance, made as many
guineas as Moran did shillings by mimicking his sayings and his songs
and his get-up upon the stage. One night this actor was at supper with
some friends, when dispute arose as to whether his mimicry was over-
done or not. It was agreed to settle it by an appeal to the mob. A forty-
shilling supper at a famous coffee-house was to be the wager. The

actor took up his station at Essex Bridge, a great haunt of Moran's, and soon gathered a small crowd. He had scarce got through "In Egypt land, contagious to the Niie," when Moran himself came up, followed by another crowd. The crowds met in great excitement and laughter. "Good Christians," cried the pretender, "is it possible that any man would mock the poor dark man like that?"

"Who's that? It's some imposhterer," replied Moran.

"Begone, you wretch! It's you'ze the imposhterer. Don't you fear the light of heaven being struck from your eyes for mocking the poor dark man?"

"Saints and angels, is there no protection against this? You're a most inhuman bla'guard to try to deprive me of my honest bread this way," replied poor Moran.

"And you, you wretch, won't you let me go on with the beautiful poem? Christian people, in your charity won't you beat this man away? He's taking advantage of my darkness."

The pretender, seeing that he was having the best of it, thanked the people for their sympathy and protection, and went on with the poem, Moran listening for a time in bewildered silence. After a while Moran protested again with: "Is it possible that none of yez can know me? Don't yez see it's myself; and that's some one else?"

"Before I can proceed any further in this lovely story," interrupted the pretender, "I call on yez to contribute your charitable donations to help me to go on."

"Have you no sowl to be saved, you mocker of heaven?" cried Moran, put completely beside himself by this last injury. "Would you rob the poor as well as desave the world? O, was ever such wickedness known?"

"I leave it to yourselves, my friends," said the pretender, "to give to the real dark man, that you all know so well, and save me from that schemer," and with that he collected some pennies and half-pence. While he was doing so, Moran started his *Mary of Egypt,* but the indignant crowd seizing his stick were about to belabor him, when they fell back bewildered anew by his close resemblance to himself. The pretender now called to them to "just give him a grip of that villain, and he'd soon let him know who the imposhterer was!" They led him over to Moran, but instead of closing with him he thrust a few shillings into his hand, and turning to the crowd explained to them he was indeed but an actor, and that he had just gained a wager, and so departed amid much enthusiasm to eat the supper he had won.

In April, 1846, word was sent to the priest that Michael Moran was dying. He found him at 15 (now 14½) Patrick Street, on a straw bed, in a room full of ragged ballad-singers come to cheer his last moments.

After his death the ballad-singers, with many fiddles and the like, came again and gave him a fine wake, each adding to the merriment whatever he knew in the way of rann, tale, old saw, or quaint rhyme. He had had his day, had said his prayers and made his confession, and why should they not give him a hearty send-off? The funeral took place the next day. A good party of his admirers and friends got into the hearse with the coffin, for the day was wet and nasty. They had not gone far when one of them burst out with "It's cruel cowld, isn't it?" "Garra ," replied another, "we'll all be as stiff as the corpse when we get to the berrin-ground." "Bad cess to him," said a third; "I wish he'd held out another month until the weather got dacent." A man named Carroll thereupon produced a half-pint of whiskey, and they all drank to the soul of the departed. Unhappily, however, the hearse was over-weighted, and they had not reached the cemetery before the spring broke, and the bottle with it.

Moran must have felt strange and out of place in that other kingdom he was entering, perhaps while his friends were drinking in his honour. Let us hope that some kindly middle region was found for him, where he can call dishevelled angels about him with some new and more rhythmical form of his old

> Gather round me, boys, will yez
> Gather round me?
> And hear what I have to say
> Before old Salley brings me
> My bread and jug of tay;

and fling outrageous quips and cranks at cherubim and seraphim. Perhaps he may have found and gathered, ragamuffin though he be, the Lily of High Truth, the Rose of Far-sought Beauty, for whose lack so many of the writers of Ireland, whether famous or forgotten, have been futile as the blown froth upon the shore.

John Barry, Father of the American Navy

It was a bright, sparkling day in April, and Captain John Barry, casting a seawise eye on the well-filled sails of his sixteen-gun brig.

By Parry Miller, in *The Irish Digest*, May, 1953, pp. 24-26. Dublin.

thanked his stars once again for a trim craft, a spirited crew, and a mission for both.

The brig was the *Lexington,* and here she was, cruising off the Virginia Capes on the look-out for English ships. For this was the year 1776, with the American Colonies in revolt and at open war with England. And Barry held a Congress commission. It made him one of the earliest naval officers to be appointed on the American side.

He was now thirty-one. He mused on all that had happened to him since that day when, a boy scarce in his teens, he had slipped away from his home in Tacumshane, County Wexford, and first gone away to sea.

Why he had done that he had never quite been able to explain. The wide, wild sea had called to his young ears, and he had been unable to resist. Not that he had ever regretted it. What he would have regretted would have been to be tied for life to the desk of a clerk in a malt-house, as his father had been.

So, as a boy, he had somehow got aboard a boat and sailed for the Golden West. He had never gone back to Wexford. At fifteen he was calling Philadelphia his home town and sailing in American ships.

By the time he was twenty-one he was master of one of them. And in the years that had followed he had built up a sound little shipping business and made a fair amount of money.

Then, in the autumn of 1775, had come this revolt against the voice of London. Barry had promptly thrown in his lot with the Americans. As a first-class shipmaster his services were snapped up. He was given the job of fitting out a fleet.

It was, of course, the first fleet of ships of war the Americans had ever had. It consisted of eight vessels, and over-all command of them was given to Captain Esek Hopkins, a merchant captain who had once been master of a privateer.

Esek had chosen for his flagship the twenty-four-gun *Alfred,* in whose fortunes John Barry had a special interest. It had been his own merchantman, the *Black Prince,* and his special pride and joy, but he had gladly turned this vessel over for conversion into a well-armed man-o'-war.

In his mind's eye Barry could see her now—with the yellow silk flag his friend John Paul Jones had hoisted at her masthead, the flag that bore the device of a pine tree and a rattlesnake, and the motto, "Don't Tread on Me."

Barry's musings were broken by a shout from the look-out. A sail away to starboard had been spotted. Barry cracked out his orders, and very soon his glass had picked up a small craft carrying English colours. He cleared his guns for action and crowded on sail to overhaul her.

She proved to be the *Edward,* mounting eight guns and carrying a crew of thirty-five, against the *Lexington's* seventy. Although outweighted, the Englishmen fought back valiantly, and there was a spirited action that lasted about an hour. Then, badly damaged, the *Edward* was forced to strike her colours. And Barry sailed proudly back to port with the first English ship-of-war to be captured by the American Navy.

This exploit won for Barry command of a new twenty-eight-gun frigate, the *Effingham,* being built at Philadelphia. Before she was ready for sea, however, English troops from Brandywine attacked and Barry was forced to run his new craft up the Delaware. There, on direct orders from George Washington, he scuttled and sank her.

Barry was now ordered to go to Boston and take command of the thirty-two-gun frigate *Raleigh.* Within a couple of days of putting to sea he was sighted by the fifty-gun English frigate *Experiment* and the twenty-eight-gun *Unicorn.* There followed a battle of wits and seamanship that was to last for the next forty-eight hours, Barry's job being to escape getting manoeuvred into a position where he would be a sitting duck for the guns of the enemy.

In the end, heavily outgunned and with every chance of escape cut off, he ran his craft fast aground on an island known as the Wooden Ball, some twenty miles from the mouth of the Penobscot River. The Englishmen, moving cautiously because of the shoaling water, went in as close as possible and opened heavy fire, to which the *Raleigh* replied with her stern guns.

While these last shots were being exchanged, Barry was speeding up preparations for landing his men and destroying his ship by setting her afire. He managed to get some of his crew ashore, but as the boats were returning for the remainder the *Raleigh's* colours fluttered down.

Barry himself had managed to get away and, with those of his men who escaped, headed for the mainland.

Things were going badly with other ships of the young American Navy. Indeed, about this time it was crushed almost out of existence. With no ships to command or sail in, Barry decided to throw in his lot with the army. He served in this capacity, with distinction, for the next couple of years.

Early in 1781 he went back to the sea, being given the thirty-two-gun frigate *Alliance,* which had just got back after a remarkable cruise round the British coast as one of John Paul Jones's squadron. His job was to carry safely to France Colonel Laurens, the new representative of the States at the Court at Versailles.

On the way back he met fresh adventures. To start with, he and the captain of a French ship captured a couple of English privateers. Then, while his craft lay becalmed off the coast of Newfoundland one May morning, she was spotted and smartly attacked by two English brigs— the sixteen-gun *Atlanta* and the fourteen-gun *Trepassy*.

For an hour the Englishmen kept up their fire with impunity. Barry himself had a shoulder badly shattered by grape-shot and had to go to his cabin for attention at the hands of the ship's surgeon. Scarce had he got there than a lucky hit from one of the brigs carried away the American flag from the masthead of the *Alliance*.

Barry heard an English hail from across the water, to know if the disappearance of the flag meant the frigate had struck. But at that moment, with everything apparently lost, Barry felt his ship suddenly lurch—lightly enough, but unmistakably. Seaman as he was, he knew well enough what it meant. That lurch meant a breeze. And sure enough, within a little while the *Alliance* had gained steerage way.

Barry knew just what to do now to turn the tables on the Englishmen. Bringing his ship smartly about, he ran her straight between the two brigs with all guns thundering. Then, his men sweating and straining and reloading, he about ship and did it again and again. The play of those powerful broadsides turned the trick. Both the brigs were compelled to strike their flags. Barry went on ranging the seas and striking shrewd blows for his adopted country.

It was Barry who fought the last sea action of the Revolutionary War. That was against the twenty-eight-gun *Sybille* which, on March 10th, 1783, tried with two other ships to intercept the *Alliance*, carrying a bullion shipment, in the Gulf of Florida.

It was because of his skill as a fighting seaman, and the reputation he had made, that in 1794 he was sent against the Algerian pirates. And in 1798, when there were hostilities with France, he was given command of the United States naval forces in West Indian waters.

In the end he became Commodore Barry and the head of the navy he had done so much to bring into being and inspire. And because of his success in the training of young officers who were later to make their mark they called him the Father of that Navy. He died at Philadelphia, in September, 1803, aged fifty-eight.

The 69th in Virginia

It was fully ten o'clock, on the mornmg of the 17th of July, when the 69th came in sight of Fairfax Court House, the road along which the regiment passed being obstructed, every half mile almost, with enormous heaps of fallen trees, which the Confederates had levelled and massed together, and which had to be cut through by our axemen, before the slightest progress could be made. In this rough and dangerous pioneering, the Engineers of the 69th, under the command of their high-spirited young Captain, did quick and clear work, splendidly maintaining their character with the regiment for usefulness, promptitude and boldness.

Arriving in sight of Fairfax Court House, and within easy cannon-shot of it, the 69th, leaving the Ohio and other regiments drawn up in line of battle along the road, striking off at right-angles to the left of the main line of march, passed on so as to flank the village and cut off the retreat of the Confederates.

Proceeding in the execution of this movement, we came in sight of a portion of the enemy, apparently from one thousand to one thousand five hundred strong, drawn up in line of battle outside the village in a field, directly fronting our line of march. The order to halt was promptly given, the right wing of the 69th was thrown into the fields to the left, and uniting there with the 2nd New York—as vigorous and spirited a body of men as any one would wish to see—moved rapidly down upon the enemy.

As they neared him, however, he retreated into the village, and then out of it towards Centreville, leaving it to be peacefully entered, a short time after, by the forces from Arlington Heights, and the encampments between that and Alexandria and beyond it.

At 12 o'clock the Green Flag was planted upon the deserted ramparts of the Confederates at Germantown; the Stars and Stripes were lifted opposite to it, at a distance of fifteen paces, and between the two beautiful and inspiring symbols—the one of their old home and the other of their new country—the 69th passed in triumph, hats and caps waving on the bayonet points, and an Irish cheer, such as never before

---

Extracts from *The Last Days of the 69th in Virginia,* by Thomas Francis Meagher, in *Memoirs of Gen. Thomas Francis Meagher,* by Michael Cavanagh, pp. 391-397. The Messenger Press. Worcester, Mass. 1892.

shook the woods of old Virginia, swelling and rolling far and wide into the gleaming air.

Defiling through the deserted earth-works at Germantown, our Brigade bore off to the left, taking position in line of battle in the open fields spreading northward from the village. Skirmishers were thrown forward, and the village also being found deserted, the march was renewed, the position of the regiments being altered—the First Wisconsin taking the right, and the 69th bringing up the rear of the Brigade.

Over the streaming bayonets, through the swaying colors and the clouds of dust rolling at the head of the 69th beside our Colonel, I saw the handful of little wooden houses, known as Germantown, rise up and dilate before us. One house, however, particularly struck me, even at that distance, and notwithstanding the dust, confusion and tumult through which I noticed it,—a two-storied house, well proportioned,—with a white, cheerful face; roses and woodbine, as I took them to be, coiling and clustering about the trellised porch; young ornamental trees in front of it; a clear and handsome feature in the clouded picture against which we were moving—it was the first pleasant object, of the quieter and friendlier order of things, we had fallen in with since we pushed on that morning from Vienna.

"That house is on fire," Father O'Reilly, the Chaplain, hurriedly observed, as he whipped his horse up beside the Colonel.

The words had scarcely fallen from his lips when a round mass of black smoke rolled out of the windows of the house and buried it in darkness. In another moment, the red flames were leaping through the smoke, and the crackling of timbers, pierced and rifted with the fire, was heard distinctly above the tramp and tumult of the march. The only ornament of the village, in hot haste and fury, was plunging into ashes. In half an hour it would be, at best, a heap of smouldering charcoal.

Whose was the scurvy and malignant hand that fired the deserted homestead? It is for the regiments of the Brigade, in advance of the 69th, to answer. With them rests the responsibility of this savage riotousness and mischief. The house was doomed irrevocably when the 69th came up. The Irish regiment swept by the blazing ruin, cursing the ruffians who had played the barbarous prank, and maddened with the thought of the disgrace it would bring on the Federal Flag.

A shout, hearty and prolonged, soon told us that Centreville, also, had been evacuated. The huts, cresting the rising ground on the left, were stripped to the very leaves and branches of which they had been built. The *redoubt* between the house and the road was emptied too, nothing falling into the possession of the Federal troops but a few ammunition boxes. It was a clean sweep the Confederates made, as they fell back, abandoning position after position, until they fiercely stood their ground in that fatal labyrinth, bristling, four miles ahead, between us and Manassas. It was there they wanted us; and their abandoned positions at Vienna, Fairfax, at Germantown, at Centreville—wherever they had been grouped between Bull Run and Falls Church, up to the evening of our advance,—were but so many artifices, elaborately arranged along our line of march, to entice us headlong, breathless and breadless, almost, to destruction.

At noon on the 18th of July, the Stars and Stripes were flying over Centreville. The regiments under Colonel Keyes, accompanied by Brigadier-General Tyler, moved down the southern slope of the hill already mentioned, and disappeared. Sherman's Brigade broke into the fields to the right of where we halted on the road—arms were stacked—haversacks and canteens were brought into play—and the sore-footed volunteers, their blankets spread above them on rails and muskets, so as to shade them somewhat, enjoyed a lunch of biscuit and hot water, and four hours' repose.

Little they seemed to heed the cannon which, at long intervals,—intervals of from ten to twenty minutes—when it first began to boom, off there in the hazy woods below,—told them that the enemy was found at last. One might have thought that every man of the 69th had been a hardened and callous veteran, so coolly, so indifferently, so lazily did they take those dread intimations that death had commenced his havoc amid the lightnings, and with all the pomp of war.

The fact is—what with the constant alarms at Fort Corcoran, forced marches and precipitate expeditions two or three times a week, being under arms upon the ramparts every second night or so, lying in ambuscade at the Alexandria and Loudon railway from midnight until dawn, and undergoing all the hardships, violences, and most of the shocks of war, the men of the 69th had become familiarized by anticipation and analogy with the scene which, at that moment, was being played out with such terrible effect amid the beautiful green trees of Virginia, and on one of the oldest high-roads to her capital. Hence the strange coolness with which they heard those bellowings of the conflict, awaiting the summons that would fling them into its fierce currents, and whirl their banner into the blackest and wildest eddies of the storm.

At four o'clock in the afternoon that summons came. Sherman's Brigade was ordered up to relieve the regiments that had been under fire for five hours and more. The 69th led the way, and, as they hurried up the hill, the elasticity and enthusiasm of their race seemed to pervade them thoroughly. Of those thousand men, sweeping on to battle, through choking clouds of dust, and under that smiting sun, there was not one but carried himself right gallantly—not one who did not feel that the honor of his race and of its military character was staked that hour upon the conduct of the 69th; and who, feeling this, and lifting his eye in rapture to the Green Flag as it danced above the rushing column, did not swear to meet the thrusts of battle with a fearless heart.

An hour's rushing—for the marching of the 69th to Bull Run that evening cannot otherwise be described—brought the regiment to the brow of the hill descending into the little meadow, where the Federal troops, regiment after regiment, had faced and stood a tempestuous fire from the batteries of rifled cannon—masked as well as naked batteries—the fire of rifle-pits—a downright torrent and whirlwind of balls and shot, all of the deadliest cunning and ripest pattern.

And here they encountered several of the 12th Regiment of New York Volunteers hurrying from the bloody arena in the woods below, some of them dragging dead or bleeding comrades along with them, others with bandaged heads or legs or arms, staggering through the dust and the vengeful storm from the rifled cannon which still pursued them. Here, too, they met the 13th of Rochester on its retreat, this fine young regiment having stood its ground until broken and overpowered.

Seeing a body of men making through the woods from where the murderous hail was pouring in upon them thick and sharp and fast, and taking them to be the Southerners in pursuit of the 12th New York, the boys of the 69th instinctively brought their bayonets to the charge, and were on the point of plunging upon the 13th, when Captain Haggerty dashed along the line and struck the bayonets upwards with his sword. It was the bold act of a cool, strong, decisive brain, and in an instant it stayed the 69th with an iron hand, as it were, and held it in a masterly suspense.

The next moment we were ordered to lie down in double file, in the wood overlooking the field of battle, with our faces and muskets to the road, and in that position, keeping perfectly silent and collected, to await further orders. For more than three quarters of an hour did the regiment keep its position there—without a word from the ranks—without a breath almost—whilst shot and shell, and every sort of hellish missile, swept and tore, whizzed and jarred, smashed and plunged through the trees all about, and close to us overhead, in hurtling and deafening showers on either flank, in front and rear.

While we lay under that torrent and hurricane of round shot, spherical ball, shell and canister, whilst we patiently submitted to this butcherly rain, Captain Haggerty stood upon our extreme right, contemplating with undisguised satisfaction, the perfect coolness and subordination of the men, the Colonel taking it just as coolly in the centre as though he had been dictating some unimportant order in his *marquee* at Fort Corcoran, with a pitcher of ice-water close at hand.

Between six and seven o'clock, General McDowell came upon the ground with a brilliant escort, including the young Governor Sprague of Rhode Island, and he, comprehending at a glance the situation of affairs, the sheer deadliness of the conflict, and the utter fatuity of attacking the hidden enemy in his lair, ordered the 69th to return to the hill overlooking the little village of Centreville, and there await further orders, which would be forthwith issued.

Were it not for the visit of Father Scully, the young and devoted Chaplain of Colonel Cass's Irish Regiment, from Boston, who, having heard of Thursday's fighting, dashed across from Washington, over five-and-thirty miles, to see and learn all about us, Saturday, despite of the glaring sunshine, would have been a gloomy day indeed. His hearty words and response lit up afresh the life and fire of the 69th; and he came in good time, and most kindly staid long enough to relieve our own beloved Chaplain, Father O'Reilly at the confessional. There were few of the 69th who failed to confess and ask forgiveness on that day. Every one, officers as well as privates, prepared for death. Sincerely and devoutly they made their peace with God. This is the secret of their courage, and the high, bright spirit with which they bore all the hardships, the privations, the terrors, and the chastisement of the battle.

It was, in truth, an affecting sight—that of strong, stalwart, rugged men—all upon their knees, all with heads uncovered, all with hands clasped in prayer and eyes cast down, approaching, one by one, the good, dear priest, who, seated at the foot of an old bare tree, against which some of our boys had spread for him an awning of green branches, heard the confessions of the poor fellows and bid them be at ease and fearless. Long as I live, I shall never forget that scene. It was not less impressive than that of Father O'Reilly's passing along our line, as we knelt within range of the enemy's batteries on one knee, with bayonets fixed, expecting every instant to be swept upon, and the final benediction was imparted.

Father O'Reilly has told me since that the earnestness and devotion with which poor Haggerty received that benediction singularly struck him, and that the attitude and expression of this truly honest and heroic soldier at that solemn moment could never leave his memory.

Of subsequent incidents and events, the world, by this time, has heard enough. Concerning the advance from Centreville, the battle, the retreat, the alarm and confusion of the Federal troops, columns and volumes have been filled. I can add nothing to the history of the day but my testimony, that wherever the Federal troops had a fair chance—wherever, indeed, they had the slightest opening even—there and then they whipped the Confederate forces, utterly overwhelmed and confounded them. In every instance where the Federal infantry came in contact with that of the seceding States, did this occur. In no one instance, not for a second, did it happen that the Federal forces were driven back by, or received the slightest check from the Southern Infantry. We yielded to their batteries, and despite of every effort and determination were compelled to do so. It was impossible for men to override that tempest. Three times did the 69th launch itself against it. Three times, having plunged head-foremost into its deadliest showers, was it hurled back. We beat their men—their batteries beat us. That is the story of the day.

Ambrose O'Higgins of Chile

There is often a touch of pleasant mystery about some of the Irish who made a great name abroad. Ambrose O'Higgins, the Mayo man— or is it the Meath man, for the books are not clear on the point, must have been one of the most forthright emigrants who ever sailed away. Who could have prophesied that the lad who ran messages for the high Lady in Meath and could there look forward to the prospect of becoming the high Lady's butler, one lucky day for him would leave his prospects behind him and land in South America on the way to become first, a market-stall keeper there, and, later, one of the great statesmen of that continent? It was he of course who as a Spanish official, after he had abandoned the market-stall, placated the Araucanian Indians of Chile who had been defying the Spaniards for twenty-four years. "Patiru Paddi" was the name that these defiant Chileans gave the Irishman—"Father Paddy," the tribute of a nickname that carried as high a compliment as a statesman ever won. The story of Ambrose O'Higgins' (the "O" adopted deliberately as an

From "Irish Empire," by D. L. Kelleher, in *The Capuchin Annual*, 1944, pp. 55-56. Dublin.

Irish identification when he achieved high Spanish rank) break later with the Spaniards and his re-creation of Chilean independence is too long to repeat. The lad who might have been a butler in the Meath parlor of the high Lady is remembered for an age instead as a famous soldier and statesman of South America. The small but memorable fact that he arranged to have a regular allowance paid to his poor relations in Ireland and committed the administration of the fund to the local parish priest stands as much to his credit perhaps as all his diplomatic and war triumphs. He was not one of these curious people too common in the world who find it rather an annoyance that poor relations exist as a reminder of their own humble origin.

His son, Bernardo O'Higgins, the son of a Chilean mother, was given command of the patriotic forces in Chile. Later he took a subordinate post with General San Martin whom he co-operated with for the organization of the army and their transportation across the Andes. Later, he took over the administration of Chile, and his firm and disinterested government is praised by historians. "Generous" is a word often used about Bernardo O'Higgins. His post of Director-General gave him dictatorial powers, but he resigned it in face of a popular manifestation. He retired to Peru where he died in 1842.

The Wandering Hawk: Chief of the Fenians

At midnight, on November 24, 1865, there was hardly a soul to be seen in the streets of Dublin City. A high wind was blowing, driving a bitter sleet before it. Policemen on duty took shelter in doorways, blowing upon their fingers and cursing the elements.

But colder even than the policemen were half-a-dozen men who were waiting, drenched to the skin, outside Richmond Jail. They were watching the high prison wall and waiting for a signal. When they spoke it was in whispers, and they dared not stamp their feet on the grass for warmth lest the sound be overheard.

In a cell within the prison a man was pacing up and down. He, too, was expecting a signal, for he knew that on this night, unless plans miscarried, an attempt would be made to rescue him. His name was James Stephens.

From *Adventures of an Irish Bookman,* a selection from the writings of M. J. MacManus, edited by Francis MacManus, pp. 24-28. The Talbot Press, Ltd. Dublin. 1952.

Stephens was the biggest prize that the Secret Service of Dublin Castle had landed for many a long day. He was the chief of the dreaded Fenian Society, a dominating, hypnotic man, the very mention of whose name would bring a hush in any Irish gathering.

A fortnight before, he had been arrested at Fairfield House in Sandymount, and a few days later was brought, under a heavy guard, before a magistrate in the Castle. In the dock he looked as cool and unperturbed as if he had been sitting in a barber's chair having a haircut. When a clerk of the court read a passage from one of his letters, in which he had declared that this should be "the year for action," Stephens startled everybody by interjecting loudly: "And so it may be!"

At the end of the proceedings the magistrate asked him if he had any observations to make. "I have," said Stephens. "If I have employed no lawyer in this case it is because by making a defence of any kind I should be recognizing British law in Ireland. Now I deliberately and conscientiously repudiate the existence of that law. I defy any punishment it can inflict on me. I have spoken."

After that short, defiant and contemptuous speech he was taken, still more heavily guarded, to Richmond Jail, where high walls, iron doors and grated windows were to keep him safe until he came up for trial on November 27. The officials in Dublin Castle felt that they need lose no sleep over him now.

But they had underestimated Fenian daring and ingenuity. One of the warders in Richmond, Dan Byrne, was a sworn member of the brotherhood. The superintendent of the hospital, John J. Breslin, was a sympathiser. With these two, the Fenian leaders still at liberty— John Devoy and Colonel Kelly—swiftly arranged a plan of rescue.

"Richmond," said a contemporary writer, "was one of the strongest jails in Ireland. At the head of one of the several stone stairs which connect the ground-floor cell system with the upper tier ran a short cross corridor of six cells. The door between the corridor and the stairway was of heavy hammered iron, nearly an inch thick. The cell doors were likewise of wrought iron, fastened with ponderous swinging bars and padlocks."

Five of these cells held Fenian prisoners—Stephens, O'Leary, Rossa, Kickham, and Luby. In the sixth, between Stephens and Kickham, the jail governor had placed an ordinary prisoner—a young lad named McLeod—with instructions to listen after locking-up time and sound a gong if he thought anything was amiss.

The night of November 24 came. The head warder went on his final round of inspection. The other warders were paraded and their keys put away in the governor's safe. Lights went out and silence descended on the prison. Hours passed by, and the city clocks had just chimed one when Stephens heard a gentle tap on his door, which in another moment was quietly opened.

Byrne and Breslin entered, each holding a revolver. No more than a nod was exchanged and Stephens followed them along the corridor, down the stone stairs and out into the yard. A ladder lying in a corner was quickly lifted and placed against the wall. Then came an unpleasant shock: it was too short!

Breslin thought quickly. Time was passing, and at any moment the alarm might be raised. McLeod might sound his gong. Beckoning Byrne, and telling Stephens to hide in an empty sentry-box, he hurried back and the two carried out a large table from the day-room. On this they placed the ladder.

Outside in the field the other rescuers, weary and famished after their long vigil, were waiting anxiously. The signal was to be a handful of gravel thrown over the wall and the "quack, quack" of a duck. About midnight—the time fixed for the signal—a real duck had quacked, as if in mockery. The watchers smiled ruefully.

Since then an hour or more had passed, and now they were growing despondent. Eventually, however, there came the quacking noise and the sound of pebbles falling. In another moment the head and shoulders of Stephens could be seen, a shadowy form in the darkness, surmounting the wall. A rope, knotted at intervals, was thrown across and seized by Breslin and Byrne at the other side.

Carefully and laboriously—for he was no light-weight—Stephens made the descent, to be greeted with fervent, but silent handshakes when he reached the ground. Everything had gone according to plan. The rope was hauled down and taken away, and Breslin and Byrne returned to the prison, the former removing the mud from his slippers before he retired to bed, the latter doing his rounds and putting off giving the alarm until he was satisfied that Stephens and his escort had had ample time to make a complete get-away.

In the morning there was wild panic in official circles in Dublin. The "Wandering Hawk" had taken wing again. Cavalry scoured the country. Squads of police and detectives were everywhere. Hundreds of suspected houses were raided; garrets and coal-holes were searched; floor-boards were torn up and wainscoting stripped. Steamers were stopped and the passengers scrutinised. Gunboats put to sea and searched fishing-smacks and coasting vessels. On all the boardings throughout the country large placards appeared with the heading in great black type: ONE THOUSAND POUNDS REWARD. At the inquisition held in the jail McLeod was asked why he did not sound the gong. "I was afraid I'd get a bullet if I did," was his simple and adequate reply.

Whilst all the commotion was going on, Stephens lay in hiding in a shabby little house in Ballybough, the home of a Mrs. Butler. She was a poor woman, but with her the Fenian leader was perfectly safe. Had the reward offered been ten times as great, she would not have betrayed him.

About seven months later a handsome open carriage, drawn by four spirited horses, drove through the streets of Dublin. It carried a postilion and footmen in livery. Two gentlemen, immaculately dressed and wearing silk hats, reclined at ease on the cushioned seats. It was a sunny afternoon in the month of June.

As the equipage passed Amiens Street Station a policeman on duty stood to attention and saluted. The gentlemen taking the air must be magistrates at least! Once the North Strand was passed, the driver whipped up his horses and they moved at a spanking pace towards Malahide and the sea. Some miles from Balbriggan the carriage halted. One of its occupants got out, bade farewell to the other, and walked to the shore, where a boat was waiting. He stepped into it and was rowed quickly out to a sailing boat anchored a few hundred yards out. The sails were set, and in a few moments the boat was speeding down the Channel bound for France.

This time the "Wandering Hawk" had spread his wings in earnest. The coachman, postilion and footman watched until the vessel was out of sight. Then they returned to the carriage and drove back quietly to Dublin. They were all picked men of the Irish Republican Brotherhood and armed to the teeth.

Charles Stewart Parnell

On Tuesday night, December 9, he started for Ireland, accompanied by many of his colleagues. A reporter from the *Freeman's Journal* asked him before his departure. "What message, Mr. Parnell, shall I send from you to the Irish people?" "Tell them," he replied, "that I will fight to the end."

From *The Life of Charles Stewart Parnell*, by R. Barry O'Brien, Vol. II, pp. 290-297. Smith, Elder & Co. London. 1898.

On Wednesday morning, December 10, he arrived in Dublin and went straight to the house of Dr. Kenny. There he received a hearty welcome, not only from the multitude collected outside but from the many friends gathered within. An eyewitness has given me an account of the scene in Dr. Kenny's breakfast-room on that eventful morning. "The room was full of men, all talking together, interrupting each other, making suggestions and counter-suggestions, proposing plans and counter-plans, and everyone too full of his own views to listen to the views of anyone else. Parnell sat silently near the fire, looking thoughtfully into it and apparently heeding nothing that was going on. Mrs. Kenny entered the room, made her way through the crowd to Parnell, and said: "Mr. Parnell, do you not want something to eat?"

"That is just what I do want," he said, with a smile.

"Why," said Mrs. Kenny, going among the agitators, "don't you see that the man is worn out and wants something to eat, while you all keep talking and debating, and making a noise."

Soon there was complete silence, and Parnell sat to the table, saying, "I am as hungry as a hawk."

Breakfast over, the Chief did not allow the grass to grow under his feet. "United Ireland," which had been founded by him, had under the direction of Mr. Matthias Bodkin, the acting editor in Mr. William O'Brien's absence, gone over to the enemy. Parnell's first order was, "Seize 'United Ireland,' expel Bodkin, and put Mr. Leamy in charge of the paper." This order was carried out on the morning of December 18, under the superintendence of Parnell himself, with characteristic vigour and despatch. Going straight to the office of the paper he removed Mr. Bodkin and his staff, placing Mr. Leamy in the editorial chair. One of Parnell's Fenian supporters has given me a brief and pithy account of what happened. "I went up to Matty Bodkin. 'Matty,' says I, 'will you walk out, or would you like to be thrown out?' and Matty walked out."

That night Parnell addressed a great meeting at the Rotunda. Miss Katharine Tynan (Mrs. Hinkson) was present, and has given a graphic account of what she saw: "It was nearly 8.30 when we heard the bands coming; then the windows were lit up by the lurid glare of thousands of torches in the street outside. There was a distant roaring like the sea. The great gathering within waited silently with expectation. Then the cheering began, and we craned our necks and looked on eagerly, and there was the tall, slender, distinguished figure of the Irish leader making its way across the platform. I don't think any words could do justice to his reception. The house rose at him; everywhere around there was a sea of passionate faces, loving, admiring, almost worshipping that silent, pale man. The cheering broke out again and again; there was no quelling it. Mr. Parnell bowed from side to side, sweeping the assemblage with his eagle glance. The people were fairly mad with excitement. I don't think anyone outside Ireland can understand what a charm Mr. Parnell has for the Irish heart; that wonderful personality of his, his proud bearing, his handsome, strong face, the distinction of look which marks him more than anyone I have ever seen. All these are irresistible to the artistic Irish.

"I said to Dr. Kenny, who was standing by me, 'He is the only quiet man here.' 'Outwardly,'' said the keen medical man, emphatically. Looking again, one saw the dilated nostrils, the flashing eye, the passionate face: the leader was simply drinking in thirstily this immense love, which must have been more heartening than one can say after that bitter time in the English capital. Mr. Parnell looked frail enough in body—perhaps the black frock-coat, buttoned so tightly across his chest, gave him that look of attenuation; but he also looked full of indomitable spirit and fire.

"For a time silence was not obtainable. Then Father Walter Hurley climbed on the table and stood with his arms extended. It was curious how the attitude silenced a crowd which could hear no words.

"When Mr. Parnell came to speak, the passion within him found vent. It was a wonderful speech; not one word of it for oratorical effect, but every word charged with a pregnant message to the people who were listening to him, and the millions who should read him. It was a long speech, lasting nearly an hour; but listened to with intense interest, punctuated by fierce cries against men whom this crisis has made odious, now and then marked in a pause by a deep-drawn moan of delight. It was a great speech—simple, direct, suave—with no device and no artificiality. Mr. Parnell said long ago, in a furious moment in the House of Commons, that he cared nothing for the opinion of the English people. One remembered it now, noting his passionate assurances to his own people, who loved him too well to ask him questions."

One sentence from Parnell's speech will suffice. It was the simple truth, and went to the heart of every man and every woman in the assembly.

"I don't pretend that I had not moments of trial and of temptation, but I do claim that never in thought, word, or deed have I been false to the trust that Irishmen have confided in me."

There were many in the Rotunda who did not look upon Parnell as a blameless man, or even a blameless politician; but all felt that in every emergency, through good report and ill report, he had been faithful to Ireland and the foe of English rule in the island. This was the bond of union between him and the men who carried the "thousands of torches" that lighted up his path that night—the men on whom he now relied to face his enemies.

While the meeting in the Rotunda was going on the Anti-Parnellites made a raid on "United Ireland," and recaptured it.

Next morning Parnell rose betimes—he had to start for Cork by an early train. But "United Ireland" was not to be left in the hands of the seceders. Dr. Kenny's carriage was quickly ordered to the door. "We must re-capture 'United Ireland' on our way to the train," said the Chief, as he finished his breakfast.

A description of the dramatic scene which followed has been given to me by a gentleman wholly unconnected with politics, who happened, by the merest chance, to be in the neighbourhood when the final battle over "United Ireland" was fought.

"I was walking down the north side of O'Connell Street, when there was a rush from all quarters in the direction of Lower Abbey Street. I followed the crowd, which stopped opposite the office of 'United Ireland.' There I witnessed a scene of wild excitement. Sticks and revolvers were being circulated freely by men who passed in and out of the dense mass, but as yet no blows had been exchanged.

"The enemy was, in fact, safe behind barred doors and windows, out of harm's way for the present, in the office of 'United Ireland.' Suddenly round the street corner dashed a pony carriage containing two gentlemen, as well as I can remember unattended; one, I was told, was Dr. Kenny, the other I knew to be Charles Stewart Parnell. I had seen him before in Ennis addressing a multitude of Clare men under the shadow of O'Connell's monument. I had been struck on that day by his power of electrifying a great multitude. I was to be even more moved and startled by him on this day. The carriage dashed on, the people making way for it, and it was as well, for no attempt was made to slacken speed. Both men seemed heedless of the crowd, thinking sternly of the seizure of the offices which they had come to make. A tremendous sensation was produced by the appearance of Parnell. They had been, doubtless, on the point of storming the citadel of the mutineers, and here was their captain come to fight in their front. Cheer after cheer filled the air, mingled with cries of hatred, defiance, and exultation. The carriage was checked so abruptly that the horse fell flat upon the road. Parnell sprang out, rushed up the steps, and knocked peremptorily at the office door. There was a pause, during which every eye regarded him and him alone. Suddenly he turned, his face pale with passion, his dark eyes flaming; he realised that obedience was not to be expected from those within, realised also the pain of being taunted and jeered at by his own countrymen, for there were indications of this from those within. He turned and spoke to some of his followers, then stood to wait. We knew by instinct that he was not going to turn away from that door, at which he had demanded admittance; he intended to storm the stronghold of the mutineers.

"I forgot everything save that there was going to be a historic fight, and that I wanted to have a good view of it. I dashed into a house opposite, and, without waiting for formal leave, ran upstairs. The windows of the first floor were crowded. I ran higher up, and soon gained a splendid point of vantage. I was in full sight of the beleaguered offices, and had a bird's eye view of the crowd in the street— a crowd of grim, determined, passionate men, many of them armed, and all ready and eager for a fray. Parnell's envoys were back by this time, bringing from some place near a crowbar and pickaxe. There was a brief discussion. Then Parnell suddenly realised that the fort might be carried from the area door. In a moment he was on the point of vaulting the railings. The hands of considerate friends restrained him by force. I heard his voice ring out clearly, impatiently, imperatively: 'Go yourselves, if you will not let me.' At the word several of those around him dropped into the area. Now Parnell snatched the crowbar, and, swinging his arms with might and main, thundered at the door. The door yielded, and, followed by those nearest to him, he disappeared into the hall. Instantly uprose a terrible noise. The other storming party, it seems, had entered from the area, and, rushing upstairs, had crashed into Parnell's bodyguard. What happened within the house I do not know, for spectators outside could only hold their breath and listen and guess. Feet clattered on the boarded stairs, voices hoarse with rage shrieked and shouted. A veritable pandemonium was let loose. At last there was a lull within, broken by the cheers of the waiting crowd without. One of the windows on the second storey was removed, and Parnell suddenly appeared in the aperture. He had conquered. The enthusiasm which greeted him cannot be described. His face was ghastly pale, save only that on either cheek a hectic crimson spot was glowing. His hat was off now, his hair dishevelled, the dust of the conflict begrimed his well-brushed coat. The people were spellbound, almost terrified, as they gazed on him. For myself, I felt a thrill of dread, as if I looked at a tiger in the frenzy of its rage. Then he spoke, and the tone of his voice was even more terrible than his look. He was brief, rapid, decisive, and the closing words of his speech still ring in my ear: 'I rely on Dublin. Dublin is true. What Dublin says to-day Ireland will say to-morrow.'

"He had simply recaptured 'United Ireland' on his way going south to Cork. The work done, he immediately entered the carriage and drove to King's Bridge terminus. After what I had witnessed I could not go tamely about my business. Hailing a car, I dashed down the quays. Many other cars went in the same direction, and the faithful crowd followed afoot. I was among the first to reach the terminus. I pushed towards the platform, but was stopped by the ticket collector. I was determined, however, not to be baulked, and I was engaged in a hot altercation with him, when I felt myself being crushed and wedged forward. With or without leave, I was being swept onto the platform, and, turning to see who was pushing or being pushed against me in the gangway, I found to my amazement that the foremost in the throng was Parnell himself. My look of angry remonstrance was doubtless soon turned, as I met his inscrutable gaze, into one of curious awe. The crowd at the station was now immense, and the spirit of 'I don't care what I do' which led me up to the room in Lower Abbey Street seemed to inspire everybody. People rushed about madly on the platform, seeking for every point of vantage to look at the Chief. Ladies got out of the first-class carriages of the train, which was waiting to start, and mingled in the throng. Parnell had entered a saloon carriage; the crowd cheered again and again, calling his name. He stood at the carriage window, looking pale, weary, wistful, and bowed graciously to the enthusiastic crowd. Many of those present endorsed the words of a young lady who exclaimed, addressing an elderly aristocrat wrapped in furs: 'Oh, father, hasn't he a lovely face!' The face disappeared from the window. The cheers again rose up, and then died away as the train passed from our sight."

Gladstone on Parnell: An Interview

I began the conversation by saying: "May I ask when you first discovered that there was anything remarkable in Parnell?"

Mr. Gladstone. "I must begin by saying that I did not discover anything remarkable in Mr. Parnell until much later than I ought to have discovered it. But you know that I had retired from the leader-

---

Ibid., pp. 356-359.

ship of the Liberal party about the time that Parnell entered Parliament, and when I came back to public life my attention was absorbed by the Eastern Question, by Bulgaria, and I did not think much about Ireland. I do not think that Mr. Parnell or Irish matters much engaged my attention until we came back to Government in 1880. You see we thought that the Irish question was settled. There was the Church Act and the Land Act, and there was a time of peace and prosperity, and I frankly confess that we did not give as much attention to Ireland as we ought to have done. Then, you know, there was distress and trouble, and the Irish question again came to the front."

"Could you say what it was that first attracted your attention to Parnell?"

Mr. Gladstone (with much energy). "Parnell was the most remarkable man I ever met. I do not say the ablest man; I say the most remarkable and the most interesting. He was an intellectual phenomenon. He was unlike anyone I had ever met. He did things and he said things unlike other men. His ascendency over his party was extraordinary. There has never been anything like it in my experience in the House of Commons. He succeeded in surrounding himself with very clever men, with men exactly suited for his purpose. They have changed since, I don't know why. Everything seems to have changed. But in his time he had a most efficient party, an extraordinary party. I do not say extraordinary as an Opposition, but extraordinary as a Government. The absolute obedience, the strict discipline, the military discipline, in which he held them was unlike anything I have ever seen. They were always there, they were always ready, they were always united, they never shirked the combat, and Parnell was supreme all the time." Then, with renewed energy: "Oh, Parnell was a most remarkable man and most interesting. I don't think he treated me well at the end, but my interest in him has never abated, and I feel an intense interest in his memory now." Then, striking the arm of his chair with his hand: "Poor fellow! poor fellow! it was a terrible tragedy. I do believe firmly that if these divorce proceedings had not taken place there would be a Parliament in Ireland to-day."

I said: "He suffered terribly during the last year of his life. The iron had entered his soul. I was with him constantly, and saw the agony of his mind, though he tried to keep it a secret from us all."

Mr. Gladstone. "Poor fellow! Ah! if he were alive now I would do anything for him."

"May I ask, when did you first speak to Parnell?"

Mr. Gladstone. "Well, under very peculiar circumstances, and they illustrate what I mean when I speak of him as being unlike anyone

I ever met. I was in the House of Commons, and it was in 1881, when, you know, we were at war. Parnell had made violent speeches in Ireland. He had stirred the people up to lawlessness. Forster had those speeches printed. He put them into my hands. I read them carefully. They made a deep impression on me, and I came down to the house and attacked Parnell. I think I made rather a strong speech (with a smile)—drew up rather a strong indictment against him, for some of the extracts were very bad. Well, he sat still all the time, was quite immovable. He never interrupted me; he never even made a gesture of dissent. I remember there was one declaration of his which was outrageous in its lawlessness. I read it slowly and deliberately, and watched him the while. He never winced, while the House was much moved. He listened attentively, courteously, but showed no feeling, no excitement, no concern. I sat down. He did not rise to reply. He looked as if he were the one individual in the House who was not a bit affected by what I said. The debate went on. After a time I walked out of the House. He rose from his seat, followed me, and coming up with much dignity and in a very friendly way, said: 'Mr. Gladstone, I should like to see those extracts from my speeches which you read. I should like particularly to see that last declaration. Would you allow me to see your copy?' I said, 'Certainly,' and I returned to the table, got the copy, and brought it back to him. He glanced through it quickly. Fastening at once on the most violent declaration, he said, very quietly: 'That's wrong; I never used those words. The report is quite wrong. I am much obliged to you for letting me see it.' And, sir (with vehemence), he was right. The report was wrong. The Irish Government had blundered. But Parnell went away quite unconcerned. He did not ask me to look into the matter. He was apparently wholly indifferent. Of course I did look into the matter, and made it right. But Parnell, to all appearances, did not care. That was my first interview with him, and it made a deep impression on me. The immobility of the man, the laconic way of dealing with the subject, his utter indifference to the opinion of the House—the whole thing was so extraordinary and so unlike what one was accustomed to in such circumstances."

"You disapproved of Mr. Parnell's action after the passing of the Land Act in 1881?"

Mr. Gladstone. "Yes; I think he acted very badly then, and unlike what one would expect from him. He proposed to get up what he called test cases, to give the Act a fair trial, as he said. But the test cases were got up really to prevent the Act getting any trial at all. Well, I then took an extreme course. I put him into gaol. It was then I said (with a smile) that the resources of civilisation were not exhausted. I felt that if I did not stop him he would have stopped the Act."

Two Whose Names Have Gone Round the World

CAPTAIN BOYCOTT*

In 1873 Captain Boycott became agent for the Lough Mask estates of Lord Erne and at the same time he leased about 1,000 acres in that area, which he farmed himself.

Captain Boycott was regarded as a domineering and exacting person, but he was respected for his courage and resourcefulness. He was a small man, but "possessed of an iron will," declared a writer who was bitterly hostile to him. He was widely known as a fearless hunter and steeplechase rider. He appeared frequently at races, sometimes as a participant, and all his life he was closely identified with the sport.

Between him and his tenants, however, there existed little sympathy or understanding. "He treated his cattle better than he did us," asserted one of his tenants in November, 1880, to a correspondent of the *Freeman's Journal*. But he experienced no difficulty in the collection of rents until August, 1879, when the tenants were not satisfied with a voluntary reduction of 10 per cent which Lord Erne made and demanded a 25 per cent abatement. Lord Erne refused to grant this, and one morning just before the rents came due Captain Boycott found a notice posted on the demesne gate, with a picture of a coffin on it, threatening him with death unless he secured for the tenants a reduction of 25 per cent. . . .

Late in September, 1880, at the instigation of the local branch of the Land League, the tenants on Lord Erne's estate submitted to Captain Boycott a schedule of what they conceived to be fair rentals for their holdings, and demanded that their rents be adjusted according to it. Lord Erne authorized his agent to allow a 10 per cent reduction from the rents of the previous November, but the tenants refused to pay anything whatsoever until their demands were met. Upon further consultation with Lord Erne, Captain Boycott offered a 20 per cent abatement, but when the tenants refused to pay he instituted ejection proceedings against them. This instant and summary action precipi-

---

*From *The Irish Land League Crisis*, by Norman Dunbar Palmer, pp. 198-210. Copyright, 1940, by the Yale University Press. New Haven.

tated a crisis. On September 22, as the process-server, escorted by several police, went forth to perform his unpleasant duty, he was met by a crowd of excited peasants, who shouted horrible threats and pelted him with mud and sticks and stones, so that after serving three processes he was forced to retreat in all haste to Lough Mask House, where Captain Boycott lived.

These events of late September were the immediate occasion for the adoption of a policy which added the word "boycott" to the English language; for Captain Boycott was soon subjected to the treatment recommended by Parnell only a few days before. The campaign was inspired and organized by the Ballinrobe branch of the Land League, of which Father John O'Malley, the priest of the parish in which Lord Erne's estate was located, was the guiding spirit.

On the morning of the 24th a crowd of peasants came to Lough Mask House and ordered all of Captain Boycott's employees to leave. The command was immediately obeyed, and the agent and his wife were left with but one old attendant whom they had brought with them from Dublin. They had no servants to do the household work, no stablemen to take care of the horses, cattle, and other animals, no laborers to harvest the crops. Their isolation was complete, for no one dared go near them or have any dealings with them. The local shopkeepers refused to fill their orders. The boy who carried the mail, upon being threatened, first resorted to clandestine visits and then ceased to deliver their letters. For a time Boycott's young nephew acted as a post-boy, but on October 2 he was stopped and threatened and thereafter the police were forced to assume this function. The bearer of a telegram was stopped and frightened away; the laundress would work no more for them; the blacksmith who shod their horses found a notice on his door warning him that if he did so again he would be shot. "My farm," wrote Captain Boycott in a letter to *The Times*, "is public property; the people wander over it with impunity. My crops are trampled upon, carried away in quantities, and destroyed wholesale. The locks on my gates are smashed, the gates thrown open, the walls thrown down, and the stock driven out on the road."

A garrison of ten men was stationed in Lough Mask House, and the harassed captain was given an armed escort to protect him from violence. Whenever he left the house, two burly members of the Royal Irish Constabulary, armed with loaded carbines, guarded his every move. "My life is not worth an hour's purchase," he told the Bessborough Commissioners, who were taking evidence on the workings of the Irish Land Act of 1870 in various parts of Ireland at this time. In all probability, however, the peasants had no intention of doing him bodily harm. Their avowed object was to isolate him, in accordance with Parnell's advice at Ennis, "as if he was a leper of old," and eventually to drive him out of the country. Occasionally they appeared before his house to hurl derisive taunts, or to trample on his crops; now and then they sent him a threatening letter; but otherwise they left him "severely alone," to carry on a "Robinson Crusoe existence" as best he could.

The most immediate problem confronting Captain Boycott was how to save his crops. Although he labored unceasingly himself, and was ably assisted by his wife, he could do little without outside help. . . . But help soon came from an unexpected source. The captain's letters to *The Times* describing his plight aroused great sympathy for his lonely struggle, and equally great indignation at the ostracism to which he had been subjected; and they attracted widespread attention to the events that were occurring in this remote part of Connaught. In the north of Ireland steps were taken to send an expedition to the relief of the besieged agent. Two Ulster gentlemen, Mr. Manning and Mr. Goddard, offered to lead such an expedition if sufficient men and money could be obtained; and the Belfast *News Letter* started a fund for this purpose. Within a few days eight hundred pounds had been raised, and hundreds of men had volunteered their services. One Ulsterman alone offered to send thirty thousand men, if need be, to the Lough Mask district!

The preparations became so formidable that the Government, fearing the results of an invasion of Land League territory by a large body of the hated Orangemen, became alarmed. A special train was arranged for November 10 to carry seventy armed laborers from Monaghan and vicinity, under the leadership of Colonel Lloyd, agent for Lord Rossmore, into Mayo, but the chief secretary for Ireland forbade the men to leave Monaghan. Captain Boycott informed the authorities that fifty men could gather his crops before the December frosts came; to send more than that number, he warned, would be unnecessary and dangerous. Accordingly, approval was given for sending an expedition of fifty volunteer Ulster laborers. . . . "The Boycott expedition," wrote *The Times'* Dublin correspondent on November 9, "is the most exciting topic of the day. It has filled the minds of the public with mingled curiosity, irritation and fear." Special correspondents and observers flocked to Ballinrobe, and settled down to report the progress of the expedition.

The news of the intended invasion of the Orangemen caused tremendous excitement in Ballinrobe and Claremorris, and indeed throughout Mayo. The excitement was enhanced by the dispatch of hundreds of additional troops and police to the Lough Mask district. On November 9 three special trains with two hundred men of the 19th Hussars and two companies of the Army Service Corps, with ammunition wagons, ambulances, and other war equipment, left Dublin for Ballinrobe; and at Athlone the last train was joined by another with four hundred of the 84th Regiment. This formidable force disembarked at Claremorris and marched the rest of the way to Ballinrobe. That night, as a correspondent of the *Freeman's Journal* wrote, "This bewildered little town" was "the headquaters of the nearest approach to an army ever beheld in Mayo since Humbert and his Frenchmen were at Castlebar in '98." The people showed no signs of hostility toward the soldiers, but all the correspondents on the spot agreed that there was grave danger of bloodshed if the Boycott relief expedition was dispatched. . . .

Meanwhile, on November 8, 9, and 10, the most extraordinary rumors were heard: that two thousand Orangemen had actually arrived in Claremorris; that five hundred armed men from the North had reached Westport by steamer and were en route for Ballinrobe; that Captain Boycott had cut his throat. And all the while extensive preparations were being made for the protection of the Ulster laborers.

On November 11 the relief expedition arrived in Mayo. At Mullingar, in County Westmeath, fifty laborers, six gentlemen and ten attendants, and large numbers of troops entered special carriages on the regular morning train from Dublin to the West. A patrol engine was sent ahead of the train, and police were stationed at key points all long the line. At every station between Athlone and Claremorris crowds gathered on the platform and cheered and groaned at the Orangemen. At Ballyhaunis the train was delayed by the hostile demonstrations. When at length, shortly before 4:00 P.M., the members of the expedition reached Claremorris, rain was falling heavily; and long before they arrived in Ballinrobe, fifteen miles away, they were thoroughly drenched.

Hundreds of soldiers and police were stationed at Claremorris; and, according to a correspondent of the *Freeman's Journal*, along the fifteen-mile route to Ballinrobe were "fully seven thousand men, military and police, more than a sixth of the whole available force of British military power in Ireland." The Land League did much to prevent disorder or conflict by issuing a manifesto to the people of Mayo, calling on them to give the Orangemen the same treatment that had been accorded to Captain Boycott; in particular they were urged not to let any conveyances to the invaders nor to give them food or shelter. The plans of the league worked perfectly. The carmen refused to convey the Northerners; Claremorris, save for the squads of troops and police and a few persons, mostly women and children, on the street-corners, was like a deserted village; and along the roadside hardly any peasants were to be seen. The long cavalcade of mounted police, hussars, dragoons, and infantry, with the Ulstermen completely surrounded by troops, must have presented a ludicrous spectacle as it moved slowly along the muddy road through the pouring rain, with a handful of jeering peasants in the rear. . . .

At 9:30 P.M. the bedraggled Ulstermen and their formidable escort at last entered Ballinrobe. The streets leading to the cavalry barracks were lined on each side with soldiers with fixed bayonets, but aside from groans and shouts of indignation from the people, there was no disturbance. By ten o'clock the laborers were safely quartered in the barracks for the night.

The following morning the cavalcade reformed and proceeded to Lough Mask House, some four miles away. In front marched about one hundred police, with loaded rifles; then came the hussars, with drawn swords; then two hundred men of the 84th Regiment, with fixed bayonets, marching in two files, with the Ulster laborers between them. In the rear were two companies of the 84th Regiment, guarding the provisions and fuel wagons. Behind the troops were the resident magistrates, constabulary officers, press correspondents, a few members of the Land League, and a small crowd of barefooted peasants, mostly women and children, who hurled taunts at the Orangemen and shouted imprecations on Captain Boycott. As on the preceding day most of the peasants were conspicuous by their absence. The procession reached Lough Mask House at 12:30 P.M., and the rest of the day was spent in making camp and in other preparations for an extended visit.

For the next two weeks the Ulster laborers dug the potatoes, mangolds, and turnips, threshed the corn and harvested the wheat, while the constables patrolled the region by day and night and the soldiers indulged in sports to keep themselves from boredom. The laborers toiled bravely under trying conditions, for the miserable weather made their task a doubly unpleasant one. . . .

On the morning of November 26 the Orangemen finished their labors, and the relief expedition prepared to depart. The scene about Lough Mask House was one of enthusiasm and rejoicing. Soldiers, police, and laborers joined in songs and cheers. From the steps of his home Captain Boycott read an address to them, in which he expressed "deep and heart-felt gratitude for the generous and timely aid," and spoke of the "unflinching determination, . . . untiring exertions, good conduct, and self-sacrifice" of the laborers, troops, and constabulary. Then he shook hands with everybody, amid loud and hearty cheers.

The retreat of the "potato warriors" was almost as farcical as was their arrival. On the day of their departure the peasants were instructed by the local Land League officials to keep out of sight; and all along the course of the march from Lough Mask House to Ballinrobe, where the expedition remained overnight, not a peasant was seen, save one old woman whom Father O'Malley accused, in mock wrath, of intimidating her Majesty's troops. As the Orangemen, escorted by troops and constabulary, left Lord Erne's estate, ahead of them strode Father O'Malley, with an umbrella over his shoulder, to see that their way was clear. He continued to march at the head of the procession "until it disappeared beyond the boundary of his parish into the records of history and of ridicule."

In the opinion of *The Times* the promoters of the Boycott expedition could "look back with satisfaction at the complete success which has attended their sympathetic enterprise." The captain's crops were saved, although at a cost of at least ten times their actual value. But the Land League and the Mayo peasantry won their battle, for with the expedition Captain Boycott, with his wife and nephew, left Mayo. He had demonstrated his courage by remaining on the estate in the face of concentrated persecution and repeated threats; now he yielded to his better judgment and gave up the hopeless struggle. He first went to Dublin, but when the proprietor of the hotel where he was staying, upon receiving a threatening notice, refused to allow him to continue on as a guest, he crossed the Channel and settled in England.

*   *   *   *

The story of Captain Boycott has a happy ending. His exile from Ireland lasted for only ten months. Save for a visit of some weeks with friends in Virginia, he remained in England until late September, 1881; then he returned to Lough Mask House. For a time he was constantly guarded by constabulary, but he experienced no further trouble. The land agitation had spent its strength, the league itself had been suppressed as an illegal organization, and most of the peasants had returned to more orderly ways. "Curiously enough," wrote a contemporary observer, "he is again at peace with his neighbors, and he is even popular, perhaps because he showed that he was a brave man."

"The case of Captain Boycott," wrote Kenward Philip in 1881, "is one of the most remarkable episodes that has ever taken place in Irish revolutionary history. Not all the Queen's horses nor all the Queen's men had been able to maintain this land agent in his beautiful home on Lough Mask after the peasants had come to a knowledge of their own strength."

JUDGE LYNCH OF GALWAY*

The name of Lynch, as either provost, portreeve, "sovereign" or mayor of Galway, occurs no fewer than ninety-five times between the years 1274 and 1654; after that year it does not appear once. One of that name is famous in history as the Irish Junius Brutus. The mere fact is sufficiently wonderful without the aid of invention; but it has, as may be supposed, supplied material for a host of romances.

The story is briefly this: James Lynch Fitzstephen was Mayor of Galway in 1493; he traded largely with Spain, and sent his son on a voyage thither to purchase and bring back a cargo of wine. Young Lynch, however, spent the money entrusted to him, and obtained credit from the Spaniard, whose nephew accompanied the youth back to Ireland to be paid the debt, and establish further intercourse. The ship proceeded on her homeward voyage, and as she drew near the Irish shore, young Lynch conceived the idea of concealing his crime by committing another, having seduced or frightened the crew into becoming participators. The [Spanish] youth was seized and thrown overboard. The father and friends of Lynch received the voyager with joy; and the murderer in a short time became himself a prosperous merchant. Security had lulled every sense of danger, and he proposed for a very beautiful girl, the daughter of a wealthy neighbour, in marriage. The proposal was accepted; but previous to the appointed day, one of the seamen became suddenly ill, and in a fit of remorse, summoned old Lynch to his dying bed, and committed to him a full relation of the villainy of his only and beloved son. Young Lynch was tried, found guilty, and sentenced to execution—the father being the judge. The wretched prisoner, however, had many friends among the people, and his relatives resolved with them that he should not die a shameful death.

The day had scarcely broken when the signal of preparation was heard among the guards without. The father rose and assisted the executioner to remove the fetters which bound his unfortunate son. Then unlocking the door, he placed him between the priest and himself, leaning upon an arm of each. In this manner they ascended a flight of steps lined with soldiers, and were passing out to gain the street when a new trial assailed the magistrate, for which he appears

---

* From *Ireland: Its Scenery, Character, Etc.*, by Mr. & Mrs. S. C. Hall, Vol. III, pp. 454-455. Virtue & Co. London. [1841?]

not to have been prepared. His wretched wife, whose name was Blake, failing in her personal exertions to save the life of her son, had gone in distraction to the heads of her own family, and prevailed on them, for the honor of their house, to rescue him from ignominy. They flew to arms, and a prodigious concourse soon assembled to support them, whose outcries for mercy to the culprit would have shaken any nerves less firm than those of the Mayor of Galway. He exhorted them to yield submission to the laws of their country; but, finding all his efforts fruitless, to accomplish the ends at the accustomed place, and by the usual hand, he, by a desperate victory over paternal feeling, resolved himself to perform the sacrifice which he had vowed to pay on the altar.

Still retaining hold of his son, he mounted with him by a winding stair within the building that led to an arched window overlooking the street, which he saw filled with the populace. Here he secured the end of a rope which had been previously fixed round the neck of his son to an iron staple which projected from the wall, and after taking from him a last embrace, he launched him into eternity. The intrepid Mayor expected instant death from the fury of the populace, but the people seemed as much overawed or confounded by the magnanimous act that they retired slowly and peaceably to their several dwellings. The unhappy father of Walter Lynch is said to have secluded himself during the remainder of his life from all society, except that of his mourning family. His house still exists in Lombard Street, Galway, which is yet known by the name of Dead Man's Lane.

How Dan Donnelly Knocked Out the British Champion

One of the most famous fights in the history of pugilism was that between the English and Irish champions, George Cooper and Dan Donnelly, which took place on the Curragh of Kildare, in the year 1815.

Dan Donnelly was one of the greatest boxers ever seen in the ring —a man who, in prowess and other characteristics, much resembled John L. Sullivan. He was born in Dublin in 1788. He was a carpenter by trade, and a man of extraordinary strength, good temper, generosity,

From *Ethics of Boxing and Manly Sport*, by John Boyle O'Reilly, pp. 56-60. Copyright, 1888, by John Boyle O'Reilly. Ticknor & Co. Boston.

and pluck. He was noted in Dublin for his skill in boxing; but he was not a professional pugilist.

In 1814, when Donnelly was twenty-six years old, one of the most famous boxers in England, named Thomas Hall, who had beaten George Cribband and other renowned fighters, went to Ireland to make a tour of the country, giving exhibits. His advent was proclaimed by an arrogantly worded challenge to "all Ireland."

He was checked by finding that his challenge was at once publicly accepted in Dublin by Dan Donnelly, who was "backed" by as much money as was needed.

The battle attracted international attention. In Ireland the excitement was very great. When the men met on the Curragh of Kildare, on the 14th of September, 1814, there were over thirty thousand persons present. Both men were cheered as they entered the ring; and the fight was fair until Hall, finding himself overmatched, fell several times without a blow, and ultimately raised a cry of "Foul" to cover his complete defeat. From the first round he had failed to make a single point on Donnelly, or to effectually stop one of Donnelly's.

Then George Cooper, the best man in England, was sent from London against the Irish champion.

Cooper had defeated the leading boxers of England, including Carter and Thomas Molineux, the Negro heavyweight, and great hopes were founded on his terrible hitting powers.

The national champions met on the Curragh of Kildare, on the same spot that had witnessed Donnelly's victory over Hall. The place was called then, and will probably be called forever, "Donnelly's Hollow." It is at the Newbridge end of the plateau on which the military huts are erected.

A Boston traveler visited the Curragh a few months ago, and was taken by a proud native to the scene of the famous battle. "The footsteps of the champions," said this gentleman the other day, "are still plainly visible. They are preserved in this way; every visitor, especially those who love the 'noble art,' puts his feet in the ancient marks, which are thus preserved and deepened in the soft green sod." The positions of the men as they began the fight are pointed out. "And over there," said the guide, "just outside the ring stood Miss Kelly, who wagered thousands of pounds on Dan Donnelly."

The battle took place on December 13, 1815, in the forenoon. In Ireland the excitement over the fight was intense, and to this day the event is a topic of common conversation. On the morning of the fight, the roads around the Curragh of Kildare were choked up with carriages and wagons of all kinds, from the four-in-hand teams of the nobility to the donkey-carts of peasants all the way from Cork or Connaught. There was a vast multitude to see the fight, and the profoundest order and good temper prevailed.

"Donnelly's Hollow" is probably one of the most perfect natural amphitheatres in the world. Here, on the sloping hill-sides, could stand or sit a hundred thousand men to behold a dramatic scene; and here, on that day, was assembled a greater crowd than had ever witnessed a boxing contest since the close of the Olympic games. An English correspondent of the press described Donnelly in these words:

"Donnelly at length stripped, amid thunders of applause, The Venus de Medicis never underwent a more minute scrutiny than did the champion of Ireland. There is nothing loose or puffy about him. He is strong and bony to all intents and purposes. He is all muscle. His arms are long and slingy, his shoulders uncommonly fine, particularly when in action, and prominently indicating their punishing quality. His head is a fighting one, his neck athletic and bold; in height nearly six feet, in weight about thirteen stone, and his *tout ensemble* that of a boxer with first-rate qualifications. Thus much for his person; now for his quality. His wind appears to be undebauched; his style is resolute, firm, and not to be denied. Getting away he either disdains or does not acknowledge in his system of tactics. *He makes tremendous use of his right hand.*"

After a stormlike cheer, the fight began amid deep silence. From the first blow, Donnelly had the advantage. He gained the usual points—first blood and first knockdown. Cooper made a brave and desperate fight, and in the fifth round he knocked Donnelly off his feet. In the seventh round Cooper was actually flung into the air by a cross-buttock, and in the eighth was dashed under the ropes by a tremendous left-hander.

For the next three rounds the result was similar, the eleventh and last round closing with a fearful right-hand blow on Cooper's mouth, which knocked him senseless.

The battle was awarded to Donnelly, amid the cheers of both Irish and English spectators. Donnelly then went to England and challenged all comers.

He attracted almost as much attention as Englishmen have recently given to Sullivan. Tom Cribb undoubtedly had been the leading boxer in his time; but he had retired from the ring several years before Donnelly's visit to England.

England was in straits for a man able to meet Donnelly. It was looked upon even by the government as dangerous, politically, to allow the Irish again to defeat a British champion.

At length a strong and able boxer, Oliver, was found to take up Donnelly's challenge. When the match was made, the chances of the fight filled the Three Kingdoms once more with matter for earnest discussion. It was said that one hundred thousand pounds (five hundred thousand dollars) were laid in bets on the battle. Every man in Ireland who had a pound to spare backed Dan Donnelly; and the "nobility and gentry" stood open-handed behind Oliver.

The national battle came off on July 21, 1819, within thirty miles of London. "Donnelly, on stripping," says the English report, "exhibited as fine a picture of the human frame as can well be imagined; indeed, if a sculptor wished a living model to display the action of the muscles, a finer subject than Donnelly could not have been found. Oliver was equally fine . . . he displayed flesh as firm as a rock . . . Oliver had never been in so good condition before."

It was a brave and desperate contest. As usual, Donnelly knocked his man down in the first round; drew his "first blood" in the second. In the seventh round, Oliver knocked Donnelly down, and this was almost his only successful point. Round after round ended in the same way—"Oliver down." In the thirteenth round, when Oliver lay helpless on the ropes, Donnelly threw up his hands, so as not to be tempted to strike him, and for this he received a great cheer. "Very handsome!" "Bravo Donnelly!" In the first hour there were thirty rounds fought, for the last four of which Oliver was gaining strength; but in the opening of the second hour Donnelly got his "second wind," and "his eye began to blaze," though, says the English report, "he was a cool as a cucumber." The next three rounds were Donnelly's, and then the Englishmen stopped betting and cheering. But they showed fair play throughout the fight; he is a poor kind of an Englishman who does not love fair play in a boxing match. Several times when "Foul" was cried against Donnelly, and when, indeed, it might have been allowed by an umpire bent on ending the fight on a technicality, both umpire and crowd shouted: "It is all right. Go on, Donnelly!" In the thirty-fourth round, Donnelly cross-countered Oliver with terrific force, striking him on the lower jaw; then while he was dazed, Donnelly whirled him over the ring with a cross-buttock; and Oliver's seconds carried him off insensible. The fight was given to Donnelly, who was scarcely marked, and who immediately dressed himself and went off to see another fight.

It was said, and believed by many, that Dan Donnelly, shortly after the fight, was knighted by the rollicking Prince of Wales. At any rate, ever afterward he was called "Sir Dan." He died in 1820, from taking a drink of cold water after a hard sparring bout. He was only thirty-two years of age.

Champion of Champions

That new champion proved to be a real champion. His testing period was over, and during the next ten years he was to win immortal renown as the gladiator *par excellence* of the nineteenth century—the great, hulking hero whose fabulous achievements elevated pugilism into the realm of epic poetry. By 1882 his method of fighting was characterized by the artless perfection that always accompanies great art. For his technique was simplicity itself: he merely kept hammering with ruthless, atavistic ferocity at his opponents until the opponents became insensible. An ardent admirer once epitomized Sullivan's pre-eminent skill in this epigram: "Other boxers begin by sparring; he begins by fighting—and he never ceases to fight."

It never seemed to occur to him that he could be beaten; indeed, he often had his rival whipped before a blow had been struck. The rival, looking fearfully across the ring, would see a burly, menacing figure just under six feet in height and weighing close to one hundred and ninety pounds. The iron muscles bulged and swelled beneath the tawny skin; black, coarse hair bristled all over the huge head; the deep, thick hairy chest and the sloping shoulders betokened a man of extraordinary strength; the broad face, the square, pile-driver jaw, and the ominous droop at the corners of the mouth were all blended into a terrifying grin; the stone gray eyes plainly showed that he wondered why anybody in the world was foolish enough to climb into a ring with him. Then time would be called, and the lithe body leaped into flaming action. He "fought like a man with a personal grievance," and utterly disdained to defend himself. There was no fancy footwork, no dancing, no side-stepping; there was only a wicked rush, a stupendous swing or two—and all was over.

From 1882 until 1892 Sullivan completely dominated the American prize ring. He was ready to fight any one—save only the redoubtable Negro, Peter Jackson—anywhere, at any time, for little money or even none. For in those sentimental days, men still fought because

From *John L. Sullivan*, by R. F. Dibble, pp. 30-61. Copyright, 1925, by Little, Brown & Co. Boston.

they liked to fight; the commercialism of sport in America had barely begun. There were, of course, plenty of blusterers who were excessively bold—on paper. Scarcely had John become the champion of America when scores of amusingly egotistical challenges were hurled at him. He quickly discovered that it was absolutely impossible to pin these braggarts down to definite engagements, and was therefore obliged to repay them in their own coin, in order to keep his escutcheon spotless.

On March 23, 1882, this notice appeared on sporting pages all through the land:

There has been so much newspaper talk from parties who state that they are desirous of meeting me in the ring that I am disgusted. Nevertheless, I am willing to fight any man in this country, for five thousand dollars a side; or, any man in the old country for the same amount at two months from signing articles,—I to use gloves, and he, if he pleases, to fight with the bare knuckles. I will not fight again with the bare knuckles, as I do not wish to put myself in a position amenable to the law. My money is always ready, so I want these fellows to put up or shut up.

John L. Sullivan

After this, Sullivan was less bothered by paperweight fighters, and was therefore able to resume what he loved to call his "series of picnics"—a guarantee that he would whip any one within four rounds or forfeit fifty dollars. Before John pounced upon his opponent in these conflicts, his manager invariably admonished him to "finish his man, but to be careful and not knock him out forever." Pat Sheedy, one of Sullivan's first managers, once did something that aroused his pupil's ire, and the pupil at once offered to beat up his teacher. Trembling with fear, Pat stuck a Derringer against John's ribs and begged for mercy. The only person who ever really managed Sullivan, in fact, was one who was strong enough to down his pupil—not by fighting, but by wrestling.

The "series of picnics" proved to be immensely popular. At every city masses of people surged in to see "The Ideal Thumper" thump his unfortunate opponent. When the national hero stepped grandly forth upon the platform, pandemonium would break loose; but occasionally individual comments became audible above the deafening roar. "Well, if he ain't just like his picture!" "Ain't he the darling?" "Oh, he's a daisy and in full bloom too!" "Look at the neck on him!" When the battle began, the mob would invariably shout for blood. Once, when John was fighting rather mildly with an antediluvian American champion, cries of "Go in and mop him up!" arose. Sullivan stood stock still, then stepped to the front of the platform, raised his hand and said, "Gentlemen, this affair tonight is just a friendly set-to. Some day I may oblige you by killing a man."

At times, before the combat had started, some spectators would shout sarcastic remarks at John, to the effect that the particular opponent of the evening would prove to be his Waterloo; but Sullivan had a set speech for such a contingency: "The bigger they are, the harder they'll fall." A favorite taunt directed against him was, "Pull off your gloves and fight like a man; the feller you're fightin' ain't wearin' no gloves." John would quietly reply, "If I don't use gloves, I'll kill him." One night, as soon as Sullivan came forth, it was painfully obvious that he had boils all over the back of his neck; and various voices charitably suggested that his opponent would be certain to direct his attack at the boils. "If he hits 'em, I'll only beat him all the quicker," John retorted; and, to the frenzied delight of the spectators, both prophecies were speedily fulfilled.

When the bell sounded time, Sullivan would sometimes stick out his head, so that his foe might imagine he had a chance to hit him; but the foe rarely dared to take such a hazardous risk, for fear that the champion was merely toying with him. Occasionally, after John had knocked his opponent out in a particularly effective fashion, the sympathy of the audience for the under dog would manifest itself in rumbling threats: "He ought to be lynched!" "Kill the big brute!" Then John would pull off his gloves, pick up his senseless rival and help to revive him; and the crowd would promptly forget its anger and cheer the victor to the roof. Thus encouraged, John would advance and make a prepared speech—though at times he would luckily forget the oration that his friends had composed for him and would improvise a much better one. When the crowd had departed it often happened, strange to say, that Sullivan and the man whom he had just pummeled would meet in the same saloon; and the vanquished man would say something like this: "John, you're a great chap. I've licked everybody in these parts; you're the first guy that ever even knocked me down." "Have a drink!" John would growl in a tone that was intended to be friendly.

* * * * *

The cutest boxer who ever faced Sullivan was doubtless Charlie Mitchell, the slippery Englishman who first fought the champion in Madison Square Garden on May 14, 1883. In the first round an unbelievable event occurred—John was knocked down—a catastrophe that had never happened before. Perhaps it will be best to let John himself explain how this calamity occurred: "My legs got crossed somehow, and just at this time Mitchell hit me, knocking me down as you would push over a chair. Then I got up and went for him like a bull at a rag." In the third round, in fact, John knocked Mitchell completely across the ring, where he tottered about, clinging feebly to the ropes. At this point the police interfered, even though Sullivan begged the police captain—a good friend of his—to let the bout go on. "Captain," he implored, "let me have just one more crack at him." "John, do you want to kill him?" the officer mildly answered.

No seats were provided for the audience at this historic affair; the whole crowd stood. Among the most notable spectators present was Roscoe Conkling. When the long black coat and the silk top hat announced his arrival, a seat was hastily built for him by laying a plank across two beer kegs; and from this place of honor he surveyed the proceedings with all his accustomed senatorial dignity. It was, indeed, a motley gathering: bankers, pickpockets, lawyers, thieves, brokers, merchants, Bowery pimps, coachmen, dudes, men about town, actors, baseball players, and millionaires—every one from Fifth Avenue to the underworld elbowed and shoved to get near the ring. Each person distrusted his neighbor; each person kept his eyes on the fighters and his hand on his purse. On account of this watchfulness, no untoward event occurred except John's awful downfall; and the whole gathering buzzed with excitement as numerous explanations were advanced. There were rumors, even at that early date, that the champion was drinking too much—for what other possible reason could he have been floored? But after the fight, when quizzed by reporters as to the truth of these insinuations, John angrily replied, "I ain't touched a drop to-day, and that report's all damned nonsense." He then proceeded to Bentley's saloon, to pass the rest of the evening as a champion should.

But when on June 30, 1884, he met Mitchell again, there was no possible doubt as to his condition. Instead of wearing his usual costume—a pair of green trunks, encircled by an American flag—he was in full evening dress. Diamond rings flashed on his fingers, and diamond studs as big as nutmegs blazed on his shirt. Yet, as he came reeling across the ring, no one could fail to see how disreputably disheveled he was: his face was swollen, blotched, and unshaven, his half-closed eyes were bloodshot, his hair was tousled. Hundreds of voices chimed together, "Sullivan's full as a goat!" As he swayed, lurched, and leered above the ropes, his trainer announced: "Gentlemen, Mr. Sullivan's doctor won't let him spar. He ain't well and can't fight." The champion's thick, husky voice hiccoughed: "Gen'l'men, thish the firs' time I ever come to New York to fight and wan't able to do it. But I been sick, an' I ain't in no condition to fight. Some may think I'm drunk, but I'm just dead sick. The doctor's certificate says so." Then Mitchell announced that he, too, had "been a 'avin' a bad time of it with malaria, and maybe it would be just as well not to fight." A man, primed for the act, rose and sheepishly threw a bouquet at Sullivan's feet; he awkwardly picked it up and staggered away as fast as he could. Several unimportant bouts followed—for the admission money was not returned. The commercialism of sport and the downfall of Sullivan had simultaneously begun.

Sickness of this particular variety became increasingly common to John. The time was rapidly approaching, in fact, when he would no longer be able to prove the truth of the two boasts he was so fond of making: that he could whip any man born of woman, and could consume any amount of liquor, in any combination, and still walk straight. In his drunken moments he was philosophical, sentimental, generous, or vicious. When philosophical, he preferred long words; he would use all that he knew, and then look up others in a dictionary. A friend once tested him with "discriminate." He glowered reproachfully and countered with the remark, "I've got a pretty good nut on me"—but the word remained undefined.

When he was sentimental, he would roar out, "Oh, White, White Moon" and "Go Tell Aunt Rhody" till the surrounding walls trembled. Once, when he was shown the skeleton of a crucifixion fish—so named because it resembled the figure of a man on a cross—John gazed at it in awestruck wonder, solemnly crossed himself, backed timidly away, and stuttered in a touchingly reverent manner, "That's almost as good as going to church. I'd give a good deal to own it." Al Smith (John's manager in 1884) was accustomed to lecture him very sternly for drinking so much; and John would be exceedingly humble and act very much like a naughty schoolboy. Swishing his large red handkerchief copiously around his red eyes, he would whimper, "I can't help it, Al. Everybody's running after me with, 'John, have a drink' here and 'John, have a drink' there. I don't like to make anybody mad by refusing. So, how can I help it?" Then Al, shaking eight monitory fingers and two angry thumbs in John's face, would snappishly reply, "See, see, you're ruining your health; see, don't you see I'm right?"

When John was feeling generous, he would whirl through the streets, throwing quantities of small change right and left at the crowds of small boys who always tagged him whenever he appeared in public. But when he was vicious, everybody gave him as wide a berth as possible. Stories—largely apocryphal, perhaps—are still told, illustrating his dreadful behavior on such occasions. He would come swaggering and swirling into some favorite saloon and whoop, "I'll lick any man in the house right here now! Them's my sentiments, John L. Sullivan, that's me!" Then he would go tearing around, smashing all the glassware in the place and afterward grandly pay for it; or he would offer to drink twice as much liquor, of any sort, as any one present, and would belch forth shouts of victorious joy as his less gifted challengers sprawled, one after another, on the floor.

* * * * *

His sprees became more and more frequent, until they began to interfere seriously with his puglistic engagements. Once, when he was scheduled to meet an unknown opponent at eight in the evening, his friends found him at seven o'clock sprawled out on a bench, wheezing and gasping in a drunken semi-slumber. The case was plainly desperate, and they therefore decided to use desperate remedies. After they had succeeded in partially arousing him, they poured this dire prophecy in to his ears: "John you don't realize what you're going to run up against to-night. We've seen the fellow and he's a regular terror." John merely grunted and told them to get out of the room; but, after a great deal of effort, they managed to drag him into his dressing room, where they put his head under a faucet, rubbed his face with bay rum and pulled him on the stage—and he promptly sank down into a chair. But when time was called, a marvelous change came over him. Leaping ferociously forward, he struck one blow—and the "regular terror" was a senseless lump. Then John retired to the dressing room, sprawled on the same bench, and promptly went to sleep again.

Very frequently, too, he was arrested for public intoxication. Indeed, the Boston police vied with each other in a friendly competition to see who could hale John before a court more frequently, for in this way an enviable notoriety was gained—their names would appear in print next day beside the name of Boston's most renowned citizen. One day John stepped on a street-car, leading his pet dog with him. The conductor, who unfortunately failed to recognize the passenger, snapped, "No dogs on here! I'll kick him off!" "If you do," retorted John, "you'll go off yourself." The conductor at once made good his promise—and so did John. A policeman near by, overjoyed at his unexpected good fortune, at once placed Sullivan under arrest. When he came before the court, the judge fined him $100 and inquired, "Anything to say, John?" "Yes," he chuckled; "let me hit him again and I'll pay you $200."

Another policeman, who hoped to make a name for himself, was less fortunate. Happening to see John cavorting around in a street to the delight of an enthusiastic audience, the officer stepped up and said, "You're drunk; you're under arrest." "That ain't true," said John, with a prodigious grin, "but even if it was I'll be sober to-morrow, while you'll be a damned fool all your life." The poor policeman was so utterly taken aback by this retort that he beat an undignified retreat, amid the jeers of the gleeful unlookers.

Drunk or sober, however, Sullivan was still the champion. From September, 1883, to May, 1884, he went with a theatrical troupe which gave exhibitions at over two hundred places. His part in this "variety show and athletic combination" was the same as of old. He fought all challengers who dared to face him, on successive nights, and when no one appeared he gave a boxing exhibition with a traveling partner. During these months, fifty-nine men tried to win the coveted $1,000, but they all met with the same woeful fate. One unfortunate, whom John disposed of in two seconds at Knoxville, Tennessee, recovered his senses in twenty minutes and inquired, "Did I win?" Sullivan thought this question was so insulting that he immediately knocked the egotist out again, for an even longer period of time.

In Indiana John once faced a ponderous caveman called "The Tripper of Cornellsville," who, according to frightful stories that had been circulated, had on various occasions "lifted over eight hundred pounds and knocked down a bull with his fists." At the beginning, the Hoosier Goliath came strutting forth in the utmost confidence that he would soon lay the champion low. His excessively vain behavior gave both Sullivan and his manager their cue: whenever a particularly formidable challenger appeared, they employed a device that would have warmed the cockles of P. T. Barnum's heart. The manager said, in a loud stage whisper, "Why, this chap'll murder you, John! I guess we'd better postpone this meeting." The audience at once went into a frenzy —for, as Sullivan later explained, "We used to pull that kind of stuff right along to get the crowd worked up." When the fight began John appeared to be very nervous, and every one howled with delight at the prospect of seeing a new champion made that night. The challenger naturally grew more and more overconfident, and smiled in a most irritating way during the first round, as he pursued his apparently discomfited rival around the ring. But in the second round Sullivan suddenly changed his tactics. The look of abject fear, carefully simulated for the occasion, was replaced by that ineffable sneer that had already given him the high distinction of being called "the toughest-looking man in America." In a flash, he smote his antagonist under the left ear; and, as a result, when time was called for the third round, "the Yahoo was still asleep." When, after a long delay, he finally came out of his slumber, he inquired whether he "had fell off a barn." Informed that something far worse than that had happened to him, he mournfully responded, "Well, I guess I never was cut out for a prize fighter."

By this time, the nation was ready to fall down at Sullivan's feet. Nothing was too good for him—there had never been anybody like him before—there never *would* be anybody like him again. His arrival at any town or city was the event of the year—almost of the century. Business was suspended and everybody went on a Roman holiday when the "Noblest Roman of Them All" came on the scene. Every schoolboy considered it a matter of honor to play hookey and follow John wherever he went. At this time the old-fashioned horse-car was still the chief means of metropolitan travel; and, to prove to the crowds that he was the veritable dare-devil that folk mythology had created, he would often run up to one of these cars when it was in full motion, seize hold and swing himself aboard, while shrieks of mingled horror and delight sounded on every side. Every neck was stretched to its utmost capacity, and every pair of eyes tried to follow him as, dressed in a big gray sweater, gray sport trousers, and a dirty-looking striped cap, he went swaggering along. Meanwhile all sorts of soulful ejaculations arose from the crowd: "That's him, ain't it?" "No, that ain't him, *that's* him!" "No, it ain't; I tell you, I seen him go up that way!" "Big?" "You bet!"

And if this was true throughout the land, how much more true was it of Boston! Conditions there soon became so bad that, whenever John ventured forth, he was in almost constant danger of being seriously injured by the worshipping thousands who mobbed him. Boston's most eminent citizens were ready to back him with any sum, "from a dollar to the Bunker Hill Monument," as one of them put it. A certain play, very popular in those days, contained this bit of dialogue between two characters: "Are you from Boston?" "Yes." "Know any big folks there?" "Yes." "Know John L.?" "Yes." "Ever shake hands with him?" "Yes." "Let me shake the hand that shook the hand of John L. Sullivan!"

* * * * *

Reporters came to see him by the dozen, and, always glad of an oppourtunity to advertise himself, he generally treated them well. . . .

A New York reporter, who was curiously strait-laced, felt moved to comment in this way on Sullivan's similarity to Socrates in the matter of corrupting the youth: "The lamentable feature of these gatherings of worshippers at the shrine of the slug-god is the presence of throngs of boys." He then cited two terrible examples. One youth, of whom a friend inquired, "Johnnny, are you going to dinner?" had peevishly retorted, "Dinner be damned! I'm going to see Sullivan." Another New York boy, an ardent admirer of Sullivan, had timorously approached him one day and asked, in a quavering tone, what sort of food he usually ate. John, who was feeling out of sorts, glared at the shaking lad and boomed: "Blood, nothing but blood! I drain a boy about your size three times a day." Logically enough, a rumor soon spread that Sullivan actually did live on blood—for the most part, the blood of cattle—and slaughter houses all through the country were forthwith besieged by anemic youths who were eager to emulate their hero's example.

* * * * *

But there was one form of notoriety that John indignantly disclaimed. Certain intense worshippers of simon-pure English and American blood had insisted that he was of Anglo-Saxon descent. Finally, a letter signed with Sullivan's name appeared, in which the hideous charge was repeated. John's righteous wrath, stirred by this low forgery, took the form of a flaming speech which was delivered at the end of one of his exhibition bouts.

"Of course I never tore off no such letter!" he roared in tones that shook the rafters. "I never knowed a Sullivan that wasn't straight Irish without any chasers to it. There may be some whitewashed Sullivans, but I don't know 'em and don't want to. In Boston, on the seventeenth of March, they celebrate Saint Patrick's Day and Evacuation Day at the same time; for the British beat it from Boston on that day when the decision went against them more than a hundred years ago. If there's any Anglo-Saxon Sullivans on the job, you bet your sweet life they cover it up, for they know the Sullivans who ain't Anglo-Saxons would do 'em up good if they got wise to it."

Public enthusiasm for John finally reached its height in the presentation of the famous diamond-and-gold belt. The illustrious ceremony took place in the Boston Theatre on August 8, 1887. Boston's mayor, her aldermen, the members of her Common Council were all there, in boxes and on the stage. Men in full evening regalia filled the orchestra, while the galleries were packed with a mob of howling rowdies. It happened that John was late, and so the gallery toughs began to screech out uncomplimentary, not to say indecent, remarks which advanced bold speculations as to the probable reasons for Sullivan's tardiness as well as the moral caliber of various individuals in the audience. Suddenly Pat Sheedy rushed to the center of the stage, shook his massive fists at the shrieking gang, and, in a voice that rose above the terrific pandemonium, roared out, "You fellows want to remember that Sullivan and myself are gentlemen with gentlemen, but among toughs we're kings!" Since not even the most disreputable brute within the range of Pat's voice dared to dispute the truth of his dictum, the din stopped at once.

When John at last appeared, no coronation ceremony ever surpassed the scene that followed. All animosities were instantly forgotten. With the precision of Junker troops, the crowd rose and spontaneously raised a series of huzzas that threatened to bring the whole building down in ruins. When, in about a quarter of an hour, comparative silence fell, there followed what was perhaps the greatest moment in a life that was an almost unbroken succession of great moments. A Councilman, who had already achieved enviable distinction by the gallantry he had shown Queen Liliuokalani during her recent visit to Boston, stepped pompously forth and clasped the $10,000 belt around the heroic torso. Next day the local papers stated that the champion "made quite a creditable speech"—a remark that was much more truthful than their characterization of the audience as "an eminently respectable gathering."

The official description of the belt ran thus: "It is forty-eight inches in length and twelve inches in width, and is the largest piece of flat gold ever seen in this country. . . . It took about three months to complete it. The panels are studded with [397] diamonds." This, however, sounds rather cold and lifeless, and John should be allowed to add the necessary personal touch: "The belt is my own personal property. My name on the belt is composed of two hundred and fifty stones. . . . The one I got from the *Police Gazette* looks like a dog collar alongside of this one."

Naturally enough, the glorious emblem was eagerly sought by collectors and crooks. At the Pan-American Exposition in Buffalo, a clever imitation of the belt was exhibited. Pat Sheedy himself, who was completely taken in, excitedly urged all of his friends to see it. Nothing in the whole place, so he swore, nothing at all—not even the two-headed fat lady—was so well worth traveling hundreds of miles to see. The fakir who showed this counterfeit made over $200 a week, and was busily devising plans to show some dozens of similar imitations throughout the land, when his trickery was detected and a just fate laid him low. A strict regard for historical truth demands the fact to be recorded that the actual career of this notorious work of art was decidedly less romantic than its illegitimate progeny. Before many years had passed, John was forced to pawn it. Then it was redeemed—and repawned—until finally poor John was compelled to surrender his treasured trophy to his creditors forever.

Gentleman Jim Corbett Defeats John L.

Meyers came down into the dining room and met us. I knew him very well and liked him very much. He had a big black eye and a cracked lip, and I started to 'kid' him about these marks of his battle. "You may look worse than I do when Sullivan gets through with you tonight," he retorted.

"No, Billy," I replied. "Sullivan won't have to hit me as many times as McAuliffe did you, to lick me. If it's done, it will be done with one punch!"

So we talked and joked with each other, and finally, about 9 o'clock, we started for the Olympic Club.

Now the following incident comes back to me as I write these words, thirty-three years afterwards:

As I was starting to put on a light summer suit, with a straw hat and a little bamboo cane to match, Delaney exclaimed, "My God! You're not going to the fight that way, are you?"

"Certainly, Mr. Delaney," I replied, examining myself in the mirror, as if I thought I looked grand.

It was too much for him. He wanted me to go to the arena like the usual short-haired, big-sweatered type of pug with a scowl that would scare people, and here I looked like a dude that a good man could break in two. For a moment, he couldn't say anything; simply looked his disgust.

"What difference does it make how I'm dressed going up?" I continued, as I gave a little extra twist to my tie. "I don't expect to fight in these clothes."

But it did make a difference to Billy, and he started to protest. I had begun the conversation in fun, but possibly I was getting a little nervous, as the hour drew nearer; anyway we had a heated argument

From *The Roar of the Crowd, The True Tale of the Rise and Fall of a Champion,* by James J. Corbett, pp. 191-202. Copyright, 1925, by James J. Corbett. Garden City Publishing Co. Copyright, 1953, by Vera Corbett. G. P. Putnam's Sons.

which lasted until I cut it short. "This is the way I'm going and that settles it," I said, and out I started, cane, straw hat and all.

The streets of the city were black with people, and as our carriage was working through, all I could bear from every side was the murmur: "Sullivan," "Sullivan," "Sullivan!" Not once did I hear the name of "Corbett"; it was all Sullivan in the air.

We reached the club and I stepped out. As I walked in at the door, right ahead of me hurried my old friend, "Mose" Guntz, from San Francisco, the one who gave Jack Dempsey a thousand dollars to second Choinyski against me. After that incident we had become great friends, and have been such ever since.

He turned around at my hail and started to speak cheerfully, but when he saw my get-up, he looked kind of embarrassed and strange, and, although he didn't *say* anything about my trimmings, I knew what effect they had on him, also that it wouldn't be but a couple of minutes before someone would tell Sullivan that Corbett came to the club with a cane in his hand and a straw hat on, like a dude! I could picture the look on Sullivan's face when he heard this news.

When I reached my dressing room, one of the club managers came in and announced, "Sullivan wants to toss up for corners."

"Let him take any corner he likes," I answered. I started to get ready. "He's going in the ring first anyway."

Word immediately came back that *I* was to go in the ring first. However, the question was settled by Brady's going down to Sullivan's dressing room and tossing a coin.

Now the only reason for my insisting that Sullivan enter ahead of me was the wonderful ovation I knew Sullivan would receive. Just then I felt quite calm, and I didn't want anything to excite me in any way, and it was possible his great reception might. But Brady had won the toss and finally it was announced that Sullivan was in the ring.

My seconds and I started down the aisle. The seats were banked circus-fashion and only a few of the audience could see us, but I could see the ring and Sullivan was not in it. The managers had lied to me. So I stopped.

Now Sullivan thought I was in the ring, because I had started and enough time had elapsed for me to get there. As I stopped and turned back I met Sullivan, for the first time since I had boxed with him in San Francisco at my benefit. I looked him in the eye and said, "You're the champion and I'm the short end. You're going in that ring first, if we stand here all night!"

This enraged Sullivan, who was always aggressive in manner, any way. He gave a roar like a wounded lion, strode down the aisle and bounded into the ring. Never before or since have I heard an ovation equal to that given him as he came through the ropes.

I said a little prayer to myself: "I hope to God I am as cool in the ring as I am now," and then, as the cheers subsided, skipped into the ring, receiving the usual reception that any fellow would get from an audience, which meant about as much as,—"Well, anyway, he showed up!"

About six months before this I had had a conversation with my dear old friend, Judge Lawlor, of the Choinyski fight days, in which he asked me how I thought I would fight Sullivan—what I thought my tactics would be. And I distinctly remember telling him the most important thing in my fight with Sullivan would be to convince him that there was one man he was going to meet who was not licked before the fight started.

"How are you going to do that?" inquired the Judge.

"I don't know myself; but I've got to do it, someway."

When I entered the ring I noticed that the floor was of turf instead of boards, on which I had always trained and fought. My shoes were of the solid sort used nowadays and I wondered how my feet would hold on turf. As soon as I entered the ring I started dancing around, and found that my feet would hold pretty well—in fact, much better than I had expected—so I was considerably relieved.

There was a reason, you see, for these jumping-jack antics that night, but I wish someone would tell me why present-day fighters do the same thing. They have been training on boards, and are fighting on boards, and using the same shoes and everything, so there is no reason for the practice unless to cover up nervousness. But it has been followed generally by fighters ever since that night. It is funny how customs and habits go down from generation to generation.

Meanwhile, Sullivan sat in his corner trying to catch my eye, his clenched fists on his knees, elbows out, and his head thrust forward in an ugly fashion. He had a wicked eye.

Now, as I had always done before, I was trying to convince him that he was the last person or thing in the world I was thinking about. I was bowing to people I didn't even see, smiling at entire strangers, waving my hand and talking to my seconds, laughing all the time.

Finally the referee, whose name was John Duffy, called us up to the centre of the ring for our final instructions. We walked up, Sullivan with his arms still folded, looking right at my eyes,—not in them, for I never met his stare,—and rising and falling on his toes without a pause. I waited for the referee, my gaze on him, and you could have heard a pin drop in the place. You wouldn't think 10,000 people could be so quiet. At last the referee got down to "hitting in clinches."

"When I tell you to break," he told us, "I want you to drop your arms."

Immediately I grasped the referee by the shoulder—mind you, all for the effect on Sullivan—and sneered, "That's very well for you to say, 'Drop your arms when I say Break!' But suppose this fellow" (even then I didn't look at Sullivan, just jerked my thumb at him) "takes a punch at *me* when *I* drop my arms?"

"If he does that, he'll lose the fight; and you'll lose, too, if you try it," Duffy answered.

"Then what about clinching like this?" I asked, and took hold of the referee and put my elbow up under his chin, pushing his head back, and repeated, "What if he does this?"

"That's a foul, of course," he answered. "The one that does it will be cautioned once. If he tries it a second time, he loses the fight."

"All right," I said, as gruffly as I could, "that's all I wanted to know."

Then, for the first time since entering the ring, I looked Sullivan square in the eye and very aggressively, too. He stopped his rising and falling on his toes and stood staring at me as if he were petrified, so surprised was he at this sudden change in my attitude, and I saw at once it had the effect I intended: I had him guessing!

In a very cocksure manner I jerked the towel from my shoulders, turned my back on him and ripped out, "Let her go!"

This piece of business had its effect not only on Sullivan, but also on the audience, for they cheered me louder then than they had when I entered the ring. They must have come to the conclusion, "Why, this fellow thinks he can whip Sullivan. We'll see a fight!"

"Time" was called, and the first round was on.

Now, I knew that the most dangerous thing I could do was to let Sullivan work me into a corner when I was a little tired or dazed, so I made up my mind that I would let him do this while I was still fresh. Then I could find out what he intended doing when he got me there. In a fight, you know, when a man has you where he wants you, he is going to deliver the best goods he has.

From the beginning of the round Sullivan was aggressive—wanted to eat me up right away. He came straight for me and I backed and backed, finally into a corner. While I was there I observed him setting himself for a right-hand swing, first slapping himself on the thigh with his left hand—sort of a trick to balance himself for a terrific swing with his right. But before he let the blow go, just at the right instant, I sidestepped out of the corner and was back in the middle of the ring again, Sullivan hot after me.

I allowed him to back me into all four corners, and he thought he was engineering all this, that it was his own work that was cornering me. But I had learned what I wanted to know,—just where to put my head to escape his blow if he should get me cornered and perhaps dazed. He had shown his hand to me.

In the second round he was still backing me around the ring. I hadn't even struck at him yet, and the audience on my right hissed me for running away and began to call me "Sprinter." Now I could see at a glance that Sullivan was not quite near enough to hit me, so suddenly I turned my side to him, waved both hands to the audience and called out, "Wait a while! You'll see a fight."

That made an awful "sucker" out of Sullivan, as the gallery-birds say, and it was quite unexpected. And since he didn't know that I knew he couldn't reach me when I pulled this stunt, he was the more chagrined. So he dashed right at me, angry as a bull, but immediately I was away again. At the end of the round I went to my corner, and said to Brady and Delaney, "Why, I can whip this fellow slugging!"

At this there was a panic in my corner, all of them starting to whine and pleading with me.

"You said you were going to take your time," they said. "What are you going to take any chances for?"

"All right," I replied, to comfort them, "but I'll take one good punch at him this round, anyway."

So far Sullivan hadn't reached me with anything but glancing blows, and it was my intention, when the third round started, to hit him my first punch, and I felt that it *must* be a good one! If my first punch didn't hurt him, he was going to lose all respect for my hitting ability.

So, with mind thoroughly made up, I allowed him to back me once more into a corner. But although this time I didn't intend to slip out, by my actions I indicated that I was going to, just as I had before. As we stood there, fiddling, he crowding almost on top of me, I glanced, as I had always done before, first to the left, then to the right, as if looking for some way to get out of his corner. He, following my eye and thinking I wanted to make a getaway, determined that he wouldn't let me out this time!

For once he failed to slap himself on the thigh with his left hand, but he had his right hand all ready for the swing as he was gradually crawling up on me. Then, just as he finally set himself to let go a vicious right I beat him to it and loosed a left-hand for his face with all the power I had behind it. His head went back and I followed it up with a couple of other punches and slugged him back over the ring and into his corner. When the round was over his nose was broken.

At once there was pandemonium in the audience! All over the house, men stood on their chairs, coats off, swinging them in the air. You could have heard the yells clear to the Mississippi River!

But the uproar only made Sullivan the more determined. He came out of his corner in the fourth like a roaring lion, with an uglier scowl than ever, and bleeding considerably at the nose. I felt sure now that I would beat him, so made up my mind that, though it would take a little longer, I would play safe.

From that time on I started doing things the audience were seeing for the first time, judging from the way they talked about the fight afterwards. I would work a left-hand on the nose, then a hook into the stomach, a hook up on the jaw again, a great variety of blows, in fact; using all the time such quick side-stepping and footwork that the audience seemed to be delighted and a little bewildered, as was also Mr. Sullivan. That is, bewildered, for I don't think he was delighted.

In the twelfth round we clinched, and, with the referee's order, "Break away," I dropped my arms, when Sullivan let go a terrific right-hand swing from which I just barely got away; as it was it just grazed the top of my head. Some in the audience began to shout "foul!" but I smiled and shook my head, to tell them, "I don't want it that way."

So the next eight rounds continued much in the fashion of toreador and the bull, Sullivan making his mad rushes and flailing away with his arms; rarely landing on me, but as determined as ever. Meanwhile I was using all the tricks in my boxing repertoire, which was an entirely new one for that day and an assortment that impressed the audience. Then I noticed that he was beginning to puff and was slowing down a little.

When we came up for the twenty-first round it looked as if the fight would last ten or fifteen rounds longer. Right away I went up to him, feinted with my left and hit him with a left-hand hook alongside the jaw pretty hard, and I saw his eyes roll. Quicker than it takes to tell it, I saw that I had then the same chance that I had had in the fight with Peter Jackson, but had failed to take—the same chance that was Firpo's when Dempsey stood helpless before him, and which he also failed to take.

This time I did not let it slip. Summoning all the reserve force I had left I let my guns go, right and left, with all the dynamite Nature had given me, and Sullivan stood dazed and rocking. So I set myself for an instant, put just a little more in a right and hit him alongside the jaw. And he fell helpless on the ground, on his stomach, and rolled over on his back! The referee, his seconds, and mine picked him up and put him in his corner; and the audience went wild.

As Sullivan struck the floor, the few people who were for me jumped up and yelled, but the mass of that vast audience were still as death; just clenched their hands, hoping their champion would rise. When the last count ended and it was over beyond doubt, then came an uproar like Niagara tumbling over the cliffs, followed by the greatest shower you ever saw, of hats, coats, canes, belts, flowers from button-holes, everything, falling on me and my seconds and all over the floor of the ring. I have often thought what a business I could have started down in Baxter Street with such an assorted stock!

So the roar of the crowd went on. I should have felt proud and dazed, but the only thing I could think of, right after the knockout, was Sullivan lying there on the floor. I was actually disgusted with the crowd, and it left a lasting impression on me. It struck me as sad to see all those thousands who had given him such a wonderful ovation when he entered the ring turning it to me now that he was down and out.

In justice to the man who had reigned so long as champion of the world, I think it is only fair to say that I was not fighting the Sullivan I had seen and admired in San Francisco at the Paddy Ryan bout, then twenty-six and in the pink of condition; but a man who had not been careful of his habits and who had enjoyed too much the good fellowship and popularity the championship brings. I got him when he was slipping; and that goes for all the champions down the line.

It is very hard to tell, as you gaze down the list at all the defeated champions of the past, which was supreme. As I got Sullivan when he was slipping, so Jeffries got Fitzsimmons; Johnson defeated Jeffries; and Dempsey, Willard. And so, too, when Dempsey starts to slip some-one is sure to get him. Like the pitcher that goes too often to the well, the champ will go once too often to the ring, and be broken in the end. And all argument as to their respective merits is foolish and futile.

After the first uproar had subsided a little, it seemed as if everybody in the audience wanted to hug me. Capt. Barrett, Chief of Police, was standing near and I said to him:—"Please don't let this crowd get hold of me. I want to go up in my room and be with the people I was with before the fight started."

Beyond Life

It is barely possible that at high noon, on February 2, 1918, some of the most renowned heroes of antiquity were gathered together in a congenial nook, located—one cannot be too sure in such matters— perhaps in Elysium, in Paradise, in Valhalla, in Hades, or even maybe in Purgatory. For, tiring of the restrictions imposed upon them in the various parts of the Unknown to which they happened to be transported after death, they had wandered to this private spot in order to brag once more about the valiant deeds they had performed in the flesh in the brave days of old. Goliath, Polyphemus, Siegfried, Hercules, Beowulf, Fafnir,—these numbered but a few of the vast throng of mighty giants on hand; while, aloft on a safe perch, Jack the Giant-Killer thumbed his nose most indecorously at the whole gathering. The talk, at first friendly, waxed more and more boisterous and raucous; vainglorious boasting and sarcastic gabbling steadily increased; louder and louder grew the rumbling threats and accusations; it seemed that a terrible and titanic combat was inevitable. Suddenly a low, muttering, awful sound broke on the air; it came nearer, ever increasing in volume; the rude talk hushed and the heroic faces grew pale. Then, as the enormous portals yawned asunder, those ancient heroes turned and fled in precipitate dismay; for through the cavernous opening there rushed a monstrous shade, moving swift as a whirlwind, brandishing a ponderous fist, and hoarsely bellowing these words into the palpable obscure: "My name's John L. Sullivan, and I can lick any son of a —— here!"

Thomas MacDonagh, Poet and Insurrectionary Leader

In that poem in which "A. E." celebrates the leaders of the Insurrection, the stanza about MacDonagh begins:

> "I listened to much talk from you,
> Thomas MacDonagh . . ."

From *John L. Sullivan*, by R. F. Dibble, pp. 208-209. Copyright, 1925, by Little, Brown & Co. Boston.

From *The Road Round Ireland*, by Padraic Colum, pp. 471-473. Copyright, 1926, by The Macmillan Co. New York.

A man of much and ready speech, a poet with a bent towards abstractions, a scholar with a leaning towards philology—that is how many in Dublin saw Thomas MacDonagh.

He came to Dublin in 1908. I had known him from the year before; then, for six years I knew him intimately. Those who saw him in the lecture-room, in his academic robe, and noted his flow of speech and his tendency towards abstractions might have carried away an image of one of those adventurous students who disputed endlessly in a medieval university. Or they might have thought of him as a scholar called into a constituent assembly. With his short figure, his scholar's brow, and his dominating nose, he looked like a man of the Gironde— a party, by the way, that he often spoke of.

And there was another MacDonagh—a MacDonagh that was a wonderfully good comrade, an eager friend, a happy-hearted companion. He had an abundance of good spirits and a flow of wit and humour remarkable even in a Munster man. He had, too, an intimate knowledge of the humours of popular life in the country and the country-town. We must regret that he put his feeling for this popular and humorous life only into one poem quite completely—into "John-John." This poem is living; it has completely, not the feeling of the countryside—other Irish poets have got that into their poems—but the feeling of the village which no other Irish poet has got:

> The fair was just the same as then,
> Five years ago to-day,
> When first you left the thimble-men
> And came with me away.
> For there again were thimble-men
> And shooting galleries,
> And card-trick men and Maggie men
> Of all sorts and degrees,
> But not a sight of you, John-John,
> Was anywhere.
>
> I turned my face to home again,
> And called myself a fool
> To think you'd leave the thimble-men
> And live again by rule,
> And go to the mass and keep the fast
> And till the little patch:
> My wish to have you home was past
> Before I raised the latch

And pushed the door and saw you, John,
Sitting down there.

He was born in Cloughjordan, a little town in Tipperary, where his
father and mother were teachers in primary schools. He was trained
by a religious order, and was indeed a religious novice in his early
youth. Afterwards he became a teacher in Kilkenny. He began to learn
Irish while he was there; afterwards he went to the Arran Islands and
to the Irish-speaking districts in Munster, and made himself fluent in
the language. While he was in Fermoy he made himself one of the
leading propagandists for the language revival in the southern counties. "The Gaelic revival has given some of us a new arrogance," he
was to write afterwards. "I am a Gael, and I know no cause but of
pride in that. *Gaedheal mé agus ni h-eol dom gur nair dom é.*" But he
was no more a pure Gael than was Padraic Pearse. His mother, born
in Dublin, was of English parentage; her maiden name was Parker;
his maternal grandfather, if I remember aright what he once told me,
was a printer connected with Dublin University. His mother became
a Catholic in her girlhood; she died only a few years before the Insurrection; at the time I knew her, she had the simplicity, the outlook,
the manner, of a fine type of Irish countrywoman.

He came to Dublin with a play that he wanted to have produced in
the Abbey Theatre, then under the brief direction of J. M. Synge.
The play was *When the Dawn Is Come*. Its scene was in a revolutionary Ireland of the future, and it was the tragedy of a leader whose
master-idea baffled his followers. Seven years afterwards he completed
a revised version of the play; he was himself then one of the leaders
in a revolutionary movement.

. . . It was in 1911, that Professor Houston, with James Stephens,
MacDonagh and myself started *The Irish Review*. MacDonagh was
associate, first, with the three of us, and, after an interregnum, with his
friend, Joseph Plunkett. They were the last editors, and the *Review*
did not survive them.

I have said that he got only once or twice into his writing the
humours and intimacies of popular life, although he could recount
these as well as any man I ever knew. I might have said, too, that he
did not get into his writing the gaiety and the good fellowship that
were his so abundantly. And because these things have not been shown,
he may be remembered as a man who was always high-minded, ideal-
istic, and austere. Really he was full of delightful extravagances. Once
I remember his telling myself and another of a career that he had
planned for himself: he would go to South America and enlist in an

army there; in a South American state with its occasional revolutions, military experience and advancement would come to him rapidly; in ten years he would be on some General Staff; then he would come back to us and organize the country for military resistance. The delightful extravagance of the project will be understood when it is told that it was made, not in the feverish days of Volunteer preparation, but in the Arcadian times when we were all concerned with Mr. Redmond's Home Rule Bill, and it was made by a man who was going back to teach a class of boys, and who would be working at a poem the next morning; it was made, too, by a man who was ready to fall in love with some Dublin girl the day after.

* * * * *

In politics, before the days of the Volunteers, he would have welcomed a reasonable settlement—or what would then have been regarded as a reasonable settlement—of Irish political conditions. Indeed, two years after its angry rejection by the National Convention he said to me that the country should have accepted the Councils Bill, with the control it gave of education and the possibility it offered of checking up on the financial relations between Great Britain and Ireland. I had a vision of my friend in a Home Rule Parliament working at social and legislative problems, and perhaps training himself to become a Minister of Education. He was, when the Home Rule Bill reached its last stages, happily married, and was the father of the child addressed in "Wishes for My Son." His second child was born six months before the Insurrection. In the end the Home Rule question became something different from an adjustment of legislations between Ireland and Great Britain. The English Conservative Party made its granting or its withdrawal depend upon a question of military preparation and racial manliness. The challenge was accepted, and the Nationalists created their Volunteers—that was in the winter of 1913. Thomas MacDonagh had a place on the Executive and the command of a corps.

I think he had been in Dublin about three years when he became associated with Joseph Plunkett. I remember his telling me that a lady had called at the school to ask him to help her son with his Irish studies. The student whom MacDonagh then took on was Joseph Mary Plunkett. The association had an influence upon both of the men. MacDonagh brought Plunkett's poems to us on the *Irish Review,* recommending them strongly. Plunkett became MacDonagh's admirer and friend; he also became an influence upon him. Joseph Mary Plunkett was a young man then; he was often ill—indeed he looked a youth who could do little more than be a reader and an onlooker. Yet he was working hard at verse and had taken up many out-of-the way studies. MacDonagh's great enthusiasm, his adventurousness of mind, his unquenchable desire to be making and shaping things, must have been vital influences upon the younger, frailer man. And on the other hand, the authentic mystical vision that Plunkett had, the conquest of the fear of death that his illness had often caused him to make, probably influenced MacDonagh to the consideration of dangerous courses.* Again I will say that what was fundamental in MacDonagh rarely went into what he wrote. That fundamental thing was an eager search for something that would have his whole devotion. His dream was always of action—of a man dominating a crowd for a great end. The historical figures that appealed straight to him were the Gracchi and the Irish military leader of the seventeenth century, Owen See O'Neill. In the lives of these three was the drama that appealed to him—the thoughtful man become a military leader; the preparation of the crowd; the fierce conflict and the catastrophe. Many things that Thomas MacDonagh said and wrote were prophetic. . . .

* * * * *

"The Gaelic revival has given some of us a new arrogance," he wrote. It was not altogether the Gaelic revival that had done this: it was the Gaelic revival plus the military movement that began with the formation of the Volunteers. Neither the Gaelic movement alone nor the Volunteer movement alone could have created the racial pride, could have brought about the challenge to a power that seemed securely entrenched in Ireland. It took both together to make the temper that was behind such a challenge. "These wars and their sequel may turn literature definitely into ways towards which I looked, confirming the promise of our high destiny here." I have said that some years before the Volunteers were formed, Thomas MacDonagh, speaking for his

---

* An account of how Joseph Plunkett, a frail and ailing youth, made himself over into a poet, a scholar, and a man of action, would be of extraordinary interest. Some of his poems have in them an exaltation which sets them apart from Irish poetry written in his generation. It must have been soon after his association with MacDonagh that he began to make the plans for a Dublin insurrection—plans which in 1915 were adoped by a military council "practically in their entirety." In the Autumn of 1915 I met him in New York: he had come to the United States from Continental Europe where, having made his way through Italy into Germany, he had had an interview with some of the German General Staff. He left some books in my charge to be given to different people; they showed how diverse his interests were: one was Edward Lear's "Nonsense Verses," the other was an abstruse work on philology—*Manual of Linguistics*, by John Clark.

everyday self, would have accepted an everyday settlement of the problems of Irish self-government. But his play *When the Dawn Is Come* and some of his poems show that there was always something fatalistic and prophetic about his vision of his own relation to the cause of Irish independence. This leader has to face a hostile tribunal. Six years after the play was produced MacDonagh, a military prisoner, faced such a tribunal. His actual speech before the British court-martial not only reproduced the thought, it reproduced the peculiar rhythms of the sentences in that play.

"This rising did not result from accidental circumstances. It came in due recurrent season as the necessary outcome of forces that are ever at work. The fierce pulsation of a resurgent pride may one day cease to throb in the heart of Ireland—but the heart of Ireland will that day be dead. . . . It will be said that our movement was doomed to failure. It has proved so. Yet it might have been otherwise. There is always a chance of success for brave men who challenge fortune."

He commanded the Volunteer force that occupied Jacob's factory, and he held his position from Monday until the following Sunday. He received from Pearse the order to surrender. "When he received the message he sat considering," said an eye-witness. "He said, 'I am thinking of my men and their position.' After a while he said, 'Well, we had better give in, there is no chance.' "

The narrator said that he went to his men and put the situation before them; they consented to surrender. He then went with some British officers to the South Dublin Union where Eamon Ceantt was in command, and he asked Ceantt to give in, and Ceantt consented. He next went to the malt house of Guinness's Brewery, and asked the Volunteer officer there to surrender. This officer, too, surrendered on MacDonagh's advice.

The military gave a quarter of an hour to his court-martial. He was called upon at midnight in Richmond Barrack and was told that he would be shot at dawn. He sent for his sister, who was a nun, and for a confessor. His wife was not able to reach him. His sister was lighted to his cell by the butt end of a candle. He confessed, made his act for Holy Communion aloud, and his thanksgiving aloud, and then sat down and wrote to his wife. When he had finished the letter he went to pray before the crucifix. His sister, when she came in, found that he had had nothing to eat or drink; there was no water for him to wash, and the sentry remained standing by them in the small cell. She turned to the sentry and said, "Will you give him some water to wash in?" The sentry said, "No."

His sister gave him their mother's rosary, and he put it around his neck. "I hope they will give me this when it is all over," she said. "Ah, no," he said quietly, "they will shoot it to bits." "But they didn't," said the narrator, "they shot four beads out of it, and his sister has the rosary now. When the time came he went quietly along the corridor to his death."

In the old heroic story Fionn is asked what music he preferred. He spoke of the song of the blackbird, the screaming of the eagle, the bay of the hounds, the deep sound of the waterfall. But the music that he preferred to all these was "the music of the thing that happens." Mac-Donagh could have made Fionn's lofty answer. He surely loved "the music of the thing that happens." He followed the music that meant the language revival, the music that meant the Volunteer movement, the music that meant insurrection and the violent breaking into a new order. And he stood up, too, to the music that was the militarist's answer to the proclamation he had signed.

Collins' Last Days

It was Friday before the Four Courts garrison surrendered. In the meantime Lynch, who had issued in Dublin a fiery proclamation calling Republicans to arms, retired to Cork "to rouse the country." He roused the country, but, instead of rushing to the relief of the Four Courts and the other buildings in which his men were besieged, he went off to Limerick. There, having engaged the garrison, he offered in the usual fashion to negotiate a truce. In the usual way it was agreed to. But Collins, having once set his face to the hard road, was having no more truces. The priest was told to clear out and the Republicans ordered to evacuate the town, which they did. It showed the temper of their resistance.

After a week of fighting they surrendered in Dublin. In the blazing wreck of the Hamman Burgess fought on like a lion. He had already nerved himself for the last ordeal. He had never retreated from the English; he would not retreat from his own countrymen. There is something about his end which recalls the old sagas. One thinks of Cuchulainn tying himself to a pillarstone by his belt and facing his enemies till the battle glory faded from his head and the bird of evil

omen perched upon the bowed shoulder. He ordered his men to surrender. Alone in the blazing building, he made his choice to die by
gunfire. Miss Macardle describes how his men, standing with their
guards in a little lane beside the hotel, anxiously asked one another
what had become of him. "Suddenly they saw him in the doorway, a
small, smoke-blackened figure, a revolver in each hand raised against
the levelled rifles of the troops. Enemies and friends cried out, 'Surrender.' But, shouting 'No!' Burgess darted forward, firing, and fell
amid a volley of shots."

When Collins heard the news he wept.

Soon enough he had cause to weep for another death, that of one
dearer to his heart. Trapped in his hotel in Skerries, Boland, always
prepared to take a desperate chance, bolted down the corridor from
his guards. A sentry raised his rifle, and he fell, shot through the
abdomen. When he died Collins came into Fionan Lynch's room crying helplessly. It seemed as though there would be no end to the
slaughter of old friends.

Collins took on his new job as commander in chief with the usual
intensity, even if there was little joy in his work. It was not the old
army which had beaten the Black and Tans: hasty recruiting had
made it in part a haphazard collection of wasters, ex-British soldiers,
people with whom he had nothing in common. They performed the
most extraordinary operations. Within a fortnight five hundred of
them had surrendered their posts and arms and were packed back to
Dublin. There was a general feeling af apathy and hopelessness. The
exchange of courtesies between old comrades went on; men changed
sides from day to day. Against this Collins warred. Devlin describes
calling on him at an early hour at Portobello and seeing him wave a
hopeless hand at the deserted barrack square. "Not a soul up yet."

When Dublin had surrendered, Kerry was the next point of attack.
Some of his old comrades pressed Collins to try and secure peace now,
before more blood was spilt and fresh passions engendered. "Let us
take Cork first," he said. He merely wanted overt evidence of victory
before opening negotiations. Cork was taken, and with it the position
of the Provisional Government was made secure. Collins set out to
inspect the occupied posts. He was in Limerick when he heard of
Griffith's death. He had been washing his face in the morning when he
collapsed, a blood vessel broken in his brain. In fear for the future
of his country, he had been going to pieces. He died a peculiarly
lonely unknown man, as poor as the first day he entered Irish politics.

While he walked in Griffith's funeral Collins knew the evening
hours were spelling the last hours on earth of Reggie Dunn and Sul-

livan. They cannot have been far from his mind that day. In Wands-
worth Prison they were awaiting the hangman and a death of infamy,
while Collins walked, with his staff behind, as head of the Irish government and the Irish army. He had never looked finer. A murmur of
delight rose from the crowds as he passed. At the same time Dunn,
who by one word of disloyalty might have saved himself, was enduring
the last utter humiliation. For each it was apotheosis: for Collins the
crowds and the adoration, for Dunn the condemned cell and the
shame. On the morning of the sixteenth of August he and Sullivan
were hanged. Collins had still a week to live.

He lived it in suffering, mental and physical. Though still full of ideas
and enthusiasm, he found it hard to work. He sat at his desk, scribbled
a few lines, then rose and left the room, not in the old dashing way
but slowly and in dejection. The shadow had begun to fall. To Cos-
grave he said, "Do you think I shall live through this? Not likely!"
He turned to a typist and asked, "How would you like a new boss?"
It was so strange, coming from him that she repeated it to O'Reilly,
who worried over it, turning the words about in his mind. Next day,
as the two of them were driving into town together, O'Reilly asked
after his health. "Rotten," replied Collins. There was a slight pause.
"How would you like a new boss?" came the question. O'Reilly's heart
sank. He replied that he would never work for anyone else. Collins
smiled, a queer half-smile, but O'Reilly saw he was gratified. Though
he still bawled down solicitude, he was obviously grateful for it.

He promised to see the peace envoys on his return from Cork. His
staff was under the impression that in his native country he hoped
to meet some old friends now in arms against him and add their influence to the cause of peace. That was also the impression he left on
Thornton, whom he sent to prepare Clonmel for a conference by with-
drawing all but old Volunteers from its garrison. Thornton was ambushed and shot down on the way.

On the night before his departure for Cork he went to bed at 7:30.
He was suffering from a bad chill. O'Reilly and his batman stuped his
stomach. O'Reilly then went for oranges and made a drink for him.
"God, that's grand!" he sighed. Encouraged by these, the first words
of gratitude which had passed between them, O'Reilly went so far as to
tuck him in for the night. But this was too much. Gathering all his
strength, Collins bawled, "Go to hell and leave me alone!"

Next morning at breakfast he was still very ill—"writhing with
pain," Mulcahy describes him—but absolute in his determination to
get to Cork. He roused a friend to say good-bye and joined him in a
farewell drink.

"You're a fool to go," said the other.

"Ah, whatever happens to me, my own fellow countrymen won't kill me," said Collins moodily.

O'Reilly woke at six and, moved by some impulse, rushed to the window. Collins was standing outside on the steps waiting for the armoured car to arrive. He wore a small green kitbag over his back, his head was bent in gloomy meditation, and O'Reilly thought he had never seen so tragically dejected a Collins as this man who, thinking himself unobserved, let himself fall slack in the loneliness and silence of the summer morning.

The instinct of devotion was strong in O'Reilly. He pulled on his trousers and, indifferent to rebuffs, dashed down stairs to say good-bye, but the car was already gone.

Ill and distraught as he was, Collins went on to Limerick and from there to Cork. On Monday he saw friends and people with whom he had business. In the evening there arrived an old friend of Frongoch days. Collins sprang to his feet, delighted, and had the room cleared. He pretended to believe that his friend had come to ask for a commission in the army. But the friend did not agree with either side. He thought they were all mad.

Collins fell serious at once. They argued, pulling the threadbare theme to and fro again. Collins' love for men was so much greater than his love for ideas that it did not weary him as it would another. His friend pleaded earnestly for agreement, any sort of agreement that would save the nation.

"Very well," said Collins. "See me tomorrow night. I may have news for you."

His friend interpreted this as a hope that he might be in a position to negotiate with some of the Republican leaders next day, or at least was in touch with someone who might. Then he noticed the old mischievous gleam in Collins' eye.

"And now," said the commander in chief, "what about a wrestle?" He pulled off his tunic with lightning glee.

"I will not," said the other, scandalized. "What would the sentries do if they saw me wrestling with you?"

"They'll do nothing at all," said Collins. In a moment the commander in chief and his friend were rolling on the floor.

Next morning, as he stood in the lounge of the Imperial Hotel chatting with Dalton, the hero of the Mountjoy attempt, he saw another old friend, Pat MacCrea, his driver, pass through the hall. MacCrea had been ambushed and wounded in Wicklow.

"Ah, Pat," he said, "your fellow countrymen nearly did for you."

It is the same theme repeated in various forms. The shadow of the end is on him, yet he cannot believe it will reach him here in his beloved Cork, among the familiar houses and fields, where nature itself should rise and shelter him.

He set out with a party under Dalton. They passed through Macroom, Bandon, Clonakilty, Rosscarbery, Skibbereen, and Sam's Cross, where years before he had recited "The Lisht" for his neighbours. They crowded in again to shake his hand as Head of the Irish government.

It was evening before they struck the back road from Bandon to Macroom. An ambush party had been waiting there since morning. Now, with the failing light, they scattered to their billets, and as Collins' convoy tore up the narrow road through the glen there were only a handful of men to dispute the way with it. They opened fire. Dalton shouted to the driver to go like hell. Collins countermanded the order. The cars screamed to a halt, and he leaped out with his rifle in his hand. For close on half an hour the fight went on; Collins continued to fire until the little group of ambushers took to flight. He followed them with his rifle. All at once Dalton and the others noticed that he had ceased to fire. They thought they heard him call. When they rushed to where he was lying they found him, his head resting on his arms, a great wound in his skull. Afterwards they thought it might have been one of the old gestures, that lightning turn of the head, which brought the wound where it was.

O'Connell whispered the Act of Contrition into his ear and dragged him across the road into shelter while Dalton continued to fight. Dalton then came and bandaged the wound. He had scarcely completed the task when he saw that Collins was dead. Darkness was coming on. O'Connell was weeping. Dalton still supported the heavy bleeding head upon his knee.

The glen was quiet again, only the wind stirred in the bushes. Over all a wild and lovely county night fell; the men came in from the fields, gathered about the fire where soon they would say the rosary; clearer in the darkness sounded the wheels of the little country cart thumping over a ledge of stone, a cart such as Collins had seen and thrilled at in the Shepherd's Bush Road. But he would hear it no longer. The countryside he had seen in dreams, the people he had loved, the tradition which had been his inspiration—they had risen in the falling light and struck him dead.

The Chieftain: Michael Collins

A woman said, "He would sit there,
Listening to songs, my mother's sheaf,
And he would charm her to regain
Songs out of note for fifty years,
(Did he remember the old songs?)
For he was of the mould of men
Who had renown in her young days,
The champions of cross-roads and field."

(His head was like the head upon
A coin when coins were minted well,
An athlete passing from the games
To take his place in citadel.)

"But once I saw a sadness come
Upon his face, and that was strange—
The song she sang had less of fret
Than all the rest—a Milking Song
(Did he remember the old songs?)
A girl's lilt as she drew streams
Into her pail at evening fall.
But you would think some great defeat
Was in his mind as she sang on."

(Some man whom Plutarch tells about
Heard in the cadence of a song
The breaking of a thread, and knew
The hold he had was not for long.)

"Only that once. All other times
He was at ease. The open door
Might show no danger lay across
That young man's path as he sat there,
Listening to songs of the old time

By the editor.

When songs were secret in their hope.
(Did he remember the old songs?)"

   (A strategist, he left behind
   Pursuit each day and thwarted death
   To plan campaign would leave no name
   To field nor to a shrine a wreath.)

But she had seen upon his face
Something that danger could not cause
Nor could she guess: the fateful glimpse
On instant opened to the man
Summoned by history. He will know
While someone outside lilts the words
That have no fret, that he must choose
Between what forceful men will name
Desertion, but that he'll conceive
As action to bring fruitful peace
And see (it could be) rifle raised
Against deserter who had led.

   (Who breaks into a history breaks
   Into an ambush frenzy-set,
   Where comrades turn to foes, and they
   The clasp of comradeship forget.)

"Did he remember the old songs?
She asks where requiem leads us on
By quays, through streets, to burial-ground.
I answer from my searching mind,
His powers made him prodigy,
But old devotions kept him close
To what was ours; he'd not forget
Threshold and hearthstone and old songs.
The requiem made for divers men
Is history; his music was
The thing that happened, as said Finn."
"No one is left on Ireland's ground

To hear that music," she intoned,
"Since Michael Collins walks no more."

(The citadel he entered in
Without procession or acclaim,
And brought a history to an end,
Setting his name 'gainst Norman name.)

John McCormack

My first meeting with John McCormack was at the house of Lady Ravensdale. I had gone there to play for a violinist whom Lady Ravensdale, always ready to encourage youthful musicians, was anxious to hear. John McCormack was present. Though I had never met him before there was no mistaking him. The thousand pictures I had seen of him with his black hair, twinkling eyes, fine head, all came to life in that imposing personality whose presence filled the room. With eagerness not unmixed with trepidation I moved over to the great man to shake his hand. I remembered feeling very small when I first met the great Chaliapin, humble when first I met Paderewski—what sort of a reception would John McCormack give me? This is what happened: he clapped me on the back and said "Let me turn over the music for you, Gerald." And that was that! Whenever I met McCormack after that, there was always friendliness, that calling me by my Christian name (it was as much as to say "I know all about you, my boy, and your work") which brought unction to the soul of a young musician.

It was not until 1938 that I accompanied John (his old partner, Edwin Schneider not feeling well enough to make the journey to Europe). This, sadly enough, was on his farewell tour of England. I went to the Dorchester Hotel to rehearse with him and after five minutes he said "What the devil do we want to rehearse for?" and this proved to be the nearest approach to a formal rehearsal we ever had.

He was in wonderful form vocally; his singing once again roused the stern music critics, always quick to detect a flaw, into superlative flights of praise. Ernest Newman wrote that when John sang *All me in gedanken* the audience should have stood up and sung it to John to express what they and music lovers the world over owed to this

By Gerald Moore, in *The Capuchin Annual*, 1946-1947, pp. 237-239. Dublin.

man for the pleasure and inspiration his singing had given. And the public? London, Liverpool, Manchester, Birmingham, Glasgow, Edinburgh, etc., all flocked to hear once again their beloved singer. It was a triumphant procession. . . . It was in his hotel that his friends and admirers would gather; there I have met great conductors, singers, violinists, pianists (I put musicians first, as they are most important); then there were ambassadors, statesmen, writers, actors and actresses, tennis players, etc., etc. To each person John would talk about their own work, to the politician politics, to the sportsman sport.

On the day of a concert, McCormack was unapproachable. He would not see anybody except his own immediate circle. Countess McCormack would see that he had all his newspapers around him and his books. He conversed in whispers (an iron restraint on John McCormack's part, for he was a vehement and explosive conversationalist). I tapped at this door when the car came to take us to the concert, he would drink a cup of black coffee and off we would go—with me doing most of the talking to monosyllabic replies from John. Arrived at the hall, he would go through a crowd of autograph hunters at the artists' room door like a knife through butter—he refused to stand out in the cold and damp signing autographs just before he was due to sing—the books could be sent in to him and he would sign them in his room.

John did not love rehearsing, as I have indicated earlier; I remember that the day before his last Albert Hall concert he had made an appointment to run through César Franck's *Panis Angelicus* at the hall with the cellist and organist—who were playing the obligati. "Why should I be going down to sing my heart out in a cold hall the day before my farewell? Sure, you go down, Gerald, you know how I sing it, you know my tempo, you know my little ways—you sing it through." And then he added with a wicked look in his eye, "Sure, I think I'll come with you for the peculiar experience it will be to hear you sing." Incidentally, that was a new sensation for me, to sing in the Royal Albert Hall. I stood near the organist but had to sing sufficiently loud for the cellist—sitting a long way off—to hear me. These two were my entire audience in that vast hall with the exception of a lady who, with a man's cap on her head, was doing some cleaning in one of the upper boxes.

This farewell tour, however, was not to be his last. Unlike many famous singers of the past, one would not ask McCormack, "How many farewell tours are you going to make?" As long as he was in good form he would have continued to make records, might be induced to make an occasional broadcast—but he would not reappear on the concert platform. Suffering humanity, however, brought him from his retirement. During the grimmest of the war years, 1941-42, he undertook a strenuous tour in aid of the Red Cross, in the course of which, and in his anxiety to swell his contribution, he gave concerts in smaller towns than any he had ever visited since he had become celebrated. We in England will always think of him with added affection for that.

Of course the man in the street went in his millions to hear him sing *I hear you calling me, Mother Machree* and *The Rose of Tralee,* and John would have been a very hardhearted man if he had not catered for this overwhelming demand. Yet, in none of his programmes did he ever neglect to give the more serious music lover a treat; there would be something from the old Italian classics, *Amarilli mia bella, O del mio dolce ardor;* from Handel, *O sleep why dost thou leave me?, Wheree'er you walk;* Schubert's *Ave Maria;* Wolf's *Herr, was tragt der Boden hier.* The two latter songs, deeply spiritual, touched the heart of John and he would imbue them with all the fervour of his religion. *To the children* by Rachmaninoff is another song which meant much to John, and through John, his listeners. Occupying the inmost recesses of John's heart as these songs may have done, it must not be thought that he could ever sing the tritest ballad with any suspicion of insincerity or carelessness. Indeed the secret of his hold on the vast public was his sincerity. If he could not sing a song with conviction he would throw it away. Every song had to have some special message for John. *When I have sung my songs to you I'll sing no more* may not be a great song—I will even go so far as to say that with any other singer it could sound banal, but when John sang it, a lump came into your throat, because you realized at once even if you were sitting at the back of the gallery—that the song meant so much to John personally. I know for a fact that whenever he sang this song he was thinking of his wife, Lily; he was paying homage to his lifelong companion, adviser and comforter.

This great minstrel will never be forgotten. He is enshrined in the hearts of the people, for his singing lifted them up and showed them beauty and romance.

Part VI

WAYS AND TRADITIONS

The Commodities of Aqua Vitae *

The soile of Ireland is very low and waterish, including diverse little islands, invironed with lakes and marrish. Highest hills have standing pooles in their tops. Inhabitants, especially new come, are subject to distillations, rheumes and fleures. For remedie whereof, they use an ordinarie drinke of Aqua Vitae, being so qualified in the making, that it drieth more and also inflameth lesse than other hot confections doo.

One Theoricus wrote a proper treatise of Aqua Vitae wherein he praiseth it unto the ninth degree. He distinguisheth three sorts thereof, simplex, composita and perfectissima. He declareth the simples and ingredients thereto belonging. He wisheth it to be taken as well before meat as after. It drieth up the breaking out of hands, and killeth the flesh wormes, if you wash your hands therewith. It scowroth all scurfe and scalds from the head, being therewish dailie washt before meales.

Being moderatlie taken, saith he, it sloweth age, it strengthneth youth, it helpeth digestion, it cutteth flegme, it abandoneth melancholie, it relisheth the heart, it lighteneth the mind, it quickeneth the spirits, it cureth the hydropsie, it healeth the strangurie, it pounceth the stone, it expelleth grauell, it puffeth away all ventositie, it keepeth and preserueth the head from whirling, the eies from dazeling, the toong from lisping, the mouth from maffling, the teeth from chattering, and the throte from ratling; it keepeth the weasan from stifling, the stomach from wambling, and the heart from swelling, the bellie from wirtching, the guts from rumbling, the hands from shivering and the sinewes from shrinking, the veines from crumpling, the bones from aking and the marrow from soaking.

Vistadius also ascribeth thereto a singular praise, and would have it to burne being kindled, which he taketh to be a token to know the goodness thereof.

And trulie it is a sovereigne liquor, if it be orderlie taken.

From "The Commodities of Aqua Vitae," a pamphlet written by an Anglo-Irish writer of the sixteenth century, Richard Stanihurst. The Dolmen Press. Dublin. 1956.

---

* The Irish *Uisge batha* (sometimes written *usquabaugh*), "Water of Life," is Latin *aqua vitae*, and has become the English *whiskey*.

The Harp

The harp is a genuine Irish emblem. Represented on the coins of our own day, displayed on the green flag that preceeded the present-day tricolor, it has a place in the oldest strata of Irish tradition where it is given a cosmic significance. Owned by the Dagda, the senior among the Divine Folk, the Tuatha de Danaan, it is taken from him by the powers of cold and darkness, the Fomorians, with whom the De Danaan are at war. Two divinities, Lugh representing Light and Ogma representing Art, penetrate the Fomorian fastness, recover the harp and restore it to the Dagda. When they come into the fastness—"There hung the harp on the wall. That is the harp in which the Dagda had bound the melodies so that they sounded not until his call summoned them forth. The young gods pronounced the harp's two secret names and at the same time called, 'Come, Summer! Come, Winter.' Having regained it, the Dagda played the harp to the Divine Folk—a wail strain, so that their tearful women wept. He played a smile strain to them, so that their women and children laughed. He played a sleep strain to them, and the company all fell asleep."* The harp with its secret or magical names is the purveyor of Sorrow, Gladness and Repose.

The harp was not only the principal musical instrument of the Irish—it was their unique instrument; they concentrated all their musical ability on the playing of it and the composition of melodies for it. Geraldus Cambrensis, the publicity man for the Norman invaders (he came into Ireland when Europe was preparing for the crusade against Saladin) placed the Irish far above the harpers of Wales, England, and France; compared with the accomplishment of the Irish, they were only at the beginning of their art. (But the professionalism of the harpers, like the professionalism of the *fili*, prevented any widening; musical scholars say that the exclusive devotion to the harp and to melodies composed for the harp halted the development of Irish music.)

The harpers lost the audience of the castle with the emigration of the leading families in the seventeenth and early eighteenth century. Their prestige declined (a factor in the decline was the coming in of Italian music) although new families of English descent were hos-

---

By the editor.
* *The Second Battle of Mag tured (Moytura)*, translated by Whitley Stokes.

pitable to such harpers as O'Carolan and O'Neill. It was a North of Ireland man, Dr. Michael MacDonnell, and an Englishman, Edward Bunting, who assembled the last harpers in Belfast in 1792. The harpers who attended were an impoverished and vagrant remnant. "There were eight men and one woman," writes a lively young lady whose letter is quoted by Mrs. Milligan Fox in her *Annals of the Irish Harpers,* "all either blind or lame, and all old but two men. Figure to yourself this group, indifferently dressed, sitting on a stage erected for them in one end of the Exchange Ballroom, and the ladies and gentlemen of the first fashion in Belfast and its vicinity looking on and listening attentively, and you will have some idea of how they looked. . . . The best performers got ten guineas, and the worst two and the rest accordingly." Some of the most distinctive of Irish melodies were in the repertoire of these harpers; they were recorded by Edward Bunting and so preserved. Outstanding amongst them was one Denis Hempson. "He played," it is recorded, "with long crooked nails, and in this performance the tinkling of the small wires under the deep tones of the bass were peculiarly thrilling. He was the only one who played the very old, the absolute music of the country, and he did it in a style of such finished excellence as persuaded the editor that the praises of the old Irish harp in Cambrensis, Fuller, and others, instead of being ill-considered and indiscriminate were no more than a just tribute to that admirable instrument and its then professors."* Hempson should have been retained to teach and so perpetuate his long cultivated art, but he was given his ten guineas and allowed to wander off. And so through a heedlessness unthinkable in any other European country, a noble accomplishment was permitted to disappear.

The last of them must have been long out of sight when the song that gives the popular presentation of the harper was made up:

BOLD PHELIM BRADY, THE BARD OF ARMAGH

Oh, list to the lay of a poor Irish harper,
And scorn not the strains of his old withered hand,
But remember those fingers they could once move sharper
To raise the merry strains of his dear native land;
It was long before the Shamrock, our green isle's loved emblem,
Was crushed in its beauty 'neath the Saxon lion's paw,
I was called by the colleens of the village and valley
Bold Phelim Brady, the Bard of Armagh.

---

* Quoted by Mrs. Milligan Fox in *Annals of the Irish Harpers.*

How I long for to muse on the days of my boyhood,
Though four score and three years have flitted since then,
Still it gives sweet reflections, as every young joy should,
That merry-hearted boys make the best of old men.
At pattern or fair I could twist my shillelagh,
Or trip through a jig with my brogues bound with straw,
Whilst all the pretty maidens around me assembled
Loved bold Phelim Brady, the Bard of Armagh.

Although I have travelled this wide world over,
Yet Erin's a home and a parent to me,
Then, Oh, let the ground that my old bones shall cover
Be cut from the soil that is trod by the free.
And when Sergeant Death in his cold arms shall embrace me,
Oh, lull me to sleep with sweet Erin go Bragh;
By the side of my Kathleen, my young wife, O place me,
Then forget Phelim Brady, the Bard of Armagh.

Set to a fine old air, "The Bard of Armagh" is popular on the
street and on the concert platform. But the picture it calls up is
altogether wrong. A harper would know that he was the custodian of
an aristocratic art and would never remind an audience that he was
once a boy of the countryside. His kind of patriotic sentiment belongs
to the Anglo-Irish and not to the Gaelic tradition. And the harper
would never have confounded his role with that of the bard; they two
were as distinct as a conservative society, rigidly adhering to professionalism, could keep them. The picture of the bearded bard harping
to his own lays *a l'Ossian* is out. Says the authority on Irish music,
Donal O'Sullivan, "The music on which Cambrensis bestowed his
encomiums was harp music, played before the heads of the noble
houses and their families as an accompaniment to the recital (or chanting) of the bardic poetry composed in their honor. The poetry was
written down and preserved in poem-books called *duanairi;* but the
same was not done with the melodies. Indeed, it is hard to imagine the
kind of music to which the bardic poems could be chanted, and this
highly stylized verse in complex, classical metres has no correspondence
with any of the Irish tunes that have come down to us. There is
nothing unhistorical about

The harp that once through Tara's halls
The soul of music shed

Only we do not know what the music was like.'*

THE HARP THAT ONCE THROUGH TARA'S HALLS

The harp that once through Tara's halls
The soul of music shed,
Now hangs as mute on Tara's walls
As if that soul were fled.
So sleeps the pride of former days,
So glory's thrill is o'er,
And hearts that once beat high for praise,
Now feel that pulse no more.

No more to chiefs and ladies bright
The harp of Tara swells;
The chord alone that breaks the night,
A tale of ruin tells.
This Freedom now so seldom wakes,
The only throb she gives
Is when some heart indignant breaks
To show that still she lives.

The Shamrock

The worst verse in the world has been written about the Shamrock.
I open Thomas Crofton Croker's *Popular Songs of Ireland* and find
this as the first of three stanzas:

There's a dear little plant that grows in our isle,
'Twas Saint Patrick himself, sure, that set it;
And the sun of his labor with pleasure did smile,
And with dew from his eye often wet it.
It thrives through the bog, through the brake, through the mireland;
And he called it the dear little Shamrock of Ireland.
  The sweet little Shamrock, the dear little Shamrock,
  The sweet little, green little, Shamrock of Ireland.

---

* In *The Journal of the Royal Society of Antiquaries of Ireland.* 1949.

By the editor.

It was first sung by a lady with the appealing name of Mrs. Mountain at the Opera House in Capel Street.

As if the above were not bad enough, we are also given the following in the same collection:

> This plant that blooms for ever,
>   With the Rose combined,
>   And the Thistle twined,
> Defy the strength of foes to sever.
> Firm be the triple league they form,
>   Despite all change of weather;
> In sunshine, darkness, calm or storm
>   Still may they fondly grow together.

Thomas Moore did a little better when he celebrated the Shamrock as

> A type that blends
> Three godlike friends,
> Love, Valour, Wit, for ever.

But besides being the begetter of bad verse, the Shamrock has also been the begetter of much argument. Crofton Croker quotes from a communication to the *Dublin Penny Journal* in which this is said:

"Other countries may boast of their trefoil as well as we, but nowhere on the broad earth, on continent or in isle, is there such an abundance of this succulent material for making fat mutton. In winter as well as in summer, it is found to spread its green carpet over our limestone hills, drawing its verdure from the mists that sweep from the Atlantic. The seed of it is everywhere. Vast lime or limestone gravel on the top of a mountain, or on the centre of a bog, and up springs the Shamrock. St. Patrick, when he drove all living things that had venom (save only *man*) from the top of Croagh Patrick, had his foot planted on a shamrock; and if the readers of your journal will go on a pilgrimage to that most beautiful of Irish hills, they will see the Shamrock still flourishing there, and expanding its fragrant honeysuckles to the western wind. I confess I have no patience with that impudent Englishman, who wants to make us believe that our darling plant, associated as it is with our religious and convivial partialities, was *not* the favorite of St. Patrick, and who would substitute in the place of that badge of our faith and our nationality, a little, sour, puny plant of wood-sorrel! This is actually attempted to be done by that stiff, sturdy Saxon, Mr. Bicheno. . . . The proof the

Englishman adduces is the testimony of one Spenser, another Saxon.
. . . But, to do Mr. Bicheno justice, he has another argument in favor
of the wood-sorrel, which is far more to an Irishman's mind. He says
that wood-sorrel, when steeped in punch, makes a better substitute for
lemon than trefoil. This has something very specious in it. if anything
would do, this would; but let the Saxon do his best. Even on his own
ground—even in London—he would find it very hard to convince our
countrymen, settled in St. Giles's, that the *Oxalis acetosella*, the sour,
puny, crabbed wood-sorrel, is the proper emblem for Ireland."

The Shamrock (Shamrog) then is not the wood-sorrel. It is a trefoil,
a clover that grows nowhere else but in Ireland; it is really a pretty
plant, growing in bunches and often with a dark stain on its green.
It was used as an emblem by the respectable Volunteers of 1777, and
subsequently as an emblem made challenging by more forward parties.
So rebellious did the wearing of the Shamrock come to seem, that in
Queen Victoria's time Irish regiments were forbidden to display it.
And this really made the Shamrock an Irish emblem, for it now spread
through the most defiant of Nationalist ballads:

THE WEARIN' OF THE GREEN

Oh, Paddy dear! and did ye hear the news that's goin' round?
The Shamrock is forbid by law to grow on Irish ground!
No more St. Patrick's day we'll keep; his color can't be seen,
For there's a cruel law agin' the Wearing o' the Green!

I met with Napper Tandy, and he took me by the hand,
And he said 'How's poor ould Ireland, and how does she stand?'
'She 's the most distressful country that ever yet was seen,
For they're hangin' men and women for the Wearin' o' the Green.'

An' if the color we must wear is England's cruel red,
Let it remind us of the blood that Ireland has shed;
Then pull the Shamrock from your hat, and throw it on the sod,
An' never fear, 'twill take root there, though under foot 'tis trod.

When law can stop the blades of grass from growin' as they grow,
An' when the leaves in summer time their color dare not show,
Then I will change the color, too, I wear in my caubeen;
But till that day, plaise God, I'll stick to the Wearin' o' the Green.

The Shamrock is a national rather than a religious emblem. How
then does it become associated with St. Patrick? The legend goes—

it is a late legend—that he held it before King Laegaire as a convincing argument for the Trinity. But St. Patrick was too good a theologian to illustrate that doctrine by such a simple-minded device. The trefoil resembles the Cross and it may have been used as a figure of it, and in that way become associated with the apostle of Christianity. It may go back to something older: the Triad was always significant for the Gaels.

A Four-Leaved Shamrock

A good many years ago a showman came to the town of Dingle and performed many tricks there. At one time he'd eat a dozen straws and then pull yards of ribbon from his throat. The strangest thing he showed me was a game-cock that he used to harness to a great log of wood. Men, women, and children were breaking their bones to see the cock, and he a small bird, drawing such a great weight of timber. One day, when the showman was driving the cock on the road towards Brandon mountain, he met a man with a bundle of grass on his back. The man was astonished to see crowds running after a cock drawing a straw behind him.

"You fool," said the people, "don't you see the cock drawing a log of timber, and it would fail any horse to draw the like of it."

"Indeed, then, I do not. I see a cock drawing a straw behind him, and sure I've seen the like many a time in my own place."

Hearing this, the showman knew there was something in the grass, and going over to the man he asked the price he was asking for the bundle. The man did not wish to sell, but at last he parted with it for eighteen pence. The showman gave the grass to his boy and told him to go aside and drop it into the river. The boy did that, and when the bundle went down the stream the man was a big a fool as another; he ran after the cock with the crowd.

That evening the same man was telling a friend how at first he saw the cock with a straw behind him, and then saw him drawing a great log of wood. "Oh, you fool," said his friend, "there was a four-leaved shamrock in the bundle of grass. While you had the shamrock, it kept every enchantment and devilment from you, and when you parted with it, you became as big a fool as the others."

From *Tales of the Fairies and of the Ghost World,* collected from Oral Tradition in Southwest Munster, by Jeremiah Curtin, pp. 154-156. Little, Brown & Co. Boston. 1895.

Fairies: The Banshee and the Leprechaun

Irish fairy lore is unlike the fairy lore of the rest of Europe in this respect: the fairy powers in Ireland have been endowed with names and personalities—they are not a nameless commonalty. And this endowment has left the fairies of Ireland more tangible and with more of a history than the fairy beings of other countries. How has it come that they have names and personalities? Alfred Nutt supposed that it was because each locality in Ireland had its special form of argicultural rites, its special name for the powers worshipped, its special version of their fortunes. He says, "Whether derived from the common Gaelic storehouse of mythic romance, or from local saga, the presence of names, of personalities, of distinctive groups of narrative connected with those personalities, gives a body, a reality, to the fairy world of Ireland lacking elsewhere."

There are two preternatural beings who have distinct existences: the Leprechaun and the Banshee: they are both solitary. It is wrong to speak of a company of Leprechauns or a company of Banshees. However, it seems that the Leprechaun began his career as a member of a community: Lu-chorpan, "The Wee Bodies." The name of his nation became corrupted, and the corruption gave rise to the idea that "brog" or shoe made part of the name. The Leprechauns then became shoemakers, and like all shoemakers they became irascible and solitary. The solitary Leprechaun is now shoemaker to the fairies. His haunts are by old castles. A very little fellow, he is always engaged in his trade of shoemaking. If you are lucky enough to come upon him, draw close to him without making a sound. Take him in your grasp. Then ask him where the crocks of gold are hidden. Insist upon his telling; do not let your mind be dissipated by his talk. In the end he will cheat you; he will say or do something that will distract your attention, and when you look again, the Leprechaun will have disappeared. "Lurikeen" seems to be the County Kildare version of his name.

The Banshee, literally the Fairy Woman (Bean Sidhe) has no abode. She comes near a house to wail for one who is about to die.

Those who know how piercing is the *caoine*, the people's lament for the dead, will realize what a dread visitant the Banshee would be. In all respects this mysterious creature is like the "keener" or mourner

By the editor.

for the dead; those who have looked upon her describe her as drawing a comb through her hair; she is probably tearing her hair out in
the manner of the ancient mourners.

The Banshee haunts only the families of the "high Milesian race,"
that is, the families whose names are Gaelic by the "O" or "Mac" or
any of the other prefixes. However, the Gaelic poets have granted a
Banshee to some of the Norman-Irish families—the Fitzgeralds have
been given one. She is a respecter of persons and haunts only those
who are authentically of noble stock.

The Shillelagh

Let us consider this curiously named object. But first we will quote
again from the old-time columnist of *The Dublin Penny Journal*
who put the wood-sorrel in its place vis-à-vis the shamrock. "The
customs of our country," he says authoritatively, "show that our people
once dwelt under the greenwood tree; for an Irishman cannot walk or
wander, sport or fight, buy or sell comfortably, without an oak stick
in his fist. If he travels he will beg, borrow or steal a shillelagh;
if he goes to play, he hurls with a crooked oak stick; if he goes to
a fair, it is delightful to hear the sound of his clohel-peen on the
cattle-horns; if he fights, as fight he must, at market or fair, the cudgel
is brought on high." This was written a century ago. The oak, available then, is not so available now; what passes for a shillelagh is a
blackthorn stick pulled out of a hedge.

The name, so attractive in its strangeness, is the name of a place
in which there was once an oak-forest. Someone who wrote *A Practical Treatise on Planting* back in the eighteenth century looked on
the survivors of a forest that had given Ireland a title to fame, the
forest of Shillelagh in County Wicklow. Here was a tree which
"measured round the forked trunk upwards of twenty seven feet;
round one of the stems, twenty feet; round the other, twelve, and is
gross timber for more than forty feet in height." To our eyes one oak
tree is very like another, provided there is some proportion between
them. But not to one who writes practical treatises on planting.
"The superior density and closeness of grain, which is the character
of the Irish oak, particularly in high situations and a dry soil, as may

---

By the editor.

appear by comparing its specific gravity with that of other oak." And
so the survivor of this particular forest is distinguished by the writer
of the treatise for "its firmness of texture as well as its stately height
and great dimensions."

Macaulay in one of his essays speaks of the applause for an oration
ringing from the rafters of Irish oak. That was in Westminster Hall.
But that is not all of it. The oak of Shillelagh was so grand that it
shared the immunity from base associations that other noble materials—gold and the unicorn's horn—have. John Banim is repeating
a piece of folklore, no doubt, when, in his dull novel, *The Croppy*,
he speaks of a room in a mansion "solidly wainscoted with Shillelagh
oak against which [as is said of the woodwork of Westminster Hall,
also reputed Irish] the venomous spider of England durst not affix his
web." And we hear, too, that "a sale was made of the finest timber of
Shillelagh into Holland for the use of the Stadthouse."

Would that one could attribute the destruction of a forest so grand
and so historic to the roofing of historic buildings! But the doom of
the forest of Shillelagh was for something much less lofty. The oaks
were sold to London dealers for pipe-staves. And why not? The new
proprietors of forfeited estates were out for quick returns, and stands
of timber were easily exploited. "It is inconceivable what destruction
was made in the course of twenty years," says our treatise-writer. And
so one of the glories of Ireland was sold at the rate of ten pounds per
thousand staves.

The place still keeps its name, and as one goes through the county
of Wicklow one comes into a railway station in which the name
"Shillelagh" is written up as if it were any other place name. Its oaks
were world-famous; the cudgel cut from one, or, in time, from outside
oaks, became "the sprig of Shillelagh," a cudgel used in man-to-man
fighting. It must be a hundred years ago since it was made an emblem
of the stage Irishman, for Crofton Croker notes, "The fearless way in
which Jack Johnstone used to sing the following song, and the dexter-
ous manner in which he accompanied it by flourishes of his shillelagh,
will long be remembered by those who have witnessed his personifica-
tion of the Irish character." And here, no doubt, we come on the root
of the shillelagh's vogue. It could be used in the gesticulation of a
vaudeville artist doing an Irish "turn."

> Oh! an Irishman's heart is as stout as shillelagh,
> It beats with delight to chase sorrow and woe;
> When the piper plays up, then it dances as gaily,
> And thumps with a whack to leather a foe.

When we bring it down to this we know that the shillelagh is not an emblem; it is really a badge.

The varnished blackthorn with green ribbons round it that the tourist brings back from "The Emerald Isle" is a simulacrum of a shillelagh. A shillelagh was an oaken cudgel; it was never swung; grasped in the middle, the knock that its knob delivered was by an arm and wrist movement. The other cudgel could guard and ward off the "whack." Skill had to come into play.

Were there, then, no knock-down fights with shillelaghs? Readers of eighteenth-century Irish novels know that there were. The most dangerous encounters were between factions that carried on some ancient family feud or between parties who, naming themselves "Old Waistcoats" and "Old Cravats" built up for themselves big and excitable followings. Theirs were stern shillelagh fights, and they make fairs loud with men's challenges and women's lamentations. "Who'll tread on the tail of my coat?" a man will challenge as he drags his coat on the ground before a crowd of men whose hands are clenched on their shillelaghs. Or, "Who'll say black is the white of my eye?" Then there are engagements. Shillelaghs strike each other, or, breaking a guard, get in a whack on a head. A woman rushes over to lift up a man who has fallen, his head bloodied. Or—and this had happened often enough—to raise a lament over a man who has been killed by a powerful stroke.

These dangerous engagements were brought to an end when the national leaders began to put a wide objective before the people—Catholic Emancipation or Repeal of the Union. The faction fights and the partisan feeling aroused by them had to be eradicted. New figures appear in the market-squares—the priest or a public-spirited gentleman on horseback riding between the factions, appealing to them in the name of their religion or their country not to carry on with such senselessness. Then the great demonstrations that O'Connell staged suspended the factions.

The Potato and the Clay Pipe

Whether or not they are emblems in any innate sense is a question, but considering the attention that has been given them on the fringes of Hibernianism, it would be wrong to relegate the potato and the clay pipe to utter obscurity in such a compilation as this. The editor's researches have enabled him to discover two pieces that can be regarded as celebrations of these good ingredients of an Irish way of life.—P.C.

THE POTATO*

Sublime potatoes! that, from Antrim's shore
To famous Kerry, form the poor man's store;
Agreeing well with every place and state—
The peasant's noggin, or the rich man's plate.
Much prized when smoking from the teeming pot,
Or in turf-embers roasted crisp and hot.
Welcome, although you be our only dish;
Welcome, companion to flesh, fowl, or fish;
But to the real gourmands, the learned few,
Most welcome, steaming in an Irish stew.

MY PIPE OF IRISH CLAY†

When I wish to solve those problems, which perplex the wisest men,
And deduce abstruse conclusions, that transcend all human ken;
When I wish to know the secrets which the pyramids infold,
Or to understand the statecraft of Rameses Great of old,
I just sit here quiet and easy, and all things seem clear as day,
When I see the smoke a-curling from my pipe of Irish clay.
But more dear to me than problems, or the Pharaohs and their kind,
Are the pictures which I then see of the land I left behind;
All the old haunts and the dear friends, all the things I used to do,
The hopes and dreams of boyhood days, they all pass me in review;
Sure I'm thinking I'm there again and beside sweet Dublin Bay,
When I see the smoke a-curling from my pipe of Irish clay.
I'm climbing up the Hill of Howth or I'm boating in the bay,
I'm strolling by the Liffey's banks or I'm bathing down at Bray;
I'm basking in the Phoenix Park, while the birds sing merrily.
The fresh winds waft the atmosphere of the mountains and the sea,
Or p'raps I'm on the Lucan road, eating berries large and ripe,
When I send the smoke a-curling from my soft clay Dublin pipe.

---

* From Thomas Crofton Croker's *Popular Songs of Ireland,* an early nineteenth-century compilation.
† From *The Gael,* September, 1904, p. 312. New York.

Potato Specialties: Traditional Recipes

I liked to sit and watch the men cutting the turf. One of the Reddins wielded the triangular slane. He had three helpers. As the dripping sods were cut, one man lifted them, two at a time, into the barrow. Mike Brophy wheeled the heavy barrow along the bank, and a fourth man went before him laying out the turf to dry. Later, the women would come to pile the turf loosely into little footings of five sods each, and when the footings had partially dried, they were erected in waist-high stacks to finish drying. Afterwards, the turf was wheeled out to the side of the road where it was built into a clamp and left there until the time came to draw it home.

Grandmother always sent me out to the bog with Judy Ryan to take the men their dinner.

We brought them stacks of round spongy griddle cakes and crusty loaves of currant bread. A whole shoulder of bacon which for the sake of extra flavour and tenderness had been cooled in the water in which it was boiled was cut up for the hungry men.

We lit a fire on the bog to make their tea. Four big sods were selected and made into a square to form a hob. In the centre we piled little branches of withered heather and scraps of flaky dry turf. When the kindling had taken, we piled on bigger pieces of turf and soon we had a glowing fire. The blackened can of brownish water from the stream was set on the hob to boil. When it was bubbling, Judy dropped in a handful of tea and sugar, lifted off the can, and set the tea to draw while the men came running in answer to her call.

They ate enormously and then lay on their backs for a little while in the heather before returning to their labour to work up an appetite for the still more enormous supper that awaited them in Gran's kitchen when day was done.

My grandmother always said that a day without potatoes was a day without nourishment. She took a great pride in feeding her employees well, and for the turf-cutters' supper she always had, not ordinary boiled potatoes, but steamed potatoes, and sometimes thump.

The potatoes to be steamed were scrubbed and put into the baker with a cupful of water. The baker was then covered, coals were piled on its lid and the potatoes were left to convert themselves into balls

From *Never No More,* by Maura Laverty, pp. 55-58. Copyright, 1942, by Maura Laverty. Longmans, Green & Co. New York and London.

of flour. Knowing that butcher's meat would be a treat for these men who rarely tasted it except at Christmas or Easter, she generally had a big joint of John Dooley's good juicy beef for them, although the men would have been well content to make their supper off the steamed potatoes, topped and buttered and eaten with a spoon like eggs.

But she gave them boiled beef as well, cooked with peas and carrots and onions and chopped cabbage, barley and dumplings. Sometimes she prepared a mock goose, spreading a great slice of steak with mashed potatoes, chopped scallions, lard, pepper and salt and a sprinkling of dried sage. The meat was rolled up, tied with tape and roasted. She basted it with milk and served it with a good brown gravy to which was added a tablespoonful of her mushroom ketchup.

The only drawback to those evenings when she made thump for the turf-cutters was that no matter how much she prepared, the men never seemed to have sufficient of the creamy fluffy potato mixture. For thump, she boiled the potatoes whole in their jackets. When they were cooked, I peeled and beetled them with the big wooden beetle, while Gran boiled a handful of scallions to tenderness in a half-pint of milk. The milk and scallions were added to the potatoes together with pepper and salt and a generous lump of butter and then the mixture was beaten until it was as white and light as freshly-fallen snow.

With thump she gave them succulent chops browned to perfection before the fire in her big Dutch oven.

Often the main dish was followed by a big rice pudding, yellow with eggs and richly spotted with raisins and sultanas, spicy cinnamon, and coated with a fragrant brown skin of nutmeg. Sometimes she unearthed a few of last year's apples from their bed of hay in the loft and made them into a dumpling.

Gran's apple dumplings, served with drawn butter, were a meal in themselves, rich, satisfying and full of flavour from the cloves and brown sugar. The tender pastry that wrapped the apples was a delight.

She took five or six freshly cooked potatoes and bruised them on the baking-board with the bottom of a big delft mug. A cup of melted butter was sprinkled over them and a good pinch of salt. Then she worked in enough flour to bind the mixture and rolled it out. When the chopped apples, cloves, brown sugar and scraps of butter had been encased in rounds of pastry, the dumplings were tied up in scalded and floured squares cut from a well-boiled flour-bag and put down to cook in boiling water.

When supper was over, the men liked to sit around the kitchen fire. Drowsy with food and their day's hard labour on the bog, they were content to sit without speaking. Whichever of the Reddin boys happened to be present would usually take a French fiddle from his pocket and play softly the plaintive old tunes of Carolan and Rose Mooney and the other Irish harpers.

His playing was good, for all the Reddins were natural musicians, but we were always relieved when he put the mouth-organ back in his pocket, and after a curt "Good-night to yez, now," set out for his home in the bog.

"He's terrible nacky with the French fiddle," Mike Brophy would say when he had gone, "but them sad tunes he plays belong to the banshee."

Donnybrook Fair

Donnybrook Fair! The acme of disorder—free-for-all ructions, shillelagh-swinging, skull-cracking all over the place! Something of this comes into one's mind on reading or seeing the name. But wild tumult was not the note of Donnybrook Fair. A German visitor of 1828, Prince Puckler-Muskau, notes the raggedness, the drunkenness, the beggary, the indecorous love-making, but says nothing of indiscriminate violence; in fact, he is surprised that the brutality that foreigners of the time expected to find at popular gatherings in English-speaking countries had no place at Donnybrook. "They were more like French people," he notes, "though their gaiety was mingled with more humour and more genuine good nature; both of which are national traits of the Irish and are always doubled by poteen (the best sort of whiskey, illicitly distilled)." He is alert to the grotesqueries of the gathering. "The lowest sort of rope-dancers and posture-masters exercised their toilsome vocation on stages of planks, and dressed in shabby finery, dancing and grimacing in the dreadful heat until they were completely exhausted." Then there were those figures "which I should have thought indigenous only to the Rio de la Plata. Two beggars were seated on a horse, that, by his wretched plight, seemed to supplicate for them; they had no saddle, and a piece of twine served as reins."

In a ballad about Donnybrook Fair in which the rags and dirt are passed over, we hear of its attendance as including

Poor painters, poor poets, poor newsmen, and knaves.

Entertainment is

By the editor.

When maidens so swift, run for a new shift,
Men muffled in sacks, for a shirt they did race there;
There jockeys well booted, and horses sure-footed,
All keep up the humours of Donnybrook Fair.

The ballad ends with

Brisk lads and young lasses can there fill their glasses
With whiskey, and send a full bumper round;
Jig it off in a tent till their money's all spent,
And spin like a top till they rest on the ground.

Donnybrook was a fair of the same kind as the English St. Bartholomew's. Its site was a mile out from the eighteenth-century city, on a common with a road through it and a little river bounding it. It was held in August. In the middle of the nineteenth century it came to an end, and part of its business was taken over by Dublin's grandiose International Horse Show, held close to Donnybrook and keeping the same date as the Fair.

In 1790 Sir Jonah Barrington, a member of the Irish Parliament, went to the Fair, and in *Personal Sketches of His Own Times* he gives a chapter to his impressions. Refreshment there was of the rough and ready order. "A pot boiling outside a tent, lumps of salt beef and cabbage." And of course, whiskey, illicit whiskey, poteen. A dozen fiddlers played for dances, making "an amalgamation of sounds most extraordinary that ever tickled the ear of a musician. Everybody drunk or sober took a share in the long dance, and I have seen a row of a hundred people laboring at the jig steps."

Across from such hilarities there was the horse fair. It, too, was hilarious. "There the jockeys were in abundance, and certainly no Fair ever exhibited as strange a mélange of the halt and blind, the sound and the rotten, the rough and the smooth. All galloping, leaping, kicking and tumbling, some in clusters, some singly; now and then a lash of a long whip and then the crack of the butt of it." Shillelagh fights were exhibitions of skill—"like sword exercises and did not appear savage. Nobody was disfigured thereby, or rendered fit for a doctor. I never saw a bone broken or a dangerous contusion from what was called 'whacks' of a shillelagh (which was never too heavy)."

Why has Donnybrook Fair a place in the lore of English-speaking people? Because of its "humours" one may guess. Back of those "humours" there was a blackguardism peculiar to low-life Dublin, "the commonality," as Sir John Barrington names them, a blackguardism that is a combination of humour, cynicism, profanity, a side of Dublin life that has its classical expression in that unforgettable street-song, *The Night Before Larry Was Stretched,* and its most magnificent embodiment in the barroom scene in Joyce's *Ulysses.* What a pity we have no presentation of characters at the Fair nor no record of the ballads that were sung there. But we can find types that must have been present, ballads that were likely to have been sung there. Biddy Moriarity with whom Daniel O'Connell had his celebrated encounter must have been amongst those present. The Gleeman that Yeats was to write about must have had his predecessor at the Fair. We can be certain that the current *Night Before Larry Was Stretched* was demanded from the ballad-singer before the tent where the pot with its salt beef and cabbage was boiling. Were *Nell Flaherty's Drake* and *Johnny, I hardly Knew You* sung there? If they were not, types related to them were. *The Beggar's Address to His Bag* belongs to a later period, but there would have been ballads celebrating the beggar's calling.

Puck Fair

The little village of Killorglin in County Kerry, built on the river Laune which flows out of the Lakes of Killarney, is each year the scene of the famous "Puck Fair and Pattern" which lasts three days: August 10th—Gathering Day; August 11th—Puck's Fair Day; August 12th—Scattering Day or Children's Day, and for these three days all West Munster converges on it. "Going home for Puck" has for Kerrymen many of the associations of "going home for Christmas." The order of the fair follows an ancient pattern.

On the evening of Gathering Day a procession in pageant assembles at the bridge end of the town and, to the accompaniment of great merriment a large Puck (male) goat, enclosed in a spacious cage and having his horns bedecked with ribbons and rosettes, is borne in triumph in a lorry through the streets to a three-story platform in the square in the center of the town. Here King Puck is enthroned for the next two days, presiding over a great cattle, sheep, and horse fair, as well as a huge throng of people, including the Baron of the Fair, a title which has been in one family for three hundred years. The title

From *The Weekly Bulletin of the Department of External Affairs,* No. 127. Dublin.

is more than an honor—with it goes the right to collect toll on every beast sold.

For three days King Puck and King Carnival reign, and for three days shops and business premises of all descriptions are open day and night. On the second day, August 11th, all the commercial transactions of the fair take place—horses, ponies, cattle, and sheep changing hands. On Scattering Day, or Children's Day, amid the gaily dressed children, they begin to dethrone the King. The ex-monarch is piped away in procession round the town and down the hill and over the bridge to where he came from. And there he is turned loose, free to wander once more in his native hills. The reign of King Puck is over for another year.

No better proof of the antiquity of the fair can be found than the variety of stories which are told to explain why the goat is honored at "Puck." No two explanations are in agreement—a Puck goat warned the inhabitants of the approach of an enemy (Cromwell is mentioned in this connection); a goat saved the town in the time of the legendary Fianna . . . and so on. These may be taken as attempts to explain something whose origin is not known.

There can be little doubt that Puck Fair was originally associated with the Festival of Lughnasa, one of the four great festivals of ancient Ireland, that of Lughnasa being the celebration of the first fruits of the harvest. Carnival celebrations were, of course, a popular feature of agricultural festivals in many countries and a feature of these was the parading and honoring of some animal. At the Mullinavat fair in Kilkenny a goat was also enthroned; at the Cappawhite fair in Tipperary a whitewashed horse was paraded and put on display on top of an earthen fort.

Wedding

"I am curious to know," he said, "who that old gentleman is?"

As he spoke, his curiosity was further excited by seeing a little boy come into the room and place a green bag on the old man's knees.

"That's the celebrated Irish piper," she replied. "I am surprised to see him here. I did not think he attended country weddings."

From *Knocknagow, or The Homes of Tipperary*, by Charles J. Kickham, pp. 215-219. James Duffy & Co., Ltd. Dublin. 1887.

"I suppose he goes round among the nobility and gentry, as we are told the harpers used to do."

"He does, and he has a beautiful little pony the countess gave him. But I suppose he's stopping at present with the priests, and Father Hannigan has brought him with him."

As he uncovered his pipes their splendor quite took Mr. Lowe by surprise. The keys were of silver, and the bag covered with crimson velvet fringed with gold; while the little bellows was quite a work of art, so beautifully was it carved and ornamented with silver and ivory. Having tied an oval piece of velvet with a ribbon attached to each and above his knee, he adjusted his instrument, and after moving his arm, to which the bellows was attached by a ribbon, till the crimson velvet bag was inflated, he touched the keys, and catching up the chanter quickly in both hands began to play. . . . The musician soon seemed to forget all mere human concerns. He threw back his head, as if communing with invisible spirits in the air above him; or bent down over his instrument as if the spirits had suddenly flown into it, and he wanted to catch their whispering there, too.

The audience, to some extent, shared in the musician's ecstasy; particularly Father Hannigan, from whose eyes tears were actually falling as the delicious melody ceased, and the old man raised his sightless eyes, and listened, as it were, for the echo of his strains from the skies. . . .

The wedding guests had been silently dropping into the room, which was now pretty well filled. Mat Donovan occasionally seized a bottle or decanter, and filled out a glass of wine, of whiskey, or "cordial" for some of them. . . . There was a hustling heard at the door, and Ned Brophy himself was seen pushing two blind pipers into the parlour with a degree of violence and an expression of countenance that led Mr. Lowe to imagine he must have caught them in the act of attempting to rob him or something of the kind. The two pipers were tall and gaunt and yellow—a striking contrast in every way to Mr. Flaherty. One was arrayed in a soldier's grey watch-coat, with the number of the regiment stamped in white figures on the back, and the other wore a coarse blue body-coat, with what appeared to be the sleeves of another old grey watch-coat sewed to it between the shoulders and the elbow. Both wore well-patched corduroy knee-breeches and bluish worsted stockings, with brogues of unusual thickness of sole, well paved with heavy nails. Their rude brass-mounted instruments were in keeping with their garments. The sheepskin bag of one had no covering whatever, while that of the other was covered with faded plaid, cross-barred with green and yellow. They dropped into two

chairs near the door, thrusting their old "caubeens" under them, and
sat bolt upright like a pair of mummies or figures at a wax-work
exhibition.

"Play that tune that the angels sang again, Mr. Flaherty," said
Father Hannigan.

Mr. Flaherty complied, a d the noise and hum of voices were at
once hushed.

"Have you that?" the piper in the watch-coat asked his companion
in a whisper, at the same time beginning to work with his elbow.

"I have," replied the other, beginning to work with his elbow, too.

A sound like snoring followed for a moment, and Mr. Flaherty
jerked up his head suddenly, and looked disturbed—as if an evil spirit
had intruded among his delicate Ariels. But as the noise was not repeated, his countenance resumed its wonted placidity, and he bent
over his instrument again.

"I think I could do it better myself," said he of the blue bodycoat,
holding his big knotty fingers over the holes of the chanter. "He didn't
shake enough."

"So could I," replied the grey watch-coat, giving a squeeze to his
bag, which was followed by a faint squeak.

"Turn him out!" shouted Mr. Flaherty, as he started to his feet, his
eyes rolling with indignation.

There was great astonishment among the company; and Miss Lloyd
jumped up in her chair and stared wildly about her, with a vague
notion that Wat Murphy's bulldog—of which interesting animal she
entertained the profoundest dread—had got into the room and seized
Mr. Flaherty by the calf of the leg.

"Come, Seumas," said Father Hannigan, "this is no place for you.
Come, Thade, be off with you," and Father Hannigan expelled the
grumbling minstrels from the parlour; but in doing so he gave each
a nudge in the ribs and slipped a shilling into his fist, which had the
effect of changing their scowl into a broad grin, as they jostled out of
the kitchen.

The Strawboys at the Wedding

We had entered a countryside which was still steeped in the old
traditions and customs, closely followed, although their origins were
often lost. The young people could not say why they danced on the

From a booklet, by Luba Kaftannikoff, sent to the editor.

great slabs covering the dolmens—those tombs of kings who lived, perhaps, four thousand years ago when the Megalithic culture of the Mediterranean countries existed also in Ireland—but dance there they did, each Midsummer's Eve, having brought with them offerings of flowers. For aeons, these dolmens were centers of fertility rites, perhaps because of some dim but universal belief that where death and decay had been, birth and growth might spring. . . .

So on an April day Nancy and Frank got married, and the Strawboys came and danced at their wedding.

"What did they look like?" I asked, when a week later I made my way up the long borheen to see the bride.

"They had high caps on them made of straw, pointed-like," said Nancy. "And masks, and straw capes round their shoulders. They'd straw tied up in the front of their legs as well. They came at sundown —about eight o'clock, new time—and stayed half an hour. They danced with all, but they never spoke."

"If they spoke 'twould break the spell," the bridegroom interjected. "They take no refreshment either."

"And it's to bring good luck?" I asked.

" 'Tis," Nancy said, as a long intimate look passed between husband and wife, and I thought of the ancient fertility rites, which always seem so near and credible in this countryside.

"Do you know where the Strawboys came from?" I asked.

"Somewhere back in the hills," Nancy said. "But Frank thought a couple of them might have been comrades of his. 'Tis years and years since the Strawboys were seen in these parts, and there was a great cheer when we seen them coming, high up across the crags, just as the sun went down."

A Wake in the Old Times

When the corpses were washed and dressed, they looked uncommonly well, considerin'. Larry indeed looked as well as Sally; but you couldn't meet a purtier corpse than she in a day's traveling. I say, when they were washed and dressed, their friends and neighbours knelt

From "Larry MacFarland's Wake," in *Traits and Stories of the Irish Peasantry*, by William Carleton, Vol. I, pp. 112-153. J. M. Dent & Co. London. 1896.

down round them, and offered up a Pater and Ave a piece for the
good of their sowls: when this was done, they all raised the keena,
stooping over them a half bend, clapping their hands, and praising
them, as far as they could say anything good of them; and indeed, the
creathurs, they were never anyone's enemy but their own, so that
nobody could say an ill word if after the first keening the friends and
neighbours took their sates about the corpse.

In a short time whiskey, pipes, snuff and tobacco came, and everyone about the place got a glass and a fresh pipe. Tom, when he held
his glass in his hand, looking at his dead brother, filled up to the
eyes, and couldn't for some time get a word; at last when he was able
to spake—"Poor Larry," says he, "you're lying there low before me,
and many a happy day we spint with one another. When we were
childher," he said turning to the rest, "we were never asunder; he was
aulder nor me by two years, and can I ever forget the leathering he
gave Dick Rafferty long ago, for hitting me with a rotten egg—
although Dick was a great dale bigger than either of us. God knows,
although you didn't thrive in life, either of you, as you might and
could have done, there wasn't a more neighbourly or friendly people
in the parish they lived in; and now, God help them both, and their
poor orphans over there. Larry *a cushla,* your health, and Sally, yours,
and may God Almighty have mercy on both your sowls."

After this, the neighbours began to flock in more generally. When
any relation of the corpses would come, as soon, you see, as they'd
get inside the door, whether man or woman, they'd raise the shout of
the keena, and all the people about the dead would begin along with
them, stooping over them and clapping their hands as before.

Well, as I said, it's it that was the merry wake, and that was only
the truth, neighbours. As soon as night came, all the young boys and
girls from the countryside about them flocked to it in scores. In a short
time the house was crowded; and maybe there wasn't laughing, and
story-telling, and singing, and smoking and drinking and crying—all
going on, helter-skelter, together. When they'd be all in full chorus
this way, maybe some new friend or relation, that wasn't there before,
would come in and raise the keena: of course the youngsters would
keep quiet; and if the person coming in was from the neighbourhood
with any of them that were so merry, as soon as he raised the shout,
the merry folks would rise up, and begin to pelt their hands together,
and cry along with him till their eyes would be red as a ferret's. That
once over, they'd be again down at the songs, and diversion, and divilment—just as if nothing of the kind had taken place: the other would

then shake hands with the friends of the corpses, get a glass or two, and a pipe, and in a few minutes be as merry as the best of them.

Well, as I was telling you, there was great sport going on. In one corner you might see a knot of ould men sitting together, talking over ould times—ghost stories, fairy tales, and the great rebelling of '41, and the strange story of Lamh Dearg, or the Bloody Hand: they'd sit smoking—their faces quite pleased with the pleasure of the pipe—amusing themselves and a crowd of people that would be listening to them with open mouth. Or, it's odd, but there would be some droll young fellow among them, taking a rise out of them; and positively he'd find them able enough for him, particularly ould Ned Mangin, that wanted only four years of a hundred. The Lord be good to him and rest his sowl in glory, it's he that was the pleasant ould man, and could tell a story with any that ever got up.

In another corner there was a different set, bent on pieces of divilment of their own. The boys would be sure to get beside their sweethearts, anyhow; and if there was a purty girl, as you may set it down there was, it was there the skroodging, and the pushing, and the shoving, and sometimes the knocking down itself, would be, about seeing who'd get her. There ould Katty Duffy, that now is as crooked as the hind leg of a dog, and it's herself was then as straight as a rush, and as blooming as a rose—Lord bless us, what an alteration time makes upon the strongest and fairest of us. It's she that was the purty girl that night, and it's myself that gave Frank MacShane, that's still alive to acknowledge it, the broad of his back upon the flure when he thought to pull her off my knee. The very gorsoons and girshas were coorting away among themselves, and learning one another to smoke in dark corners. . . .

After that time the house got too throng entirely, and couldn't hould half of them, so, by jing, off we set, maning all the youngsters of us, out to Tom's barn that was red up for us, there to commence the plays. When we were gone the ould people had more room, and they moved about on the sates we had left them. In the mane time, lashings of tobacco and snuff, cut in plate fulls, and piles of fresh new pipes, were laid on the table for any one that wanted to use them.

When it drew near the morning, every one of us took his sweetheart and, after convoying her home, we went to our own houses to get a little sleep—so that was the end of poor Larry MacFarland and his wife Sally Lowry.

A Husband Laments His Wife

O poor Josie, you are laid out now by the women, and there is fear upon my heart lest my tread should break your rest. And I have a strong belief that you are in the country of quiet now, but I shall never lay my eye till the butt of my life again on one who will break the ice like you. You used to be at market and fair with me, and indeed not like many another woman with your hood down over your eyes, but 'twas it that was fastened tightly at the back of your neck. It's well I remember the morning that the little man came from the South with the sweet tongue who thought to get the two calves from us from an old tune of Mary Bun; but, if he thought it, you put the fire on his coat-tails going, and you put the fleas jumping in the hair of the Kerryman. And it's well I remember the morning of the Christmas fair, when that other schemer came seeking for two fat pigs for the fasting-bite of a donkey; but, if he came, you put him in as much of a scurry as Red Beston was in the day he tried to pull his wife out from the band of the wheel, when she couldn't put a foot under her with drink, and fear was upon his heart that he'd be arrested by the peelers for putting her neck under the wheel himself. I never came in from the garden to you but the little gate was open, the ass fed, and the little stirabout-pot ready beside the fire, but now the gate will be shut, the ass unfed, and the stirabout-pot on its mouth outside the door, and you'll never take hold of the iron spoon again. And if anyone came short in their share it would be yourself, O woman of the great heart, and if the white goat ran dry the black goat didn't know it. You would play a tune on your tongue and dance to it, and maybe there would be puckers in your belly at the same time, and if there was another woman in your shoes it's often her husband wouldn't have the life of a black cat the day he didn't kill any rat. When the neighbour used to come with the horse to plough up the garden for you, he used to go out from you with his belly bursting, you used to give him potatoes and salt pork and white cabbage, and you used to give him a loaf and tea and a duck-egg, and you used to give him a little quart of porter you had brought with you to be ready for the day you went to the market. He used to be off then to the neighbours bellows-ing your praise, and he'd say that any poor man who had a good lucky wife, that his hen was on the nest, and his rent in his pocket. And now, my

From *The Face and Mind of Ireland*, by Arland Ussher, p. 150. Copyright, 1950, by the Devin-Adair Co. New York.

dear love, I must take your hand for the last moments—and I shall have to do it behind my back—for the poor women are here to settle you sweetly in your coffin, and you look so neat that you will be making cajolery up in the other world. And I see their heads bent, and the drop falling from their eyes, for they say they won't see a woman the like of you taking a clean shirt from the line ever again, for you never tore a rib of anyone's hair, and if you couldn't fill the cup, you didn't spill it. But I see the blue light now shining on you, and as content as we always were I have a strong belief that you will be a thousand times richer now possessing the Graces, for there won't be any itching on your mind to know where'll you get your breakfast on Easter Sunday morning. The angels will lay a soft bed for you, and you need have no fear that any wind will blow the little stack of barley out of the corner of the garden ever again. I will make the Sign of the Cross over you now between yourself and the Tempter, and God will direct you straight to the end of every crooked lane, into the strange Blessed Land—the place where the harvest is ready cut and threshed, and the barn filled to the top with the grain that will never fail.

Charms

A CHARM TO WIN LOVE

"O Christ, by your five wounds, by the nine orders of angels, if this woman is ordained for me, let me hold her hand now, and breathe her breath. O my love, I set a charm to the top of your head, to the sole of your foot, to each side of your breast, that you may not leave me nor forsake me. As a foal after the mare, as a child after the mother, may you follow and stay with me till death comes to part us asunder. Amen."

ANOTHER CHARM TO WIN LOVE

A charm of most desperate love, to be written with a raven's quill in the blood of the ring finger of the left hand:

"By the power that Christ brought from heaven, mayst thou love me, woman! As the sun follows its course, mayst thou follow me. As light to the eye, as bread to the hungry, as joy to the heart, may thy presence be with me, O woman that I love, till death comes to part us asunder."

From *Ancient Legends, Mystic Charms and Superstitions of Ireland*, by Lady Wilde, pp. 79-89. Ticknor & Co. Boston. 1887.

ANOTHER CHARM TO WIN LOVE

This is the charm I set for love; a woman's charm of love and desire; a charm of God that none can break:

"You for me and I for thee and for none else; your face to mine, and your head turned from all others."

This to be repeated three times secretly, over a drink given to the beloved.

ANOTHER CHARM FOR LOVE

Golden butter on a new-made dish, such as Mary set before Christ. This to be given in the presence of a mill, of a stream, and the presence of a tree, the lover saying softly:

"O woman, loved by me, mayst thou give me thy heart, thy soul and body. Amen."

A CHARM TO CAUSE ENMITY BETWEEN LOVERS

Take a handful of clay from a new-made grave, and shake it between them, saying:

"Hate ye one another! May ye be as hateful to each other as sin is to Christ, as bread eaten without a blessing is to God."

A CHARM AGAINST SORROW

A charm said by Mary for her Son, before the fair man and the turbulent woman had laid Him in the grave:

> The charm of Michael with the shield;
> Of the palm-branch of Christ,
> Of Brighid with her veil.

The charm that God set for himself when the divinity within him was darkened.

A charm to be said by the cross when the night is black and the soul is heavy with sorrow.

A charm to be said at sunrise, with the hands on the breast, when the eyes are red with weeping and the madness of grief is strong.

A charm that has no words, only the silent prayer.

A CHARM AGAINST FEVER

"God save thee, Michael, archangel! God save thee!
What aileth thee, O man?

A headache and a sickness and a weakness of the heart. O Michael, archangel, canst thou cure me, O angel of the Lord?

May three things cure thee, O man. May the shadow of Christ fall on thee! May the garment of Christ cover thee! May the breath of Christ breathe on thee! And when I come again thou wilt be healed."

These words are said over a patient while his arms are lifted in the form of a cross, and water is sprinkled on his head.

A Charm for a Pain in the Side

"God save ye, my three brothers, God save ye! And how far have ye to go, my three brothers?

To the Mount of Olivet, to bring gold for a cup to hold the tears of Christ.

Go then. Gather the gold, and may the tears of Christ fall on it, and thou wilt be cured, both body and soul."

These words must be said while a drink is being given to the patient.

A Few Prayers

Before Eating

May the blessing of the five loaves and two fishes, which God divided amongst five thousand men, be ours; and may the King who made division put luck in our food and in our portion. Amen.

On Kneading Bread

The luck of God and the prosperity of Patrick on all that I shall see, and on all that I shall take. The luck that God put upon the five loaves and upon the two fishes, may he put it upon this food.

On Milking a Cow

The blessing of Mary, and the blessing of God,
The blessing of the sun and moon on their road,
Of the Man in the East and the Man in the West,
And my blessing with thee, and be thou blest.

From *Amhrain Diadhe Chuige Connacht, The Religious Songs of Connacht,* translated by Douglas Hyde, Vol. II. p. 49 ff. M. H. Gill & Co. Dublin. [1906.]

On Going on a Journey

Seven prayers, seven times over told,
Mary left to her son of old,
Bride left to her mantle's length,
God left to his own great strength.
Between us and the Fairie kind,
Us and the People of the Wind,
Us and the water's drowning power,
Us and temptation's evil hour,
Us and the world's all blighting breath,
Us and the bondsman's cruel death.

On Raking the Ashes Over the Fire at Night

With the staff of the sons of Patrick,
The fire now I am raking,
Awaken let God's good angels,
But enemies none be waking.
Eight steeds are about the house,
A house not clouded a minute,
May no dead ever leave it,
Nor living be wounded in it.

Saint Patrick's Breastplate

Patrick with eight companions advances on Tara, Easter 433. The
hymn chanted in Irish is known in Irish as "The Deer's Cry" and in
Latin as "St. Patrick's Breastplate."

I arise to-day
Through the strength of heaven:
Light of sun,
Radiance of moon,
Splendour of fire,
Speed of lightning,
Swiftness of wind,

From *Selections from Ancient Irish Poetry*, translated by Kuno Meyer, pp. 25-26.
Constable & Co. Ltd. London. 1911.

Depth of sea,
Stability of earth,
Firmness of rock.

I arise to-day
Through God's strength to pilot me:
God's might to uphold me,
God's wisdom to guide me,
God's eye to look before me,
God's ear to hear me,
God's word to speak for me,
God's hand to guard me,
God's way to lie before me,
God's shield to protect me,
God's host to save me
From snares of devils,
From temptation of vices,
From everyone who wishes me ill
Afar and anear
Alone and in a multitude.

I summon to-day all these powers between me and those evils:
Against every cruel merciless power that may oppose my body and
     soul;
Against incantations of false prophets
Against black laws of Pagandom
Against false laws of heretics,
Against craft of idolatry,
Against spells of women and smiths and wizards,
Against every knowledge that corrupts man's body and soul.

Christ to shield me to-day
Against poison, against burning,
Against drowning, against wounding,
So that there may come to me abundance of reward.
Christ with me, Christ before me, Christ behind me,
Christ in me, Christ beneath me, Christ above me,
Christ on my right hand, Christ on my left,
Christ when I lie down, Christ when I sit down, Christ when I arise,
Christ in the heart of every man who thinks of me,
Christ in the mouth of everyone who speaks of me,
Christ in every eye that sees me,
Christ in every ear that hears me.

I arise to-day
Through a mighty strength, the invocation of the Trinity:
Through belief in the Threeness,
Through confession of the Oneness
Of the Creator of Creation.

A Few Riddles

A bottomless barrel,
It's shaped like a hive,
It is filled full of flesh,
And the flesh is alive.
    (tailor's thimble)

As I went through the garden
I met my uncle Thady,
I cut the head of his neck,
And left his body aisy.
    (a head of cabbage)

My daddy on the warm shelf,
Talking, talking to himself.
    (pot simmering on the hob)

Up in the loft the round man lies,
Looking up through two hundred eyes.
    (a sieve)

Snug in the corner I saw the lad lie,
Fire in his heart and a cork in his eye.
    (bottle of whisky)

'Tis round as dish was ever known,
And white as snow the look of it,
'Tis food and life of all mankind,
Yet no man e'er partook of it.
    (breast-milk)

Out she goes and the priest's dinner with her.
    (hen with an egg)

From *Beside the Fire*, edited, translated and annotated by Douglas Hyde, p. 172 ff. David Nutt. London. 1910.

The Toast

Slan agus seaghal agat;	Health and life to you;
Bean ar do mhein agat;	The woman of your choice to you;
Talamh gon chios agat,	Land without rent to you,
Agus bas in Eirinn.	And death in Eirinn.

A Few Sayings

The south wind is soft and mild,
And is very good for the seeds.

The north wind is cold, and when
It blows the lambs are born.

The west wind is a generous wind
And fills the fisherman's nets.

The east wind is dark and gloomy
And is the harbinger of frost.*

*   *   *   *   *

Three blows that support Ireland: The blow of the hammer on the anvil, the blow of the axe on the block, the blow of the flail on the floor.†

*   *   *   *   *

There is a tradition that the knitting which is done after dark is always the best because the sheep are asleep. There are plenty of crickets round the hearth, and the islanders never molest them, for they say that if you injure a cricket his friends will eat your socks in revenge.‡

*   *   *   *   *

The beginning of a ship is a board; of a kiln, a stone; of a king's reign, salutation; and the beginning of health is sleep.

Given to the editor by Reverend Patrick S. Dinneen.

* From *The Gael*, April, 1901. † From oral tradition. ‡ From *Islands of Ireland*, by Thomas H. Mason, B. T. Batsford Ltd. London. 1936.

Lie down with the lamb,
And rise up with the bird
From the time you see a harrow and a man behind it
Until you see stacks of turf and cocks of hay.§

*   *   *   *   *

An aged woman of the grey locks, may eight hundred blessings twelve times over be on thee! Mayst thou be free from desolation, O woman of the aged frame! And may many tears fall on thy grave!¶

Oaths, Curses, Blessings

There are some mock oaths among Irishmen which must have had their origin amongst those whose habits of thought were much more elevated than could be supposed to characterize the lower orders. "By the powers of death" is never now used as we have written it; but the ludicrous travesty of it, "By the powdhers o' delft," is quite common. Of this and other mock oaths it may be right to observe that those who swear by them are in general ignorant of their proper origin. There are some, however, of this description whose original form is well known. One of these the Irishman displays considerable ingenuity in using. "By the cross" can scarcely be classed under the mock oaths; but the manner in which it is pressed into asseverations is amusing. When the Irishman is affirming a truth he swears "by the crass" simply, and this with him is an oath of considerable obligation. He generally, in order to render it more impressive, accompanies it with suitable action, that is, he places the forefinger of each hand across, that he may assail you through two senses instead of one. On the contrary, when he intends to hoax you by asserting what is not true, he ingeniously multiplies the oath, and swears "by the five crasses," that is, by his own five fingers, placing at the same time his four fingers and his thumbs across each other in a most impressive and vehement manner. Don't believe him then—the knave is lying as fast as possible, and with no remorse. "By the crass o' Christ" is an oath of much solemnity, and seldom used in a falsehood. The Irishman also often places two bits of

§ From oral tradition. ¶ From *Ancient Cures, Charms and Usages of Ireland*, by Lady Wilde. Ward & Downey. London. 1890.

From "An Essay on Irish Swearing," in *Traits and Stories of the Irish Peasantry*, by William Carleton, Vol. I, pp. 203-219. J. M. Dent & Co. London. 1896.

straw across, and sometimes two sticks, upon which he swears with an appearance of great heat and sincerity—*sed caveto*.

Irishmen generally consider iron as a sacred metal. In the interior of the country the thieves (but few in number) are frequently averse to stealing it. Why it possesses this hold upon their affections it is difficult to say, but it is certain that they rank it among their sacred things; consider that to find it is lucky, and nail it over their doors when found in the convenient shape of a horseshoe. It is also used as a medium of asserting truth. We believe, however, that the sanction it imposes is not very strong. "By this blessed iron!" "By this blessed an' holy iron!" are oaths of an inferior grade; but if the circumstance on which they are founded be a matter of indifference, they seldom depart from truth in using them.

The Irishman, when engaged in a fight, is never at a loss for a weapon, and we may also affirm that he is never at a loss for an oath. When relating a narrative, or some other circumstance of his own invention, if contradicted, he will corroborate it, in order to sustain his credit or produce the proper impression, by an abrupt oath upon the first object he can seize. "*Arrah,* nonsense! by this pipe in my hand, it's as thrue as"—and then, before he completes the illustration, he goes on with a fine specimen of equivocation—"By the stool I'm sittin' an, it is; an' what more would you have from me, barrin' I take my book oath of it?" Thus does he, under the mask of an insinuation, induce you to believe that he has actually sworn it, whereas the oath is always left undefined and incomplete.

Sometimes he is exceedingly comprehensive in his adjurations, and swears upon a magnificent scale; as, for instance, "By the contints of all the books that ever wor opened an' shut, it's as thrue as the sun to the dial." This certainly leaves "the five crasses" immeasurably behind. However, be cautious, and not too confident in taking so sweeping and learned an oath upon trust, notwithstanding its imposing effect. We grant, indeed, that an oath which comprehends within its scope all the learned libraries of Europe, including even the Alexandrian of old, is not only an erudite one, but establishes in a high degree the taste of the swearer, and displays on his part an uncommon grasp of intellect. Still we recommend you, whenever you hear an alleged fact substantiated by it, to set your ear as sharply as possible; for, after all, it is more than probable that every book by which he has sworn might be contained in a nutshell. The secret may be briefly explained. The Irishman is in the habit of substituting the word never for ever. "By all the books that never were opened or shut," the reader perceives, is only a flourish of trumpets—a mere delusion of the enemy.

In fact, the Irishman has oaths rising gradually from the lying ludicrous to the superstitious solemn, each of which finely illustrates the nature of the subject to which it is applied. When he swears "by the contints o' Moll Kelly's Primer, or "by the piper that played afore Moses," you are perhaps as strongly inclined to believe him as when he draws upon a more serious oath—that is, you almost regret the thing is not the gospel that the Irishman asserts it to be. In the former sense, the humorous narrative which calls forth the laughable burlesque of "by the piper o' Moses" is usually the richest lie in the whole range of fiction.

The next thing which occurs to us in connection with the present subject is cursing; and here again the Irishman holds the first place. His imprecations are often full, bitter and intense. Indeed, there is more poetry and epigrammatic point in them than in those of any other country in the world.

We find it a difficult thing to enumerate the Irish curses so as to do justice to a subject so varied and so liable to be shifted and improved by the fertile genius of those who send them abroad. Indeed, to reduce them into order and method would be a task of considerable difficulty. Every occasion and every fit of passion frequently produce a new curse, perhaps equal in bitterness to any that has gone before it.

Many of the Irish imprecations are difficult to be understood, having their origin in some historical event, or in poetical metaphors that require a considerable process of reasoning to explain them. Of this twofold class is that general one—"The curse of Cromwell on you!" which means, "May you suffer all that a tyrant like Cromwell would inflict!" and "The curse o' the crows upon you!" which is probably an allusion to the Danish invasion, a raven being the symbol of Denmark; or it may be tantamount to "May you rot on the hills, that the crows may feed upon your carcass!" Perhaps it may thus be understood to imprecate death upon you or some member of your house—alluding to the superstition of rooks hovering over the habitations of the sick, when the malady with which they are afflicted is known to be fatal. Indeed, the latter must certainly be the meaning of it, as is evident from the proverb of "Die, an' give the crow a puddin'."

"Hell's cure to you!" "The divil's luck to you!" "High hanging to you!" "Hard feeding to you!" "A short coorse to you!" are all pretty intense, and generally used under provocation and passion. In these cases the curses just mentioned are directed immediately to the offensive object, and there certainly is no want of the *malus animus* to give them energy. It would be easy to multiply the imprecations belonging to this class among the peasantry, but the task is rather unpleasant.

There are a few, however, which in consequence of their ingenuity we cannot pass over; they are, in sooth, studies for the swearer. "May you never die till you see your own funeral" is a very beautiful specimen of the periphrasis: it simply means, may you be hanged; for he who is hanged is humorously said to be favoured with a view of that sombre spectacle, by which they mean the crowd that attends an execution. To the same purpose is "May you die wid a caper in your heel!" "May you die in your pumps!" "May your last dance be a hornpipe on the air!" These are all emblematic of hanging, and are uttered sometimes in jest, and occasionally in earnest. "May the grass grow before your door!" is highly imaginative and poetical. Nothing, indeed, can present the mind with a stronger or more picturesque emblem of desolation and ruin. Its malignity is terrible.

There are also mock imprecations as well as mock oaths. Of this character are "The divil go with you and sixpence, an' thin you'll want neither money nor company!" This humorous and considerate curse is generally confined to the female sex. When the Irishman happens to be in a romping mood, and teases his sweetheart too much, she usually utters it with a countenance combating with smiles and frowns, whilst she stands in the act of pinning up her dishevelled hair, her cheeks, particularly the one next to the Irishman, deepened into a becoming blush.

"Bad scran to you!" is another form seldom used in anger; it is the same as "Hard feeding to you!" "Bad win' to you!"; as "Ill health to you!" it is nearly the same as "Consumin' [consumption] to you!" Two other imprecations come under this head, which we will class together because they are counterparts of each other, with this difference, that one of them is the most subtly and intensely withering in its purport that can well be conceived. The one is that common curse, "Bad 'cess to you!" that is, bad success to you; we may identify it with "Hard fortune to you!" The other is a keen one indeed—"Sweet bad luck to you!" Now, whether we consider the epithet sweet as bitterly ironical, or deem it as a wish that prosperity may harden the heart to the accomplishment of future damnation, as in the case of Dives, we must in either sense grant that it is an oath of powerful hatred and venom. Occasionally the curse of "Bad luck to you!" produces an admirable retort, which is pretty common. When one man applies it to another, he is answered with "Good luck to you, thin; but may neither of them ever happen!"

"Six eggs to you, an' half a dozen o' them rotten!" like "The divil go with you an' sixpence!" is another of those pleasantries which mostly occur in the good-humoured badinage between the sexes. It implies disappointment.

There is a species of imprecation prevalent among Irishmen which we may term neutral. It is ended by the word bit, and merely results from a habit of swearing where there is no malignity of purpose. An Irishman, when corroborating an assertion, however true or false, will often say, "Bad luck to the bit but it is!" "Divil fire the bit but it's thruth!" "Damn the bit but it is!" and so on. In this form the mind is not moved, nor the passions excited; it is therefore probably the most insipid of all their imprecations.

Some of the most dreadful maledictions are to be heard among the confirmed mendicants of Ireland. The wit, the gall, and the poetry of these are uncommon. "May you melt off the earth like snow off the ditch!" is one of a high order and intense malignity; but it is not exclusively confined to mendicants, although they form that class among which it is most prevalent. Nearly related to this is "May you melt like butter before a summer sun!" These are, indeed, essentially poetical: they present the mind with appropriate imagery, and exhibit a comparison perfectly just and striking.

* * * *

There is a strange opinion to be found in Ireland upon the subject of curses. The peasantry think that a curse, no matter how uttered, will fall on something, but that it depends upon the person against whom it is directed whether or not it will descend on him. A curse, we have heard them say, will rest for seven years in the air, ready to alight upon the head of the person who provoked the malediction. It hovers over him, like a kite over its prey, watching the moment when he may be abandoned by his guardian angel; if this occurs, it shoots with the rapidity of a meteor on his head, and clings to him in the shape of illness, temptation or some other calamity.

They think, however, that the blessing of one person may cancel the curse of another; but this opinion does not affect the theory we have just mentioned. When a man experiences an unpleasant accident they will say, "He has had some poor body's curse"; and, on the contrary, when he narrowly escapes it, they say, "He has had some poor body's blessing."

There is no country in which the phrases of goodwill and affection are so strong as in Ireland. The Irish language actually flows with the milk and honey of love and friendship. Sweet and palatable is it to the other sex, and sweetly can the Irishman, with his deluding ways, administer it to them from the top of his mellifluous tongue, as a dove feeds her young, or as a kind mother her babe, shaping with her own pretty mouth every morsel of the delicate viands before it goes into that of the infant. In this manner does the Irishman, seated behind a ditch, of a bright Sunday, when he ought to be at Mass, feed up some innocent girl, not with "false music," but with sweet words, for nothing more musical or melting than his brogue ever dissolved a female heart. Indeed, it is of the danger to be apprehended from the melody of his voice that the admirable and appropriate proverb speaks; for, when he addresses his sweetheart under circumstances that justify suspicion, it is generally said, "Paddy's feedin' her up wid false music."

What language has a phrase equal in beauty and tenderness to *cushla machree*—the pulse of my heart? Can it be paralleled in the whole range of all that are, ever were, or ever will be spoken, for music, sweetness, and a knowledge of anatomy? If the Irishman is unrivaled at swearing, he fairly throws the world behind him at the blarney. In professing friendship and making love, give him but a taste of the native, and he is a walking honeycomb, that every woman who sees him wishes to have a lick at; and heaven knows that frequently, at all times, and in all places, does he get himself licked on their account.

Another expression of peculiar force is *vick machree*—or, son of my heart. This is not only elegant, but affectionate beyond almost any other phrase except the foregoing. It is, in a sense, somewhat different from that in which the philosophical poet has used it, a beautiful comment upon the sentiment of "the child's the father of the man," uttered by Wordsworth.

We have seen many a youth, on more occasions than one, standing in profound affliction over the dead body of his aged father, exclaiming, *"Ahir, vick machree-vick machree-wuil thu marra wo'um? Wuil thu marra wo'um?"* "Father, son of my heart, son of my heart, art thou dead from me—art thou dead from me?"—an expression, we think, under any circumstances, not to be surpassed in the intensity of domestic affliction which it expresses; but, under those alluded to, we consider it altogether elevated in exquisite and poetic beauty above the most powerful symbols of Oriental imagery.

A third phrase peculiar to love and affection is *Manim astheee hu* —or, "My soul's within you." Every person acquainted with languages knows how much an idiom suffers by a literal translation. How beautiful, then, how tender and powerful, must those short expressions be, uttered, too, with a fervour of manner peculiar to a deeply feeling people, when, even after a literal translation, they carry so much of their tenderness and energy into a language whose genius is cold when compared to the glowing beauty of the Irish.

Mavourneen dheelish, too, is only a short phrase, but coming warm and mellowed from the Irishman's lips into the ear of his *colleen dhas,* it is a perfect spell—a sweet murmur to which the *lenis susurrus* of the Hybla bees is, with all their honey, jarring discord. How tame is "My sweet darling," its literal translation, compared to its soft and lulling intonations. There is a dissolving, entrancing, beguiling, deluding, flattering, insinuating, coaxing, winning, inveigling, roguish, palavering, come-over-ing, comedhering, consenting, blarneying, killing, willing, charm in it, worth all the philtres that ever the gross knavery of a withered alchemist imposed upon the credulity of those who inhabit the other nations of the earth—for we don't read that these shriveled philtre-mongers ever prospered in Ireland.

No, no—let the Irishman alone. If he hates intensely, effectually, and *inquestingly,* he loves intensely, comprehensively, and gallantly. To love with power is a proof of a large soul; and to hate well is, according to the great moralist, a thing in itself to be loved. Ireland is, therefore, through all its sects, parties and religions, an amicable nation. Their affections are indeed so vivid that they scruple not to kill each other with kindness; and we very much fear that the march of love and murder will not only keep pace with, but outstrip, the march of intellect.

Ireland and Scotland Exchange Instruments

We cannot find that the bagpipe was indigenous to the Irish. To the Caledonians, we believe, they must be content to owe it. We got it, as it were, in exchange for the harp. The early history of this instrument is enveloped in the mist that hangs over the Dark Ages. According to Aristides Quintilianus, it prevailed in the very first times in the Highlands of Scotland. The genius of the Highlanders seems to favor this opinion. Ever a warlike people, ardent in the field of battle, and impatient of control in time of peace, the sound of the bagpipe must have been peculiarly grateful to their ear. Hence their hasty adoption of it, on its introduction amongst them by the Romans. A Scottish writer, speaking of this instrument, says, "it is the voice

From *Historical Memoirs of the Irish Bards,* by Joseph C. Walker, pp. 77-78. Printed for the author by Luke White. Dublin. 1786.

of uproar and misrule, and the music calculated for it seems to be that of rude passion." Even in very late times, the Scots used the bagpipe to rouse their courage to battle, to alarm them when secure, and to collect them when scattered; purposes to which they taught the Irish to apply it.

Irish Pipes and Pipers

The Irish pipes of today are the result of an evolution of the military, or marching, pipe, which, as near as I can learn, resembled the present Scotch pipe. Its beginning dated from the latter part of the sixteenth century. History is silent as to the name of the ingenious individual who transformed the pipe from its primeval state into a superior musical instrument, which has been called the "Irish organ" and "the sweetest of all reed instruments."

THE SOFT IRISH PIPES

As comparatively few know the difference between the Scotch and Irish pipes, I will endeavor to describe both. The Irish union pipes is a parlor or social instrument, not louder than a violin. The player must be in a sitting position so that the lower end of the chanter may rest on his knee. The wind is furnished by a bellows held under the right arm and is conveyed by a tube to an airtight leather bag held under the left arm, which controls the pressure of the reeds and quills in the different parts of the pipes. The chanter is the flutelike part, played by the fingers. It has two chromatic octaves and is in musical terms a "C" instrument, the same as a violin or piano—that is, the "A" on the chanter tunes with theirs. It is also supplied with seven keys, giving it full scope for sharps and flats. An accompaniment to the chanter is provided for in what is technically known as the "regulators," a series of twelve keys, which are placed conveniently under the right hand of the player and played with the wrist, thus giving a second violin effect. The whole is harmonized by a set of drones, which consists of three notes, basso, alto, and tenor, tuned to the chanter. These sound one continuous blended note.

As the reconstruction of the Irish pipes was coincident with the

By Thomas Ennis, Chicago Pipers Club, in *The Gael*, February, 1902, pp. 33-38. New York.

period which produced Ireland's sweetest bands, its well-timed conception gave it adaptability and power to reproduce Irish music with all its original flavor unequaled by any other instrument of the present day.

"Swirl" and Drone

The Scotch pipes is a martial instrument, adapted to simple marching tunes. The player may be standing or walking. It is also a reed instrument, the wind is blown by the mouth through a tube which leads to a bag held under the left arm. The pipes are of simple construction, having one chanter and three drones. The chanter has only nine notes altogether and tunes with no other instrument. It is incapable of playing correctly any tune not confined to one octave. Its notes are exceedingly loud and harsh, necessitating a corresponding loudness in the drones, so that the effect, when in close proximity or in the hands of an unskilled player, is extremely unpleasant to the untrained ear. But with all its shortcomings the Scot reveres it, cherishes it, loves it. He has danced his picturesque reels and strathspeys to its music in its native glens. He has marched to victory on many a hard-fought battlefield, spurred on by its thrilling inspiration, and whether in bonnie Scotland or in exile its skirling reverberations are constantly in his ear and he is ever ready to uphold and proclaim it his national instrument.

For more than 200 years the Irish pipes enjoyed uninterrupted popularity. It was the music of rich and poor alike. The "gentry," notably in the province of Connacht, by individual subsidy, patronized it— that is, each had a piper, paid and provided for, attached to his household. This custom is still upheld by some, notably the Duke of Leinster at the magnificent ducal residence, Cartron, near Maynooth. The most brilliant member of this great Geraldine family, the heroic, patriotic, and unfortunate Lord Edward, was a sweet player of the Irish pipes and the set he used is to be seen to this day in the Dublin Museum.

Some Notable Pipers

The best performer of whom we have any record was John Crump, the famous Munster piper, who was considered by James Hardiman the best player in Ireland.

Hardiman had a magnificent set of pipes especially constructed which he presented to Crump.

After the death of Crump the pipes became the property of Paddy Coneely, the famous Galway piper, Paddy, who was totally blind, lived in Galway about sixty years ago, and was a noted character in his day.

The pipes found its devotees even among the clergy and professional men in Ireland, and some among the former were renowned players. Bishop O'Connor, of Limerick, taught Ferguson all he knew about the pipes. When Catherine Hayes visited the United States and Canada, she was accompanied by Ferguson, who played at nearly all her concerts. It was during that celebrated tour that he had the honor of playing the sacred music at Mass in a church in Brooklyn. Carleton, the novelist, tells us of Talbot, who was a celebrity about the latter part of the eighteenth century. He received high honors from the music lovers of London on the occasion of his visit there and was "commanded" to play before the king. He had peculiar notions about his music, as he could not be induced to play for dancing. Carleton quotes him as saying: "My music is for the ears, not for the heels." With the death of Canon Goodman, which occurred about ten years ago, the list, in all probability a long one of "Gentlemen" pipers, passed away. He was an Episcopalian minister, and resided at Skibbereen, in County Cork. The reverend gentleman was not only a professor of the Gaelic language, but a high authority on Irish music and a skilled performer on the Irish pipes as well.

FROM REELS TO WALTZES

There has been much conjecture as to the causes that brought about the decadence of the once popular Irish pipes. Some put the blame on the clergy, who in their zeal for better moral conditions suppressed the time-honored dance gatherings in their respective jurisdictions, not knowing that in so doing they were driving the people from the enlivening reel, jig, and hornpipe of the cross-roads and barn to the enervating and insipid waltz, polka, and two-step of the parlor and public hall. If indiscretions resulted from these dance gatherings of the young people, the piper was seized on by the local pastor as the tempter from whose influence arose all the immorality of the time. Through the enmity of those misdirected but well-meaning conservators of the public morals, the piper became disreputable. His profession was gradually taken up by the blind and those physically incapacitated for hard labor, and in a short time the once honored piper's profession became synonymous with mendicancy.

The great famine of 1847 almost extinguished the last vestige of the people's customs. That calamitous period, when starvation, disease, death, and emigration absorbed the people's minds, and its long aftermath of years of despondency almost obliterated the aspirations, musical and otherwise, of that generation. The succeeding generation was more susceptible to the Anglicizing methods of England's representatives in Ireland. The "snobbery" germ entered the hearts of the people and propagated a race of nondescripts who were neither Irish nor English. Everything Irish became repugnant to them, the pipes, the dances, the language, the music itself, everything was discarded but the "brogue," which, happily, was unshakable, as if stamped on their tongues by Providence as a reminder of their infidelity.

Pilgrims

I think it was in the midsummer of 1832 that I joined a party of the peasantry of my native village who were en route to the "pilgrimage" at St. John's Well, near the town of Kilkenny. The journey (about twenty-five Irish miles) was commenced early in the afternoon, and it was considerably after sunset when we reached our destination. My companions immediately set about the fulfilment of their vows, whilst I, who was but a mere boy, sat on the green grass, tired and in an ill humour, after my long and painful tramp over a hundred stony hills and a thousand rugged fields, under the burning sun of midsummer afternoon. I was utterly unable to perform any act of devotion, nor, I must confess, was I very much disposed to do so, even were I able; so I seated myself quietly amid the groups of beggars, cripples, "dark people," and the other various classes of pilgrims who thronged around the sacred fountain.

Among the crowd I had marked two pilgrims, who, from the moment I saw them, arrested my particular attention. One of these was an aged female, decently clad—the other was a very fine young girl, dressed in a gown, shawl, and bonnet of faded black satin. The girl was of a tall and noble figure—strikingly beautiful but stone-blind. I learned that they were natives of the County Wexford; that the girl had lost her sight in brain fever, in her childhood; that all human means had been tried for her cure, but in vain; and that now, as a last resource, they had traveled all the way to pray at the shrine of St. John, and bathe her sightless orbs in the healing waters of his well. It is believed

Written by John Keegan as a preface to his poem "The Dark Girl by the Holy Well," in *Irish Literature*, edited by Justin McCarthy, Vol. V, pp. 1766-1767. De Bower Elliot Co. Chicago. 1904.

that when Heaven wills the performance of cures, the sky opens above the well, at the hour of midnight, and Christ, the Virgin Mother, and St. John descend in the form of three snow-whites, and descend with the rapidity of lightning into the depths of the fountain. No person but those destined to be cured can see this miraculous phenomenon, but everybody can hear the musical sound of their wings as they rush into the well and agitate the waters. I cannot describe how sad I felt myself, too, at the poor girl's anguish, for I had almost arrived at the hope that, though another miracle was never wrought at St. John's Well, Heaven would relent on this occasion and restore the sweet Wexford girl to her long-lost sight. She returned, however, as she came, a "dark girl," and I heard afterwards that she took ill and died before she reached home.

The Ploughman

The peasant's name was Donovan, but he was universally known as Mat the Thrasher. He excelled in all kinds of work as a farm labourer, and never met his match at wielding a flail. As a consequence, he was in great request among farmers from October to March; and, indeed, during all the year round—for Mat could turn a hand almost to anything, from soling a pair of brogues to roofing and thatching a barn. His superiority as a ploughman was never questioned. As a proof of his skill in this line, we may mention that when Maurice Kearney was about running what in Ireland is called a "ditch" through the centre of his "kiln field," the difficulty presented itself—how to make the fence perfectly straight. And, as a matter of course, Mat Donovan was immediately sent for.

"Now," said Mat, after looking at the ground, "where do you want to run it?"

"From this bush," his employer replied, laying his walking-stick on a whitethorn bush in the fence, "to the ash-tree at the left side of the gap," pointing to a tree at the opposite side of the field. "In a straight line," he added, looking at Mat as if the problem were worthy to be grappled with even by his genius.

Mat walked away without uttering a word, leaving Mr. Kearney and the half dozen workmen, who, leaning on their spades, were waiting

. From *Knocknagow, or The Homes of Tipperary*, by Charles J. Kickham, pp. 23-24. James Duffy & Co., Ltd. Dublin. 1887.

the order to begin at the construction of the new ditch, but altogether unable to conjecture how he intended to proceed; but with unshaken faith in his ultimate success.

Mat walked leisurely back to the "gurteen" where he had been at work, and was soon seen coming through the gap near the ash-tree with his plough and horses. With one huge hand he leant on the handle of the plough, thereby lifting the irons, so that they might glide over the ground without cutting through it, till he came to the ash-tree. Facing his horses towards the whitehorn bush at the opposite side of the field, he fixed his eye steadily on that object.

Mr. Kearney and his workmen heard his "Yo-up!" to the horses, and on he came, nearer and nearer, slow but sure, till they could catch the air of the song which he commenced to chant with as great a solemnity of look and intonation as if its accurate rendering were a necessary condition of the success of his undertaking. They soon had the benefit even of the words, and as Mat pulled his horses to one side as their breasts touched the whitehorn bush, he continued while he reined them in:

> Oh, had I the lamp of Aladdin,
> And had I his geni also,
> I'd rather live poor on the mountain,
> With colleen dheas cruiteen namo.
> [With a pretty girl milking her cow.]

"There it is for you," he exclaimed, as he folded his arms, after flinging down the reins, "as straight as the split in the poll of a peeler."

Some readers may, perhaps, require an explanation of Mat's allusion to "the split of a peeler's poll." The fact is, that respectable force now known as the Royal Irish Constabulary have always been noted for the extreme care bestowed by them on the hair of their heads. At the time of which we write, a "crease" down the back of the head was one of the distinguishing marks of a policeman in country districts, and to such a perfection had the "force" attained in the matter of this crease, that Mat the Thrasher could find nothing in art or nature capable of conveying a just idea of straightness of the line he had marked out but "the split in a peeler's poll."

Luck's Way in the Morning

"Well," says the poet, throwing himself down on a tussoc, "isn't it a pity for you to be cutting turf on such a hot day? Sit down a bit, the day is long and it'll be cool in the afternoon."

I didn't care much for what he had to say, but I was rather shy of refusing to sit down with him. Besides, I knew that if the poet had anything against me, he would make a satire on me that would be very unpleasant, especially as I was just about coming out in the world. So I sat down beside him.

"Now," says the poet, "perhaps you haven't got the first poem ever I made. 'The Blackfaced Sheep,' that was my first, and I had good reason for making it as far as provocation goes."

Would you believe it—he started to recite every word of it, lying there stretched out on the flat of his back! There was a hummock of soft heather under him, and the scorching heat of the sun was flaming down from the cloudless, deep blue sky over our heads, toasting the side of the poet that was uppermost.

I praised the poem to the skies, though it was vexing me sorely from another point of view—keeping me back from the profitable work that I had promised myself that morning should be done. The poet had put a stop to that with his babbling.

"The poem will be lost," says he, "if somebody doesn't pick it up. Have you anything in your pocket that you could write it down with?"

If a man isn't in luck's way in the morning and God's favour with him, the poor wretch can't hope to do much.

Service in Scotland

When I was sixteen years old I went to Scotland with a crowd, of whom Charlie, Jimmie and I were about the same age. We walked from Cleendra to Letterkenny, a distance of thirty-six miles, and

From *The Islandman*, by Tomás O'Crohan, translated from the Irish, with an Introduction, by Robin Flower, pp. 115-116. Chatto & Windus. London. 1934. The Clarendon Press. Oxford. 1951.

From *Paddy the Cope*, an Autobiography, by Patrick Gallegher, with an Introduction by Dorothy Canfield Fisher, pp. 16-25. Copyright, 1942, by the Devin-Adair Co. New York.

trained from Letterkenny to Derry on the Londonderry and Lough
Swilly Railway, built a few years previously. We arrived at Derry in
good time for the Glasgow boat. I paid four shillings for my ticket.
I suppose we were in the same steerage compartment in which my
father often travelled. In any case the cattle and pigs were in the
same flat. There was a bench or seat along the side of the ship, not
enough sitting room for all the women and men in the compartment.
There was no lavatory. (If it came hard on you, you had to go in
among the cattle.) It was a bit tough on the big women, as there was
not much room. We landed at the Broomielaw at about 12 noon on
the following day, and broke up into squads. The squad I was with
(six of us in all) went to Queen's Street Station, and took our tickets
for Jadeborough, Roxboroughshire, and as far as I can remember
the ticket was six shillings and sixpence. We reached Jadeborough late
that night, and got lodgings in Muldoon's Model, fourpence each for
a bed. John Biddy and Hughdie Micky collected one shilling from
each of us for the supper and breakfast. They went out to a small shop
and got bread, bacon, tea, sugar and milk, the whole lot coming to
four shillings and a halfpenny. I remember the price because we
divided the change, fourpence each for five, threepence halfpenny for
the sixth, and cast lots. John Biddy got the threepence halfpenny.

Next morning we went out amongst the farmers looking for work.
We had no luck. All of us had a few shillings left, but there were no
shops on our travels. When we began to get hungry, Frank Pat led
the way to Stevenson's farm to cadge food. Frank and John knocked
at the kitchen door. Mr. Stevenson asked them what they wanted.
They said that they were looking for work. "Come out in the morning
if it is dry and I will start you two. Are you hungry?" They said that
they were a little hungry. He went into the house and the girl came
out with a big basket of pieces of bread and a fine can of skim milk
with a big ladle stuck in it. She told us that we could go over the field
and that when we were finished to bring back the basket, can and ladle.
We went into the field, sat on our bundles and had a great feed. We
brought back the dinner set. The steward came to us and asked what
two did Mr. Stevenson engage. Frank and John made a fast rush to
him, taking off their caps. Frank said, "It is me and him, sir."

"Well, come with me and I will show you your bothey," said the
steward.

We four that were left travelled on, calling on other farmers, but
failed to get employment. As it was getting dark we went to a farmhouse. Hughdie knocked at the door. A middle-aged lady opened it and
asked what did we want at that hour of the night. Hughdie said that

we were looking for work. She said that the master was not at home but she did not think he wanted any Irishmen. "Are you hungry?" she said.

Hughdie said, "Middling."

"Wait a minute," she said. She and a girl came back again with a bucketful of scraps of bread, a large jug of milk, and a cup. We ate a bellyful and were well satisfied. Hughdie and I went back to the door with the bucket, the jug and the cup. Hughdie knocked again at the door and the same lady opened it. He handed her the utensils and said, "Thank you, lady. May God bless you. Maybe you would let us sleep in the barn for the night. We are very tired and none of us smoke." (This was a lie, as he smoked himself and so did Manus Johnny, but they did not smoke that night until all the lights in the farmhouse were out.) "Well, you can sleep in the barn if none of you smoke," she said. We went into the barn, and made ourselves comfortable, and we were feeling happy. Charlie sang "The Banks of Clady," Manus sang, "The Bonnie, Bonnie Banks of Loch Lomond," and I told a story about Oisin and after that we said the Rosary. There was plenty of straw to put under and over us, and we had a good sleep.

Next morning we were off again. Hughdie and Manus got work at the first farm we came to. I think if Charlie and I were a bit stronger the farmer would have started us. Hughdie told the master that the two boys were hungry, and he went into the house. When he came out again he looked at us, and said, "We have nothing to give you, but if you like to wait the porridge will soon be ready." We were glad to wait and get a fine feed of porridge and milk. Hughdie and Manus were real sorry for us. They did not know what would happen to us, and they said if we did not get work to come back to them that night. Each of them gave us a shilling, and they had very few shillings left. We walked on over a big moor, but we could see no farmhouse, and one said to the other, "We are astray," and we got frightened. There was a mist rising on the moor and we decided to turn back to Manus and Hughdie, but no matter how far we travelled we could not get out of the moor. As it was getting dark, we came across a cart-track, we knew it would lead us somewhere. We happened to follow it in the right direction. We were very hungry, tired, and downhearted. We lay down, and put our bundles under our heads: there was no cold and the heather was warm. Charlie said to me, "We forgot to say our prayers." We went on our knees, and when we had our prayers said a sharp breeze arose, and the night got colder. Charlie said, "Paddy, look at the light!" I looked in the direction Charlie was pointing, and

I thought the light was coming towards us. I concluded that it was
some of the fairies we left at home in the glen in Cleendra, and I felt
delighted. I said, "Charlie, the wee princes of Cleendra to our aid are
advancing."

"Ay, you bloody fool," said Charlie, "you know damn well no fairies
would live in Scotland. Look again, the light is not moving; it is a
house." I did not think so. Charlie put his bundle on his shoulder
and he said to me, "If you do not come, you can stay. I am going to
that house anyway," and off he went. I was not long in following him.
It was a house all right, and when we were within ten yards of it the
light went out. Heavy drops of rain were falling. We decided that our
best plan would be not to knock, but try and get into some of the out-
houses until morning. After a while searching, we got into one of the
byres where there were no animals, but there was plenty of hay. The
wind was still increasing, and then came the lightning and thunder,
and soon the rain was coming down in bucketfuls, but we were so
fagged out we were soon fast asleep.

It must have been near one o'clock the next day when I awoke. It
was still raining, and I shook up Charlie. I had a sore head, and was
very hungry. Charlie was just as bad. Nobody about the farmhouse
knew we had slept there all night, and we picked up courage and went
to the door. I knocked, but no answer. We then went around to the
back of the house, and met an old man with a long beard, and as
many patches on his trousers as you would see on any old man at
home. He looked at us, and we looked at him. "What are you laddies
doing here?" he said. Charlie answered, "We are looking for the
master to see if he would give us work."

"I am Sam Douglas, master of the Crow's Farm; always was, and
always will be," he said. "I have a field of turnips ready for singling.
Can any of you lads single?"

We both said that we could. We had been practising with small rows
of stones before we left home.

Hughdie spent a week training us to knock four stones off the top
of a drill and leave the next in its bed without touching it. The day
before we left for Scotland we were carefully examined by our fathers,
Hughdie and the others. We satisfied the examiners, who told us it
would be no shame for us to say we could single turnips. The other
four in our squad were in Scotland often before. Charlie and I were
the only new hands in the squad.

The master told us we could start in the morning. "I will give each
of you seven bob a week until the harvest if you are worth it; if not, off
you go," he said. "I have no blankets until I get into Kelso next

market day, and if you are worth the money I will get a new blanket
for you. You can sleep over the horses, and I will give you plenty of
bags to get into. It will not be always raining and blowing like this.
Oh! does either of you lads smoke?"

We said, "No," which was the truth.

He then had another look at us, and said, "It is wonderful how
you Irishmen can always find Mr. Douglas' farm. How did you come?
I did not see you coming up the road, and you are as dry as a pin-
cushion."

One waited for the other to answer. I thought Charlie should answer because he was older than I.

The old man spoke again. "Did you no hear what I asked ye? What
road did ye come, and how is it you are so dry? It is raining since
Jane and I went to bed last night."

I was still waiting for Charlie to answer, but he never spoke. Then
I said, "We got lost on the moor last night, and we saw your light
and made for it. As we were coming to the door the light went out,
and when we saw the lightning and heard the thunder and then the
rain, we got frightened, and we went into the byre, where we were
sleeping until a wee while ago."

"Well, well, I dinna think I can blame ye: under the same circumstances I might hev done the same thing meself. One never kens what
he will do when he hes tae dae it. Get into the barn yonder, or ye'll
get wet. I am wet now standing talking to ye. When Jane has the
dinner ready, Mary will gie ye a call, and one of ye will come doon
for it."

Off we went to the barn. Although we were wet we were quite
happy knowing that we were going to work in the morning. We were
not very long in the barn until we heard the shout: "Paddies, let one
of you come down to the kitchen for your dinners."

Charlie insisted that I should go. He always bossed me. When I
went to the kitchen door I heard somebody say, "Come in," and in I
went. There were two women in the kitchen, one of them was as ugly
as sin, about twenty-five years of age, with a bit of a moustache, and
a tuft of long hairs growing out of her chin. Her eyes were as red as
herrings that would be going sick.

Sam, in addition to being an old man, was no beauty. God knows, I
immediately felt sorry for him. I thought it must be a bit tough to
sleep with such an ugly-looking woman. The other was a very nice girl.
She spoke first, and said, pointing to the table where there were two
small loaves of bread and a jug of milk, "This is your dinner, laddie;
take it up to the barn, and when you are finished bring the jug back

to Mary." When I went up to Charlie I told him about the ugly woman, whom I thought was Sam's wife, and the nice servant girl. Charlie said, "I am glad I did not go down. I have a weak stomach, and an ugly sight like that would put me off my meat."

We finished the dinner, and I went back to Mary with the jug. I came back to Charlie and told him I met Mary at the door and gave her the jug: I thought she was more ugly now than when I saw her at first. Then Charlie said, "Mary is not Sam's wife; sure he said it was raining since Jane and himself went to bed last night, and Jane must be Sam's wife."

"Well," I said, "my goodness, if that nice woman is Sam's wife I am damn sorry for her. Charlie! wait until you see her. She is the most handsome girl I have ever seen. She has lovely golden hair, blue eyes, and her skin is as white as the lilies we used to get on the lough at home, and she has beautiful teeth. She has as good a figure as your sister Nellie. She is beautiful."

It rained all that day. We stayed in the barn. We saw two other men and a lump of a boy going about the yard, feeding the horses and doing other things. We got to know afterwards that they were employed all the year round by Sam. They were called hinds, and the boy was the flunkey that did handy jobs about the house.

About seven o'clock we heard Mary again calling, "Paddies, your porridge is ready." Charlie ordered me to go for the porridge. I went to the kitchen door, and ugly Mary gave me a flat dish of porridge with a small well of skim milk right in the centre and two horn spoons stuck in the porridge. I carried the dish most carefully to the barn lest I should spill the milk. As soon as I entered the barn I said, "She is worse-looking every time I see her."

Charlie said, "For God's sake do not talk of that woman again until I get my supper."

I did not say another word about her that night. I lifted the dish and spoon and went back to the kitchen with them. There was no person to be seen. I left them on the table and turned to walk out when a door opened at the side and Jane stepped out. I looked at her. I think I must have watched her for about a minute or two. As I was going out she said to me, "Did you get enough supper?" I do not remember what answer I made, as I know I got very excited, but I certainly must have told her that we had enough as there was some porridge left in the dish. She then said, "Wait a minute." She went through the same door from the kitchen and came back in a second or two, handed me a small parcel and said, "Put that in your pocket; do not open it until you go to the barn; do not let Mary, the servant, see it; do not tell the hinds or anyone else I gave it to you."

When I went back to the barn I opened the paper and in it were two nice cuts of bread and two slices of beef. We did not taste it until we thought it was bed-time. We then had a nice feed. Our clothes were dry and we were quite happy. We had plenty of straw to make a good bed. Each of us got two sacks, put one into the other, said our prayers and slipped into the sacks. Charlie sang, "Come Back to Erin'; I commenced to tell a story, but before I was half-way through we were both asleep, and slept as sound as two dogs until we were called by one of the hinds about half-past five in the morning.

When we came to the street, the hind whose name was Robert handed each of us a hoe and asked us to follow him. He took the first drill, Charlie the second and I the third. Charlie could easily single as much as Robert, but it was a hard struggle for me to keep up. At eight o'clock the "flunkey" came to us with coffee and bread. The day was good and we sat at the top of the field while taking our breakfast. The we singled again until twelve noon, when we got an hour for dinner, which consisted of a small loaf and a bottle of beer. Charlie and I tasted the beer. Oh! it was bitter. We spat it out. Robert was delighted. He was not long slugging our beer as well as his own. After dinner Robert slowed down. He did not go half as fast as in the morning. We stopped work about six o'clock, and got a fine dish of porridge and skim milk.

A Boy Wins the Farmers' Race

"Where's your father?" Mr. Murray asked me one morning when I was hitching up Charlie.

"He's out tending the sheep," I told him.

"Well, then," said Mr. Murray, "I'd like to have you drive me into the town of Roscommon. What do you say, shall we take Charlie?"

"I'd be glad to, Mr. Murray," I said. That's the least I could do after him giving our horse the free grass.

Now Charlie was used to common carts, but never before had he been in a side-car. I was scared for what he might do, but he paid no

From *And That's No Lie*, by Beatrice Bill Talbot, pp. 44-52. Copyright, 1946, by Houghton, Mifflin & Co. Boston.

attention when I put Mr. Murray's harness on him, and when he felt the side-car behind him, Charlie thought it was a baby carriage after the big loads he'd been hauling.

It was twelve mile to the town of Roscommon, and Charlie drove fine. Starting back, Mr. Murray said, "Johnny, stop a minute. I see my friend, Mr. O'Connor. Maybe he'd like a ride home."

So Mr. O'Connor got in the side-car. He was a man who owned a great many horses, a man I'd often seen, a millionaire, but what we called an "everyday" man, for he liked the poor as well as the rich. I'll tell you what his business was. Did you ever see those white clay pipes? Well, he had a factory for making them. I don't see how they did it, but they was made, anyhow.

Mr. O'Connor lived in Knockeroghery, which was about halfway between the towns of Roscommon and Athlone. We hadn't gone very far when he said to Mr. Murray, "Where did you get your horse?"

"He isn't mine," Mr. Murray told him. "This is my herder Patsy Linehan's horse and it's his boy that's driving him."

"Well," say Mr. O'Connor, "that horse is a beautiful stepper."

A few minutes later, we heard someone coming at a good clip down the road behind us. Mr. O'Connor turned around to find out who it was.

"Look," he cried, "see who's coming. If it isn't Mr. Gubbins driving his trotter!"

That was the gentleman's name, but my father would have said, "Here comes 'Splatter the Beggars,' " for that's what the farmers called him. Now Mr. Gubbins wasn't a hair better than me. When they was boys his father and my father worked together in the fields, but he'd made millions, that was the differ, and now he was independent and thought he was above everyone. Mr. Gubbins didn't care who it was or who it wasn't, he'd always take the road just like an automobile. He'd never stop for no man, no woman, no one. Why, he wouldn't give the road to the King of England if he could take it from him. You know how the poor has to walk to church on a Sunday? Well, when they see Mr. Gubbins coming, they'd hurry to get off the road, for he never avoided a puddle. Small wonder they called him "Splatter the Beggars."

The nearer Mr. Gubbins was to us, the more excited Mr. O'Connor got.

"Boy," he yelled at me, "shut him off, shut him off!"

So, of course, I pulled Charlie across the road.

"What's up?" called out "Splatter the Beggars" when he finds himself stopped by our side-car. "What's up?"

"Will you take a fair trotting bet from here to Knockeroghery?" Mr. O'Connor asked him.

"Yes," says "Splatter the Beggars," "I'll take any bet that you want." For well he knew that he had the best trotter in the Parish of Kiltoon, and 'twas easy to see that Charlie was a young horse and me a green boy.

"The bet is twenty-five pounds on the first horse that reaches my avenue without breaking his trot," said Mr. O'Connor, "and I'm riding with Johnny."

Then Mr. Murray speaks up, "Wait a minute," he said, "Johnny here is only a boy, and his father is poor. This horse of his is no more than a four-year-old and he's never raced before. It's all of six mile to Knockeroghery, and the horse might drop dead before he ever got there."

"I don't care," says Mr. O'Connor; "if anything happens to the horse, I'll pay this boy's father more than he is worth."

So the bet was made, but Mr. Murray was not in it, for he was riding with Mr. Gubbins.

I knew the race would be won by the longest stepping horse and the quickest, and that did Charlie get a good start he'd have the advantage. Roads is narrow in County Roscommon, so we had to find a place wide enough for the two side-cars to start side by each. Finally we was off with hardly the width of a thumb between the two hubs. I hadn't to touch Charlie with the whip to have him keep pegging his feet, but just tighten the reins, and the more I tightened them the more Charlie would depend on me. A horse you know depends on you same as you depend on him.

I never looked nowhere but straight down the road, and when I see it begin to narrow, I pulled on the reins, and if ever you see Charlie peg those legs! He took the lead. He done wonderful, 'twas music to hear "Splatter the Beggars" pounding behind us.

"We're gaining, Johnny, we're gaining," whispered Mr. O'Connor, but I never looked nowhere but straight ahead and just kept praying that Charlie would keep going and not break his trot.

You'll think it a lie, but as sure as the sky is over your head, when we turned in Mr. O'Connor's driveaway, "Splatter the Beggars" wasn't even in sight!

"Honest to God, Charlie is a beauty!" cried Mr. O'Connor, and he grabbed my hand and shook it. "You done fine, Johnny—just fine; now you can go home and tell your father what a wonderful trotter he has."

When we got in the stable yard, Mr. O'Connor said to his groom,

"This horse is in a terrible heat, walk him around until he cools off, then rub him down well." And all the time I just stood there watching them. When "Splatter the Beggars" come trotting in, one of the stable boys took his horse and everybody shook everybody's hand except Mr. Gubbins, he didn't shake mine. Then the three gentlemen walked toward Mr. O'Connor's house for to get their supper. Just before they got out of sight, Mr. O'Connor turned round, "Come on, Johnny," he called, "you come, too."

"No, thank you, sir," I said, for I'd sooner go into the kitchen and make jokes with my own sort. But they dragged me in with them.

I think it was a good-sized dining room, but I can't remember it well. I was only a lad of fifteen and there have been so many ups and downs since then to put things out of my mind. I know I sat at a long table and done the best I could to handle the knives and forks, but I never said a word except that they asked me a question.

"Johnny, who'd you get your horse by?" Mr. O'Connor wanted to know.

"By Charles, the runaway stud horse," I told him.

Then Mr. Murray told them all about Fannie, our brood mare, and how she was half hunter and half draft.

And after that up jumps Mr. O'Connor with a glass of wine in his hand. "Gentlemen," he says, "here's to Charlie, the four-year-old, and I think the betting money should go to the boy that drove him." And didn't he give me the twenty-five pounds!

"My father will be after thanking you himself," I said. I didn't know what else to say.

"Say, Johnny," says Mr. O'Connor, "there's going to be a farmers' race down here in a little while. Wouldn't you like to have Charlie run in it?"

"Oh," I says, "I couldn't tell. You'd have to ask my father. The horse doesn't really belong to me."

"Well," says Mr. O'Connor, "you tell your father there's going to be a prize of twenty-five pounds for winning the race, besides a brand-new set of farm harness that is worth, I should say, between forty and fifty pounds."

"Ah, yes," speaks up "Splatter the Beggars," "I have one of my horses entered for that farmers' race."

"Then, maybe," Mr. O'Connor says to him, "maybe you'll get at that race what you got this afternoon." Then all the gentlemen laughed; they was having a good time same as anyone would.

When Mr. Murray and I was leaving, Mr. O'Connor come out with us. He stood with one of his feet on the steps of our side-car. "Johnny,"

he says, "now don't forget, you ask your father if Charlie can go in
the farmers' race. Tell him if he agrees I'll take the horse and feed
him and train him."

"If you do that, Mr. O'Connor," I says, "on the day of the race will
I be riding him?"

"No, Johnny," he said, "I'm afraid you are too young."

"I'll die if I don't ride him," I made so bold as to tell him.

"Have you ever taken a jump?" Mr. O'Connor then asked me.

"No, sir," I said, "and neither did Charlie."

"Have you ever ridden on a saddle?"

"No, sir," I tells him, "but I never see a horse that could take me
off without a saddle."

"Well, then," Mr. O'Connor said, "I'll pay your carfare and you
come down here as often as you can and learn the jumps and we'll try
you out."

When I got home, I told my father about driving Mr. Murray to the
town of Roscommon.

"Did Charlie do all right?" asks my father.

"Yes," I says, "he done better than that."

So I tell him about how he beat the trotting horse belonging to
"Splatter the Beggars," but I didn't say anything about the betting
money.

"I'm pleased that he won," said my father, "but it's easy for a young
horse to get hurt in a race, and I'm glad nothing happened to Charlie."

So then I shows him the twenty-five pounds Mr. O'Connor gave me.
After counting the money, my father says, "You done fine by us,
Johnny."

"Now we can pay the store what we owe them," and he hands me
money to my mother. She counted it twice and kept saying, "I'm glad
nothing happened to Charlie," then she got up and put it in the teapot
on the top shelf of the dresser.

So then I put it up to my parents how Mr. O'Connor wanted to have
Charlie run in the farmers' race. I told them all about the prizes, even
so they didn't like the idea. My father wasn't quite so agin it as my
mother, for he knew what a good horse Charlie was. Still he said, "No,
I'll not be letting Mr. O'Connor have the horse to learn to jump stone
walls. Supposing something happened to Charlie!"

I felt awful bad, but what could I say? For, believe me, the old
people in Ireland wouldn't take any back talk from their children.
Mr. Murray, he felt bad too, when he found out Charlie wasn't going
in the farmers' race. He tried to talk my father into it. "Johnny might
come in third or fourth and get some money," he said, but my father

said, "No, I'm afeared the horse will get hurt." He was twice as worried about Charlie as he was about me.

Now Mr. Murray had an old horse that he thought the world of. He was a relative of our horse and his name was Charlie too. I guess they was stepbrothers or something; anyway, it was the same as if a man got married the second time.

"Patsy," Mr. Murray says to my father, "your Charlie reminds me of when my old horse was in his prime, and 'twould tickle me to see another Charlie in a race."

So finally my father said "Yes," and the next day one of Mr. O'Connor's men come and took Charlie, and I cut across the fields to the station at Kiltoon, and caught the two-o'clock train to Knockeroghery. I stayed there two hours, and one of the grooms started to learn me to ride and jump with the saddle on Charlie. Mr. O'Connor was watching us, but he didn't say nothing; but, after I had gone there four or five times, he said, "Johnny, you'll do." So then I was happy. But when I was alone with them, I suffered a lot with my parents. They didn't like me going off to Knockeroghery. They missed me and the work Charlie and I did on the farm. You know how it was; besides, they was old-fashioned people and they thought I might kill the horse.

Now "Splatter the Beggars" was a clever one. When he found I was going to ride Charlie in the farmers' race, didn't he take out the work-horse he had entered and put in Jack-the-Ripper, a well-known hunter in them parts, and a horse to be afraid of! 'Twas easy to see that "Splatter the Beggars" wanted to get back at me.

When Patsy, my father, heard about this, he got ugly; he said he wasn't going to have a farm horse break his neck trying to beat a thoroughbred. He said I couldn't go to Knockeroghery no more. My heart was broke. I didn't care about living if I couldn't go in the farmers' race, so, when my father wasn't looking, I ran to the station. It took all the spunk I'd got, but I had to ride Charlie! I was afeared of my life when I got home that evening, but all my father said was, "Is Charlie jumping well?"

At last the day of the race come. It was held on some farm land on Mr. O'Connor's estate, and just white stones was let down in the fields to show us where to go, and there was nineteen walls for us riders to jump. The crowd stood on a little hillside where they could see most of the race and at the foot of it was a low wooden grandstand just big enough for the judges to sit on. I wouldn't want to be telling you a lie or anthing, but I'm sure over a thousand people came to that race. Maybe they'd walk three Irish mile or it might be five cross-cutting through the fields they come. Hundreds of them had never seen me before and never seen me since; they was interested in other riders and other horses, but Mr. Murray and Miss Georgina and all the Parish of Kiltoon was there—every one of them, girls and all. Everybody that knew us went but my mother. Old women in Ireland are funny; she got the feeling I was going to be killed, so she couldn't bear to see the race.

There were fourteen entries and all of them farm horses except the one belonging to "Splatter the Beggars," and I was in fears of that horse. Mr. Gubbins had a man named Dexter to ride his hunter, Jack-the-Ripper. He was older than me and was out to win, no matter what.

Charlie and me got a good start; so did Dexter and Jack-the-Ripper. From the first we kept close together and one would be clearing the stone wall as the other approached it, and I could tell by the shouts of the crowd that soon the race was between us. We was what you call neck and neck—tearing along we was, past eighteen jumps with just one stone wall left to get over. As we came close to it, Dexter came nearer to me and quick-like he give me the foot to knock the stirrup off of me, but his trickery didn't do him no good, for I never left the saddle. God was good. Charlie leaped ahead. He run like a rabbit and won by a head. So I beat "Splatter the Beggars" twice with the same horse.

And if ever you heard the cheering and clapping of hands, for of course no one really thought I had any chance when Jack-the-Ripper was put in the race, and wasn't Charlie the big shot!

Mr. O'Connor came running up to us. "I knew that horse was a winner!" he cried. "I want to buy Charlie!" And right then and there he told my father he'd give him sixty pounds for the horse, and Patsy, my father, said, "Thank you, Mr. O'Connor, the money will come in mighty handy."

Now I suppose it looks bad for me to be telling you all that Charlie brought us. There was twenty-five pounds for the trotting race, and twenty-five pounds more for the farmers' race, then the sixty pounds Mr. O'Connor paid to my father, that's one hundred and ten, besides the new harness.

That money gave my parents a fresh start in life; it paid all their debts, and they was put in a way to live comfortable. But when I hear Mr. O'Connor say to one of his grooms, "Put Charlie in the stable, he is my horse now," I felt awful bad. Over there, when you're fond of an animal, it's like parting with one of your children. First you see them most every hour of every day—then you have to go on living without them.

Throwing the Sledge Hammer

Barney soon appeared with the sledge upon his shoulder, and Mat Donovan, after balancing it in his mind, laid it at Captain French's feet.

The captain stripped with the look of a man sure to win, and handed his coat and vest to his servant. A murmur, partly of admiration and partly of anxiety for the result of the contest, arose from the crowd of men, women, and children around, as he bared his arms; for compared with them Mat Donovan's appeared almost slight and attenuated.

"I never saw the like of him," someone was heard to exclaim in a low, solemn tone, but which was distinctly audible in the dead silence.

He took the heavy sledge, and placing his foot to the mark, swung it backwards and forwards twice, and then wheeling rapidly full round, brought his foot to the mark again, and, flying from his arm as from a catapult, the sledge sailed through the air, and fell at a distance that seemed to startle many of the spectators.

It was then brought back and handed to Mat Donovan, who took it with a quiet smile that somewhat reassured his friends. Mat threw the sledge some three feet beyond the captain's mark, and many of those round drew a long breath of relief; but there was no applause.

But the captain's next throw was fully six feet beyond Mat Donovan's, and several of his father's tenants and retainers cried, "More power, Captain!"

Mat Donovan, however, cleared the best mark again by three feet. The captain now grasped the sledge, clenching his teeth, and looking so fierce and tigerlike, his eyes flashing from under his knitted brows, that the women at the front of the crowd involuntarily pressed back, appalled. With every muscle strained to the utmost, he hurled the huge sledge from him, falling forward on his hands; and as the iron ploughed up the green sward far beyond Mat Donovan's throw, the shout of the captain's partisans were drowned by something like a cry of pain from the majority of the spectators.

"Begor, Captain," said Mat Donovan, surveying his adversary with a look of thoroughly genuine admiration, "you're good!"

From *Knocknagow, or The Homes of Tipperary*, by Charles J. Kickham, pp. 460-462. James Duffy & Co., Ltd. Dublin. 1887.

Taking his place again at the stand, he laid down the sledge, and, folding his arms, fell into deep thought. Many a tear-dimmed eye was fixed upon him, for all imagined he was beaten.

"His heart'll break," Bessy Morris heard a girl near her murmur.

"The captain is a good fellow," thought Mat Donovan, "an' I'd like to lave him the majority—if I could do it honorable."

He looked at the anxious faces around him; he looked at Bessy Morris; but still he was undecided. Someone struck the big drum a single blow, as if by accident, and, turning round quickly, the thatched roofs of the hamlet caught his eye. And, strange to say, those old mud walls and thatched roofs roused him as nothing else could. His breast heaved, as, with glistening eyes, and that soft plaintive smile of his, he uttered the words, "For the credit of the little village!" in a tone of the deepest tenderness. Then, grasping the sledge in his right hand, and drawing himslf up to his full height, he measured the captain's cast with his eye. The muscles of his arms seemed to start out like cords of steel as he wheeled slowly round and shot the ponderous hammer through the air.

His eyes dilated, as, with quivering nostrils, he watched its flight, till it fell so far beyond the best mark that even he himself started with astonishment. Then a shout of exultation burst from the excited throng; his hands were convulsively grasped, and hats sent flying in the air; and in that wild joy they crushed around him and tried to lift him upon their shoulders.

"O boys, boys," he remonstrated, "be 'asy. Sure 'tisn't the first time ye saw me throw a sledge. Don't do anything that might offend the captain afther comin' here among us to show ye a little diversion."

The remonstrance had the desired affect, and the people drew back and broke up into groups to discuss the event more calmly. But Mat's eye lighted with pride when he saw Miss Kearney upon the fence with her handkerchief fluttering in the breeze above her head, and Hugh waving his hat by her side. Even the ladies in the phaeton caught the enthusiasm and displayed their handkerchiefs; while Grace ran to the doctor and got him to lift her up in his arms in order that she might have a better view.

"Donovan," said Captain French, "your match is not in Europe. I was never beaten before."

"Well, it took a Tipperary man to beat you, Captain," returned Mat Donovan.

"That's some consolation," said the captain. "I'm a Tipperary boy myself, and I'm glad you reminded me of it."

These Dogs Are Older than History

The history of the Irish wolfhound is the history of the dogs of Ireland, for while Irish dogs have made history, history in her turn has made the Irish wolfhound.

Hunting and fighting filled the life of the early Irish, and master and hound alike excelled on the hunting ground and in the battlefield. The dogs were fed on the flesh of the red deer, the stag and the boar, and they slept on their master's bed on the skins of the wild animals they had brought to bay.

White seems to have been a favourite colour for the Irish wolfhound of the heroic age, but we have proof that dogs and horses were dyed. Blue evidently was the height of fashion for dogs' coats, but we also read about white horses and dogs with purple ears.

The dogs reproduced in early Irish art were obviously of the large hound type. We are, however, left in doubt as to whether these illustrations show rough or smooth-coated dogs; but it stands to reason that dogs exposed to the hardships of the chase, the adversity of the weather and the attacks of wild beasts are more inclined to grow a shaggy protective coat than the hounds of sunny Greece and Rome.

The gigantic size of these hounds, combined with their swiftness and courage, brought forth admiring comments from anyone who saw them. In 1571 the Blessed Edmund Campion, S.J., in his *Historie of Ireland,* describes the Irish greyhounds as higher of bone and limb than a colt.

Comparisons were constantly drawn between the great hounds and their masters. In 1594 Camden informs us in his *Brittania* that in Ireland animals are smaller than in England, except men and those hunting dogs we call greyhounds. Fynes Moryson, in his account of the Rebellion under Shane O'Neill, mentions the cattle as little and only men and greyhounds of Ireland as of great stature, while in 1681 Dineley's *Tour in Ireland* maintains that "all the breed of the country except women and greyhounds are less than the breed of England."

The same Rebellion is mentioned in connection with wolfhounds in a letter from Sir Walter Sentleger to Walsyngham, in which Sentlegger asks Walsyngham for three brace of Irish greyhounds, adding that the Rebellion had worn out the breed of them.

There was a large export of Irish hounds between the 16th and

---

Condensed from *The Dogs of Ireland,* by Anna Redlich, in *The Irish Digest,* January, 1950, pp. 73-75. Dublin.

18th centuries. Correspondence concerning these transactions would fill a medium-sized volume, were we to collect all the imploring, cajoling, threatening and blackmailing epistles connected with the acquisition of wolfdogs.

The export ban of 1652 on wolfhounds seems to have been completely ignored by those involved in these transactions.

The wolfhounds of that time sometimes wore a "garland," consisting of two iron hoops crossing each other and hanging before the dogs' legs to prevent them running after sheep and cattle.

About 1770 Oliver Goldsmith gives a highly complimentary description of the Irish wolfhound in *Animated Nature*. It is interesting to note that Goldsmith comments on the dog's ear carriage, which is that of a greyhound. Many specialists of the breed have argued as to whether the wolfhound of the past resembled a greyhound or mastiff, but we can rest assured that the huntsmen of that time were not concerned with such trivial "points," provided their hounds showed courage, strength and speed.

From the 16th century, when illustrations of Irish and other greyhounds became more plentiful, we find many smooth-coated dogs on paintings and tapestries.

The destruction of the last wolf in Ireland is mentioned by Captain Graham in a letter to the *Field* in 1885. A Mr. Watson of Ballydarton, a well-known Master of the Hounds, kept a pack of wolfhounds which killed the last wolf at Myshall near Ballydarton in 1786.

Gradually the large hounds developed from necessity into a pure ornament. Some of the descendants of the old Irish chieftains had parted with many commodities of life but had retained their hounds, though as wolf-hunting disappeared even these diminished in size. Lord Altamont of Westport in County Mayo kept eight large dogs which stood 28½ inches high. Their coats were smooth, their colour black and white, and they were delicate and hard to rear.

Towards the beginning of the 19th century the O'Toole family and the Earl of Caledon both owned wolfhounds. Sir Walter Scott, who already possessed some large deerhounds of the Glengarry strain, was offered a wolfhound, but declined, saying that there was no occupation for it as the only wolf was in the menagerie. Another adherent of the breed was Sir John Browne, of The Neale, County Mayo.

These enthusiasts were few and far between and people had already forgotten what these dogs looked like and were apt to call anything from a Newfoundland to a Great Dane a true Irish wolfhound.

But history repeats itself and seventeen centuries after Finn Mac Cumaill's immortal Bran, a dog of the same name and race was destined to revive the breed and bring fame to a new generation of Irish wolfhounds.

Towards the end of the 18th and in the early part of last century a gentleman was seen walking through the streets of Dublin, accompanied by three enormous dogs, among them a huge, grey, shaggy hound, called Bran, which from every description was a pure wolfhound, one of the last of his race. This dog figures in the famous Kilfane and Ballytobin strains, and can, therefore, be called one of the ancestors of the present hound.

About 1863 an Englishman, Captain George Augustus Graham, took up the breed with so much enthusiasm that he not only saved it from oblivion, but brought it back into the limelight of international dogdom.

He also had been a breeder of deerhounds, and, belonging to the observant kind, soon noticed that some of his deerhounds invariably threw back to the large type of Irish wolfhound. He experimented with the material at his disposal until he obtained dogs of the Kilfane and Ballytobin strains, the only pure wolfhound blood still existing in Ireland at that time. From then on it was comparatively plain sailing, which fact, however, does not reduce the debt of gratitude we owe to this pioneer of the breed. He collected the pedigrees of 300 wolfhounds, published those of hundreds of deerhounds, and would travel any distance to inspect a specimen reported to be a true Irish wolfhound.

* * * * *

A wolfhound marks the Belleek china, and the Irish sixpenny piece portrays International Champion Finbarr.

In Ireland at the present time there are about thirty wolfhounds.

The Otter Hunter's Story

. . . Just then a human figure turned the rock abruptly, and the old otter-killer stood beside us. The rushing of the stream prevented us from noticing his approach. He had been examining his traps, and as the way was rugged, he was delayed till now. The old man's appear-

From *Wild Sports of the West, with Legendary Tales and Local Sketches,* by W. H. Maxwell, Vol. I, pp. 134-139. Richard Bentley. London. 1832.

ance in this place, and at that hour, was picturesque. His dark dress, his long white hair, falling down his shoulders, the sealskin wallet, the fish spear, and the rough terrier, his companion, all were in perfect keeping.

"Well, Antony, what sport?"

"Little to speak of, Master Julius. I expect the trap wants oiling, for there was otter's spraints* everyplace about it. I went to the lake yonder, and while the breeze kept up, the fish took well. I killed a dozen red trout."

"Did you meet any of the 'gentlefolk,'† friend Antony? This is *just* the night that one would expect to find them *quadrilling* upon some green and mossy hillock."

The old man smiled and turned to me. "Well, well, the master won't believe in them; but if he had seen them as I did—"

"And did you *really* see them?"

"God knows, I tell you truth, sir." Then, resting himself on a rock, he thus continued: "It will be eleven years next month, when I was hunting otters at Lough na Mucka—the master knows the place, for many a good grouse he shot beside it. I then had the best two *tarriers* beneath the *canopy;* this poor *crater* is their daughter," and he patted the dog's head affectionately. "Well, I had killed two well-sized cubs, when Badger, who had been working in the weeds, put out the largest bitch I ever saw; I fired at her, but she was too far from me, and away she went across the Lough, and Badger and Venom after her. She rose at last; Badger gripped her, and down went dog and otter. They remained so long under water that I was greatly afraid the dog was drowned; but, after a while, up came Badger. Though I was right glad to see my dog, I did not like to lose the beast; and I knew, from the way that Badger's jaws were torn, that there had been a wicked struggle at the bottom. Well, I encouraged the dog, and when he had got his breath again, he dived down, nothing daunted, for he was the best *tarrier* ever poor man was master of. Long as he had been before at the bottom, he was twice longer now. The surface bubbled, the mud rose, and the water became black as ink: 'Ogh! murder,' says I, 'Badger, have I lost ye?' and I set-to clapping my hands for trouble, and Venom set up the howl as if her heart was broke. When, blessed be the Maker of all! up comes Badger with the otter gripped by the neck. The bitch swam over to help him, and I waded to the middle, and speared and landed the beast. Well, then I examined her, she had her mouth full of

---

* Marks or traces left by the animal. † Fairies.—W.H.M.

ould roots and moss, for she had fastened on a stump at the bottom, and the poor dog was sorely put-to to make her break her hold. I mind it well: I sold the skin in Galway, and got a gold guinea for it."

"Was that the night you met the fairies?"

"Stay, Master Julius, I'm coming to that. Well, three otters were a heavy load, and I had four miles to travel before I could reach Morteein Crassagh's.* The master knows the house well. The night was getting dark, and it's the worst ground in Connaught. Well, I was within a mile of Morteein's, when it became as black as pitch; and I had the shaking bog to cross, that you can hardly pass in daytime, where, if a man missed his way, he would be swallowed up in a moment. The rain began, and the poor dogs were famished with cold and hunger. God! I was sure I must stay there, starving till the morning; when, on a sudden, little lights danced before me, and showed me the hard tammocks as plain as if the sun was up. I was in a cruel fright, and the dogs whimpered, and would not stir from my foot. I was afraid to stay where I was, as I knew the *gentle-people* were about me; and I was unwilling to attempt the quagh,† for fear the light would leave me, and then I would get neither back nor forward. Well, the wind began to rise; the rain grew worse; I got desperate, and resolved to speak to the fairies civilly. 'Gentlemen and ladies,' says I, making a bow to the place where the lights were dancing, 'may be ye would be so obliging as to light me across the bog.' In a minute there was a blaze from one end of the quagh to the other, and a hundred lights were flashing over the bogs. I took heart and ventured; and wherever I put my foot, the place was as bright as day, and I crossed the swamp as safely as if I had been walking on a graveled road. Every inch the light came with me, till I reached the boreein‡ leading to Morteein Crassagh's; then, turning about, I made the fairies a low bow; 'Gentlemen and ladies,' says I, 'I'm humbly thankful for your civility, and I wish ye now a merry night of it.' God preserve us! The words were hardly out when there was a roar of laughter above, below, and around me. The lights vanished, and it became at once so dark that I could scarcely make out my way. When I got fairly inside Morteein's kitchen, I fainted dead; and when I came to, I told them what had happened. Many a time fairy candles are seen at Lough na Mucka; but sorrow mortal was ever lighted across the quagh by the *gentle-people* but my-

---

* Martin with the rough face. † A morass. ‡ A horsepath leading into bogs.— W.H.M.

self, and that the country knows. Well—the master is laughing at me; but I'll hobble to the cabin, or they'll think the *gentle-people* have carried me off at last, as they did Shamus Bollogh,* from Ballycroy."

The Old Fox Hunter

Dr. Kiely was astonished to find his patient in a chair on the lawn, propped up with pillows. His son, a tall, cadaverous-looking man with grizzled hair and beard, stood on one side of the chair, and a saintly-looking though somewhat spruce young clergyman at the other.

"Blow, Rody, blow," muttered the poor old invalid. And the horn sounded, and the woods gave back the echo.

"O sweet Woodlands, must I leave you?" exclaimed the old fox hunter in tones of the deepest grief.

"You're going to a better place," said the clergyman impressively.

"Yoix! Tallyho!" cried the invalid faintly. "Blow, Rody, blow!"

"Don't ax me, sir," returned the huntsman, after putting the horn to his lips and taking it away again. "My heart is ready to burst."

"O sweet Woodlands, must I leave you?" his master exclaimed again.

"My dear sir," the clergyman repeated, stooping over him and placing his gloved hand gently upon his shoulder, "my dear sir, you are going to a better place."

The invalid turned round and looked earnestly into the young clergyman's face, as if he had until then been unconscious of his presence.

"You're going to a better place; trust me, you're going to a better place," the clergyman repeated fervently.

"Ah," said the old fox hunter, with a sorrowful shake of his head, and looking earnestly into the parson's face, "ah, by God, I doubt you."

The dying foxhunter seemed to drop into a doze, from which a low fretful whine from one of the hounds caused him to awake with a start. "Poor Bluebell; poor Bluebell," he murmured. The hound named wagged her tail, and coming close to him, looked wistfully into his face. The whole pack followed Bluebell, waving their tails, and with

---

* James the Stutterer.—W.H.M.

From *Knocknagow, or The Homes of Tipperary,* by Charles J. Kickham, pp. 160-161. James Duffy & Co., Ltd. Dublin. 1887.

their trustful eyes appeared to claim recognition, too, from their old master. But his head drooped, and he seemed falling asleep again. He roused himself, however, and gazed once more upon the fine landscape before him, and again called on his huntsman to sound the horn. The huntsman put it to his lips, and his chest heaved as he labored for breath; but no sound awoke the echoes again.

"God knows I can't sir," he cried, bursting into tears.

The Tavern

Its immunity

'Neath one fir tree, a shelter scant,
Beside the roadside heather
Stands Barney's slated tavern gaunt,
The sport of wind and weather;
'Tis there from town and village far,
Afar from Guard officious,
With nothing near the view to mar
Should aught approach suspicious.

Its patrons

Through decades Barney's favored pub,
All hampering 'hours' defying,
For topers hard had been the hub
From districts wide outlying;
Here round the brightly blazing hearth,
Replenished bowls before them,
They lingered long, oft loth to part
Till day was dawning o'er them.

Nor were there round this fireside set
But sots and tipplers only;
Dear social souls here too were met

From *The Cork Accent* (Some echoes from the Rebel County), by P. Barry, pp. 14-18. [No publisher, no date.]

Mid sad and soured and lonely;
'Twas here, a haven safe from strife,
Poor Jimeen Joe retreated
When he and Cait, his worthy wife
Had arguments o'erheated.

And card-playing fans o'er "forty-fives"
In weather cold and murky
Spent cheery nights in hard-fought Drives
For choicest goose and turkey;
In sugawn corner-chair at ease
Shawn Dubh, in long orations,
Poured censure stern on Guards, T.D.'s,
Boards, Courts and Corporations.

An unexpected raid

One night as Maudlin Meehaul Moor
Lay in a corner snoring,
And Norry's Ned, from shrews secure,
Some Murphy's Best was lowering.
While, sotto voce, Jimeen Joe
His Cruskeen Laun was lauding,
And Theigeen Tim forgot his woe,
Shawn Dubh was loud applauding.

As card-players o'er the latest Trick
Were sharp and high disputing,
And some in hiccupped voices thick
Their stormier friends were soothing;
Lo! as the earliest cock had crowed,
Through opened doors two figures strode
'Neath snowflakes deeply shrouded.

The welcome warmth from radiant blaze
These sheeting snows soon melted,
And there before each startled gaze
Stood Guards in great-coats belted!
From blank amazement's shock severe
The gamblers, swiftly waking,
Tumultuous rushed for doorways near
O'er all that barred them breaking.

The stakes and scores all now forgot,
O'er tierce and tub they vaulted,
The doorways gained, were free—had not
Strong hands their hurry halted;
Glass beakers meanwhile crashed and broke,
And chairs and stools kept falling,
And Meehawl Moor from dreams half woke,
Was loud on Fanny calling.

But 'frighted most, as Guards appeared,
Was he who match had lighted,
When not his pipe but Barney's beard
He nervously ignited;
While riot reigned thus round the floor,
The Guards, cool pencils plying,
Stood, each beside a bolted door,
All egress stern denying.

The prosecution

The Court took, when each case was tried,
Good records long pre-dating
And close approach of Christmastide
As pleas extenuating;
Except that when Jimeen was named
By duteous guard attendant,
The Justice, strangely stern, declaimed
Against the mute defendant.

Reminded him he'd wed his spouse
For worse as well as better,
That nights left long in lonely house
Were bound to fright and fret her,
Which Cait, the better half, all ears,
With pleased approval tittering,
And on Jimeen, nigh shamed to tears,
Throws gloating glances withering.

"Unkindness could," he added, "kill
A gentle wife's devotion,"
(His kerchief here concealed but ill
His risible emotion);

"Though wives, in truth, are all not saints,
They've rights to be corrective,
And—if compelled—to make complaints
To sergeant or detective."

"Now take, Jimeen, these words to heart,"
(He spoke in tone more tender)
And from the Court you may depart
Dismissed as first offender."

The sequel

Jimeen and those within the hall
Saw clear from this oration
That Cait had basely sold them all
By secret information;
And circling round her close about,
With threats and tempers rising,
"Informer!" o'er and o'er they shout
With gestures terrorizing.

The sergeant saw, and heard, and smiled;
No more reports vindictive,
No midnight raids in weather wild
Enforcing "Hours" restrictive;
He blessed the jovial Justice, too,
Who took the tip collusive,
And who, an old-time neighbour, knew
Cait's tendencies abusive.

Now Barney's pub its course pursues,
No Guards its guests e'er troubling,
All day and night for crowding queues
The brimming bowls are bubbling;
In laun-a-walla all may share,
And, doubt it as thou mayest,
Jimeen is of all the happiest there,
The merriest and the gayest.

The Cruiskeen Lawn

Let the farmer praise his grounds,
Let the huntsman praise his hounds,
   The shepherd his dew-scented lawn;
But I, more blest than they,
Spend each happy night and day
   With my charming little cruiskeen lawn, lawn, lawn,
  My charming little cruiskeen lawn.
     Gra ma chree ma cruiskeen,
     Slainte geal mavourneen,
     Gra machree a coolin bawn.

     Gra machree ma cruiskeen,
     Slainte geal mavourneen,
     Gra machree a coolin bawn, bawn, bawn,
     Gra machree a coolin bawn.

Immortal and divine,
Great Bacchus, god of wine,
   Create me by adoption your son:
In hope that you'll comply
My glass shall ne'er run dry,
   Nor my smiling little cruiskeen lawn, &c.

And when grim death appears,
In a few but pleasant years,
   To tell me that my glass has run;
I'll, say, Begone, you knave,
For bold Bacchus gave me leave,
   To take another cruiskeen lawn, &c.

Then fill your glasses high,
Let's not part with lips a-dry.
   Though the lark now proclaims it is dawn;
And since we can't remain,
May we shortly meet again,
   To fill another cruiskeen lawn, lawn, lawn,

From *The Dublin Book of Irish Verse*, 1728-1909, edited by John Cooke, pp. 741-742. Hodges, Figgis & Co., Ltd. Dublin. 1909.
See page 609 for music.

To fill another cruiskeen lawn.
   Gra ma chree ma cruiskeen,
   Slainte geal mavourneen,
   Gra machree a coolin bawn.

   Gra ma chree ma cruiskeen,
   Slainte geal mavourneen,
   Gra machree a coolin bawn, bawn, bawn,
   Gra machree a coolin bawn.

Beside the Fire

Where glows the Irish hearth with peat
There lives a subtle spell,
The faint blue smoke, the gentle heat,
The moorland odours tell

Of white roads winding to the edge
Of bare, untamed land,
Where dry stone wall or ragged hedge
Runs wide on either hand.

The cottage lights that lure you in
From rainy western skies;
And by the friendly glow within
Of simple talk and wise,

And tales of magic, love or arms
From days when princes met
To listen to the lay that charms
The Connacht peasant yet.

There honour shines through passions dire,
There beauty blends with mirth,
Wild hearts, ye never did aspire
Wholly for things of earth!

From *An Anthology of Irish Verse*, edited by Padraic Colum, pp. 46-47. Copyright, 1922, by Boni & Liveright. New York.

Cold, cold this thousand years—yet still
On many a time-stained page
Your pride, your truth, your dauntless will,
Burn on from age to age.

And still around the fires of peat
Live on the ancient days;
There still do living lips repeat
The old and deathless lays.

And when the wavering wreaths ascend
Blue in the evening air,
The soul of Ireland seems to bend
Above her children there.

Folkways in Aran

The chief handicrafts of the islands (Aran) are: spinning and weaving, basket-making, boat-building, and carpentry work.

When the sheep are shorn, the women wash the fleece and put it in the sun to dry, and, in order to facilitate the drying, they tease it with their fingers. When dry, it is further teased into a loose woolly mass by means of two carders which are somewhat like very large hairbrushes, having, instead of bristles, wire hooks which loosen the hairs of the wool which is now ready for spinning.

The spinning-wheels in Aran are the same type as those in Connemara, but they are quite different from those used in County Donegal. The latter are more ornamental and are worked by a foot treadle which is manipulated by a woman sitting in a chair. In Aran the worker generally stands, whereas on the Blasket Islands, where the spinning-wheels are the same type as in Aran, but smaller in size, with shorter legs to the base, the operator sits down when working.

* * * * *

Weaving is done by hand; the cloth wears for years and is almost impervious to rain, as the natural oil of the wool has not been removed by chemical processes.

Oisiers are grown for basket work, which consists of creels for carry-

From *The Islands of Ireland,* by Thomas H. Mason, pp. 82-84. B. T. Batsford, Ltd. London. 1936.

ing turf and seaweed, skibs, which are round shallow baskets used for draining the water from boiled potatoes or cabbage, and long, oval, shallow baskets called "ribhs" which are used for carrying the baited fishing-lines.

The carpenter on Inishere was very busy but he kindly consented to make me a couple of baskets and to allow me to take photographs during the process, for, as he remarked to my son, "He did not like to disappoint the gentleman"; and on another occasion, "The ould man is great for the photographing. I don't know could ye stop him if ye tried." In making a creel the thick ends of the sally rods are stuck in the ground, the spaces being carefully measured by a straw. When watching the process I thought that this method was probably identical with that pursued by our early ancestors from whom the art has descended down to the present day. Basket-making is one of the earliest handicrafts practiced by mankind.

The tools used in making the framework of a currach are a plane, a saw, an auger, a hammer, and a chisel. The bracket which helps to fasten the seat to the gunwale is generally a forked bough from a tree, which is much stronger than a bracket cut out of timber since the latter is liable to split on account of the grain in the wood.

There is plenty of bird life on the islands; the sea-fowl nest on the cliffs, waders on the sandy shores and larks and other small birds are numerous. One sees the chough and the sparrow hawk; swans nest on the lake on Inishere, and, strange to say, the thrushes only came to the islands about forty years ago when, driven from the mainland by an unprecedented hard and continued frost, they took refuge on the islands where the climate is milder and frosts seldom occur.

I was perplexed when I heard the cry of a curlew, evidently close at hand. Investigating, I found that a starling, perched on the gable of a cottage, was responsible. For some time he continued with his perfect imitation, which was not so loud, but identical in every other respect with the plaintive note of the curlew.

The Last Fortress of the Celt

On an island in the Atlantic, within a day's journey from Dublin, there is still a people who live in conditions older than the Middle Ages, and have preserved in an extraordinary degree the charm of primitive man.

By J. M. Synge, in *The Gael*, April, 1901, pp. 109-113. New York.

Inishmaan, the middle, and least sophisticated of the Arran group of County Galway, has no harbor worthy of the name, no real roads, no carts, no post office, and, what is rare in Ireland, no police barrack. The population, about three hundred and fifty, depend for their meagre livelihood on net and line fishing, which they carry on in curraghs, or canvas canoes, with the greatest enterprise and daring.

The visitor usually reaches this lonely rock from Kilronan, the principal village in the great Arran Island, whence he is borne to his destination in the stern of a long, light-oared curragh. The sound is not much more than a mile wide at the narrowest part, yet the voyage from Kilronan takes almost an hour, and the unfamiliar company of the lithe islanders dressed in grey homespun flannels, together with the leaping oscillation of the canoe, gives one a strange sense of novelty. A landing is effected at a small pier, and after a half hour's walk between flat sheets of naked limestone, where a few goats nibble a repast of blue gentian and maiden-hair, one reaches a straggling settlement of about seventy cottages. It is only when one has spent months in one of these, and grown, so to speak, into one's place on the chimney corner, that the full charm of the people can be realized.

Lodgings in the ordinary sense are not, of course, to be had, but I was fortunate enough to find a room, sometimes used by Gaelic scholars, which was tolerably comfortable. My hostess was an elderly woman who wore the short red petticoat, indescribable shawl, and raw cow-skin shoes, which form the national costume. Like most of the older women she was quite ignorant of English, but her daughter could both read and understand it, though she never used a Saxon word except when speaking to her pigs, a curious habit which is common on the island, and may be explained in more ways than one. This girl was dressed exactly as her mother except that when she went out on Sunday she put an elaborate shawl over her head, while the elder woman, indeed all the married women, are satisfied with an extra red petticoat, worn with the waistband around the face.

Their cottage was one of the most important in the Island, and there were numerous visitors from early morning till bedtime. All were received with the usual Gaelic salutation, "That God may bless thee," given a stool by the fire, and drawn into conversation with unconscious yet admirable courtesy. Shoes and stockings were still regarded as a thing put on as extra, and when the day's work was done the women generally laid them aside, showing finely formed feet and ankles under their short petticoats, while they did the honors of their kitchen.

At first the men spoke English for my convenience, expressing themselves more correctly than the ordinary peasant, though some used the
Gaelic idioms continually, and substituted the "he" or "she" for "it,"
as the neuter pronoun is not found in modern Irish. Their vocabulary
was, of course, very limited, which gave rise at times to curious nomenclature. Thus one evening when my comb had been mislaid, my old
host came to me and asked if I had found my "little rake"!

The faces of the men were somewhat unlike the Irish type, and
showed traces of the Pre-Celtic blood, which has lingered in the west
of Europe, while among the women were some curiously Mongolian
features, rather resembling the Bigoudennes of the south coast of
Brittany.

The kitchen where we sat was a marvel of unconscious decoration.
The deep glow from the garments of the women who clustered round
the fire on their stools lent a color of almost oriental richness, and the
white-washed walls were toned by the turf smoke to a delicate brown
which harmonized as by design with the hard earthen floor. On one
side of the fire stood the spinning-wheel, and on the other a large
pot of indigo for dying wool. Round the walls, or among the open
rafters, one could see many sorts of fishing tackle, with the oilskins
of the men, and right over head, under the thatch, a whole red cowskin
destined for the primitive shoes, or pampooties, as they are called in
English.

* * * * *

When they talk with strangers, language is a favorite subject. As all
outsiders who spend any time upon the island are philologists, the
islanders have concluded that linguistic studies—particularly Gaelic
studies—are the chief object in a life of moneyed leisure.

"We have seen," said one of my visitors, "Frenchmen, Danes, and
Germans, and there was not one of them without books of Irish, which
they could read better than ourselves. Believe me, there are no rich
men now in the world who are not studying the Irish."

They think little of the stranger who cannot claim mastery over
five or six idioms, and as they are themselves bi-lingual, they realize in
a way the ordinary peasant cannot do, what it means to think and
speak in several languages. In spite of their simplicity they are not
easy to deceive, weighing what is told them with much deliberation.
One day I heard a heated discussion under my door as to whether I
had written with my own hand the Irish letters I had sent them in
my absence: the doubt, of course, was raised because I write the language more correctly than I speak it. The schoolmaster has an ingeni-

ous test for his philological visitors. When a newcomer is announced, he invites him into his parlor, and pours out a glass of the national beverage. Then he leads the conversation to linguistic matters, and when the foreigner has committed himself to a not always modest statement of his learning, he produces an advertisement of some patent medicine, printed in about twenty different tongues, and requests the visitor to demonstrate his attainments.

The youngest son of the household where I lodged was appointed as my teacher and guide, and whenever he was not at work, he led me about the island or took me out fishing in a curragh, teaching me Irish all the time. The rough fossiliferous limestone which abounds in some places soon destroyed my shoes, so I was compelled to adopt the pampooties of the natives. They consist simply of a piece of cowskin laced round the heel and toe, with the hair outside. In the evening when they are taken off, they are placed in a basin of water, as the rough hide cuts the foot and stocking if it is allowed to harden—then about midday, if occasion offers, the wearer steps into the surf, up to his ankles, so that the feet are continually moist. At first I threw my weight upon my heels, as is done naturally in a boot, and was a good deal bruised, but, after a day or two, I learned the natural elastic walk of primitive man, and could follow my companion in any portion of the island. Sometimes one goes for a mile or more jumping from rock to rock without a single ordinary step. This exercise soon taught me that toes have a definite employment, for I found myself jumping by instinct onto any tiny crevice in the rock before me, and clinging with an eager grip in which ten individual muscles ached with their unusual exertion.

One day a steamer came out from Galway with a party of police and land agents, who had long been expected, as evictions were impending on the island. Till then no islander had consented to act as bailiff, so it had been impossible to find, or identify, the cattle of the defaulters. On this occasion, however, a man undertook the dishonorable office, and many lean cows fell into the hands of the law. In the evening, when the last policeman had embarked, an old woman come forward from the crowd, and, mounting on a rock near the boatslip, began a fierce rhapsody in Gaelic, waving her withered arms with extraordinary passion.

"This man," she said, "is my own son. It is I that ought to know him. He is the first ruffian in the whole big world."

During my first visit to the island an old man used to come up and tell me stories in the kitchen and was generally followed by some of the neighbors who knew his custom and came in to listen also. One story he told me was of peculiar interest: the old folk tale which unites the "pound of flesh" theme, used by Shakespeare in the *Merchant of Venice,* and the "wager on the faithful wife," given by Boccaccio, and again by Shakespeare in *Cymbeline.* These stories are, of course, very widely distributed, yet I listened with a strange feeling of wonder while this illiterate native of a wet rock in the Atlantic told the same tales that had charmed the Florentines by the Arno. Once his stories were so Boccaccian in their flavor that I blushed to hear them in the company of girls and women. He gave me also a very full account of the fairies and their proceedings. He had often seen them, he said, playing ball in the evening by the boatslip, and they were about a yard high, with caps like the peelers (policemen). Once he saw a woman who was "away" with them, looking over a wall toward the north, but she did not speak to him. Another night he heard a voice crying out in the Irish, "Oh, mother, I'm killed," and in the morning there was blood upon the wall, and a child in the house not far away was dead.

He advised me earnestly not to linger in certain portions of the island after nightfall, for fear "the good people" might "do me a mischief." When I knew him better he took me aside and said he would tell me a secret he had never yet told to living man. "Take a sharp needle," he said, "and stick it in under the collar of your coat, and not one of them will be able to have power on you." Iron is a common talisman with barbarians, but in this case the idea of exquisite sharpness was also present, and, perhaps, the traditional sanctity of the instrument of toil, a belief which is common in Brittany. He shed tears when I went to his hovel to see him before my departure, as he said he would never see me again. Then, with a curious change of thought, he urged me to "put insurance on him," as his death was certainly approaching, and I might win five hundred pounds. He was buried between the following Christmas and the new year.

An old woman died in the cottage next to mine while I was on the island, and I was enabled to witness the curious lamentations for the dead. I did not go to the wake, as I feared my presence might jar upon the mourners, but all the evening before the funeral I could hear the strokes of a hammer in the yard, where the next of kin labored at the coffin. Next day, a few minutes before the start, poteen—the illicit whiskey of western Ireland—was served liberally to the men who stood about upon the road, and a portion was brought to me in my room. Then the coffin was carried out, and the procession, composed for the most part of old men and women, moved off to the graveyard, in the low eastern district of the island. While the grave was being opened, all the women sat down among the flat tombstones bordered by a pale fringe of early bracken, and began the wild keene, or lamentation. Each aged crone, as she took her turn of the leading recitative, seemed possessed for the moment with a profound ecstasy of grief, swaying to and fro, and bowing her withered forehead to the stone before her, while she called out to the dead with a perpetual recurring chant of sobs. All around the graveyard old wrinkled women, looking out from under their deep red petticoats, rocked themselves with the same rhythm, and intoned the half articulate wail which is sustained as an accompaniment. The morning had been beautifully fine, but as they lowered the coffin into the grave thunder rumbled overhead, and hailstones hissed among the bracken.

The tendency to drink is the only vice upon the island, and it cannot be severely censured. When storm and fog come up from the Atlantic, and beat for weeks upon the cliffs, the sense of desolation that grows on one is indescribable. Nothing can be seen but a mass of wet rock, then a strip of surf, and then a tumult of grey waves. The inhabitants do not seem at first to pay much attention to the dismal fury that is around them, but after a few days they begin to talk about their pigs, or cattle, with the voice of men telling stories in a haunted house, and the bottle of poteen is drawn from its hiding-place. In some circumstances an anaesthetic is needful, and a storm in Inishmaan is one of these.

Leaving Home

He was a singularly handsome young man, with a fresh, clear complexion and light blue eyes. His crisp golden curls, like his sister's, had a tinge of red in them, and it was a common remark among the neighbours that Jimmy Hogan was "too handsome for a boy." He certainly appeared delicate and effeminate to strangers; but such a thought never occurred to his acquaintances, for it was well known that he could do as good a day's work as any man in the parish except Mat Donovan; and that at the hurling he was often the first, and always among the first, to be "called" when the match was making. He was generally good-humoured and amiable; but it was remarked

From *Knocknagow, or The Homes of Tipperary*, by Charles J. Kickham, pp. 202-204. James Duffy & Co., Ltd. Dublin. 1887.

that when strongly moved, all color would fly from his lips, which were of so bright a red as to make the paleness of his face more striking, and his white, regular teeth seem literally all of pearl.

His sister, who bore a strong resemblance to him, looked at him now with the deepest sympathy, the tears welling into her gentle eyes, and seemed at a loss for something to say that might cheer him. She approached him almost timidly, and laid the tips of her fingers lightly on his shoulder. He took no notice, and after a moment's hesitation, she pulled one of his hands from under his chin, and, sitting in his lap, looked playfully into his face.

"Tell me something about the fair," she said. "Did you meet many people you knew?"

"I didn't meet any wan you'd care to hear about," he replied.

"Did you call into Mrs. Burke's?"

"I did; an' I don't know what business I have to call in anywhere."

Her countenance fell at this, but forcing a smile, she said, "How is Alice?"

"She's very well," he replied, with assumed indifference.

"Oh, yes! Pretend you don't care which!"

"You know very well, Nancy," he said, after a short silence, " 'tis no use for me to be thinkin' uv any wan."

"Well, maybe you're too young to think uv gettin' married yet a while, but that's no raison why you wouldn't be thinkin' uv somebody. An' if you knew how light they are about you," she added laughingly.

"That's all nonsense," he replied, trying to look displeased, while a smile of gratified vanity played upon his red lips.

"Nancy," he said, after a pause, "I have my mind made up."

"For what?"

"Not to stay here any longer."

"Oh, Jimmy, don't talk that way."

"Where is my use in stayin' here? My father don't want me. An' what am I betther than a common labourer?—nor so good. So there's no use in talkin'; go I will. An', for God's sake, don't say anything to throuble me, for 'tis throuble enough that's on me."

"Oh, Jimmy!" she wailed, resting her head upon his shoulder, and trembling violently. "Oh, Jimmy! I'd rather be dead."

"That's all foolishness," he replied. " 'Twill be the best for all of us. You know yourself you never could be settled if I stopped at home, unless I got married and got a fortune to give you; an' the Lord knows when that might be. So 'tis better for you to have the place; an' then there'll be enough comin' to look for you."

"I'll never marry, Jimmy. All I'd ever ask is to have us all live together as long as God spared us to each other. An' oh! how happy we'd be. An' wouldn't you take a delight in improvin' the place, like my father? An' afther a time you'd have some money uv your own. You might have a few heifers or cows—I'll give you my lamb!" she exclaimed suddenly, as if she were sure that the lamb, beyond all doubt, would banish discontent from his mind forevermore.

"You'll never have sinse," he replied, smiling. "But why do you say you'll never marry? Is id on account of that blackguard, Ned Brophy? I don't know what kep me from—well, no matther."

"Don't blame him, Jimmy. Maybe he couldn't help it."

"Didn't he know all along what he had to expect?" Jimmy asked indignantly. "An' when he knew he couldn't marry widout a fortune, why was he keepin' gaddin' afther you, an' makin' you the talk uv the counthry?"

"I don't care about the talk uv the counthry," his sister replied, with tears in her eyes. "Let 'em talk away."

"But why do you say he's not to be blamed?"

"Well, I don't say he's not; only not so much as a person might think. I think," she continued with a sigh, "it was partly my mother's fault. She was so anxious for him that the minute she saw he took notice of me, she was always huntin' him, an' pressin' him, an' nearly makin' him come whether he'd like it or not. I know I was foolish myself. But when everyone used to be jokin' about him, an' when I see him so fond of me, I couldn't help it," poor Nancy added, blushing deeply, and struggling to keep down the sob that swelled up in her throat. "'Tis all over now," she continued plaintively, but more calmly, "an' my mind is at rest, an' I'm satisfied. But don't think I could ever care for wan again—that way."

"I'm thinkin' uv it this long time. Don't be a fool. Sure I can write to ye, an' maybe I might come home afther a few years in flyin' colors."

Do You Remember?

> Do you remember that night
> That you were at the window,
> With neither hat nor gloves,

From *An Anthology of Irish Verse*, edited by Padraic Colum, pp. 60-61. Copyright, 1922, by Boni & Liveright. New York.

Nor coat to shelter you;
I reached out my hand to you,
And you ardently grasped it,
And I remained in converse with you
Until the lark began to sing?

Do you remember that night
That you and I were
At the foot of the rowan tree,
And the night drifting snow;
Your head on my breast,
And your pipe sweetly playing?
I little thought that night
Our ties of love would loosen.

O beloved of my inmost heart,
Come some night, and soon,
When my people are at rest,
That we may talk together;
My arms shall encircle you,
While I relate my sad tale
That it is your pleasant, soft converse
That has deprived me of heaven.

The fire is unraked,
The light is extinguished,
The key under the door,
And do you softly draw it.
My mother is asleep,
And I am quite awake;
My fortune in my hand,
And I am ready to go with you.

A "Wake" for the Emigrant

A girl whom I knew came into the shop I frequented. Her greeting was constrained and she stood silent and apart, with a shawl across her head. She had taken me to many festivities during the months I was in that place. I came over and spoke to her in Irish: "When will there be a dance in your village?" I asked. "There's a dance tonight," she said, "if you would care to come." "Is it at the Stone's?" "No, it's at our house. It's the night of my own wake."

She did not use the word in its generally accepted sense. In some of the Irish-speaking districts the word "wake" has come to signify the last gathering around the boy or girl who is leaving the village for Boston or New York. Grania was in the shop, to buy provisions for her American wake. I had seen another part of peasant Ireland denuded of its vitality—by emigration, and I thought of Grania as typical of the robust and high-spirited youth who go away and are lost to the country, or return to Ireland for a while, changed and dissatisfied. She bade good-bye to those in the shop and gave me the word to come with her. Our path was between walls of loose stones that went across a country strewn with boulders. On account of these bare surfaces of rock the landscape was toned with greyness. There was no luminary in the early night; the full moon was gone and the new moon had not made its appearance. It is customary in this part of the country to use the English word "Village" as the equivalent of their area of community. But the picture brought up by the word has no relation to their scattered hamlet. The houses were scattered through miles of uneven territory, and no roof was visible from the door of another house.

We met Grania's mother before we came to the house. She was one of those women who smile as though they did not understand what was happening or what was being said. She was silent and smiled as though speech had been frightened from her. The father greeted me at the door and brought me to the circle that was round the fire. He was a stolid and silent man. Another old man at the fire spoke eloquently and passionately in Irish. "Every man has his rearing, except the poor Irishman. This is the way with him. When his children grow up, they scatter from him like the little birds." Grania had taken off her shawl and was busy in the household duties. There was some intensity in her manner, but she made herself pleasant and capable. While I waited, a remarkable person engaged me in polite conversation. She had the manners of an aristocrat and the faculty of being amused by her fellow-creatures. Her manners were designed to show an overwhelming interest in the person whom she addressed, but it was hard to say whether she laughed with you or laughed at you. There was salt in her conversation, and she was witty in two languages.

Tea was served in the upper room, and I went there as the young people were beginning to arrive. This sleeping room was expressive of the influences that are changing Irish rural life. There was an open American trunk, and dresses sent from New York or Boston were lying on the bed. On the wall was a fine mirror that would have been in its place in the dressing-room of an actress. Visitors had been coming, singly and in couples, and on going back to the kitchen, I encountered something like a mob. People were standing three-deep from the walls. I heard a discord of music and song, the clash of grave speaking with loud-tongued humour, of gossip and boisterous flirtation, of American nasals and full-sounding Gaelic vowels. The children crowded together in the recess of the wide chimney, and the old people kept going into and coming out of the inner room. People were speaking of a dance, but a stranger would wonder whether there was room for a dance between the dresser and the fire on the hearth, between the table and the meal bins. Grania drew out the partners for the girls, arranged the dance, and induced a quiet man to play on the flute. The figures in the dance were complicated, but even the swinging of the partners was accomplished with safety.

After some rounds of dancing, songs were given. English words were most in the fashion. Some of the songs were in the Irish tradition, some had been brought home by the workers in Scotland and England, and some had come from America. I pressed for one of their own traditional songs. I could not make an advance in kind, but I recited a poem of my own, and after that the company were inclined to my request. A young man whom I had noticed for his satirical powers stoods up for the song. It was of the locality and it satirized a person whose character had comic associations for the company.

The narrative begins in the house of Shaun, the person satirized. It is in the middle of the night, and Shaun and his dependents are in their beds. Someone gives the alarm—the cow has gone astray. Shaun rises and in the dark gropes for his garments. And Shaun and his adherents are off on the quest. Alone he finds the cow. He waits till dawn, and then takes the homeward trail. Now he is in need of rest and refreshment. He comes to a lonely house and is admitted. A single woman entertains him, and a district, awakened by the commotion of the search, sees Shaun, the guileless man, leave the house at an ambiguous hour. To save the good name of the district he and the woman marry. In this way Shaun gets his wife. The song set forth in a comedy of manners and it was received with applause. When it was over I discovered that the singer was the maker, and that he was noted through the countryside for his stinging ranns. A young and handsome boy sang another ballad in Irish. It was the lament of a man who had been put in prison, "Not for killing not for stealing, but for making the brew that pays no duty." "My hair was cropped round my ears, and ugly clothes were put upon me. For nine months I was there, without company, without music." The last phrase was a flash of the Celtic spirit. It brought to my mind a romance of the Heroic Age, in which one of the Fianna complains, "For three days we were in the pit without food, without drink, without music."

The night wore on with dance and song, with challenge and repartee. Grania left us and stayed in the upper room for a while. When she returned she was in wild spirits and set about forming another dance. The orchestra was changed for this. She brought down a fiddle and a young man undertook to play. Only the wildest spirits were in this last dance that was on the skirts of the creeping day. Before the dance ended, Grania's brother went from us, and we saw him take the harness down from the wall. It was an action as significant as anything in drama. The dance went on, but we heard the stamp of the awakened horse and the rattle of the harness as the conveyance was made ready for the journey. The dance fluttered out. Through the window the trees became visible, then we saw colour, the green of the grass and the green of the leaves. Grania left the revellers and went into the room where her mother was busy. All of us who were in the kitchen went outside, so that those who were parting would have the place to themselves. In the morning world the corncrakes were crying through the meadows. They were quiet in the house now, and the chill of dawn made me wish for the overcoat I had left within. I went inside. After the vivid life I felt the emptiness of the kitchen; the fire had burned to ashes and the broad light through the window was on the flame of the lamp. As I was going out, Grania came down, dressed for the journey. The poor girl was changed. She was dazed with grief.

She sat on the cart that went down to the stony road, and the remnant of the company followed. Farther on they would meet more carts with other emigrants, boys and girls. The cart jogged itself onto the main road; as yet there was only a single figure on the way, a man driving a cow to some far-off fair. We bade good-bye to Grania and separated. On my way back I passed her house; it was soundless and closed in as if the house had not yet wakened into life.

Part VII

FIRESIDE TALES

In Memory of the Story-Teller,
Padraic O'Conaire

They'll miss his heavy stick and stride in Wicklow—
His story-talking down Winetavern Street,
Where old men sitting in the wizened daylight
Have kept an edge upon his gentle wit;
While women on the grassy streets of Galway,
Will hearken for his passing—but in vain,
Shall hardly tell his step as shadows vanish
Through archways of forgotten Spain.

Ah, they'll say: Padraic's gone again exploring;
But now down glens of brightness, O he'll find
An alehouse overflowing with wise Gaelic
That's braced in vigour by the bardic mind,
And there his thoughts shall find their own forefathers—
In minds to whom our heights of race belong,
In crafty men, who ribbed a ship or turned
The secret joinery of song.

From *Arable Holdings,* by F. R. Higgins. Cuala Press. 1933.

Introduction

Stories, to a great many people, are the main ingredient in folklore. The stories given here are from different parts of Ireland, written down at different times and published with different intentions. Within the selection there are contrasts: the stories taken down in Irish and given in translation belong to a different world from those whose rendering is in English. There are two stories about the Goban Saor: in the first, written down in the southeast where the language for many generations has been English, he appears as the shrewd craftsman; in the second, taken down in Irish from a west Ireland story-teller, he is obviously a character in a fragment of a mytho-logical cycle. Such a story as "The Shee an Gannon and the Gruagach Gaire," also taken down in Irish, is a hero tale. But the stories taken down in the English-speaking counties have lost their primeval quality: they are humorous and a bit mocking. The two very different stories, "The Horned Women" and "Little Fairly" need a comment. "The Horned Women" is authentically a folk tale, and was written down in Irish by Sir William Wilde; in retelling it, Lady Wilde has given it a literary, but not an inappropriately literary, form. "Little Fairly" is by a literary man, Samuel Lover.—P.C.

The Way of the Leprecaun

The . . . Leprecauns had ceased work and were looking at the children. Seumas turned to them.

"God bless the work," said he politely.

One of the Leprecauns, who had a grey, puckered face and a thin fringe of grey whisker very far under his chin, then spoke.

"Come over here, Seumas Beg," said he, "and I'll measure you for a pair of shoes. Put your foot up on that root."

The boy did so, and the Leprecaun took the measure of his foot with a wooden rule.

"Now, Brigid Beg, show me your foot," and he measured her also. "They'll be ready for you in the morning."

"Do you never do anything else but make shoes, sir?" said Seumas.

"We do not," replied the Leprecaun, "except when we want new clothes, and then we have to make them, but we grudge every minute spent making anything else except shoes, because that is the proper work for a Leprecaun. In the night time we go about the country into people's houses and we clip little pieces off their money, and so, bit by bit, we get a crock of gold together, because, do you see, a Leprecaun has to have a crock of gold so that if he's captured by men folk he may be able to ransom himself. But that seldom happens, because it's a great disgrace altogether to be captured by a man, and we've practised so long dodging among the roots here that we can easily get away from them. Of course, now and again we are caught; but men are fools, and we always escape without having to pay the ransom at all. We wear green clothes because it is the color of the grass and the leaves, and when we sit down under a bush or lie in the grass they just walk by without noticing us."

The Kildare Lurikeen

A young girl that lived in sight of Castle Carberry, near Edenderry, was going for a pitcher of water to the neighboring well one summer

From *The Crock of Gold*, by James Stephens, pp. 56-57. Copyright, 1912, by The Macmillan Co. New York.

From *Legendary Fiction of the Irish Celts*, by Patrick Kennedy, pp. 130-131. Macmillan & Co. London. 1866.

morning, when who should she see sitting in a sheltery nook, under an old thorn, but the Lurikeen, working like vengeance at a little old brogue only fit for the foot of a fairy like himself. There he was, boring his holes, and jerking his waxed ends, with his little three-cornered hat with gold lace, his knee-breeches, his jug of beer by his side, and his pipe in his mouth. He was so busy at his work, and so taken up with an old ballad he was singing in Irish, that he did not mind Breedheen till she had him by the scruff of the neck, as if he was in a vice.

"Ah, what are you doing?" says he, turning his head round as well as he could. "Dear, dear! to think of such a purty colleen ketching a body, as if he was after robbing a hen's roost! What did I do to be treated in such an undecent manner? The very vulgarest young ruffian in the townland could do no worse. Come, come, Miss Bridget, take your hands off, sit down, and let us have a chat, like two respectable people."

"Ah, Mr. Lurikeen, I don't care a wisp of borrach for your politeness. It's your money I want, and I won't take hand or eye from you till you put me in possession of a fine lob of it."

"Money, indeed! Ah! Where would a poor cobbler like me get it? Anyhow there's no money hereabouts, and if you'll only let go of my arms, I'll turn my pockets inside out, and open the drawer of my seat, and give you leave to take every halfpenny you'll find."

"That won't do; my eyes will be going through you like darning needles till I have the gold. Begonies, if you don't make haste, I'll carry you, head and pluck, into the village, and there you'll have thirty pair of eyes on you instead of one."

"Well, well! was ever a poor cobbler so circumvented! and if it was an ignorant, ugly bosthoon that done it, I would not wonder; but a decent, comely girl, that can read her 'Poor Man's Manual' at the chapel, and—"

"You may throw your compliments on the stream there; they won't do for me, I tell you. The gold, the gold, the gold! Don't take up my time with your blarney."

"Well, if there's any to be got, it's under the ould castle it is; we must have a walk for it. Just put me down, and we'll go on."

"Put you down, indeed! I know a trick worth two of that; I'll carry you."

"Well, how suspicious we are! Do you see the castle from this?" Bridget was about turning her eyes from the little man to where she knew the castle stood, but she bethought herself in time.

They went up a little hillside, and the Lurikeen was quite reconciled, and laughed and joked; but just as they got to the brow, he looked up over the ditch, and shouted as if a bugle horn was blew at her ears. "Oh, murder! Castle Carberry is afire!" Poor Bridget gave a great start, and looked up towards the castle. The same moment she missed the weight of the Lurikeen, and when her eyes fell where he was a moment before, there was no more sign of him than if everything that passed was a dream.

The Shannon Mermaid

"Sure, [said the old woman], 'twas over there beyond the corner where the river is that the mermaid was caught, and Deny Duggan described her to me, and he the oldest man in Foynes. The man that caught her was one of those who watched the weir over on the Island. They were forever seeing a woman on the point, and they knew it was the mermaid that was ever living in the river, and one day the man saw her sitting on a big stone on the point and she a-combing her fine golden hair back from the forehead of her, and combing it from the rack. And he faced round and crept up behind her when she was not knowing it, and caught her by the two shoulders of her, and brought her to his house, where his mother lived.

"It was the beautifullest woman ever you see'd, with the golden hair and fair skin of her. Now after a time he took her as his wife, and she had three children to him, and all the time she was doing all the work a woman might do, but never a smile or a laugh out of her, except one day when he was a-doing something with the child on the floor, playing with it, and then she let the sweetest laugh out of her that ever you heard. Now the man had taken the covering from her that she had the day sitting on the rock, a sort of an oily skin, and he had been told to keep it from her and put it away by way of luck.

"And the house was built so that the fireplace had piers like on each side of it, as in the country houses, and on the top a shelf, and 'twas on this that the man had put away the covering among the nets and sacks. For—she was going about the house doing all the work that a woman might do, but that she could never climb up on a thing, and she afeared even to stand on a chair to reach a thing as might be. But one day—it was seven years from the day he had caught her on the stone and brought her home—she was sitting by the fire with the

From *The Gael*, November, 1899, pp. 238. New York.

child, and he just able to walk. He was on her knee sitting, when the man came in looking for the net, and he began to throw things about on the shelf looking for it. Well, he threw down an old sack out of the way of him, and with it sure the covering fell down, and he never seeing it, and it fell behind her so as she couldn't lay hand to it with the child on her knee; so she looked over her shoulder and saw it, and she put the child to stand with the chair, went and took the covering and out of the door with it before the man had time to get down and stop her, and down to the shore she went with a laugh as never you heard with the ringing in it, and into the sea, and she never came back again.

"And the three children of her were reared on the island over beyond Deny Duggan's, and 'tis three ages [generations] ago now, for Deny he is the oldest man in Foynes, and when he was young he knew the children of her, and heard of her from a friend of the man that worked with him on the weir."

The Kerry Mermaid

A tinge of gray faintly illuminating the mottled clouds in the eastern sky was heralding the approach of dawn just as Donal More and his men were coming ashore after having been all night to sea. No sooner had those bronzed fishermen landed than they proceeded to store the fish temporarily—their night's catch—in a hut on the beach, and this task completed they secured their boat in a sheltered cove in close proximity to the hut.

Tired, sleepy, and hungry, the natural impulse of those men was to reach home as quickly as possible, and by the easiest and most direct route. Their way lay along the strand for a mile and from the strand to the public road that led to their homes there was a short, narrow, rocky path between a tall cliff, and at high water this path was impassable. The passage was called Aghgar, the alternate way was a difficult path over a steep mountain, and to avoid this circuitous route, many a desperate risk was taken and many a life was sacrificed in crossing the short but dangerous path of Aghgar.

On coming to Aghgar it was yet dark but not too dark for the men to discern that the tide was receding—a condition that made it possible for stalwart men such as they were to cross with comparative

By Michael O'Reilly, in *The Gael*, June, 1903, pp. 185-186. New York.

safety. They clasped hands, Donal leading as usual, and no sooner had they entered the passage than they saw before them seated on a rock a woman adjusting her tresses. As soon as she beheld them she seemed to get alarmed, and quick as lightning she disappeared into the water. In her great anxiety to get away, she forgot her mantle, and Donal instantly seized it and held it firmly in his grasp.

"That was the mermaid, or sea-nymph, about which we have heard so much," said Donal, "but this is the first time I ever laid eyes on her, though I have been to sea early and late."

Scarcely had he spoken these words and while yet beneath the cliff, the woman returned and demanded her cloak. With this demand Donal refused to comply, and the mermaid threatened that she would send a mighty wave against the cliff that would overwhelm them and sweep them into the depths of the ocean. This threat did not in the least alarm Donal, for he had often heard that a mermaid had no more power than any other woman after having parted with her mysterious mantle. When the men reached the road she was still following them and ceaselessly imploring Donal to return the garment, but her cries and screams and supplications did not in the least weaken his resolve to retain the cloak, and he folded it carefully and secured it inside his overcoat.

The woman's great distress moved the other men to pity—pity, perhaps, not unmingled with fear. Old Donough acted as spokesman and remonstrated with Donal.

"It is not lucky for you, Donal," said he, "to keep such a strange thing, and it is not safe and wise for you to bring it into your fine house, and the mermaid, the poor thing, will drop dead if you keep that cloak."

"Luck, or ill-luck," said Donal, "I will not part with the cloak, and as soon as I reach home, I will lock it in the large trunk."

The men were pained at Donal's strange behavior, but save an exchange of ominous looks they did not venture any further persuasion.

When the mermaid understood that there was no prospect of obtaining her cherished garment, she regained her composure and followed Donal meekly to his house where she henceforth took up her abode.

Donal was at this time about thirty years of age, and though there were hundreds of modest, good-looking, amiable young women within the circle of his acquaintance, he was yet a bachelor. For a man of his station in life, he was possessed of considerable wealth, in fact, he was the richest man in the barony. It was not necessary for him to follow fishing as a means of livelihood, but he always accompanied his men, and he was passionately fond of the sea. There was not from Valentia to Cape Clear an abler boatman than Donal; in the severest storm he could always manage to steer his boat to safety, and he was stalwart, clear-headed, and fearless.

As already stated, the mermaid made Donal's home her abode, and there was not any maid as skillful, as deft, or as zealous in the discharge of her duties. She was a beautiful young woman and Donal first became enamoured of her when he saw her seated on that rock beneath the cliffs at early dawn passing her shapely fingers through her bewitching ringlets.

Shortly a great transformation came over Donal's temperament, he was no longer to be seen with his fishermen and he absented himself from most of the social gatherings of the district. He appointed Donough captain of the boat, and although Donough, too, was an able seaman the men did not have the same confidence in him nor did they give him the same unquestioned obedience that they had unreservedly given to Donal.

"What is coming over Donal at all?" queried Diarmuid. "He cares for us no more. We miss him very much, and it is many a long night he shortened for us with his stories and songs and pleasant words."

"I am afraid," replied Donough, "that we won't see him very often again in this boat. It was a bad day for us all when he met that mermaid or whatever she is. He is so much in love with her that he has no thought for anyone or anything else. There is a rumor that they are to be married next Sunday."

"This is queer," said Diarmuid, "nobody ever heard of anything like it before. I can't understand how a man of Donal's standing can ever stoop to marry a mermaid that he knows nothing about, and that is not akin to any good old family. However, she is such a beautiful creature that it is hard to blame him for falling in love with her. We all know why Donal was so stony-hearted on the morning that he first met her and why he refused to part with the cloak."

The attachment of Donal to the mermaid was discussed far and near and many ventured to predict that the mermaid would take Donal to Tirnanog as Niad had taken Ossian a thousand years before.

Donal and the mermaid were married and there was not in all Kerry a more loving couple than they. Nor had he any reasons to regret his choice, for the mermaid was a dutiful wife and an exemplary mother, and time only still more enhanced her in his esteem. She had an aversion to certain drinks and foods, she never tasted broths or roasted meats, and she would not allow fish of any kind to be brought into the house.

They had been married over thirty years and they were blessed with a large grown-up family. The daughters were like the mother, remarkably handsome, and there were not living at that time any women who approached them in beauty, and they had qualities more enduring than beauty which endeared them to their neighbors and acquaintances. Their sons were tall and stalwart and they inherited their father's passion for the sea. They were leaders in every manly exercise, and there were not in all Ireland more skilled and fearless seamen. Sons and daughters were verily a credit to their parents and their happy home was the rendezvous of scholars, seannachies, and musicians.

Everything prospered with this worthy family, and with wealth came a desire for social distinction. To satisfy this desire they purchased a fine residence in the capital city of the province. All arrangements having been completed, the moving day arrived; and moving was then even a more formidable task than now, for the vans of over two hundred years ago were rather primitive, and the ideal roads of today were then unknown.

It was long past midday when the heavy-laden wagons were ready to proceed to the city. The family were seated in their coaches ready for the journey when the mother alighted from her coach and returned to the house presumably for something she had forgotten, or perhaps to take another look at the interior of a home in which she had lived so long, where she had spent the happy days of youth, where the children were born, and where she had resided until arrived at serene and contented old age.

On passing through one of the now almost empty rooms—empty of everything worth removing—she noticed that a large trunk that contained miscellaneous old articles had fallen in pieces, and the contents were scattered broadcast on the floor.

She stooped and picked up what appeared to be an old, dust-covered, well-worn garment, and no sooner did she grasp it than she laughed so loudly that her laugh was heard all over the village—if Donal had forgotten the magic mantle, not so had the mermaid— In an instant she regained her former youth and beauty, she no longer cared for husband and children, and swifter than the velocity of the March winds she returned joyfully to her beloved Tirnanog on the blue rim of the western ocean.

Daniel Crowley and the Ghosts

There lived a man in Cork whose name was Daniel Crowley. He was a coffinmaker by trade, and had a deal of coffins laid by, so that his apprentice might sell them when he himself was not at home.

A messenger came to Daniel Crowley's shop one day and told him that there was a man dead at the end of the town, and to send up a coffin for him, or to make one.

Daniel Crowley took down a coffin, put it on a donkey cart, drove to the wakehouse, went in, and told the people of the house that the coffin was there for them. The corpse was laid out on a table in a room next to the kitchen. Five or six women were keeping watch around it; many people were in the kitchen. Daniel Crowley was asked to sit down and commence to shorten the night—that is, to tell stories, amuse himself and the others. A tumbler of punch was brought, and he promised to do the best he could.

He began to tell stories and shorten the night. A second glass of punch was brought to him, and he went on telling tales. There was a man at the wake who sang a song; after him another was found, and then another. Then the people asked Daniel Crowley to sing, and he did. The song that he sang was of another nation. He sang about the good people, the fairies. The song pleased the company, who desired him to sing again, and he did not refuse.

Daniel Crowley pleased the company so much with his two songs that a woman who had three daughters wanted to make a match for one of them, and get Daniel Crowley as a husband for her. Crowley was a bachelor, well on in years, and had never thought of marrying.

The mother spoke of the match to a woman sitting next to her. The woman shook her head, but the mother said: "If he takes one of my daughters, I'll be glad, for he has money laid by. Do you go and speak to him, but say nothing of me at first."

The woman went to Daniel Crowley then, and told him that she had a fine, beautiful girl in view, and that now was his time to get a good wife; he'd never have such a chance again.

Crowley rose up in great anger. "There isn't a woman wearing clothes I'd marry," said he. "There isn't a woman born that could bring me to make two halves of my loaf for her."

The mother was insulted now and forgot herself. She began to abuse Crowley.

From *The Gael*, April, 1899, pp. 43-44. New York.

"Bad luck to you, you hairy little scoundrel," said she, "you might be a grandfather to my child. You are not fit to clean the shoes on her feet. You have only dead people for company day and night; 'tis by them you make your living."

"Oh, then," said Daniel Crowley, "I'd prefer the dead to the living any day if all the living were like you. Besides, I have nothing against the dead. I am getting employment by them, and not by the living, for 'tis the dead that want coffins."

"Bad luck to you, 'tis with the dead you ought to be, and not with the living; 'twould be fitter for you to go out of this altogether and go to your dead people."

"I'd go if I knew how to go to them," said Crowley.

"Why not invite them to supper?" retorted the woman.

He rose up then, went out, and called: "Men, women, children, soldiers, sailors, all people that I have made coffins for, I invite you to-night to my house, and I'll spend what is needed in giving a feast."

The people who were watching the dead man on the table saw him smile when he heard the invitation. They ran out of the room in a fright and out of the kitchen, and Daniel Crowley hurried away to his shop as fast as his donkey could carry him. On the way he came to a public-house, and, going in, bought a pint bottle of whiskey, put it in his pocket, and drove on.

The workshop was locked and the shutters down when he left that evening, but when he came near he saw that all the windows were shining with light, and he was in dread for the building or that robbers were in it. Then right there Crowley slipped into a corner of the building opposite, to know could he see what was happening, and soon he saw crowds of men, women, and children walking towards his shop and going in, but none coming out. He was hiding some time when a man tapped him on the shoulder and asked: "Is it here you are, and we waiting for you? 'Tis a shame to treat company this way. Come now."

Crowley went with the man to the shop, and as he passed the threshold he saw a great gathering of people. Some were neighbors, people he had known in the past. All were dancing, singing, amusing themselves. He was not long looking on when a man came up to him and said: "You seem not to know me, Daniel Crowley."

"I don't know you," said Crowley. "How could I?"

"You might then, and you ought to know me, for I am the first man you made a coffin for, and 'twas I gave you the first start in business."

Soon another came up, a lame man. "Do you know me, Daniel Crowley?"

"I do not."

"I am your cousin, and it isn't long since I died."

"Oh, now I know you well, for you are lame. In God's name," said Crowley to the cousin, "how am I to get these people out of this? What time is it?"

" 'Tis early yet; it's hardly eleven o'clock, man."

Crowley wondered that it was so early.

"Receive them kindly," said the cousin; "be good to them, make merriment as you can."

"I have no money with me to get food or drink for them; 'tis night now, and all the places are closed," answered Crowley.

"Well, do the best you can," said the cousin.

The fun and dancing went on, and while Daniel Crowley was looking around, examining everything, he saw a woman in the far-off corner. She took no part in the amusement, but seemed very shy in herself.

"Why is that woman so shy—she seems to be afraid?" asked he of the cousin. "And why doesn't she dance and make merry like the others?"

"Oh, 'tis not long since she died, and you gave the coffin, as she had no means of paying for it. She is in dread lest you'll ask her for the money, or let the company know that she didn't pay," said the cousin.

The best dancer they had was a piper by the name of John Reardon, from the City of Cork. The fiddler was one John Healy. Healy brought no fiddle with him, but he made one, and the way he made it was to take off what flesh he had on his body. He rubbed up and down on his own ribs, each rib having a different note, and he made the loveliest music that Daniel Crowley had ever heard. After that the whole company followed his example. All threw off what flesh they had on them and began to dance jigs and hornpipes in their bare bones. When by chance they struck against one another in dancing, you'd think it was Brandon Mountain that was striking Mount Eagle, with the noise that was in it.

Daniel Crowley plucked up all his courage to know could he live through the night, but still he thought daylight would never come. There was one man, John Sullivan, that he noticed especially. This man had married twice in his life, and with him came the two women. Crowley saw him taking out the second wife to dance a breakdown, and the two danced so well that the company were delighted, and all the skeletons had their mouths open, laughing. He danced and knocked so much merriment out of them all that his first wife, who was at the end of the house, became jealous and very mad. altogether. She ran down to where he was and told him she had a better right to dance with him than the second wife.

"That's not the truth for you," said the second wife. "I have a better right than you. When he married me you were a dead woman and he was free, and, besides, I'm a better dancer than what you are, and I will dance with him whether you like it or not."

"Hold your tongue!" screamed the first wife. "Sure, you couldn't come to this feast at all but for the loan of another woman's shinbones."

Sullivan looked at his two wives, and asked the second one: "Isn't it your own shinbones you have?"

"No, they are borrowed. I borrowed a neighboring woman's shinbones from her, and 'tis those I have with me tonight."

"Who is the owner of the shinbones you have under you," asked the husband.

"They belong to one Catherine Murray. She hadn't a very good name in life."

"But why didn't you come on your own feet?"

"Oh, I wasn't good myself in life, and I was put under a penalty, and the penalty is that whenever there is a feast or a ball I cannot go to it unless I am able to borrow a pair of shins."

Sullivan was raging when he found that the shinbones he had been dancing with belonged to a third woman, and she not the best, and he gave a slap to the wife that sent her spinning into a corner.

The woman had relations among the skeletons present, and they were angry when they saw the man strike their friend. "We'll never let that go with him," said they. "We must knock satisfaction out of Sullivan!"

The woman's friends rose up, and, as there were no clubs or weapons, they pulled off their left arms and began to slash and strike with them in terrible fashion. There was an awful battle in one minute.

While this was going on, Daniel Crowley was standing below at the end of the room, cold and hungry, not knowing but he'd be killed. As Sullivan was trying to dodge the blows sent against him, he got as far as Daniel Crowley, and stepped on his toes without knowing it. Crowley got vexed and gave Sullivan a blow with his fist that drove the head from him, and sent it flying to the opposite corner.

When Sullivan saw his head flying off from the blow, he ran, and, catching it, aimed a blow at Daniel Crowley with the head, and aimed so truly that he knocked him under the bench; then, having him at a disadvantage, Sullivan hurried to the bench and began to strangle him. He squeezed his throat and held him so firmly between the benches and the floor that the man lost his senses and couldn't remember a thing more.

When Daniel Crowley came to himself in the morning his apprentice found him stretched under the bench with an empty bottle under his arm. He was bruised and pounded. His throat was sore where Sullivan had squeezed it. He didn't know how the company broke up, nor when his guests went away.

The Student Who Disappeared

There came a number of young people from the County of Galway to a great college, to learn and gain instruction, so as to become priests. I often heard the name of the college from my mother, but I do not remember it. It was not Maynooth. There was a man of these of the name Patrick O'Flynn. He was the son of a rich farmer. His father and mother desired to make a priest of him. He was a nice, gentle lad. He used not to go dancing with the other boys in the evening, but it was his habit to go out with the grey light of day, and he used to be walking by himself up and down under the shadow of the great trees that were round about the college, and he used to remain there thinking and meditating by himself, until some person would come to bring him in to his room.

One evening, in the month of May, he went out, as was his custom, and he was taking his walk under the trees when he heard a melodious music. There came a darkness or a sort of blindness over his eyes, and when he found his sight again he beheld a great high wall on every side of him, and out in front of him a shining road. The musicians were on the road, and they playing melodiously, and he heard a voice saying, *"Come with us to the land of delight and rest."* He looked back and he beheld a great high wall behind him and on each side of him, and he was not able to return back again across the wall, although he desired to return. He went forward then after the music. He did not know how long he walked, but the great high wall kept ever on each side of him and behind him.

He was going and ever-going, until they came to a great river, and water in it as red as blood. Wonder came upon him then, and great fear. But the musicians walked across the river without wetting their

From *Amhrain Diadhe Chuige Connacht, The Religious Songs of Connacht,* translated by Douglas Hyde, Vol. II, pp. 123-133. M. H. Gill & Co. Dublin. [1906.]

feet, and Patrick O'Flynn followed them without wetting his own. He thought at first that the musicians belonged to the Fairy Host, and next he thought that he had died and that it was a group of angels that were in it, taking him to heaven.

The walls fell away from them, then, on each side, and they came to a great wide plain. They were going then, and ever-going, until they came to a fine castle that was in the midst of the plain. The musicians went in, but Patrick O'Flynn remained outside. It was not long until the chief of the musicians came out to him and brought him in to a handsome chamber. He spoke not a word, and Patrick O'Flynn never heard one word spoken as long as he remained there.

There was no night in that place, but the light of day throughout. He never ate and he never drank a single thing there, and he never saw anyone eating or drinking and the music never ceased. Every half-hour, as he thought, he used to hear a bell, as it were a church-bell, being rung, but he never beheld the bell, and he was unable to see it in any place.

When the musicians used to go out upon the plain before the castle, there used to come a tribe of every sort of birds in the heavens, singing the most melodious music that ear ever heard. It was often Patrick O'Flynn said to himself, "It is certain that I am in heaven, but is it not curious that I have no remembrance of sickness, nor of death, nor of judgment, and that I have not seen God, nor His Blessed Mother, as is promised to us!"

Patrick O'Flynn did not know how long he was in that delightful place. He thought he had been in it only for a short little time, but he was in it for a hundred years and one.

One day the musicians were out in the field and he was listening to them, when the chief came to him. He brought him out and put him behind the musicians. They departed on their way, and they made neither stop nor stay until they came to the river that was as red as blood. They went across that, without wetting their foot-soles, and went forward until they came to the field near the college where they had found him at first. Then they departed out of his sight like a mist.

He looked round him, and recognized the college, but he thought that the trees were higher and that there was some change in the college itself. He went in, then, but he did not recognize a single person whom he met, and not a person recognized him.

The principal of the college came to him, and said to him, "Where are you from, son, and what is your name?"

"I am Patrick O'Flynn from the County of Galway," said he.

"How long are you here?" said the principal.

"I am here since the first day of March," said he.

"I think you are out of your senses," said the principal. "There is no person of your name in the college, and there has not been for twenty years, for I am more than twenty years here."

"Though you were in it since you were born, yet I am here since last March, and I can show you my room and my books."

With that, he went up the stairs and the principal after him. He went into his room and looked around him, and said, "This is my room, but this is not my furniture, and those are not my books that are in it." He saw an old Bible on the table and he opened it, and said, "This is my Bible, my mother gave it to me when I was coming here, and, see, my name is written in it."

The principal looked at the Bible, and there, as sure as God is in heaven, was the name of Patrick O'Flynn written in it, and the day of the month that he left home.

Now there was great trouble of mind on the principal, and he did not know what he should do. He sent for the masters and the professors and told them the story.

"By my word," said an old priest that was in it, "I heard talk when I was young, of a student who went away out of the college, and there was no account of him since, whether living or dead. The people searched the river and the bog holes, but there was no account to be had of him, and they never got the body."

The principal called to them then to bring him a great book in which the name of every person was written who had come to that college since it was founded. He looked through the book, and see! Patrick O'Flynn's name was in it, and the day of the month that he came, and this (note) was written opposite to his name, that the same Patrick O'Flynn had departed on such a day, and that nobody knew what had become of him. Now it was exactly one hundred and one years from that day he went until the day he came back in that fashion.

"This is a wonderful and a very wonderful story," said the principal, "but, do you wait here quietly, my son," said he, "and I shall write to the bishop." He did that, and he got an account from the bishop to keep the man until he should come himself.

At the end of a week after that the bishop came and sent for Patrick O'Flynn. There was nobody present except the two. "Now, son," said the bishop, "go on your knees and make a good confession." Then he made an act of contrition, and the bishop gave him absolution. Immediately there came a fainting and a heavy sleep over him, and he was, as it were, for three days and nights a dead person. When he came to himself the bishop and priests were round and about him.

He rose up, shook himself, and told them his story, as I have told it, and he put excessive wonderment upon every man of them. "Now," said he, "here I am alive and safe, and do as ye please."

The bishop and the priests took counsel together. "It is a saintly man you are," said the bishop then, "and we shall give you holy orders on the spot."

They made a priest of him then, and no sooner were holy orders given him then he fell dead upon the altar, and they all heard at the same time the most melodious music that ear ever listened to, above them in the sky, and they all said it was the angels who were in it, carrying the soul of Father O'Flynn up to heaven with them.

The Strange Tale of O'Neill's Son

In the time when there were kings in Ireland it was their custom to be taking spoils from each other. O'Connor took a spoil from O'Neill. Repentance overtook him and he sent a message to O'Neill and his son to come to a feast and that he would give back the spoil. They went west to O'Connor. O'Connor met them and gave them good welcome. They were walking towards the house, O'Neill's son behind them. He saw a nice hazel rod. He pulled out a pocket-knife and cut it. He was cutting a point on the rod and he did not notice until he was at O'Connor's house. He bethought himself that it would be an unmannerly thing to go in to the company with a knife in his hand, and he thrust it into the eave of the house. When he entered he saw his father lying on the ground, bleeding and wounded. He pulled him out and put him on his back and took him to a house of healing on the other side of the river. It was a year and a day before the father recovered.

At the end of the year and the day they set out to go home and when they came to the river it was in flood, and the son put the father on his back to carry him across the river. In the middle of the river he slipped on a stone and fell. The father was carried off by the flood and vanished from sight.

O'Neill's son was greatly distressed then. He did not know what to do. He thought he would go home. As he was passing O'Connor's

From "Mac ui Neill," collected by Enri O Muirgheasa, in *Béaloideas*, Journal of the Folklore of Ireland Society. Dublin. 1927. Translated by Maire Mac Neill for the editor.

house on the way home he saw the knife he had thrust in the eave a year ago. He said to himself he would not give them the satisfaction of having it, and he pulled out his knife, closed it and put it in his pocket. Walking past the door he looked in and saw his father and the nobles sitting round the table.

"My son," said the father, "what delayed you? The nobles are waiting for you, and the food is getting cold."

"Oh, Father," said O'Neill's son, "is it you? If it is, there is something odd in the case."

"It is I," said O'Neill, "and there is nothing wrong, and what is coming over you?"

"Come hither, Father," said the son, "until I tell you that they made a murderous attack on you a year ago, and that I took you to a house of healing and that you were carried off from me in the flood."

"Och, Son," said he, "there was nothing of that."

"If that is true," said the son, "I will not return home nor any other place, and I will not sleep two nights in the same house until I see if the like of what happened to me ever happened to anyone else."

Off he went, following his head, and he was wandering away for years. Late one evening he came into a house and asked, and was given, a night's hospitality. When he had eaten his supper, the man of the house asked him where he was going and how far he had walked. He told him, as I have told you, what happened to him.

The man of the house said, "You will have no need to go farther. A much stranger thing happened to me than happened to you."

The king's son was filled with joy when he heard that. The man of the house told him that he had a big field of oats and that he got twelve reapers to cut the oats. "I myself was binding in their wake," said he, "and when the woman of the house called out for them to go in to dinner, I told the men to go in, and I remained to bind what they had reaped. When I had the last sheaf bound I went to the house and I met the men coming out, and when I entered all the bread was eaten. My wife asked me to go to the well for a *pigin* [piggin] full of water so that she could make me a little loaf and bake it on the embers.

"I went down to the well and I took a *pigin* full of the water and set it standing on a stone which was above the well. I looked out on the sea and saw the nicest little *curach* coming in on the wave-tops. I went down to the shore and put one foot into the *curach* and the *curach* went out. I had to draw my other foot in. The *curach* went out to sea from wave to wave, and I was in fear I would be drowned.

"The *curach* landed me at an island I had never seen. As quick as my soles could go, I was ashore. I was dressed in woman's clothes from throat to ankle and I had become a woman.

"I walked on until I went into a house. I asked and was granted a night's hospitality. They asked me where I was going and how far I had come. I could not tell them. I had lost my memory. They told me the king of the place was offering a big reward to any woman who would bring up his child. The next morning I went to the king and I told him I would bring up his child. This I did until the child was reared. I was walking one day beside the sea with the child on my shoulder and I saw a little *curach* coming in on top of the waves. I went down and put one foot in it to pull it in, but the *curach* floated out, and I and the child with it. It did not stop from wave to wave until it left me in the same place where it had found me. As I got out of it, my own clothes were on me and I was a man again. On my way up I saw the *pigin* full of water on the stone over the well, and I thought I would bring it to the house. When I went in, my wife was standing at the table with her hands down in the flour bin.

" 'You were in a great hurry an hour ago,' " she said, "and you are in no hurry now. Wherever you found that child, you could have left it with its own mother."

" 'Woman o,' said I, 'there is more than that to the story,' and I told her what I have told you. She was greatly amazed.

"And, man," said he to O'Neill's son, "that is the same girl there standing on the floor as the child I reared."

His wife testified to O'Neill's son that it was all true.

As soon as O'Neill's son saw the light of day next morning he went home to his father and stayed with him ever after. And that is the marvel that happened to O'Neill's son.

The Woman Who Went to Hell

There was a woman coming out of her garden with an apron-full of cabbage. A man met her. He asked her what she would take for her burden. She said it was not worth a great deal, that she would give it to him for nothing. He said he would not take it, but would buy it. She said she would only take sixpence. He gave her the sixpence. She threw the cabbage towards him. He said that was not what he bought,

From *West Irish Folk-Tales and Romances*, collected and translated by William Larminie, pp. 188-195. Elliot Stock. London. 1898.

but the burden she was carrying. Who was there but the devil? She was troubled then. She went home and she was weeping. It was a short time until her young son was born. He was growing till he was eighteen years old. He was out one day and fell, and never rose up till he died. When they were going to bury him, they took him to the people's house (*i.e.*, the chapel). They left him there till morning.

There was a man among the neighbors who had three daughters. He took out a box of snuff to give (the men) a pinch. The last man to whom the box went round left the box on the altar. They went home. When the man was going to bed he went looking for his box. The box was not to be got. He said he had left it behind him in the people's house. He said he would not sleep that night until he got a pinch. He asked one of his daughters to go to the people's house and bring him the box that was on the altar. She said there was loneliness on her. He cried to the second woman, would she go? She said she would not go; that she was lonely. He cried to the third, would she go? And she said she would go; that there was no loneliness on her in his presence (*i.e.*, of the corpse).

She went to the people's house. She found the box. She put it in her pocket. When she was coming away she saw a ring at the end of the coffin. She caught hold of it till it came to her. The end came from the coffin. The man that was dead came out. He enjoined on her not to be afraid.

"Do you see that fire over yonder? If you are able, carry me to that fire."

"I am not able," said she.

"Be dragging me with you as well as you can."

She put him on her back. She dragged him till they came to the fire.

"Draw out the fire," said he, "and put me lying in the midst of it; fix up the fire over me. Anything of me that is not burnt put the fire on it again."

He was burning till he was all burnt. When the day was coming she was troubled on account of what she had seen during the night. When the day grew clear there came a young man, who began making fun with her.

"I have not much mind for fun on account of what I have seen during the night."

"Well, it was I who was there," said the young man.

Three quarters (of a year) from that night she dressed herself up as if she was a poor woman. She went to his father's house and asked for lodging till morning. The woman of the house said that they were not giving lodging to any poor person at all. She said she would not ask but a seat by the fire. The man of the house told her to stay till morning. She sat by the fire. In the course of the night she went into the room, and there she had a young son. He, *i.e.*, her husband, came in at the window in the shape of a white dove. He dressed the child. The child began to cry. The woman of the house heard the crying. She would wager the lady had left a baby after her. She rose to get out of bed. Her husband told her to lie quiet and have patience. She got up in spite of him. The door of the room was shut. She looked in through the keyhole. He was standing on the floor. She perceived it was her son who was there. She cried to him, was it he that was there? He said it was.

"One glance of your eyes has sent me for seven years to hell."

"I will go myself in your place," said his mother.

She went then to go to hell. When she came to the gate, there came out steam so that she was burnt and scalded. It was necessary for her to return. "Well," said the father, "I will go in your place." It was necessary for him to return. The young man began to weep. He said he must go himself. The mother of the child said that she would go.

"Here is a ring for you," said he. "When thirst comes on you, or hunger, put the ring in your mouth; you will feel neither thirst nor hunger. This is the work that will be on you—to keep down the souls; they are stewing and burning in the boiler. Do not eat a bit of food there. There is a barrel in the corner, and all the food that you get throw into the barrel."

She went to hell then. She was keeping down the souls in the boiler. They were rising in leaps out of it. All the food she got she threw into the barrel till the seven years were over. She was making ready to be going then. The devil came to her. He said she could not go yet awhile till she had paid for the food she had eaten. She said she had not eaten one morsel of his share: "All that I got, it is in the barrel." The devil went to the barrel. All he had given her was there for him.

"How much will you take to stay seven years more?"

"Oh, I am long enough with you," said she; "if you give me the all that I can carry, I can stay with you."

He said he would give it. She stopped. She was keeping down the souls during seven years. She was shortening the time as well as she could till the seven years were ended. Then she was going. When the souls saw she was going they rose up with one cry, lest one of them should be left. They went clinging to her; they were hanging to her hair all that were in the boiler. She moved on with her burden. She had not gone far when a lady in a carriage met her.

"Oh! great is your burden," said the lady; "will you give it to me?"

"Who are you?" said she.

"I am the Virgin Mary."

"I will not give it to you."

She moved on with herself. She had not gone far when a gentleman met her.

"Great is your burden, my poor woman; will you give it to me?"

"Who are you?" said she.

"I am God," said he.

"I will not give my burden to you."

She went on with herself another while. Another gentleman met her.

"Great is the burden you have," said the gentleman; "will you give it to me?"

"Who are you?" said she.

"I am the King of Sunday," said he.

"I will give my burden to you," said she. "No rest had I ever in hell except on Sunday."

"Well, it is a good woman you are; the first lady you met it was the devil was there; the second person you met it was the devil was there, trying if they could get your burden from your back. Now," said God, "the man for whom you have done all this is going to be married to-morrow. He thought you were lost since you were in that place so long."

She did not know till she was at home. The house was full of drinking and music. She went to the fire. Her own son came up to her.

The ring that her husband gave her she put in the glass.

"Put your hand over the mouth of the glass; give it to no one at all till you hand it to your father."

The lad went to his father. He gave him the glass. The father looked into it, and saw the ring. He recognized the ring.

"Who has given you this?" said he.

"A poor woman by the fire," said the lad.

The father raised the child on his shoulders that he might point out to him the woman who had given him the ring. The child came to the poor woman.

"That is the woman," said he, "who gave me the ring."

The man recognized her then. He said that hardly did he know her when she came so worn and wasted. He said to all the people that he would never marry any woman but this one; that she had done everything for him; that his mother sold him to the devil, and the woman had earned him back; that she had spent fourteen years in hell, and now she had returned.

This is a true story. They are all lies but this one.

The Palace in the Rath

Everybody from Boncady to Enniscorthy knows the rath (a fortified place surrounded by a wall or ditch) between Tombrick and Munfin. Well, there was a poor, honest, quiet little creature, that lived just at the pass of Glenamoin, between the hill of Coolgarrow and Kilach-diarmid. His back was broken when he was a child, and he earned his bread by making cradles, and bosses, and chairs, and beehives, out of straw and briers. No one in the barony of Bantry or Scarawalsh could equal him at these. Well, he was a sober little fellow enough, but the best of us may be overtaken. He was coming from the fair of Enniscorthy one fine summer evening, up along the beautiful shady road of Munfin; and when he came near the stream that bounds Tombrick, he turned into the fields to make his road short. He was singing merrily enough, but by degrees he got a little stupefied; and when he was passing the dry, grassy ditch that surrounds the rath, he felt an inclination to sit and rest himself.

It is hard to sit awhile, and have your eyes a little glassy, and the things seeming to turn round you, without falling off asleep; and asleep my poor little man of straw was in a few minutes. Things like droves of cattle, or soldiers marching, or big flakes of foam on a flooded river were pushing on through his brain, and he thought the drums were playing a march, when he woke up, and there in the face of the steep bank that was overgrown with bushes and blackthorn, a passage was open between nice pillars, and inside was a great vaulted room, with arches crossing each other, a hundred lamps hanging from the vault, and thousands of nice little gentlemen and ladies, with green coats and gowns, and red sugar-loaf caps, dancing and singing, and nice little pipers and fiddlers, perched up in a little gallery by themselves, and playing music to help out the singing.

He was a little cowed at first, but as he found no one taking notice of him, he stole in, and sat in a corner, and thought he'd never be tired looking at the fine little people figuring, and cutting capers, and singing. But at last he began to find the singing and music a little tedious. It was nothing but two short bars and four words, and this was the style:

> Yae Luan, yae Morth—
> Yae Luan, yae Morth.

From *Legendary Fiction of the Irish Celts*, by Patrick Kennedy, pp. 100-104. Macmillan & Co. London. 1866.

The longer he looked on, the bolder he grew, and at last he shouted at the end of the verse:

Agus Dha Haed-yeen.

Oh, such cries of delight as rose up among the merry little gentry! They began the improved song, and shouted it until the vault rang:

Yae Luan, yae Morth—
Yae Luan, yae Morth
Yae Luan, yae Morth,
   Agus Dha Haed-yeen*

After a few minutes, they all left off the dance, and gathered round the boss maker, and thanked him for improving their tune. "Now," said the chief, "if you wish for anything, only say the word, and, if it is in our power, it must be done." "I thank you, ladies and gentleman," says he, "and if you'd only remove this hump from my back, I'd be the happiest man in the Duffrey." "Oh, easy done, easy done!" said they. "Go on again with the dance, and you come along with us." So they went on with:

Yae Luan, Yae Morth,
Yae Luan, Yae Morth,
Yae Luan, Yae Morth,
   Agus Dha Haed-yeen.

One fairy taking the new friend by the heel, shot him in a curve to the very roof, and down he came the other side of the hall. Another gave him a shove, and up he flew back again. He felt as if he had wings; and one time when his back touched the roof, he found a sudden delightful change in himself; and just as he touched the ground, he lost all memory of everything around him.

Next morning he was awakened by the sun shining on his face from over Slieve Buie, and he had a delightful feel down along his body instead of the disagreeable *cruith* he was accustomed to. He felt as if he could go from that to the other side of the stream at one step, and

---

* Monday, Tuesday
  Monday, Tuesday,
  Monday, Tuesday,
   And Wednesday.
Correctly: Dia Luain, Dia Mairt, Dia Ceadoin.—P.K.

he burned little daylight till he reached Glenamoin. He had some trouble to persuade the neighbours of the truth of what had happened; but the wonder held only nine days; and he had like to lose his health along with his hump, for if he only made his appearance in Bally-carney, Castle Dockrell, Ballindaggin, Kilmeashil, or Bonclody, ten people would be inviting him to a share of a tumbler of punch, or a quart of mulled beer.

The news of the wonderful cure was talked of high and low, and even went as far as Ballynocrish, in Bantry, where another poor *anga-shore* of a humpback lived. But he was very unlike the Duffrey man in his disposition; he was as cross as a brier, and almost begrudged his right hand to help his left. His poor old aunt and a neighbour of hers set out one day, along with him, along the Bunclody road, passing by Killanne and the old place of the Colcoughs at Duffrey Hall, till they reached Temple-shambo. Then they kept along the hilly by-road till they reached the little man's house near the pass.

So they went up and told their business, and he gave them a kind welcome, and explained all the ins and outs of his adventure; and the end was, the four went together in the heel of the evening to the rath, and left the little lord in his glory in the dry, brown grass of the round dyke, where the other met his good fortune. The little ounkran never once thanked them for all the trouble they were taking for him. He only whimpered about being left in that lonesome place, and bade them to be sure to be with him at the flight of night, because he did not know what way to take from it.

At last, the poor cross creature fell asleep; and after dreaming about falling down from the rocks, and being held over the sea by his hump, and then that a lion had him by the same hump, and was running away with him, and then that it was put up for a target for soldiers to shoot at, the first volley they gave awoke him, and what was it but the music of the fairies in full career. The melody was the same as it was left them by the hive-maker, and the tune and dancing was twice as good as it was at first. This is the way it went:

Yae Luan, yae Morth—
Yae Luan, yae Morth—
Yae Luan, yae Morth—
Agus Dha Haed-yeen.

But the new visitor had neither taste nor discretion; so when they came about the third time to the last line, he croaked out:

Agus Dha-Yaerd-yeen,
Agus Dha Haen-ya.*

It was the same as a cross fiddler that finds nobody going to give him anything, and makes a harsh back-screak of his bow along one of the strings. A thousand voices cried out, "Who stops our dance? Who stops our dance?" and all gathered round the poor fellow. He could do nothing but stare at them with his poor, cross, frightened face; and they screamed and laughed till he thought it was all over with him.

But it was *not* over with him.

"Bring down that hump," says the king; and before you could kiss your hand it was clapped on, as fast as the knocker of Newgate, over the other hump. The music was over now, the lights went out, and the poor creature lay till morning in a nightmare; and there the two women found him, at daybreak, more dead than alive. It was a dismal return they had to Ballynocrish; and the moral of my story is, that you should never drive till you first try the virtue of leading.

The Meanest Man in Munster

The Galbally farmers are the meanest men in Munster! Whoever knows anything knows that. It was a priest who gave out that saying on them, and he never spoke a truer word. It is a sight to look at them in the market or at a fair. At Cahirmee the whole world knows them for a blister and a blemish on the five countries. There they are all for *airgead sios,* and luck pennies back, and neither pedigree, nor blood, nor learning, nor Latin, has any sway with them, nothing but the ready lucre and the yellow gold. And the price they'd offer for a horse one would think it was how you stole him. Even the young children despise them, and going on along the road would show never a one of them a bird's nest for fear the *bodoch* would rob it against night came.

But bad as they are now, their fathers before them were a sight worse in the old times. 'Tis how one of them used to be coming across the hills into the country when the mills are grinding at Killavullen and Castletown. Well, he was the mean man. If he ever had a name of his own even the women disremembered it. But they had a song on

---

* Correctly: Dia Daoin, Dia Aoine—Thursday, Friday.—P.K.

By John Shandon, in *The Gael,* February, 1903, pp. 46-47. New York.

him and a bye-word, and the "Trencherman" was the name they put
on him. 'Tis that he was long of leg and long of step, a tall, thin, and
lathy man. If he was anything at all 'tis one of the White Knights'
people he was, and curse-bound like the whole box and dice of them.

Well, he was the mean man. His endeavours were forever to be eating and drinking. The worst of it was that nothing would fatten him.
My hand to you but he could eat and drink for a month of Sundays
and be still lean and hunger-bitten. He vexed many a hospital house
and spluttered over many a good table. As soon as ever the miller sat
down to his bit of sup, morn, noon or night who throws his long sack
of a body across the half door but my bould Trencherman. Never
abashed comes in my boyo, with his puss all mouth only for the two
little slits of eyes he got from a weasel forever on the hunt for meat
and drink.

You should see him at a "patron" humming about from booth to
booth. Full of talk to men he never saw before though in truth he was
befamed in every parish. 'Tis queer things were heard tell of him. He
once plucked a poor red ousel and ate her without salt, and they made
a joke of his cuteness, saying he's drown an eel in an eggcupful of
water, and so on.

Wake or wedding he was always on the make till he was counted the
curse of the country—dragging it down—and men began to aggravate
themselves against him. As for the women—they found him out entirely. With them he was no good for King or Kilbeeny county. He
was once at a funeral and when all was over, and the sod spread with
boys and girls beginning to amuse themselves slashing one another
with nettles, didn't they discover that someone had eat the priest's
breakfast, and his reverence not yet at the Munda Cor Meum of the
Mass, and the Book not passed. 'Twas how he went into the kitchen
tracing relations and when the good woman of the house ran out to
say a few prayers, he out with the meat in the maw like the mean
mongrel he was. Well, the women fell on him and the whole congregation were at him trying to make him behave himself.

After that not a bit would he get for love or money or God-sake
in the world, so he was minded to put the length of Ireland between
himself and the people. He cut his stick and greased his brogues and
off beyond the hills to Galbally and nothing with him but a dish cover
he stole. He crossed the Funcheon by Athaneen and spent the night
in a haggard east of Kildoorrery, with no other companions than the
owl and the wildcat—kind for him. He made three parts of that night,
one cursing the country for turning sour to him, one contriving to be

venged on them, and one making a moan for the emptiness of this
world.

There is a well hard by there under the mountain ash blessed for
healing by St. Molaga; the water is so mellifluent that people say the
bees be washing golden honey in it. There is a little white trout do be
in that well from oldtime out of mind. He was the Saint's own little
storeen and pet, and came from beyond seas with him. He is blessed
too, and shines in the dark places of the water, and at night, like a
star through the trees. Moreover, he is most knowledgeable and no one
ever envies him on his happy swimmingness. The children that see him
will never lose sight of their eyes nor do the cattle get murrain.

They saw many things of that Molaga trout, that are too wonderful
to remember. Time is a good story-teller but he is getting old. Once
a little otter that had been ginned and hurted before her escape could
not go to a hunting that day, nor the other day, and her five whelpeens
were like to starve.

"My dear, love to you forever," said the otter in Irish to the trout.
"Comradeen of the clear water, my children are small and 'tis food
they want. Help me, for Molaga's sake, and in the Long Day, at the
Latter End, by the Brink of Judgment, I will stand by you."

"No sooner said than done," made answer the Blessed Trout, and
he opened his veins and gave his ripe rich blood to whet the weeny
water dogs.

Another time, a little *mionnan** got beyond the tight tether of the
spancel and reached and grasped a groundsel on the high rock. One
of the Sons of the Rock—a small echo—gave a shout out of him, scared
the *mionnan,* and she slipped down deep into the well. She was like to
drowned having sank the third time, when as God would have it, she
saw the little trout.

"My dear, love to you forever," says the *mionnan.* "Sweet sire, save
me for Molaga's sake, or I perish, and those that need my milk in the
bimeby will wither away."

"No sooner said than done," said the little trout, and he spread forth
his fins, very wonderful to look upon—a rarey show. The goat stepped
on their gold edges and climbed on the dry land.

When the Trencherman saw this little trout he hungered for him
and he got his dirty dish cover and put it deep in the well and cajoled
the little fellow into it. Then he made himself a fire and put the dish
cover upon it, filled it with water and the little trout swimming and
sparkling inside.

* Pronounced meenawn—a little goat, a kid.—P.K.

Then he said in his heart: "Gillaroo you're mine now or never," and he smacked his thick lips.

Well, it was never! Because he boiled and watched and watched and boiled until the night was coming and the trout began to shine. Just as the Trencherman, wonderstruck, looked into the pot, the trout gave a shake out of his joints, slapped his fins and jumped back with himself into the well. The first bubbles splashed into the Trencherman's eyes and knocked the sight from him. Out rushed the otter and her five young ones and stuck their teeth in him till they heard every bone in his body crack. That is their nature. Down jumped the goat and put her horns through him and let in the east wind, and it blew the life out of him. And there he lay on the bed of nettles beside the four big stones, food for crows, and all that was left of him was a bye-word for gentle and simple.

John Connors and the Fairies

There was a man named John Connors, who lived near Killarney, and was the father of seven small children, all daughters and no sons. Connors fell into such rage and anger at having so many daughters, without any sons, that when the seventh daughter was born he would not come from the field to see the mother or the child.

When the time came for christening he wouldn't go for sponsors, and didn't care whether the wife lived or died. A couple of years after that a son was born to him, and some of the women ran to the field and told John Connors that he was the father of a fine boy. Connors was so delighted that he caught the spade he had with him and broke it on the ditch. He hurried home then and sent for bread and meat, with provisions of all kinds to supply the house.

"There are no people in the parish," said he to the wife, "fit to stand sponsors for this boy, and when night comes I'll ride over to the next parish and find sponsors there."

When night came he bridled and saddled his horse, mounted, and rode away toward the neighbouring parish to invite a friend and his wife to be godfather and godmother to his son. The village to which he was going was Beaufort, south of Killarney. There was a public-

From *Tales of the Fairies and of the Ghost World,* collected from Oral Tradition in Southwest Munster, by Jeremiah Curtin, pp. 6-17. Little, Brown & Co. Boston. 1895.

house on the road. Connors stepped in and treated the bystanders, delayed there a while, and then went his way. When he had gone a couple of miles he met a stranger riding on a white horse, a good-looking gentlemen wearing red knee-breeches, swallow-tailed coat, and a Caroline hat (a tall hat).

The stranger saluted John Connors, and John returned the salute. The stranger asked where was he going at such an hour.

"I'm going," said Connors, "to Beaufort to find sponsors for my young son."

"Oh, you foolish man," said the stranger; "you left the road a mile behind you. Turn back and take the left hand."

John Connors turned back as directed, but never came to a cross-road. He was riding about half an hour when he met the same gentleman, who asked: "Are you the man I met a while ago going to Beaufort?"

"I am."

"Why, you fool, you passed the road a mile or more behind. Turn back and take the right hand road. What trouble is on you that you cannot see a road when you are passing it?"

Connors turned and rode on for an hour or so, but found no side road. The same stranger met him for the third time, and asked him the same question, and told him he must turn back. "But the night is so far gone," said he, "that you'd better not be waking people. My house is near by. Stay with me till morning. You can go for the sponsors to-morrow."

John Connors thanked the stranger and said he would go with him. The stranger took him to a fine castle then, and told him to dismount and come in.

"Your horse will be taken care of," said he, "I have servants enough."

John Connors rode a splendid white horse, and the like of him wasn't in the country round. The gentleman had a good supper brought to Connors. After supper he showed him a bed and said, "Take off your clothes and sleep soundly till morning."

When Connors was asleep the stranger took the clothes, formed a corpse just like John Connors, put the clothes on it, tied the body to the horse, and leading the beast outside, turned its head towards home. He kept John Connors asleep in bed for three weeks.

The horse went towards home and reached the village next morning. The people saw the horse with the dead body on its back, and all thought it was the body of John Connors. Everybody began to cry and lament for their neighbour. He was taken off the horse, stripped, washed, laid out on the table. There was a great wake that night, everybody mourning and lamenting over him, for wasn't he a good man and the father of a large family? The priest was sent for to celebrate mass and attend the funeral, which he did. There was a large funeral.

Three weeks later John Connors was roused from his sleep by the gentleman, who came to him and said:

"It is high time for you to be waking. Your son is christened. The wife, thinking you would never come, had the child baptized, and the priest found sponsors. Your horse stole away from here and went home."

"Sure then I am not long sleeping?"

"Indeed, then, you are: it is three whole days and nights that you are in that bed."

John Connors sat up and looked around for his clothes, but if he did he could not see a stitch of them. "Where are my clothes?" asked he.

"I know nothing of your clothes, my man, and the sooner you go out o' this the better."

Poor John was astonished. "God help me, how am I to go home without my clothes? If I had a shirt itself, it wouldn't be so bad; but to go without a rag at all on me!"

"Don't be talking," said the man; "take a sheet and be off with yourself. I have no time to lose on the like of you."

John grew in dread of the man, and taking the sheet, went out. When well away from the place he turned to look at the castle and its owner, but if he did there was nothing before him but fields and ditches.

The time as it happened was Sunday morning, and Connors saw at some distance down the road people on their way to mass. He hurried to the fields for fear of being seen by somebody. He kept the fields and walked close to the ditches till he reached the side of a hill, and went along by that, keeping well out of sight. As he was nearing his own village at the side of the mountain there happened to be three or four little boys looking for stray sheep. Seeing Connors, they knew him as the dead man buried three weeks before. They screamed and ran away home, some of them falling with fright. When they came to the village they cried that they had seen John Connors, and he with a sheet on him.

Now, it is the custom in Ireland when a person dies to sprinkle holy water on the clothes of the deceased and then give them to poor people or to friends for God's sake. It is thought that by giving the clothes in this way the former owner has them to use in the other world. The person who wears the clothes must wear them three times to mass one

Sunday after another and sprinkle them each time with holy water. After that they may be worn as the person likes.

When the women of the village heard the story of the boys some of them went to the widow and said:

" 'Tis your fault that your husband's ghost is roaming around in nakedness. You didn't give away his clothes."

"I did, indeed," said the wife. "I did my part, but it must be that the man I gave them to didn't wear them to mass, and that is why my poor husband is naked in the other world."

Now she went straight to the relative and neighbour who got the clothes. As she entered the man was sitting down to breakfast.

"Bad luck to you, you heathen!" said she. "I did not think you the man to leave my poor John naked in the other world. You neither went to mass in the clothes I gave you nor sprinkled holy water on them."

"I did, indeed. This is the third Sunday since John died, and I went to mass this morning for the third time. Sure I'd be a heathen to keep a relative naked in the other world. It wasn't your husband that the boys saw at all."

She went home then, satisfied that everything had been done as it should be.

An uncle of John Connors lived in the same village. He was a rich farmer and kept a servant girl and a servant boy. The turf bog was not far away, and all the turf at the house being burned, the servant girl was told to go down to the reek and bring home a creel of turf. She went to the reek and was filling her creel, when she happened to look towards the far end of the reek, and there she saw a man sticking his head out from behind the turf, and he with a sheet on him. She looked a second time and saw John Connors. The girl screamed, threw down the creel, and ran away, falling every few steps from terror. It was to the reek that Connors had gone, to wait there in hiding till dark. After that he could go to his own house without any one seeing him.

The servant girl fell senseless across the farmer's threshold, and when she recovered she said: "John Connors is below in the bog behind the reek of turf, and nothing but a sheet on him."

The farmer and the servant boy laughed at her and said: "This is the way with you always when there's work to do."

The boy started off to bring the turf himself, but as he was coming near the reek John Connors thrust his head out, and the boy ran home screeching worse than the girl. Nobody would go near the creek now, and the report went out that John Connors was below in the bog minding the turf. Early that evening John Connors' wife made her children go on their knees and offer up the rosary for the repose of

their father's soul. After the rosary they went to bed in a room together, but were not long in it when there was a rap at the door. The
poor woman asked who was outside. John Connors answered that it
was himself.

"May the Almighty God and His Blessed Mother give rest to your
soul!" cried the wife, and the children crossed themselves and covered
their heads with the bedclothes. They were in dread he'd come in
through the keyhole; they knew a ghost could do that if it wished.

John went to the window of two panes of glass and was tapping at
that. The poor woman looked out, and there she saw her husband's
face. She began to pray again for the repose of his soul, but he called
out:

"Bad luck to you, won't you open the door to me or throw out some
clothes? I am perishing from cold."

This only convinced the woman more surely. John didn't like to
break the door, and as it was strong, it wouldn't be easy for him to
break it, so he left the house and went to his uncle's. When he came
to the door all the family were on their knees repeating the rosary for
the soul of John Connors. He knocked, and the servant girl rose up to
see who was outside. She unbolted and unlatched the door, opened it a
bit, but seeing Connors, she came near cutting his nose off, she shut it
that quickly in his face. She bolted the door then and began to scream:
"John Connors' ghost is haunting me! Not another day or night will I
stay in the house if I live to see morning!"

All the family fastened themselves in in a room and threw themselves
into bed, forgetting to undress or to finish their prayers. John Connors
began to kick the door, but nobody would open it; then he tapped at
the window and begged the uncle to let him in or put out some clothes
to him, but the uncle and children were out of their wits with fear.

The doctor's house was the next one, and Connors thought to himself, "I might as well go to the doctor and tell all to him; tell him that
the village is gone mad." So he made his way to the doctor's, but the
servant boy there roared and screeched from terror when he saw him,
ran to his master, and said, "John Connors' ghost is below at the door,
and not a thing but a sheet on him."

"You were always a fool," said the doctor. "There is never a ghost in
this world."

"God knows, then, the ghost of John Connors is at the door," said
the boy.

To convince the boy, the master raised the upper window. He looked
out and saw the ghost sure enough. Down went the window with a slap.

"Don't open the door!" cried the doctor. "He is below; there is some mystery in this."

Since the doctor wouldn't let him in any more than the others, John Connors was cursing and swearing terribly.

"God be good to us," said the doctor. "His soul must be damned, for if his soul was in purgatory it is not cursing and swearing he'd be, but praying. Surely, 'tis damned he is, and the Lord have mercy on the people of this village; but I won't stay another day in it; I'll move to the town to-morrow morning."

Now John left the doctor's house and went to the priest, thinking that he could make all clear to the priest, for everybody else had gone mad. He knocked at the priest's door and the housekeeper opened it. She screamed and ran away, but left the door open behind her. As she was running towards the stairs she fell, and the priest, hearing the fall, hurried out to see what the matter was.

"Oh, Father," cried the housekeeper, "John Connors' ghost is below in the kitchen, and he with only a sheet on him!"

"Not true," said the priest. "There is never a person seen after parting with this world."

The words were barely out of his mouth when the ghost was there before him.

"In the name of God," said the priest, "are you dead or alive? You must be dead, for I said mass in your house, and you a corpse on the table, and I was at your funeral."

"How can you be foolish like the people of the village? I'm alive. Who would kill me?"

"God, who kills everybody, and but for your being dead, how was I to be asked to your funeral?"

" 'Tis all a mistake," said John. "If it's dead I was it isn't here I'd be talking to you to-night."

"If you are alive, where are your clothes?"

"I don't know where they are or how they went from me, but I haven't them, sure enough."

"Go into the kitchen," said the priest. "I'll bring you clothes, and then you must tell me what happened to you."

When John had the clothes on he told the priest the day the child was born he went to Beaufort for sponsors, and, being late, he met a gentleman, who sent him back and forth on the road and then took him to his house. "I went to bed," said John, "and slept till he waked me. My clothes were gone from me then, and I had nothing to wear but an old sheet. More than this I don't know: but everybody runs from me, and my wife won't let me into the house."

"Oh, then, it's Daniel O'Donohue, King of Lochlein, that played the trick on you," said the priest. "Why didn't you get sponsors at home in this parish for your son as you did for your daughters? For the remainder of your life show no partiality to son or daughter among your children. It would be a just punishment if more trouble came to you. You were not content with the will of God, though it is the duty of every man to take what God gives him. Three weeks ago your supposed body was buried and all thought you dead through your own pride and wilfulness."

"That is why my wife wouldn't let me in. Now, your Reverence, come with me and convince my wife, or she will not open the door."

The priest and John Connors went to the house and knocked, but the answer they got was a prayer for the repose of John Connors' soul. The priest went to the window then and called out to open the door.

Mrs. Connors opened the door, and seeing her husband behind the priest she screamed and fell: a little girl that was with her at the door dropped speechless on the floor. When the woman recovered, the priest began to persuade her that her husband was living, but she wouldn't believe that he was alive till she took hold of his hand: then she felt of his face and hair and was convinced.

When the priest had explained everything he went away home.

No matter how large his family was in after years, John Connors never went from home to find sponsors.

Why the Weariness of the Blacksmiths Falls upon the Cowherds

On a certain day as the Virgin Mary was traveling the road, a gust of wind came and blew the cloak off her. She put it around her again, but failed to find the pin that fastened it. With her hand she held the cloak to her and she was not pleased to be going that way along the road.

On she went and the wind was not abating. She passed a field in which there were cattle and a man herding them.

"Would you kindly throw a thorn down to me from the branch over head," said she to him.

Told by Tomás O'Criomhthain, in *Béaloideas,* Journal of the Folklore of Ireland Society. Dublin. 1927.

"I should have very little to do to employ myself that way," he said.

She left him there and went on until she met another who was doing as the first. She asked of him what she had asked from the other.

"You have not so much to do that you cannot keep your hand to your cloak," he told her. Thus did the two cowherds treat her.

Then she came to a forge. As she went by, the blacksmith who was standing before it said to her, "Why have you not a pin to hold your cloak instead of your hand?"

"I have lost it," she said, "and I am ashamed that it is with my hand I have to hold it."

"I will find you something," said he. "Come inside and rest yourself."

Putting his hand into his pocket the blacksmith took out a piece of silver. He fashioned it into a brooch the like of which was never seen before nor since. While he was making it she never took her eyes off him. Then she thanked him and went on her way. The brooch was so made that it could not, without a hand taking it out, be detached from the cloak. For all this the Virgin Mary was so grateful that she prayed God that the blacksmith nor his descendants should not suffer from weariness: their weariness was put upon the cowherds. And this explains the saying *"Bionn tuirse na ngaibhne ar na buachailli bo"*—"The blacksmiths' fatigue falls on the cowherds."

The Piper and the Puca

In the old times there was a half-fool living in Dunmore, in the County Galway, and although he was excessively fond of music, he was unable to learn more than one tune and that was the "Black Rogue." He used to get a great deal of money from the gentlemen, for they used to get sport out of him.

One night the piper was coming home from a house where there had been a dance, and he half drunk, when he came to a little bridge that was up by his mother's house, he squeezed the pipes on, and began playing the "Black Rogue."

The Puca (a goblin) came behind him, and flung him on his own back. There were long horns on the Puca, and the piper got a good grip on them, and then he said, "Destruction on you, you nasty beast, let me go home. I have a ten-penny piece in my pocket for my mother, and she wants snuff."

By Douglas Hyde, in *The Gael*, October, 1900, p. 273. New York.

"Never mind your mother," said the Puca, "but keep your hold. If you fall, you will break your neck and your pipes."

Then the Puca said to him, "Play up for me the Shan Van Vocht."

"I don't know it," said the piper.

"Never mind whether you do or you don't," said the Puca. "Play up and I'll make you know."

The piper put wind in his bag, and he played such music as made himself wonder.

"Upon my word, you're a fine music-master," says the piper, then: "But tell me where you're bringing me."

"There's a great feast in the house of the Banshee, on the top of Croagh Patric, tonight," says the Puca, "and I'm for bringing you there to play music, and, take my word, you'll get the price of your trouble."

"By my word, you'll save me a journey, then," says the piper, "for Father William put a journey to Croagh Patric on me, because I stole the white gander from him last Martinmas."

The Puca rushed him across hills and bogs and rough places, till he brought him to the top of Croagh Patric. Then the Puca struck three blows with his foot, and a great door opened, and they passed in together into a fine room.

The piper saw a golden table in the middle of the room, and hundreds of old women sitting around it. The old women rose up and said, "A hundred thousand welcomes to you, you Puca of November. Who is this you have with you?"

"The best piper in Ireland," says the Puca.

One of the old women struck a blow on the ground, and a door opened in the side of the wall, and what should the piper see coming out but the white gander which he had stolen from Father William.

"By my conscience, then," said the piper, "myself and my mother ate every taste of that gander, only one wing, and I gave that to Moyrua [Red Mary], and it's she told the priest I stole his gander."

The gander cleaned the table, and carried it away, and the Puca said, "Play up music for these ladies."

The piper played up, and the old women began dancing, and they were dancing until they were tired.

Then the Puca said to "Pay the piper," and every old woman drew out a gold piece, and gave it to him.

"By the tooth of Patric," said he, "I'm as rich as the son of a lord."

"Come with me," says the Puca, "and I'll bring you home."

They went out then, and just as he was going to ride on the Puca, the gander came up to him, and gave him a new set of pipes. The Puca was not long until he brought him to Dunmore, and he threw the piper off at the little bridge, and then he told him to go home, and says to him, "You have two things now that you never had before—you have sense and music."

The piper went home, and he knocked at his mother's door, saying, "Let me in, I'm as rich as a lord, and I'm the best piper in Ireland."

"You're drunk," said the mother.

"No indeed," says the piper, "I haven't drunk a drop."

The mother let him in, and he gave her the gold pieces, and "Wait now," says he, "til you hear the music I'll play."

He buckled on the pipes, but instead of music, there came a sound as if all the geese and ganders in Ireland were screeching together. He wakened the neighbors, and they were all mocking him, until he put on the old pipes, and he played melodious music for them; and after that, he told them all he had gone through that night.

The next morning when his mother went to look at the gold pieces, there was nothing there but the leaves of a plant.

The piper went to the priest, and told him the story, but the priest would not believe a word from him, until he put the pipes on him, and then the screeching of the ganders and geese began.

"Leave my sight, you thief," says the priest.

But nothing would do the piper till he put the old pipes on him to show the priest that his story was true.

He buckled on the old pipes, and he played melodious music, and from that day till the day of his death, there was never a piper in the County Galway was as good as he was.

How Little Fairly Outwitted His Commoch Brother

You see owld Fairly was a mighty dacent man that lived, as the story goes, out over the back o' the hills beyant there, and was a thrivin' man ever afther he married little Shan Ruadh's daughter and she was little,

---

From *Legends and Stories of Ireland,* by Samuel Lover, Second Series, pp. 276-315. Baldwin & Cradock. London. 1837.

Lover makes a distinction between the stories and the legends in these volumes: the legends are in dialect and were evidently told him. "Though the village crone and mountain guide," he notes, "may have many hearers, still their circle is so circumscribed, that most of what I have ventured to lay before my readers is, for the first time, made tangible to the greater portion of those who do me the favour to become such."

like her father before her, a dawnshee craythur, but mighty cute, and industhered a power always, and a fine wife she was to a sthrivin' man, up early and down late, and shure if she was doin' nothin' else, the bit iv a stocking was never out iv her hand, and the knittin' needles goin' like mad. Well, sure they thruv like a flag or a bulrush, and the snuggest cabin in the counthry side was owld Fairly's. And, in due coorse, she brought him a son (throth she lost no time about it either, for she was never given to loiterin') and he was the picthur o' the mother, the little ottomy that he was, as slim as a ferret and as red as a fox, but a hardy craythur. Well, owld Fairly didn't like the thoughts of havin' sitch a bit iv a brat for a son, and besides he thought he got on so well and prospered in the world with one wife, that by gor, he determined to improve his luck and get another. So with that, he ups and goes to one Doody, who had a big daughter—a wopper, by my soul, throth she was the full of a door, and was called by the neighbors *garran more,* for in throth she was a garran, the dirty dhrop was in her, a nasty stag that never done a good turn for any one but herself, the long-sided jack that she was; but her father had a power o' money, and above a hundher head o' cattle, and devil a chick nor child he had but herself; so that she was a great catch for whoever could get her, as far as the fortin' went; but throth the boys did not like the looks iv her, and let herself and her fortin' alone. Well, as I was sayin', owld Fairly ups and goes to Doody and puts his *comether* an the girl, and faix she was glad to be ax'd, and so matthers were soon settled, and the ind of it was they wor married.

Now maybe it's axin' you'd be, how he could marry two wives at wanst; but I towld you before, it was long ago, in the good owld ancient times, whin a man could have plinty of everything. So home he brought the dirty garran, and sorra long was she in the place whin she began to breed (arrah, lave off and don't be laughin' now; I don't mane that at all), whin she began to breed *ructions* in the fam'ly and to kick up *antagions* from mornin' till night, and *put betune* owld Fairly and his first wife. Well, she had a son of her own soon, and he was a big boss iv a divil, like his mother—a great fat lob that had no life in him at all; and while the little dawnshee craythur would laugh in your face and play wid you if you cherrup'd to him, or would amuse himself, the craythur, crawlin' about the flure and playin' wid the sthraws, and atein' the gravel, the jewel—the other bosthoon was roarin' from mornin' till night, barrin' he was crammed wid stirabout and dhrownded a'most wid milk. Well, up they grew, and the big chap turned out a *gommoch,* and the little chap was as known' as a jailor; and though the big mother was always puttin' up her lob to malthrate and abuse little Fairly, the dickens a one but the little chap used to sarcumvint him, and gev him no pace, and led him the life iv a dog wid the cunnin' thricks he played an him.

Now, while all the neighbors a'most loved the ground that little Fairly throd on, they cudn't abide the garran more's foal, good, bad, or indifferent, and many's the sly malavoguein' he got behind a hedge, from one or another, when his father or mother wasn't near to purtect him, for owld Fairly was as great a fool about him as the mother, and would give him his eyes a'most to play marbles, while he didn't care three thraneens for the darlint little chap. And 'twas the one thing as long as he lived; and at last he fell sick, and sure many thought it was a judgment an him for his unnathrel doin's to his own flesh and blood, and the sayin' through the parish was from one and all, "There's owld Fairly is obleeged *to take his bed with the weight of his sins.*" And sure enough off o' that same bed he never riz, but grew weaker and weaker every day, and sint for the priest to make his sowl, the wicked owld sinner, God forgive me for sayin' the word, and sure the priest done whatever he could for him; but afther the priest wint away he called his two wives beside his bed, and the two sons, and says he, "I'm goin' to lave yiz now," says he, "and sorry I am," says he, "for I'd rather stay in owld Ireland than go anywhere else," says he, "for a raison I have—heigh! heigh! heigh!— Oh, murther, this cough is smotherin' me, so it is. Oh, wurra! wurra! but it's sick and sore I am. Well, come here yiz both," says he to the women, "you wor good wives both o' ye; I have nothin' to say agin it—(Molly, don't forget the whate is to be whinny'd the first fine day) and ready you wor to make and to mend (Judy, there's a hole in the foot of my left stockin'), and—"

"Don't be thinkin' o' your footin' here," says little Judy, the knowledgeable craythur, as she was, "but endayvour to make your footin' in heaven," says she, "mavourneen."

"Don't put in your prate 'till you're ax'd," says the owld savage, no ways obleeged that his trusty little owld woman was wantin' to give him a helpin' hand tow'rds puttin' his poor sinful soul in the way o' glory.

"Lord look down an you!" says she.

"Tuck the blanket round my feet," says he, "for I'm gettin' very cowld."

So the big old hag of a wife tucked the blankets round him.

"Ah, you were always a comfort to me," says owld Fairly.

"Well, remember my son for that same," says she, "for it's time I think you'd be dividin' what you have bechuxt uz," says she.

"Well, I suppose I must do it at last," says the owld chap, "though—

hegh! hegh! hegh! Oh, this thievin' cough—it's hard to be obleeged to lave one's hard airnins and comforts this a-way," says he, the unfort'nate owld thief, thinkin' o' this world instead of his own poor sinful sowl.

"Come here, big Fairly," says he, "my own bull-boy, that's not a starved poor ferret, but worth while looking at. I lave you this house," says he.

"Ha!" says the big owld sthrap, makin' a face over the bed at the poor little woman that was cryin', the craythur, although the owld villain was usin' her so bad.

"And I lave you all my farms," says he.

"Ha!" says the big owld sthreel again.

"And my farmin' *ingraydients*," says he.

"Ha!" says he again, takin' a pinch o' snuff.

"And *all* my cattle," says he.

"Did you hear that, ma'am?" says the garran more, stickin' her arms akimbo, and lookin' as if she was goin' to bate the woman.

"All my cattle," says the owld fellow, "every head," says he, "barrin' one, and that one is for that poor scaldcrow there," says he, "little Fairly."

"And is it only one you lave my poor boy?" says the poor little woman.

"If you say much," says the owld dyin' vagabone, "the divil recaive the taste of anything I'll lave him or you," says he.

"Don't say divil, darlin'."

"Howld your prate I tell you and listen to me. I say, you little Fairly—"

"Well, Daddy," says the little chap.

"Go over to that corner cupboard," says he, "and in the top shelf," says he, "in the bottom of a crack'd taypot, you'll find a piece of an owld rag, and bring it here to me."

With that, little Fairly went to do as he was bid, but he could not reach up so high as the corner cupboard, and he ran into the next room for a stool to stand upon to come at the crack'd taypot, and he got the owld piece iv a rag and brought it to his father.

"Open it," says the father.

"I have it open now," says Little Fairly.

"What's in it?" says the owld boy.

"Six shillin's in silver, and three farthin's," says little Fairly.

"That was your mother's fortune," says the father, "and I'm going to behave like the hoighth of a gentleman, as I am," says he; "and I hope you won't squandher it," says he, "the way that every blackguard now thinks he has a right to squandher any decent man's money he is heir to," says he, "but be careful of it," says he, "as I was, for I never touched a rap iv it, but let it lay gotherin' in that taypot, ever since the day I got it from Shan Ruadh, the day we sthruck the bargain about Judy, over beyant at the 'Cat and Bagpipes,' comin' from the fair; and I lave you that *six* shillings, and *five* stone o' mouldy oats that's no use to me, and *four* broken plates, and that *three*-legged stool you stood upon to get at the cupboard, you poor *anharrough* that you are, and the *two* spoons without handles, and the *one* cow that's gone back of her milk."

"What use is the cow, Daddy," says little Fairly, "widout land to feed her on?"

"Maybe it's land you want, you pinkeen," says the big brother.

"Right, my bully boy," says the mother, "stand up for your own."

"Well, well," says the owld chap, "I tell you what, big Fairly," says he, "you may as well do a dacent turn for the little chap, and give him grass for his cow. I lave you all the land," says he, "but you'll never miss grass for one cow," says he, "and you'll have the satisfaction of bein' bountiful to your little brother, bad cess to him for a starved hound as he is."

But, to make a long story short, the ould chap soon had the puff out iv him; and when the wake was over, and that they put him out to grass—laid him asleep, snug, *with a daisy quilt over him*—throth that minit the poor little woman and her *little* offsprig was turned out body and bones, and forced to seek shelter any way they could.

Well, little Fairly was a cute chap, and so he made a little snug place out back iv a ditch, and wid moss, and rishes, and laves, and brambles, made his mother snug enough, until he got a little mud cabin built for her, and the cow gave them milk, and the craythurs got on pretty well, until the big dirty vagabone of a brother began to grudge the cow the bit o' grass, and he ups and says he to little Fairly one day, "What's the raison," says he, "your cow does be thresspassin' on my fields?" says he.

"Sure and wasn't it the last dyin' words o' my father to you," says little Fairly, "that you would let me have grass for my cow?"

"I don't remember it," says big Fairly—the dirty naggur, who was put up to all by the garran more, his mother.

"Yiv a short memory," says little Fairly.

"Yis, but I've a long stick," says the big chap, shakin' it at him at the same time, "and I'd rekimmind you to keep a civil tongue in your head," says he.

"You're mighty ready to bate your little brother, but would you fight your match?" says little Fairly.

"Match or no match," says big Fairly, "I'll brake your bones if you give me more o' your prate," says he, "and I tell you again, don't let your cow be threspassin' an my land, or I warn you that you'll be sorry," and off he wint.

Well, little Fairly kept never mindin' him and brought his cow to graze every day on big Fairly's land, and the big fellow used to come and *hish* her off the land, but the cow was as little and cute as her masther—she was a Kerry cow, and there's a power o' cuteness comes out o' Kerry. Well, as I was sayin', the cow used to go off as *quiet* as a lamb; but the minit the big bosthoon used to turn his back, *whoo!* my jewel, she used to leap the ditch as clever as a hunter, and back wid her again to graze, and faix good use she made of her time, for she got brave and hearty, and gev a power o' milk, though she was goin' back of it shortly before, but there was a blessin' over Fairly and all belongin' to him, and all that he put his hand to thruv with him. Well, now, I must tell you what big Fairly done—and the dirty turn it was; but the dirt was in him ever and always, and kind mother it was for him. Well, what did he do but he dug big pits all through the field where little Fairly's cow used to graze, and he covers them up with branches o' threes and sods, makin' it look fair and even, and all as one as the rest o' the field, and with that he goes to little Fairly, and says he, "I tould you before," says he, "not to be sendin' your little blackguard cow to threspass on my fields," says he, "and mind I tell you now, that it won't be good for her health to let her go there again, for I tell you she'll come to harm, and it's dead she'll be before long."

"Well, she may as well die one way as another," says little Fairly, "for sure if she doesn't get grass she must die, and I tell you again, divil an off your land I'll take my cow."

"Can't you let your dirty cow graze along the roadside?" says big Fairly.

"Why then do you think," says little Fairly, answering him mighty smart, "do you think I have so little respect for my father's cow as to turn her out a beggar an the road to get her dinner off the common highway? throth I'll do no sitch thing."

"Well, you'll soon see the end iv it," says big Fairly, and off he wint in great delight, thinking how poor little Fairly's cow would be killed. And now wasn't he the dirty, threacherous, blackhearted villain, to take advantage of a poor cow, and lay a thrap for the dumb baste?— but whin the dirty dhrop is in, it must come out. Well, poor Fairly sent his cow to graze next mornin', but the poor little darlin' craythur fell into one o' the pits and was kilt, and when little Fairly kem for her in the evenin' there she was cowld and stiff, and all he had to do now was to sing *drimmin dhu dheelish* over her, dhrag her home as well as he could, wid the help of some neighbors that pitied the craythur and cursed the big bosthoon that done such a threacherous turn.

Well, little Fairly was the fellow to put the best face upon everything and so, instead of givin' in to fret, and makin' lamentations that would do him no good, by dad he began to think how he could make the best of what happened, and the little craythur sharpened a knife immediately and began to skin the cow, "and anyhow," says he, "the cow is good mate, and my owld mother and me'll have beef for the winther."

"Thrue for you, little Fairly," said one of the neighbors was helpin' him, "and besides, the hide'll be good to make soles for your brogues for many a long day."

"Oh, I'll do betther with the hide nor that," says little Fairly.

"Why, what better can you do nor that wid it?" says the neighbor.

"Oh, I know myself," says little Fairly, for he was as cute as a fox as I said before, and wouldn't tell his saycrets to a stone wall, let alone a companion. And what do you think he done with the hide? Guess now—throth I'd let you guess from now till Christmas, and you'd never come inside it. Faix it was the complatest thing you ever heard. What would you think but he tuk the hide and cut six little holes in partic'lar places he knew av himself, and then he goes and he gets his mother's fortin, the six shillin's I told you about, and he hides the six shillin's in the six holes, and away he wint to a fair was convenient, bout three days afther, where there was a great sight o' people, and a power o' sallin' and buyin', and dhrinkin' and fightin', by course, *and why not?*

Well, Fairly ups and he goes right into the very heart o' the fair, an' he spred out his hide to the greatest advantage, and he began to cry out (and by the same token, though he was little he had a mighty sharp voice, and could be heard farther nor a bigger man), well he began to cry out, "Who wants to buy a hide?—the *rale* hide—the owld original goolden bull's hide that kem from furrin parts—who wants make their fortin' now?"

"What do you ax for your hide?" says a man to him.

"Oh, I only want a thrifle for it," says Fairly, "seein' I'm disthressed for money, at this present writin'," says he, "and by fair or foul manes I must raise the money," says he, "at wanst, for if I could wait, it's not the thrifle I'm axin' now I'd take for the hide."

"By gor, you talk," says the man, "as if the hide was worth the King's ransom, and I'm thinkin' you must have a great want of a few shillin's," says he, "whin the hide is all you have to the fore, to dipind on."

"Oh, that's all *you* know about it," says Fairly, "shillin's indeed! by gor, it's handful o' money the hide is worth. Who'll buy a hide—the rale goolden bull's hide!"

"What do you ax for your hide?" says another man.

"Only a hundher guineas," says little Fairly.

"Is it takin' llave of your siven small senses you are?" says the man.

"Why, thin indeed I b'lieve I am takin' lave o' my sinses sure enough," says Fairly, "to sell my hide so chape."

"Chape," says the man, "arrah thin listen to the little mad vagabone," says he to the crowd that was gother about by this time, "listen to him askin' a hundher guineas for a hide."

"Aye," says Fairly, "and the well-laid out money it 'ill be to whoever has the luck to buy it. This is none o' your common hides—it's the goolden bull's hide—the Pope's goolden bull's hide, that kem from furrin parts, and it's a fortune to whoever 'ill have patience to bate his money out iv it."

"How do you mane?" says a snug owld chap that was always poachin' about for bargains—"I never heerd of batin' money out of a hide," says he.

"Well, then, I'll show you," says Fairly, "and only I'm disthressed for a hundred guineas, that I must have before Monday next," says he, "I wouldn't part with this hide; for every day in the week you may thrash a fistful o' shillin's out iv it, if you take pains, as you may see." And wid that, my jew'l, he ups wid a cudgel he had in his hand, and he began leatherin' away at the hide; and he hits it *in the place he knew of himself,* and out jump'd one o' the shillin's he hid there. "Hurroo!" says little Fairly, "darlint you wor, you never desaived me yet!" and away he thrashed agin, and out jumped another shillin'. "That's your sort!" says Fairly, "the devil a stitch wages any o' yiz ever got for thrashin' as this"—and then another whack, and away wid another shillin'.

"Stop, stop!" says the owld craving chap. "I'll give you the money for the hide," says he, "if you'll only let me see can I bate money out iv it." And wid that he began to thrash the hide, and, of course, another shillin' jumped out.

"Oh, it's yourself has the rale twist in your elbow for it," says Fairly, "and I see by that same, that you're above the common, and desarvin' of my favour."

Well, my dear, at the word *"desarvin' o' my favour,"* the people that was gother round (for by this time all the fair a'most was there), began to look into the rights o' the thing, and, one and all, they agreed that little Fairly was one o' the *"good people";* for if he wasn't a fairy, how could he do the like? and besides he was sitch a *dawnshee craythur* they thought what else could he be? and says they to themselves, "That owld divil, Mulligan, it's the likes iv him id have the luck iv it, and let alone his gains in *this* world, and his scrapin' and screwin', and it's the fairies themselves must come to help him, as if he wasn't rich enough before." Well, the owld chap paid down a hundher guineas in hard goold to little Fairly, and off he wint wid his bargain.

You may be sure the poor owld mother of little Fairly was proud enough when she seen him tumble out the hard goold on the table forninst her, and "my darlint you wor," says she, "an' how did you come by that sight o' gold?"

"I'll tell you another time," says little Fairly, "but you must set off to my brother's now, an ax him to lind me the loan iv his scales."

"Why, what do you want wid a scales, honey?" says the owld mother.

"Oh, I'll tell you *that* another time, too," says little Fairly; "but be aff now and don't let the grass grow undher your feet."

Well, off wint the owld woman, and maybe you'd want to know yourself what it was Fairly wanted wid the scales. Why, thin, he only wanted thim just for to make big Fairly curious about the matther, that he might play him a trick, as you'll see by-an-by.

Well, the little old woman wasn't long in bringing back the scales and whin she gave them to little Fairly. "There, now," says he, "sit down besides the fire, and there's a new pipe for you and a quarthen o' tobaccy, that I brought home for you from the fair, and do you make yourself comfortable," says he, "till I come back." And out he wint and sat down behind a ditch, to watch if big Fairly was comin' to the house, for he thought the curiosity o' the big gommoch and the garran more would make them come down to spy about the place, and see what he wanted wid the scales; and, sure enough, he wasn't there long when he see them both crassin' a stile hard by, and in he jumped into the gripe o' the ditch, and ran along under the shelter o' the back iv it, and whipped into the house and spred all his goold out an the table, and began to weigh it in the scales.

But he wasn't well in, whin the cord o' the latch was dhrawn, and in marched big Fairly and the garran more, his mother, without "by your lave," or "God save you," for they had no breedin' at all. Well, my jewel, the minit they clapped their eyes an the goold, you'd think the sight id lave their eyes: and indeed not only their eyes, let alone, but their tongues in their heads was no use to them, for the divil a word either o' them could spake for beyant a good five minutes. So, all that time little Fairly kept never mindin' them, but wint an a weighin' the goold, as busy as a sailor, and at last, when the big brute kem to his speech, "Why thin," says he, "what's that I see you doin'?" says he.

"Oh, it's only divertin' myself I am," says little Fairly, "thryin' what weight o' goold I got for my goods at the fair," says he.

"Your goods indeed," says the big chap, "I suppose you robbed some honest man an the road, you little vagabone," says he.

"Oh, I'm too little to rob anyone," says little Fairly, "I'm not a fine big able fellow, *like you,* to *do the same.*" "Then how did you come by the goold?" says the big savage. "I towld you before, by sellin' my goods," says the little fellow. "Why, what goods have *you,* you poor unsignified little brat?" says big Fairly. "You never had anything but your poor beggarly cow, and she's dead."

"Throth then, she is dead, and more by token, 'twas yourself done for her complate, anyhow, and I'm behoulden to you that same the longest day I have to live, for it was the makin' of me. You wor ever and always the *good brother to me;* and never more than whin you killed my cow, for it's the makin' o' me. The divil a rap you see here I'd have had if my cow was alive, for I wint to the fair to sell her hide, brakin' my heart to think that it was only a poor hide I had to sell, and wishin' it was a cow was to the fore; but, my der, when I got there, there was no ind to the demand for hides, and the divil a one, good, bad or indifferent was there by my own, and there was any money for hides, and so I got a hundher guineas for it, and there they are."

"Why then do you tell me so?" says the big chap. "Divil a lie in it," says little Fairly—"I got a hundher guineas for the hide. Oh, I wish I had another cow for you to kill for me, throth would I!"

"Come home, Mother," says big Fairly, without sayin' another word, and away he wint home, and what do you think he done but killed every individual cow he had, and "By gor," said he, "it's the rich man I'll be when I get a hundher guineas apiece for all their hides," and accordingly off he wint to the next fair hard by, and he brought a carload o' hides, and began to call out in the fair, "Who wants the hides?—here's the chape hides—only a hundher guineas apiece!"

"Oh, do you hear that vagabone that has the assurance to come chatin' the country again?" says some people that was convaynient, and that heard o' the doin's at the other fair, and how the man was chated by a *sleveen* vagabone—"and think of him to have the impudence to come *here,* so nigh the place to take in *uz* now! But we'll be even wid him," says they, and so they went up to him and says they to the

thievin' rogue, "Honest man," says they, "what's that you have to sell?"
"Hides," says he.

"What do you ax for them?"

"A hundher and ten guineas apiece," says he—for he was a greedy crathur and thought he never could have enough.

"Why, you riz the price on them since the last time," says they.

"Oh, these are better," says big Fairly, "but I don't mind if I sell them for a hundher apiece, if you give me the money down," says he.

"*You shall be ped on the spot,*" says they—and with that they fell on him and thrashed him life a *shafe,* till they didn't lave a *spark* of sinse in him, and then they left him sayin', "*Are you ped now, my boy?*—faix you'll be a warnin' to all rogues for the futhur, how they come to fairs, chatin' honest min out o' their money, wid cock-and-bull stories about their hides; but in trooth I think your own hide isn't much the better of the tannin' it got today—faix and it was the rale *oak bark* was put to it, and that's the finest tan stuff in the world and I think it'll sarve you for the rest of your life." And with that they left him for dead.

But you may remark it's harder to kill a dirty noxious craythur than anything good, and so by big Fairly—he conthrived to get home, and his vagabone mother sawdhered him up afther a manner, and the minit he was come to his strength at all, he detarmint to be revenged on little Fairly for what he had done, and so off he set to catch him while he'd be at brekquest, and he bowlted into the cabin wid a murtherin' shillelah in his fist—and "Oh," says he, "you little mischievious miscrayant," says he, "what made you ruinate me by making me kill my cows?" says he.

"Sure I didn't bid you kill your cows," says little Fairly—and that was all thrue, for you see, *there* was the cuteness o' the little chap, for he didn't *bid* him kill them sure enough, but he *let an* in that manner, that deludhered the big fool, and sure divil mend him.

"Yes, you did bid me," says big Fairly, "or all as one as bid me, and I haven't a cow left, and my bones is bruck all along o' your little jackeen manyewvers, you onlooky sprat that you are, but by this and that I'll have my revenge o' you now." And with that he fell on him and was goin' to murther poor little Fairly, only he run undher a stool, and kept tiggin' about from one place to th' other, and that the big botch couldn't get a right offer at him at all at all, and at last the the little owld mother got up to put a stop to the ruction, but if she did, my jew'l, it was the unlooky minit for her, for by dad she kem in for a chance tap o' the cudgel that big Fairly was weltin' away with, and you know there's an owld sayin' "a chance shot may kill the divil," and why not an owld woman?

Well, that put an end to the *skrimmage*, for the phillilew that little Fairly set up whin he seen his owld mother kilt would ha' waked the dead, and the big chap got frekened himself, and says little Fairly, "By gor, if there's law to be had," says he, "and I think *I have* a chance o' justice, *now that I have money to spare*, and, if there's law in the land, I'll have you in the body o' the jail afore tomorrow," says he, and wid that the big chap god cowed, and wint off like a dog without his tail, and so poor little Fairly escaped bein' murthered that offer, and was left to cry over his mother, an' indeed the craythur was sorry enough, and he brought in the neighbors and gev the owld woman a dacent wake, and there was few pleasanther evenin's that night in the county than the same week, for Fairly was mighty fond of his mother, and faix he done the thing ginteely by her, and good reason he had, for she was the good mother to him while she was alive, and by dad, by his own cuteness he conthrived she should be the useful mother to him afther she was dead, too.

For what do you think he done? Oh! by the Piper o' Blessintown you'd never guess, if you wor guessin' from this to Saint Tib's eve, and that falls neither before nor afther Christmas we all know. Well, there's no use guessin', so I must tell you. You see the owld mother was a nurse to the Squire, that lived hard by, and so, by coorse, she had a footin' in the house any day in the week she pleased, and used often to go over and see the Squire's childhre, for she was as fond o' them a'most as if she nursed *thim* too; and so what does Fairly do but he carried over the owld mother stiff as she was, and dhressed in her best, and he stole in, *unknownst*, into the Squire's garden, and he propped up the dead owld woman stan'in hard by a well was in the gardin, wid her face forninst the gate, and her back to the well, and wid that he wint into the house, and made out the childhre, and says he, "God save you, Masther Tommy," says he, "God save you, Masther Jimmy, Miss Matty and Miss Molshee," says he, "an' I'm glad to see you well, and sure there's the owld mammy nurse come to see yiz, childhre," says he, "and she's down by the well in the garden, and she has ginger-bread for yiz," says he, "and whoever o' yiz runs to her first 'ill get the most gingerbread; and I rekimmind yiz to lose no time but run a race and sthrive who'll win the gingerbread."

Well, my dear, to be sure off set the young imps, runnin' and schreechin', "Here I am, mammy nurse, here I am," and they wor brakin' their necks a'most to see who'd be there first, and wid that they run with sitch *voylence* that the first o' thim run whack up agin the poor owld woman's corpse, and threw it over plump into the middle o' the well. To be sure the childhre was frekened, as well they might, and back agin they ran as fast as they kem, roarin' murther, and they riz the house in no time, and little Fairly was among the first to go see what was the matther (by the way) and he set up a *hullagone,* my jewel, that ud split the heart of a stone and out kem the Squire and his wife and, "What's the matther?" says they. "Is it what's the matther?" says Fairly. "Don't yiz see my lovely owld mother is dhrowned by these devil's imps o' childhre?" says he. "Oh, Masther Jemmy, is that the way you thrated the poor owld mammy nurse, to go dhrownd her like a *rot* afther that manner?" "Oh, the childhre didn't intind it," said the Squire. "I'm sorry for your mother, Fairly, but—"

"But what?" says little Fairly, "sorry—inthroth and I'll make you sorry, for I'll rise the counthry, or I'll get justice for such an unnath'ral murther, and whoever done it must go to jail, if it was even Miss Molshee herself."

Well, the Squire did not like the matther to go to that, and so says he, "Oh, I'll make it worth your while to say nothing about it, Fairly, and here's twenty golden guineas for you," says he.

"Why thin do you think me such a poor blooded craythur as to sell my darlin' owld mother's life for twenty guineas? No, in throth, tho' if you wor to make it fifty I might be talkin' to you."

Well, the Squire thought it was a dear morning's work, and that he had very little for his money in a dead owld woman, but sooner than have the childhre get into throuble and have the matther made *a blowin' horn* of, he gev him the fifty guineas, and the owld mother was dhried and waked over agin, so that she had greather respect ped to her than a Lord or a Lady. So you see what cleverness and a *janius* for cuteness does.

Well, away he wint home afther the owld woman was buried wid his fifty guineas snug in his pocket, and so he wint to big Fairly's to ax for the loan of the scales once more, and the brother ax'd him for what? "Oh, it's only a small thrifle more o' goold I have," says the little chap, "that I want to weigh."

"Is it *more* goold?" says big Fairly, "why, it's a folly to talk, but you must be either a robber or a coiner to come by money so fast."

"Oh, this is only a thrifle I kem by at the death o' my mother," says little Fairly.

"Why, bad luck to the rap *she* had to lave you, anyway," says the big chap.

"I didn't say she left me a fortin," says little Fairly.

"You said you kem by the money by your mother's death," says the big brother.

"Well, an' that's thrue," says the little fellow, "an' I'll tell you how it was. You see, afther you killed her, I thought I might as well make the most I could of her, and says I to myself, faix and I had great good luck wid the cow he killed for me, and why wouldn't I get more for my mother nor a cow? and so away I wint to the town and I offered her to the docthor there, and he was greatly taken wid her, and by dad he wouldn't let me lave the house without sellin' her to him, and faix he gev me fifty guineas for her."

"Is it fifty guineas for a corpse?"

"It's thruth I'm tellin' you, and was much obleeged into the bar-gain, and the raison is, you see, that there's no sitch thing to be had for love or money as a dead owld woman—there's no killin' them at all at all, so that a dead old woman is quite a curiosity."

"Well, there's the scales for you," says big Fairly, and away the little chap wint to weigh his goold (as he let on) as he did before. But what do you think, my dear—throth you'll hardly b'lieve me when I tell you. Little Fairly hadn't well turned his back whin the big savage wint into the house where his owld mother was, and tuck up a rapin' hook and kilt her an the spot—divil a lie in it. Oh, no wondher you look cruked at the thoughts of it, but it's morially thrue, faix he cut the life out ov her, and he determined to turn in his harvist for that same, as soon as he could, and so away he wint to the docthor in the town hard by, where little Fairly towld him he sowld *his* mother, and he knocked at the door, and walked into the hall with a sack on his shouldher, and settin' down the sack, he said he wanted to spake to the docthor.

Well, when the docthor kem and heard the vagabone talkin' o' fifty guineas for an old woman, he began to laugh at him, but whin he opened the sack and seen how the poor owld craythur was murdhered, he set up a shout, "Oh, you vagabone," says he, "and now you come to *rape* the fruits o' your *murdher*." Well, the minit big Fairly heerd the word *murdher* and *rapin'* the reward, he thought the doctor was up to the way of it, and he got frekened, and with that the docthor opened the hall-door and called the watch, but Fairly bruk loose from him, and ran away home, and when once he was gone, *the docthor thought there would be no use in rising a ruction* about it, and so he shut the door and never minded the police. Big Fairly to be sure was so frekened he never cried stop antil he got clean outside the town and with that the first place he wint to was little Fairly's house, and, burstin' in the door, he said, in a tarin' passion, "What work is this you have been at now, you onlooky miscrayant?" says he.

"I haven't been at any work," says little Fairly. "See yourself," says he, *"my sleeves is new,"* says he, howldin' out the cuffs av his coat to him at the same time, to show him.

"Don't think to put me aff that-away with your little kimmeens, and your divartin' capers," says the big chap, "for I tell you I'm in airnest, and it's no joking matther it 'ill be to you, for, by this an' that, I'll have the life o' you, you little spidhogue of an abortion as you are, you made me kill cows. Don't say a word, for you know it's thrue."

"I never made you kill your cows," says little Fairly, no ways daunted by the fierce looks o' the big bosthoon.

"Whisht! you vagabone!" says the big chap. "You didn't bid me do it out o' the face, in plain words, but you made me sinsible."

"Faix an' that was doin' a wondher," says little Fairly, who couldn't help having the laugh at him though he was sore afeard.

"Bad luck to you, you little sneerin' vagabone," says the big chap again, "I know what you mane, you long-headed schkamer that you are, but, by my sowl, your capers 'ill soon be cut short, as you'll see to your cost. But before I kill you, I'll show you to your face, the villian that you are, and it is no use your endayvourin' to consale your bad manners to me, for if you had a veil as thick as the shield of A-jax, which was made o' siv'n bull hides, it would not sarve for to cover the half o' your inni—quitties."

"Whoo! that's the owld schoolmasther's speech you're puttin' an us now," says little Fairly, "and faith it's the only thing you iver larned, I b'lieve, from him."

"Yis, I lerned how fine a thing it is to bate a little chap less than myself, and you'll see with a blessin', how good a scholar I am at that time, and you desarve it, for I towld you just now before you in-therrupted me how you made me kill all my cows (and that was the sore loss), and afther that whin you could do no more, you made me kill my mother, and divil a good it done me, but nigh and got me into the watch-house; and so now I'm detarmint you won't play me any more thricks, for I'll hide you snug in the deepest bog-hole in the bog of Allen, and if you throuble me afther that, faix I think it'll be the wondher," and with that he made a grab at the little chap, and while you'd be sayin' "thrap stick," he cotch him, and put him body and bones into a sack, and he threwn the sack over the back of a horse was at the door, and away he wint in a tairin' rage, straight for the Bog of Allen.

Well, to be sure, he couldn't help stoppin' at a public house by the roadside, *for he was dhry with rage,* an' he tuk the sack where little Fairly was tied up and he lifted it aff o' the horse an' put it standin' up beside the door goin' into the public-house, an' he wasn't well gone in whin a farmer was comin' by, too, and he was as dhry wid the dust as ever big Fairly was with the rage (an' indeed it's wondherful how aisy it is to make a man dhry) and so, as he was goin' by he sthruck agin the sack that little Fairly was in, and little Fairly gev a groan that you'd think kem from the grave, and says he (from the inside o' the sack), "God forgive you," says he.

"Who's there?" says the farmer, startin', and no wondher.

"It's me," says little Fairly, "and may the Lord forgive you," says he, "for you have disturbed me and *I halfway to heaven.*"

"Why, who are you at all?" says the farmer. "Are you a man?" says he.

"I am a man now," says little Fairly, "though if you didn't disturb me I'd have been an angel of glory in less than no time," says he.

"How do you make that out, honest man?" says the farmer.

"I can't explain it to you," says little Fairly, *"for it's a mysthery,* but what I tell you is truth," says he, "and I tell you that whoever is in this sack at this present," says he, "is as good as halfway to heaven, and indeed I thought I was there a'most, only you sthruck agin me, and disturbed me."

"An do you mane for to say," says the farmer, "that whoiver is in that sack will go to heaven?"

"Faix they are on their road there at all events," says little Fairly, "and if they lose their way, it's their own fault."

"Oh, thin," says the farmer, "maybe you'd let me get into the sack along wid you, or to go to heaven, too."

"Oh, the horse that's to bring us *doesn't carry double,*" says little Fairly.

"Well, will you let me get into the sack instead of you?" says the farmer.

"Why, thin, do you think I'd let anyone take sitch a dirty advantage o' me as to go to heaven afore me?" says little Fairly.

"Oh, I'll make it worth your while," says the farmer.

"Why, thin, will you ontie the sack," says little Fairly, "and jist let me see who it is that has the impidence to ax me to do the like?" And with that the farmer ontied the sack and little Fairly popped out his head. "Why, thin, do you think," says he, "that a hangin'bone lookin' thief *like you* has a right to go to heaven afore me?"

"Oh," says the farmer, "I've been a wicked sinner in my time, and

I haven't much longer to live, and to tell you the truth, I'd be glad to get to heaven in that sack, if it's thrue what you tell me."

"Why," says little Fairly, "don't you know it is by *sackcloth and ashes* that the faithful see the light o' glory?"

"Thrue for you indeed," says the farmer. "Oh, murdher, let me get in there, and I'll make it worth your while."

"How do you make that out?" says little Fairly.

"Why, I'll give you five hundher guineas," says the farmer, "and I think that's a power o' money."

"But what's a power o' money compared to heaven?" says little Fairly, "and do you think I'd sell my soul for five hundher guineas?"

"Well, there's five hundher more in an owld stockin' in the oak box in the cabin by the crass-roads at Dhrunsnookie, for I am owld Tims o' Dhrumsnookie, and you'll inherit all I have if you consint."

"But what's a thousand guineas compared to heaven?" says little Fairly.

"Well, do you see all them heads o' cattle there?" says the farmer. "I have just dhruv them here from Ballinasloe," says he, "and every head o' cattle you see here shall be yours also if you let me into that sack that I may go to heaven instead o' you."

"Oh, think o' my poor sowl!" says Fairly.

"Tut, man," says the farmer, "I've twice as big a sowl as you have and besides I'm owld, and you're young, and I have no time to spare and you may get absolution aisy and make your pace in good time."

"Well," says little Fairly, "I feel for you," says he, "an' I'm half inclined to let you overpersuade me to have your will o' me."

"That's a jewel," says the farmer.

"But make haste," says little Fairly, "for I don't know how soon you might get a refusal."

"Let me in at wanst," says the farmer. So, my dear, Fairly got out and the farmer got in and the little chap tied him up and says he to the farmer, "There will be great *norations* made agin you all the way you're goin' along and you'll hear o' your sins over and over agin and you'll hear o' things you never done at all," says little Fairly, "but never say a word or you won't go where I was goin'. Oh, why did I let you persuade me?"

"Lord reward you!" says the poor farmer.

Well, just at that minit little Fairly heerd big Fairly comin' and away he run and hid inside iv a churn was dhryin' at the ind o' the house, and big Fairly lifted the sack was standin' at the door, and feelin' it more weighty nor it was before, he said, "Throth, I think you're growin' heavy with grief, but here goes anyhow," and with that he hoist it up on the horse's back, an' away he wint to the bog iv Allen.

Now, you see big Fairly, like every blackguard that has the bad blood in him, the minit he had the sup o' dhrink in, the dirty turn kem out, and so, as he wint along he began to wollop the poor baste, and the sack where his little brother was (as he thought, the big fool) and to jibe and jeer him for his divarshin. But the poor farmer did as little Fairly towld him, an' never a word he said at all, though he could not help roaring out every now and thin, when he felt the soft ind of big Fairly's shillelah across his backbone, and sure the poor fool thought it was his bad conscience and the seven deadly sins was tazin' him, but he wouldn't answer a word for all that, though the big savage was *aggravatin'* him every fut o' the road antil they kem to the bog; and when he had him there, faix he wasn't long in choosin' a big hole for him—and, my jewel, in he popped the poor farmer neck and heels, sack and all; and as the soft bog-stuff and muddy wather closed over him, "I wish you a safe journey to the bottom, young man," says the big brute, grinnin' like a cat at a cheese, "and as clever a chap as you are, I don't think you'll come back out o' that in a hurry, and it's throubled I was with you long enough, you little go-the-ground schkamer, but I'll have a quiet life for the futhur."

And wit that he got up on his horse, and away he wint home, but he had not gone over a mile, or there-away, whin who should he see but little Fairly mounted on the farmer's horse, dhrivin' the biggest dhrove o' black cattle you ever seen, and by dad, big Fairly grewn as white as a sheet whin he clapt his eyes an him, for he thought it was not himself at all was on it, but his ghost; and he was goin' to turn and gallop off, whin little Fairly called out to him to stay, for that he wanted to speak to him. So, when he seed it was himself, he wondhered to be sure and small blame to him—and says he, "Well, as cute as I know you wor, by gor, this last turn o' yours bates Bannagher—and how the divil are you here at all, whin I thought you wor cuttin turf wid your sharp little nose in the bog of Allen? for I'll take my affi-downdavy, I put you into the deepest hole in it, head foremost, not half an hour agon."

"Throth you did sure enough," says little Fairly, "and you wor ever and always the good brother to me, as I often said before, but by dad you never done rightly for me antil today, but you made me up now in airnest."

"How do you mane?" says big Fairly.

"Why, do you see all these cattle here I'm dhrivin'?" says little Fairly.

"Yes, I do, and whose cattle are they?"

"They're all my own—every head o' them."

"An' how did you come by them?"

"Why, you see, when you threwn me into the boghole, I felt it mighty cold at first and it was mortial dark, and I felt myself goin' down and down, that I thought I'd never stop sinking, and wondhered if there was any bottom to it at all, and at last I began to feel it growin' warm and pleasant and light and whin I kem to the bottom there was the loveliest green field you ever clapped your eyes on, and thousands upon thousands o' cattle feedin', and the grass so heavy that they wor up to their ears in it—it's thruth I'm tellin' you—O divil sitch meadows I ever seen, and when I kem to my self, for indeed I was rather surprised and thought it was dhramin' I was—whin I kem to myself, I was welkim'd by a very ginteel spoken little man, the dawnshiest craythur you ever seen, by dad I'd have made six iv him myself, and says he, 'You're welkim to the undherstory o' the bog iv Allen, Fairly.' 'Thank you kindly, sir,' says I. 'And how is all wid you?' says he. 'Hearty, indeed,' says I. 'And what brought you here?' says he. 'My big brother,' says I. 'That was very good iv him,' says he. 'Thrue for you, sir,' says I. 'He is always doin' me a good turn,' says I. 'Oh, then, he never done you half so good a turn as this,' says he, 'for you'll be the richest man in Ireland soon.' 'Thank you, sir,' says I, 'but I don't see how.' 'Do you see all them cattle grazin' there?' says he. 'To be sure I do,' says I. 'Well,' says he, 'take as many o' them as your heart desires and bring them home wid you.' 'Why, sure,' says I, 'how could I get back myself, up out of the boghole, let alone dhraggin' bullocks afther me?' 'Oh,' says he, 'the way is aisy enough, for you have nothin' to do but dhrive them out the back way over there,' says he, pointin' to a gate. And sure enough, my darlint, I got all the bastes you see here and dhruv them out and here I'm goin' home wid 'em and maybe I won't be the rich man—av coorse I gev the best o' thanks to the little owld man and gev him the hoighth o' good language for his behavior. And with that, says he, 'You may come back again and take the rest o' them,' says he—and faix sure enough I'll go back the minit I get these bastes home and have another turn out o' the boghole."

"Faix and I'll beforehand wid you," says big Fairly.

"Oh, but you shan't," says little Fairly, "it was I discovered the place, and why shouldn't I have the good iv it?"

"You greedy little hound," says the big fellow, "I'll have my share o' them as well as you." And with that he turned about his horse and away he galloped to the boghole, and the little fellow galloped afther him, purtendin' to be in a desperate fright, afeard the other would get there first, and he cried, "Stop the robber," afther him, and when he came to the soft place in the bog they both lit, and little Fairly got before the big fellow and purtended to be makin' for the boghole in a powerful hurry, crying out as he passed him, "I'll win the day! I'll win the day!" and the big fellow pulled foot afther him as hard as he could, and hardly a puff left in him he ran to that degree, and he was afeard that little Fairly would bate him and get all the cattle, and he was wishin' for a gun that he might shoot him, when the cute little divil, just as he kem close to the edge of the boghole, *let an* that his foot slipped and he fell down, cryin' out, "Fair play! Fair play!—wait till I rise!" but the words wasn't well out of his mouth when the big fellow kem up. "Oh, the divil a wait," says he, and he made one desperate dart at the boghole, and jumped into the middle of it. "Hurro!" says little Fairly, gettin' an his legs agin and runnin' over to the edge o' the boghole, and just as he seen the great splaw feet o' the big savage sinkin' into the sludge, he called afther him, and says he, "I say, big Fairly, don't take all the cattle, but lave a thrifle for me. *I'll wait, however, till you come back,*" says the little rogue, laughin' at his own cute conthrivance, "and I think now I'll lade a quiet life," says he, and with that he wint home, and from that day out he grewn richer and richer every day and was the greatest man in the whole counthryside, and all the neighbors gev in to him that he was the most knowledgeable man in thim parts, but they all thought it was quare that his name should be *Fairly,* for it was agreed, one and all, *that he was the biggest rogue out*—barrin' Balfe, the robber.

The Goban Saor

It's a long time since the Goban Saor was alive. Maybe it was him that built the Castle of Ferns; part of the walls are thick enough to be built by any goban, or gow, that ever splintered wood, or hammered red-hot iron, or cut a stone. If he didn't build Ferns, he built other castles for some of the five kings or the great chiefs. He could fashion a spear-shaft while you'd count five, and the spear-head at three strokes of a hammer. When he wanted to drive big nails into beams that were ever so high from the ground, he would pitch them into their place, and, taking a fling of the hammer at their heads, they would be drove

From *Legendary Fiction of the Irish Celts,* by Patrick Kennedy, pp. 67-72. Macmillan & Co. London. 1866.

in as firm as the knocker of Newgate, and he would catch the hammer when it was falling down.

At last it came to the King of Munster's turn to get his castle built, and to the Goban he sent. Goban knew that, in other times far back, the King of Ireland killed the celebrated architects Rog, Robog, Rodin, and Rooney, that way they would never build another palace equal to his, and so he mentioned something to his wife privately before he set out. He took his son along with him, and the first night they got lodging at a farmer's house. The farmer told them they might leave their beasts to graze all night in any of his fields they pleased. So they entered one field, and says Goban, "Tie the beasts up for the night." "Why," says the son, "I can't find anything strong enough." "Well, then, let us try the next field. Now," says he, "tie up the horses if you can." "Oh, by my word, here's a thistle strong enough this time." "That will do."

The next night they slept at another farmer's house, where there were two young daughters—one with black hair, very industrious; the other with fair complexion, and rather liking to sit with her hands across, and listen to the talk round the fire, than to be doing any work. While they were chatting about one thing and another, says the Goban, "Young girls, if I'd wish to be young again, it would be for the sake of getting one of you for a wife; but I think very few old people that do be thinking at all of the other world, ever wish to live their lives over again. Still I wish that you may have good luck in your choice of a husband, and so I give you three bits of advice. Always have the head of an old woman by the hob; warm yourselves with your work in the morning; and, some time before I come back, take the skin of a newly killed sheep to the market, and bring itself and the price of it home again." When they were leaving next morning, the Goban said to his son, "Maybe one of these girls will be your wife some day."

As they were going along, they met a poor man striving to put a flat roof over a mud-wall round cabin, but he had only three joists, and each of them was only three-quarters of the breadth across. Well, the Goban put two nicks near one end of every joist, on opposite sides; and when these were fitted into one another, there was a three-cornered figure formed in the middle, and the other ends rested on the mud wall, and the floor they made was as strong as anything. The poor man blessed the two men, and they went on. That night they stopped at a house where the master sat by the fire, and hardly opened his mouth all evening. If he didn't talk, a meddlesome neighbor did, and interfered about everything. There was another chance lodger besides the

Goban and his son, and when the evening was half over, the Goban said he thought he would go farther on his journey as it was a fine night. "You may come along with us, if you like," says he to the other man; but he said he was too tired. The two slept in a farmer's house half a mile farther on; and the next morning the first news they heard, when they were setting out, was that the man of the house they left the evening before was found murdered in his bed, and the lodger taken up on suspicion. Says he to his son, "Never sleep a night where the woman is everything, and the man nothing." He stopped a day or two, however, and by cross-examining and calling witnesses, he got the murder tracked to the woman and the busy neighbor.

The next day they came to the ford, where a dozen of carpenters were puzzling their heads about setting up a wooden bridge that would neither have a peg nor nail in any part of it. The king would give a great reward to them if they succeeded, and if they didn't, he'd never give one of them a job again. "Give us a hatchet and a few stocks," says the Goban, "and we'll see if we have any little genius that way." So he squared a few posts and cross-bars, and made a little bridge on the sod; and it was so made, that the greater weight was on it, and the stronger the stream of water, the solider it would be.

Maybe the carpenters weren't thankful, except one envious little, ould bastard of a fellow, that said any child might have thought of the plan (it happened he didn't think of it, though), and would make the Goban and his son drink a cag of whiskey, only they couldn't delay their journey.

At last they came to where the King of Munster kept his court, either at Cashel or Limerick, or some place in Clare, and the Goban burned very little daylight till he had the palace springing up like a flagger. People came from all parts, and were in admiration of the fine work; but as they were getting near the eaves, one of the carpenters that were engaged at the wooden bridge came late one night into the Goban's room, and told him what himself was suspecting, that just as he would be setting the coping-stone, the scaffolding would, somehow or other, get loose, himself fall down a few stories and be killed, the king wring his hands, and shed a few crocidile tears, and the like palace never be seen within the four seas of Ireland.

"*Sha gu dheine* [that's it]," says the Goban to himself; but next day he spoke out plain enough to the king. "Please, your Majesty," says he, "I am now pretty near the end of my work, but there is still something to be done before we come to the wall-plate that is to make all sure and strong. There is a bit of a charm about it, but I haven't the tool here—it is at home, and my son got so sick last night, and is lying so bad, he is not able to go for it. If you can't spare the young prince, I must go myself, for my wife wouldn't intrust it to anyone but of royal blood." The king, rather than let the Goban out of his sight, sent the young prince for the tool. The Goban told him some out-landish name in Irish, and bid him make all the haste he could back.

In a week's time, back came two of the poor attendants that were with the prince, and told the king that his son was well off, with the best of eating and drinking, and chess-playing and sword exercise, that any prince could wish for, but that out of her sight Goban's wife nor her people would let him, till she had her husband safe and sound inside of his own threshold.

Well, to be sure, how the king fumed and raged! But what's the use of striving to tear down a stone wall with your teeth? He couldn't do without his palace being finished, but he couldn't do without his son and heir. The Goban didn't keep spite; he put the finishing touch on the palace in three days, and, in two days more, himself and his son were sitting at the farmer's fireside where the two purty young girls were.

"Well, my colleen bawn," says he to the one with the fair hair, "did you mind the advice I gave you when I was here last?" "Indeed I did, and little good it did me. I got an old woman's skull from the churchyard, and fixed it in the wall near the hob, and it so frightened everyone, that I was obliged to have it taken back in an hour." "And how did you warm yourself with your work in the cold mornings?" "The first morning's work I had was to card flax, and I threw some of it on the fire, and my mother gave me such a raking for it, that I didn't offer to warm myself that way again." "Now for the sheep-skin." "That was the worst of all. When I told the buyers in the market that I was to bring back the skin and the price of it, they only jeered at me. One young buckeen said, if I'd go into the tavern and take share of a quart of mulled beer with him, he'd make the bargain with me, and that so vexed me that I turned home at once." "Now my little *ceann dhu* [dark head], let us see how you fared. The skull?" "Och," says an old woman, sitting close to the fire in the far corner, "I'm a distant relation that was left desolate, and this," says she, tapping the side of her poor head, "is the old woman's skull she provided." "Well, now for the warming of yourself in the cold mornings." "Oh, I kept my hands and feet going so lively at my work that it was warming enough." "Well, and the sheep-skin?" "That was easy enough. When I got to the market, I went to the crane, plucked the wool off, sold it, and brought home the skin."

"Man and woman of the house," says the Goban, "I ask you before this company, to give me this girl for my daughter-in-law; and if ever her husband looks crooked at her, I'll beat him within an inch of his life." There were very few words, and no need of a black man to make up the match; and when the prince was returning home, he stopped a day to be at the wedding. If I hear any more of the Goban's great doings, I'll tell 'em some other time.

The Gloss Gavlen

The Gobaun Seer and his son went eastward to the eastern world to Balar Beimann to make for him a palace. "Shorten the road, my son," said the father. The son ran out before him on the road, and the father returned home on that day. The second day they went traveling, and the father told his son to shorten the road. He ran out in front of his father the second day, and the father returned home.

"What's the cause of your returning home like that?" said the wife of the young Gobaun.

"My father asked me to shorten the road. I run out on the road before him, and he returns."

"Do you begin tomorrow at a story he has never heard, and I'll go bail he will not return. And do you never be in any place that the women are not on your side."

They went traveling the third day, and the young Gobaun began at a story his father never heard, and he returned no more till they came to the eastern world. Then they made the palace for Balar Beimann, and he did not wish to let them go back, for fear they should make for another man a palace as good as his.

"Take away the scaffolding" (said he) ; for he wanted to let them die on the top of the building. Balar Beimann had a girl, who went by under the building in the morning.

"Young Gobaun," said she, "go on thy wisdom. I think it is easier to throw seven stones down than to put one up as far as you."

"That's true for you," said young Gobaun.

They began to let down the work. When Balar Beimann heard that they were throwing down the works, he ordered back the scaffolding till they were down on the ground.

From *West Irish Folk-Tales and Romances,* collected and translated by William Larminie, pp. 1-9. Elliott Stock. London, 1898.

"Now," said the old Gobaun Seer, "there is a crookedness in your work, and if I had three tools I left after me at home, I would straighten the work, and there would not be any work in the world to compare with it. The names of the tools are—Crooked against Crooked, Corner against Corner, and Engine against deceit,* and there is not a man to get them but your own son. You will find," said he, "a woman with one hand, and a child with one eye, in the house, and a stack of corn at the door."

The father then gave him a ship and sent him over to Erin. He was traveling ever till he found out the house; and he went into it. He asked if that was the house of young Gobaun. The woman said it was.

"He said to me there was a woman with one hand, and a child with one eye in the house, and a stack of corn at the door."

"Don't you see," said she, "that I have only one hand, and don't you see this stick in the hand of the child? I don't know what moment he won't put it in his eye and take the eye out of himself; and don't you see the stack of corn outside at the door?"

He asked then for the three tools.

"What three tools?" said she.

"They are Crooked against Crooked, Corner against Corner, and Engine against deceit."

She understood then that they (i.e., her husband and his father) would never come home, if she did not understand these words.

"The three tools that are called Crooked against Crooked, Corner against Corner, and Engine against deceit, they are down in this chest."

She went then and opened the chest, and told him to stoop down to the bottom, that she was not tall enough. He stooped, and when she got him bent down, she threw him into the chest and closed it, and told him he should stay there till young Gobaun and old Gobaun came home and their pay for their service with them.

She sent word to Balar Beimann that she had his son in confinement, till young Gobaun and old Gobaun came home. He gave them a ship and sent them home with their pay; and she let Balar's son go back. Balar asked Gobaun what smith would he get to put irons on his palace.

"There is no smith in Erin better than Gavidjeen Go."

When the old Gobaun came home, he told Gavidjeen Go to take no pay from him for putting the irons on his palace, except the Gloss.†

---

* Or, perhaps, "trick against treachery."   † A champion cow.—W.L.

"If twenty barrels were put under her, she would fill twenty barrels."

Balar Beimann then wrote to the Gavidjeen Go that he would give him the Gloss if he would make irons for his palace. But when he sent the Gloss, he did not give the byre-rope, and he knew that when he did not give that, she would go from him.

This is the bargain that Gavidjeen Go made then with every champion that came to him: to mind the cow and bring her safe home to him at evening; he would make a sword for every champion who would mind her. She would pasture in the daytime at Cruahawn, of Connaught, and drink at Loch Ayachir-a-Guigalu, in Ulster, in the evening.

Kian, the son of Contje, came to him to have a sword made. He told him he would make it, but that the bargain would be to mind the Gloss that day.

"If she is not home with you to me in the evening, you must lay down your head on the anvil, that I may cut it off with your own sword."

Kian, the son of Contje, went then and took hold of her by the tail. When he came home in the evening, "Here is the Gloss outside," said he to Gavidjeen Go. There was a champion inside in the forge, whose name was the Laughing Knight. He ran out and said to Kian: "The smith is about to put tempering on your sword, and unless you have hold of it, there will be no power in it when you wield it."

When Kian, the son of Contje, went in, he forgot to drive in the Gloss. Gavidjeen Go asked him, "Where is the Gloss?"

"There she is, outside the door."

When he went out she was gone.

"Lay down your head upon the anvil, that I may cut it off."

"I am asking of you the favour of three days, to go and seek her."

"I will give you that," said he.

He went with himself then, and was following her tracks till he came to the sea. He was up and down the shore, plucking his hair from his head, in trouble after the Gloss. There was a man out on the sea in a currach. He rowed in to him. It was the tawny Mananaun, the son of Lir. He asked him: "What is the matter with you to-day?"

He told him: "How much will you give to any one who will leave you in the place where the Gloss is?"

"I have nothing to give him."

"I will ask nothing of you, but the half of all you gain till you come back."

"I will give you that," said Kian, son of Contje.

"Be into the currach."

In the winking of an eye he left him over in the kingdoms of the cold; nor on that island was a morsel cooked ever, but they ate every kind of food raw. Kian, son of Contje, made a fire, and began to cook his food. When Balar Beimann heard the like was there, he took him to be his cook, his story-teller, and his fireman. Well, Balar Beimann had one daughter, and a prediction was made that she would have a son, who would kill his grandfather. He then put her into prison for fear a man would come near her; and it was he himself who would go to her with food, and the companion with her was a dummy woman. Mananaun left this enchantment with Kian, son of Contje, that any lock he laid his hand on would open and shut after him. He was looking at Balar Beimann going to this house, to his daughter, with food for her, and he went himself after him to the house, and he laid his hand on the lock and opened the door, and found none but the two women there. He made a fire for them. He was coming there ever, till a child happened to her. He was then going to depart, when the boy was born. He went to the king and told him he must depart.

"Why are you going?" said he.

"It is because accidents have happened to me since I came into this island. I must go."

"What is the accident?" said he.

"A child has happened to me."

Balar had two sons on another island learning druidism. They came home to the palace to their father.

"Father," said a man of them, "your story-teller, your cook, and your fireman will give you your sufficiency of trouble."

Kian, son of Contje, was listening to them speaking. He went to the daughter of Balar Beimann, and told her what her brother said.

"Well," said she, "it is now time for you to be going. That is the byre-rope of the Gloss, hanging on the wall. She will be as quick as you; and take with you the boy."

He went then till he came to the place where Mananaun put him out. Mananaun told him, when he was in difficulty, to think of him and he would come. He now came on the instant.

"Be in the currach," said Mananaun, "and make haste, or Balar Beimann will drown us, if he can. But greater is my druidism than his," said the tawny Mananaun, the son of Lir.

He jumped into the currach, and the Gloss jumped in as soon as he. Balar Beimann followed them, and raised the sea in a storm before them and behind them, nor did Mananaun aught but stretch out his hand and make the sea calm. Balar then set fire to the sea before them in hopes of burning them, but Mananaun threw out a stone, and extinguished the sea.

"Now, Kian, son of Contje, you are safe and sound home, and what will you give me for it?"

"I have nothing but the boy, and we will not go to make two halves of him, but I will give him to you entirely."

"I am thankful to you. That is what I was wanting. There will be no champion in the world as good as he," said Mananaun.

This is the name that Mananaun baptized him with—the Dul Dauna. He and Mananaun were out one day on the sea, and they saw the fleet of Balar Beimann sailing. The Dul Dauna put a ring to his eye, and he saw his grandfather on the deck walking, but he did not know it was his grandfather. He took a dart from his pocket and flung it at him and killed him. The prophecy was then fulfilled.

The Shee an Gannon and the Gruagach Gaire

The Shee an Gannon* was born in the morning, named at noon, and went in the evening to ask his daughter of the king of Erin.

"I will give you my daughter in marriage," said the king of Erin; "you won't get her, though, unless you go and bring me back the tidings that I want, and tell me what it is that put a stop to the laughing of the Gruagach Gaire,† who before this laughed always, and laughed so loud that the whole world heard him. There are twelve iron spikes out here in the garden behind my castle. On eleven of the spikes are the heads of kings' sons who came seeking my daughter in marriage, and all of them went away to get the knowledge I wanted. Not one was able to get it and tell me what stopped the Gruagach Gaire from laughing. I took the heads off them all when they came back without the tidings for which they went, and I'm greatly in dread that your head'll be on the twelfth spike, for I'll do the same to you that I did to the eleven kings' sons unless you tell what put a stop to the laughing of the Gruagach."

The Shee an Gannon made no answer, but left the king and pushed away to know could he find why the Gruagach was silent.

From *Myths and Folk-Lore of Ireland*, by Jeremiah Curtin, pp. 114-128. Copyright, 1889, by Jeremiah Curtin. Little Brown & Co. Boston.

* Shee an Gannon, in Gaelic "Sighe an Gannon," the fairy of the Gannon.   † The laughing Gruagach.—J.C.

He took a glen at a step, a hill at a leap, and traveled all day till evening. Then he came to a house. The master of the house asked him what sort was he, and he said: "A young man looking for hire."

"Well," said the master of the house, "I was going tomorrow to look for a man to mind my cows. If you'll work for me, you'll have a good place, the best food a man could have to eat in this world, and a soft bed to lie on."

The Shee an Gannon took service, and ate his supper. Then the master of the house said: "I am the Gruagach Gaire; now that you are my man and have eaten your supper, you'll have a bed of silk to sleep on."

Next morning after breakfast the Gruagach said to the Shee an Gannon: "Go out now and loosen my five golden cows and my bull without horns, and drive them to pasture; but when you have them out on the grass, be careful you don't let them go near the land of the giant."

The new cowboy drove the cattle to pasture, and when near the land of the giant, he saw it was covered with woods and surrounded by a high wall. He went up, put his back against the wall, and threw in a great stretch of it; then he went inside and threw out another great stretch of the wall, and put the five golden cows and the bull without horns on the land of the giant.

Then he climbed a tree, ate the sweet apples himself, and threw the sour ones down to the cattle of the Gruagach Gaire.

Soon a great crashing was heard in the woods—the noise of young trees bending, and old trees breaking. The cowboy looked around, and saw a five-headed giant pushing through the trees; and soon he was before him.

"Poor miserable creature!" said the giant; "but weren't you impudent to come to my land and trouble me in this way? You're too big for one bite, and too small for two. I don't know what to do but tear you to pieces."

"You nasty brute," said the cowboy, coming down to him from the tree, "'tis little I care for you"; and then they went at each other. So great was the noise between them that there was nothing in the world but what was looking on and listening to the combat.

They fought till late in the afternoon, when the giant was getting the upper hand; and then the cowboy thought that if the giant should kill him, his father and mother would never find him or set eyes on him again, and he would never get the daughter of the king of Erin. The heart in his body grew strong at this thought. He sprang on the giant, and with the first squeeze and thrust he put him to his knees in the hard ground, with the second thrust to his waist, and with the third to his shoulders.

"I have you at last; you're done for now!" said the cowboy. Then he took out his knife, cut the five heads off the giant, and when he had them off he cut out the tongues and threw the heads over the wall.

Then he put the tongues in his pocket and drove home the cattle. That evening the Gruagach couldn't find vessels enough in all his place to hold the milk of the five golden cows.

After supper the cowboy would give no talk to his master, but kept his mind to himself, and went to the bed of silk to sleep.

Next morning after breakfast the cowboy drove out his cattle, and going on farther than the day before, stopped at a high wall. He put his back to the wall, threw in a long stretch of it, then went in and threw out another long stretch of it.

After that he put the five golden cows and the bull without horns on the land, and going up on a tree, ate sweet apples himself, and threw the sour ones to the cattle.

Now the son of the king of Tisean set out from the king of Erin on the same errand, after asking for his daughter; and as soon as the cowboy drove in his cattle on the second day, he came along by the giant's land, found the five heads of the giant thrown out by the cowboy the day before, and picking them up, ran off to the king of Erin and put them down before him.

"Oh, you have done good work!" said the king. "You have won one-third of my daughter."

Soon after the cowboy had begun to eat sweet apples, and the son of the king of Tisean had run off with the five heads, there came a great noise of young trees bending and old trees breaking, and presently the cowboy saw a giant larger than the one he had killed the day before.

"You miserable little wretch!" cried the giant; "What brings you here on my land?"

"You wicked brute!" said the cowboy, "I don't care for you"; and slipping down from the tree, he fell upon the giant.

The fight was fiercer than his first one; but towards evening, when he was growing faint, the cowboy remembered that if he should fall, neither his father nor mother would see him again, and he would never get the daughter of the king of Erin.

This thought gave him strength; and jumping up, he caught the giant, put him with one thrust to his knees in the hard earth, with a second to his waist, and with a third to his shoulders, and then swept the five heads off him and threw them over the wall, after he had cut out the tongues and put them in his pocket.

Leaving the body of the giant, the cowboy drove home the cattle, and the Gruagach had still greater trouble in finding vessels for the milk of the five golden cows.

After supper the cowboy said not a word, but went to sleep.

Next morning he drove the cattle still farther, and came to green woods and a strong wall. Putting his back to the wall, he threw in a great piece of it, and going in, threw out another piece. Then he drove the five golden cows and the bull without horns to the land inside, ate sweet apples himself, and threw down sour ones to the cattle.

The son of the king of Tisean came and carried off the heads as on the day before.

Presently a third giant came crashing through the woods, and a battle followed more terrible than the other two.

Towards evening the giant was gaining the upper hand, and the cowboy, growing weak, would have been killed; but the thought of his parents and the daughter of the king of Erin gave him strength, and he swept the five heads off the giant, and threw them over the wall after he had put the tongues in his pocket.

Then the cowboy drove home his cattle; and the Gruagach didn't know what to do with the milk of the five golden cows, there was so much of it.

But when the cowboy was on the way home with the cattle, the son of the king of Tisean came, took the five heads of the giant, and hurried to the king of Erin.

"You have won my daughter now," said the king of Erin when he saw the heads, "but you'll not get her unless you tell me what stops the Gruagach Gaire from laughing."

On the fourth morning the cowboy rose before his master, and the first words he said to the Gruagach were: "What keeps you from laughing, you used to laugh so loud that the whole world heard you?"

"I'm sorry," said the Gruagach, "that the daughter of the king of Erin sent you here."

"If you don't tell me of your own free will, I'll make you tell me," said the cowboy; and he put a face on himself that was terrible to look at, and running through the house like a madman, could find nothing that would give pain enough to the Gruagach but some ropes made of untanned sheepskin hanging on the wall.

He took these down, caught the Gruagach, fastened his two hands behind him and tied his feet so that his little toes were whispering to his ears. When he was in this state the Gruagach said: "I'll tell you what stopped my laughing if you set me free."

So the cowboy unbound him, the two sat down together, and the Gruagach said: "I lived in this castle here with my twelve sons. We ate, drank, played cards, and enjoyed ourselves, till one day when my sons and I were playing, a wizard hare came rushing in, jumped on our table, defiled it, and ran away.

"On another day he came again; but if he did, we were ready for him, my twelve sons and myself. As soon as he defiled our table and ran off, we made after him, and followed him till nightfall, when he went into a glen. We saw a light before us. I ran on, and came to a house with a great apartment, where there was a man with twelve daughters, and the hare was tied to the side of the room near the women.

"There was a large pot over the fire in the room, and a great stuirk* boiling in the pot. The man of the house said to me: 'There are bundles of rushes at the end of the room, go there and sit down with your men!'

"He went into the next room and brought out two pikes, one of wood, the other of iron, and asked me which of the pikes would I take. I said 'I'll take the iron one'; for I thought in my heart that if an attack should come on me, I could defend myself better with the iron than the wooden pike.

"The man of the house gave me the iron pike, and the first chance of taking what I could out of the pot on the point of the pike. I got but a small piece of the stuirk, and the man of the house took all the rest on his wooden pike. We had to fast that night; and when the man and his twelve daughters ate the flesh of the stuirk, they hurled the bare bones in the faces of my sons and myself.

"We had to stop all night that way, beaten on the faces by the bones of the stuirk.

"Next morning, when we were going away, the man of the house asked me to stay a while; and going into the next room, he brought out twelve loops of iron and one of wood, and said to me: 'Put the heads of your twelve sons into the iron loops, or your own head into the wooden one'; and I said: 'I'll put the twelve heads of my sons in the iron loops, and keep my own out of the wooden one.'

"He put the iron loops on the necks of my twelve sons, and put the wooden one on his own neck. Then he snapped the loops one after another, till he took the heads off my twelve sons and threw the heads and bodies out of the house; but he did nothing to hurt his own neck.

"When he had killed my sons he took hold of me and stripped the

---

* Stuirk is a half-grown sheep. Jeremiah Curtin, the American collector of these stories, wrote "stork," overlooking the fact that there are no storks in Ireland. Apparently someone who was translating localisms for him gave him a word which he heard as "stork."

skin and flesh from the small of my back down, and when he had done that he took the skin of a black sheep that had been hanging on the wall for seven years and clapped it on my body in place of my own flesh and skin; and the sheepskin grew on me, and every year since then I shear myself, and every bit of wool I use for the stockings that I wear I clip off my own back."

When he had said this, the Gruagach showed the cowboy his back covered with thick black wool.

After what he had seen and heard, the cowboy said: "I know now why you don't laugh, and small blame to you. But does that hare come here still to spoil your table?"

"He does indeed," said the Gruagach.

Both went to the table to play, and they were not long playing cards when the hare ran in; and before they could stop him he was on the table, and had put it in such a state that they could not play on it longer if they had wanted to.

But the cowboy made after the hare, and the Gruagach after the cowboy, and they ran as fast as ever their legs could carry them till nightfall; and when the hare was entering the castle where the twelve sons of the Gruagach were killed, the cowboy caught him by the two hind legs and dashed out his brains against the wall; and the skull of the hare was knocked into the chief room of the castle, and fell at the feet of the master of the place.

"Who has dared to interfere with my fighting pet?" screamed he.

"I," said the cowboy; "and if your pet had had manners, he might be alive now."

The cowboy and the Gruagach stood by the fire. A stuirk was boiling in the pot, as when the Gruagach came the first time. The master of the house went into the next room and brought out an iron and a wooden pike, and asked the cowboy which would he choose.

"I'll take the wooden one," said the cowboy; "and you may keep the iron one for yourself."

So he took the wooden one; and going to the pot, brought out on the pike all the stuirk except a small bite, and he and Gruagach fell to eating, and they were eating the flesh of the stuirk all night. The cowboy and the Gruagach were at home in the place that time.

In the morning the master of the house went into the next room, took down the twelve iron loops with a wooden one, brought them out, and asked the cowboy which would he take, the twelve iron or the one wooden loop.

"What could I do with the twelve iron ones for myself or my master? I'll take the wooden one."

He put it on, and taking the twelve iron loops, put them on the necks of the twelve daughters of the house, then snapped the twelve heads off them, and turning to their father, said: "I'll do the same thing to you unless you bring the twelve sons of my master to life, and make them as well and strong as when you took their heads."

The master of the house went out and brought the twelve to life again; and when the Gruagach saw all his sons alive and as well as ever, he let a laugh out of himself, and all the Eastern world heard the laugh.

Then the cowboy said to the Gruagach: "It's a bad thing you have done to me, for the daughter of the king of Erin will be married the day after your laugh is heard."

"Oh! Then we must be there in time," said the Gruagach; and they all made away from the place as fast as ever they could, the cowboy, the Gruagach, and his twelve sons.

They hurried on; and when within three miles of the king's castle there was such a throng of people that no one could go a step ahead. "We must clear a road through this," said the cowboy.

"We must indeed," said the Gruagach; and at it they went, threw the people some on one side and some on the other, and soon they had an opening for themselves to the king's castle.

As they went in, the daughter of the king of Erin and the son of the king of Tisean were on their knees just going to be married. The cowboy drew his hand on the bridegroom, and gave a blow that sent him spinning till he stopped under a table at the other side of the room.

"What scoundrel struck that blow?" asked the king of Erin.

"It was I," said the cowboy.

"What reason had you to strike the man who won my daughter?"

"It was I who won your daughter, not he; and if you don't believe me, the Gruagach Gaire is here himself. He'll tell you the whole story from beginning to end, and show you the tongues of the giants."

So the Gruagach came up and told the king the whole story, how the Shee an Gannon had become his cowboy, had guarded the five golden cows and the bull without horns, cut off the heads of the five-headed giants, killed the wizard hare, and brought his own twelve sons to life. "And then," said the Gruagach, "he is the only man in the whole world I have ever told why I stopped laughing, and the only one who has ever seen my fleece of wool."

When the king of Erin heard what the Gruagach said, and saw the tongues of the giants fitted into the heads, he made the Shee an Gannon kneel by his daughter, and they were married on the spot. Then the son of the king of Tisean was thrown into prison, and the next day they put down a fire, and the deceiver was burned to ashes The wedding lasted nine days, and the last day was better than the first.

The Horned Women

A rich woman sat up late one night carding and preparing wool, while all the family and servants were asleep. Suddenly a knock was given at the door, and a voice called: "Open! Open!"

"Who is there?" asked the woman of the house.

The mistress, supposing that one of her neighbors had called and required assistance, opened the door, and a woman entered, having in her hand a pair of wool carders, and bearing a horn on her forehead, as if growing there. She sat down by the fire in silence, and began to card the wool with violent haste. Suddenly she paused and said aloud: "Where are the women? They delay too long."

Then a second knock came to the door, and a voice called as before: "Open! Open!"

The mistress felt herself constrained to rise and open to the call, and immediately a second woman entered, having two horns on her forehead, and in her hand a wheel for spinning the wool.

"Give me place," she said, "I am the Witch of the Two Horns," and she began to spin as quick as lightning.

And so the knocks went on, and the call was heard, and the witches entered, until at last twelve women sat round the fire—the first with one horn, the last with twelve horns. And they carded the thread, and turned their spinning wheels, and wound and wove, all singing together an ancient rhyme, but no word did they speak to the mistress of the house. Strange to hear and frightful to look upon were these twelve women, with their horns and their wheels; and the mistress felt near to death, and she tried to rise that she might call for help, but she could not move, nor could she utter a word or cry, for the spell of the witches was upon her.

Then one of them called to her and said: "Rise, woman, and make us a cake."

Then the mistress searched for a vessel to bring water from the well that she might mix the meal and make the cake, but she could find none. And they said to her: "Take a sieve and bring water in it."

And she took the sieve and went to the well; but the water poured from it, and she could fetch none for the cake, and she sat down by the well and wept. Then a voice came by her and said: "Take yellow clay and moss and bind them together and plaster the sieve so that it will hold."

From *Ancient Legends, Mystic Charms and Superstitions of Ireland,* by Lady Wilde, pp. 18-21. Ticknor & Co. Boston. 1887.

This she did, and the sieve held the water for the cake. And the voice said again: "Return, and when thou comest to the north angle of the house, cry aloud three times and say, 'The Mountain of the Fenian Women and the sky over it is all on fire.'"

And she did so.

When the witches inside heard the call, a great and terrible cry broke from their lips and they rushed forth with wild lamentations and shrieks, and fled away to Slieve na mon, where was their chief abode. But the Spirit of the Well bade the mistress of the house to enter and prepare her home against the enchantments of the witches if they returned again.

And first, to break their spells, she sprinkled the water in which she had washed her child's feet (the feet-water) outside the door on the threshold; secondly, she took the cake which the witches had made in her absence, of meal mixed with the blood drawn from the sleeping family. And she broke the cake in bits, and placed a bit in the mouth of each sleeper, and they were restored; and she took the cloth they had woven and placed it half in and half out of the chest with the padlock; and, lastly, she secured the door with a great crossbeam fastened in the jambs, so that they could not enter. And having done these things she waited.

Not long were the witches in coming back, and they raged and called for vengeance.

"Open! Open!" they screamed. "Open, feet-water!"

"I cannot," said the feet-water, "I am scattered on the ground and my path is down to the Lough.'

"Open, open, wood and tree and beam!" they cried to the door.

"I cannot," said the door, "for the beam is fixed in the jambs and I have no power to move."

"Open, open, cake that we have made and mingled with blood," they cried again.

"I cannot," said the cake, "for I am broken and bruised, and my blood is on the lips of the sleeping children."

Then the witches rushed through the air with great cries, and fled back to Slieve na mon, uttering strange curses on the Spirit of the Well, who had wished their ruin; but the woman and the house were left in peace, and a mantle dropped by one of the witches in her flight was kept hung up by the mistress as a sign of the night's awful contest, and this mantle was in possession of the same family from generation to generation for five hundred years after.

Part VIII

THE FACE OF THE LAND

Ireland Delineated

"Ireland is at all poynts like a young wench that hath a green sickness . . . She is very fayre of visage, and hath a smooth skinn of tender grasse. Indeed she is somewhat freckled (as the Irish are) some partes darker than others. Her flesh is of a softe and delicate mould of earth, and her blew vaynes trayling through every part of her like rivulets. She hath one master vayne called the Shannon, which passeth quite through her, and if it were not for one knot (one mayne rock) it were navigable from head to foot. She hath three other vaynes called the sisters—the Suir, the Nore and the Barrow which, rising at one spring, trayle through her middle parts and joyne together in their going out.

Her bones are of polished marble, the grey marble, the black, the redd, and the speckled, so fayre for building that their houses show like colledges, and being polished, is most rarely embellished. Her breasts are round hillockes of milk-yielding grasse, and that so fertile, that they contend with the vallyes . . . Of complexion she is very temperate, never too hott, nor too could, and hath a sweet breath of favonian winde.

She is of gentle nature. If the anger of heaven be agaynst her, she will not bluster and storme, but she will weep many days together, and (alas) this summer she did so water her plants that the grass and the blade was so bedewed, that it became unprofitable, and threatens a scarcity.

Justice Luke Gernon (1620)

From *Ireland from the Flight of the Earls to Grattan's Parliament*, compiled and edited by James Carty. C. J. Fallon. Dublin. 1949.

Irish Landscape

Ireland is as regards landscape especially favoured among areas of moderate size on account of the wide variety of its physical and also its human interests. As to its actual frontiers, the turbulent ocean on the one side and the less formidable Irish Sea on the other provide round their margin an inexhaustible variety of no-man's-land where the waves have eaten into the rocks, forming dark cliffs or sandy bays; also the less conspicuous reverse condition where the sea had been forced back owing to the rising of the coast, resulting in new land planed smooth by the former action of the defeated ocean, and now carrying a population of land animals and land plants. Inside the shifting coast-line lies the main mass of our island. Though the surface of Ireland is on the whole smooth, it has passed during its history through great and long-continued periods of stress, when gigantic internal forces have crumpled the rocks from which erosion has produced ridges and hollows, giving the delightful variety of form which we call scenery. Streams have deepened their courses, carving our valleys, sometimes wide and fertile, sometimes narrow and gorge-like.

In a rainy country like Ireland, all hollows, large and small, are filled with water, so that Ireland is indeed a land of lakes. The central parts have for a long time suffered little from large earth-movements, so that much of the surface forms a great plain of limestone still retaining much of the horizontality which characterised the muds as which it was originally laid down under the ocean. At present raised some few hundreds of feet above the level of the sea, it forms a land surface much older than that of most countries of Europe. And a further point— the decayed rocks modified by the Ice Age, mixed with the remains of thousands of years of grassy vegetation, have produced a soil singularly suitable for the food of grazing animals. So Ireland is, and has been since man and his flocks first arrived, pre-eminently a cattle country. That is its destiny and, in the absence of extensive mineral deposits, so it will remain.

The Limestone Plain of Central Ireland, the most dominant physical feature of the country, is covered in the main with either grass or bog. Peat-bog is a very characteristic feature of Ireland and the Irish land-

---

A selection of short extracts from R. Lloyd Praeger's booklet, "The Irish Landscape," published by the *Comhar Cultúra Eireann* (the Cultural Association of Ireland). Dublin.

549

scape, about one-seventeenth of the whole surface of the country being covered by this strange vegetable blanket. Out in the Central Plain the wide treeless, purplish, flat or convex, surfaces of the bogs give a quite unusual aspect to the wider views. This spreading peat is a very recent happening from the geological point of view. Our great bogs are only a few thousand years old, the operating conditions being the oncoming of wet coldish climate subsequent to the Ice Age. In many areas the growth of the peat has now lessened or ceased. The bacteria which cause the decay of vegetable matter lost their vigour under the wet cold conditions, and in consequence decay lessened, acidity increased, and the accumulation of dead plants resulted, until forty or fifty feet of peat may remain, useless except for fuel (when dried).

Next as regards conditions affecting Irish landscape must be placed the abundant rainfall. Owing to its position against the Atlantic seaboard with its mild moisture-laden westerly winds, Ireland is a wet country, and the frequent rain falls at all times of the year. The surface receives annually a precipitation of forty to fifty inches over most of its area, and much more in the wettest parts. The driest parts near Dublin receive thirty inches of rain per annum; even in summer growth is seldom interrupted by droughts, and there is in consequence justification for Ireland's name of the Emerald Isle. The presence of golf-courses verdant in August on light sandy soil excite astonishment in the minds of visitors from the United States or from the greater part of the European mainland. Rivers maintain an almost average outflow throughout the year, and the level of the innumerable lakes seldom allows of an extensive fringe of mud or sand. On the roads, even before the arrival of the invaluable tarmac, dust was rarer in summer than in most regions of macadam; but the roads of the past were famous for their mud.

Wind dominates the Irish landscape everywhere. Even where actual exposure is slight, you have only to glance at the eastern inclination of the trees if you wish to obtain your compass-bearings, and the height of the tree-line, seldom great in Ireland, decreases as one goes westward till along the Atlantic coast it drops to sea-level; many Irish islands can scarcely boast even a shrub. In exposed areas the effect can be quite fantastic. Along the west coast in particular the trimming effected by the wind on young trees is accentuated by the presence of salt in the air, and dense dwarf growth results, in spite of the warmth.

The trees which decorate the Irish countryside are still mainly old native species—ash, oak, birch, alder, holly, willow, mountain-ash, hazel, blackthorn—much preferable and more conformable to the general vegetation and aspect of the island than the close-ranked masses of foreign species that the professional forester, horrified at the relative sparsity of trees, pours into Ireland incessantly. Looked on as a crop— and an invaluable one—the "regimented rows of incongruous conifers" which are ousting the native vegetation are of highest importance; but the day may come when we shall long for the open view, not for merely a tall hedge on either hand with a lovely prospect over mountain and valley gone—and as a palliative clouds of midges and horseflies which are the real and only pests in this Ireland of ours.

The native trees and shrubs are mostly of only medium height and any of them are crammed with blossom in their appointed season— gorse, broom, blackthorn, hawthorn, rowan—and they regenerate naturally from seed, which the many imported kinds seldom do—so we may be sure that at least on poor soils and in wind-swept places they will continue to delight the eye, despite the advancing menace of Sitka spruce and all the other foreign invaders.

The rather unsophisticated native birds that lend life to the Irish landscape are a great joy to those who appreciate wild life—and, one may add, who possess the ability to see them. It is an experience to spend a day in the country with a birdman. He sees a dozen different kinds to each one that you see, and every one of them full of beauty and interest and character. In Ireland with its open landscape and frequent absence of cover, there are plenty of birds to see. Rook villages full of noise and bustle in the early half of the year are, I fancy, commoner than human villages. What open view fails to show, if the trees are bare, the high-placed dark dome which signifies last year's nest of a magpie? In hedge and field the birds are with us everywhere.

But in Ireland it is to the sea-shore and lakes that one should go in early summer to see the birds in their glory. The sea-cliffs are their citadel, and the sight of thousands of gulls, guillemots, razorbills, cormorants, puffins, tight-packed on rocky ledges or grassy slopes, is one of the most remarkable our island affords. The lordly gannet is elusive, and favours the coast of Kerry; but most are widespread.

In contrast to the native birds, the higher animals which belong to Ireland are usually not conspicuous. Of deer we have only one native, the red deer, which is a rare and shy inhabitant of Kerry. Then we come to the badger, hare and otter, and after them smaller creatures like the squirrel and stoat and the rare marten; but all are shy, and do not affect the general lay-out of the animal kingdom as seen by the average men.

The birds of the wilder places have a special charm about them, partly no doubt due to association. It is not to the crowds of birds of certain of the cultivated areas—what we may call the mob-birds (rooks, jackdaws, starlings, as well as sea-gulls and other abundant species)—that we turn for interest, but rather to the rarer inhabitants of the less frequented parts of the country, where are found living less conspicuously what we may call the aristocracy of the bird world—ring ouzels and woodcock and snipe on the moors, dippers and grey wagtails and kingfishers by the streams, great crested grebes on the lakes, and a whole lot of others seldom seen, though they are often present, except by those who know how and where to look. These are for the observant visitor; but who cannot get rare joy from the presence of our common birds of the roadside—blackbirds and thrushes, bullfinches and chaffinches, robins and swallows, and the dainty tits. Then there are a number of higher animals familiar to observers on the other side of the Irish Sea, which he will *not* see in Ireland, but it is doubtful if he will miss them much—the mole, the voles, the common toad, and everything in the way of snakes, and similar beasts. Zoologists say they were never here, while the people prefer to believe that Saint Patrick drove them all out—believe whichever explanation suits your mental make-up.

Killarney

The tourist on approaching the lakes of Killarney is, at once, struck by the peculiarity and the variety of the foliage in the woods that clothe the hills by which on all sides they are surrounded. The effect produced is novel, striking, and beautiful; and is caused chiefly by the abundant mixture of the tree-shrub (*Arbutus Unedo**) with the forest-trees. The Arbutus grows in rich profusion in nearly all parts of Ireland; but nowhere is it found of so large a size, or in such rich luxuriance, as at Killarney. The extreme western position, the mild and humid atmosphere (for, in Ireland, there is fact as well as fancy in the poet's image,

> "The suns with doubtful gleam
> Weep while they rise,")

From *Ireland: Its Scenery, Character, Etc.*, by Mr. & Mrs. S. C. Hall, Vol. III, pp. 180-251. Virtue & Co. London. [1841?]

* Pliny says it is called "Unedo" because, having eaten one, you will never desire to eat another. It is said, however, that an agreeable wine is made from the berry in the south of Europe.—S.C.H.

and the rarity of frosts, contribute to its propagation, and nurture it to an enormous growth, far surpassing that which it attains in any part of Great Britain; although, even at Killarney, it is never of so great a size as it is found clothing the sides of Mount Athos. In Dinis Island there is one, the stem of which is seven feet in circumference, and its height is in proportion, being equal to that of an ash-tree of the same girth which stands near it; and on Rough Island, opposite O'Sullivan's cascade, there is another, the circumference of which is nine feet and a half. Alone, its character is not picturesque; the branches are bare, long, gnarled, and crooked; presenting in its wild state a remarkable contrast to its trim, formal, and bush-like figure in our cultivated gardens. Mingled with other trees, however, it is exceedingly beautiful; its bright green leaves happily mixing with the light, or dark, drapery of its neighbours—the elm and the ash, or the holly and yew, with which it is almost invariably intermixed. It strikes its roots apparently into the very rocks—thus filling up spaces that would otherwise be barren spots in the scenery. Its beautiful berries, when arrived at maturity, are no doubt conveyed by the birds, who feed upon them, to the heights of inaccessible mountains, where they readily vegetate in situations almost destitute of soil. Its most remarkable peculiarity is, that the flower (not unlike the lily-of-the-valley) and the fruit—ripe and unripe—are found at the same time, together, on the same tree. The berry has an insipid though not an unpleasant taste, is nearly round, and resembles in colour the wood-strawberry; whence its common name—the Strawberry-tree. It appears to the greatest advantage in October, when it is covered with a profusion of flowers in drooping clusters, and scarlet berries of the last year; and when its gay green is strongly contrasted with the brown and yellow tints which autumn has given to its neighbours. . . .

Before we proceed to visit the Upper Lake—to which we shall first conduct the reader—it will be desirable to lay before him a brief history of the most interesting and the most celebrated portion of Ireland—a scene which far surpasses, in natural beauty, aught that nature has applied elsewhere in Great Britain; for, with scarcely an exception, the devoted worshippers of Loch Katrine and the fervid admirers of the northern English lakes have yielded the palm to those of Killarney; some, however, having qualified the praise they bestow upon "the Pride of Ireland," by admitting only that "the three lakes, considered as one—which they may naturally be, lying so close to each other—are, together, more important than any *one* of the lakes of Cumberland and Westmoreland." A glance at the map will show that the three are separated but by very narrow channels; and that two of them have scarcely any perceptible division. They have, nevertheless, very distinctive characteristics: the Lower Lake is studded with islands, all richly clothed with evergreens; the Upper Lake is remarkable for its wild magnificence, the mountains completely enclosing it; and the Middle Lake is conspicuous for a happy mingling of both—yet inferior to the one in grace and beauty, and to the other in majestic grandeur.

The romantic beauties of the Killarney lakes were celebrated ages ago; in a very ancient poem they are classed as "the tenth wonder" of Ireland. The Irish name is Loch Lene—"the Lake of Learning," according to some authorities—a name by which it is still recognised among the peasantry, and which it is presumed to have derived from the number of "bookish monks" by whom its monasteries of Innisfallen, Mucross, and Aghadoe were at one time crowded. The lakes are formed and supplied by numerous minor lakes that exist in the surrounding mountains, and may be described as an immense reservoir for the several rivers that also flow into them, having received on their way the waters of innumerable tributary streams. The only outlet for the waters thus collected is the narrow and rapid river Laune, a channel along which they proceed to the Atlantic through the beautiful bay of Dingle. The origin of these lakes—covering an extensive valley—is, therefore, self-evident; but fiction has assigned to them one of a far less obvious nature; for, as will be readily supposed, the scene is full of wild legends and marvellous traditions, harmonising with the poetical character of the locality.

The legends which account for the existence of the lakes vary in some respects; but all have one common source—the neglecting to close the entrance to an enchanted fountain, which caused an inundation, and covered, in a single night, fair and fertile fields, and houses and palaces, with water. One of them attributes the misfortune to the daring impiety of an O'Donoghue, who, full of scepticism—and wine, scorned the tradition which doomed to destruction the person who should displace the stone over the well-head, and resolved to expose its falsity, by removing it to his castle: his subjects, with whom his word was law, awaited the result in fear and trembling—all but his favourite jester, who fled to the summit of a neighbouring mountain. When the morning sun broke, he looked down into the valley and saw nothing but a broad sheet of water. Another legend throws the responsibility of the awful event on a fair young peasant girl, who was wont to meet her lover—a stranger ignorant of the mystic spell—by the fountain-side: one night they were lulled to sleep by the music of its flow; at day-break the girl awoke screaming "The well! the well!" It was too late; the water was rushing forth, and overtook them as they ran. They were drowned, and involved in their fate the inhabitants of the whole district.

The Upper Lake will require no very detailed description. Its length is somewhat more than two miles; it is in no place more than a mile in breadth: its circumference being about eight miles. It is narrow and straggling; the islands it contains, though small, are numerous and gracefully wooded; but its chief value is derived from the mountains— the most conspicuous being "the Reeks"—by which it is, on all sides, surrounded; and which throw their dark shadows upon the water, so as to give it a character of gloom, in perfect keeping with the loneliness of the scene. One feels as if the sound of a human voice would disturb its solitude; and wishes the oars, that row him over it, were muffled. The more prominent of the islands are "Oak Island or Rossburkie," "Stag Island," "Eagle's Island," "Ronayne's Island," and "Arbutus Island"; and nearly in the centre the fine and beautiful cascade of Derricunnihy sends its abundant tribute to the lake. Its superabundant waters are discharged through the pass which commences at "Colman's Eye"—a promontory that juts into the lake, and limits the passage to a breadth of about thirty feet.

There are three modes of visiting the upper lake—one by water, another by the Kenmare road, crossing the old Weir bridge, and the other by proceeding through the Gap of Dunloe; the latter is to be recommended, as affording the tourist who is willing to rise early, an opportunity of examining, in one day, the most remarkable points in the scenery, proceeding by land and returning by water through the three lakes.

* * * * *

The entrance to the Gap is a sudden introduction to its marvels; the visitor is at once convinced that he is about to visit a scene rarely paralleled for wild grandeur and stern magnificence; the singular character of the deep ravine would seem to confirm the popular tradition that it was produced by a stroke of the sword of one of the giants of old, which divided the mountains and left them apart for ever. Any where, and under any circumstances, this rugged and gloomy pass would be a most striking object; but its interest and importance are, no doubt, considerably enhanced by the position it occupies in the very centre of gentle and delicious beauty. The varied greenery of the pleasant glades that skirt the lakes, or line the banks of their tributary rivers, has hardly faded from the eye, before the bleak and barren rocks, of forms as varied and fantastic as they are numerous, are placed before it; and the ear, in lieu of the mingled harmony of dancing leaves, and rippling waters, and songs of birds, is compelled to listen only to the brawling and angry stream rushing onwards, wasting its strength in foam, but continually changing its form—here a creeping rivulet—here a broad lake—and there a fierce cataract. Along the banks of the river is a narrow and, of course, circuitous, path. On the right, the Reeks, with their grand-master, Carran-tuel—"the inverted sickle" —the highest mountain in Ireland, look down upon the dark glen; while, on the left, Tomies and the Purple mountain rise above it, and with a more gracious countenance; for their sides are not so steep but that the goat finds sure footing and pleasant pasture; and the cow—if it be Kerry born—may also wander and ruminate at leisure. The road, or rather bridle track—the pony that treads it must not be a stranger— often passes along the brinks of precipices, and then descends into absolute pits; the roar of the rushing torrent is heard plainly all the while— now and then in the depths below, and now and then as a talkative and warning guide by the side of the wayfarer. The dark stream is the Loe; and in its limited course through the Gap it expands at several points into lakes of various and unequal magnitude, and again contracts itself to gather force for a new rush through the valley. The rocks along the pass are of forms the most grotesque; and each has received some distinguishing name from the peasantry. Although the mountains on either side are for the most part bare, they present occasionally patches of cultivation, "few and far between"; but sufficient to show that even in this savage region the hand of industry may be employed with advantage. From some crevices, too, peep out the gay evergreens—high up, and often so far distant that the eye cannot distinguish the arbutus from the prickly furze. Occasionally, too, the deep gloom of the pass is dispelled by the notes of Spillane's bugle—waking the echoes of the mighty hills; and now and then the eagle soars above the valley. Still it would be impossible for the very lightest-hearted to be otherwise than sad while passing through this dark and deep ravine; it oppresses the spirits with exceeding melancholy. Yet it has its own peculiar sources of pleasure; and, strange as it may seem, nothing at Killarney afforded us so much intense enjoyment.

When the Pass terminates, and the tourist is, as will be supposed, wearied in heart and foot, he suddenly comes upon a scene of unrivalled beauty. A turning in the narrow pathway, brings him just over the Upper Lake; and hanging above "the black valley"—the Coom Duv. . . . It was with an uncontrollable burst of enjoyment that we gazed upon the delicious scene. A short time before we had thus indulged in a luxuriant draught of nature, we had examined one of the most singular relics of very ancient art. On the side of a lofty hill is the

"Logan Stone"—about twenty-four feet in circumference. The peasants call it the "balance rock," and it is doubtless a druidical remain of remote antiquity. Moore likens it to the poet's heart, which

> "The slightest touch alone sets moving,
> But all earth's power could not shake from its base."

Leaving "the Black Valley," with the white cataract that crowns it, the tourist passes through "Lord Brandon's demesne;" and having found his boat waiting in one of the sweet and lonely creeks, of which there are so many, he takes his seat, and prepares for pleasure of a less fatiguing character—the oars rapidly convey him through the Upper Lakes.

The narrow and tortuous channel, about four miles in length, that leads from the Upper to the Middle, or Torc lake, is full of interest and beauty; the water is clear and rapid; and on either side it is amply wooded; the "patrician trees" happily mingling with the "plebeian underwood"; through which glimpses of the huge mountains are occasionally caught.

About midway is the far-famed Eagle's Nest, the most perfect, glorious, and exciting of the Killarney echoes. The rock, (for in comparison with the mountains that look down upon it, it is nothing more, although, when at its base, it appears of prodigious height), derives its name from the fact that for centuries it has been the favoured residence of the royal birds, by whose descendants it is still inhabited; their eyrie being secured by nature against all human trespassers. The rock is of a pyramidical form, about 1700 feet high, thickly clothed with evergreens, but bare towards the summit; where the nest of the bird is pointed out, in a small crevice nearly concealed by stunted shrubs. We put into a little creek on the opposite side of the river; but remained in our boat, having been recommended to do so. Our expectations of the coming treat had been highly raised, and we were in breathless anxiety to enjoy it. The bugle-player, Spillane—to whose skill and attention we gladly add our testimony to that of every traveller who has preceded us—landed, advanced a few steps, and placed the instrument to his lips—the effect was MAGICAL—the word conveys a poor idea of its effect. First he played a single note—it was caught up and repeated, loudly, softly, again loudly, again softly, and then as if by a hundred instruments, each a thousand times more musical than that which gave its rivals birth, twirling and twisting around the mountain, running up from its foot to its summit, then rolling above it, and at length dying away in the distance until it was heard as a mere whisper, barely audible, far away. Then Spillane blew a few notes—ti-ra-la-ti-ra-la: a multitude of voices, seemingly from a multitude of hills, at once sent forth a reply; sometimes pausing for a second, as if waiting for some tardy comrade to join in the marvellous chorus, then mingling together in a strain of sublime grandeur, and delicate sweetness, utterly indescribable. Again Spillane sent forth his summons to the mountains, and blew, for perhaps a minute, a variety of sounds; the effect was indeed that of "enchanting ravishment"—giving

"resounding grace to all Heaven's harmonies."

It is impossible for language to convey even a remote idea of the exceeding delight communicated by this development of a most wonderful property of Nature; sure we are that we shall be guilty of no exaggeration if we say that this single incident, among so many of vast attraction, will be sufficient recompense to the tourist who may visit these beautiful lakes. When Spillane had exhausted his ability to minister to our enjoyment—and the day was declining before we had expressed ourselves content—preparations were made for firing off the cannon. As soon as they were completed, the match was applied. In an instant every mountain for miles around us seemed instinct with angry life, and replied in voices of thunder to the insignificant and miserable sound that had roused them from their slumbers. The imagination was excited to absolute terror; the gnomes of the mountains were about to issue forth and punish the mortals who had dared to rouse them from their solitude; and it was easy for a moment to fancy every creek and crevice peopled with "airy things." The sound was multiplied a thousand-fold, and with infinite variety; at first it was repeated with a terrific growl; then a fearful crash; both were caught up and returned by the surrounding hills; mingling together, now in perfect harmony, now in utter discordance; while those that were nearest became silent, awaiting the on coming of those that were distant; then joining together in one mighty sound, louder and louder; then dropping to a gentle lull, as if the winds only created them; then breaking forth again into a combined roar that would seem to have been heard hundreds of miles away. It is not only by these louder sounds the echoes of the hills are awakened; the clapping of a hand will call them forth; almost a whisper will be repeated—far off—ceasing—resuming—ceasing again.

At Dinis Pool the current divides; one branch, turning to the right, enters Torc Lake; the other, turning to the left, runs between Dinis Island and Glenà mountain, and joins the Lower Lake at the Bay of Glenà—beautiful Glenà! . . .

There is, we think, nothing at Killarney, where nature is everywhere charming to absolute fascination, to equal this surpassingly lovely spot. The mountain of Glenà, clothed to luxuriance with the richest evergreens, looks down upon a little vale endowed with the rarest natural gifts, and which the hand of taste has touched, here and there, without impairing its primitive character. . . . Glenà—although we have described it here—properly belongs to the Lower Lake.

The Torc, or Middle, or Mucross, Lake, for it is known by each of these names, is more sheltered, and less crowded with islands than the other lakes. The entrance into it from the upper lake we have described; that from the lower lake is either round by Dinis Island (a course seldom taken) or under Brickeen Bridge, a bridge of a single arch, which connects Bricken Island with the Peninsula of Mucross. Upon this Peninsula is the far-famed Mucross Abbey; and the great tributary to the lake is the beautiful Torc cascade, supplied from the "Devil's Punch-Bowl," in the mountain of Mangerton, conveyed through a narrow channel, called "the Devil's Stream." The cascade is in a chasm between the mountains of Torc and Mangerton: the fall is between sixty and seventy feet. The path that leads to it by the side of the rushing and brawling current, which conducts it to the lake, has been judiciously curved so as to conceal the full view until the visitor is immediately under it; but the opposite hill has been beautifully planted—Art having been summoned to the aid of nature—and the tall young trees are blended with the evergreen arbutus, the holly, and a vast variety of shrubs. As we advance, the rush of water gradually breaks upon the ear, and at a sudden turning the cataract is beheld in all its glory. It is exceedingly beautiful. At times the torrent is very great; but not unfrequently the supply is so limited, that it dwindles, by comparison, into a mere mill stream.

*   *   *   *   *

The Lower Lake is, as we have said, much larger than either Torc Lake or the Upper Lake; and tourists generally prefer it to either of its sister rivals. It is more cheerful, and in parts more beautiful; but, as we have intimated, less graceful than the one, and far less grand than the other.

There islands, small and large, in the Lower Lake, to the number of about five-and-thirty, including those of all sizes and proportions, that are not merely bare rocks; and nearly the whole of them are luxuriantly clothed in the richest verdure and foliage. The principal in extent and the most distinguished for beauty are Ross, Innisfallen, and Rabbit Island; but among the lesser "stars of earth," there are several that surpass their comparatively giant neighbours in natural loveliness and grace;—such, for example, is Mouse Island, the tiny speck that lies between Ross and Innisfallen. . . .

As we have observed, from all parts of the lake, and from every one of the adjacent mountains, the castle of Ross is a most interesting and attractive point in the scenery; and it amply repays the honour it receives by enabling the visitor to obtain, from the summit of its tower, a commanding view of every important object by which it is surrounded. . . .

INNISFALLEN

Ross Island is nearly in the centre of the Lower Lake; the next in importance is Innisfallen—sweet Innisfallen! It receives from all tourists the distinction of being the most beautiful, as it is certainly the most interesting, of the lake islands. Its peculiar beauty is derived from the alternating hill and dale within its small circle; the elegance of its miniature creeks and harbours; and the extraordinary size as well as luxuriance of its evergreens; and it far surpasses in interest any one of its graceful neighbours, inasmuch as here, twelve centuries ago, was founded an Abbey, of which the ruins still exist, from which afterwards issued "the Annals of Innisfallen"—among the earliest and the most authentic of the ancient Irish histories. On approaching it, we seem to be drawing near a thick forest; for the foliage is remarkably close, and extends literally into the water, many of the finest trees having their roots under the lake. On landing, however, we find that the lofty elm and magnificent ash, mingled with hollies of gigantic growth, and other evergreens of prodigious height and girth, only encircle a green sward, of so pure and delicious a colour as to demand for Innisfallen, beyond every other part of Ireland, the character of being pre-eminently "the Emerald Isle." Vistas have been skilfully formed through the trees, presenting on one side a view of the huge mountains, and on the other of the wooded shores of Ross. Of the abbey a few broken walls alone remain; it is said to have been built in the seventh century by Saint Finian Lobhar (the Leper), the descendant of one of the most renowned of the Munster kings; and it was subsequently appropriated to the use of the regular canons of St. Augustin. A far more ancient structure, the small Oratory or Chapel, is an object of considerable interest; its situation is picturesque; and its appearance,

"Being all with ivy overspread,"

is in happy keeping with the ancient character of the island. . . .

We cannot quit the subject, however, without requiring the reader to make with us the ascent to the summit of Mangerton; or, if he be in rude health and strength, and time be not of much value, he may encounter Carran Tuel—the highest mountain of Ireland—from the top of which he will see, still more gloriously pictured, the magnificent panorama of the lakes at the foot, the Atlantic Ocean in the distance, and, between them both, a trace of country unparalleled for rude grandeur and gentle beauty.

* * * * *

The view from the mountain-top defies any attempt at description; it was the most magnificent sight we had ever witnessed—and one that greatly surpassed even the dreams of our imagination. In the far away distance is the broad Atlantic, with the river of Kenmare, the bay of Dingle, and the storm-beaten coast of Iveragh. Midway are the mountains—of all forms and altitudes, with their lakes and cataracts, and streams of white foam. At our feet lie the three Killarney lakes, with Glenà, and Torc, and even Tomies, looking like protecting walls girdling them round about. The islands in the upper and lower lake have, some of them, dwindled into mere specks, while the larger seem fitted only for the occupation of fairies. . . . We had scarcely reached the top, when the clouds came suddenly around us—around, above and below; we could not see our companions although they were but a few yards from us, and the rough play of the wind prevented us from hearing their voices. . . . The dark light, for it is scarcely paradoxical to say so, continued about us for many minutes. It was a bright white mist in which we were enveloped; and, as we attempted to peer through it, we could compare it to nothing but lying on the ground and looking upwards when the sky is unbroken by a single cloud. After a time, however, the clouds gradually drifted off; and the whole of the magnificent panorama was displayed beneath us. The effect was exciting to a degree; the beautiful foreground, the magnificent midway, and the sublime distance, were all taken in by the eye at once. While we gazed, however, the clouds again passed over the landscape, and all was once more a blank; after a few minutes they departed, and gave to full view the whole of the grand and beautiful scene; and in this manner above an hour was occupied, with alternate changes of darkness and light. On our way down the mountain, we deviated from the accustomed track to visit Coom-na-goppel—"the Glen of the Horse." The glen may be likened to a gigantic pit, surrounded on all sides by perpendicular mountain rocks, in which the eagle builds his nest without the fear of man: it is inaccessible except from one particular spot, where its super-abundant waters have forced a passage into a still lower valley. To reach it from the heights above would be almost impossible.

Loch Salt in Donegal

Ascending the steep side of the Kilmacaennan Mountain, we at length reached the top of the mountain (or rather the summit of the pass through the "ridge"), and suddenly turning the point of a cliff that jutted out and checked the road, we came abruptly into a hollow something like the crater of an extinct volcano, which was filled almost entirely by a lovely lake, on the right hand of which rose the high peak of the mountain, so bare, so serrated, so tempest-worn, so vexed at the storms of the Atlantic, that if matter could suffer we might suppose that this lofty and precipitous peak presented the appearance of ma-terial endurance: not one tint of shadowing that decks and paints a mountain brow was wanting. Here was the brown heath, grey lichen, green fern, and red cranesbill; and there, down the face of the cliff, from the top to the water's edge, the black, seared streak of a meteoric stone, which had shattered itself against the crest of the mountain, and rolled down in fiery fragments into the lake, was distinctly visible. On the other side, a fair, verdant bank presented itself, courting the traveler to take rest; gentle and grassy knolls were here and there in-terspersed, on which sheep of a most picturesque leanness—some black, some white—were grazing. But the lake! Not a breath was abroad on its expanse; it smiled as it reflected the grey mountain and the azure face of heaven; it seemed as if on this day the spirit of the Atlantic had fallen asleep, and air, and earth, and ocean were celebrating the festival of repose; the waters of the lake, of the color and clearness of he sky, were: *Blue, darkly, deeply beautifully blue.* You could look down a hundred fathoms deep and see no bottom. Speckled trout, floating at immense depths, seemed as if they soared in ether. Then the still-ness of the scene: you seemed lifted, as it were, out of the turmoil of the world into some planetary paradise.

From *Sketches in Ireland Descriptive of Interesting Portions of the Counties of Donegal, Cork and Kerry,* by Caesar Otway, pp. 6-8. William Curry, Jun. & Co. Dublin. 1839.

The Bright Dwellings and the Legend
of Pope Gregory

I set my face to the hill again, and now took my way against the slope, ascending slowly to the summit of the Island [Blasket, off Kerry]. There, almost on the highest ridge, where the land breaks abruptly towards the sea, an ancient people in days before any history had built their high place. Using the cliff edge for the seaward front of their dun, they had drawn a semi-circular trench to fence off their dwelling towards the land. And through a gap in the inner wall of this trench they had run a lesser ditch, dividing the inner space into two equal portions. The whole forms a cliff fort of the kind familiar along the range of the seawall of southern and western Ireland.

Let us leave it to the historians of the time before history to inquire who were the dark and strange people before the coming of the Celts who, vanishing, have left little more than these vast shells in which they lived to be their memorials. . . .

The dun has known other inhabitants than those, its first builders. Roughly shaped stones hidden in the earth bear witness to later buildings, and these may well have been the homes of men of religion whose constructions still remain elsewhere on the Island and in the other islands of the group. There may be some truth, too, in the tradition of the islanders which claims so confidently that the Danes dwelt here. That the Northmen were on the Island we may be confident, and they can hardly have failed to make use of this strong place commanding both the landward and seaward slopes. But history has nothing to tell us of that occupation, and no monuments remain to fill the gap of the written record.

Below the fort the sharp wall of the cliff drops to a flat space, overgrown with heath, and fern, and sea-pink, and I know not what of the delicate and faint-hued island flowers. This space the Islanders with a happy instinct call the garden of the dun. A path leading out of it to the left wanders down the cliff, and, if you have the head for heights, you may follow it and come at last to a hole under a flat ledge of rock called Sgairt Phiarais, Pierce's Cave, where, says the tradition, Pierce Ferriter, poet and warrior, hid from his enemies. . . .

From *The Western Island, or The Great Blasket*, by Robin Flower, pp. 33-36. Copyright, 1945, by Oxford University Press, New York, Inc.

Another path leads along the brink of the cliffs and climbs to the summit of An Cro, the highest point of the Island. Beneath to the sea are the "bright stone dwellin's" (*na clochain gheala*). . . . Loose stones lie about all over the ground, and it is plain that there must at one time have been a considerable settlement here. It may be that excavation would reveal the foundations of a church, but a cursory inspection does not yield any evidence of such a building to the inexperienced eye. Further down to the sea there is a little group of ruins the form of which is still discernible. These have been beehive huts of the customary Irish type. Of one there are still considerable remains, of a very interesting form. The building is half buried in the earth, and when you come to examine it you find that it was originally two-roomed, the rooms divided off from each other by an interior wall with a low doorway. Other remains in the neighborhood are too fragmentary for description.

No record or tradition remains to tell what manner of men dwelt here when these buildings were new. But other such clochans are to be found on Inis Tuaisceart and Iniscileain, and there can be little doubt they had an ecclesiastical purpose. This is the country of St. Brendan. There across the water is the great mountain named after him, where the country people go on painful pilgrimages for the cure of all their ailments. And away beyond Sybil Head is the bay from which in their tradition he set out on his wild journey into the Atlantic, voyaging among marvelous islands, and coming at last to that icy peak where Judas Iscariot once in every year finds a day's solace from the pains of Hell.

There is another story, found in a fifteenth-century manuscript, that a pilgrim from these parts in the old time went to Rome and remained there, marrying a daughter of Rome, and begetting a son who afterwards came to be the great Pope Gregory, Gregory of the Gael, Gregory Goldenmouth. The natives of the papal city, we know, have a different opinion in this matter, but that, no doubt, is mere local partiality. In any case, when Pope Gregory was near his end, he gave instructions that, when the breath had left his body the empty corpse should be enclosed in a coffin with his name legibly inscribed thereon, and that the coffin should be committed to the Tiber. So it was done. And Tiber carried the rich freight to the Mediterranean Sea, the current swept it through the Pillars of Hercules, and after long travel it was cast up on the shores of Aran, and there the goldenmouthed Pope found burial, an Irishman in Irish earth. In witness of which fact, one of the sounds of Aran has the name of Gregory Sound to this day.

Everywhere on the shores of Dingle Bay are sacred spots: the oratory of Gallarus, a marvel of building, still whole and unimpaired, the church of Kilmalcadar, and the holy pyramid of Skellig Michael. One suspects some connection between the ruins on the Blasket and the more perfect remains on the Great Skellig, which a local tradition says were a penitential settlement from a monastery on the mainland dedicated to St. Michael. It may be so, but one thinks rather of the other high places under the invocation of St. Michael of Monte Gargano, St. Michael in peril of the sea on the Breton coast, and the mount of St. Michael in Cornwall. Here, in these rocky fastnesses devoted to the warrior angel, the hermits may well have thought that their long battle against the demon hosts might best be carried to a conclusion. Cut off from all the easy ways of the world, with all the issues of life simplified in that savage isolation to an unrelenting conflict of prayer and fasting, they offered themselves up for their fellows in a white martyrdom of utter privation.

A Dream of Inishmaan

Some dreams I have had, in a cottage near the Dun of Conchubar, on the middle island of Aran, seem to give strength to the opinion that there is a psychic memory attached to certain neighborhoods.

One night after moving among buildings with strangely intense light upon them, I heard a faint rhythm of music beginning far away from me on some stringed instrument.

It came closer to me, gradually increasing in quickness and volume with an irresistibly definite progression. When it was quite near, the sounds began to move in my nerves and blood, and to urge me to dance with them.

I knew, even in my dreams, that if I yielded to the sounds I would be carried away to some moment of terrible agony, so I struggled to remain quiet, holding my knees together with my hands.

The music increased again, sounding like the strings of harps tuned to a forgotten scale, and having a resonance as searching as the strings of the cello.

Then the luring instrument became more powerful than my will, and my limbs moved in spite of me.

In a moment I was swept away by a whirlwind of notes. My breath

By J. M. Synge, in *The Gael*, March, 1904, p. 93. New York.

and thoughts and every impulse of my body became a form of the dance, till I could not distinguish any more between the instruments and the rhythm, and my own person or consciousness.

For a while it seemed an excitement that was filled with joy; then it grew into an ecstasy where all existence was lost in a vortex of movement. I could not think there had ever been a life beyond the whirling of the dance.

At last, with a sudden movement, the ecstasy turned into an agony and rage. I struggled to free myself, but seemed only to increase the passion of the steps I moved to. When I shrieked I could only echo the notes of the rhythm.

Then, with a moment of incontrollable frenzy, I broke back to consciousness, and awoke.

*　*　*　*　*

I dragged myself, trembling, to the window of the cottage and looked out. The moon was glittering across the bay, and there was no sound anywhere on the island.

The Ruins Speak

One of the peculiar features of that part of Ireland is the ruined castles which are so thick and numerous. The face of the country appears studded with them, it being difficult to choose any situation from which one, at least, may not be described. They are of various ages and styles of architecture, some of great antiquity, like the stately remains which crown the crag of Cashel; others built by early English conquerors; others, and probably the greater part, erections of the time of Elizabeth and Cromwell. The whole speaking monuments of the troubled and insecure state of the country, from the most remote periods to comparatively modern time. . . .

I diverged from the road, and crossing two or three fields, came to a small grassy plain, in the midst of which stood the castle. . . . A kind of awe came over me as I approached the old building. The sun no longer shone upon it, and it looked so grim, so desolate and solitary; and here was I in that wild country, alone with that grim building before me. . . . The interior of the walls was blackened, as by fire, and a few pro-

From *Lavengro*, by George Borrow, pp. 82-84. T. N. Foulis. London, Edinburgh and Dublin, 1914.

jected stumps of beams, which seemed to have been half burnt. . . .
There were echoes among the walls as I walked about the court. . . . I
entered the keep by a low and frowning doorway, the lower floor consisting of a large dungeon-like room with a vaulted roof; on the left
hand was a winding staircase the thickness of the wall; it looked anything but inviting; yet I stole softly up, my heart beating. . . . There
was an object at the farther end. She was an old woman, at least eighty.
She was seated on a stone, cowering over a few sticks burning feebly
on what had been a right noble and cheerful hearth. . . .

"Is this your house, mother?" I at length demanded, in the language
which I thought she would best understand.

"Yes, my house, my own house, the house of the broken-hearted . . .
my own house, the beggar's house, the accursed house of Cromwell."

Life in the Castles

Writers on domestic and defensive architecture, alluding to these
castles erected in Ireland between the fourteenth and sixteenth centuries, are too much in the habit of looking upon our castellated mansions as mere guard rooms for the security and defence of the soldiery
by which they were garrisoned, without taking into consideration the
artistic skill and taste with which many of them were adorned; nor
remembering the ladies bright and accomplished who "walked in silk
attire"; the bards and minstrels, with their harps, and songs, and
legends; the scholars learned, the clerics pious, as well as the valiant
knights and nobles, in their burnished armour and nodding plumes,
by whom they were tenanted but of whose social life and habits we
know little.

In looking back upon those ages, it is scarcely possible to disassociate
from skill, taste, and refinement in architecture, similar personal culture and costume; but until some gifted poetic child of Eire, with an
eye to see, and a pen to paint the beauties of both nature and art—
observation to appreciate and display the workings of the human heart
—dramatic—learned in the history of the past—antiquarian in knowledge, and patriotic in feeling—and, above all, possessing the rare gift
of fusing fiction with fact, and weaving the romance with the legend,
as Scott did for the history and monuments of his native country—the

From [Sir William R. W.] *Wilde's Loch Coirib, Its Shores and Islands*, edited
by Calm O Lochlainn, pp. 49-50. Dublin. 1936. Original publication, Dublin, 1867.

castle may crumble, the abbey moulder, the warrior lie unremembered, and the fair lady unwept for, in this land so fertile in imagination, and so profound in pathos. And until the proprietors who own these castles feel proud of their heritage or their acquisition, and the clerics who claim by transmitted hereditary right these abbeys, and who perhaps hope to claim them on a future day, take some interest in their preservation, the most the modern writer can do is to invoke public opinion; while the tourist will still have, for yet many a day, to grope his way among those crumbling walls, through mud and briars, and to disturb the bullock calves and fat wethers, that may almost invariably be found desecrating the tombs that pave these sacred aisles; and disturb the goats that take occasional shelter even underneath their high altars.

Blarney

The famous Blarney Castle and the magic Blarney Stone with its traditional power of conferring eloquence on all those who kiss it are known to the world. The word "Blarney" has long ago found a place in the English Dictionary and is supposed to have originated in the dealings of Queen Elizabeth's government with the then Lord of Blarney, Cormac MacDermott Carthy. Repeatedly he was asked by the Queen's deputy, Carew, to renounce the traditional system by which the clans elected their chief, and to take the tenure of his lands from the Crown. But, while seeming to agree to this proposal, he put off the fulfilment of his promise from day to day "with fair words and soft speech," until Elizabeth declared: "this is all Blarney; what he says he never means." Thus "Blarney" came to mean pleasant talk intended to deceive without offending.

Blarney Castle

The best way to get to Blarney Castle is to walk there—to walk there, I mean, from the town of Cork. You will go to Patrick's Bridge. You

From *The Blarney Annual of Fact and Fancy*, p. 14. Woodlands Press. Blarney, 1951.

From *Cross Roads in Ireland*, by Padraic Colum, pp. 306-312. Copyright, 1930, by The Macmillan Co. New York.

will walk along the quays. You will pass Shandon Church whose bells
a poet has made famous. You will come to a second bridge. Then you
will turn up Blarney Street. You will go on until you come to a place
named Clougheen. And the valley which Blarney Castle dominated is
then before you.

But you should stay for a while upon Patrick's Bridge and take in
the scene and the people. Across the way is Shandon Church with its
turret.

> White and brown is Shandon's steeple,
> Parti-coloured like the people.

Two sides of the turret are of white stone, two of brown stone. The
white stone is used again in the embankment of the river; the Lee
flows along the quays built of limestone. This, the central part of Cork,
is a very little way from the countryside. Turn off the bridge along
the quayside, and the ass-cart filled with cabbages, the country cart
loaded with peat are the vehicles you see. Gulls flying over the river.
And the people who give Ireland her journalists, schoolmasters, and
civil-servants are passing by.

They are a merchant-folk primarily—ready of tongue, shrewd of
mind, good at bargaining. They have soft and rippling speech and
are ready to engage in long conversations with one another. Lots of
young men seem to be detached from any employments—strolling
about, or pushing barrows, or carrying baskets. Several monks pass,
brown-garbed and with sandles on their feet. Sometimes one sees an
old woman who has on the voluminous hooded cloak that was worn
everywhere in Munster a century ago. The girls look as if they all had
personality—a fresh, clear, but unvivid personality; the younger they
are the prettier they are; the girls seem to be at their prettiest around
fourteen. But when you go along the quaysides and come to the second
bridge you see more of the folk-life of Cork. They are real types, these
old women who are selling gooseberries, apples, blackthorn-sticks. I
went to buy withered apples from one of them. Both she and her
charming granddaughter were so eager to serve that I bought gooseberries, too; they measured them out for me in a pewter mug, and
I'm sure they gave me an extra ha'-penny worth for good measure. And
so, eating gooseberries, I turned up Blarney Street.

'Tis a long street that begins in an undistinguished part of the town
and ends in a lane. But then I am out of the town and in the county
of Cork. Clougheen—"the little stones"—is not a village; there is a
church there and a few houses, a pump, and that is all. And the road
to Blarney is before me.

I go to Blarney by the fields that are the greenest of all the green
fields of Eirinn. Yonder field is a green mirror for the clouds to make
shadows upon. And I pass a field that has yellow dandelions and grass
so soft and smooth that I think that only the cattle of a king have
any right to graze there—no other cattle would be worthy of such a
sward. Passing these fields I come to Blarney village with its factory,
a dull little place. And then I go through the gate and enter the
grounds of Blarney's old castle, grounds overgrown with shrubs.

Near the gate, under the trees, with a shawl over her head for
shelter from the showers, is a simple-faced old woman. She returns my
salutation, and I go over and talk to her. She has a simple and rambling mind. She tells me that her husband was employed on this
property, and that she has permission to come here and sit under the
trees. She likes the air here and she likes to watch the flowing water.
She does not say it to me, but I gather from her rambling allusions
that she nurses the hope that some of the visitors will make her some
sort of offering—something that would give her an allowance of tea,
or snuff, or tobacco. There are wild children in the house she lives in;
there are bad neighbors all around her; she does not sleep. So she
likes being here, within the gate and under the trees. And over and
over again she tells me that she likes to watch the flowing water from
where she sits. There are handsome trout in that stream that never
were caught and that never can be caught. She tells me a legend of the
castle that has as much to recommend its authenticity as any of the
half-dozen legends that are current. And as I go away from her she
says, "May God carry you every road safe."

* * * * *

The legend of the castle that my old woman told me had to do with
water and a fairy woman, and, although the woman in it is old, not
young, I imagine it is a fragment of a Melusina story. The King of
Munster saved an old woman who was about to drown in the lake.
She had nothing to give him by way of reward. She told him, however, that if he would mount the topmost wall of his castle, and kiss
a stone which she described to him, he would gain a speech that would
win friend or foe to him, man or woman. There is a lake that might
well be the scene for an encounter for a Melusina: it is about a mile
from the castle.

But, as the friend who meets me here, a poet and a scholar, reminds me, Blarney was famous for its groves before the stone and its
lake were ever heard of. The place-name itself means "groves." And it
is for its groves that Blarney is celebrated in what is the most diverting

of Irish poems. As we walk amongst the trees, my poet-friend from
Cork, Frank O'Connor, repeats the poem and comments upon it. Imitations of Gaelic verse, he holds, should not be intentional; there should
be no striving for the effect of Gaelicism—it should come indeliber-
ately. He instances "The Bells of Shandon," written by a Latin scholar
who wrote for the sake of mystification, and "The Groves of Blarney"
which was made up to parody a song made in schoolmaster's English.
The structure and the sound of Gaelic poetry are reproduced in it:
the "a" sound of "Blarney" is woven through every stanza, but every
word that has the sound seems to have gone into its place smilingly:

> The groves of Blarney, they are so charming
> Down by the purling of sweet silent streams,
> Being banked with posies that spontaneous grow there,
> Planted in order by the sweet rock close.
> 'Tis there the daisy and the sweet carnation,
> The blooming pink and the rose so fair,
> The daffydowndilly, likewise the lily,
> All flowers that scent the sweet fragrant air.
>
> There's gravel walks there for speculation
> And conversation in sweet solitude;
> 'Tis there the lover may hear the dove, or
> The gentle plover in the afternoon;
> And if a lady would be so engaging
> As to walk alone in these shady bowers,
> 'Tis there the courtier he may transport her
> Into some fort or all underground.
>
> For 'tis there's a cave where no daylight enters,
> But cats and badgers are forever bred;
> Being mossed by nature that makes it sweeter
> Than a coach and six of a feather bed.
> 'Tis there the lake is, well stored with perches
> And comely eels in the verdant mud;
> Besides the leeches, and groves of beeches
> Standing in order for to guard the flood.
>
> There's statues gracing this noble place in—
> All heathen gods and nymphs so fair,
> Bold Neptune, Plutarch, and Nicodemus,
> All standing naked in the open air!

So now to finish this brief narration,
Which my poor genius could not entwine;
But were I Homer, or Nebuchadnezzar,
'Tis every feature I would make it twine.

This is the poem which James Stephens, as he told me once, would rather have written than anything else in an Irish anthology.

Malahide

The town of Malahide is situated in the Barony of Coolock, about seven miles north-northeast of the City of Dublin, and about half a mile distant stands the ancient seat of the Talbot family.

A number of suggestions have been put forward as to the derivation of the name Malahide, perhaps the most probable being that it comes from Baile-atha-id, signifying the "town of Id's ford."

The present castle is almost square in form, with a Gothic entrance on the southeast. This side of the fortress is flanked at each angle by a round tower, one of them at least having been added during the last century. The whole effect is much enhanced by the building being largely covered with ivy.

During the early part of the eighteenth century the stronghold was enlarged and modernized by its owner, Colonel Talbot. It had at that time lost its castellated character, which was restored, while the moat that surrounded it was filled in and planted.

The former entrance was by drawbridge, protected by a portcullis and barbican. The old tower of the barbican now gives entrance to the stable yard.

The hall is flagged and vaulted, and the walls are hung with interesting martial relics, while a handsomely carved chair is said to have belonged to King Robert Bruce.

A circular flight of stairs leads to the next floor, which contains the famous "Oak Room." The timber for its ornamentation is said to have been brought from the "faire green commune of Ostomanstoune," which was not so far away, and from which King William Rufus is said to have obtained the oak to roof Westminster Hall. The panels in Malahide Castle are of an ebony black, and are richly carved in

From *Castles of Ireland, Some Fortresses, Histories and Legends,* by C. L. Adams, pp. 292-295. Elliot Stock. London. 1904.

relief with scriptural subjects. The ceiling is cross-beamed with oak, and a wide mullioned window gives light to this beautiful apartment. It is said to have once been the castle chapel, and that behind a double panel, carved with scenes from the Garden of Eden, is a recess still occupied by the altar.

Here amongst other interesting objects is the suit of armour traditionally supposed to have been worn by Sir Walter Hussey, who was the first husband of the Hon. Maud Plunkett, and was killed on his wedding day.

The dining hall is said to date from the Tudor period, and it has a pointed ceiling of stained wood with a gallery at one end. In this room is displayed a very fine collection of historical and family portraits by many celebrated artists, amongst whom are Lely, Titian, Reynolds, Kneller, and others.

The portraits include those of "Handsome Dick Talbot," Duke of Tyrconnel, favourite of Charles II and James I, the Duchess of Portsmouth and her son the Duke of Richmond, the Earl of Lucan, Ireton, Myles Corbet, and several royal personages.

The "saloon" has also some art treasures, the chief being an altarpiece by Albert Durer, which once belonged to Mary Queen of Scots, and was purchased by Charles II for the Duchess of Portsmouth for the then enormous sum of £2,000.

The lands of Malahide were granted to the Talbot family in 1174 by Henry II, in whose train was Chevalier Richard Talbot, when the king came to Ireland in 1172. This grant was confirmed to Sir Richard Talbot by Edward IV in 1475.

The foundations of the castle were laid by the first Richard Talbot in Henry II's reign upon the gentle elevation of limestone rock where it stands today. It was enlarged during Edward IV's reign.

Sir Richard Edgecomb landed at Malahide in 1488 as Lord Justice, and writes that "there was a gentlewoman called Talbot received and made me right good cheer," until the Bishop of Meath and others came later in the day to escort him to Dublin.

During the rebellion of Lord Offaly or the "Silken Thomas," the O'Tooles and O'Byrnes ravished the country north of Dublin, and having plundered Howth, they "went to Malahyde and burst open the gates till they came to the hall-doors, when as they were resisted with great difficulty," they returned homeward.

After the rising had been suppressed, the unfortunate young leader executed, and his family attainted, Gerald, afterwards twelfth Earl of Kildare, only escaped from the English Government through the assistance of his aunt, the Lady "Aleanora" FitzGerald, and for the protection she had afforded her nephew she was detained at Malahide Castle awaiting the King's pleasure. From here, in 1545, was dated her petition for pardon to Henry VIII, which he granted.

Lord Strafford tried to gain some of the Talbot possessions and privileges in 1639, but without success.

John Talbot was banished to Connaught for taking part in the rebellion of 1641, and his castle and 500 acres were granted on a seven-year lease in 1653 to Miles Corbet, who was Chief Baron. His house in Dublin had been visited by plague, and he took up residence at Malahide about Christmas time. Here he lived until obliged to fly for his life, and he was afterwards executed as a regicide.

There is a tradition that Cromwell was his guest at Malahide during his tenancy.

A picture appearing on the Down Survey Map (1655-56) represents the castle as having a large tower at one end, and the notes describe it as "a good stone house therein, with orchards and gardens and many ashtrees, with other outhouses in good repair."

Upon the Restoration the Talbot family came again into possession. . . . Richard Talbot was created Lord Talbot de Malahide in 1831, and the present peer is fifth Baron.

Maynooth Castle

At the time of the Anglo-Norman invasion the ancient territory of *Ui Faolain,* comprising the northern portion of Kildare, in which was the district of Magh Nuadhat, the ancient name of Maynooth, was ruled over by the O'Connors and the Byrnes; but in the conquest under Strongbow these warlike chieftains were, after a long and strenuous resistance, driven from their holdings, and forced to seek refuge in the mountain fastness of Wicklow.

To Maurice Fitzgerald, the foremost of the adventurous band that came over with Strongbow and the progenitor in Ireland of the princely race that "channeled deep old Ireland's heart by constancy and worth," was granted the Manor of Maynooth, and here in the year 1176 he erected a large fortress castle, chiefly to serve as a protection against the inroads of the ousted native clans. This castle, as it then stood, consisted of a large defensive keep, of early Norman structure, with massive walls of stone, opening towards the town by

By J. W. Kavanagh, in *The Gael,* November, 1902, pp. 341-344. New York.

a large embattled gateway. It formed a powerful fortress, for its proximity was close to the junction of two rivers, which filled the surrounding fosse with water.

The Castle of Maynooth became the chief residence of the Kildare Fitzgeralds, and had much need of being well fortified; for, with the increasing possessions and honors of its possessors, the envy of the ruling chieftains was naturally aroused and their hostility directed against them. And so there opened to the Fitzgeralds the scene of many a fierce conflict, through all of which their war-worn banner was bravely borne, at one time in triumph—at another time in defeat. Thus with varied fortune, withstanding the attacks of many onslaughts, and "braving all the angry fury of the skies," the original fortress stood, until in the year 1426 it was greatly enlarged and in part rebuilt by John, the sixth Earl.

The ruins of this rebuilt castle still exist in a state of good preservation, and show it to have been of great size and strength. Standing beside the picturesque town of Maynooth, and shadowing the famous college, its grey, ivy-covered walls tower in stately grandeur towards the heavens. . . .

In 1477, Gerald, the eighth Earl, succeeded to the titles. He was one of the greatest of the Kildare Earls, and merits, therefore, a more than passing word. Surnamed Gerald the Great, or "Garrett More," he is described as "a mightie man of stature, full of honor and courage, milde in government, and to his enemies sterne." It was this Earl who founded the old college of St. Mary, Maynooth, assigning for the purpose a portion of his lands as an endowment.

The erection of this college had, however, to await the time of the succeeding Earl. At different periods for a long span of years, extending over the reign of five English sovereigns, Gerald the Great was Lord Deputy of Ireland; but during the reign of Henry VII, several accusations, notably that of having burned the Cathedral of Cashel, were brought against him, and he was arrested and committed a prisoner to the Tower of London.

This event, it is said, broke the too-feeling heart of his wife, the Countess Alicia. For two long years he remained a prisoner in the Tower, until, in 1496, he was at length summoned to trial before the King. In the midst of his traducers he stood alone in answer to their charges, yet, not a whit dismayed, he faced them all, and by the very ingenuousness of his answers saved himself.

"Not all Ireland can rule this Earl," said his enemies.

"Is that so?" said the King; "then he is the finest person to rule all Ireland," and he therewith reappointed him his deputy.

Returning to Ireland, Gerald afterward resided mostly at the Castle of Maynooth, where his zeal in discharging his duties as Lord Deputy had him at almost continuous warfare with one or other of the native chieftains. In 1513, whilst engaged on one of his expeditions, he received a wound from the effects of which he died in a short time. He lived a long life, and was honored as a wise statesman, and a true and noble-hearted man.

In 1521 the ninth Earl, "the brave and handsome Gerald," having obtained from the Archbishop of Dublin a license to erect the college originally designed by his father, "then," according to the state papers of the time, "built the college in a most beautiful form, and placed there a provost, vice-provost, five priests, two clerks, and three choristers, to pray for his soul and the soul of his wife."

The college was called the "College of the Blessed Virgin of Maynooth," and the prebend of Maynooth and his successors were to be the provosts. It was suppressed in 1538 by Henry VIII. (Its chapel was renovated by the Duke of Leinster in 1770, and has since served as the Protestant church of the parish.) Shortly after his succession to the earldom, Gerald, the younger, like so many of his ancestors, was vested in the high office of Lord Deputy, but although the regent thereby of the English sovereign in Ireland, he was in truth an Irish chieftain at heart.

On many occasions he had to clear himself of grave charges, which his enemies at court, incessantly plotting to secure his downfall, preferred against him, and at length, a conspiracy having been got up, he was in 1534 summoned to London on an impeachment of disloyalty. Before leaving Ireland he was ordered to nominate a vice-deputy to act for him during his absence. Convening the council for the purpose, he, with their approval, intrusted the office to his eldest son, the Lord Thomas (known in history as Silken Thomas, from the silken banner carried by his standard bearer), a brave, chivalrous, but inexperienced youth of only twenty-one years.

Misfortune, alas, was on the trail of the noble Geraldines, and the fate that had so long weathered their old stronghold of Maynooth through many a dark and troubled scene was at last about to meet with reverse.

Meanwhile the enemies of the Fitzgeralds still continued to intrigue against them. Not content with having secured the imprisonment of the Earl, they strove also to bring about the downfall of the son. For this end they gave currency to a report, bearing it out with forged letters, that the Earl was beheaded in the Tower, and that a like fate awaited the vice-deputy, as well as his brothers and uncles. The effect of such news, they well knew, on the high-spirited, impetuous young Geraldine, would be to incite him to rash deeds of vengeance, the outcome of which would be disaster.

Nor were they wrong in their conjecture, for on hearing the news, Lord Thomas, aroused with intense grief and passion, gathered his followers around him, and hastened to the council chamber in St. Mary's Abbey, where the council under the presidency of Cromer, the Chancellor, were assembled.

On entering the chamber, way was immediately made for him to preside, but, motioning to the Chancellor to resume his seat, he said he did not come there to preside, but to tell them of a bloody tragedy that was enacted in London, and of injuries perpetrated against his house. "This sword of state," he added in an impassioned tone, "is yours, not mine; take it back. I should stain honor if I used it to your hurt. Now I need my own sword, which I can trust. The common sword is already bathed in this Geraldine's blood, and thirsteth for more. I am none of Henry's deputies. I am his foe. I have more mind to meet him in the field than to serve him in office." Then casting his sword on the table with a resounding force, he left the chamber followed by his cheering supporters.

In vain Cromer, the staunch adherent of the Geraldines, sought with tears in his eyes to dissuade him from carrying out his rebellious intention. But Silken Thomas was not to be dissuaded. He had cast down the gauntlet, and, as befitted the Geraldine, would abide by the same.

Sir William Skeffington was now appointed deputy, and the Chancellor and other supporters of the Geraldines holding office were replaced by their known adversaries.

Having defeated a small force which attacked him near Clontarf, Silken Thomas proceeded to fortify strongly his different strongholds, but particularly that of Maynooth, which was then described as being so almost impregnable, that "nothing equal to its strength had been seen in Ireland since the English first held rule in the land." He then marched with his army into Connacht to collect the troops already promised to him by his allies, leaving in the meantime the command of the garrison of Maynooth in the hands of his foster-brother, Christopher Parese.

The deputy, taking advantage of his absence, advanced his army against Maynooth on March 15th, 1535. . . .

The siege was then opened. Against the north side of the castle the ordnance was directed, and for a fortnight continued to batter its walls. In all probability the besieged would have held out until the return of Silken Thomas with his augmented forces, had it not been for the treachery of Parese. Actuated by the desire of securing a rich reward, this traitor secretly made terms with the deputy, by which he agreed to betray the castle into his hands, receiving "a summe of money for his paynes, and a competent stay during his life."

The opportunity of carrying out the treachery soon presented itself. Having captured a field-piece from the enemy in a sally against them, Parese ordered the occasion to be given to festivities. In the night when the garrison, intoxicated after the feast, were in heavy slumber, Parese gave signal to the enemy, who without delay scaled the walls, and receiving but little resistance, captured the castle, immediately advancing their standard on its highest turret to apprise the deputy of their success. . . .

Within the castle were Dean of Kildare; Donald O'Wogan, Master of the Ordnance; Sir Symon Walshe, a priest, and Nicholas Wafer, with other gunners and archers, to the number of thirty-seven. They were all taken prisoners, and on the noon of the following day twenty-five of them were beheaded and one hanged before the castle gate.

Parese lost no time in appearing before the deputy to receive his promised award. The deputy received him in a cold manner, but heartily thanked him on behalf of the King for the great service he had rendered to the state, and then, by way that he might better reward him as he ought, inquired the favors his master bestowed on him. Lured by these plausible words, Parese enlarged upon his master's generosity, thinking that he would thus increase accordingly the value of his reward. "How then, Parese," asked the deputy, "could you find it in your heart to betray the castle of a master who has been so good to you? Truly, when you were hollow to him, you will never be true to us." Then turning to his officers, he ordered them to pay him the stipulated sum of money, and afterwards to chop off his head.

So fell the old fortress of Maynooth, to be followed in a short time by the downfall of its noble chief.

Already proclaimed a rebel by the council, deserted by many of his followers, outnumbered and harassed by powerful levies, Silken Thomas was ultimately forced to surrender. In the hands of his relentless foes he was shown no quarter. Immediately sent a prisoner to the Tower of London, he was in the beginning of 1537 executed with his five uncles at Tyburn. During his imprisonment we are told that he was treated with great cruelty, which the following letter, still extant in the state papers, which he wrote to one of his old faithful servants, would show:

"My trusty servant, I heartily recommend me unto you. I pray that you will deliver thys othyr letter unto O'Bryen. I have sent to him for 20 pounds [symbol] sterling, which if he take you, as I trust he will, then I will that you come over, and bring it unto my Lord Crumwell, that I may so have it. I have never had enny money since I came into prison, but a nobull, nor I have had neither hosyn, dublet, nor shoys, nor shyrt but one; nor any other garment, but a single fryse gown, for a velvet furryd wythe bowge, and so have gone wolward, and barefoot, and barelegged diverse times (when it had not been very warme) ; and so I should have done still, and now, but that poor prisoners of their gentleness hathe sometyme given me old hosyn, and shoys, and old shyrts. This I wryte to you, not as complaining on my friends, but for to show you the trewthe of my great need, that you should be the more dylygent in going unto O'Bryen, and in bringing me the aforesaid 20 pounds, whereby I might the sooner have here money to by me clothys, and also for to amend my slender comyes and fair. I will you take out of what you bring me for your cost and labor. I pray you have commended me unto all my lovers and friends, and shew them that I am in gude health—by me, THOMAS FITZGERALD."

Thus we see him, true and noble-hearted to the last, without even a word of resentment for his stern captors; faithful to his friends away in the land that he loved; generous even in his need—anxious to reward the little service of his trusted servant from his own paltry share; and grateful, too, for the rude favors of his fellow prisoners. . . .

The possessions of all the Fitzgeralds were now forfeited to the crown, and the Castle of Maynooth, becoming "Ye Kynge's Cashell of Mynoth," became the residence of his Deputy, Sir William Skeffington, who died there in 1535, and afterwards of his successors, Lord Leonard Gray and Sir Anthony St. Leger.

At length, in 1552, Gerald, the eleventh Earl, brother of Silken Thomas, and the sole survivor of the Geraldines, was restored to the Manor and Castle of Maynooth by Edward VI; and, subsequently, in the time of Queen Mary received back the ancient titles of his house.

After his death his widow, the beautiful Countess Mabel, continued to live in the "Fair House of Minuth" until her death in 1610, when her nephew Gerald, the fourteenth Earl, took up his residence there. At this time Maynooth had the strange distinction of having one of the only two deer parks in Ireland, the other being on the Earl of Ormonde's estate in Munster.

During the minority of George, the sixteenth Earl, who succeeded to the titles at the early age of eight years, the Castle of Maynooth fell into a state of great dilapidation; but it was enlarged and repaired by Richard, the famous Earl of Cork, who was guardian of the young Earl, on the occasion of his daughter's marriage with him in 1630.

During the Civil War which broke out in 1641, Maynooth Castle was captured and spoiled on more than one occasion, and on one of them its library was destroyed. . . . In 1647 the troops of Owen Roe O'Neill besieged and captured the castle, taking much booty and many prisoners, of whom they hanged twenty-six. This was the last siege—the

> "Last scene of all,
> That ends the strange, eventful history."

Henceforth it became uninhabited, and by degrees fell into ruin.

A BIT OF THE NORTH

In northeast Ulster where the country people speak—or, until recently, spoke—the Lallans or Lowlands Scots, there is a particular tradition. The examples from that tradition given here are few, not because there is not a great deal to select from, but because much of it blends with the lore of the rest of the country. To come on a couple of striking poems in Lallans is for this editor a particularly fortunate circumstance—they do not come in the usual Irish publications. In reading "Winter" and "To a Hedgehog," the one by a schoolmaster and the other by a weaver, one might be left with the impression that they derive from Burns. This would be wrong. They are "phrased in their own idiom," say John Hewitt, the idiom being "a branch of the great Lallans tree which still flourishes across the Moyle."—P.C.

Once Alien Here

So I, because of all the buried men
in Ulster clay, because of rock and glen
and mist and cloud and quality of air
as native in my thought as any here,
who now would seek a native mode to tell
our stubborn wisdom individual,
yet lacking skill in either scale of song,
the graver English, lyric Irish tongue,
must let this rich earth so entrance the blood
with steady pulse where now is plunging mood
till thought and image may, identified,
find easy voice to utter each aright.

Winter

The green warl's awa, but the white ane can charm them
Wha skate on the burn, or wi settin dogs rin;
The hind's dinlin hans, numb wi snaw baas, to warm them
He claps on his hard sides, whase doublets are thin.

From *No Rebel Word,* poems by John Hewitt, p. 10. Frederick Muller. London. [1951.]

By James Orr, collected by John Hewitt, in The Ulster Quarterly of Poetry, *Rann,* Winter, 1950, p. 6. Lisburn.

How dark the hail-shower maks yon vale, aince sae pleasin!
How laigh stoops the bush that's owre-burdent wi drift!
The icicles dreep at the half-thawt house-easin,
Whan blunt the sun beams frae the verge o the lift.

The hedge-hauntin blackbird, on ae fit whiles restin,
Wad fain heat the tither in storm-rufflet wing;
The silly sweelt sheep, ay the stifflin storm breastin,
Are glad o green piles at the side of the spring.

This night wi the lass that I hope will be kin' soon,
Wi Sylvia, wha charms me, a wee while I'll stap:
Her ee is as clear as the ice the moon shines on,
As gentle her smile as the snaw-flakes that drap.

To a Hedgehog

Thou grimmest far o grusome tykes
Grubbin thy food by thorny dykes
Gude faith, thou disna want for pikes
        Baith sharp an rauckle;
Thou looks (Lord save's) arrayed in spikes,
        A creepin heckle.

Sure Nick begat thee, at the first,
On some auld whin or thorn accurst;
An some horn-fingered harpie nurst
        The ugly urchin;
Then Belzie, laughin like to burst,
        First caad thee Hurchin.

Fowk tell how thou, sae far frae daft,
Whan wind-faan fruit be scattered saft,
Will row thysel wi cunning craft
        An bear awa
Upon thy back, what fares thee aft,
        A day or twa.

By Samuel Thompson, *ibid.*, p. 11.

But whether this account be true
Is mair than I will here avow;
If that thou stribs the outler cow,
    As some assert,
A pretty milkmaid, I allow,
    Forsooth thou art.

Now creep awa the way ye came,
And tend your squeakin pups at hame;
Gin Colly should oerhear the same,
    It might be fatal,
For you, wi aa the pikes ye claim,
    Wi him to battle.

The Battle of the Boyne

July the first, in Oldbridge town,
    There was a grievous battle
Where many a man lay on the ground,
    By cannons that did rattle.
King James he pitched his tents between
    the lines for to retire;
But King William threw his bomb-balls in,
    And set them all on fire.

Thereat enraged they vowed revenge
    Upon King William's forces,
And oft did vehemently cry
    That they would stop their courses.
A bullet from the Irish came,
    And grazed King William's arm,
They thought his majesty was slain,
    Yet it did him little harm.

Duke Schomberg then, in friendly care,
    His King would often caution
To shun the spot where bullets hot
    Retained their rapid motion;

From an old ballad-sheet.

But William said, he don't deserve
    The name of Faith's defender,
Who would not venture life and limb
    To make a foe surrender.

When we the Boyne began to cross,
    The enemy they descended;
But few of our brave men were lost,
    So stoutly we defended;
The horse was the first that marched o'er,
    The foot soon followed after;
But brave Duke Schomberg was no more,
    By venturing over the water.

When valiant Schomberg he was slain,
    King William he accosted
His warlike men for to march on
    And he would be the foremost;
"Brave boys," he said, "be not dismayed,
    For the loss of one commander,
For God will be our king this day. . . .

*   *   *   *

Come let us all with heart and voice
    Applaud our lives' defender,
Who at the Boyne his valour showed
    And made his foe surrender.
To God above the praise we'll give
    Both now and ever after;
And bless the glorious memory
    Of King William that crossed the water.

The Ould Orange Flute

In the County Tyrone, near the town of Dungannon,
Where many a ruction myself had a han' in,
Bob Williamson lived, a weaver by trade,
And all of us thought him a stout Orange blade.

From an old ballad-sheet.

On the Twelfth of July, as it yearly did come,
Bob played on the flute to the sound of the drum—
You may talk of your harp, your piano or lute,
But nothing could sound like the ould Orange flute.

But this treacherous scoundrel he took us all in,
For he married a Papish called Bridget McGinn;
Turned Papish himself and forsook the old cause
That gave us our freedom, religion and laws.
Now the boys in the townland made some noise upon it,
And Bob had to fly to the province of Connacht,
He flew with his wife and fixings to boot,
And along with the others the ould Orange flute.

At chapel on Sundays to atone for his past deeds,
He'd say Pater and Aves and counted his brown beads,
Till, after some time, at the priest's own desire,
He went with that ould flute to play in the choir.
He went with that ould flute to play in the loft,
But the instrument shivered and sighed and then coughed
When he blew it and fingered it and made a strange noise,
For the flute would play only "The Protestant Boys."

Bob jumped up and started and got in a flutter,
And he put the ould flute in the bless'd holy water;
He thought that it might now make some other sound,
When he blew it again it played "Croppies Lie Down!"
And all he did whistle, and finger, and blow,
To play Papish music he found it "no go".
"Kick the Pope," "The Boyne Water" and such like 'twould sound,
But one Papish squeak in it couldn't be found.

At a council of priests that was held the next day,
They decided to banish that ould flute away;
As they couldn't knock heresy out of its head,
They bought Bob another to play in its stead.
So the ould flute was doomed and its fate was pathetic,
It was fastened and burned at the stake as heretic,
While the flames roared around it they heard a strange noise,
'Twas the ould flute still whistlin' "The Protestant Boys."

Johnny's the Lad I Love

As I roved out on a May morning,
Being in the youthful spring,
I leaned my back close to the garden wall
To hear the small birds sing;

And to hear two lovers talk, my dear,
To know what they would say,
That I might know a little of her mind
Before I would go away.

"Come, sit ye down, my heart," he said,
"All on this pleasant green,
It's full three quarters of a year and more
Since together you and I have been."

"I will not sit on the grass," she said,
"Now nor any other time,
For I hear you're engaged with another maid,
And your heart is no more of mine," she said,
"And your heart is no more of mine."

"Oh, I'll not believe what an old man says,
For his days are nearly done,
Nor will I believe what a young man says,
For he's fair to many a one," she said,
"He's fair to many a one."

"But I will climb a high, high tree,
And rob a wild bird's nest,
And I'll bring back whatever I do find
To the arms I love the best," she said,
"To the arms I love the best."

From an old ballad-sheet.

Part IX

BALLADS AND SONGS

The Minstrel's Invitation

I am of Ireland,
And of the holy land
   Of Ireland.
Good sir, pray I thee
For of *Saint Charité*
Come and dance with me
   In Ireland.

Fragment of a dance song, composed by an Anglo-Irish minstrel of the early fourteenth century. From *Anglo-Irish Literature 1200-1582*, by St. John D. Seymour. Cambridge University Press. 1929.

Introduction

In a collection so brief as the present one has to be, many readers will look in vain for favorite songs. Several have been left out because they are available in many other collections: it would be superfluous to give here "The Minstrel Boy," "The Last Rose of Summer" or "In Dublin's Fair City," and there are many others in the same category.

Of those included in this section, a few need some words of explanation. "The Lamentation of Hugh Reynolds" is a street song that goes back to the time when the abduction of a girl with the intention of a forced marriage was a capital crime. It became a hanging matter if the girl went into the witness box where the man was up for trial and swore that it was against her will she was carried off. The girl who did this was generally regarded as a betrayer—"She swore his life away," was how the public judged her. Hugh Reynolds' refrain is "She's the dear maid to me," meaning "She cost me dearly." With its assonance and internal rhymes this song has a Gaelic form.

"Johnny I Hardly Knew Ye" is masterly in its cynical acceptance of the woes of war for the poverty-stricken slum-dweller. There's nothing before the maimed private soldier but beggary. And this very popular street song is in dramatic contrast to "The Girl I Left Behind Me," where a recruit off to the wars sings of his girl at home; in "Johnny," a soldier has come home and his girl sings of what the wars have done to him.

"Mollie Brannigan" or "Mollie Bralligan" is the comedian's parody of the sentimental song. It has so much gusto that it creates a genre of its own.

And then we come to the most famous of Irish street songs, "The Shan Van Vocht." The title means "The Poor Old Woman" and it is a "secret" name for Ireland. The tone is exultant. The Poor Old Woman is being informed that the boys are ready, and this time they will have help, for a French fleet has set out for Ireland. As a footnote: the French leader, Hoche, did not have Lafayette's luck. The fleet was broken up by a storm and the troops could not land in Bantry.

" 'Thank You, Ma'am,' Says Dan"—one does not know whether this is a parody or a genuine celebration of a simple heart, as "I Know My Love" is a genuine lament of a simple heart. " 'Thank You, Ma'am' " was first sung in literary circles in Dublin by the poet and revolutionist, Thomas MacDonagh, who probably had obtained it in the County Kilkenny. The present writer prevailed on him to publish it in a literary weekly, and thus it got into circulation.

For her cooperation in selecting and annotating the music for these songs, the editor thanks Maire O'Scannlain.—P.C.

———

John O'Dwyer of the Glens

Oh!__ oft at pleas-ant morn-ing,__ Sun-shine all a - dorn-ing,__

I've heard horns give warn-ing, With bird's__ mel - low call.

Badg - ers flee be - fore us,__ Wood-cocks star - tle o'er us,__

Guns' make ring- ing chor-us, A - mid the e - choes all; The

fox run high__ and__ high-er__ Horse-men shout - ing nigh-er The

maid - en mourn - ing__ o'er__ her fowl he left in gore. But__

now, they fell the wild-wood__ Fare-well home of child-hood.__ . Ah,

Shaun O'Dwyer a' - Glean- na,__ Thy day is o'er.

It is my sorrow sorest!	The antler'd noble-hearted—
Woe, the falling forest,	Tall stags are never started,
The north wind gives me no rest,	Are never chased nor parted
And death's in the sky.	From their fuzzy hills.
My faithful hound's tied tightly,	If peace came but a small way,
Now never sporting brightly,	I'd journey down to Galway,
Who'd make a child laugh lightly,	And leave, tho' not for alway,
With tears in his eye.	My Erinn of ills.

The Shan Van Vocht

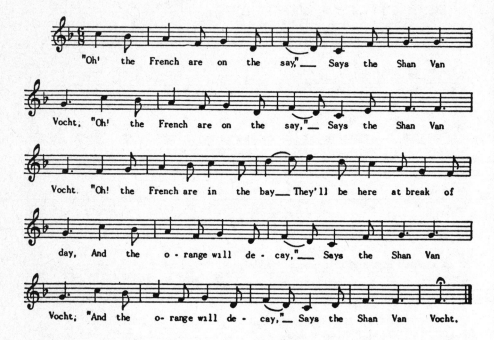

"Oh! the French are on the say,"— Says the Shan Van Vocht; "Oh! the French are on the say,"— Says the Shan Van Vocht. "Oh! the French are in the bay— They'll be here at break of day, And the o-range will de-cay,"— Says the Shan Van Vocht; "And the o-range will de-cay,"— Says the Shan Van Vocht.

"And where will they have their camp?"
  Says the Shan Van Vocht;
"And where will they have their camp?"
  Says the Shan Van Vocht.
"On the Curragh of Kildare,
  And the boys will all be there,
With their pikes in good repair,"
  Says the Shan Van Vocht;
"With their pikes in good repair,"
  Says the Shan Van Vocht.

"And what colour will be seen?"
  Says the Shan Van Vocht;
"And what colour will be seen?"
  Says the Shan Van Vocht.
"What colour should be seen
  Where our fathers' homes have been
But our own immortal green,"
  Says the Shan Van Vocht;
"But our own immortal green,"
  Says the Shan Van Vocht.

"Will old Ireland then be free?"
  Says the Shan Van Vocht;
"Will old Ireland then be free?"
  Says the Shan Van Vocht.
"Old Ireland shall be free,
  From the centre to the sea—
Then hurrah for liberty!"
  Says the Shan Van Vocht;
"Then hurrah for liberty!"
  Says the Shan Van Vocht.

Ballynure Ballad

As I was goin' to Bal - ly - nure, the day I well— re - mem-ber,— For to view the lads and lass - es on— the fifth day of No- vem - ber, With a ma - ring - doo - a - day, With a ma - ring - a - doo - a - dad - dy oh.———

As I was goin' along the road
   when homeward I was walking,
I heard a wee lad behind a ditch-a
To his wee lass was talking,
With a ma-ring-doo-a-day,
With a ma-ring-a-doo-a-dad-dy, oh!

Said the wee lad to the wee lass,
"It's will ye let me kiss ye,
For it's I have got the cordial eye
   that far exceeds the whiskey,"
With a ma-ring-doo-a-day,
With a ma-ring-a-doo-a-dad-dy, oh!

This cordial that ye talk about
   there's very few o' them gets it,
For there's nothin' now but crooked combs
   and musilin gowns can catch it.
With a ma-ring-doo-a-day,
With a ma-ring-a-doo-a-dad-dy, oh!

Molly Brannigan

Ma'am dear, did ye ne-ver hear of pret-ty Mol-ly Bran-ni-gan? In troth,— then, she's left me and I'll ne-ver be a man a-gain. Not a spot on my hide will a sum-mer's sun e'er tan a-gain, Since Mol-ly's gone and left me here a-lone for to die. The place where my heart was you'd ai-sy rowl a turn-ip in, 'Tis as large as all Dub-lin, and from Dub-lin to the Div-il's glen. If she wish'd to take an-oth-er, Sure she might have left mine back a-gain, And not have left me here — all a-lone for to die.

Ma'am dear, I remember when the milking time was past and gone,
We walked thro' the meadow, when she swore I was the only one
That ever she could love, but oh! the base and cruel one,
For all that she's left me here alone for to die.

Ma'am dear, I remember when coming home the rain began,
I wrapt my frieze-coat round her an' ne'er a waistcoat had I on;
My shirt was rather fine-drawn, but oh! the false and cruel one,
For all that she's left me here alone for to die.

The left side of my carcase is as weak as water gruel, ma'am,
There's not a pick upon my bones, since Molly's proved so cruel, ma'am;
Oh! if I had a blunder gun, I'd go an' fight a duel, ma'am,
For sure I'd better shoot myself than live here to die.

I'm cool an' determined as any Salamander, ma'am.
Won't you come to my wake when I go the long meander, ma'am?
I'll think myself as valiant as the famous Alexander, ma'am,
When I hear ye crying o'er me, "Arrah, why did ye die?"

I Know Where I'm Goin'

I know where I'm go-in', __ And I know who's go-in' with me,

I know who I love   But the dear knows who I'll mar- ry!

I have stockings of silk,
Shoes of fine green leather,
Combs to buckle my hair,
And a ring for every finger.

Some say he's black,
But I say he's bonny,
The fairest of them all
My handsome, winsome Johnny.

Feather beds are soft,
And painted rooms are bonny,
But I would leave them all
To go with my love Johnny.

'Tis Pretty to Be in Ballinderry

1. 'Tis   pret - ty   to   be   in   Bal -   lin - der - ry,   'Tis
2.   Oh,   that   I   was   in   lit - tle Rams   Is -   land!

pret - ty   to   be   in   Ag -   ha -   lee,   'Tis   pret-tier to   be   in
Oh,   that   I   was   with Phe - ly my   di - a-mond!   He   would whistle, and

bon - ny Rams Is -   land,   Sit - ting un - der an   i - vy - tree.
I __ would sing,   Till   we __ would make the whole   Is - land   ring.

Och   hone!   Och   hone!   Och   hone!   Och   hone!
Och   hone!   Och   hone!   Och   hone!   Och   hone!

The Snowy Breasted Pearl

There's a — col-leen fair as May, For a year and for a day. I have
tried in ev'-ry way her heart to gain. There's no — trick of tongue or eye, Fond —
youths with mai - dens try, But I've tried with cease-less sigh — and —
tried in vain If to far off France or Spain. She crossed the rag-ing main, Her
face to see a - gain, The seas I'd brave, But — if 'tis heav'ns de-cree, That —
mine she may not be, May the son of Ma - ry, me, in mer - cy save.

Oh, snowy milk white dove
    To whom I've given my love,
Ah, never thus reprove
    My constancy.

There are maidens would be mine,
    With wealth in land and kine,
If I would but incline
    To turn from thee.

But a kiss with welcome bland
    And touch of thy fair hand,
Is all that I demand,
    Did thy love burn.

But if not mine, dear girl,
    Oh, snowy breasted Pearl,
May I never from the fair
    With life return.

The Paisteen Fionn (The Fair-Haired Child)

My Pais - teen Fionn is my soul's de - light Her__
heart_ laughs_ out__ in her blue eyes bright, The bloom of the ap - ple her
bo - som white, Her__ neck like the March swan's in white - ness. Oh'__
you____ are my dear,__ my dear__ my dear;__ Oh!
you__ are my dear and my fair love! You__ are my own__ dear, and my
fond - est hope here__ And__ oh that my cot - tage you'd share, _ love'

Love of my bosom, my fair Paisteen,
Whose cheek is red like the roses' sheen;
My thoughts of the maiden are pure, I ween,
    Save toasting her health in my lightness!

        Oh! you are my dear, etc.

From kinsfolk and friends, my fair, I'd flee—
From all the beautiful maids that be;
But I'll never leave you, sweet gramachree,
    Till death in your service o'ertakes me!

        Oh! you are my dear, etc.

Eileen Aroon

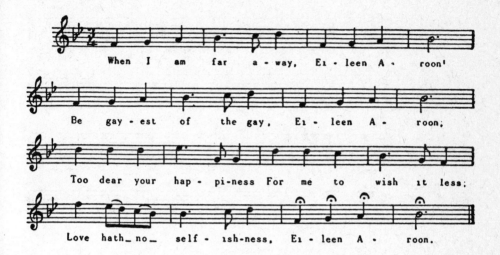

When I am far a-way, Eileen A-roon!
Be gay-est of the gay, Eileen A-roon;
Too dear your hap-pi-ness For me to wish it less;
Love hath no self-ish-ness, Eileen A-roon.

And it must be our pride, Eileen Aroon,
Our trusting hearts to hide, Eileen Aroon;
   They wish our love to blight;
   We'll wait for Fortune's light;
   The flowers close up at night,
             Eileen Aroon.

And when we meet alone, Eileen Aroon,
Upon my bosom thrown, Eileen Aroon,
   That hour with light bedecked
   Shall cheer us and direct
   A beacon to the wrecked,
             Eileen Aroon.

Fortune, thus sought, will come, Eileen Aroon,
We'll win a happy home, Eileen Aroon;
   And as it slowly rose,
   'Twill tranquilly repose,
   A rock 'mid melting snows,
             Eileen Aroon.

She Moved Through the Fair

My young love said to me "My mother won't mind And my father won't slight you for your lack of kind." And she stepp'd a-way from me and this she did say "It will not be long love, till our wed-ding day."

She stepp'd away from me
and went thro' the fair,
And fondly I watch'd her
move here and move there,

And then she went homeward
with one star awake,
As the swan in the evening
moves over the lake.

Last night she came to me,
she came softly in,
So softly she came
that her feet made no din.

And she laid her hand on me
and this she did say,
"It will not be long, love,
till our wedding day."

I Know My Love

"I _____ know my love by his way o' walk- in', And I know my love by his way o' talk- in', And I know my love drest in a suit o' blue, And if my love leaves me what will I do - o - o?" And still she cried "I love him the best and a troubled mind sure can know no rest"__ And still she cried "Bon - ny boys are few And if my love laves me what will I do - o - o?"

There is a dance house in Mara dyke,
And there my true love goes ev'ry night.
He takes a strange one upon his knee
And don't you think now that vexes me.

And still she cried "I love him the best," etc.

If my love knew I could wash and wring,
If my love knew I could weave and spin,
I'd make a coat all of the finest kind,
But the want of money sure laves me behind.

And still she cried "I love him the best," etc.

The Coolin

This very ancient air has been included in collections from 1786 on; it was also used in an opera, *The Mountains of Wicklow,* in 1798, but was called "The Coolin" for the first time about a hundred years ago. The title is a corruption of the Gaelic original "An Chuilfhionn," meaning, "the maid of the flowing fair locks." It is best known throughout Ireland as "Tho' the Last Glimpse of Erin," by Thomas Moore.

"Thank You, Ma'am," Says Dan

"What brought you in-to my room, to my room, to my room, What brought you in-to my room?" said the mis-tress un-to Dan. "I came here to court your daugh-ter, Ma'am, I thought it no great harm,—Ma'am!" "Oh, Dan me dear, you're wel-come here!" "Thank you, Ma'am," says Dan. ___

"How came you to know my daughter, my daughter, my
  daughter,
How came you to know my daughter?" says the mistress
  unto Dan.
"Going to the well for water, Ma'am, to raise the can I
  taught her, Ma'am!"
"Oh, Dan, 'tis you're the handy man!" "Thank you,
  Ma'am," says Dan.

"Oh, you can have my daughter, my daughter, my daughter,
Yes, you can have my daughter," says the mistress unto Dan,
"But when you take my daughter, Dan, of course you'll
  take me also, Dan!
Oh, Dan me dear, you're welcome here!" "Thank you,
  Ma'am," says Dan.

This couple they got married, got married, got married,
This couple they got married, Miss Elizabeth and Dan;
And now he keeps her mother and her father and her brother
  and . . .
"Oh, Dan, 'tis you're the lucky man!" "Thank you,
  Ma'am," says Dan.

The Girl I Left Behind Me

Come— all ye— hand-some come-ly maids That live near Car-low—
dwell-ing Be-ware of— young men's flat-t'ring tongue When love to you they're—
tell-ing. Be-ware of the kind words they say, Be
wise and do not mind——— them, For— if they were talk-ing
till they die They'd leave you all be-hind them.

In Carlow town I lived I own
All free from debt and danger.
Till Colonel Reilly listed me
To join the Wicklow Rangers.
They dressed me up in scarlet red
And they used me very kindly
But still I thought my heart would break
For the girl I left behind me.

I was scarcely fourteen years of age
When I was broken-hearted,
For I'm in love these two long years
Since from my love I parted.
These maidens wonder how I moan
And bid me not to mind him
That he might have more grief than joy
For leaving me behind him.

"Johnny I Hardly Knew Ye"

While going the road to sweet Ath-y, Hur-roo! ___ Hurroo! ___ While going the road to sweet Ath-y, Hur-roo! ___ Hurroo! ___ While ___ going the road to sweet Ath-y; A
stick in my hand, and a drop in my eye, ___ A dole-ful dam-sel
I heard cry: "Och John-ny, I hard-ly knew ye!"

CHORUS

With their drums and guns and guns and drums The
en-em-y near-ly slew ye, ___ Och, John me dear, you
look so queer, John-ny I hard-ly knew ye!

Where are your eyes that looked so mild? Hurroo! Hurroo!
Where are your eyes that looked so mild? Hurroo! Hurroo!
Where are your eyes that looked so mild,
When my poor heart you first beguiled?
Arah, why did you run from me and the child?
Och, Johnny I hardly knew ye!   (*Chorus*.)

Where are the legs with which you run? Hurroo! Hurroo!
Where are the legs with which you run? Hurroo! Hurroo!
Where are the legs with which you run
When first you went to carry a gun?
Indeed your dancing days are done! Och, Johnny, I hardly
    knew ye!   *(Chorus.)*

It grieved my heart to see you sail, Hurroo! Hurroo!
It grieved my heart to see you sail, Hurroo! Hurroo!
It grieved my heart to see you sail,
Though from my heart you took leg-bail;
Like a cod you're doubled up head and tail,
Och, Johnny, I hardly knew ye!   *(Chorus.)*

You haven't an arm and you haven't a leg, Hurroo! Hurroo!
You haven't an arm and you haven't a leg, Hurroo! Hurroo!
You haven't an arm and you haven't a leg,
You're an eyeless, noseless, chickenless egg,
You'll have to be put in a bowl to beg:
Och, Johnny, I hardly knew ye!   *(Chorus.)*

I'm happy for to see you home, Hurroo! Hurroo!
I'm happy for to see you home, Hurroo! Hurroo!
I'm happy for to see you home,
All from the Island of Sulloon;
So low in flesh, so high in bone,
Och, Johnny, I hardly knew ye!   *(Chorus.)*

But sad it is to see you so, Hurroo! Hurroo!
But sad it is to see you so, Hurroo! Hurroo!
But sad it is to see you so
And to think of you now as an object of woe,
But your Peggy will keep you as her beau;
Och, Johnny, I hardly knew ye!

The Lamentation of Hugh Reynolds

My — name it is Hugh Rey-nolds — I came of hon - est par - ents, Near Ca-van I was born — as you may plain-ly see For the lov-ing of a maid One Cath - er - ine Mc - Cabe — My life has been be - trayed — She's the dear — maid to me. The — coun - try was be - wail-ing — my dole-ful sit - u - a - tion, — But still I'd ex - pec - ta - tion this maid would set me free, But — O, she was un - grate-ful — Her par-ents prov'd de - ceit - ful An' tho' I lov'd her faith-ful, she's the dear — maid to me. —

Young men and tender maidens, throughout this Irish nation,
Who hear my lamentation, I hope you'll pray for me;
The truth I will unfold, that my precious blood she sold,
In the grave I must lie cold; she's the dear maid to me.

The Leprehaun

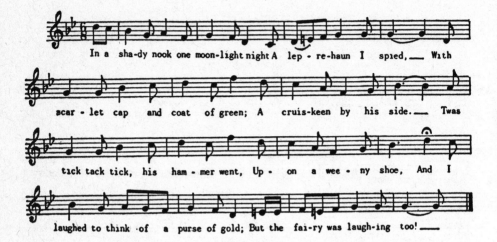

In a sha-dy nook one moon-light night A lep-re-haun I spied,— With scar-let cap and coat of green; A cruis-keen by his side.— Twas tick tack tick, his ham-mer went, Up-on a wee-ny shoe, And I laughed to think of a purse of gold; But the fai-ry was laugh-ing too!—

With tip-toe step and beating heart,
    Quite softly I drew nigh:
There was mischief in his merry face;—
    A twinkle in his eye.
He hammered and sang with tiny voice,
    And drank his mountain dew;
And I laughed to think he was caught at last:—
    But the fairy was laughing too!

As quick as thought I seized the elf;
    "Your fairy purse!" I cried;
"The purse!" he said—" 'tis in her hand—
    "That lady at your side!"
I turned to look: the elf was off!
    Then what was I to do?
O, I laughed to think what a fool I'd been;
    And the fairy was laughing too!

The Cruiskeen Lawn

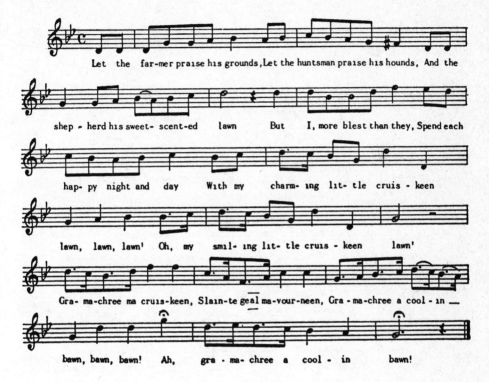

Let the far-mer praise his grounds, Let the huntsman praise his hounds, And the

shep - herd his sweet- scent-ed lawn   But   I, more blest than they, Spend each

hap- py night and   day   With my   charm- ing lit- tle cruis - keen

lawn,   lawn,   lawn! Oh,   my   smil- ing lit- tle cruis - keen   lawn!

Gra- ma-chree ma cruis-keen, Slain-te geal ma-vour-neen, Gra - ma-chree a cool - in __

bawn, bawn, bawn!   Ah,   gra - ma- chree   a   cool - in   bawn!

"The Cruiskeen Lawn" means "The Little Full Jug"—the translation of the chorus is:

> Little jug, my heart's love,
> Bright health to my own dove;
> Little jug, my own heart's love, love, love,
> Oh! Little jug, my own heart's love!

This song dates back to antiquity—the author and composer being unknown. In Ireland and Scotland the air has been known for many centuries, in the latter country as "John Anderson My Jo."

See page 458 for full text.

The Star of the County Down

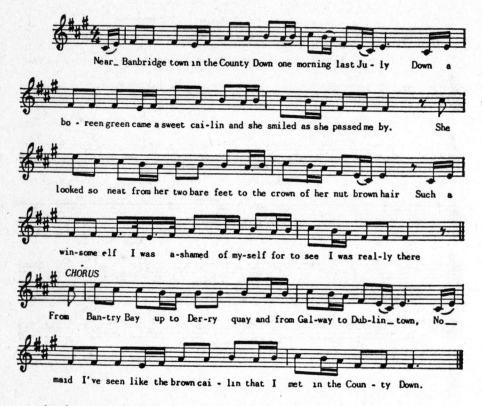

Near_ Banbridge town in the County Down one morning last Ju-ly   Down a
bo-reen green came a sweet cai-lin and she smiled as she passed me by.   She
looked so neat from her two bare feet to the crown of her nut brown hair   Such a
win-some elf I was a-shamed of my-self for to see I was real-ly there

CHORUS

From Ban-try Bay up to Der-ry quay and from Gal-way to Dub-lin_ town, No_
maid I've seen like the brown cai-lin that I met in the Coun-ty Down.

As she onward sped sure I scratch'd my head and I looked with a
feeling rare,
And I says, says I, to a passer by, "Who's the maid with the
nut brown hair?"
He smiled at me and he says to me, "That's the gem of
Ireland's crown,
Young Rosie McCann from the banks of the Bann, she's the star
of the County Down."

At the harvest fair she'll be surely there, so I'll dress in
my Sunday clothes;
With my shoes shone bright and my hat cocked right for a
smile from the nut brown Rose.
No pipe I'll smoke, no horse I'll yoke till my plough is a
rust coloured brown,
Till a-smiling bright by my own fireside is the star
from the County Down.

Finnegan's Wake

Tim Fin-ne-gan liv'd in Wal-kin Street a gen-tle-man Ir-ish

might-y odd. He had a tongue both rich and sweet, an' to

rise in the world he car-ried a hod, Now Tim had a sort of a

tip-plin' way With the love of the li-quor he was born, An' to

help him on with his work each day, He'd a drop of the cray-thur ev-'ry morn.

CHORUS

Whack fol the dah, dance to your part-ner Welt the flure yer trot-ters shake,

Was-n't it the truth I told you, Lot's of fun at Fin-ne-gan's Wake.

This song is American-Irish: it goes back to the time when the Irish immigrants were the house builders in New York, mounting ladders, their hods on their shoulders. In the song, Finnegan falls, is considered dead, is waked, and revives when he gets hold of the whiskey that is being passed round at his wake. James Joyce found in this song a comic statement of universal mythology—the Fall of Man, the Partaking of the Water of Life, the Renewal of Existence—and used it for the title of his last and enigmatic book.

The Maid of the Sweet Brown Knowe*

Come all ye lads and lass-es and hear my mourn-ful tale, Ye
ten-der hearts that weep for love to sigh you will not fail, 'Tis
all a-bout a young man and my song will tell you how He
late-ly came a-court-ing of the Maid of the Sweet Brown Knowe.

Said he, "My pretty fair maid, could you and I agree,
To join our hands in wedlock bands, and married we will be;
We'll join our hands in wedlock bands, and you'll have my
    plighted vow,
That I'll do my whole endeavours for the Maid of the Sweet
    Brown Knowe."

Now this young and pretty fickle thing, she knew not what to
    say,
Her eyes did shine like silver bright and merrily did play;
Says she, "Young man, your love subdue, I am not ready now,
And I'll spend another season at the foot of the Sweet Brown
    Knowe."

---

* A little hill (pronounced N-yoe).

The Derry Air

Suantree (Hush Song)

Sweet babe, a gold en cra - dle holds thee; Soft a snow - white
fleece_ en-folds thee; Fair-est flow'rs are strewn_be-fore_thee; Sweet birds war - ble
o'er thee: Sho - heen_ sho lo!_____ Sho - heen_sho lo lo!

Oh! sleep, my baby, free from sorrow,
Bright thou'lt ope thine eyes to-morrow;
Sleep while o'er thy smiling slumbers
Angels chant their numbers:
Shoheen sho lo!

"The Derry Air" is one of the most ancient of Irish melodies. Several different verses have been set to it, including Catherine Tynan Hinkson's poem "Would God I Were the Tender Apple Blossom." The most widely sung version is "Danny Boy," by Fred E. Weatherly.

Index